A NEW CATECHISM

A NEW CATECHISM

CATHOLIC FAITH FOR ADULTS

WITH SUPPLEMENT

CROSSROAD · NEW YORK

1986
The Crossroad Publishing Company
370 Lexington Avenue, New York, NY 10017

Nihil Obstat: Leo J. Steady, Censor Librorum
Imprimatur: ✠ Robert F. Joyce, Bishop of Burlington
September 29, 1969

The original edition of this book,
De Nieuwe Katechismus,
was commissioned by the Hierarchy of the Netherlands and
produced by the Higher Catechetical Institute at Nijmegen
in collaboration with numerous others.
Imprimatur for the original Dutch edition:
Utrecht, March 1, 1966. Bernardus Cardinal Alfrink.

The Scripture quotations are from the *Revised Standard
Version of the Holy Bible, Catholic Edition*
Copyright © 1965 and 1966 by the Division of Christian
Education of the National Council of the Churches of Christ
in the U.S.A. and used by permission

This translation was made by Kevin Smyth
© 1967 and 1969 Herder and Herder, Inc.

Printed in the United States of America

Library of Congress Cataloging in Publication Data

Nieuwe katechismus. English.
  A new catechism.

  Translation of: De nieuwe katechismus.
    1. Catholic Church—Catechisms and creeds—English.
I. Title.
BX1961.N5313 1982   238'.2   81-22159
ISBN 0-8245-0331-7   AACR2
ISBN 0-8245-0332-5 (pbk.)

FOREWORD

Peace to this house and to all who live in it!

In the following pages we hope to present anew to adults the message which Jesus of Nazareth brought into the world, to make it sound as new as it is. As such this book is an attempt to render faithfully the renewal which found expression in the Second Vatican Council. That is why it is called *A New Catechism*.

But "new" does not mean that some aspects of the faith have been changed while all the rest remains as before. Had that been our object, we could simply have changed a few pages of the old catechism. But this is not the case. The whole message, the whole of the faith remains the same, but the approach, the light in which the faith is seen, is new. Everything that lives has both to remain itself and to renew itself. The message of Christ is a living thing, and hence this new type of catechism tries to present the faith of our fathers in a form suitable to the present day.

This required a new type of book. Earlier catechisms looked for brief formulations which could easily be memorized. But the object of this book is to preach Christ's message through ordinary language, to set out its background at leisure, and to throw light on present-day questions by means of the gospel.

We hope that this catechism will inspire the sense of true fellowship which is God's great work. Life with God is a very personal thing, but it is not a task to be fulfilled in isolation. It always brings fellowship with it.

Thus we hope that this catechism will, above all, make us one in heart and soul with the whole, wonderful Catholic Church in which men live together, in spite of differences of race, culture and mentality. And we also hope that the catechism will play its part in strengthening the progress of unity among all Chris-

V

tians, for the message of this book is the Kingdom for which all Christians pray. Finally, we hope that this book will help to reinforce our union with all our fellowmen, who live in the same world as we do and share the same cares and yearnings. For it is to this world with its cares and yearnings that the message of this book is addressed. Denominational differences, which shall not be blurred or ignored in this book, need not be barriers. We hope that they may lead to discussions where the human existence we share will receive further elucidation.

The Bishops of the Netherlands

HOW TO USE THIS BOOK

The aim of this catechism is to serve the reader by showing him the Christian message as a connected whole. But at the same time, it tries to answer a multitude of particular questions. For this reason we have tried to make each chapter complete in itself. As a result the catechism is not just one book, but a small library of little books of three to thirty pages in extent dealing with the various subjects on which the reader may seek advice. The reader can open the book wherever he likes. There are three means to facilitate reference work. First of all the table of contents, then the index of words at the end of the book and finally the small numbers in the margin of the text which refer one to pages where a more extensive treatment may be found or where the subject is viewed in a different light.

For a summary of the message of faith in shorter form, we refer the reader first and foremost to the twelve articles of the Apostles' Creed, and the longer Creed which is used at Mass, the ancient confessions in which the Church proclaimed its faith. The table of contents also provides a short summary, if the chapter titles are read in sequence.

When not in use, this book's proper home is beside your Bible, for our constant object is to lead the believer to the source of his faith, ever ancient and ever new, the word of God.

The themes treated were chosen to provide matter of reflection for mature believers. As far as possible all technical language has been avoided so as to facilitate reading and discussion.

Finally, we have a request to make both of Catholics and non-Catholics. Misunderstandings are always possible, and a book which covers as many subjects as this one can give rise to many of them. We ask our readers to try to see each word in the context of the whole gospel message. This means that no passage can be read properly unless the preceding and following pages are taken into account. Sometimes what is missing on one page is said and elaborated on another. It would be wrong to take any one statement and read it in isolation in a book which for the most part does not aim at hard and fast definitions but at an approximation to the unfathomable mystery.

The heart of this preaching is the message of Easter. If the news of Jesus' resurrection were removed, not one page of the book would have any value. The *New Catechism* is an expression of firm faith in this message and an effort to enunciate God's ineffable mystery in the language of our times.

TABLE OF CONTENTS

X

TABLE OF CONTENTS

XII

God—Our powerlessness to save ourselves—Our
struggle against sin and misery—"The lifter of my
head" (Ps 3:4)—Redeemed by Jesus' death—Summary
—The other doctrines elevated by Christ?—Christians
evangelized by non-Christians—Election

in the cycle of the year—Not an isolated element—
The duration of the Eucharistic presence—The reservation of the Eucharist—The holy and the profane

PART ONE

THE MYSTERY OF EXISTENCE

In A.D. 627 the monk Paulinus visited King Edwin in northern England to persuade him to accept Christianity. He hesitated and decided to summon his advisers. At the meeting one of them stood up and said: "Your majesty, when you sit at table with your lords and vassals, in the winter when the fire burns warm and bright on the hearth and the storm is howling outside, bringing the snow and the rain, it happens of a sudden that a little bird flies into the hall. It comes in at one door and flies out through the other. For the few moments that it is inside the hall, it does not feel the cold, but as soon as it leaves your sight, it returns to the dark of winter. It seems to me that the life of man is much the same. We do not know what went before and we do not know what follows. If the new doctrine can speak to us surely of these things, it is well for us to follow it."

They found the answer they sought in the message of Jesus. Does this mean that questions about the meaning of existence ceased to be put? No. Every generation and every man must ask them. It is natural for man to question the meaning of life.

This book, therefore, begins by asking what is the meaning of the fact that we exist. This does not mean that we begin by taking up a non-Christian attitude. It simply means that we, too, as Christians, are men with enquiring minds. We must always be ready and able to explain how our faith is the answer to the question of our existence.

When man ceases to take things for granted

The growing child puts question after question. For the moment, it seems satisfied with the answers given it. But the grown man still keeps on putting questions. And then he comes to the question which is always greater than any answer which man can find of himself: Who am I? What is man? What is this creature that comes into the brightness and warmth of the human day, hurrying on his way from the mystery of his origin to the mystery of his end? What is the meaning of life? What is the point of this world? The question can be posed in various terms but it remains the same question.

We sometimes hear ourselves asking it in a quiet moment, when we cease to take our everyday life for granted. The sense of bewilderment can be very unnerving in the years between twelve and twenty as childhood patterns are broken and the young mind gradually awakens to responsibility, or whenever one first has real sight of oneself and the world as something strange, marvellous and terrifying. Age does not silence the question, but merely poses it in new ways.

The young father whose children are asleep upstairs while he relaxes in the company of his wife after the strain of the day, puts the question differently from the man who is hated and abandoned by his children and whose life is humanly speaking a failure. The undergraduate at an evening's discussion sees the question-mark from a different angle than the workman waiting for his bus in the cold morning air. The woman suffering in hospital puts the question differently from the woman sunning herself on the beach. The religious-minded man puts it differently from the man whose tastes are more "worldly". The unbeliever puts it differently from the believer, and the man who tries to follow his conscience differently from one who does not. The question sounded differently in the nineteenth century. But in the twentieth, it is still the same enigma which man is always asked to solve, not a game which one can stand aside from, but the question of each man's happiness and of his aim in life. And whether life itself has a goal.

Or is the question academic? Something to occupy a leisure hour, more a reverie than a serious challenge? A man fully occupied with work and family will surely have something better to think about?

What we do contains both question and answer

But in fact, all our work and all our family affairs, all that we do be it pleasant or tiresome, expresses the same question. It is so vast and deep that we also put it with our heart and hands. It is not just something to which we give occasional thought. Everything we do is a tender, strong and urgent request put to existence. We want it to be kind to us, to be meaningful for us, in a word, to reveal its purpose.

But the question we put in these various ways also contains an answer. An answer takes shape in our hands and in our love. Work accomplished, good health and happy children are already a fulfilment of our demand that life should have meaning. Happiness is of itself meaningful.

THE GRANDEUR AND MISERY OF MAN

Let us pause here a moment to consider briefly our life on this earth. We shall try to sum it up by naming four essential elements of our existence: (1) We live together with others; (2) On this earth; (3) Ourselves part of this world; (4) But endowed with a certain freedom and spiritual quality. These are also the main elements of which our happiness is composed.

Life in common

We do not live isolated from one another. Our life is lived in common and this is one of the most inescapable elements of our existence. Man cannot exist without his fellows. He could not speak or think or love otherwise. He could not even survive his birth. We need each other and we love each other. The child's mother is not there simply to look after him. In the long run, child-care could perhaps be mechanized. But the child needs his mother as a human being. Society is a tissue of personal relationships expressed through mutual confidence and love. Within this love all people are included and without it society degenerates. Life in common is one of the great answers to the quest for meaning and happiness. Love and solidarity mean fulfilment. A long day behind a counter may only make sense for somebody if he can go home in the evening to his wife and children and so be together with those who matter to him above all others.

In the world

Such is our existence—along with others. But it is also along with the things of this world. From our very first cry we make contact—touching, grasping, feeding, playing. We work at things and build, we calculate, ponder and admire. Man fills his life with efforts to change the world, whether he is washing the dishes or building rockets. But it is not a meaningless pastime. It is a joyful task. A man provides a house for his family, and his wife provides him with a home. They work together to construct an environment in which a child can feel secure. They provide a world of love for their children.

What we do as a family we also work for as a nation and indeed on a universal scale, striving always to make the world human and livable, to master it by our work. In doing so, we not only develop the material world but our own selves. We grow and become men through our work.

As part of the world

The third element of our existence is that we ourselves form part of the material world. We seem to be made of the same material as the earth and plants and animals around us. The fibres of our being are so much part of the universe that we cannot think or make a decision without the processes at work in our braincells, without the matter of this world. This is not a humiliation. It is the way we are and it is our glory.

Growing freedom

The fourth main element is that man is also more than his body. Through their senses animals take stock of their surroundings but they do not "come to themselves" and hence do not question their existence. Their reactions are determined by stimuli and reflexes and so are not free. We, too, live by sense-impressions but we have a certain clearness of mind that can consciously survey and consider everything, even our own thought. This is the irreducible mystery of our personal consciousness. And here lies our responsibility. We are not simply at the mercy of stimuli and reflexes like the animals. We also have a certain freedom. This is also part of the fulfilment of existence, that we are a thinking, conscious, responsive part of the world, that in growing freedom we can choose the good.

Misery

This picture of existence is not yet complete. For all the elements of our happiness and glory are permeated by our misery.

Take our life in common. We can sour each other's life as well as sweeten it. We can be sadly disappointed when we trust each other and it need not be the other man's fault. And how much spontaneity is quenched by the simple fact that we live together! A docker once wrote to a friend of his, a priest celebrating his jubilee: "Most people are born originals, but they end as copies."

The loving attraction between the sexes can become a passion which turns into hateful cruelty, even between man and wife. Just because they are so close to each other, they can misunderstand, disappoint and hurt each other. So, for the same reason, can parents and children. Many a young family seemed to be a sound answer to life – but did not remain so.

It is the same with the joy of work in the world. It helps man to develop, but it also limits him. Work can be hard, monotonous and depressing. The body of man, the radiance of the whole personality, can be degraded so that lust replaces joy. There is fatigue and sickness. And if we suffer pain or see it, how can we speak of the glory of the body?

Even consciousness and freedom, man's crown that places him above the animals, are weak and obscured and limited. What do we really know? How free are we really under our impulses? And sadder still, we can knowingly and willingly do what our true knowledge and real will forbid. There is sloth, malice, selfishness and guilt. No matter how often life says "Yes" to our request for happiness, the answer also contains a constant "Not yet" and "No". That is why our longings are endless.

The flight of time

There is an unrest that is still deeper. It is there even when life says "Yes", when work humanizes man and the world, when love is full and true. That which is truly good demands to remain so. But nothing lasts in this world. At the very moment that something unique and enchanting has come about, man knows that it must pass away. An Old Testament writer felt 55 this sharply in the midst of his joy, and expressed it thus:

7

"For everything there is a season, and a time for every
matter under heaven:
a time to be born, and a time to die;
a time to plant, and a time to pluck up what is planted;
a time to kill, and a time to heal;
a time to break down, and a time to build up;
a time to weep, and a time to laugh;
a time to mourn, and a time to dance;
a time to cast away stones, and a time to gather stones
together;
a time to embrace, and a time to refrain from embrac-
ing;
a time to seek, and a time to lose;
a time to keep, and a time to cast away;
a time to rend, and a time to sew;
a time to keep silence, and a time to speak,
a time to love, and a time to hate;
a time for war, and a time for peace" (Eccles. 3:1–8).

It is true that the fruits of our work remain. Man can leave
behind him immortal works of art. Our knowledge and our
love live on in our children and grandchildren, in the race of
man as it proceeds on its way. But can all this assure the dying
man that his life had a purpose? His consciousness, his "selfhood", vanishes from the earth. Can the uncertain twilight of
his end make complete sense of his earlier struggles, of the good
that he did and the injustice that he suffered? If the unique "I"
with its unbounded hopes is blotted out completely in death,
how can the purpose of its existence be completely fulfilled in it?

Believers in Old Testament times tried hard to be clear on
the point. They hardly envisaged a hereafter. Earthly existence
had to be given a meaning. They tried to see it in happiness and
the blessing of children. But this was not entirely satisfactory, as
Ecclesiastes testifies:

"For the fate of the sons of men and the fate of beasts is the
same; as one dies, so dies the other. They all have the same
breath, and man has no advantage over the beasts; for all is
vanity. All go to one place; all are from the dust, and all turn
to dust again. Who knows whether the spirit of man goes
upward and the spirit of the beast goes down to the earth?"
(Eccles. 3:19–21).

THE EVOLUTION OF THE WORLD

Let us proceed with our search. Sometimes the meaning of a phenomenon is revealed when we examine its beginnings. "How did it start?" is a question which may cast light on its significance and purpose.

My beginnings

How did our life begin? Where does it come from? From our parents, of course. Every year there are new discoveries about the processes of fertilization and heredity. But we are still not able to predict with certainty that a birth will take place, or whether it will be a boy or a girl. Still less can we foretell what type of person it will be. We can imagine that there will be progress in this direction, but the birth of a new person, a new centre of thought and love, will always remain something that neither parents nor scientists can fully explain. There is something unique and unaccountable about each man, and it cannot be deduced from a microscopic examination of tissues or glands. With the coming of each new person, there is a consciousness, an "I" that was never there before. And its origin is shrouded in mystery. There is no clear answer here.

Our origin

But if the birth of the individual throws no light on our problem, what of the origin of mankind? Let us look at our past.

We know our parents, our grandparents – but then only a few names and events in a past growing ever dimmer. For most people, the beginning of the nineteenth century is as far back as they can trace their families, though there are a few "old" families whose names find some echoes in the Middle Ages.

The history of the nations can be carried back for five thousand years only in some parts of the world. Older than this there are a few cave-paintings, a few small fertility-symbols, the remains of camp-fires buried deep in the earth. And then there is nothing more than a handful bones from the skeletons of our ancestors.

Evolution

Is there no answer here? There is undoubtedly something. The skulls and bones that have been found tell us something that we had not known, that the further back we delve into the past, the more primitive is the type of man we find. Before *homo sapiens*, present-day man, science distinguishes Neanderthal man, his forehead and chin receding somewhat. Earlier still, over two hundred thousand years ago, there were the various forms of hominids, with strongly receding facial angles, but walking upright. They had crude stone tools and they hunted, though exactly how, we do not know. Three hundred thousand years earlier, half a million years ago, a still more primitive type can be vaguely discerned, the Australopithecos, an ape-like being, but more human than present-day apes. Nearly everything is uncertain—the dates, the families, the links between the various phases. One thing only stands out clearer and clearer, the marvellous fact that a species of animal living in plains and forests mounts a long, slow line of evolution to reach—us.

The life in my body comes from the beasts. This is something that many people once found shocking. Not perhaps because they thought it undignified, because Scripture had allotted man a still lower origin, the clay. The real cause of offence was rather the contrast with the Bible story. Up to very recently, the Bible was regarded too much as a sort of scientific manual, and not enough as story written to throw God's light on the existing world. The difficulty was solved by a better understanding of the Bible. And richer and richer finds showed still more clearly the great drama of the spine that slowly straightened up, and the skull that took on a greater volume, as the beast developed into man.

All this seems to point to some sort of answer. Life has a direction and some sort of meaning. But the answer is not a clear one. The origin of man lies outside our grasp. When did man begin? Was the Australopithecos already one of us? Or the other hominids? No doubt mankind had a beginning. The transition is hard to trace externally, but man is such a new type of existence that somewhere or other a living being must have 382 been called "who" and not "it". But when and where is completely lost in the mists of prehistory.

The evolution of the universe

Science tells us that the history of man is preceded by a very much longer ascent, the coming of life. Its origin takes us back to incalculably remote ages, when somewhere on this cooled-off globe of stone, air and water the carbon compounds appeared which now form the cells of all living matter. Ancient as life may be, it is still very young compared with the inanimate matter before it, whose origins are lost in the endless ages during which the galaxies have been expanding in a universe of which the limits are still undiscovered. Where did matter come from? Or did it not come from anywhere?

What does it mean that all this exists and grows? In the growth of life hazard and selection play a large role. But do they explain it? Is it an accident that things strive upwards through such new and wonderful phases—existence, life, feeling, thought? What has been going on? Can we see any meaning in it?

It is also true that life never flourishes without pain for men and beasts, fear, mutilation and decay. The back grows straighter and the forehead fuller, but it is still the backbone of a skeleton, and the sockets lose their eyes. Why has my life begun? Is it just a brief period of light between two unknowns? The past has nothing clear to say. Can we learn anything from the future?

The future of man

It seems as though the ascending line of history will go on. We teach our children more than our forefathers knew or needed to know. Most of the great epidemics have been banished from the earth. Many seemingly incurable diseases have yielded to medicine. We till the earth, so to speak, with less sweat and toil. There is more leisure, more travel, more means of communication. We are reaching out into space.

And we are less barbarous than of old. Taking revenge on evil-doers and enemies, the rack, blindings and public executions are gone or decried. We have even more pity for the beasts than formerly. This progress is nourished by a constant hope. Every child that is born is haloed by happier expectations. Wars end with new children playing on the ruins. When we survey our planet it sometimes seems that we are taking a firmer grip of the world.

But after centuries of progress we have seen mass-murders in the most civilized regions of the earth, the like of which had been unknown to history. Men found means of combatting illness, but they also invented new ways of killing. Rockets are sent into space, but there are other rockets capable of destroying all life on earth. The future is uncertain.

My future too. Shall I be a good man or an evil one? And what currents will sweep my children along? Then there is death that casts a shadow on every yearning. Men may have a happier future, and build a strong city of freedom and brotherhood, but it will still have a gate opening on the dark, through which men will go all the more sadly, the happier the city, the better mankind. And even if science finds ways of prolonging life, anything can happen on this earth. Life is uncertain. So is happiness, and the meaning of life.

Are we then to believe that human history, past, present and future, the whole evolution of the universe, with its pain and anxiety, its loves and its joys, and its final end, is a meaningless jest? Is it an aimless trajectory, coming from nowhere, going nowhere, as the universe perhaps contracts and expands indefinitely? There is nothing in the world that can answer us.

THE IMMENSE LONGING

Is there anything that can be my all?

But if this is existence why do we not grow used to it? Why do we go through life with a question that goes further than any answer we find? Why are our hopes pitched so high that every answer seems too mean?

Our heart remains set on total security, a love that lasts, an unclouded happiness. This longing has never been fulfilled, but it stays with us whatever we may do, and sets the tone for every day of our lives.

This is true down to the most ordinary details. Any minute of any day is built on unfulfilled longings. A woman is working in the house. She says to herself: I'll have a tea-break at half-past ten. The time comes, and she sits down and relaxes. And then she thinks: It would be nice if so and so dropped in. Or she says to herself: I'd like to do the ironing, but the clothes aren't quite dry. And then she thinks: It would be nice if the sun came out, everything would dry faster. Or she remembers a television programme which she is looking forward to in the evening. Or she worries about some minor illness of a child. There is always something else she wants.

But is there never a moment when I am fully content? It seems at times that I am, when I have obtained something that I longed for very dearly and then at last can enjoy it. Suppose I am parched with thirst on a long hot day. My mouth grows drier and drier. There is nothing I want more than water. Water is "my all". And then I find it and drink and drink. It seems that I am totally satisfied, completely happy. And then at once I notice other things that are wrong. I have a blister on my hand. I need something again. Nothing can satisfy me totally.

But perhaps some person can be all things to me? Man and wife can be all in all to each other, and ask nothing more than the precious love that they possess and from which they live. Is that the final goal, the fulfilment of our desires?

May there not be moments when we feel something of what the woman said in one of Claudel's plays: "I am the promise that can never be kept, and that is just my charm"? There can be paralysing and even shattering disappointments—on both sides.

But there is something still more marvellous than the tragedy of dissatisfaction. It is the experience of the joy of mutual fulfilment which in spite of this, or rather through this, opens up wider perspectives. This happens for instance when we are filled with a great joy. It seems that it has overtones—the conviction that this is not just an accident. Must not something so splendid be in the safe keeping of something that is perfectly secure, good and eternal? Two young people ask themselves: "How did we come to know one another? By sheer chance? Whom do we thank for the fact that our first unforgettable romance grew into love? We thought that we gave each other our love. But sometimes we find ourselves thinking that we were given to one another, that it was not an accident, that it had to be so. Why? And through whom?"

At such moments it seems as though something in us answered "Yes" when we asked the meaning of life. "Yes, there is a meaning. Our longings are meant to be fulfilled. We are safe and sure, founded on something that is greater and dearer than anything on earth." It is the thought that beyond the limits we know, there is something boundless for our hearts. Men have said so in a thousand ways, like the poets who wrote of the deep truth and the insuperable distance of communication in love— "to see each other and not to be each other" (M. Vasalis), or like the husband who wrote of his dead wife: "In any case, marriage did one thing for me. I can no longer believe that religion comes from our subconscious wishful thinking and is only a sublimation of sex. In our years together, H. and I enjoyed love as a festival, in all possible ways, solemnly and happily, romantically and realistically, sometimes as dramatic as a storm, sometimes as comfortable as a pair of slippers. We were contented fully, in heart and head and life. If God was only a substitute for love, we should have lost all interest in him. Why should we have cared for a substitute when we had the thing itself? But it was not that way. We both knew that we needed something besides the other, something totally different. You might as well say that if two people are in love they have no need of reading, eating—or breathing" (C. S. Lewis). The deeper promise in the world of love and beauty can be heard in Belloc's poem:

> Mortality is but the stuff you wear
> To show the better on the imperfect sight.
> Your home is surely with the changeless light
> Of which you are the daughter and the heir.
>
> For as you pass, the natural life of things
> Proclaims the Resurrection; as you pass
> Remembered summer shines along the grass
> And somewhat in me of the immortal sings.
>
> You were not made for memory, you are not
> Youth's accident I think but heavenly more;
> Moulding to meaning slips my pen's poor blot
> And opening wide that long forbidden door
>
> Where stands the Mother of God, your exemplar.
> How beautiful, how beautiful you are!

In our happiness as in our pain we have a hint of something beyond our finite bounds. We should not let the deep simplicity of this hope be argued away by superficial explanations that do not reach the level of this essential question itself. We must not say that we have to be content with our beautiful, touching, human, finite life, because it is simply not true that we are. All that we do is impelled by a desire within which there is a surmise that something infinitely secure and good and beautiful buoys us up.

THE DESIRE OF OUR CONSCIENCE

We spoke of our longing for happiness. But there is also our desire to be good. We know that we may not snatch at happiness at any price. If we did, it would not be even happiness. We wish to live *well*. A man may be in love with a woman, but if it would mean misery for her husband and her children, it cannot be. Men put "goodness" above happiness, if they try really to be happy. We have a conscience.

All men, believers and unbelievers, know the voice of conscience. Efforts have often been made to reduce it to "more intelligible" realities and so explain it. A natural inhibition has been suggested. Just as the instinct of self-preservation (fear of death) keeps men within the bounds where life is possible, so too, in its way, does conscience. It has also been explained in terms of self-respect, fear of public opinion, inherited custom, education and environment. No doubt all these elements play a part. They explain the applications of conscience—why the boundary between good and evil is placed differently by various peoples or various men. There are, after all, great differences in human judgments of what conscience allows or forbids. But we all agree in placing the difference between good and bad on a deeper level than between useful and useless, pleasant or painful.

Even when no one sees the bad I do, even when no one is directly harmed by it, my conscience warns, accuses and troubles me, but above all, encourages me and guides me to what is good and right. Others can help me to discover *what* exactly is the good thing to do and what is not. But in my responsibility, my sense of being ashamed, my remorse, my desire to be good, in a word, in the certainty *that* I ought to do the right thing—or ought to have done it—I stand alone. Remorse I experience alone. No one is close enough to me to help. I hear another voice. My self-respect? No, it is not myself that I see as judge. I experience something greater. Is it that I unconsciously feel the eyes of all men upon me? No, it seems to me that I stand alone with my guilt.

The verdict of conscience is accompanied by profound feelings. Sometimes there is fear and anxiety—fear of missing one's truest goal in life. But above all, conscience is the source of profound joy—the joy of being at one with one's true destiny, one's final, perfect goal.

Has my life, then, a goal and a meaning? Our desire for goodness tells us that finite and weak though we be, we are shaped and destined for an absolute goodness.

THE CALL FOR THE INFINITE

Seen by reason

Our partial goodness calls for the existence of the perfect good. Our feeble strength calls for the omnipotent. Our humanness calls for the divine. My finite being stands out—indeed, can only be known as finite—against the infinite which is revealed in my desires and thoughts. If the world and our life is not to be meaningless, a mere jest, we must confess that the Infinite is present. Hence St Paul could say: "Ever since the creation of the world God's invisible nature has been perceived in the things that have been made" (Rom. 1:20).

A whole life's look

But the Apostle makes it clear that reason speaks out of the fulness of life. He is especially insistent on sin as an impediment to reason. But he does not mean that it is always personal sin that prevents men's minds from accepting something that intervenes so clearly and powerfully. Environment, education and psychological structure often make it nearly impossible to accept the stringent force of all that points to the Infinite. Experience shows that in general, men must first be familiar with God through faith before they can accept the rational evidence. Hence the believer cannot pride himself on knowing what gives sense to human life. He has not learned it through his cleverness or talents. He has received it as a gift.

Scholars can expand the insight of the ordinary heart into a scientific proof, though not after the manner of the natural sciences, since it is not a truth of science. Even history cannot be given in scientific formulae, since it takes in the whole of life. Still less can the most profound questions of existence be comprised within fixed formulae. They are too great for that, too closely linked with all that man is. Nonetheless, systematic reflection on this profound level is "scientific", and philosophy can use the light of reason to show that in every assertion about life we refer to the Infinite, as *the* truth, *the* reality, *the* goodness and *the* joy.

THE CHALLENGE TO REASONING

Not finite—finished

But no matter how clearly life and thought lead us to surmise an infinite Origin (and no matter how vaguely), and no matter how effectively a profound philosophy can show that in all our thought and language there is a resonance of the Infinite, as its deepest background, there is a fierce challenge to all our peaceful reflection. The challenge is the misery of the world. How can we harmonize all the sickness, disappointments and cruelty of this world with an infinitely good origin? We are not merely finite—which is a quality which does in fact call for the presence of the Infinite—we are also finished, failures. Our whole existence is marred by guilt and death.

How can this be? How is it to be explained? The perfect being that we have discovered through reflection gives no answer to absurdity, pain and death. How are we to imagine an Infinite who preserves in being all that is good and beautiful, and at the same time all that is hateful and repugnant?

> "The night racks my bones,
> and the pain that gnaws me takes no rest.
> With violence it seizes my garment;
> it binds me about like the collar of my tunic.
> God has cast me into the mire,
> and I have become like dust and ashes.
>
> I cry to thee and thou dost not answer me;
> I stand, and thou dost not heed me.
> Thou hast turned cruel to me,
> with the might of thy hand thou dost persecute me.

Thou liftest me up on the wind, thou makest me ride
  on it,
and thou tossest me about in the roar of the storm.

Yea, I know that thou wilt bring me to death,
and to the house appointed for all living.
Yet does not one in a heap of ruins stretch out his hand,
and in his disaster cry for help?
Did I not weep for him whose day was hard?
Was not my soul grieved for the poor?

But when I looked for good, evil came;
and when I waited for light, darkness came.
My heart is turmoil, and is never still;
days of affliction come to meet me.
I go about blackened, but not by the sun;
I stand up in the assembly, and cry for help.
I am a brother of jackals,
and a companion of ostriches.
My skin turns black and falls from me,
and my bones burn with heat." (Job 30:17–30)

And death is the end.

"But the mountain falls and crumbles away,
and the rock is removed from its place;
the waters wear away the stones;
the torrents wash away the soil of the earth;
so thou destroyest the hope of man.
Thou prevailest for ever against him, and he passes;
thou changest his countenance, and sendest him away."
  (Job 14:18–20)

Encounter with the Absolute?

Does it not seem absurd? An immeasurable longing, which is
always brought up short by the wall of death and guilt?

"Surely I am too stupid to be a man.
I have not the understanding of a man.
I have not learned wisdom,
nor have I knowledge of the Holy One.

Who has ascended to heaven and come down?
Who has gathered the wind in his fists?
Who has wrapped up the waters in a garment?
Who has established all the ends of the earth?
What is his name, and what is his son's name?
Surely you know!" (Prov. 30:2–4)

You know it all so easily, as the seeker who simply does not see says to the pious. You find you can pass at once from creation to a supreme being. Very well, granted that it is unthinkable that the world could exist without an infinite, perfect, first cause, how do you explain so much suffering and misery?

Perhaps the Infinite will speak. Perhaps the Absolute will join us, explain himself, defend himself—against Job, against us. Perhaps he will show us the meaning of our grand and painful existence!

"THE MESSAGE WE HAVE HEARD FROM HIM"

The word of God

The word has gone out in the world that in Jesus of Nazareth the Infinite has revealed himself.

> "That which was from the beginning, which we have heard, which we have seen with our eyes, which we have looked upon and touched with our hands, concerning the word of life—the life was made manifest, and we saw it, and testify to it, and proclaim to you the eternal life which was with the Father and was made manifest to us—that which we have seen and heard we proclaim also to you, so that you may have fellowship with us; and our fellowship is with the Father and with his Son Jesus Christ. And we are writing this that our joy may be complete.
> This is the message we have heard from him and proclaim to you, that God is light and in him is no darkness at all." (1 Jn 1:1–5)

Jesus is the answer, more marvellous than man could have dreamt of. The Son of God himself is submerged in our misery.

God himself suffers with us in the greatest act of love. God has so loved the world.

This is not an answer that makes the ultimate why and wherefore clear. The mystery of existence is not solved. But faith in Christ indicates the direction in which truth is to be found. God does not simply cast a cold eye on evil and pass by. Evil is not from him. He fights against it. He feels its weight. In one of the most cruel deaths human ingenuity has devised he shows himself to us as saviour. We see a stake and a crossbeam and in the man stretched out upon it God himself appears to us. The cross, like a man with outstretched arms, is the sign-post that points to the unfathomable mystery of God. It points in the gloom to the heart of the mystery. Through the cross God has opened his heart to reveal his deepest mystery—God at one with the victim.

492–498 Further on in the book there will be more about the existence of evil and our inclination to use our own ideas too readily to draw a picture of divine omnipotence. Very often, we think we know exactly what God "could have" done or prevented. And in this way we turn him into a powerful ruler who is content to leave us in our misery. But God's omnipotence is more profound, more profoundly different and indescribable than we can comprehend. We must deepen our conviction that we only really know and meet him in Jesus. In every question about God, we must ask ourselves what has been revealed in Jesus. His life shows us now how God, in his true omnipotence, fights with sin and suffering, in a different way, more mysterious, fiercer, more involved and more triumphantly than our ideas of omnipotence could have imagined. His is the final victory over our guilt and our mortality. Why it was accomplished precisely in this way we do not know. What we do know is that it is a mystery of light and goodness. Faith in Jesus Christ means that we see, to some extent, with the eyes of God.

"You have made us for yourself"

The objection is sometimes made that faith is something we have thought out to soothe the anxieties of existence; that it is only a search for some sort of reassurance in face of the difficul-
36 ties of life; that it is simply a "projection" of our desires into
38 an image outside us.

But the fact that men seek security, and that given the appa-

rent meaninglessness of life, anxiety plays a part in this search,
is of itself no argument against the existence of God who can
shelter and protect us. And still less does it prove that anxiety
is the sole and the deepest motive. When a child looks for his
mother in a crowd, he does so perhaps because he is afraid.
He cannot do without her. But does this mean that he looks
for her only because he is afraid? Can it not also be because
he loves her? This also seems to be true of man's desire of God,
because it persists even when he has found joy.   14

But there is something more to be noted about "projecting".
Much has been learned in recent years about how greatly
man's idea of God is influenced by his psychology, culture and
environment. But this does not make us any clearer about
whether God exists or not. Granted that we do "project",
that is, give our thoughts and desires an independent existence
outside us, the question still remains as to whether man is not
"more" than himself. (Our faith tells us that he is. The Christian
vision has always recognized the more than human orientation
of humanity. "You have made us for yourself, O Lord, and
our heart can never rest until it rests in you" [St Augustine,
Confessions].)

No doubt the existence of our projections tells us something
about our search for the Infinite. They may help us to see how
often we are merely pretending to seek God, along illusory
paths. Scripture often speaks of such ways, as for instance
Jeremiah 7 and John 16:1–3. We often attribute to God, more
or less culpably, what are to some extent our own ambiguous
fantasies. And then when we discover how much of our picture
of God is drawn according to our own wrong ideas, how often
we have seen him where he is not to be found, we may feel
that we stand there empty-handed. The divinity that we thought
to see has vanished from our horizon, and we are left with a void
in which we ask with anguish: does God exist?

But when we shed our illusions, our false gods, we are not
left with nothing. What remains is the truth that survives the
test of the experience of human realities, the truth that is not
a flight from reality but the way to the fullest development   270-286
of man. We recognize this truth in the man Jesus of Nazareth.
Jesus, the Son of Man, is most truly and fully man, and as such
is the way by which the living God comes to us. "No one has
ever seen God. The only Son, who is in the bosom of the Father,
he has made him known" (Jn 1:18).

Thus we have followed once more the path sketched in the preceding pages, which takes us from the distant unknown to the revelation of him who is with us now. This is what Jesus meant when he said: "The kingdom of God is at hand; repent, and believe in the gospel" (Mk 1:15). As we call out to God in our darkness, Jesus our brother stands among us and says: "Come and see" (Jn 1:39). The whole aim of this book is to be an answer to this invitation.

Because the manifestation of God's glory took place in human history, the order followed by the book will be that of history, the history within which our own lives are set.

PART TWO

THE WAY TO CHRIST

A. THE WAY OF THE NATIONS

PRIMITIVE RELIGIONS

From the very beginning of known history the human family has been divided and dispersed among countless peoples and tribes, each group a stranger to the other.

On an earth still uncultivated, in the forests and on the tundras, human speech began to be heard—not just the instinctive cries of animals excited or in pain, but sounds which were formed as distinctive signs of realities: what we call words. Man considered the world, and gave the parts of it their names, not just to satisfy himself, but to share things with others. It is not good for man to be alone.

The first common thought and language were naturally concerned with the most obvious things, the objects of sense-perception: other men, animals, the parts of the body, natural objects, atmospheric phenomena. All that was perceived was considered as one great whole, so much so that it was only with difficulty that thought took the form of reasoning and precise distinctions. Nonetheless, in managing his tools and his life man already showed powers of practical and logical thought. And it also seems that men everywhere sought for the causes behind the phenomena, and reflected on the origins of things and of man.

This search went on everywhere and in countless ways. Between fears and hopes, between joys and sorrows, and—being men—between good and evil as well as they could apply the notions, men found themselves on an endless quest, which they pursued not just with their minds, but with their whole being. The creature began to respond to the work of his creator. "He made . . . every nation of men to live on all the face of the earth, . . . that they should seek God, in the hope that they might feel after him and find him" (Acts 17:26–7).

In and behind things men saw forces, which could be personified as spirits and gods. Men tried to influence the higher world, sometimes by magical rites, but also by prayer and sacrifice. Death was hardly considered an event which formed part of the natural course of things. It was therefore believed that the whole man was not affected by it. Part of the personality survived. This conviction, in many different forms, was general. The belief that one of the gods was the highest is not always present, but can be traced even in the most primitive cultures. There is no stage of culture and no part of the earth in which it does not occur.

The form that man's "groping" took was greatly influenced by his manner of life. Where men relied so much on nature that they subsisted by hunting and gathering wild produce, the animal world played a great part. Higher beings were sometimes thought of as lords of the beasts or in the form of animals, and so on. The thought of one supreme God, especially as the provider of food, was often present.

In more developed stages of culture, where the ground was tilled, natural objects like the sun, moon and storms were often personified as important divine figures. Fertility rites and human as well as animal sacrifice appear. Sometimes there is one supreme God. In the religion of the pastoral cultures, however, great stress is laid on one supreme Sky-God.

THE GREAT CULTURES OF THE PAST

It is only comparatively recently, some five thousand years ago, that men produced the civilizations in which a State united on an ideological basis a great number of men. These civilizations are characterized by a division of labour, so that not all were wholly occupied with food production. Centres of government, worship and culture grew up, the first large cities. Language was given visible expression through the development of written forms of communication.

This took place in the Near East, in Mesopotamia, where the Sumerian civilization existed about 3000 B.C. There were great centres of civilization on the Nile about 2800, on the Indus about 2500, in China about 1500 B.C. Then civilizations appeared in Mexico about 1000 and in Peru about 800 B.C.

It is generally assumed that there was some connection between the origins of these primary major civilizations. Their finest achievements in architecture, sculpture and song went to enhance their religious ceremonies.

The great civilizations are characterized in general by polytheism. This may have arisen in various ways, as for instance, by giving independent existence to attributes or local forms of the highest god, by worship of his heavenly progeny or by adding the gods of conquered peoples to one's own. A king of the gods was generally acknowledged as the most high among them. In Genesis 14, Melchizedek is "priest of the 286 Most High".

Sometimes there were noble philosophies to crown the human religions, as for instance among the Greeks.

Thus the groping quest went on. Though mixed with sin, such as despotism and licentiousness, and with error, such as fatalism, these religions were the way in which millions of men experienced the mystery of God in their lives. Deep human wisdom was sought after painfully, with great concentration and self-sacrifice. And we may be sure that our Lord Jesus Christ, the eternal Word, was at work in the wisdom of these religions, through his Holy Spirit: not manifestly, as God 33 revealed him among the Jews, but no doubt really and profoundly.

There are three major religions which exist today along with Judaism and the Christian revelation, and which evoke admiration. They are Hinduism, Buddhism and Islam. Something must also be said of Chinese "universism".

HINDUISM

Hinduism or Brahmanism (the two terms are used in the same sense here) is the religion which developed in India after the coming of the Aryans (about 1500 B.C.), using elements provided by the conquerors and the conquered. It did not present itself as a revealed religion. It grew up gradually out of human experience, as an endless search for the depths of the self, a continuous meditation, anxious to lose nothing of the richness of experience.

"Hinduism", as Gandhi said, "is a tireless quest for truth.

It is the religion of the truth. The truth is God. We have known denial of God, but never of truth." The openness, flexibility and tolerance of Hinduism is endless. There is room in it for primitive polytheism and for the most refined philosophy. Hence it cannot be said that any particular god is the God of this religion.

All earthly reality, life, joy, personality and love, is regarded as illusion and the source of suffering. These may be escaped through detachment and recollection (in the *Advaita-Vedanta*) or by certain practices of recollection (in *Samkhya* and *Yoga*). Emancipation is the escape of the "I" *(Atma)* into the "All" *(Brahma)*. In other words, it is the truth (of which one does not become conscious, strictly speaking, since consciousness is here absorbed), that *Atma* is the same as *Brahma*. Freed from consciousness, feeling, love and personality, in perfect unity with the "All", one escapes from the vicissitudes of existence.

Those who do not ascend so high must be re-born after death, according to the law of their *Karma* (the actions of their lives) on a higher or a lower plane, either as beasts or a higher type of man. The doctrine implies that man can take the wrong way, but not that this is ingratitude or an offence against love. Hence 449-450 the notion of sin does not really exist except in the sense of an act with strictly automatic consequences. The doctrine of the transmigration of souls entailed a strict division of society into castes (1. priests or Brahmans; 2. warriors; 3. merchants and farmers; 4. menial workers—and lower still and without caste, the pariahs). The concentration on the spiritual and the inner life is impressive.

271 In the chapter on redemption, more will be said about 283-284 Hinduism, and about a feature of it through which it surpasses its own principles. It should be obvious that such a great and ancient religion cannot be described as briefly as has been done here. (How inadequate would be the picture of Christianity if it were attempted in so short a space!) However, some of the main features of Hinduism have been indicated.

BUDDHISM

Only a small group of privileged persons can follow out fully the strict way of life of Brahmanism. This left the masses dissatisfied, especially the lower castes. A more acceptable way

28

was pointed out by a man born about 560 B.C., Siddharta Gautama, called the Buddha, that is, the enlightened one. Deliverance does not come by the uttermost self-renunciation, but by equilibrium, the equilibrium between the full life and self-denial. This brings serenity and peace, here and now. Doctrines which Buddhism shares with Hinduism are the transmigration of souls and absorption into *Nirvana* (the cessation of individual existence). But Buddhism is extremely practical: "Follow the way, and do not ask what may yet exist after what exists. Do it, by your own strength alone." Buddhism is self-liberation from one's own actions, from *Karma*. Its purpose is to escape from pain. Life itself is pain. It is related that the Buddha was brought up in palaces and gardens from which all sight of suffering was banished. But then he suddenly thought of pain, old age and death. Pain, he said, comes from the desire of sense-perception and life. Man must strive to rid himself of such desires and so to escape from the flux of painful, changing and insubstantial things of which the world, including man himself, is composed. This is the way to *Nirvana* where there is no pain. The eight "ways" that lead to *Nirvana* show how noble the doctrine of Buddhism can be. The first is the way of pure knowledge, that is, insight into the vision of things described above. The second is that of correct behaviour, benevolence and unselfishness and the wish to harm no one. The "ways" go on thus to develop a pure and lofty morality. The self-liberation by one's own strength is sought along sober, practical ways based on experience, in contrast to the more ritualist and liturgical tendencies of Hinduism. Nothing is said of God. Buddhism refuses to say yes or no on this point.

Here too sin and love are not really components of existence. Man's actions, *Karma*, must be directed in practice, so to speak, to the good. Repentance as we understand it, i.e. the realization of having offended against love, plays here a less significant role. Benevolence is a way to tranquillity. It does not mean being moved by the misery of others, going out of oneself towards God and one's fellows—not what Christians mean by love. 271 449–450

Nonetheless, there was a development in Buddhism which went beyond its basic inspiration and which resembles the doctrine of charity. It is found in *Mahayana* Buddhism (the "Great Vehicle"). More will be said of this in the chapter on redemption. The *Mahayana* spread chiefly to Tibet, China and Japan. An older and classical form of Buddhism (*Hinayana*, the 284–285

"Small Vehicle") spread over south-east Asia. In India itself, however, since the seventh century, Buddhism has been gradually disappearing, so that Hinduism remains the most widespread religion there. But in recent years the way of the Buddha has been gaining much ground among the pariahs.

CHINESE UNIVERSISM

Something should be said about the attitudes to life which developed in the vast regions of ancient China. Some of these attitudes were rather polytheistic, in others a more philosophical trend dominated. A general feature of Chinese thought is that it is a doctrine concerned with the structure and harmony of the universe, from which the general description "Chinese universism" is derived.

The fundamental notion is that the primal unity is composed of two forces: *Yang* (bright, warm, active, productive, male) and *Yin* (receptive, calm, cold, dark, female). They need each other. Everything comes from the harmony and tension between them. The sky came from *Yang* and the earth from *Yin*, and then all other beings from both together. The seasons, for instance, come as *Yang* (summer) and *Yin* (winter), so that first one and then the other is dominant. In cycles of a hundred and twenty-nine thousand six hundred years, the primal unity passes through creation and back to unity, beginning again perpetually at the end of each cycle. The power which directs all this is called *Tao* (the way). It is already present in the primal unity and brings about the harmony of creation. The quest for *Tao* is the quest for the true way of life.

Confucius (Kung-Futse), born 551 B.C., drew on ancient traditions and his own reflections to teach such a way of life. The main points are reverence for ancestors, self-control, humaneness and kindness. It is a very practical doctrine, aimed at action. There is another form of the Chinese religion which is more contemplative, aiming rather at ridding oneself of desire and finding repose by uniting oneself with the deepest grounds of being. This is *Taoism*, which goes back to the profound thinker, Lao-Tse, perhaps a contemporary of Confucius. It is not certain that these two doctrines still form part of the vital interests of men today. Outside China they have little impact.

In their country of origin they are undergoing the harsh test of Marxism, with what success we do not know.

ISLAM

But the powers of expansion of Islam cannot be doubted. Along with Hinduism and Buddhism it is the greatest of non-Christian religions. It arose about A.D. 600 among Arabian tribes who 217 had been hitherto polytheist. They might perhaps have accepted the Christian faith which existed on the frontiers of their territories. But at this time Mahomet appeared, from the Arabian city of Mecca. He appealed to visions which he had received from God (Allah) in a near-by cave. He was convinced by his visions that he was the "Seal of the Prophets", he who was to complete definitively all the revelations of God from Abraham on, up to and including Jesus. The heart of his doctrine is God's absolute oneness, unity and power. The book in which he recorded his revelations is called the *Koran*, which is regarded as having been literally dictated by God.

The religious obligations of Islam are: (1) to acknowledge Allah by a confession of faith; (2) to pray five times a day in the direction of Mecca; (3) to give certain contributions to the poor; (4) to fast during the month of Ramadan from sunrise to sunset; (5) to make the pilgrimage to Mecca at least once in a lifetime. On Fridays there is an assembly in the mosque, if there are at least forty worshippers. Music and images are forbidden in divine service. The duty of the holy war is not incumbent on the individual Muslim, but on the community when it is ready for it. At present the war is regarded above all as a spiritual combat. Polygamy is permitted. Those who die in the holy war go straight into paradise. Other good men reach it at the end of the world. The wicked are punished in hell. Many Muslims think that the end of the world will be heralded by the coming of Jesus. The most impressive element in this religion is the deep reverence for God's absolute power. Doctrines and duties are clear and simple, and hence missionary work and instruction can be brief. The passage from Islam to Christianity remains rare. More will also be said about Islam 271–272 in the chapter on redemption.   285, 286

HUMANISM AND MARXISM

There remain two great currents of thought among modern men, humanism and Marxism, which claim the allegiance of some of own countrymen, neighbours and friends. Neither of the two is a religion, though both undoubtedly comprise an attitude towards the Absolute. The starting-point of humanism is that either the Absolute does not exist or that it does not make itself known clearly enough for us to base our lives on it. Humanists think that man himself is sufficient reason for a life of goodness. A Humanist Society has been formed to vindicate the value of this attitude. Many Christian elements are implicitly present in the humanist ethic and approach to life.

264–274
285–286

Up to the present, at any rate, it has been asserted very clearly in the Marxist creed that God does not exist. Belief in God is said to be harmful to man. Belief in the Absolute is a "projection" whereby a man puts part of himself outside himself, and thus loses part of himself ("alienation"). "Religion is the sigh of creation in torment, the soul of a heartless world, a mentality formed on mindless objects. It is the opium of the people" (Marx).

274–277
285–286

This doctrine took shape at a time when in fact a faith not fully grasped was hindering men from working for a juster distribution of food, clothing and shelter. It is a permanent reminder that Christians must examine their conscience on the way they are putting their religion into practice. Having originated in a Jewish-Christian world, Marxism took over certain elements from it, in spite of its absolute rejection of it. One instance is its expectation of a bright future, and of the "little man" as the bearer of salvation. For many, such elements in Marxism may point the way to a renewed Christianity. In this sense perhaps Marxism may be considered not merely as a post-Christian development, but as a pre-Christian one. The faith which inspires this book tells us that Christ is always the fulfilment of God's plan for mankind. Hence we may still see in post-Christian religions and ideologies such as Islam, humanism and Marxism, an unconscious longing and a roundabout search for the true image of Christ which we Christians so often obscure.

THE SPIRIT OF GOD IN THE WHOLE WORLD

It is not for us to pass precise judgments on the elements of sin or Satanic evil which may also be found in these forms of thought. Hinduism and Buddhism set men's minds on *Nirvana*. Islam imprisons men in a doctrine which does not call God father. Humanism teaches children not to turn to God. Marxism holds out a future that will never come. There is some wickedness and corruption in all this. But we must trust in the Spirit of God, who leaves no man untouched, and concentrate on the truth and goodness which they offer to men. And then they can also be helpful to us. The gleam of truth in another way of life can help Christians to gain a deeper and more vital conviction of Jesus' truth. As St Thomas Aquinas said in the thirteenth century, repeating the words of St Ambrose in the fourth, "all truth, no matter by whom it is uttered, comes from the Holy Spirit". Humanity's groping quest for God is animated by God's quest for man. 286

In Israel and on behalf of all mankind, our creator linked himself with our human destiny to prepare the way for his greatest glory which is that: "God so loved the world that he gave his only Son." This process was a very gradual one and did not proceed without reference to human development and circumstances. On the contrary, the people among whom he revealed himself shared the vicissitudes and mentality of the other peoples of the ancient East. But precisely here something strange and original stands out, which is an enigma to unbelievers but to believers a sign that in this people the creator sought out man in a unique way. "Attaching himself freely and almost imperceptibly to mankind on its pilgrimage, the divine travelling companion enters the conversation as he finds it. He intervenes to give it a new direction. Then there is a new beginning whose effects are gradually but inexorably felt" (Renckens). 489–492

B. THE WAY OF ISRAEL

Somewhere between the Nile and the Euphrates there lived a group of nomad tribes who had fled from cultured Egypt, a land where they could neither live as a group or practise their religion. After a dramatic escape, they had reached Kades in the desert. The name of their God was Yahweh. Reduced to bare subsistence level, in the void between two worlds, they were spiritually virgin soil. As they struggled between the urge to go on and the temptation to return to the "flesh-pots" of Egypt, God sought them out, to make them "his own possession among all peoples" (Exod. 19:5). The story of this revelation is to be read in the books which form the Old Testament.

The pages that follow present some general guidelines as a help to the reading of the Old Testament itself. The order followed is: (1) that God's revelation came to Israel through events, (2) through words about these events, and (3) through the fact that these words were committed to writing.

GOD'S WONDERFUL WORKS

Phase 1: The Hebrew shepherds, c. 1800–1200 B.C.

The events themselves are a silent revelation of God. Hebrew shepherds fly from Egypt. And in an ordinary human situation, the struggle for existence, for food, clothing and shelter; in forms already partly in existence; and perhaps even with a divine name already known, the truly divine breaks through. A charismatic figure, Moses, plays a special role in these events. Of the four hundred years before this, we know nothing, except that the Hebrew people were held captive in Egypt. But

34

before 1700 B.C. there were people of the same stock in Canaan, the land between the Jordan and the Mediterranean, whom the Hebrew recognized as their ancestors. Among their number were the "patriarchs" Abraham, Isaac and Jacob, the last also known as Israel. Through these men God first entered our history. Though at this distance there is very little we can say about what exactly took place, it is remarkable how closely customs and names which occur in the stories of the patriarchs agree with what modern research has deciphered in the cuneiform writings of the period.

Phase 2: The settlement, 1200–1000 B.C.

After Moses' time, the nomadic Hebrew tribes entered the more fertile land of Canaan. War ensued between the invaders and the city-dwellers of the land. The number killed was considerably smaller than we read in the Bible. In the end, the land was occupied. Some names have been preserved from these centuries: Joshua and then the "judges", such as Samson, Gideon and Jephthah. It was a savage period, as the Bible shows clearly enough. The tribes spread out over the land, 61–62 Judah to the south of Jerusalem, as also the tribe of Simeon, which disappeared in time, the other tribes to the north. Jerusalem itself remained unconquered, forming a wedge between the two groups. The only bond between the tribes was the common worship of Yahweh.

Something remarkable happened when the tribes entered the country. Comparative religion tells us that normally when a nomadic, pastoral people settles down to agriculture and cattle-raising, as Israel did, there is a marked change in its religion. The one god of the tribe is absorbed eventually into the local pantheon of nature and fertility gods. But this did not happen in Israel's case. It was undoubtedly tempted to adopt the local fertility cults of the Baals and Astartes who were the gods of the fields in their new home. But the people as a whole did not yield to the temptation. Though now cultivating fertile ground they remained true to the revelation of the desert. And what they had learned about Yahweh stood them in good stead. He brought them strength, unity and peace.

Phase 3: The ancient oriental kingdom, c. 1000–587 B.C.

The same phenomenon may be observed in the next phase of the people's development. About 1000 B.C., Israel's existence as a settled people reached a highpoint, when it became a kingdom. King David conquered Jerusalem. King Solomon built a temple there. According to the ordinary laws of comparative religion, a State religion should have developed, in which the godhead was the personification of the power of the State. The god should have been a sort of celestial reflection ("projection") of the State, doing and saying what the State wanted, like Marduk, the god of Babylon, who was the heavenly reflection of Babylon's ambitions. But when Israel became a monarchy Yahweh became the God of king and nation. Life and religion were at one. This was the warm, tranquil midday of Yahwism, with no clashes between society and religion, between prosperity and worship. But this was not because Yahweh was shaped by the State. Contrary to what happened among the neighbouring peoples, the State was made by Yahweh. No doubt there was the temptation to make him the slave of the State. But he was a living God. Through the prophets who appeared throughout the whole of the monarchy period, he made his revelation clearer and clearer.

The more the monarchy declined, after Solomon, into the despotism typical of neighbouring nations, the more clear-cut became the task of these prophets. They ensured that a kernel of true worshippers of Yahweh, a "Remnant," was preserved. As a consequence State and religion ceased to be identified.

The exile, 587–39 B.C.

The exile was the salvation of Israel's message. For the State disappeared, as the prophets had predicted. The kingdom, split in two after Solomon, was a little buffer-state which was crushed between the great powers of Mesopotamia and Egypt. In 721 B.C. the northern kingdom ("Israel", with Samaria as its capital) went into exile in Assyria, and in 587 the people of the southern kingdom ("Judah", with Jerusalem as capital) were transported to Babylon.

Once again, if at this point religious history had taken its normal course, allegiance to Yahweh would have ceased with the break-up of the State. But in the new "desert" of the exile

Yahweh was experienced anew by his people. There, among foreigners, the Hebrews saw more clearly that he was the creator of heaven and earth. Through the words of the prophets, he led a remnant back to their homeland when Babylon fell to the Persians in 539 B.C.

Judaism, from c. 500 B.C. on

The majority of those who returned were the former inhabitants of Judah. This is why the next five centuries are called the period of Judaism. Jerusalem was re-built. But little of political importance could be accomplished. In the second century B.C., the Jews rebelled under the leadership of the Maccabees against their Greek overlords who had succeeded the Persians in 332 B.C. Then in 63 B.C. they came finally under Roman occupation. But the strength of the people did not lie in political independence. Jerusalem became the centre for a people that was spread over the whole of the ancient world but did not lose its identity. The Jewish communities living outside Palestine are termed the diaspora ("dispersion"). Among the Jews of these centuries there were many men of deep and simple faith who recognized their own insufficiency and put all their hopes in the coming of God. These are termed "the poor of Yahweh". Jesus, the hope of all mankind, was to come from a group of such people who lived near Jerusalem.

74, 84–85
88, 99
351, 415

Such is in outline the story of the Old Testament, the people of the ancient covenant. They progressed from a nomadic pastoral way of life to a settled agricultural one, formed themselves into a nation and became ultimately a scattered spiritual community. These are processes such as any emerging nation could undergo. But it was through the history of the Jewish people that God chose to reveal himself and his fidelity. (On God's faithfulness to Israel after the coming of Jesus of Nazareth, see the chapter on the early Church.)

204–205

THE WORD OF GOD

The word of revelation

So far we have confined ourselves as far as possible to the historical events as such. We shall now consider *the word* which was at work in Israel from the start. The liturgical feasts included music and dancing and recitation, with songs, prayers and above all stories. Here the meaning of the events began to be manifest. It was only through the word that reality could become truly real. The work of Yahweh could only be seen when a man of great faith pointed it out in the events.

The actual form of this spoken word has mostly vanished in the mists of the past. But there is one clearer period that throws light on the task of the word throughout the whole of Israel's history. This is the period of the prophets. They spoke to the people in the name of Yahweh. Enlightened by faith, they dedicated themselves to God's plan. But Israel did not accept uncritically everyone who claimed to speak in the name of Yahweh. There were also false prophets. The true prophets established their credentials by the very message which they gave. It was at one with pure faith in Yahweh, with the liberating experience of God's true nature. The message was formulated in increasingly spiritual terms as age succeeded age. It refused to accommodate itself to a comfortable, lukewarm religion, or to the wishful thinking of king and people. It often took the form of hard sayings which forced men to take sides. The pure of heart found a new joy as they recognized the authentic call to the true Israel.

Covenant

Is it possible to sum up in one word the revelation which was given to Israel? Perhaps the term "covenant" will do. Covenant implies fellowship and friendship. But between whom? Here it means between all members of the people and also between the people and God. The two things cannot be separated. The people were staunchly united among themselves through being united to Yahweh. By preserving unity among themselves they remained united to Yahweh. The word of revelation was always concerned with this covenant. It was the revelation that the deepest reality of history and of each individual life is God's

281
376–379

offer of friendship and faithfulness, friendship and loyalty to 472
one another.

This brought with it at once the revelation of another reality, 277
a revelation reserved for Israel and Christianity, that of sin. 449, 462
This means ultimately that wrong-doing is not merely an
inevitable imperfection, or the domination of an evil, external
power, but personal infidelity to personal friendship. Evil is
always something personal. Human history is revealed to
Israel as the history of a love, and hence something to be taken
seriously.

The word in the history of Israel   45–47

It is difficult to trace the exact form in which the word of 34–35
revelation was spoken to the patriarchs. We can divine something
of it from such ancient names of God as "the Mighty One of
Jacob" (Gen. 49:24). The name indicates a bond between God
and Jacob. The covenant began in a way with Abraham, Isaac
and Jacob. Combined though it was to some extent with a
primitive image of God and the world, it was still something
unique, which came into the world once and for all. Abraham's
manner of life and thought was no doubt very different from
ours. But he experienced what we experience with God,
friendship with the same God. Hence this half-barbarian
nomad is rightly called the father of our faith (cf. Rom. 4:11).

From the time of the exodus from Egypt, when the tribal 34–35
covenant begins to stand out clearly, we have such ancient
words as the "ten commandments". The first three of these
speak of the bond with Yahweh, the other seven of the bond
between one man and another. Here we see once more how
closely connected are human fellowship and fellowship with
Yahweh.

In the time of the Judges, songs, stories and treaties mould and
remould the covenant, which is still in a primitive form.

Under the reign of David, when the covenant was acclaimed
as the natural heritage of Israel, the word also took on the form
of liturgical chants: the psalms. But the warnings of the prophets 38
also began to make themselves heard, growing more urgent, as
we saw, as the period of the monarchy went on. They signalled
the grim counterpart to the covenant, infidelity to Yahweh,
harshness towards the neighbour. When the prophets speak of

Yahweh's love and anger and of his determination never to abandon the covenant he has forged with his people, they use the tragic image of the beloved wife who abandons her husband who, in his turn, is unable to forget her.

During the miseries of the exile, God's inexhaustible fidelity stands out very strongly, with its message of courage and consolation. A very pure notion of the covenant was reached at this time, as Israel, deprived of land and temple, had to preserve its contact with God in spite of the seductive and impressive religions encountered in Babylon.

36–37 This attitude was maintained during the restoration and the dispersion after the exile. To be loyal to Yahweh was to create history and to grow towards a great future. This faith was expressed in many forms.

51 *The story of the first men*

261–263 In the years before and after the exile, words were uttered which
425 threw divine light not merely on the meaning of Israel's history but also on that of all mankind. The stories of our origins, which are now found at the beginning of the Bible (Gen. 1–11, about Adam and Eve, Cain, Noah, Babel), were then given form. We shall explain elsewhere how these chapters do not ultimately intend to relate actual historical facts. They express in their own way the conviction that what took place between God and Israel also takes place between God and mankind: a covenant established by God, but thwarted by our sin. This is the profound message of these imperishable stories. They concern us all.

Unique phenomena in Israel

Messianism

The revelation of God's loyalty led in Israel to a phenomenon unique in the world: men expected something from God. All men, of course, long for a redemption, and all religions are religions of redemption. But only in Israel was there the conviction that this redemption is deliverance from our human faithlessness and hence from sin.

Israel, too, was alone in the conviction that redemption was being accomplished in history. The world had a destiny. From the time of David onwards this destiny took on a very definite form. God was to remain true to the house of David, according to the pronouncements of the prophets. The future held a predestined figure who would emerge from David's line and bring deliverance in the name of Yahweh. Israel waited for someone from Yahweh: the Messiah.

Sense of history

83

Knowledge of the living God also gave Israel a feeling for 51, 212–213 history. Here too Israel stands alone in the ancient East. This tiny people, with a culture inferior to that of its mighty neighbours, produced historical writing which was completely unique. Other peoples, no doubt, had their stories and annals. But Israel alone had a sense of the deeper background of the facts and their inter-connection. Israel's interest came from the conviction that the living God was at work in history.

Monotheism

Hope in the promises and a sense of history are connected with another feature of Israel's religion: the adoration of the one and only God.

No doubt there were forms of monotheism elsewhere, as in the sun-worship of the Pharaoh Echnaton, and in religions where one of the gods was supreme. But such forms never showed the consistency, concentration and force which the revelation of the true God had in Israel. Monotheism in Israel was not above all a matter of counting. It was something more comprehensive and vital: the truth that God was unique, incomparably active in the work of salvation. There is nothing 270–286 in the least like this in any of the religions which then existed.

The experience of the closeness of God

God present in his word

The word was the means whereby God's work was made clear to Israel. But thus the word itself was something more than a word. It was itself a manifestation of Yahweh, a work wrought by him. Through it the creator of the universe appeared to lowly man.

> "Surely the people is grass . . .
> but the word of our God will stand for ever" (Is. 40:7–8).

These are the words of "Deutero-Isaiah" at the end of the exile. And again we read:

"For as the rain and the snow come down from heaven,
and return not thither but water the earth,
making it bring forth and sprout,
giving seed to the sower and bread to the eater,
so shall my word be that goes forth from my mouth;
it shall not return to me empty,
but it shall accomplish that which I purpose,
and prosper in the thing for which I sent it"
(Is. 55:10–11).

The Law

371-375 God is near in his word and also through a certain form of his word, the law, the explicit conscience of the people. In the law the people encountered God. "That will be your wisdom and your understanding in the sight of the peoples, who, when they hear all these statutes, will say, 'Surely this great nation is a wise and understanding people'. For what great nation is there that has a god so near to it as the Lord our God is to us, whenever we call upon him? And what great nation is there that has statutes and ordinances so righteous?" (Deut. 4:6–8).

The commandments of the law are "not in heaven, that you should say, 'Who will go up for us to heaven, and bring it to us . . .?' But the word is very near you; it is in your mouth and in your heart" (Deut. 30:12–14).

Wisdom

There is also a third term to describe how close God was to Israel: "Wisdom". The word occurs chiefly in the later books of the Old Testament, when God's presence is contemplated.

"All wisdom comes from the Lord
and is with him for ever.
The sand of the sea, the drops of rain,
and the days of eternity—who can count them?
The height of heaven, the breadth of the earth,
the abyss, and wisdom—who can search them out?
Wisdom was created before all things,
and prudent understanding from eternity.
The source of wisdom is God's word in the highest
heaven,
and her ways are the eternal commandments"
(Ecclus. 1:1–5).

There are a few points we could usefully think about here. Our starting-point will be the modern world.

One may well be filled with profound admiration when one considers the discoveries man has made and the way in which he has systematized them so as to bring them within his service. We are amazed at what the human mind is capable of discerning. Indeed its ability is amazing but in fact our scientists are only observing patterns, structures and properties that already existed, that formed a part of the nature of things as originally conceived by a pre-existing wisdom.

Amazing things have come to light about the migration of birds. And then we think of how great is the wisdom of the creator who caused all the refined instincts to develop in the migrant birds.

We all know some people for whom we at once developed a warm affection. They know how to make us feel at ease. They are never at a loss for a warm and cheering word. But what of the wisdom that thought of such a heart, and of the other heart so readily open to it? Preceding all that exists is a subtle, acute and commanding wisdom which brings about structure, life, insight and wisdom in the world. This wisdom is of God. Israel sometimes speaks of it as a created reality, at other times as an aspect of God himself. It is God in so far as he turns to the world and mingles with us men. Gratitude and admiration sometimes went so far that this wisdom was spoken of as a person. This does not mean that it was thought of as a person. It was poetic imagery, such as we find in the following, where wisdom is made to speak:

> "When there were no depths I was brought forth . . .
> When he established the heavens, I was there . . .
> When he marked out the foundations of the earth,
> then I was beside him like a master workman . . .
> rejoicing in his inhabited world . . ." (Prov. 8:24–31).

And we read in the Book of Wisdom:

> "In her there is a spirit that is intelligent, holy,
> unique, manifold, subtle,
> mobile, clear, unpolluted,
> distinct, invulnerable, loving the good, keen,
> irresistible, beneficent, humane,

> steadfast, sure, free from anxiety,
> all-powerful, overseeing all,
> and penetrating through all spirits
> that are intelligent and pure and most subtle . . .
> For she is a breath of the power of God,
> and a pure emanation of the glory of the Almighty;
> therefore nothing defiled gains entrance into her.
> For she is a reflection of eternal light,
> a spotless mirror of the working of God,
> and an image of his goodness" (Wis. 7:22–23, 25–26).

A modern scientist once remarked that in the constant change and flux of matter, the only permanent and inflexible factor seemed to be the laws of nature. We may use this to illustrate how God's wisdom was displayed and revealed to Israel. The Book of Wisdom goes on to say: "Though she is but one, she can do all things, and while remaining in herself, she renews all things" (7:27).

The supreme manifestation of this wisdom is in man. It does not appear only in his intelligence. It is in his whole life, in his goodness and holiness. The text continues:

> "In every generation she passes into holy souls
> and makes them friends of God and prophets" (7:27).

There is nothing greater on earth:

> "I loved her and sought her from my youth,
> and I desired to take her for my bride" (8:2).

"Word", "Law", "Wisdom"—these are all ways of saying that the living God concerned himself closely with Israel, and with the world. We have considered the term "wisdom" at some length. This is because little is said of it in our ordinary teaching. But chiefly because Wisdom and Word were revealed in the New Testament as a person. And in the epistles of St Paul, Christ is spoken of in terms which are used of Wisdom in the Old Testament: "He reflects the glory of God" (Heb. 1:3); "All things were created through him and for him. He is before all things, and in him all things hold together" (Col. 1:16–17). Thus God's activity in turning to us was to be a person: the

Word made flesh. In word, law and wisdom a first, veiled contact was made between the Son of God and humanity. They were a preparation for the incarnation of the Word, for the visible manifestation of Wisdom. It is well to return at times to these "cosmic" statements of the Old Testament, so that we can remind ourselves how thoroughly the whole of reality is penetrated by Christ's work for us.

77-78

499-500

HOLY SCRIPTURE

Much of the word of God which was spoken in Israel is heard no more. But some of it, and indeed the kernel, was crystallized in writing. God's word was noted down, and we have this holy thing within our grasp. The revelation given by God in the desert is now to be found on our bookshelves. It is the word of God which has been handed down to us.

When did the writing take place? From about the time of David on (*c.* 1000 B.C.), and all through the history of Israel. The Old Testament is a collection of books spread over a thousand years. And very often the individual books were not the product of a single effort. Some of them only took shape gradually. The book of Exodus is a typical example. It is interspersed with laws from before David's time as well as with others which date from after the exile. It is a code that grew along with the people. The Book of Psalms is another book that took centuries to develop fully. Between the oldest and the latest psalms there is an interval of eight hundred years. The Old Testament reflects the whole of the long existence of a people.

The origin of the Bible

39-40
53-57

Investigation of the language and style has enabled us to establish with ever increasing precision the various phases of the development of Scripture. As many readers will be interested in these findings there follows a brief survey of them, with apologies to those who find that it interrupts the message of the chapter.

The first phase is that of the writers known as the Yahwist and the Elohist (J and E) from the period of the early monarchy (*c.* 1000–750 B.C.) These produced some contemporary historical narratives, such as 2 Samuel 9 to 1 Kings 2, "the succession to the throne", one of the earliest large literary fragments, and a masterpiece at that. These circles also committed to writing a number of oral traditions which had been formed in ancient times. These include such very ancient items as the Ten Commandments, Psalm 29 and the Song of Deborah in Judges 5. The story of paradise and the fall, Genesis 2 and 3, is also an example of ancient narrative matter which was written down in Jahwist and Elohist circles. We may say in general that the basic elements of the Pentateuch (the first five books of the Old Testament) took shape in this period.

The second phase in the constitution of Scripture is connected with the prophetic movement and may be dated to *c*. 750–500. The prophetical books were composed for the most part in this period, as were also Joshua, Judges, 1 and 2 Samuel, 1 and 2 Kings. In addition, the literature mentioned earlier was collected and worked over afresh. The most striking example is the rewriting of the Law in prophetic language, the "Second Law" or Deuteronomy. Hence the literature of this period is said to belong to the Deuteronomic school (D).

Finally, there is the religious literature from the time after the exile. This was mostly a product of priestly circles, whence the name "priestly writings" (P). The writing of the national history was continued (1 and 2 Chronicles, Ezra and Nehemiah). This school also gave final form to some other books that had already existed for a long time. (The story of creation in Genesis 1 is from this period.) Many laws, psalms and proverbs were written down at this time.

About 200, the Greek edition of the Scriptures took shape within the authentic Jewish community of faith. This version was called the Septuagint, and was the Bible the Apostles normally used.

To characterize briefly the styles of the various schools one might perhaps say that J and E are fresh and original, D full of ardour and P clear. The life of a whole people was thus embodied in the Scriptures.

60   We must not imagine that the writers were conscious of the fact that they were producing "Holy Scripture": the divine inspiration of the books will be discussed later.

210–211   We must now say something about the various phases in which the Scriptures came to be recognized as canonical (official) sacred writings. We know that when the Samaritans broke away, about 450 B.C., they took with them the Pentateuch ("the Law"). From this we may deduce that only the Pentateuch was then regarded as canonical.

It is practically certain that the prophetical books, and the historical books from Joshua to Kings inclusively, were also recognized as canonical about 300 B.C. The Jews called these "the Prophets". For the other books, which they called "the Writings" the boundaries of the canon were not so clear. The Greek translation of the Bible included some books which are not in the Hebrew Bible. These are Tobit, Judith, parts of Esther, 1 and 2 Maccabees, Wisdom, Ecclesiasticus, Baruch and parts of Daniel.

Till about A.D. 200, these books were accepted without question by the Church. But in discussions with the Jews, who by A.D. 100 had fallen back on the "Hebrew" canon, there seemed to be no point in citing books they did not have in their Bible. This made them the subject of controversy. But Catholic tradition has retained them as part of the Bible, while the Calvinist reform excludes them and Lutherans puts them at the end for edifying reading. The question is not so important as it may appear. The fact that these books, which are, incidentally, often very beautiful, are part of Scripture does not mean that they are as important as the rest. And they add no new message.

In the spelling of biblical names there has been a difference between Catholics and Protestants. Catholics followed the Septuagint, and hence used the forms as given in Greek transcription about 200 B.C. The Reformers chose to follow the pronunciation as it was fixed by the Jews in the early Middle Ages, when the vowel signs were added to the text. (Hebrew has no real vowel signs.) This Catechism uses a spelling agreed upon by Catholics and Protestants.

The literary genre and the literal sense 146

After noting these historical facts—which are not necessary for an understanding of Scripture—we may now discuss more closely a point which is of more immediate importance for a proper understanding of the Bible: the fact that a number of different "literary genres" occur in the Old Testament. Let us try to see what this means.

A "literary genre" is a "way of using language", a style. A

47

law or a specification is written in a different form of language from poetry. The former are concerned with describing something very exactly, the latter aims at evoking something. A novel is a different genre from an official record. The novel is a story that tries to be true to life, to show what "man" is, but does not imply that the events really happened. An official record is concerned with giving an exact summary of the facts, with no interest in making "human beings" appear true to life.

We ourselves use various genres when we write or speak, often without noticing it. The witness of an accident in which a child is killed will tell the story one way when reporting the accident to the police, and another if he has to break the news to the parents, and yet a third way when describing it to his wife. There would be three genres, in each of which the event is described differently, with some things left out and others emphasized. Different persons often produce different "literary genres". One man tells a story as precisely and baldly as a police report, the other tries to capture something of real life, perhaps by exaggerating certain things. If we do not know the speakers, we might make mistakes. We might think that the first man was not interested in what he had to say, or that the second was telling lies. In fact, each is using a different genre.

Whatever we read or hear should be judged according to the genre used in each case. Otherwise misunderstandings must arise. The genre may vary from family to family, from group to group and from region to region. We all know how some words can vary their meaning according to the part of the country in which they are used. But only if one knows all these words and understands the significance of all regional variations of speech can potential misunderstanding be avoided.

The literary genre can also vary from period to period. A short word used now may mean as much as a whole sentence that thirty years ago was needed to express the same thing. If one is not "with it", one mistakes the real meaning.

Many mistakes have in fact occurred in the interpretation of the Old Testament. If within the area of one small country or within the short space of thirty years misunderstandings can arise, we must allow for many possibilities of wrong interpretations between Old Testament times and today. The Old Testament was written in a land very different from anything we know, and between two and three thousand years ago.

Particularly as regards the writing of history misunderstandings have arisen; many of them are still with us. We are inclined to approach the Bible stories with the habits of mind of the present day, taking them as more or less literal reports. But this is by no means always the genre used in the Bible. The account of creation, for instance, with its six days, is in poetic form. What it wishes to convey is that all things come from the hand of God. The form used is that of noble poetic imagery, not that of reporting. As early as the thirteenth century St Thomas Aquinas, for instance, pointed this out.

It is only recently that it has been recognized that the story of Adam and Eve was not to be taken as a piece of reporting. It deals, as we have seen, with man. This much was also known long ago. But for lack of other sources, it was thought that the names and details were also historical; so too Genesis 2–11. 40
261–263
425–426

The story from Genesis 12 onwards deals with a historical process. But it does so in the way in which the Hebrews wrote history. What was important to Israel was that the basic traits of the great events should be brought out. We have already seen what they are: God's creative covenant, human infidelity, divine restoration. This Israel experienced in history. The events, like all great human events, went hand in hand with great inward experiences. These too formed part of the facts. An event is like an iceberg in the ocean, one tenth above water, nine tenths below the surface. The inward experience is the major part of the event. A group of harried nomads escapes its oppressors through a dried-up waterway, a branch of the Red Sea. It was an overwhelming experience, which a whole people never tired of telling. But the psychology of the inward experience they could not describe, as the modern novelist can. This literary genre did not exist.

But then how could the nine tenths of the iceberg, the conviction of Yahweh's aid, be properly rendered? The great experience was put into words through a great story. This was their literary genre. The external facts were exaggerated in order to do justice to the grandeur of the experience. In this way, imperishably beautiful stories were told, which by their very hyperbole evoke the historical events better than mere documentation could have done.

In Exodus 17:8–13, for instance, we have a description of the battle which the people had to fight against the Amalekites. Moses stood on the mountain with outstretched arms. When he let his arms fall, Israel was driven back. When he raised them,

Israel had the advantage. Towards evening he was so tired that two men had to support his arms. This is a striking way of telling what happened, namely that the leader appointed by Yahweh brought them victoriously through the battle. The whole inward and outward experience is compressed into the picture of a man with outstretched arms.

But the Old Testament is full of such magnificent imagery. We have seen that the books were worked over for centuries in the course of their production. Hence it sometimes happened that two renderings of the one event were juxtaposed. We read for instance in the account of the passage through the Red Sea that an east wind blew and dried it up (Exod. 14:21). God intervened through a well-known natural event. But later psalmists and story-tellers found another means of expressing the same experience: the waters stood like a wall on the right hand and the left. This also found its rightful place in the narrative, immediately after the first statement (Exod. 14:22). The re-telling of the story in greater dimensions turned it into an image of all salvation.

We may perhaps be astonished at the liberties that were taken in such narratives. But that was their literary genre, though it is not ours. This freedom was connected with a deep sense of the unity of history. Men were profoundly convinced that the same God who was at work in their own day was also at work in the past. Hence they could incorporate into the ancient stories conditions under which they themselves were living. For instance, the apostasy in the desert is described as "dancing round the golden calf". This was in fact what the writer under the monarchy saw precisely as apostasy: the worship offered to the divinity in Israel, under the form of calves. There was no better way of making this clear to his readers. In doing so, he created a symbol of apostasy valid for all times.

We may say in general that it was Israel's literary genre, as we have seen, to be ready to turn internal events into external happenings. There is an excellent example in the story of the call of the young Samuel. A young man is not sure that he has been called. He thinks over his vocation. At one moment it seems clear. And then again it is not. He lies awake at night examining his conscience. He consults others. A modern writer could describe the whole inward process. But Israel made it into the sublimely simple story which we read in 1 Samuel 3.

If one is not alert to the special literary genre one imagines that God always spoke in actual words when one reads, "God spoke"—to Jeremiah, to Moses, to Abraham. But God need not necessarily express himself verbally. What matters is that he communicated the certainty of faith. Abraham is the father of believers.

In saying all this, we may perhaps seem to have minimized God's revelation in Israel. As regards the miracle stories, we have suggested that they often looked much more ordinary from outside. As regards God's speaking, we have said that it was mostly within the heart.

But why should this be considered minimizing? We gain a clear vision of *the* great miracle of Israel, *its whole history*, the 40–41 truth that an ordinary people with an ordinary history was in fact so fundamentally different. That was precisely God's way of leading them. The stories of miraculous rescue are the small change in which the great treasure is counted out before our eyes.

The miracle is not that God spoke to Israel in sentences, but that from this small people the divine voice rings out to all mankind. This is the significance of all the passages in which we read, "God spoke". Within Israel's events and through Israel's voice and testimony we are able to discern the presence of God. We must not be misled by nineteenth-century Bible illustrations, with their clouds and shafts of light and triangles in the sky. In Israel's eventful history and through the words she spoke as that history unfolded, God gave us his unique revelation.

In all this there is something to be carefully noted. We are 40–41, 365 talking of actual events. Israel was truly guided by happenings 207–210 and words along the path of her history. It is not a matter of myths or the vague "once upon a time" of fairy-tales. Even 328 the narratives of Genesis 1–11, which relate no particular 40 happenings, undoubtedly affirm that humanity is something active and evolving, making its own history.

At this stage the reader of the Old Testament will feel that an important question must now be answered before he can make headway with his reading. How far should any story be taken literally? There are in general three answers to this question. The first is this. In the history of the patriarchs the persons are historical and many of the features go back to patriarchal times. In the Exodus, the main line and many details of it go back to the time in which the Exodus occurred. In the subsequent history, the main movement of the story does in fact correspond to the facts.

The second answer is this. If one consults scholarly works, one can find more detailed discussion about the degree of literal accuracy to be attributed to the various narratives. But here even the most careful scholarship must admit to many uncertainties. Once we are dealing with a literary genre which is alien to us there must be some margin of doubt. Compared with fifty years ago, we may today be going too far in the opposite direction, and allowing less literalness to many stories than they really deserve. Possibly many more unusual things happened, even externally, than we often think. After all, 107 why should such extraordinary things happen at Lourdes and 475 not in ancient Israel? Possibly God did in fact make men hear the sound of words when giving revelation, so that many stories should be taken more literally.

And then there is the third answer, which gives a very essential aspect of the matter. It is not very important to know exactly 208 the degree of literal, external accuracy. We can give ourselves 328–329 over to the story as it stands. We may read it without distracting questions, confident that the authentic truth of the event, the nine tenths of the iceberg, will come through to us. To re-live the story is to re-live the history of Israel. This is why it is no great harm that the literary genre was not recognized for such a long time, and that so many stories, such as that of the fall, were taken too literally. Even then the message came through, the message of the story of creation, of paradise and the fall, of the tower of Babel. The real message remains the same whether one thinks that God spoke to Abraham in a human voice or not. Even if we take the scene extremely literally, we know that this is not ultimately the important thing, but that what counts is that God called to the heart of man.

The relevance of the literary genres of the Bible

One further question arises. We have seen how remote from our way of thinking is the literary genre of the Bible. This being so, how is modern man to be really at home with it? Can he take it seriously?

Here we see how great a blessing it was that Israel had such a deep feeling for the unity of history. When recounting the ancient events, Israel could thereby bring out the very factors which are still valid today—the broad lines which tell us the way God works. Hence the whole literary genre is such that it brings out something of universal human import in every story. It is a mirror of man, in which we too can see ourselves reflected. And hence the stories are not alien to us.

Another reason for this is that they are often so splendidly told. Thus they have also the permanent human value of great art. It is like the great statues in the Egyptian desert. The Pharaohs who appear there are not always exactly portrayed. But these ancient sculptures show us more of man—and hence of the Pharaohs—than the exact likenesses in Madame Tussaud's waxworks. So too the biblical stories can sometimes tell us more about man before God than many a present-day story of this type. Further, the biblical language and imagery are very human and universally recognizable. They cannot become outworn as long as man has a body. The Bible speaks in terms of water, rock, depths, light, hand, ear, death, life and so on—words that can be as readily understood by the man in the spacecraft as by the housewife in her kitchen.

The books of the Old Testament

The titles of the books of the Old Testament often sound strange. A list of them, together with a brief statement of their main themes, will be helpful. The order followed is the order in which we find them in the Bible. This is not a chronological 45 order and neither is it based on the dates when their canonicity 46 was recognized. On the whole, however, it is a systematic order. The question of spelling has already been mentioned. Older 47 Catholic titles are given in brackets.

The Pentateuch

The Bible begins with the book of Genesis, which means the book of origins. After the opening chapters on "primitive history", the story of the patriarchs follows.

Exodus, meaning the going forth, starts almost immediately with the call of Moses, after which come the ten plagues of Egypt, the start of the exodus itself, the story of Sinai, and a number of laws.

Leviticus is so called because of the Levites who play such a large part in the liturgical worship. Many a Bible reader's enthusiasm has been destroyed through battling with this book. Apart from some stories about Aaron and his sons, it is mostly made up of innumerable prescriptions for the liturgy. (In any case, it is not recommended that one starts with Genesis and reads on through each book in turn: one does not necessarily read through the contents of a book-shelf from left to right).

Numbers is so called because of the census of the people which the book contains. The Jews at this stage are still in the desert, and some of their adventures there are narrated, and yet more laws are enumerated.

Deuteronomy, that is, the second law, sums up once more, in ardent tones, the story of the law and the exodus. It was written under the monarchy, and the spirit of the prophets breathes through its pages. It is prophet's vision of the exodus. It ends with Moses' death. These five books (called "the Law" or the Pentateuch) were ascribed traditionally to Moses. This does not mean that he wrote them. The ascription implies that he was the great figure when the law was first codified.

The historical books

Joshua (Josue) describes episodes from the conquest of Canaan It ends with the covenant of the tribes at Schechem.

Judges deals with the period when there was no king in Israel At times of great distress a Judge, that is, a deliverer, came forward. None of the books in the Bible has preserved so faithfully the primitive and barbarous traits of the people with whom God joined hands. It was only by a gradual process that he was to transform them.

The short book of *Ruth* then follows, telling the touching story of David's great-grandmother as a young girl.

In 1 and 2 *Samuel* (1 and 2 Kings or Kingdoms) we have the story of the beginnings of the monarchy. 1 and 2 *Kings* (3 and 4 Kings or Kingdoms) give the succeeding rulers down to the exile.

1 and 2 *Chronicles* (1 and 2 Paralipomena) recount once more the history from David to the exile. This is preceded by lists of names extending from Adam to David. The style of the book is more refined, less powerful and colourful than that of Samuel

and Kings. Particular attention is paid to liturgical worship. The book comes from post-exilic priestly circles.

Ezra and *Nehemiah* (1 and 2 Esdras or Esdras and Nehemias) are relatively short. They tell how the exiles returned to the ruins of Jerusalem, and how they re-built the city and re-established the community.

Then come three stories of divine deliverance, the books of *Tobit* (Tobias), *Judith* and *Esther*.

At the end of the historical books come 1 and 2 *Maccabees*, telling of the guerilla warfare conducted by the Maccabean brothers in the second century B.C. against the Greek occupation.

Poetic and Wisdom literature

The historical books are followed by a quite different type of literature, the "poetic" and "sapiential" (Wisdom) books.

First there is a great dramatic poem about human suffering, which poses the question of God's justice, the book of *Job.* 17–18 It asks "why?", and demands that God should show himself definitively. God then reveals himself in the grandeur of nature, as one whose thoughts man cannot follow. It was as much of an answer as could be given until Jesus came. After Job, come the *Psalms*, the most widely read collection of poems in the 319 world. Just as a whole landscape can be reflected in a pool of water, so too in the Psalms one can re-discover the whole of Scripture, in the form of prayer and song. And they give us an insight *into* Old Testament man. Many of the Psalms are ascribed to David, but this is rather like ascribing the Pentateuch to Moses. David is the figure active in the early stages of this literary form, and hence psalms composed later were attributed to him. It seems certain that there are some psalms in the psalter that really are David's, but we do not precisely know which these are. They are probably to be found among the first forty—Psalm 18 (17), for instance, is possibly one of his.

Just as David is the psalmist and Moses the legislator, the wise sayings are ascribed to Solomon. Hence he is said to be the author of the next book, *Proverbs*, a set of rules for day-to-day life given in the form of short sayings. They are preceded by a hymn in which the divine origin of wisdom is acclaimed.

Ecclesiastes is also a Wisdom book, but much shorter, and in a very different mood. It shows the inadequacy of attitudes that occur elsewhere in the Old Testament. It has sometimes been described as the bankruptcy of the Old Testament. In its own peculiar way this well-written book, critical and somewhat pessimistic, is a preparation for the New Testament.

302
388 *The Song of Solomon* (Canticle of Canticles) follows. It is also known as the Song of Songs. It is a collection of beautiful lovepoetry.

The Book of Wisdom sings the praises of God's wisdom and its role in Israel's history.

Ecclesiasticus, or the Wisdom of Jesus the Son of Sirach, a collection of wisdom sayings put together about 200 B.C. by a certain Jesus ben (son of) Sirach. The Latin title means the "Church book". It is remarkable how much of its sober, practical wisdom is still relevant, though the book was composed for a very different type of society, much more patriarchal in nature.

38 The prophets

It is in these Old Testament books that emotions run highest, where the struggle for loyalty to Yahweh is vividly depicted at its most intense. Here are the words which rang out in the streets and market-places of Jerusalem and elsewhere.

The "great prophets" come first, so called because their books are the longest. *Isaiah* (Isaias) wrote a hundred and fifty years before the exile, the classical prophet of rebuke and consolation. Chapters 40 to the end, so full of hope and encouragement, are by later disciples from his school. The section 40–55 ("Deutero-Isaiah") is particularly impressive.

Jeremiah (Jeremias) may be styled "the vulnerable"—a poet with a sensitive eye for men, plants and beasts. Torn between his need of tenderness and the direness of his message, he had to live through the terrible epoch preceding and at the onset of the exile. After this book come (five) *Lamentations*, probably a liturgy to be chanted over the ruins of Jerusalem. They are not by Jeremiah himself. Then follows a prophecy ascribed to Jeremiah's disciple *Baruch*, and then a *Letter of Jeremiah*, addressed to the exiles (not by the prophet). The titles of these last three books show how warmly the memory of Jeremiah was cherished.

With *Ezekiel* (Ezechiel) we are in the period after the exile. The riches of this book are almost inexhaustible: symbolic actions, visions, similes worked out in detail. It ends with a hopeful vista of the new age and the new temple.

Daniel is quite different from the three other great prophets.

The first part contains narratives, the second visions in which the great forces of history are portrayed in mysterious dream images. Two stories follow, Susanna, and Bel and the Dragon.

Then come the twelve "minor prophets", so called because their books are much shorter. *Hosea* (Osee), the man deserted by his wife, recognizes through his own unhappy marriage the dramatic situation between Yahweh and Israel. *Joel* spoke at the time of a terrible plague of locusts. *Amos*, the countryman from the North, stern and uncompromising, is the most ancient prophet whose words have come down to us in book form. *Obadiah* (Abdias) is represented only by a single page, breathing vengeance, which must not, however, be isolated from the whole prophetic movement. *Jonah* (Jonas) is a short book which is rightly placed among the minor prophets, though very different from the rest. It is a non-historical tale, giving the message of God's mercy for all men. *Micah* (Micheas) was a contemporary of Isaiah. His prophecy contains the oracle about the Davidic dynasty from Bethlehem, from which a saviour was to come. Very short books follow, the oracles of *Nahum* against Nineveh, the oracles of *Habakkuk* (Habacuc), with the powerful canticle at the end, and the oracles of *Zephaniah* (Sophonias), about the day of Yahweh.

At the end there are three prophets from the time of the restoration after the exile. *Haggai* (Aggaeus); *Zechariah* (Zacharias) difficult but rewarding, who mentions the coming saviour who is to be meek and to come riding on an ass; and finally *Malachi* (Malachias), who speaks of the coming of God who is to sweep away what is unseemly.

No ordinary "pious book"

We have now compiled a certain amount of information about the Old Testament. It is clearly not a piece of light reading but rather a library of imposing splendour, as awesome as an Alpine landscape. The reader can easily be very bewildered by it. Possibly he expects a pious and edifying book, that is, moralizing writing which does no more than put virtuous deeds before us. But the story of the patriarchs already contains a number of crude and savage deeds, or things that we find immoral, all told quite dispassionately. The reader has then to admit that the Bible is not a "pious" book, but the echo of reality, as God joins a very primitive humanity on its march.

A refinement of morality is brought about only gradually. In the story of Abraham, we are not invited to copy all he did, but to be attentive to the basic message: how he remained true to Yahweh in everything. We must, so to speak, take the broader view when we read the Old Testament, and bear in mind that ours is not the only way of doing things.

This is not so difficult when certain things are branded as evil, like the sins of Sodom, or when they are simply narrated, like the deceit practised by the daughters of Lot. But sometimes it seems as if God approved of what was done, as in the case of Jacob's trickery, and still more in that of the extermination of the inhabitants of Canaan. Yahweh is said to have commanded it.

But these cases must also be regarded as the defects of primitives. When trying to preserve the worship of Yahweh in its purity, they knew no better than to use the methods of their times and culture. God's mentality had not yet penetrated deeply enough. That they remained true to Yahweh was already something.

How imperfect and faulty things were under the Old Testament may be seen from Jesus' comment on the fact that a man could divorce his wife without more ado. According to Jesus, this was "because of the hardness of their hearts". It was not God's real will. This is also true of the massacres in the book of Joshua (which were, in any case, much less extensive than the numbers given suggest, and also on a considerably smaller scale than the losses inflicted on many countries during modern colonization).

The growth of the moral sense

233-234

We may observe in the Old Testament a growing refinement of morals, a gradual leavening by the spirit of Yahweh. Contact with him was never fruitless. This is what makes the Old Testament so stimulating. We must always watch out for where it is going. Something is growing and developing, from below to above, always straining upwards and outwards. This was felt even then. The history of Israel is charged with the implicit hope that it is moving towards a great Day. Thus a word uttered in the name of Yahweh is also a word about the future, obscure but certain. The prophets above all, who had to speak of punishment and malediction, also spoke of this future. This is why the word "prophet", which really means "one who speaks out",

40-41

38

often came to mean in our languages "one who predicts the future". For Israel, to speak out meant to say that salvation was to come, the Day of the Yahweh. The truest salvation is that man should grow in goodness, and it is in that direction that the ascending line moves, slowly and painfully, in Israel. And hence the summit of Old Testament prophecy are the words of Jeremiah and Ezekiel:

> "Behold, the days are coming, says the Lord, when I will make a new covenant with the house of Israel and the house of Judah . . . I will put my law within them, and I write it upon their hearts" (Jer. 31:31–33). "A new heart I will give you, and a new spirit I will put within you; and I will take out of your flesh the heart of stone and give you a heart of flesh" (Ezek. 36:26).

The Spirit

There is a passionate intensity in the Old Testament, a strong, lofty and vital impulse. This is not lacking elsewhere in the noble urges of humanity. But it is close at hand in Israel, pure and strong, throughout all impurity and weakness. This breath of life is called "the Spirit". When the Spirit of Yahweh is with someone, he is carried out of himself. Initial expressions of this were primitive. When the Spirit of Yahweh came upon Samson, 194 he was given strength to fight.

The coming of God's Spirit could be manifested by phenomena indigenous to the culture of the time, such as ecstasies and dancing. But these are not essential, and they disappear as the Spirit is made manifest in higher ways. The classical prophets are no longer carried away by their transports. Ecstasy in their case means that all their forces are concentrated in a heightened freedom. This is the purer form in which inspiration increasingly 196–197 appears. It develops in the direction of the ordinary. 317–318

Israel awaited with longing the king on whom the Spirit of the Lord was to rest (Is. 11:2). Indeed, the whole people was 92 to share in the Spirit (Joel 2:28). The crowning gift of the Spirit came with Jesus, as may be seen, for instance, from the story of Pentecost.

Scripture through the Spirit

But in the Old Testament the Spirit was already at work as the vital impulse, as the force which animated everything. He was in the events. He was behind the words. And he caused them to be committed to writing. The book of the Old Testament which we take into our hands is the work of the Spirit.

This is not to be taken to mean that the Spirit dictated the books, or that he inspired the writers with ideas unconnected with the life and faith of the people. The biblical writers interpreted the faith of Israel with the resources of their own style, through their own personalities and with the limitations of view imposed by their times. The writing of the sacred books was simply a privileged element of a whole fabric of Spirit-guided events. The inspiration of the books should not be detached from the workings of the Spirit in the whole "event" which was Israel.

This might suggest that Scripture was partly man's work, and partly the work of the Spirit. But it is, in fact, all from man and all from the Spirit of God, just as music is wholly, say, from the piano, and yet wholly from the pianist. When the Spirit of God is at work, man is not, so to speak, disconnected from his real self, but most fully himself.

95, 176
205–206
327–328
485–486

The spiritual sense of Scripture

All this is also true of the writings of the New Testament. The whole Bible is given a marvellous unity by the fact that it is all animated by the one Spirit. Primitive elements which were struggling upwards in the Old Testament, appear spiritualized and pure in the New. And when we survey the whole, as we now can do after the coming of Christ, we can sense already in the old what the Spirit will do with the same reality in the new. We can feel in the old stories all the purpose and pressure of the Spirit as it moves on to the New Testament. When we read of enemies engaged in battle, we know that Christ has turned this into the battle against evil. When we read of the sacrificed lamb, we cannot but remember the pierced body of Jesus. When we see how the Israelites were rescued from the bondage of Egypt, we recognize that deliverance from sin and its enfeebling oppression lies in the same line. The old stories become symbols of the new salvation.

It is legitimate to read Scripture in this way, because the one

Spirit breathes through it all. All parts of Scripture are akin. Along with their literal meaning, the stories, seen as a whole, have a deeper, spiritual meaning. They are prefigurations of Christ and of our life in Christ. In most cases, the Old Testament writer was not conscious of this. But he undoubtedly shared the general conviction of Israel, that God was going to reveal himself in some new way. In this sense, the deeper, spiritual meaning of a book did not lie entirely outside the scope or 176 intention of the writer. We have been taught by our Lord himself, and the Apostles, to read the old stories as symbols of our life with Christ.

This ascent from the old to the new is a joyful re-discovery of Christ. With each reading we feel ourselves carried along by the great upward impulse which was at work in Israel. With each reading we turn anew to Christ, who might otherwise perhaps become too ordinary for us. This is a way in which we can experience the newness of the New Testament. Even the coarseness and cruelty of the stories take on a special significance. We can leave them behind and say with relief: happily, the Spirit intended something else in the long run. We read 327-328 of Joshua's battles, and we know that ultimately we are concerned with the battle which Jesus fought and which we must fight along with him, for love, joy and peace, the fruit of the Spirit.

Levels of life in faith 58

Does this mean that we can feel ourselves superior to the men of those days? No—because it has been granted to us as a grace, that we are perhaps in a more developed stage of civilization. And what matters for each of us is not the stage of development he is in, but with what faith, loyalty and goodness he lives on his actual level.

Each period in Israel's history had its own way of achieving the good. Let us trace this briefly.

Up to and including the time of David, it may perhaps be 34-36 said that God was experienced above all as the giver of earthly blessings—the promised land flowing with milk and honey, which could only be reached and held if the Israelites were true to Yahweh and to one another. The others, the enemies, were excluded. This attitude can be seen at its most characteristic in the Book of Judges, where much heroism is displayed along with a sturdy devotion to religion.

36-37 In the time of the prophets, the connection between the
38-39 covenant and the material welfare of the nation became looser.
Now it was more a matter of being true to Yahweh for his
own sake. And men began to feel more concern for the needs
of their fellows. To serve Yahweh meant to be kind to the
oppressed, the widow and the orphan. At the same time, they
began to take an interest in other peoples, as men who also had
a conscience. Ultimately, "well-being" was seen not as material
prosperity, but as goodness and justice.

36-37 After the exile, there were those who discovered a still closer
unity with mankind and hence with God. They felt their own
inadequacy, and hence that they were not different from the
other members of the human race. We read in the Book of
Wisdom:

> "Thou dost overlook men's sins, that they may repent,
> For thou lovest all things that exist,
> and hast loathing for none of the things which thou
> hast made,
> for thou wouldst not have made anything if thou
> hadst hated it.
> How would anything have endured if thou hadst not
> willed it?
> Or how would anything not called forth by thee have
> been preserved?
> Thou sparest all things, for they are thine, O Lord
> who lovest the living" (Wis. 11:23–26).

The sense of their own insufficiency often brought with it
an intense desire for a saviour.

Hence we may distinguish three phases. In the first (under the
Judges) the dominant interest was common loyalty and the
welfare of the nation. In the second (under the prophets), individual life and personal conscience were in the foreground.
In the third (after the exile) there was a sense of fellowship with
all men and an expectation of a deliverer whom God was to
send. At any of these stages men could serve God well.

These three steps still have a certain relevance for our Christian
world. There are periods and cultural levels and groups in which
Christianity can only be lived to a limited extent, so to speak,
in terms of wellbeing (God is good to our family, our nation).
Others pay great attention to a pure and conscientious life.

Finally there are men whose hearts are open for all human beings. Indeed, the three phases can to some extent co-exist in each man. One can lead a good life in any of the three phases, provided one is always striving—like the kernel of Israel—to grow into the next phase and burn one's boats behind one. To refuse such readiness is to wither away in a given phase.

One can discern the same stages in the general outlook of humanity as a whole. Some groups are further advanced than others. They cannot all be reduced to the same denominator. First there is an exclusive religion within a closed group; there a development of the individual conscience and regard for others; finally, there comes the recognition that one is a member of humanity sharing in a responsibility for its affairs and one looks out purposively for a saviour. These are the ascending stages through which we believe that the whole world is advancing towards Christ.

This took place in a unique way in Israel, the people among whom Christ was born, who were favoured with a clearer view 33 489–492 of the relationship between God and the world. But groping along a thousand threads, through mazes and sometimes into cul-de-sacs, but ever searching, mankind goes forward always. Wherever men are true to the good Spirit, they live in familiarity, consciously or unconsciously, with the human manifestation of God. To this we shall now turn.

PART THREE

THE SON OF MAN

The word "gospel"

From the beginning the events which now follow were comprised by the narrators under the title of "gospel". The word means "good news" (Greek: *evangelion*), "joyful proclamation" —something like the welcome letter or telegram that brings total relief to the anxious heart.

The word gospel did in fact come into use in times of great distress. It was addressed to the exiles in Babylon. They were 36 captives in a strange land. Jerusalem was far away, on the other side of the desert, a heap of ruins. But after many years the political situation took a favourable turn. The Persian Cyrus began his march of liberation through the Babylonian empire. Then a prophet (from the school of Isaiah) recognized that God was going to lead his people back to Jerusalem, through the desert. He perceived what was probably an inward voice calling out:

> "In the wilderness prepare the way of the Lord,
> make straight in the desert a highway for our God.
> Every valley shall be lifted up,
> and every mountain and hill be made low ..."
> (Is. 40:3–4).

This stirring cry, in the splendid imagery of the ancient East, depicts the majestic progress of God through the desert to Jerusalem, in the midst of his people—just as he had once led them out of Egypt.

In the vision, a herald is sent on ahead to Jerusalem. He is to stand on a hill-top in sight of the ruins.

> "Get you up to a high mountain,
> O herald of *good tidings* to Zion;
> lift up your voice with strength,
> O herald of *good tidings* to Jerusalem" (Is. 40:9).

Here is the origin of the word gospel, good tidings. It is a shout of joy ringing out over abandoned ruins:

> "Behold, the Lord God comes with might . . . .
> He will feed his flock like a shepherd,
> he will gather the lambs in his arms . . . .
> For I, the Lord your God,
> hold your right hand . . ." (Is. 40:10, 11; 41:13).

Such promises were never totally fulfilled in the Old Testament. No doubt God led Israel by the right hand through tribulations under which another people would have perished, but Israel knew that it was still to look forward to a final fulfilment, to the great manifestation of the kingship of God and all its joys. But this had not yet come, and the people were longing for a prophet, a bringer of good news, who would change their lives.

John the Baptist

All four gospels begin with a certain John who is called the Baptist. He appeared in the desert, and thus awakened memories of the times of grace—the return from Babylon, the exodus from Egypt.

John came forward in the fifteenth year of the reign of the Roman emperor Tiberius, that is, between October A.D. 27 and September A.D. 28 (or perhaps 28/29). His food and clothing were the simplest possible. This is not without significance. For it is a reminder of Elijah. The scene of his preaching was not far from the rocky shore of the Dead Sea, where, in recent years, scrolls have been found which belonged to religious communities that once lived there. It is certainly not impossible that John had contact with them.

The imminence of the Kingdom of God

John was more than a reminder of ancient times of grace and deliverance. He announced a new era of grace, the fulfilment of all that had gone before. The exodus from Egypt and Babylon were only prefigurations compared with what was to happen now. Now God really comes. John is really the voice in the desert, calling men to build straight roads for God. The way that is to be made ready is no longer a desert track which can be blown away in a year or so, but an inward way in the heart of man, and one that must be lasting. This way is called conversion.

"Repent!" was John's cry; literally, change your hearts, start to think differently, develop fresh attitudes concerning your behaviour. There are two wrong ways of understanding repentance. One is to think that purely external acts of penance are envisaged. The other is to confine it to a purely internal attitude. It really means a change so deep and inward that the whole of the external life is also changed. In Luke, John gives a number of very straightforward examples: to give away a garment, if one has several and another none, to take a stand against accepted professional abuses (Lk. 3:10–14).

John's message is joyful. It announces the time of God's grace. But it is also very serious, because men can still say "yes" or "no" to the coming grace. John is dominated by the notion that "He who comes" will be "for the fall and rising" of men. He describes his coming as the moment when the roots of the tree are laid bare and the axe is lying on them ready for the first stroke. He who comes is one with a winnowing-fan in his hand, who has a fire kindled to consume the chaff. He is one who will "baptize with the Holy Spirit and with fire" (Mt. 3:11). John, inspired by Old Testament thoughts, must have meant by fire not only a refining fire to purify the good, but also the fire of judgment for the wicked. He announced the coming of the world's judge.

To prepare men for this awesome "baptism" he administers an ablutionary baptism with water. This gives them the opportunity of showing their readiness for conversion. It is a sign of being open for what is to come, but is not entry into the Kingdom of God, like Christian baptism. "From the days of John the Baptist until now the kingdom of heaven has been coming violently, and men of violence take it by force" (Mt. 11:12). This obscure saying may also be translated "the kingdom of heaven has suffered violence", so that the "men of violence" may be the wicked who try to harm the kingdom, or the good who are strong enough to enter it. But in any case it clearly affirms that with John an event of world-shaking proportions has been set in motion. This is what distinguishes him from all Old Testament figures. His call is, "It is close at hand". In this way he is a part of the New Testament: "The law and the prophets were until John" (Lk. 16:16). He belongs to it as the man at the turning-point: a boundary-mark between two ages, the old and the new. He is a part of the way to Christ.

And this is not something which was only true once, long ago in the past. It is always true, because the repentance which he preached always remains the way into the kingdom which he announced. He is not a figure that we can forget now that Jesus, the true light, has appeared. John is always relevant because he calls for a preparation which all men need to make. Hence every year there are four weeks in the life of the Church in which it listens to the voice of the Baptist. These are the weeks of Advent.

Advent

Advent means a (solemn) coming. From the fourth Sunday before Christmas until Christmas itself, the Church recalls the approach of the Lord. A liturgical remembrance is not a mere piece of memory-work. It deals with events which are still relevant for us. To remember means in this case to re-enact. But even this is perhaps not clear enough. It could be taken in the sense of what happens when we remember the dead—we re-live in our minds what happened long ago. But liturgical celebration re-enacts the event, not just in thought, but in reality. Every event recalled by the liturgy was a meeting of God with man. But God is ready to make what was decisive in this event, its grace, take place once more among those who celebrate it. They experience the same encounter with God as did those who with receptive hearts lived through the event in the past. Indeed, they experience it better than those who were only present in the body, like someone who passed by where John was preaching, but did not pause.

Thus the celebration of Advent means that we share once more the longing for God's coming and the conversion which prepared for it. It is a way of experiencing more and more fully how God comes to us in our darkness. For this reason, many of the liturgical readings of the season are taken from the prophets, 38 those great watchmen. The liturgy draws especially on Isaiah, 56 the most monumental of the prophets, who is so rich in messianic texts. Isaiah's firm belief that God was to send his anointed and his salvation helped him to find words which can still express man's longing for God today. "Have courage, fear not, behold your God." Isaiah is one of the three great figures of the Advent liturgy. The magnificent Advent chant, *"Rorate coeli desuper"*, "Rain down, O heavens, from on high", is also taken from Isaiah.

We have already spoken of the second great figure, John the Baptist. The Christian people comes to stand in spirit on the banks of the Jordan and lives once more, with an intensity corresponding to its devotion, the time of joyful expectation, and also of earnest warning, which abides for all ages.

Finally, the liturgy also takes up the story of the immediate human preparation: how the mother of the longed-for saviour experienced the coming: in her womb and, as Scripture notes, in her faith (Lk. 1:45) and in the messianic joy of the *Magnificat*.

These three figures point onwards to the one who has not yet appeared. Their moods are different, varying from the painful nostalgia of a prophet to the happy expectancy of a young mother. So too the liturgy mingles a sense of desolation and abandonment with hopefulness and joy.

Advent means every coming of Jesus. Primarily, it means the coming of the Lord into the world, which took place once and for all. But it also means his coming into our human fellowship here and now. And this again is seen in conjunction with his great coming—his manifestation at the end of time. Advent begins in fact with this, in the readings of the first Sunday of the season.

Advent is also celebrated by some household customs, such as the Advent wreaths with their four candles, one more of which is lit every Sunday, to symbolize the approach of the Light.

THE BIRTH OF JESUS

No one noticed it, but one day, among the crowds who came to be baptized by John, the long-awaited Messiah appeared.

Who was he? Where did he come from?

He probably spoke the dialect of Galilee, since he came from this northern province, which was in fact half-pagan and held in little esteem. A little village nestling on a hill was his home town—Nazareth. "Can anything good come out of Nazareth" was the reaction of one Jew when he heard of it (Jn 1:46). His age was "about thirty" (Lk. 3:23), and his name not particularly striking, Yehoshua, or as we say, Jesus.

The infancy narratives

Who is he?

The first announcement made about him, as we can see from the earliest strata of the New Testament, was not concerned with his youth or even the course of his life, but with the high-point of his existence: his death and his deliverance from it by God, the resurrection. This divine event outshines all else. What was first proclaimed about him was that he lives.

When his words and his life-story later became part of the preaching, they were viewed from the standpoint of faith in who he is. When finally his childhood was recounted—working upstream to the source—this was not done to collect matter for a "life of Jesus" which would satisfy mere curiosity. Undoubtedly, the infancy narratives (Mt. 1 and 2, Lk. 1 and 2) were not composed without the aid of historical reminiscences. But their chief aim was to put before men who believed that he lived—and were experiencing it in life and prayer—the profound significance of his coming; that God's promises began to be fulfilled, that the light broke through. The infancy narratives are truly "evangel", that is, "good news".

For more discussion of such questions, one may read the chapter entitled "Who is this Man?" and also, "The Origins of the Gospels" and "The most ancient Accounts of Jesus".

145–151
206–209
209–210

Is it so regrettable, after all, that when we examine the accounts of Jesus' infancy, we find ourselves so ill-informed about many of the historical details? This lack of concrete detail seems to have bothered some people, as may be seen from the fact that in earlier times Christians felt the need of inventing stories about Jesus' childhood—how as a child he made little birds out of mud, and how these then flew away when he clapped his hands. Something of the same mentality appears in the endeavours of our own times to discover as much as possible of the concrete circumstances from every historical allusion. It is a curiosity inspired, by love, the symptom of an effort to learn to know him better.

But is this the right method to attain this end? Can any accumulation of precise detail reveal to us the saving deeds of the living Lord as effectively as the gospel narratives inspired by faith? The infancy gospels of Matthew and Luke are truly good tidings in themselves, reflecting clearly, for all their simplicity, the real greatness of his manifestation. They do it so well that we can celebrate along with them the great feastdays—Christmas, Epiphany and Candlemas (Purification).

In what we have to say in this book about the life of Jesus, we hope to be faithful to the attitude of the gospels. We shall not try to reconstruct a biography from the data of the gospels, as though we were looking for information about someone who has passed away. We shall try to allow the gospels to speak for themselves, with their clear message about one who lives.

Born of woman

The stories about Jesus' origin tell us clearly that he comes from the human race and that he comes from God. The unity of the human and the divine in him, which faith was later to express in the terms used by the Council of Chalcedon *(see below)*, is already given in the first pages of Matthew, Mark, Luke and John.   77–82

Matthew and Luke use the most solemn way possible to proclaim that Jesus is rooted in humanity. They give a genealogy (Mt. 1:1–17; Lk. 3:23–28). The impact of this summary is felt most strongly in Matthew, who opens his gospel with it. It begins with the words, "The book of the genealogy", which in Greek is the same as "The book of Genesis". The list is composed of three equal parts, showing a literary re-moulding which takes them beyond the region of precise information. The idea is to produce an overture which will call the reader's attention to some significant high-points. The genealogy from David onwards is not clear, on account of some differences between Matthew and Luke, which could perhaps be solved by assuming somewhere along the line a levirate marriage (cf. Deut. 25:6). The intention of the author is better realized by noting that

Luke stresses a further line of descent, the descent from Adam, which underlines the fact that Jesus belongs to the whole of mankind.

The genealogy of Matthew includes four women, Tamar, Rahab, Ruth and the wife of Uriah. Why were only these four women mentioned? Possibly because they were all foreigners. If so, Matthew is indicating, as Luke did by mentioning Adam, that the birth of Jesus belongs to all mankind. Did Matthew also mention them because the Old Testament ascribes a sinful situation or a sinful calling to three of them? This is also possible. But in any case they are there (along with many sinful men) as unmistakable signs that Jesus comes from sinful humanity. The two lists end with Joseph. Through him, they show that Jesus is linked to mankind. This modest figure at the dawn of the history of salvation, one of the "poor of Yahweh" was in the sight of the law Jesus' link with the people of Israel. He was "the last of the Patriarchs".

Born of God

As well as Jesus' human origin, the gospels also give his divine origin.

There are several figures in the Old Testament of whom it is said that their birth was an answer to prayer. A human marriage which was at first childless finally bore fruit after much longing, prayer and a divine promise. This was the way with Israel's ancestors Isaac and Jacob, and also Samson, Samuel and the child from the house of Achaz, who was the sign of God's fidelity in a time of deep distress. Such was the birth of John the Baptist. In these stories something that is true of all parenthood is brought out with particular emphasis: that a new human being—every time something unique—is ultimately from God. The child is "a gift" from God, as we often read in the "births" column of the newspapers—much more than something that the parents have "had".

Jesus is the climax of all the promises of children fulfilled in Israel. When he came into the world, he was being prayed for by a whole people and promised by a whole history. He was a child of promise in a unique sense, and the profoundest desire of the whole of mankind. He was born wholly of grace, wholly of promise—"conceived of the Holy Spirit". He was *the* gift of God to mankind.

This the evangelists Matthew and Luke express when they proclaim that Jesus' birth was not due to the will of a man. They proclaim that this birth, does not depend on what men can do of themselves—infinitely less so than in other human births. That is the deepest meaning of the article of faith, "born of the virgin Mary". There is nothing in the bosom of mankind, nothing in human fruitfulness that can procreate him, from whom all human fruitfulness, all the begetting of our race depend: for all things were made in him. Mankind has ultimately no one to thank but the Holy Spirit for the coming of this promised one. His origin is not of blood nor of the will of the flesh nor of the will of a man, but from God: from the Most High.

Matthew

All this is said by Matthew and Luke in simple and ordinary terms in which the newness of Jesus is expressed. In Matthew we read: "Now the birth [again 'genesis'] of Jesus Christ took place in this way. When his mother Mary had been betrothed to Joseph, before they came together she was found to be with child of the Holy Spirit; and her husband Joseph, being a just man and unwilling to put her to shame, resolved to divorce her quietly. But as he considered this, behold, an angel of the Lord appeared to him in a dream, saying, 'Joseph, son of David, do not fear to take Mary your wife, for that which is conceived in her is of the Holy Spirit'" (Mt. 1:18–20).

Luke

And then we have the magnificent pages from the most subtle of the evangelists: the annunciation narrative of Luke (Lk. 1:26–38). He does justice, as well as may be, to the truth that the grace of Jesus' coming was an event of world-wide significance.

The messenger of God is called Gabriel, the angel who in the book of Daniel is the announcer of the last days. Hence the fact that Gabriel is named indicates that the time of God's final mercy is at hand. The message itself is also full of allusions to God's earlier promises. The very greeting of the angel opens up a world full of assurance of salvation from the Old Testament: "Hail, full of grace." Every people has its own type of greeting. We wish people "good morning". One of the forms used in

Greek was, "Rejoice!". This is what Luke has—literally, "Rejoice, O favoured one". But at the same time, the summons is more than an ordinary Greek greeting. It is the echo of such prophetic promises as that of Zephaniah:

> "Sing aloud, O daughter of Zion;
> shout, O Israel!
> Rejoice and exult with all your heart,
> O daughter of Jerusalem! . . .
> The King of Israel, the Lord, is in your midst"
> (Zeph. 3:14f.);

and

> "Rejoice greatly, O daughter of Zion!
> Shout aloud, O daughter of Jerusalem!
> Lo, your king comes to you;
> triumphant and victorious is he" (Zech. 9:9).

Such invitations were addressed to the "daughter of Zion". This is the people of Israel, Jerusalem in particular, personified in the symbolic image of a maiden.

This jubilation is now fulfilled in the girl who is there in person as the representative of the whole people. Israel is there in Mary and hears the message, that God is sending the king, the Messiah, into their midst.

Mary said to the angel, "How can this be, since I have no husband?" This question is there as an introduction to the second part of the message: "The Holy Spirit will come upon you, and the power of the Most High will overshadow you" (Lk. 1:35). The word "overshadow" is taken from the Old 191 Testament. It recalls the luminous cloud which descended on the tent in the desert or on the temple of Jerusalem as a sign of God's presence (Exod. 40:34–35; Num. 9:15; 10:34; 2 Chr. 7:2). There are many other allusions to the Old Testament in the Annunciation narrative.

73-74 *The mother of the Lord*

80, 88 89 But let us continue for a moment to consider the young woman
93, 172 to whom God did such mighty things, in whom one age of the
200, 212 world comes to an end and another begins. She embodies
268 Israel's expectations at their finest, and she becomes the type
475 476 of the Church who receives Jesus. Unlike the Baptist or the

Apostles, she has no task in the preaching of the gospel. She is not an official herald. And hence the gospel of Mark, which only treats of Jesus' public ministry, pays little special attention to Mary. But Matthew, Luke and John discover more and more of her task. This is more than her blood-relationship to Jesus (cf. Lk. 8:19–21). Her whole person is involved in the events. Mary "kept these things in her heart and pondered them all" (Lk. 2:19, 51). She was one "who believed" (Lk. 1:45). "Prius mente concepit quam ventre"—she conceived him in her heart before conceiving him in her womb. It is entirely in keeping with the gospel spirit to honour her special place in the mystery of Christ.

Jesus was her first-born. The gospels do not say that she had other children after him. The fact that Jesus' "brothers and sisters" (Mt. 13:55–56) are mentioned need mean nothing in this connection. In Hebrew and Aramaic more distant relatives are also given this title. And this is still the custom in Nazareth. That Jesus' "brothers and sisters" need not be children of Joseph and Mary may be seen from the fact that the two brothers named first in Mt. 13:55 appear in Mt. 27:56 as sons of another Mary. It is highly improbable that this James and Joseph would be mentioned without some note, if they were not the same as those already spoken of. Further, Jn 19:27 makes it highly improbable that Mary had other sons. It is significant that Mary is nowhere represented in Christian art, including that of the Reformation, with other children.

The Church celebrates the annunciation to Mary on 25 March, nine months before Christmas. There is also the custom of saying the Angelus three times a day, at 6 a.m., midday and 6 p.m., when the church bells are rung. It is a prayer which recalls the incarnation.

The Word was made flesh

45
499–500

Did Mary fully understand whom she was bringing into the world? No, it was only Jesus' resurrection that showed clearly who he was. But then the Church very soon composed such hymns as:

> "He is the image of the invisible God,
> the first-born of all creation;
> for in him all things were created" (Col. 1:15–16).

And another hymn runs:

> "Though he was in the form of God,
> he did not count equality with God a thing to be
> grasped,
> but emptied himself,
> taking the form of a servant,
> being born in the likeness of men" (Phil. 2:6,7).

These are New Testament texts written down even earlier than the gospels. They are not the only ones. Later texts also speak of the mystery of Jesus' origin from God. Thus, for instance, in the prologue of John we read:

> "In the beginning was the Word,
> and the Word was with God,
> and the Word was God.
> He was in the beginning with God" (Jn 1:1–2).

He who is born was already there at the origin, "in the beginning" of which Gen. 1:1 speaks.

> "All things were made through him,
> and without him was not made anything that was
> made" (Jn 1:3).
> "All things were created through him and for him"
> (Col. 1:16).

Thus the New Testament proclaims that he who is born has already been at work in the world from the start. This is indicated by the title used by John, "the Word". It is an echo of the expression, "God spoke", in the account of creation. It is a reminder of the Word of God which through prophets and holy men created Israel. It is a recollection of the life-giving Wisdom of God, "a pure emanation of the glory of the Almighty" (Wis. 7:25). Hence the Epistle to the Hebrews says, "he reflects the glory of God" (Heb. 1:3).

This divine condescension, of which strong intimations were already given in the Old Testament, now appears as man on earth. God is no longer distant: "The Word became flesh" (Jn 1:14).

To think of it is to be brought up sharp in silent admiration.

There can be only one reason for the mystery of the incarnation of the Son of God: "Only love does such things." "God so loved the world that he gave his only Son" (Jn 3:16).

The image of God's being

This is a mystery so divine that man dare scarcely believe it. Perhaps the best way of penetrating its depths is to examine men's efforts to minimize it. From the very first centuries of Christianity men have been reluctant to accept it in all its majesty. Three times the Church had to make a solemn pronouncement to keep the fullness of the mystery intact.

What is this inclination to restrict the meaning of the incarnation?

We may perhaps describe it as follows. On the basis of our own ideas, and also on the basis of a wrong-headed and partial understanding of the Old Testament, we have formed certain preconceptions of God, of his invisible nature, his power and his inaccessibility. We then compare these concepts spontaneously with Jesus and say that he cannot be God.

As though we really knew who God is! As though our pre- 18–19
conceived notions of God were an exhaustive representation of God! In point of fact, we only know who God is through Jesus. It is not through (our idea of) God that we learn to know Jesus. 90–91
But it is through Jesus that we learn to know God. His manifesta- 497–498
tion is the only true view of God's revelation.

About A.D. 300, the inclination we have spoken of showed itself in the doctrine of an Alexandrine priest, Arius. He compared a God, principally thought out by men, with Jesus' appearance and pronounced that Christ was not God, though undoubtedly a creature of a very high order. The first great council of the Church, that of Nicaea in 325, was convoked on this occasion. It declared solemnly that in Jesus God really appeared on earth as a person, as the person of the Son.

The confession of faith drawn up by the Council of Nicaea is the creed which is still said or sung after the gospel at Mass: 332
"God from God, light from light, true god from true God; begotten, not made, one in substance with the Father." "Begotten, not made": there is truly generation (being born) in and from God, which is not creation. 498–502

Thus the Son proceeds from the Father by way of generation, not creation.

But men still had questions. They still had difficulties in harmonizing their own more or less self-made notions of God with God's actual manifestation in Jesus.

About 400, this led to the theory that the Son of God in heaven and the man Jesus on earth were really two distinct persons. They were admittedly united to one another, but they remained distinct. This was a way, it was thought, of guarding a certain notion of God in its purity. The theory is linked to the name of Bishop Nestorius, who lived in the fifth century. But for signs of this way of thinking we can also look nearer home. It can still exist in practice in our notion of Christ, especially among those of scientific or semi-scientific bent. On the one hand we believe that Jesus is the Son of God, but once we have acknowledged this we feel able to push it aside in all further consideration of Jesus. We go on to consider him as a rabbi who lived two thousand years ago. We speak of him as a great man. We do not really see *in* his human life the person of the Son of God, the radiance of the eternal light.

To counteract this tendency, the Council of Ephesus proclaimed in 431 that in spite of the difference between divine and human nature, there is one person in Christ. We find God in the man Jesus. To express forcibly this mystery of Christ, the Council gave Mary the title of *Theótokos*, Mother of God.

But there still remained another way of safeguarding the preconceived notion of God. At the time of the Council of Ephesus this solution was put forward by the Monophysites. They recognized very reverently—there were many monks in their ranks—the unity in the person of Christ, but they saw it in such a way that he possessed only a divine nature. Behind all the humanity of Christ there was no real human nature. The Son of God only acted as if there were. He was not really man. God lived on earth with only the outward appearance of man.

These incorrect views can still affect our own notion of Christ, especially in the case of pious people. The divinity of Jesus is made so dominantly central that nothing further is seen. Hence we can sometimes read descriptions of the Christ-child where he merely behaves *as if* he were a baby. Jesus, so to speak, only pretends to live a human life. But he does not grow up like a human being, he does not think and feel like a man. He is infinitely perfect, merely appearing outwardly with human form.

Hence after the council which defined Christ's divinity (Nicaea) and the council which defined his unity (Ephesus), another synod was necessary to safeguard Christ's humanity. The pronouncement was made, in admirable and definitive words, at the Council of Chalcedon, only twenty years after Ephesus, in 451. It declared that in the person of Christ not only the divine but also the human nature existed in its entirety. The real God appears in a real man. The majesty of God is as close to us, as kind, pitiful, majestic and involved in the struggle with evil, as is Jesus. Away, then, with our elaborate human explanations. How God is, we can find in Jesus, who was born, died and rose again, and lives on through his Spirit in his Church.

Away with our fears also. In him who has fought for us against evil, "unto the shedding of blood", we find the true path into the reality of God's mystery. The human heart of Christ is the heart of God. 496–498

How this involves man

In these three councils, which were accepted unreservedly by the founders of the Reformation in the sixteenth century, the uniqueness and novelty of Jesus' manifestation to man were safeguarded. The councils were held under circumstances of the greatest possible difficulty. But through them God brought mankind to a new level of development and understanding.

This may be seen to some extent from the following consideration. As the history of language shows, our concept of "person", in the profoundly human sense of the word, was only clarified on the occasion of these councils.

The Romans had the word "*persona*", which they used as a legal term to describe the free citizen. This meant that a slave was not a *persona*. The Greeks had the concept of the "individual", that is, the realization of universal human nature in the single, independent unit. But the irreplaceable selfhood which each man is, with his special and incalculable dignity—all that is expressed in the term "human person"—only became clear during these great councils. Because the Son of God was really man, every human person possessed a priceless dignity. Hence came the conviction of the dignity and rights of man, including the incapacitated, the seemingly unproductive members of society. Once the existence of the other as a person was rec- 220
ognized, slavery had really lost its worst sting, even before the 233

58, 60–63 actual abolition of it had been brought about on the economic
233–234 and social level. It takes centuries for such truths to penetrate
249–278 humanity. We cannot know what state mankind would have
been in without the coming of Christ. Neither Christian nor
humanist nor Marxist can do so. It may be said that two thousand
years of Christianity have been to no purpose. But how can one
know this? No one can fully understand what God's revelation
has accomplished in the world.

Some effects may be seen in art. This has been pointed out
by a writer well acquainted with the arts of mankind, André
Malraux, who is not himself a Christian. The faces in Roman
art, as he sees it, are primarily "natures", representations of
human nature in general, while the visage of a medieval statue
is the history of a life. "And the finest Gothic mouths are like
the scars left by life."

These considerations may seem to have taken us away from
our subject, which is the incarnation. But they help us to see
how closely God's becoming man is connected with man's
becoming man—in the way that God meant him to be. Indeed,
with his divinization, as was said at the time of the great
councils: God truly became man in order that we might become
truly divine. The whole man is involved.

334 Dogmas are not merely words, they are values—values which
352 enlarge our horizons. The great achievement of the three
365–366 Christological councils was to broaden our narrow paths as
448 much as possible. They reject nothing. All they do is to reject
human negations. They unfold the mystery which is disclosed
in the gospels.

The celebration of Jesus' birth

We do not know the day of Jesus' birth. In early times there was
no great interest in the date of Christmas. The only feast
celebrated was that of Easter, which commemorates the whole
mystery of Christ. But in the third century Christians began to
feel a wish to celebrate Christ's birth by itself. It is the same
phenomenon as we have noted in the telling of the gospel. First
came the great salvific events as accomplished by Christ in his
maturity, and only then the desire to "work upstream" to see
the first stages.

The fact that Jesus' birthday was unknown left Christians

free to choose the most meaningful date. Spontaneously, the time of year when the days began to lengthen was chosen. Hence from time immemorial, 25 December and 6 January have been taken as the dates of Jesus' first manifestation. This meant adopting pagan feast days. But this was incidental. The basic reason is much simpler and one which appeals to human nature in general. When a new brightness appeared in nature, Christians began to celebrate the coming of the new Light that will never fail. It is a spiritual light, and hence it is no great harm that in our modern cities which are always lighted, or in the southern part of the globe, the climb of the sun, the natural symbol in question, is hardly noticeable or indeed entirely absent. Christian faith does not hold aloof from nature; it gladly associates itself with its course, but it is not a nature religion attached to the cycle of the seasons. It is based on historical facts which remain eternally relevant. 40–41 51, 182–183 207, 213

The birth of Jesus is a fact in history. All history has been dated according to it. The year one is the year of the birth of Jesus. This was the splendid vision with which Dionysius Exiguus (Denis the Small—a monk of the sixth century) replaced the ancient enumeration, which counted the years from the foundation of Rome. No doubt he paid too little attention to the word "about" in Luke's phrase, "about thirty years of age", speaking of the age of Jesus at the beginning of his ministry (Lk. 3:23). The result was that Denis was probably from four to seven years out in his reckoning. But this is not very important. Even if Jesus was born some years earlier, the dating by "anno Domini" (A.D.), "the year of the Lord", retains its profound significance: that a new age began with Jesus.

The historical event of God's manifestation for our salvation remains close to us in the liturgy. Hence this chapter is written from the standpoint of our own annual celebration of his coming, which takes in the matter very well, since the liturgy from 25 December to 2 February covers all the important events. 343

In the darkest night of the year, the Church recalls the birth of Jesus. This is done by celebrating the Eucharist three times— at midnight, about dawn and during the day, each time with new chants and prayers. This custom comes from Jerusalem. First the vigil was kept at Bethlehem. At dawn, the procession reached Jerusalem. During the day, Christians came together in the great church of the city. Hence we, the Church, still celebrate three Masses on Christmas Day.

By midnight, when the faithful gather, the contemplative orders all over the world have already chanted the very long Matins of Christmas night, two hours of psalms, readings from Isaiah and from Pope Leo the Great, Gregory the Great, Augustine and Ambrose—a prolonged hymn of admiration. Thus the contemplative Church prepares for Jesus' coming, while most of us are making the last preparations among our families, on this night when the prophecies were fulfilled and when Mary and Joseph made their practical preparations for the birth.

Midnight Mass begins with a chant which tells of the eternal birth of the Son from the Father. "The Lord said to me, 'You are my Son, today I have begotten you'" (from Psalm 2). The epistle is from St. Paul to Titus: "The grace of God has appeared for the salvation of all men" (Tit. 2:11–15). After chants from the royal psalms, the liturgy of the word comes to a climax this night with the simple story of the birth—how a census brought Joseph and Mary to the town from which David had come, Bethlehem. "While they were there, the time came for her to be delivered. And she gave birth to her first-born son and wrapped him in swaddling cloths, and laid him in a manger, because there was no place for them in the inn" (Lk. 2:6–7).

A manger or crib is a receptacle for fodder. This is how the Light appeared—as a poor person, someone for whom there was no room. No doubt the place of his birth was some indication of his greatness. It was the royal city of Bethlehem, in which the promises to David were at last fulfilled.

And we are also told of an apparition of angels. God's glory breaks through. The angels' song is given as follows:

> "Glory to God in the highest,
>   and on earth peace to men of good will" (Lk. 2:13;
> cf. also R. S. V., Catholic edition).

What is meant is the men of God's good will. And hence it can also be translated, men with whom God is pleased (cf. R. S. V., Catholic edition). God's good will, his benevolence from which he excludes nobody, is the great theme of this night: "In this is love, not that we loved God but that he loved us and sent his Son to be the expiation for our sins" (1 Jn 4:10).

After this story of the birth comes a sermon on the mystery which is being celebrated, and then the Eucharist itself.

The Mass at dawn is full of symbols of light. The epistle is again from Paul to Titus. It speaks of God's goodness, his good will and his initiative: "He saved us, not because of deeds done by us in righteousness, but in virtue of his own mercy" (Tit. 3:5–7).

The gospel continues the narrative of Luke from the point reached at the midnight Mass. It describes the first choice of God—poor shepherds, who were led to find the child. Shepherds were not only poor, they were also despised. These are now 88 the representatives of the whole people, as appears from the angel's words: "I bring *you* good news [literally, gospel] of a great joy which will come to all the people" (Lk. 2:10). At the first moment when salvation ceases to be a thing of the future, and begins to be a glorious "Today", the gospel already sees all values reversed. The despised, and not the honoured and respected, now represent the people. With the gospel of the Mass at dawn the re-telling of the story of the birth ends.

The daytime Mass is the real festal Mass of Christmas. The most solemn proclamation of the eternal birth of the Son is reserved for this Mass. The opening psalm begins with the simple-seeming words, "A child is born to us . . ." but then follow immediately the words, "The government is upon his shoulders, and his name is called, Angel of great counsel" (Is. 9:5, according to the Greek text). The epistle is the masterly opening of the epistle to the Hebrews (Heb. 1:1–12). For the gospel, the beginning of St John is chosen:

> "In the beginning was the Word,
> and the Word was with God,
> and the Word was God.
> He was in the beginning with God;
> all things were made through him,
> and without him was not anything made that was made.
> In him was life,
> and the life was the light of men.
> And the light shines in the darkness,
> and the darkness did not accept it . . .

The true light that enlightens every man was coming
into the world.
He was in the world,
and the world was made through him,
yet the world knew him not.
He came to his own home,
and his own people received him not.
But to all who received him, who believed in his name,
he gave power to become children of God;
who were born, not of blood, nor of the will of the flesh,
nor of the will of man, but of God.
And the Word became flesh and dwelt among us . . .
We have seen his glory, glory as of the only Son
from the Father,
full of grace and truth" (Jn 1:1–5, 9–14).

Such are the exalted terms in which the Church liturgy celebrates the mystery. If we join in with heart and soul, we receive
the grace of Christmas: the encounter with the whole Christ,
seen in the form of the Christ-child.

This celebration is echoed in our families and in the other
forms of social life. The crib, the carols—even on the wireless
or the gramophone—the holly and ivy, the melody of the
church bells, make the birth of Jesus a feast which has a unique
impact in the home and elsewhere.

For non-believers, 25th December is the mid-winter festival.
It is a rest after the work of the autumn, a time to enjoy the
intimacy of family life. This is a function which Christmas also
fulfils for Christians. It means that the feast contains strangely
contrasting elements, as St Francis of Assisi already felt and
as has often been underlined by modern poets. Christmas is, on
the one hand, a feast of poverty, of stepping outside one's
own circle, a time of love. And on the other hand it is a feast
of abundance, of remaining within one's own circle, of intimacy
preserved, and hence too of love there. One of the tasks of
Christians must be to remain ready and welcoming towards
all neighbours outside the closed family circle. Only in this
way can our celebration of Christmas correspond at all to the
marvellous condescension of Jesus.

Eight days after the birth of the child came the circumcision,
as Luke narrates. This is also recalled by the Church a week

after Christmas, on New Year's Day. Through the sign of circumcision, as prescribed by the law, Jesus became a member of the people of Israel.

This was the day that the child was given the name which had already been pronounced over him before his birth: Jesus, that is, Yahweh saves. It is the name borne by the man who led the people into the promised land: Joshua (in its Greek form).

The epiphany of the Lord

The cycle of Christmas is not yet closed. The liturgy of the sixth of January is a new climax. It is a feast which in ancient times was celebrated even more splendidly than Christmas. Even at the present day it has the place in the eastern Church which Christmas has for us. It celebrates a magnificent concept, that of the epiphany or manifestation of the Lord.

For this, three events of the history of salvation are taken together: the homage of the wise men from the East, the baptism of Christ in the Jordan and the marriage feast of Cana—three initial manifestations of his glory.

For the epistle one of the most jubilant texts of the book of Isaiah was chosen, 60:1-6, "Arise, shine, Jerusalem". Yahweh is to make his brightness shine forth in Jerusalem, so that the heathen nations are drawn to it. Through Jesus, the salvation of God did in fact appear in Jerusalem and Palestine.

The gospel takes the first of the three saving events. It is a story which Matthew places at the beginning of his gospel, Jesus' first manifestation to non-Jews, which is an indication that the world outside Israel is also affected by Jesus' coming. By means of a sign among the stars and a Jewish prophecy, some "wise men" from the East (perhaps Persia or Babylon or Arabia) discover the child with his mother Mary and offer him royal homage. Since the time of the catacombs, paintings of the scene have been one of the favourite ways of depicting Jesus' manifestation to the whole world. In some countries, like Holland and Germany, it is called the feast of the three kings.

The story of the wise men has an aftermath in the slaughter of the children at Bethlehem and the flight into Egypt. The death of these children who unknowingly gave their blood for Jesus is celebrated close to Christmas, 28 December, which is called the Feast of the Holy Innocents.

The significance of the flight into Egypt is that Jesus, on his return, followed in the footsteps of the people which had come up from Egypt long ago. Matthew calls attention to it by saying, "This was to fulfil what the Lord had spoken by the prophet, 'Out of Egypt have I called my son'" (Mt. 2:15). Jesus is *the* Son, much more than the people was. In him, the people will return from the house of bondage, to be slaves no more.

Jerusalem for the first time

Luke has still another journey of Jesus to mention: the Lord goes up to Jerusalem for the first time. This saving event is celebrated on 2 February, the "Feast of the Encounter" *(Hypapánte)* or the Purification (formerly known as Candlemas). Forty days after Jesus' birth his parents went to Jerusalem. To fulfil the law, Mary had to undergo a ritual purification. Jesus, as the first-born, had to be given to God. (The first-born, in such cases, was then "redeemed". Since the parents were poor, a pair of doves was sufficient.)

From the many meanings which come together in this scene, the liturgy has chosen one in particular. It is the meaning which was also central to Luke, according to modern exegesis, namely, that the city of the promises, Jerusalem, was receiving in its arms for the first time the promised deliverer. The liturgical setting, which comes from the East, is here of an un-Roman exuberance: "Put on your bridal adornments, O Zion, and receive Christ the King; embrace Mary who is the gate of heaven; for she it is who bears the King of glory of the new light." So begins the introductory chant in honour of the child and his mother.

The epistle, from Malachi 3:1–4, speaks of God coming to purify his temple. The gospel is part of the narrative from Luke (2:22–32).

It is also profoundly significant that those who greet him in Jerusalem are not the official religious leaders of the people, but an old man and an old woman. They undoubtedly represent the "poor of Yahweh", those who waited patiently for "the consolation of Israel".

37, 74
85, 99

Their names were Simeon and Anna. The former sings a hymn about the child who is "a light for revelation to the Gentiles, and for glory to thy people Israel". The choice falls on Gentiles as well as Jews. Once again the whole of Jesus' work is symbolized in one of the early events—including the

tears which this child, thirty years later, was to shed over Jerusalem (Lk. 19:41–44). Simeon speaks to the young mother of
the fall of many as well as of the rising of many. This child 102–104
will be such that men will be inwardly unmasked. For Mary, 149, 150
this will mean that a seven-fold sword of sorrow will pierce 157, 172
her heart.

Childhood in Nazareth

Jesus grew up in Nazareth. Joseph was a carpenter (Mt. 13:35).
Jesus also practised this trade (Mk 6:3). Hence, till he was
nearly thirty years of age, his activities were limited to the
framework of a social task and he lived in an ordinary family.

Our Christian predecessors, a century ago, contemplated
lovingly the family life of Nazareth. They were moved by the
model of peace, obedience and love that could be imagined in
Nazareth. Hence, in 1892, the Feast of the Holy Family was
instituted, to be celebrated on the first Sunday after Epiphany.

But Jesus did more in his hidden life than leave us a good
example. His life in that village reveals how God is and how
he acts. Nazareth signifies that the Son of God has manifested
himself to us through the ordinary life of mankind. Out of
the life that men lead, from the hunter of pre-history to the
city-dweller and countryman of today, the bread-winner, the
school-boy, the housewife; life in family and group, with the
burden and the joy of work; life that seemingly has no history—
out of such life the Son of God makes himself manifest. This
helps us once more to know God better. He is the God who
has willed to appear in common things, the hidden God who
has always shared the ordinary life of man, the "God close by"
to us in our own lives which do not attract attention and do not
make history. Nazareth shows God with us, in our work, in our
family life. This meaning is certainly also present in the feast
of Jesus' hidden life, which is celebrated on the Sunday after
Epiphany.

Jerusalem for the second time

No incidents are recorded from the years at Nazareth, except
this one story. When Jesus was twelve years old, he went to
Jerusalem with his parents for the Feast of the Passover, and
as Luke relates, remained behind unobserved, in the Temple.

Mary and Joseph found him on the third day among the teachers. These rabbis were amazed at the intelligence of his answers, but Mary uttered a mother's reproof: "Son, why have you treated us so? Behold, your father and I have been looking for you anxiously'" (Lk. 2:48). Jesus takes up the word "father" and tells Mary that he must be concerned with the things that concern his Father. By "his Father", he means God. His parents do not understand. Mary keeps the words in her heart.

What is the meaning of this incident? To explain it, we must 88 ask why Luke recounts it. As we have already said, it is always 114 of great importance to this evangelist that Jesus reveals himself 155–156 in Jerusalem. God had promised to appear to men there. The first time was the offering in the temple. Jesus could not yet speak. Jerusalem spoke, in the person of Simeon and Anna. It was meeting its Lord for the first time. In the story of the twelve-year-old child, Jesus speaks. Now the Lord meets Jerusalem for the first time. We see God's promises coming true before our eyes.

This fulfilment of prophecy is used by Luke to end the story of Jesus' youth. He told therefore this very human story of the boy from the country town of Nazareth who suddenly finds himself in the great capital which is the city of God and feels with all the fibres of his being: "Here I am at home." Jesus is so absorbed by this sight of the majesty of God his Father, and by this first intimation of his task in life, that he forgets his parents.

An intelligent boy discovers his vocation. That is the way in which God comes to his temple. The prophecies are fulfilled in an unexpected and very human way. God appears to us in a growing child. "And Jesus increased in wisdom and in years, and in favour with God and man" (Lk. 2:52).

Jesus' consciousness

The question might now be asked: "how can he be Son of God, and hence know all things, and at the same time man, and hence grow in knowledge?" It is the same question as was discussed 79 in the previous chapter, but put more precisely and acutely with regard to Jesus' consciousness. Here too the answer must be that we must be careful not to start from our human ideas of God, as though apart from Jesus we knew God fully. Jesus is not for those who (think they) know who God is, but for those who seek to know who God is. All we can do is fix our eyes on the man Jesus. Only by thus paying attention to him can we begin to realize something of the God who reveals himself in him. God is much greater than all the ideas we have of "greatness". 497–498

God's consciousness is much more living and warm than we can imagine an "absolute consciousness" to be, with the aid of our own concepts. *In* Jesus' truly human knowledge (in which, for instance, the world dawned on him as on any other human being) something of his likeness to God radiates. In Jesus God has become accessible to us.

BAPTISM AND TEMPTATION

It is to be expected that Jesus' first public appearance will be described in such a way that the whole kernel of his mission will become apparent.

The vocation of men of God in the Old Testament is often described at the beginning of their history. Magnificent external images—a throne-hall with an altar of fire (Is. 6:1–7), an almond tree in blossom (Jer. 1:11)—are used to express 47, 53
profound internal experiences. 317

The gospels start Jesus' public life with an event which was handed down and emphasized from the oldest tradition: his baptism by John in the Jordan. This is the second of the initial saving acts which are celebrated at the Epiphany—it is read as the gospel a week later, 13 January.

In the story, outward images are the expression of a reality which cannot be fully put into words. The reality is the contact of the Father with Jesus, and the power of the Holy Spirit. This contact is summed up in words from the Old Testament: "Thou art my Son, my beloved; with thee I am well pleased" (Mk 1:11).

This evokes the figure of the Servant of the Lord, the suffering Servant, to whom a number of chants are devoted in Isaiah. There we read: "Behold my servant . . . my chosen, with 279–283
whom I am well pleased" (Is. 42:1), and again, ". . . the Lord has laid on him the iniquity of us all" (Is. 53:6).

Hence the baptism is a sign of Jesus' role as servant, of his submission and suffering, indeed, of his death. Twice Jesus was later to describe his death by the word "baptism" (Mt. 20:22; Lk. 12:50). The beloved Son dedicates himself as servant, sets 156

246 out on his path of lowliness, to be the lamb who bears all sin. This is his vocation.

The gospel goes on: "He saw the heavens opened and the Spirit descending on him like a dove" (Mk 1:10), just as the Servant Song continues: "I have put my Spirit upon him" (Is. 42:1).

59 The men of God in earlier times who were animated by the Spirit experienced this as something strange, a higher force taking hold of them. But as Jesus goes on with his public mission, his being filled with the Spirit seems to have a certain naturalness about it, almost as if he did not need the Spirit. This is of course not literally true. It would be more correct to say that he does not possess the Spirit as something foreign to him. It is a force which belongs to him, which he possesses as his own Spirit. "He whom God has sent utters the words of God, for it is not by measure that he (God) gives (him) the Spirit" (Jn 3:34; cf. also Is. 11:2 and Jn 1:33).

The water-baptism of John is given a new significance by 242, 252 this Spirit-baptism. It becomes a symbol of the baptism with the Spirit which will be conferred on future believers. Hence the Eastern liturgy sings on the vigil of Epiphany: "Today the Lord bows his head under the hand of his precursor; today John immerses him in the depths of the Jordan; today the Lord buries the sins of men in the waters; today he is proclaimed from on high as Son of God and beloved Son; today the Lord himself comes to sanctify the nature of the waters. He plunges himself into the flood of the Jordan, not because he needs to be cleansed, but to prepare in his own person the re-birth which is meant for us."

As to the consequences which Jesus' life-work entailed, the gospels leave no possibility of mistake. They tell of temptations against his vocation. "In every respect he has been tempted as we are, yet without sinning" (Heb. 4:15).

There were temptations in the course of his ministry. For instance, when he first revealed how his life was to end, when he spoke of the final baptism of death, "Peter took him and began to rebuke him, saying, 'God forbid, Lord! This shall never happen to you'. But he turned and said to Peter, 'Get behind me, Satan! You are a hindrance to me; for you are not on the side of God, but of men'" (Mt. 16:22–23). Peter's insistence was very human and well-intentioned. But Jesus saw in it the

great danger—the opposite of his baptism, the temptation of the 109
adversary, the Satan.
482

The gospels tell of temptations in the desert. Whether the
place, the appearance of the devil and the three-fold form of the
temptation are an exact report or a stylization, neither adds to
nor takes away from the salvific event. But it is very significant
that the desert is mentioned. It is the place of encounter with
God and of temptation. Jesus is re-making the journey of the
Israelites through the desert, where the people was also tempted.
The people succumbed, but Jesus resists, as naturally as he
possesses the Spirit. He uses three sayings taken from the story
of Israel in the desert (Deut. 8:3; 6:16; 6:13). Where Israel,
and with it all mankind, forgets its task in life and longs in its
wretchedness to return to the flesh-pots of Egypt, Jesus affirms
that man also lives by every word that comes forth from the
mouth of God. Where Israel tempts God and tries to force a
miracle from him, Jesus refuses to stage an impressive spectacle.
Where Israel abandoned itself to the worship of worldly idols,
Jesus refuses earthly lordship, which the devil offers him in
exchange for a genuflection.

To work a miracle for his own benefit; to demand some
imposing spectacle from God; to gain worldly dominion:
these were precisely the three ways which he refused to adopt.
They seem to be obviously desirable for anyone who aims at
success. But Jesus knew that he had come to bring about a
reversal of values. What men set their hearts on, as he was to
say to Peter, what the world regards as wisdom and glory,
that was what he had to avoid. His baptism signified readiness
to submit and suffer, to share the common lot, to be a servant,
even unto death. In a word, he chose not success but service.
To be faithful to his task was his joy, and it brought a new joy
into the world. "And behold, angels came and ministered to
him" (Mt. 4:11).

THE KINGDOM OF GOD

Cana

In out-of-the-way Galilee Jesus revealed his glory for the first
time. The Gospel of John begins here with a marriage which is
celebrated in Cana, a village near Nazareth. Jesus changed

water—which was there for Jewish rites of purification—into excellent wine. This is a prefiguration of the messianic joy of the "Hour" of Jesus' death and resurrection which was to replace the old by the new, water by wine. The evangelist notes that Mary requested this sign. Jesus' reaction seems to be a refusal. He refers Mary to his (last) Hour, which it is the Father's, not Mary's, to determine. Nonetheless, he accedes to her request. This is certainly not without significance in John's presentation, all the more so since later on he expressly mentions Mary's presence at the Hour itself (Jn 19:26).

172

The marriage at Cana is the third of the events which are celebrated as the Epiphany of the Lord on 6 January. The story is read at the gospel of the second Sunday after Epiphany.

A great light

Galilee was the first to hear Jesus' message. This frontier region was constantly overrun by Assyria in the time of the prophet Isaiah. But even then, in his faith in God's grace, the prophet had predicted for it a glorious future. The prophecy comes true when this province is granted the privilege of being the first to hear the gospel. Matthew, having stated that Jesus went to live in Capernaum, continues:

> "[This was] that what was spoken by the prophet Isaiah
> might be fulfilled:
> 'The land of Zebulon and the land of Naphtali,
> toward the sea, across the Jordan,
> Galilee of the Gentiles—
> the people who sat in darkness
> have seen a great light,
> and for those who sat in the region and shadow of death
> light has dawned'" (Mt. 4:14–16).

Wine at a marriage, light in the darkness—this is how the gospels see his appearance in Galilee.

The message now delivered by Jesus can be summed up in one word: the kingdom of heaven. "From that time Jesus began to preach, saying, 'Repent, for the kingdom of heaven is at hand'" (Mt. 4:17).

The meaning of "kingdom of heaven"

What Jesus actually said was, "the kingdom of God", as three of the four evangelists record. But Matthew writes consistently, "the kingdom of heaven". He conforms to the rabbinical custom of replacing "God" by "heaven", out of reverence.

It is therefore the kingdom of God. But kingdom is not understood here as the region or realm where God is king, but as God's kingship. Hence "Kingship, reign of God", or "Lordship of God" would also be a very good translation. It was a word full of meaning for its hearers. It did not need to be explained to them, any more than "health" to those who are ill or "peace" to those who are at war. It was the consummation which they all longed for. The notion had been built up in the Old Testament, and the term crystallized the belief that God was Lord of this world and hence that he would one day manifest himself to banish injustice and misery from this life, so full of tormented questionings. This is the true kernel of the hope. 38 40 68 155–156

But in the course of time, the expectation had taken on various forms, many of which were less pure and noble ... There were men prepared to reach for their swords at the first mention of the word. They thought of the reign of God as the subjugation of the heathen, a national revival, a State where God would rule. Others saw the coming of the kingdom as a divine irruption which would shake the pillars of heaven and resurrect a new world. They often indulged in speculations as to the exact day on which the world was to come to an end. The descriptions of it were often highly fantastic. This vein in literature and tradition is called apocalyptic.

Both views rested on an often very materialistic and literal interpretation of the imagery of the prophets. What these had left open was given a fixed and definite form—nationalistic or apocalyptic. The pure kernel of the expectation of the reign of God was surrounded by less worthy feelings, above all, resentment. 60

The kingdom of God in Jesus' work

The first words which Jesus cried out to the world were: "Repent, for the kingdom of heaven is at hand." Men understood the terms he used. But how and in what form did Jesus understand the kingdom? No swords were drawn and no stars fell from heaven. This is the first strange thing about his preaching, that nothing of the sort occurred.

He also refused to indicate any date. "Watch therefore, for you do not know on what day your Lord is coming." Thus he condemned the human wish, which still exists, to find out the day on which the world will end. Such a precise date no doubt provides the faith with something exciting, and apparently fortifying, by fixing attention on something external and definite. But Jesus wished to convey a deeper truth.

He also avoids the imaginative descriptions which were then usual. No doubt he means to announce a divine intervention of world-wide import, but he does not think that the "end of the world" coincides with the first manifestation of the kingdom. Furthermore, his picture of the end is sober and restrained, compared to the apocalyptic tradition of the times. His message concentrates strongly not on any external event, but on the fact of God's rule.

This brings us to the most striking element of his message. He announces the kingship which has already begun. The kingdom is there—in Jesus' own work and preaching.

> "Then turning to the disciples he said privately, 'Blessed are the eyes which see what you see! For I tell you that many prophets and kings desired to see what you see, and did not see it, and to hear what you hear, and did not hear it'" (Lk. 10:23–24). And again:
> "Blessed is he who takes no offence at me" (Mt. 11:6).

No doubt, at the beginning, he kept the mystery of his person well in the background, and spoke only of God's lordship. But this does not hide the fact that this lordship was there through his own presence.

Whereas the apocalyptic seers spoke of events and things which were outside themselves, Jesus brings the kingdom along with him. For him, it is no distant vision. He is at the very centre, involved in a battle with another kingdom. "If it is by the finger of God that I cast out demons, then the kingdom of God has come upon you" (Lk. 11:20).

But there is nothing world-shattering to be seen. To those who ask for the exact date, Jesus answers: "The kingdom of God is not coming with signs to be observed; nor will they say,

'Lo, here it is!' or 'There!' for behold, the kingdom of God is in the midst of you" (Lk. 17:20–21). There is no national uprising, there are no signs in the heavens, but only something of God and heaven which is hidden in daily life, in the workaday world of man.

The parables

Jesus takes up a way of speaking which is in similes or "parables". Parables are stories which illustrate a point. The doctors of the law also used them at the time. But Jesus' use of them is quite different. The doctors of the law were concerned with explaining an existing text. On Jesus' lips, the parables themselves are the message. They relate in a simple and striking way incidents from daily life which everyone can follow. Sometimes they are events so strange that they rarely happen, like a banquet to which no one comes. But even these stories can be understood at once.

Jesus often begins his story with the simple, direct and engaging question, "Which of you ...?" This opening is characteristic of Jesus' personal style. It was used by no other rabbi of Jesus' time.

Jesus used these parables in order to make his meaning clear. Thus Mark writes: "With many such parables he spoke the word to them, as they were able to hear it" (Mk 4:33), that is, in such a way that they could understand it.

But there is something that must be present beforehand, if men are to understand. Jesus often cries out after a parable, "If any man has ears to hear, let him hear". What is indispensable is the inner readiness to give oneself, to be converted, a receptivity, an ear for the hidden message. Anyone without this readiness hears only the story. The misunderstood parable then becomes a sign that the hearers remain outside. The parable which was meant to be understood becomes a sign of reprobation. This is the meaning of Mark 4:10–13, a saying which should not be read except in the light of verse 33 of the same chapter, which we have just quoted.

The parables of the hidden kingdom

It is not surprising that some of Jesus' parables deal with the unexpected element of the kingdom: its hiddenness.

> "The kingdom of heaven is like leaven which a woman took and hid in three measures of meal, till it all was leavened" (Mt. 13:33).

> "Another parable he put before them, saying,
> 'The kingdom of heaven is like a grain of mustard-seed which a man took and sowed in his field; it is the smallest of all seeds, but when it has grown it is the greatest of shrubs and becomes a tree, so that the birds of the air come and make nests in its branches'" (Mt. 13:31–32).

There is a marvellous contrast between the beginnings of everyday things and their end, and Jesus uses this trait from nature to illustrate the apparent insignificance of the kingdom of God at the beginning. The little parable of the seed growing of itself also shows how modestly the kingdom makes its way, though also how supremely independent it is of men.

> "And he said, 'The kingdom of God is as if a man should scatter seed upon the ground, and should sleep and rise night and day, and the seed should sprout and grow, he knows not how. The earth produces of itself, first the blade, then the ear, then the full grain in the ear. But when the grain is ripe, at once he puts in the sickle, because the harvest has come'" (Mk 4:26–29).

These parables were certainly an answer to the doubters who were wondering—is this really the reign of God? We see 92–93 here the consequences of what Jesus undertook at his baptism. He was not to seek the external pomp which dazzles men without really helping them. His works were to be ordinary, unpretentious, unspectacular. The kingdom too was to have the form of a servant.

The eight beatitudes

This appears most strikingly in the introduction to the Sermor. 129–131 on the Mount, the discourse on a hill in Galilee in which Matthew collects many of Jesus' sayings:

"Blessed are the poor in spirit, for theirs is the kingdom of heaven.

Blessed are those who mourn, for they shall be comforted.

Blessed are the meek, for they shall inherit the earth.

Blessed are those who hunger and thirst for righteousness, for they shall be satisfied.

Blessed are the merciful, for they shall obtain mercy.

Blessed are the pure in heart, for they shall see God.

Blessed are the peacemakers, for they shall be called sons of God.

Blessed are those who are persecuted for righteousness' sake, for theirs is the kingdom of heaven" (Mt. 5:3–10).

Jesus did not mean to designate eight different classes of men by the beatitudes. They all mean one and the same group. It is not easy to define it. It would be wrong to see in it a definite social group such as the "have-nots". What the gospel says is the poor *in spirit*. It is not a matter of just having nothing, it is a mentality. On the other hand, it would be wrong to understand only those who had acquired the virtues of self-renunciation and peaceableness. Hence the beatitudes do not speak of any particular social class, nor are they just a summary of virtues.

Their meaning may be described as follows. They have in view men who have nothing to hope for from the world and look to God for everything; men who are cold-shouldered by the world but who bear no rancour and are wholly open to God. In a word, they are men whose lives resemble the way of submissiveness and loving service which Jesus himself adopted at his baptism. It is an attitude which throws all "worldly" rules into confusion. Thus the Son of God pronounces as blessed those who live such a life as he chose for himself. They are in an ideal position to await the kingdom of God, indeed, to receive it already here on earth as a deep joy in an existence which often seems to be far from attractive. God will comfort them and fill them with good things and make them his children.

Sometimes they will be poor men, sometimes men of virtue. But they can include such men as the tax-collector in the Temple (cf. Lk. 18:9–14), who was neither poor nor virtuous, but became conscious of his inadequacy, and hence hungered and thirsted seriously after righteousness, fully ready to reform. The beatitudes do not speak of something that is already complete and achieved, but of the great and stirring truth, that God will be there for all who feel their need of him and hope in him. And it also appears that God's verdict on success and failure, high and low, joy and sorrow, is different from ours.

In Israel in the time of Jesus there were very distinct groups of good people, who imagined themselves to be the pure "remnant" of the people. And in a certain sense they were— they were loyal to the law and the faith. One of these groups were the Pharisees ("the separated"). Jesus does not link up with an existing "pure remnant" of this type. He collects quite a different class of men. He looks to the lost sheep of Israel. No Pharisee need be excluded, but he must be the sort of person described in the beatitudes. This was what was shocking. "Many that are first will be last, and the last first" (Mk 10:31). "Blessed is he who takes no offence at me" (Mt. 11:6). In fact, most of the Pharisees and the doctors of the law remained aloof, while many insignificant people joined him.

"Desegregation"

How familiar boundaries could be displaced by Jesus' message may be seen from the fact that he constantly demonstrated God's benevolence towards the Samaritans, a people with some unorthodox beliefs who lived between Judea and Galilee. Nonetheless, he does not appear to have placed their heresy on the same footing as Judaism (cf. Jn 4:22).

Jesus probably did not preach outside Palestine, but it was a foreigner, the centurion of Capernaum, who gave him occasion to speak of the many who were to come from East and West and sit at table with Abraham, Isaac and Jacob (cf. Mt. 8:11). Hence even the boundaries of Israel are no longer valid. No doubt, salvation begins with the Jews, but the people which is to be gathered for the kingdom comes from all over the world. This too was found shocking.

87 But what was most bewildering was the way he overstepped the boundaries in his dealings with public sinners. When he is invited to dine by a Pharisee, one of the "respectable people", he accepts (Lk. 7:36). But he also accepts the invitation of a tax-collector working for the Romans, a swindler and a deserter from his people. Indeed, he even invites himself to his house

(Lk. 19:5–6). This was unheard of. A religious teacher never stooped to eat with sinners.

It would be a superficial view of the matter to take Jesus' behaviour merely as a deliberate disregard of conventions. Still less did he intend to be just the good companion who would leave these sinners as they were. They were in misery, and he brought the kingdom of God: His eating with them was part of the coming of the kingdom. The repast in common was for Jesus a symbol of the joys of messianic times and of unity with God. This he was to demonstrate for all times at his last supper, 163–164 but these other meals we read about were pointers in the same direction. To eat along with sinners meant that he was bringing them God's loving lordship, and hence liberation from sin.

Such incidents radiate a profound happiness. They show how the coming of God's kingdom was embodied in his work— and also what sort of men Jesus intended by his beatitudes. Here is one of such happy moments:

> "He entered Jericho and was passing through. And there was a man named Zacchaeus; he was a chief tax-collector, and rich. And he sought to see who Jesus was, but could not, on account of the crowd, because he was small of stature. So he ran on ahead and climbed up into a sycamore tree to see him, for he was to pass that way. And when Jesus came to the place, he looked up and said to him, 'Zacchaeus, make haste and come down; for I must stay at your house today'. So he made haste and came down, and received him joyfully. And when they saw it they all murmured, 'He has gone in to be the guest of a man who is a sinner'. And Zacchaeus stood and said to the Lord, 'Behold, Lord, the half of my goods I give to the poor; and if I have defrauded anyone of anything, I restore it fourfold'. And Jesus said to him, 'Today salvation has come to this house, since he is also a son of Abraham. For the Son of Man came to seek and to save the lost'" (Lk. 19:1–10).

Joy

The coming of the kingdom is God's grace decreed and given. But grace demands that we should give ourselves up to it. How is this to be done?

Our Lord has told us: "Whoever does not receive the kingdom of God like a child shall not enter it" (Mk 10:15). This does not mean, as is sometimes thought, rather romantically, that Jesus holds up the innocence of the child as an ideal. It means "to feel small", to accept being given something, and also, no doubt, the lowliness of a new start. It corresponds to what Jesus says to Nicodemus in the gospel of John: "Unless one is born anew, he cannot see the kingdom of God" (Jn 3:3). It is the same attitude as that called for in the beatitudes.

Those who thus become as little children, who allow themselves to be given grace, and who surrender themselves in turn, receive the joy that comes from God. To refuse is to miss this joy. The gospel often notes the deep sadness of those who cling to their old way of life and refuse to allow God entrance. It breaks out in "murmurs" or groans of disapproval when Jesus eats with sinners (Lk. 19:7), when he heals the sick (Mk 3:6), and when the children dance for joy in the Temple (Mt. 21:15). The workers who had been in the vineyard before the eleventh hour (Mt. 20:11) and the elder brother of the prodigal are also joyless. "But it was fitting to make merry and be glad, for this your brother was dead, and is alive; he was lost, and is found" (Lk. 15:32).

The joy is the joy of those who do not feel sure of their own excellence, but of God's grace. They are men who know that much has been given them. Hence perhaps the grimmest example of refusal of the messianic joy is given in the parable of the man released from a debt bigger probably than anyone in Palestine could pay (more than three million pounds). He goes and throttles a fellow-servant for the sake of a five pound note. He forgets all that God forgave him, and the joy of his release, and goes over to the attack like somebody standing on his rights (Mt. 18:21–35). To refuse to forgive others, according to Jesus, is to forget one's own guilt and pardon and joy.

453–454
479–481

Judgment

Jesus' message is a very serious one. Take the parable of the sower (Mt. 13:3–23). He who encounters the kingdom is either stony or good earth. Indeed, the ground can be good to start with, but the growth can be choked by "the cares of the world and the delight in riches" (Mt. 13:22). "Enter by the narrow gate; for the way is wide and easy that leads to destruction, and those who enter by it are many" (Mt. 7:13; cf. Lk. 13:23). This is a terrifying warning. Jesus makes no pronouncement on the *number* of the saved. But he does say that there are very many who refuse to respond or who spoil the gift of themselves by their half-heartedness, and that they thereby refuse joy, perhaps their eternal joy. He sees the way as narrow.

We should not go on talking about the saying till it has lost its awe-inspiring seriousness. But we should always think rather of our own personal case than of mankind in general. This seems to be Jesus' intention, according to Luke 13:23f. He is asked, "Lord, will those who are saved be few?". This is a question about humanity in general, but he replies with a warning addressed to the bystanders: "Strive to enter by the narrow door; for many, I tell you, will seek to enter and will not be able." What each one must do is to try to enter. Each individual has the real possibility in his grasp. We can make no judgment about the number.

The kingdom is something for which all should be given:

> "The kingdom of heaven is like treasure hidden in a field, which a man found and covered up; then in his joy he goes and sells all that he has and buys that field" (Mt. 13:44).

Jesus says the same thing in the Sermon on the Mount, but with such seriousness and urgency that eternity seems very close:

> "If your right eye causes you to sin, pluck it out and throw it away; it is better that you lose one of your members than that your whole body be thrown into hell. And if your right hand causes you to sin, cut it off and throw it away; it is better that you lose one of your members than that your whole body go into hell" (Mt. 5:29–30).

Again and again Jesus calls for watchfulness:

> "Let your loins be girded and your lamps burning, and be like men who are waiting for their master to come home from the marriage feast, so that they may open to him at once when he comes and knocks.

> Blessed are those servants whom the master finds awake when he comes; truly, I say to you, he will gird himself and have them sit at table, and he will come and serve them" (Lk. 12:35–37).

160 Jesus explains in Matthew 25:31–46 the kind of deeds which he demands. There men are acquitted or condemned for the good that they have done or omitted towards "one of the least of these" whom Jesus calls his brothers.

The kingdom in the course of time

The kingdom of God is sublime and divine, yet it never loses touch with the everyday world, with the here and now, with us. We are constructing eternity now. The date of the kingship is "today", the moment of Jesus' presence. But, as we have seen in the many parables of growth, it is to penetrate all things more and more. It grows towards a manifestation in the future.

The first manifestation is Jesus' resurrection. Hence Jesus says: "Truly, I say to you, there are some standing here who will not taste death before they see the kingdom of God come with power" (Mk 9:1). This is the great moment when God is to demonstrate his lordship by raising Jesus from the dead and by giving the Spirit to men. Then began a time when God's lordship was to extend over the world. Jesus chose disciples for this work: "Fear not, little flock, for it is your Father's good pleasure to give you the kingdom" (Lk. 12:32). He even left behind him "the keys of the kingdom of heaven". In a word: to make his kingdom live in the world, he formed for himself a people. This people is called by him "his Church". The Church 144 is not yet the kingdom, but "it forms the embryonic and initial stage of the kingdom on earth, during which the Church grows gradually, yearning for the consummation of the kingdom, hoping and praying with all its might to be united with its king in glory" (Vatican II, Constitution on the Church, no. 5).

"Then comes the end, when he delivers the kingdom to God the Father after destroying every rule and every authority and power. For he must reign until he has put all his enemies under his feet. The last enemy to be destroyed is death . . . When all things are subjected to him, then the Son himself will also be subjected to him who put all things under him, that God may be everything to every one" (1 Cor. 15:24–29). The kingdom which was first manifested in simplicity and love in the country-side of Galilee, is to reach its fulfilment in a great love among all that exists.

To receive the kingdom means to be ready to hear this message. To believe in the kingdom means to believe in this immortal unity of man in the joy of the Father.

The Church proclaims Jesus

Many things have remained unsaid about the kingdom in this chapter. Nothing has been said of the Father, though the Father is the centre of Jesus' thoughts, the sun which radiates through his spirit. But it is no great harm that so much has been omitted, because we shall have to speak again many times of God's lordship in the course of the book. Indeed, there is not a page of this book that does not in some way speak of it.

Nonetheless, we do not use the term "kingdom of God" as often as Jesus did. Nor did the Church do so, from the earliest times. Some have said that this was because the Church spoke too much of the Church. But this is not the real reason. The real reason is that with Jesus' resurrection and glorification came the revelation of who he was. This humble figure is not merely the preacher of the kingship, he is also the king. This rabbi is not merely the herald of the lordship, he is also the Lord. Indeed, as Origen said, "he is himself the kingdom". To see him is to see 150–151 the Father. Hence to proclaim him is to proclaim the kingdom, and this is what the Church has, tried to do. Throughout all the ages during which it preached Jesus, it was preaching the king-dom.

It is well to return again and again to Galilee to hear the message. One of the ways in which we do this is through the liturgy. At many of the Sunday Masses, one of the parables of the kingdom of heaven is read as the gospel of the day. And no day goes by without the prayer going up to God from the Christian family: "thy kingdom come".

58–59   *Prophecies fulfilled*

Jesus made the kingdom manifest in his preaching and *in his signs*. "If it is by the finger of God that I cast out demons, then the kingdom of God is come upon you" (Lk. 11:20).

When John the Baptist sent messengers from his prison to ask Jesus about his Messiahship, Jesus answered: "Go and tell John what you hear *and see*: the blind receive their sight and the lame walk, lepers are cleansed and the deaf hear, and the dead are raised up and the poor have the Good News preached to them" (Mt. 11:4–5).

This was a reference to the prophetic words of Isaiah about the coming of God:

> Say to those who are of a fearful heart,
> "Be strong and fear not!
> Behold, your God—
> he will come with vengeance, with the recompense
>   of God.
> He will come and save you.
> Then the eyes of the blind shall be opened,
>   and the ears of the deaf unstopped;
> then shall the lame man leap like a hart,
>   and the tongue of the dumb sing for joy.
> For waters shall break forth in the wilderness,
>   and streams in the desert" (Is. 35:4–6).

(It should be noted that the promise of vengeance and recompense in the prophecy is simply the promise of liberation, put in Old Testament terms.) Jesus' signs show him as the promised bringer of God's joy. Possibly these wonders appeared less breath-taking, more amiable, than the prophets had suggested. John had undoubtedly expected the blasts of the winnowing-fan, the judge coming to baptize the world with fire. But even in the signs there seems to have been something that marked them as Jesus' own—something unexpectedly mild and gracious. This does not make them in any way less marvellous. On the contrary, it makes them very special signs of God's majesty in its intimacy with men's misery.

The nature of miracle

It is well to consider for a moment what the Bible understands by miracle. A miracle, according to Scripture, is something in which man sees God at work. Thus one of the psalms says of the starry heavens: "Let the heavens praise thy wonders, O Lord" (Ps. 89:6). But the word is used above all for events in which God's saving power is very specially manifest. They occur in the New Testament in connection with Christ's goodness, striking events which arouse wonder and have a definite significance. They are called "miracles", "signs", "works", "mighty deeds". It is quite natural that as men of modern times, whose knowledge of nature and its laws increases yearly, we should put the question: Are these signs events which are "outside the laws of nature"? This approach, as has already been shown, is not that of the Bible. And even for ourselves, the question is steadily losing its meaning. After all, what do we know of the relationship between the new creation, which is here breaking through, and the laws of nature?

The one thing that we can say with certainty is that—always linked with salvation and judgment, and above all, always linked with Christ—mighty forces are released for man's benefit. There is no reason to regard this as an arbitrary and extrinsic intervention on the part of God, as though God were thwarting his own work of creation. On the contrary, the miracles do not resist the forces of nature. They leave them to act with marvellous success and effectiveness, in keeping with the "longing" and the "groaning" which lives deep within nature itself (Rom. 8:22f.). "My Father is working still, and I am working" (Jn 5:17).

We should not therefore speak of "exceptions to the laws of nature". We must rather say that miracles teach man that he does not know what can happen within himself and in the world—"There are more things in heaven and earth, Horatio, Than are dreamt of in your philosophy" *(Hamlet)*.

Man is filled with wonder when the world gives him a glimpse of its real purpose and perfection. In the miracle, the believer senses the initial effects of the new creation: of the new world into which the Risen Lord has entered.

Jesus' miracles: characteristics

The miracles narrated of Jesus have on the whole such original and characteristic traits that there is only one conclusion possible: that Jesus did in fact work miracles.

The first notable thing about them, in the eyes of the biblical scholar, is that they are so few. They are by no means the main content of the gospels, as they are in many of the biographies of great men of the time.

Another remarkable thing is the unselfishness of Jesus' signs. 93 This was already noticeable in the temptations in the desert. Jesus refused to perform a miracle for his own benefit or to put on a spectacle. And in fact none of the miracles which he wrought was for his own benefit. They cease with his passion.

He avoided just as deliberately anything that might bring the miracle into the sphere of the show-piece or that might make of 443–445 it a mere demonstration of power. One need only compare Jesus' life with that of many magicians, wonder-workers and practitioners of occult sciences, to be struck by the simplicity, sobriety and impressive dignity of his work. Even when he adopts a particular ritual, an ablution, for instance, everything remains very simple. In a word, the miracles were not performed before a public, but directed to persons.

Then there is the effortlessness with which Jesus wrought his signs: no hypnotism, no irrelevant ceremonial, no complicated preparations or teams of helpers. There is only a simple, authoritative word, sometimes spoken at a great distance. His miracles have the tranquillity of God's creative action.

There is not the slightest trace of "magic" in Jesus' miraculous powers. Magic is the effort to bring divine power under one's control by certain operations, without giving oneself to God, without personal relationship. But Jesus prays expressly before his miracles: "Father, I thank thee that thou heard me" (Jn 11:41). As the Son, he works in a personal relationship along with the Father, and does not really need to ask. "I knew that thou hearest me always, but I have said this on account of the people standing by" (Jn 11:42).

The fact that Jesus' miracles were signs of his mission does not mean that the men on whom they were worked were indifferent to him. The living, human being was not the chance object on which he exercised his power. He worked his miracles "out of compassion" (Lk. 7:13). It is part of the very sign that God's help is seen to be personal and genuinely kind. It is part of the sign that even the healing of a sickness is a genuinely salvific work.

It is highly instructive that not one of Jesus' signs is punitive. 494–495 This may be contrasted with the Old Testament, where there are stories of how God's "judgment" sometimes works in a miraculous manner. This is never the case with Jesus himself. When the "sons of thunder" demand fire from heaven, Jesus turns on them and rebukes them severely (Lk. 9:55). The withering of the fig-tree (Mk 11:12–14, 20) was not a punishment, but a warning. And we can see from Luke, who gives a parable instead of this miracle (Lk. 13:6–9), how gentle and patient this warning was.

Cures

Jesus' miracles are mostly bodily cures. God meant his envoy to be seen as one who could heal, as one who overcomes death. This is then made fully clear in the three instances of the dead being raised to life. It is hard to say which of these stories is the most beautiful (Mk 5:21–43; Lk. 7:11–17; Jn 11). Jesus sees his struggle against sickness and death as a struggle against evil, indeed, against the evil one.

Of the woman so crippled that she was bent double and unable to stand up straight, Jesus says that she was fettered by Satan— 92–93 like a tethered beast which cannot go to the drinking-trough 482 (Lk. 13:15–16). Jesus came to heal a deeper wound. Those who are cured of a bodily sickness must one day die. Jesus' work is to bring about a healing which will endure through death. He heals the wounds of sin, and the bodily cures are signs of this. 111–112 They are a sign that the kingdom is at war—against evil.

Exorcisms

This is made still clearer by another type of miracle. Jesus sometimes meets men who are "possessed by the devil". In the gospels, the possessed are not to be understood as sinful men, but as men who are not themselves and give visible and audible signs of insanity and even frenzy. Some of the possessed are described as afflicted by illness, as in Matthew 17:15, where we read that the boy tormented by the demon was "an epileptic". Thus the gospels do not make such a distinction as we imagine between being ill and being possessed. Jesus saw something of the Adversary in both: in the deformed backbone (Lk. 13:16) and in the lonely cries "among the tombs and on the mountains" (Mk 5:5). But in the latter case Jesus confronted evil more directly: here man's spirit and not his body was affected. Jesus' power to bring deliverance in such need was one of the clearest signs of the kingdom.

Jesus speaks of Satan as a personal power. The gospel records a number of occasions on which the possessed cried out that Jesus was "the holy one of God" (Mk 1:24) or "Son of the Most High God" (Mk 5:7). What powers were at work here we do not know.

Jesus once showed his majesty very clearly by freeing a sadly tormented victim and then allowing the evil power (called "Legion") to go into a herd of pigs, which then rushed down the mountainside into a lake. In this way, through an event in nature, we are given a glimpse of the fierceness with which the struggle is waged. But it is not the stampede of the pigs that is the real sign, but the fact that "they (the Gerasenes) came to Jesus and saw the demoniac sitting there, clothed and in his right mind" (Mk 5:15). This is the real sign: a man healed.

Miracles in nature

Finally, there are the miracles which Jesus worked upon natural objects. They are not described as random demonstrations of strength, but as signs, directed to persons in their own familiar surroundings. The stilling of the storm signifies the security of those who follow him. The wonderful catch of fish is the unexpected gift after wasted effort—and also a sign of the task of being fishers of men. The miraculous multiplication of the loaves is the stilling of hunger, and a symbol of the messianic banquet, which is to be given a fuller manifestation in the eating of Jesus' flesh and the drinking of his blood (Jn 6).

In the service of the word

Once, when some people sought him out because he was able to perform miracles, he said: "Let us go on to the next towns, that I may preach there also; for that is why I came out" (Mk 1:38).

Jesus' preaching is his main task. This preaching is "the sign of Jonah", the prophet (Lk. 11:29). Where there is no connection

with the preaching, Jesus works no miracles, as for instance
when he finds himself faced with unresponsive men—his fellow-
townsmen in Nazareth, the Pharisees, Herod. And though we
read in one place, "Believe me . . . or else believe for the sake
of the works themselves" (Jn 14:11), we also read that Jesus had
little confidence in those who only believed on account of the
works (Jn 2:23–24). And speaking of the brothers of the rich
miser, he said, "If they do not hear Moses and the prophets,
neither will they be convinced if some one should rise from the
dead" (Lk. 16:31).

Faith and miracle

Thus there is an initial faith which precedes the miracle. The
miracle strengthens and stabilizes it. Sometimes Jesus himself
calls for a strong faith. This perhaps surprises us. It was in such a
situation that the prayer was uttered, "I believe; help my
unbelief!". The demand for an initial faith does not, however,
mean that the miracle is worked by faith—as sometimes happens
in the case of the "faith-healers". Faith, the surrender of self, is
a preliminary requirement, but it is God who heals. Hence it need
not be the sick man himself who has faith. In Mark 9:24 it is the
father of the sick boy. If the miracle was due to an intense effort
of faith, it would be a feat performed by the sick person himself,
and not a sign of the kingdom. The miracle is a work of God
which points to a deeper deliverance: the acceptance of God's
reign.

Signs

Jesus' signs are not merely an adjunct to his preaching. They also
speak for themselves. "The deeds of the Word are themselves
words" (St Augustine).

Hence Jesus once healed a cripple as a sign of the forgiveness 328
of sins (Mt. 9:6–7). The healing was not merely the external
proof that Jesus could accomplish the invisible action of forgiving
sin. It was also meant as an outward sign of what happened
within. The well-being of the man as he went home with his
pallet on his back signifies forgiveness, a cure that reaches out
beyond death. Hence the Christians of the catacombs depicted
this "bed-porter" on the graves of their dead friends. The
healing signified forgiveness through baptism, and eternal joy.

111

252-255   The sacraments are, in fact, the most authentic prolongation
164   of Christ's signs. The Gospel of St John pays particular attention
to this point. It was written in a community which had already
had more than half a century's experience of the Lord in the
207-208   sacraments. Thus for instance the multiplication of the loaves
(Jn 6) points to the Eucharist as food, and the healing of the man
born blind (Jn 9) to baptism as illumination.

But though the sacraments are the most authentic continuation of Jesus' signs, he also decreed that his earthly wonders
should live on in his Church as signs. "The Lord worked with
them and confirmed the message by the signs that attended it"
as the ending of Mark says. In the life of the Church the
miracle is so "ordinary" that for many centuries no one has been
canonized unless at least two miracles can be ascribed to his
intervention, as a sign that the Lord did in fact "work with
him".

But what is true of Jesus' earthly life is also true of his work
in the Church. The miracles, which affect only a few, are not
his greatest gift. The great realities are his word and his Eucharist
and his forgiveness and the other sacraments—the signs of him
which are there for all.

304-319   THE TEACHER OF PRAYER

We must now turn to Jesus' direct contact with the Father who
was always the centre of his thoughts. Jesus was a man who
prayed. He did not confine himself to any one form of prayer.
We see him active on every level on which man tries to make
contact with God. He celebrated the prescribed liturgy of a feast
with his disciples (Mt. 26:30). And when he went to the syna-
gogue, he joined in the psalms and prayers. There is no reason
to believe that he did otherwise. He found the Father along
with his people. We are told that on one occasion he intoned
an Old Testament psalm (Mk 15:34), which he probably recited to the end.

But this most original of all men mostly used his own words.
97   They are found in the prayer which is most characteristic of
him. We could already surmise from the parables that it would
be simple and direct. And in fact he prays to the Father with
the utmost simplicity (see for instance Lk. 10:21). This is the
way we must imagine that he prayed on the occasions when

"all night he continued in prayer to God", alone on the hills (Lk. 6:12). Jesus may of course have prayed without words, but this is nowhere said.

Prayer and mission

It is easy to recognize that Jesus' prayer is always spoken of in connection with his mission. His withdrawal into the desert— the "retreat" to which he was impelled by the Holy Spirit— is described as a preparation for his task. Later, he also took refuge in isolation, when the world tried to force a worldly Messiahship upon him, and this is in the same line. He goes to the desert to make contact with his Father and so fulfil his vocation in all its purity. Before choosing the Apostles, he passes the night in prayer. Each of his fellow-workers is given him by his Father in prayer. His miracles were prayed for, and performed by virtue of his personal relationship to the Father.

Mark has preserved for us a little episode which shows in unexpectedly sharp contours the place which prayer held in Jesus' life.

> "And in the morning, a great while before day, he rose and went out to a lonely place, and there he prayed. And Simon and those who were with him followed him, and they found him and said to him, 'Every one is searching for you'. And he said to them, 'Let us go on to the next towns that I may preach there also; for that is why I came out'" (Mk 1:35–38).

The Christian of today, who knows that every good work done out of charity is also a prayer, is surprised to read this. He sees how Jesus withdraws to pray. It shows how much we should reproach ourselves if we neglect our intercourse with God and devote *all* our time to work, housekeeping or charitable works. 311–312

And the little incident also tells us why. After a night of prayer, Jesus realizes still more profoundly what his real task is, where his true service to man lies, and hence moves on. It is through prayer that the compass which directs our activities remains true.

And the prayer itself is a force which sustains others. "Simon, Simon, behold, Satan demanded to have you all, that he might sift you all like wheat, but I have prayed for you [Simon], that your faith may not fail; and when you have turned again, strengthen your brethren" (Lk. 22:31–32).

Transfiguration

Thus Jesus' life and work is penetrated by prayer. The gospels show how the glory of his intercourse with the Father was once revealed in all its brightness. As he was praying on a mountain, a voice was heard, a luminous cloud appeared and his face and garments were suffused with light. These outwards symbols were a manifestation of the inward event—the presence of the Father to the Son in the Spirit. It was a glorious witness to his baptism and vocation. It was also a revelation of the world of warmth and love in which the Father and the Son were united to one another.

But even at this heavenly moment the earthly task is extraordinarily close. Two toilers who had preceded him, Moses and Elijah, also appear, and he speaks to them of his Exodus (this is the word used for "departure", meaning death) "which he was to accomplish at Jerusalem" (Lk. 9:31). Thus Jesus' prayer is not a flight from life or an evasion of his task, but an essential part of it.

Last prayers on earth

We can read in John 17 of the prayer which Jesus uttered at the Last Supper, as it was recalled by the disciple who at that meal leaned on Jesus' breast, and written down by him many years later, in the form inspired by the Spirit of Jesus. Jesus prays for his Church in "the high priestly prayer". Behind this fervent address to the Father we hear the voice of the glorified Lord with particular clarity. We encounter in it the whole reality of Jesus.

But the most moving prayer of Jesus is undoubtedly the cry which he uttered in the Garden of Olives, "Abba, Father, all things are possible to thee; remove this cup from me; yet not what I will, but what thou wilt" (Mk 14:36).

Hand in hand with the Father he trod his path. The head of the new people of God, he gave his life its greatness by making it a life of prayer.

"*Abba*"

There is a term in Jesus' vocabulary which sums up everything.
It is the word "Abba". This is what Jesus calls God. It means
"Father". The unfathomable depths of the love between the
Son and the Father are revealed in this very human word. It
denotes a wealth of familiarity and simplicity—since God is
utterly simple, and the word "Abba" signifies something even
more intimate than "Father". It is the expression of confident 382–383
familiarity used by children, the sort of sound most readily
formed by an infant's lips—like "dada". The Aramaic *abba* is
itself a diminutive. And this is how Jesus addresses God. And
he also taught us to say "Abba!". He did so during his life,
and also by his Spirit after his resurrection.

"We do not know how to pray as we ought, but the Spirit
himself intercedes for us with sighs too deep for words." "You
have received the spirit of sonship. When we cry, 'Abba,
Father!' it is the Spirit himself bearing witness with our spirit
that we are children of God" (Rom. 8:26, 15–16). These words
refer to the early Christian community, where prayer inspired
by the Spirit was offered, sometimes in ecstasy. Greek-speakers 195–196
could be heard pronouncing the Aramaic word "Abba".

The difficult words of Paul just quoted can be understood
at once when we understand the kernel of his thought, which is
the word "Abba". The Spirit of Jesus impelled Christians to be
bold enough to address God by the familiar term "Father".
That same Spirit impels us now to do the same.

God is also addressed solemnly as Father a number of times
in the Old Testament. He is Father of the people, of the chosen
king, of the pious. But just as Jesus' preaching of the kingdom
of God was new, and brought it close to men, so, too, he makes
the Father known in a new and more intimate way. He speaks
from the standpoint of the Son. We must turn to the Father as
normally and permanently as the Son, along with the Son.
This is infinitely richer than the title of father in the Old Testament.

But Jesus' way of speaking also makes it clear that he himself
has a more profound relationship to the Father than we. Jesus
never says "Our Father" (except when putting these words
on our lips). He says "my Father and your Father". God is not
our Father in the same way as he is Father of Jesus. Sonship 153
does not accrue to him. He possesses it from the beginning. 77–82

115

495-502 Our sonship is an event which is accomplished in us through Jesus. This event is the coming of the kingdom of heaven.

If we wish to know exactly what Jesus understood by the word Father in our regard, we must look at the place where he himself explains it—the story of the merciful father. Traditionally this story is generally given the less appropriate title of "the prodigal son", but the main figure is the Father. For those who are ready to understand, Jesus gives in this parable his description of God as Father (Lk. 15:11–32).

Thus he made use of something as simple and natural as fatherhood in order to name God. Those who have a faulty notion of "Father" have a long way to go before they can approach God with uninhibited heart and say, "The Spirit which I have received is not the spirit of slavery, to fall back into fear, but I have received the spirit of sonship through which I cry, 'Abba, Father!'" (cf. Rom. 8:15). But since the Son is man, and our brother, each of us has Jesus as his brother on his way through life, and hence makes loving contact with God's mystery. And the effort to visualize God's Fatherhood can lead to a clear and unambiguous attitude of sonship towards the one unique Father.

296-297 appear in left margin

119 *Confidence and persistence*

Jesus teaches us that man may come as he is to God, with all his needs and desires, in his daily round of ordinary duties. The Father knows that we have very great need of ordinary things. Hence Jesus says that we must not be long-winded in our prayers, as the heathens are (Mt. 6:7–8), and also counsels us insistently to continue to ask again and again for what we need. The word "to badger" seems hardly too strong when we read in Luke 11:5–13 and 18:1–7 of the neighbour who arrives late in the evening to ask for a loan of food, and of the widow petitioning the judge.

The two directives seem to contradict one another. We must not use many words, and we must indeed use many words. But if we consider Jesus' intention, they envisage the same thing: to deal with God as our Father. On the one hand, the favourable answer is not a sort of recompense which can be calculated as a sort of *quid pro quo* for a well-phrased request, in the way in which the heathens counted on an answer which would be a fair compensation for human effort. On the other hand, it is

God's will that we importune him in season and out of season. Both directives are therefore an invitation to limitless confidence.

Jesus' counsel, that we should retire into an inner room to pray, is also based on God's Fatherhood. "Your Father who sees in secret will reward you" (Mt. 6:6).

Jesus ascribes particular value to the prayer which is offered in common by men as brothers and sisters:

> "Again I say to you, if two of you agree on earth about anything they ask, it will be done for them by my Father in heaven. For where two or three are gathered in my name, there am I in the midst of them" (Mt. 18:19–20).

Confidence, sincerity, watchfulness

The bold confidence which Jesus urges on us is not irreverence. The Father whom we wish to approach is the Father who is in heaven, the holy God from whose presence all falsehood and impurity is banished. Prayer, as described by Jesus, is offered up by men who are in all respects needy and deficient. But at the same time Jesus demands that we should not be hypocrites in the presence of the Father. "Not every one who says to me, 'Lord, Lord', shall enter the kingdom of heaven, but he who does the will of my Father who is in heaven" (Mt. 7:21).

> "So if you are offering your gift at the altar and there remember that your brother has something against you, leave your gift there before the altar and go; first be reconciled to your brother, and then come and offer your gift" (Mt. 5:23–24).

Hence Jesus also says: "Watch and pray." Prayer, he teaches, is something to be done with attentiveness, with preparedness, with a watchful eye on the kingdom's coming:

> "Take heed to yourselves lest your hearts be weighed down with dissipation and drunkenness and cares of this life, and that day come upon you suddenly like a snare; for it will come upon all who dwell upon the face of the whole earth. But watch at all times,

praying that you may have strength to escape all these things that will take place, and to stand before the Son of man" (Lk. 21:34–36).

Or as Jesus said in the garden: "Watch and pray that you may not enter into temptation" (Mk 14:38). And hence the Lord's Prayer says: "Lead us not into temptation, but deliver us from evil."

The expectant readiness for God's coming is also supposed in the petition, "Hallowed be thy name", which asks that God may show his power and glory. We must not underestimate the meaning of this petition. It is a request that God may appear in our world and in our life—the same as in the petition, "Thy kingdom come".

"Forgive us our trespasses"

This basic attitude of reverent expectancy explains how Jesus could speak in a very surprising way when dealing, so to speak, with the question of how God can permit so much evil, if he is a Father. This question, by which men try to call God to account, is turned back upon the questioner by Jesus. This may be seen from his reaction to two public disasters.

There were some present at that very time who told him of the Galileans whose blood Pilate had mingled with their sacrifices. And he answered them, "Do you think that these Galileans were worse sinners than all the other Galileans, because they suffered thus? I tell you, No; but unless you repent you will all likewise perish. Or those eighteen upon whom the tower in Siloam fell and killed them, do you think that they were worse offenders than all the others who dwelt in Jerusalem? I tell you, No; but unless you repent you will all likewise perish" (Lk. 13:1–5).

Thus Jesus opposes the Old Testament view, which saw in a calamity a sign of someone's guilt. This is not a New Testament view, and we should rid ourselves of it entirely. But Jesus' attitude also shows that he does not consider man as such guiltless. And hence "forgive us our trespasses" is included in the prayer that he taught. He considers man to be in the state of the debtor in the parable, whose debt of ten thousand talents (three million pounds) was forgiven (Mt. 18:23–27).

This, of course, does not answer all questions about suffering. Later on in this book we shall discuss how the gospel message shows us that God does not passively permit evil and suffering, but fights against them actively. But here something of supreme importance is determined by Jesus' words: our attitude to God. It is not God who is to be called to account, but we. God shows his attitude in his love and patience with regard to us men who are evil. This is magnificently demonstrated by Jesus' whole life and passion. It is also revealed in the admonitory parable which follows:

492
501–502

> A man had a fig tree planted in his vineyard; and he came seeking fruit on it and found none. And he said to the vinedresser, "Lo, these three years I have come seeking fruit on this fig tree, and I find none. Cut it down; why should it use up the ground?" And he answered him, "Let it alone, sir, this year also, till I dig it about and put on manure. And if it bears fruit next year, well and good; but if not, you can cut it down" (Lk. 13:6–9).

The answer to prayer

495–497

Jesus also gives a surprising answer to another of man's questions. This is the question of unanswered prayer: "I have prayed, but nothing happens." Jesus simply says: "Whatever you ask in prayer, believe that you will receive it, and you will" (Mk 11:24). Matthew gives the saying in a less paradoxical form: "And whatever you ask in prayer, you will receive, if you have faith" (Mt. 21:22). The meaning is the same—that the answer is certain. This is Jesus' only reply to the question.

Hence those who have really understood the call to prayer will not fall silent if they receive no answer, but continue to pray. Jesus tells us to ask and ask: "Ask, and it will be given you; seek and you will find; knock, and it will be opened to you" (Lk. 11:9).

If we persevere thus, we shall be led to a point where the greatest prayer of all will begin to make itself heard in our contact with God: "Thy will be done on earth as it is in heaven." The will of God is something heavenly and majestic. But,

> "As the heavens are higher than the earth,
> so are my ways higher than your ways
> and my thoughts than your thoughts" (Is. 55:9).

We often fail to see how God hears us. The answer is always in the line of what we ask (since Jesus says, *all* that you ask), but it is often higher than what we ask.

The clearest instance is Jesus in the Garden of Olives. He prayed that his sufferings should pass him by—the most human and urgent of all prayers. But his sufferings came upon him. Nonetheless, he was heard in the line of his prayer, though on a higher level. As we read in the epistle to the Hebrews, written long after the resurrection:

> "In the days of his flesh, Jesus offered up prayers and supplications, with loud cries and tears, to him who was able to save him from death, and he was heard for his godly fear. Although he was a Son, he learned obedience through what he suffered" (Heb. 5:7–8).

Jesus begged to escape the sufferings of Good Friday, but was given the glory of Easter Sunday. Indeed, even during his prayer he had already included the proviso: not my will but thine be done. The will of God is heavenly, glorious, decisive. And hence we must rejoice inwardly and outwardly at Jesus' promise: ask and you shall receive. The great example of an answer to prayer, which was so sublime that it was not recognized, is the kingdom of God which Jesus brought. It was the answer to prayer—including the prayers of the Pharisees—to the plea for the coming of the kingdom. The answer was more heavenly, profound and simple, and closer to the heart's desire than they had expected. And hence they did not recognize it.

We need faith abounding and growing, not only to pray, but to be alert enough to see the answer to prayer. The crudest forms of blindness can occur. Sometimes we can have an abundance of earthly goods to prove that our prayer for our daily bread has been heard, and still we can say—all my prayers are unheard. We need faith to recognize the answer. We can constantly catch ourselves turning a blind eye to the hearing of our prayers.

Jesus also tells us to pray in his name (Jn 16:24). This means that we must make him our intercessor and that it is along with

Jesus our brother that we must approach the Father. But it also means that we must pray as he did, in the very same spirit, and this means always implying the words, "but not my will but thine be done". But this can only be learnt slowly. It is the task of a lifetime.

The Apostle who leaned on Jesus' breast and then lived on for some seventy years in the Spirit of Jesus, sums all this up in the words: "This is the confidence which we have in him, that if we ask anything according to his will he hears us. And if we know that he hears us in whatever we ask, we know that we have obtained the requests made of him" (1 Jn 5:14–15).

And Jesus says that the greatest gift is the good Spirit:

> "What father among you, if his son asks for a fish, will instead of a fish give him a serpent; or if he asks for an egg, will give him a scorpion? If you then, who are evil, know how to give good gifts to your children, how much more will the heavenly Father give the Holy Spirit to those who ask him?" (Lk. 11: 11–13).

The Our Father

All the foregoing is summed up in the prayer which Jesus gave us: "Pray then like this:

> Our Father who art in heaven,
> hallowed be thy name,
> thy kingdom come,
> thy will be done
> on earth as it is in heaven.
> Give us this day our daily bread,
> and forgive us our trespasses,
> as we forgive them that trespass against us;
> and lead us not into temptation,
> but deliver us from evil."

This is the form given by Matthew, as it has been rendered for many centuries by Catholics and Protestants with little difference in the translation. But Protestants generally add another clause, which is also added by the liturgies of the East. This ancient liturgical conclusion, which has also found its way into some

121

manuscripts of the Bible (and the Authorized Version used by English-speaking Protestants) is not part of the original text of Scripture. But it is very beautiful, and runs as follows: "For thine is the kingdom, the power, and the glory, for ever and ever. Amen."

The originality of the Our Father

Some clauses of the *Our Father* resemble parts of Jewish prayers of the time. But the *Our Father* as a whole is as different as is the kingdom which Jesus brought. First of all, there is the unheard-of simplicity of the form, which does not include any of the long preambles then usual, and, as we have just seen, has no solemn conclusion. Another unique characteristic is that the prayer for God's name and kingdom and will is completely detached from all nationalism; and it also comes at the start, before the prayer for our own needs. These latter petitions are characterized by their extreme realism and naturalness.

149   This prayer, for all its simplicity, brings the most human and everyday affairs into harmony with the tremendous divine future. It is too short and pregnant to be recited quickly. Catholics can learn something from Protestants in this matter.

We end this chapter with the comment given by the gospel
456–457 itself on the *Our Father*. It is brief and to the point. "For if you forgive men their trespasses, your heavenly Father will also forgive you; but if you do not forgive men their trespasses, neither will your Father forgive your trespasses" (Mt. 6:14–15).

THE WILL OF THE FATHER

The one desire of Jesus

89–91 Jesus, when he was still only twelve years old, startled those around him by revealing the one passionate longing of his heart: "Did you not know that I must be about my Father's business?" (Lk. 2:49). Thus, from the very first words that he speaks, the gospel describes him as a man completely taken up with the will of the Father. The inward unity between the Father
153–154 and his only-begotten Son who is God from God, Light from
77–82 Light, now becomes manifest in a human life.

122

And what this life shows is obedience. As the epistle to the 497-502
Hebrews says:

> "Consequently, when Christ came into the world,
>   he said,
> 'Sacrifices and offerings thou hast not desired,
> but a body thou hast prepared for me;
> in burnt offerings and sin offerings thou hast taken
>   no pleasure.'
> Then I said, 'Lo, I have come to do thy will, O God',
> as it is written of me in the roll of the book"
>   (Heb. 10:5–7).

Jesus did not find his task in life sombre or trying. It was his joy, as is magnificently described by St John in Jesus' conversation with the Samaritan woman at the well. After Jesus had opened the eyes of one of his fellow-men to the truth, "the disciples besought him, saying, 'Rabbi, eat'. But he said to them, 'I have a food to eat of which you do not know'. So the disciples said to one another, 'Has any one brought him food?' Jesus said to them, 'My food is to do the will of him who sent me, and to accomplish his work'" (Jn 4:31–34).

To sum up Jesus' personal "spirituality" in one word, one could say simply: the will of God. His "vocation" at the Jordan is a vocation to *service*. His preaching is God's *reign*. His deepest prayer is: Thy *will* be done. It all comes to the same thing—perfect obedience.

His life was not what might have been expected. Much of what might seem to be part of a full human existence was absent from this most perfect human life. Indeed, it might be asked whether this life could be called truly great. Is it not too limited in scope, too one-sided, too truncated? Jesus built up no fortune, did not marry and had no children. Man's greatest glory, his own will, was identified by Jesus with the will of Another.

But here there was in fact a life of grandeur and of many dimensions. He who possessed nothing, brought treasures which rust and moth could not consume. He who had no wife or child was brother and giver of new life to all who came to him. He made Another's will his own—but was there ever a freer man on earth than he?

Jesus lived a life before the eyes of men such as they had scarcely dreamt of. A life directed to the following out of God's

will is shown to be the richest, fullest and simplest that is possible in this world. This is God's kingdom and God's lordship.

236–241   *Faith*

289–297 Jesus has summoned us to live a life of the same obedience.
"Repent, and believe in the gospel"—the Good News.

    Faith comes first. The knowledge of the glad tidings is
gained by the surrender of the whole person, by going out of
111 oneself. This attitude is called faith. We saw above that Jesus'
miracles could be a way to faith, but we also saw that the
miracles never occurred apart from what was more important
and essential, Jesus' words. In John 6, our Lord asks the Apostles
whether they, too, wished to go away, like the others. Peter
answers, "Lord, to whom shall we go? You have the words of
eternal life" (Jn 6:68). There is nowhere man can go where he
will find more truth than in Jesus' words—truth not only for
his intellect but for his whole personal being.

    And his words, likewise, must not be seen in isolation.
All the majesty and simplicity of his person goes with them.
149–151 They have heavenly authority which does not hypnotize, but
makes each heart find and know itself. And finally, these three
things—Jesus' miracles, words and personality—must not be
isolated from the testimony of the Father, of which the gospel
of John speaks. Jesus was once asked, according to St John,
to produce his attestation, and he replied:

    "'In your law it is written that the testimony of two men is
true; I bear witness to myself, and the Father who sent me
bears witness to me'. They said to him therefore, 'Where is
your Father?' Jesus answered, 'You know neither me nor my
Father; if you knew me, you would know my Father also'"
(Jn 8:17–19).

    By knowing Jesus truly, by surrendering oneself and giving
oneself to him, one acquires also an inward testimony. The
Father gives one the inward knowledge that the right way to
truth and life has been found.

    The way to Jesus is not irrational. Nonetheless, the final step
is an act of confidence. And even this is not done indeliberately.
But it is a way of knowing which is something more than pure
292 reasoning. It is something deeper. For no matter how highly
one esteems the analytical work of the intellect, this is not what
is deepest and most total in man, nor even in his knowledge.

124

The core of man's being

There is a level of our being which is deeper than the intellect, more personal than feelings, more human than the subconscious. It is the level on which the unity of the two great aspects of our being, knowledge and love, exists. There man's effort to lay hold of truth is inseparable from his striving after goodness. In this primal unity, knowledge is not a cold light and love is not a blind urge. Knowledge is full of love, and love itself has vision.

It is the level of our being on which we love, where conscience resides, where we can be deeply and simply happy, where we are most truly human—a living "I", a living "You".

To this core of our being Jesus addresses himself when demanding faith. Our knowledge, our aspiration after truth, is combined with our striving for the good, by means of this primal unity. This orientation takes place in the self-evident conviction that what is totally good is also totally true. To give a full and true assent to the Lord is a judgment of value, committing directly the whole of one's being.

This does not mean that the intellect is excluded or ignored. It remains in complete harmony with all that we are. 236-238 445-449

We should be careful not to describe this central unity as "feeling"—since words like feeling, emotion and instinct are used to describe many shallower and less central human reactions.

Even "intuition" will not do, since in ordinary language it means something different. The word "conscience" would come closer. "Knowledge through connaturality with the desire for the good" is too long and complicated. "Personal dedication" is too artificial for so fundamental an act. And so we come back to the good old word with which the biblical term was translated long ago: belief, that is, faith. The word "belief" is etymologically connected with "love".

Faith and intellectual endowments

Since God draws faith from the deepest core of man's being, its degree and vitality are not tied to intellectual endowments, like philosophy, for instance, which is much more dependent on them. If the way of faith was that of pure reasoning the cleverest and most cultured people would find God most easily. The less learned and the less gifted would be less enlightened than they as regards the final end of life. But the knowledge through which God is found stems rather from man's inner orientation than from his talents. "In that same hour he rejoiced in the Holy Spirit and said, 'I thank thee, Father, Lord of heaven and earth, that thou hast hidden these things from the wise and understanding and revealed them to babes; yea, Father, for such was thy gracious will'" (Lk. 10:21).

This black-and-white contrast, typical of oriental language, does not mean that the intelligent are rejected by the Father, but simply that "brains" alone are no passport to knowledge of him. The way taken by faith is described in the first two chapters of the First Epistle to the Corinthians. "Where is the wise man? Where is the scribe? Where is the debater of this age? Has not God made foolish the wisdom of the world? For since, in the wisdom of God, the world did not know God through wisdom, it pleased God through the folly of what we preach to save those who believe" (1 Cor. 1:20–21). "For the foolishness of God is wiser than men, and the weakness of God is stronger than men" (1:25). "God chose what is low and despised in the world, even things that are not, to bring to nothing things that are, so that no human being might boast in the presence of God" (1:28–29). "Yet among the mature we do impart wisdom, although it is not a wisdom of this age ... But we impart a secret and hidden wisdom of God, which God decreed before the ages for our glorification" (2:6–7).

Unbelief

The whole man stands or falls by his faith. "He who does not believe is condemned already. ... This is the judgment, that the light has come into the world, and men loved darkness rather than light, because their deeds were evil. For every one who does evil hates the light, lest his deeds should be exposed. But he who does what is true comes to the light, that it may clearly be seen that his deeds have been wrought in God" (Jn 3:18–21).

Such trenchant texts occur most frequently in John, and they make it terrifyingly clear that one cannot with impunity evade or disregard the greatest thing to be found on earth. Throughout the whole of the gospels we find this condemnation of the "cares of this world" (Mt. 13:22), the indifference, the insincerity, the conceitedness, through which so many men turn away from Jesus, their conscience still nagging them fitfully. What Jesus demands is no small thing.

"Now great multitudes accompanied him; and he turned and said to them, 'If any one comes to me and does not hate his own father and mother and wife and children and brothers and sisters, yes, and even his own life, he cannot be my disciple. Whoever does not bear his own cross and come after me, cannot be my disciple'" (Lk. 14:25–27).

That Jesus knew well that faith is constantly menaced, is clear from the parable of the sower, in which so much of the seed fails to take root. There is also a saying in Luke, rather loosely linked to its context, which points in the same direction: "Nevertheless, when the Son of man comes, will he find faith on earth?" (18:8). There is a similar saying in Matthew: "Because wickedness is multiplied, most men's love will grow cold" (24:12).

Does this mean that all who are ignorant of the faith are condemned from the start? This is not necessarily so. An assertion of unbelief may sometimes come from a heart ready to believe. All that is wanting is the opportunity of discovering Christ truly in the Church. It may be that the message about Christ has not yet become something real in a man's life. 241 293–297 408–409

There is much that we men shall never know, whether of goodness or of evil. This means that we may never break off contact with anyone, a member of the family or our local society, who has given up the fellowship of Christ's Church. This would not be right, even if we could pass a valid judgment. Because which of us can claim to be without sin? On the other hand, if one sees a friend or acquaintance leaving Christ out of his life, one certainly may not conclude that that is the right thing for him personally to be doing. We may perhaps think that we fully understand why he cannot believe, but it would be wrong to form a settled judgment that he is where he is meant to be. We may suspect this to be so, but we cannot be certain. All we can do is to think as highly of each other as possible.

Jesus and the law

When calling for faith, Jesus speaks with an authority which fills us with amazement. He speaks with equally great authority when he calls men to live according to the will of God. In him 150–151

God himself was present, the giver of the law. Hence he could abolish at one stroke all the complications that marked the observance of the sabbath. This he did with a wonderfully appealing human argument (Mk 2:27), and thus changed the tradition of the ancients.

But we can also see that on two occasions he changed Scripture itself. The great change was in the prescriptions on ritual purity. According to the law, one could become "pure" or "impure" through various actions or various foods. The main classifications are found in the book of Leviticus. But the situation had been aggravated by tradition.

"And he called the people to him again, and said to them, 'Hear me, all of you, and understand: there is nothing outside a man which by going into him can defile him; but the things which come out of a man are what defile him. If any man has ears to hear, let him hear.'"

"And when he had entered the house, and left the people, his disciples asked him about the parable. And he said to them: 'Then are you also without understanding? Do you not see that whatever goes into a man from outside cannot defile him, since it enters, not his heart but his stomach, and so passes on?' Thus he declared all foods clean. And he said, 'What comes out of a man is what defiles a man. For from within, out of the heart of man, come evil thoughts, fornication, theft, murder, adultery, coveting, wickedness, deceit, licentiousness, envy, slander, pride, foolishness. All these evil things come from within, and they defile a man'" (Mk 7:14–23).

389   His reinforcement of the marriage bond is expressed very clearly. In the Old Testament it was easy enough for the husband to divorce his wife:

"And Pharisees came up and in order to test him asked, 'Is it lawful for a man to divorce his wife?' He answered them, 'What did Moses command you?' They said, 'Moses allowed a man to write a certificate of divorce, and to put her away.' But Jesus said to them, 'For your hardness of heart he wrote you this commandment. But from the beginning of creation, God made them male and female. For this reason a man shall leave his father and mother and be joined to his wife, and the two shall become one. So they are no longer two but one. What therefore God has joined together, let not man put asunder'. And in the house the disciples asked him again about this matter. And he said to them, 'Whoever divorces his wife and marries another, commits adultery against her, and if she divorces her husband and marries another, she commits adultery'" (Mk 10:2–12).

Matthew adds the dismayed reaction of the disciples. "If such is the case of a man with his wife, it is not expedient to marry" (Mt. 19:10). This shows how little they were prepared for this teaching which restored in fact the woman to her proper place of honour and consecrated married love as a highly personal giving of self between man and woman.

(The words "except for unchastity", which are found only in Matthew [Mt. 19:9] probably mean "except in the case of an illegitimate marriage", as for instance one contracted within the forbidden degrees of kinship according to Jewish law.)

Faithfulness to the law

On the whole, Jesus starts from the existing law. It is important not to lose sight of this. We would be taking a wrong view of him if we regarded him as a fanatical revolutionary, a mere iconoclast. "Think not that I have come to abolish the law and the prophets; I have come not to abolish them but to fulfil them" (Mt. 5:17).   371–374 Disobedience and lawlessness he condemns, and the law of God he welcomes and affirms.

The law at its most radical

On the other hand, Jesus brings about a breakthrough with   374–376 regard to this law. The words "It was said to the men of old . . . but I say to you" occurs six times in the Sermon on the Mount.   98–100

All the changes that are here made have the effect of turning something external into something internal—without, however, abandoning the external precept. They could be summed up in the words, "not only . . . but also". Not only murder is forbidden, but also the thought in which hatred is cherished and the word through which hatred is expressed. Not only divorce outside due form of law is forbidden, but any divorce at all. The same idea lies behind the demand for veracity without oaths, the command never to contemplate revenge, and finally the call for a love which like God's sunshine and God's rain is bestowed impartially on all men, including enemies. At the end, his hearers were struck dumb with amazement. Even in the very language and style, so concise and to the point, with such power to strike terror and to heal, they could perceive that God was there.

379–380   The demands of the Sermon on the Mount are not precisely-formulated laws, not a network of regulations—in which, after all, each mesh forms a gap through which to escape the law. For though precepts are necessary in human life, so that one knows where one stands, precepts alone cannot make a good man. In the Sermon on the Mount, we do not meet an impersonal code of law, but the living God. We are face to face with God's authentic and unmitigated will.

Our first reaction to it is awe and delight: yes, this is how things are, this is how things ought to be, this is goodness, this is life, God's rule and kingdom.

But immediately afterwards we ask ourselves: can I do it? As for instance when our Lord says, "Do not resist one who is evil" (Mt. 5:39). And then the answer is, no—to fulfil it entirely
303   is impossible. And that is why it is not to be made into a law. Nonetheless, it is the will of God and the joy of the kingdom that such heroic and selfless non-resistance be practised more and more. But we never know wholly how it is done or to be done.

Hence we *pray* "thy kingdom come" and "thy will be done". In these petitions, we ask for the strength to carry out the demands of the Sermon on the Mount on earth as in heaven. We ask that these commandments may be a leaven to transform the world.

The Church has made the non-juridical character of the Sermon on the Mount clear by not transcribing any of its precepts in the form of laws. There is no law about turning the other cheek, nor about not taking oaths. But the believer would be wrong to think that the demands of Christ and his Church are exhausted in the well-defined commandments. Each one of us is still faced with the demands of the Sermon on the Mount, not as suggestions which we may apply if we wish, but as serious demands, according to which we are judged. They are for all people. According to Matthew, the Sermon on the Mount was addressed "to his [Jesus'] disciples". In Matthew this means: listen carefully, for it is of the utmost importance that what I am about to say be handed on to the Church. Thus the Sermon on the Mount is not a sort of honours course for those who have passed the test of the Ten Commandments. It is not for the "perfect" but for everybody: even for those who feel they have not yet lived up the Ten Commandments. All are called to rest, in the spirit, on that hill in Galilee and listen to that declaration of the will of God being thus articulated on their behalf and for their ears; and they must try to pray that God's royal lordship may come true in all men.

It might seem rather discouraging to be given a set of precepts which cannot be fully obeyed. It would indeed be so, if the Sermon on the Mount consisted of laws with well-defined bounds of the "thus far and no further" type. But this is not the case. The Sermon on the Mount comprises commandments which tell us to do our utmost, and to put our whole heart and soul into the effort. This means that each of us can be sure that God will regard the dedicated will rather than the external accomplishment—though our will must sooner or later express itself in action, in a better life.

Thus when we find we are not yet able, not yet ready, to fulfil such precepts, this is not a reason for discouragement or anxiety, but for humility. It is the humility enshrining the joy of which Jesus spoke when he said: "When you have done all that is commanded you, say, 'We are unworthy servants; we have only what was our duty'" (Lk. 17:10).

Judgment and reward

None of this should leave the impression that there is no judgment. On the contrary. But the judgment is God's verdict on our heart. And such a judgment is much more severe than any standard which a mere set of laws could apply. But if we try to love one another, we may be sure, even if our heart accuses us, that God is greater than our hearts (cf. 1 Jn 3:19f.). 102–104
379–380

Nor should we conclude that there is no reward. Jesus ends the beatitudes by saying, "Rejoice and be glad, for your *reward* is great in heaven" (Mt. 5:12). This reward is not a carefully calculated payment in return for efforts made. God is not to be imagined as a sort of divine partner to a contract with mankind. He will never default and, indeed, gladly gives much more than might have been expected—as the brother of the prodigal son and the disappointed workers in the vineyard discovered. Thus God's rewards are not "payment". The reward consists in being taken up into his love, and this love is the "treasure in heaven" (cf. Mt. 6:19–21). "Blessed are those servants whom the master finds awake when he comes; truly, I say to you, he will gird 301–302
481–487
172 himself and have them sit at table, and *he will come and serve them*" (Lk. 12:37).

No one knows how much merit he has acquired. Hence no one can live simply for the sake of acquiring merit, but only for love. And so we must not only obey the Ten Commandments, but struggle to meet the disturbing yet compelling demands of the Sermon on the Mount, in our lives and family and work. The Sermon on the Mount is in Matthew 5 to 7.

196
300–304
376–380   *The greatest commandment*
405–406
434–438   Jesus was once asked by one of the doctors of the law:
501–502

> "Teacher, which is the great commandment in the law?" And he said to him, "You shall love the Lord your God with all your heart, and with all your soul, and with all your mind. This is the great and first commandment. And a second is like it, You shall love your neighbour as yourself. On these two commandments depend all the law and the prophets" (Mt. 22:36–40).

By combining two texts of the Old Testament, and making them the heart of the law, our Lord gave a new commandment which was the most radical in the changes it brought about. It is the commandment of an all-embracing love which takes in God and man, including the man himself who keeps it: the commandment supposes that we also love ourselves. It is truly a love that takes in all.

That Jesus is here affirming the most important thing in human life may be seen from the words, "with all your heart, and with all your soul, and with all your mind". These are the very words which one might choose to describe a passionate and consuming love. As the Old Testament so bluntly says—God is a jealous God. He loves us so dearly that he demands to be loved by us. "The Lord lives" (Ps. 18:46). To refuse him 310 311 our heart is to turn the image of the Father into a spectre and make it impossible to encounter and love our neighbour properly.

It would also be self-deception to neglect the second commandment for the sake of the first. This would be to fail to encounter God. "If any one says, 'I love God', and hates his brother, he is a liar; for he who does not love his brother whom he has seen, cannot love God whom he has not seen" (1 Jn 4:20).

Are we then to make of our neighbour a sort of cipher on whose shoulders we climb so as to meet God? No—our neighbour is not just an insubstantial spectre in Jesus' doctrine. He is not just a useful means through which to exercise the love of God. Our neighbour himself is there in person, with his needs, his humanity, his own individual quality. We must think of Jesus and the widow of Naim, where he was "moved by compassion". The good Samaritan, too, is said to have been "moved by compassion". Here in fact the unfortunate victim is so much the centre of interest that the whole story is told from his point of view. It is almost through his ears that we hear the footsteps approaching and then dying away.

Jesus has promised to bring men to heaven to live with him because they have sheltered the homeless and visited the sick. They did not have to feel they were doing it to him. Nonetheless, he regards it as done to himself, just because men have loved their neighbours so personally and generously for their own sakes. God is in man. He makes them men. To be sincerely for man, is to be for God.   376–378

As yourself

How strongly we are to identify ourselves with our fellow-men is clearly stated by Jesus in the words taken from Leviticus: love your neighbour as yourself. This has been commented on as follows: "If the commandment of brotherly love were expressed otherwise than in the little phrase, 'as yourself', which is so easily used and yet so infinitely far-reaching, the commandment could not master self-love so thoroughly as it does. It is impossible to twist or distort the words, 'as yourself'. With all the sharp discernment of eternity, they penetrate into the recesses of the heart, where man loves himself. They leave self-love without the smallest excuse or the least way of escape. It is wonderfully done. There could be endless and closely-argued discussions about how the neighbour is to be loved, and self-love would always be able to find excuses or ways of escape, on the grounds that the matter had not been treated exhaustively or that an instance had been overlooked, some point not laid down clearly or forcibly enough. But once the words 'as yourself' have been pronounced, the commandment has a strangle-hold on self-love from which it can never twist itself free."

On the word "neighbour" as used by Jesus the same writer says: "Yes, we all know our neighbour at a distance. But at a distance, he remains a figment of the imagination, because the very term 'neighbour' means that he is 'nigh' and near to us—anyone we meet, all men without exception. At a distance the neighbour is a shadow, like a fleeting fancy in men's thought. Unhappily, they do not notice that the man who just went by was in fact their neighbour."

But these profound words of the writer Kierkegaard should not be taken to mean that love is joyless. In a world which, according to St Paul, was "heartless" (Rom. 1:31) this command-

233-234 ment signalled happiness and peace, and that new level of heart-felt humaneness, which we now take so much for granted. It signalled a new world.

"Love"

Consequently, Christian love made its way through the world of those days under a new name, which was taken from the Greek translation of the Old Testament. It occurred frequently there, in contrast to profane usage. The word for Christian love was "*agape*". It was undoubtedly chosen in order to avoid another word which had been "too often profaned" in the course of time—*eros*. The latter term was in fact very often used in the sense of merely sensual egoism, as the word "love" is now sometimes used in the lower reaches of the cinema. It is, there-fore, noteworthy that the word *eros* does not occur at all in the New Testament. The good news of *agape* resounds there, giving a sense of liberation.

But it would be wrong to conclude that this heavenly *agape* is devoid of all the traits of earthly love. The Greek word *agape* can be used of all types of love; not just for the altruistic love which consists of giving, but also for the desire for the humanly attractive which makes demands. And the New Testament also uses it in this sense. The longing of the Father for the prodi-gal son, and of the son for the Father, is described in very warm and human colours.

Hence the fact that Christian love is pure, selfless and liberat-
382-384 ing does not mean that the attraction and the longings that
405-408 human beings feel with regard to one another are ruled out as

134

worthless. On the contrary, the love which is preached by Christ looks very human indeed. It joins with human love and raises it to a higher plane.

Like the sun and the rain

The most far-reaching change wrought by Jesus in the under- 172
standing of love was that he extended it to take in enemies: "I say to you, Love your enemies and pray for those who persecute you, so that you may be sons of your Father who is in heaven; for he makes his sun rise on the evil and on the good, and sends rain on the just and the unjust. For if you love those who love you, what reward have you? Do not even the tax collectors do the same? And if you salute only your brethren, what more are you doing than others? Do not even the Gentiles do the same? You, therefore, must be perfect, as your heavenly Father is perfect" (Mt. 5:44–48).

These last words refer to God's example in giving the sun and the rain which rises and falls on all people indiscriminately. Thus for Jesus the profoundest reason for love is not in any given view of man or of the world, but is based on the root and ground of all existence, God. Love is part of God's lordship, because 501–502
"God is love" (1 Jn 4:8).

THE MESSIAH AND HIS COMMUNITY   348–370

A new people

Did Jesus imagine that the kingdom of God would come as the sanctification of isolated persons, called by God but without any mutual links?

Having become man, he behaved towards his fellow-men in a human way. Men must live together. So he did what God had done in the Old Testament. He gathered a people.

Though initially a small group, it was the possessor of a magnificent promise. "Fear not, little flock, for it is your Father's good pleasure to give you the kingdom" (Lk. 12:32). The kingdom of God takes shape among men.

There are many indications that Jesus not only foresaw this new people, but provided for it in advance. It would, of course, be wrong to think that by the time of his death he had set up an extensive organization. As a prophetic teacher, it was man's heart he sought. But it would be to misunderstand his character if one thought of him as an idealistic prophet scattering his words heedlessly abroad, making no effort on the human level to ensure that a human community resulted. A new people stemmed from him, to which the whole of mankind is called. In it nation and race count for nothing. What counts is the 98–102 realization of one's own insufficiency and the readiness to receive the kingdom of God.

The gathering of "Apostles"

The clearest sign that Jesus wanted a community to develop is that he deliberately gathered disciples around him. Every rabbi had disciples. But just as Jesus was no ordinary teacher, so, too, 148 his group of followers was no ordinary one. The disciples of the rabbis chose their teacher themselves, gradually learned his interpretation of the law, and so in the end themselves became masters.

In Jesus' case, it is noticeable that they do not choose him, but that he calls "those whom he desires" (cf. Mk 3:13)—without beating about the bush, and with sovereign authority. (It is fascinating to compare the various stories of the calling of the disciples in the different gospels.)

Jesus demands everything from his disciple:

> As they were going along the road, a man said to him, "I will follow you wherever you go". And Jesus said to him, "Foxes have holes, and birds of the air have nests; but the Son of man has nowhere to lay his head". To another he said, "Follow me". But he said, "Lord, let me first go and bury my father". But he said to him, "Leave the dead to bury their own dead; but as for you, go and proclaim the kingdom of God". Another said, "I will follow you, Lord; but let me first say farewell to those at my home". Jesus said to him, "No one who puts his hand to the plough and looks back is fit for the kingdom of God" (Lk. 9:57–62).

These words, which describe the choice of a wider circle of disciples, should not be taken as prescribing indifference towards one's parents. Jesus reproached the Pharisees with such indifference (Mk 7:9–13), and he might possibly make the same reproach to some groups of religious today. With oriental terseness, as may be seen for instance in the play on the meaning of "dead", he shows how radical the new beginning is. To leave the old behind is part of the happiness of the kingdom. Indeed the whole history of salvation begins with the words: "The Lord said to Abraham, 'Go from your country and your kindred and your father's house . . . And I will make of you a great nation'". (Gen. 12:1–2).

Together, Jesus' disciples formed a "little flock", which he initiated into the mysteries of the kingdom of God. But he paid special attention to the formation of twelve of them. He taught them to baptize (Jn 4:2). As regards the message they were to proclaim, he taught them much more than the rabbis taught their disciples. These were instructed only in the interpretation of the law. But Jesus made his Apostles heralds of an *event*, the coming of the kingdom of God and the will of God.

Their mission was one great authority. As Matthew writes, "He called to him his twelve disciples and gave them authority over unclean spirits, to cast them out, and to heal every disease and every infirmity" (Mt. 10:1). The very name "Apostle" indicates great authority. *Apostolos* is Greek for "he who is sent" —an "envoy". It is a translation of the Hebrew *shaliach*. In the time of Jesus this meant an envoy with full powers rather than a mere spokesman or messenger. Thus the Apostles are more than the ordinary disciples of the rabbis. But in another sense they are less. A disciple could become a rabbi, but an Apostle could never become what Jesus is. Jesus, and he alone, is the Lord. The Apostles receive their authority by delegation from Jesus, to whom it belongs.

The missionary discourse

The tenth chapter of Matthew, the "missionary" (or "apostolic") discourse, contains directives given by the Lord to his Apostles. Here is part of it:

> Behold, I send you out as sheep in the midst of wolves; so be wise as serpents and innocent as doves. Beware of men; for they will deliver you up to councils, and flog you in their synagogues, and you will be dragged before governors and kings for my sake, to

bear testimony before them and the Gentiles. When they deliver you up, do not be anxious how you are to speak or what you are to say; for what you are to say will be given to you in that hour; for it is not you who speak, but the Spirit of your Father speaking through you. Brother will deliver up brother to death, and the father his child, and children will rise against parents and have them put to death; and you will be hated by all for my name's sake. But he who endures to the end will be saved. When they persecute you in one town, flee to the next: for truly, I say to you, you will not have gone through all the towns of Israel, before the Son of man comes.

A disciple is not above his teacher, nor a servant above his master; it is enough for the disciple to be like his teacher, and the servant like his master. If they have called the master of the house Beelzebub, how much more will they malign those of his household. So have no fear of them; for nothing is covered that will not be revealed, or hidden that will not be known. What I tell you in the dark, utter in the light; and what you hear whispered, proclaim upon the housetops. And do not fear those who kill the body but cannot kill the soul; rather fear him who can destroy both soul and body in hell. Are not two sparrows sold for a penny? And not one of them will fall to the ground without your Father's will. But even the hairs of your head are all numbered. Fear not, therefore, you are of more value than many sparrows. So every one who acknowledges me before men, I also will acknowledge before my Father who is in heaven; but who ever denies me before men, I also will deny before my Father who is in heaven.

Do not think that I have come to bring peace upon earth; I have not come to bring peace but a sword. For I have come to set a man against his father, and a daughter against her mother, and a daughter-in-law against her mother-in-law; and a man's foes will be those of his own household.

He who loves father or mother more than me is not worthy of me; and he who loves son or daughter more than me is not worthy of me; and he who does not

take his cross and follow me is not worthy of me. He
who finds his life will lose it, and he who loses his
life for my sake will find it (Mt. 10:16–39).

The ecclesiastical discourse

The eighteenth chapter of Matthew is called his "ecclesiastical
discourse", because it contains directives for the life of the
Church. Here is one passage from it:

> What do you think? If a man has a hundred sheep,
> and one of them has gone astray, does he not leave the
> ninety-nine on the hills and go in search of the one
> that went astray? And if he finds it, truly, I say to you,
> he rejoices over it more than over the ninety-nine that
> never went astray. So it is not the will of your Father
> who is in heaven that one of these little ones should
> perish.
>
> If your brother sins against you, go and tell him his
> fault, between you and him alone. If he listens to you,
> you have gained your brother. But if he does not
> listen, take one or two others along with you, that
> every word may be confirmed by the evidence of two
> or three witnesses. If he refuses to listen to them, tell it
> to the church; and if he refuses to listen even to the
> church, let him be to you as a Gentile and a tax
> collector. Truly, I say to you, whatever you bind on
> earth shall be bound in heaven, and whatever you
> loose on earth shall be loosed in heaven (Mt. 18:12–18).

Delegation from heaven   197

These last words show very clearly the great authority given to
the Apostles. The terms bind and loose mean both to declare
something permissible or forbidden, and to ban (excommunicate)
someone or to admit him once more to the fellowship. Thus the
authority in question is that which is essential in a community—
to be able to say what may or may not be done, and who belongs
to it and who does not.

The word "whatever" shows how wide are these powers. In
Matthew, the word "heaven" is a substitute for "God". Hence
anything that the Apostles bind or loose is bound or loosed in
the reality of the divine sphere. The authority thus conferred on

men is sublime. It is a power for salvation, life and forgiveness, as can be seen from the words of our Lord in the gospel of St John: "If you forgive the sins of any, they are forgiven; if you retain the sins of any, they are retained" (Jn 20:23). (This point 357–370 will be further discussed later on.)

362
368–369

The pastors and their responsibilities

To grasp the life-giving character of these powers, it is well to read the whole of the "ecclesiastical discourse" in Matthew (ch. 18). It will be seen that the wielders of authority are not on a different and higher plane with regard to God than the ordinary faithful. On the contrary, their situation lays upon them greater responsibilities, for which they will have to answer to their Master. Hence we read in Luke:

> But know this, that if the householder had known at what hour the thief was coming, he would have been awake and would not have left his house to be broken into. You also must be ready; for the Son of man is coming at an hour you do not expect. Peter said, "Lord, are you telling this parable for us or for all?" And the Lord said, "Who then is the faithful and wise steward, whom his master will set over his household, to give them their portion of food at the proper time? Blessed is that servant whom his master when he comes will find so doing. Truly I tell you, he will set him over all his possessions. But if that servant says to himself, 'My master is delayed in coming', and begins to beat the menservants and the maidservants, and to eat and drink and get drunk, the master of that servant will come on a day when he does not expect him and at an hour he does not know, and will punish him, and put him with the unfaithful. And that servant who knew his master's will, but did not make ready or act according to his will, shall receive a severe beating. But he who did not know, and did what deserved a beating, shall receive a light beating. Every one to whom much is given, of him will much be required; and of him to whom men commit much they will demand the more" (Lk. 12:39–48).

140

Jesus chose twelve Apostles. He meant this number to be symbolic. Just as the ancient people stemmed from the twelve sons of Israel, making the twelve tribes, so, too, the new people begins with twelve men. He himself alluded to the connection between the two (Mt. 19:28).

It is noteworthy that the Apostles included in their number a former tax-gatherer, that is, a "collaborator", Matthew, and a "zealot", a resistance fighter against the Romans, Simon—men who by nature should have been deadly enemies. They also included some fishermen from Galilee, whom Jesus had summoned to the apostolate in terms that might not strike us as particularly elegant—that they should be fishers of men. Of course, fishing, as used here, does not mean killing, but rescuing and giving life, as the word used for it in Luke 5:10 clearly shows. The term is the same as that used in the Old Testament to speak of an anathema being lifted, and hence of men being delivered from death (cf. e. g. Jos. 6:25).

There is also a disciple who will betray Jesus. Jesus' words about the responsibility of those in authority were not a rhetorical flourish, but were dictated by bitter necessity.

Peter

The figure who stands out most clearly is a fisherman called Simon Bar-Jona, which means son of Jona (John-son). In this impetous and mercurial man of the people Jesus laid a solid foundation of loyalty and love:

"Simon, Simon, behold, Satan demanded to have you [plural], that he might sift you [plural] like wheat, but I have prayed for you [singular] that your faith may not fail; and when you have turned again, strengthen your brethren" (Lk. 22:31–32).

He is given the surname "Rock", *Petros* in Greek. He may have wavered for a while, but he was still the man who was to be the leader of the Church, the little flock, after Jesus' death. The Acts of the Apostles show beyond all doubt that this in fact is what happened.

The gospels of Matthew and John and also Luke record in striking terms the charge which was given to Peter. In all the lists of the Apostles he is always named first. In Luke, the phrase "fisher of men" is addressed only to him (5:10). What is said in Matthew 18 about the authority of the Twelve in general is addressed, surprisingly enough, to Peter alone in Matthew 16. 140

141

Before going on to discuss the consequences that follow from what was said to Peter, let us try to read the words afresh, as though for the first time, and note the marvellous power for salvation which is here conferred on a human being.

> Now when Jesus came into the district of Caesarea Philippi, he asked his disciples, "Who do men say that the Son of man is?" And they said, "Some say John the Baptist, others say Elijah, and others Jeremiah or one of the prophets". He said to them, "But who do you say that I am?" Simon Peter replied, "You are the Christ, the Son of the living God". And Jesus answered him, "Blessed are you, Simon Bar-Jona! For flesh and blood has not revealed this to you, but my Father who is in heaven. And I tell you, you are Peter; and on this rock I will build my church, and the powers of death shall not prevail against it. I will give to you the keys of the kingdom of heaven, and whatever you bind on earth shall be bound in heaven, and whatever you loose on earth shall be loosed in heaven" (Mt. 16:13–19).

These words of Jesus have sometimes been regarded as an interpolation, on the grounds that he could not possibly have said them. But modern scholarship has shown that they are to be found in all the manuscripts, even the most ancient ones. And the language itself, highly charged with metaphor, is so full of Semitic elements that there are few texts in Matthew that are so surely part of the gospel as this one. Thus, for instance, the play on the words Peter and Rock is only complete in the basic Aramaic text: Kepha—kepha (as it is, accidentally, in the French Pierre—pierre). The Greek translation showed the pun as Petros—petra. This was preferred to the other possible translation, Petros—petros, because petra means the live, unquarried rock or bed-rock, which was what Jesus meant, whereas petros would normally mean stone or boulder, something that could be thrown. For the proper name, however, Petros was chosen, since it would have been awkward to call a man Petra, the word for rock being feminine in Greek.

It is generally recognized today, even by Protestant writers, that the ordinary and obvious interpretation of the text is the most authentic. Thus the well-known Protestant exegete Günther Bornkamm writes: "In the interpretation of the saying about Peter and the Church, Roman Catholic and Reformed theologians are much closer to each other than they were in former times. The 'Rock' is not Christ, as was held long ago by Augustine, followed by Luther, nor the faith of Peter or the preaching office, as the Reformers held, but Peter himself as leader of the Church."

Some Protestants, however, find it questionable that Jesus himself should have spoken so definitely about the Church. Here there is a difference among Protestant writers. What they all deny is that the words also apply to Peter's successors. (For further discussion of this point, see the chapter on the hierarchy.) 366–368

We should not be tempted, as a result of the difficulties that have always been raised about this text, to reduce it to a mere "proof text" for use as a weapon in debate. We must try to be receptive to the strength and consolation the text offers. Jesus will build his Church. The word "church" *(qahal)* is often used in the Old Testament for the people of Israel in the desert. This is also what Jesus means: a new people.

"The powers of death" or "the gates of hell" (Hades, the underworld) mean the powers of evil. They will never overcome the Church of God.

Heaven, too, has its gates, and their invisible keys are in Peter's hands. He is the steward with full authority, with the function of regent as described in Isaiah 22:21–22.

Then come the words which in Matthew 18 are also addressed 140 to the Apostles in general, "to bind" and "to loose", that is, to declare right or wrong, also to excommunicate or to lift the ban—with effect "in heaven", that is, "with God". This power is here bestowed on Peter alone, the weak, impulsive and very ordinary Peter, the rock which still has to be hewn and chiselled by Jesus with many a hard word. Even at his weakest moments, he will still receive a call from the Lord: "And the Lord turned and looked at Peter" (Lk. 22:61). That was very soon after Jesus had said to him, "And when you have turned again, strengthen your brethren" (Lk. 22:32).

John places the election of Peter after Jesus' death. This shows that the foundation of the Church is provided for primarily in the time following Jesus' earthly existence:

> When they had finished breakfast, Jesus said to
> Simon Peter, "Simon, son of John, do you love me
> more than these?" He said to him, "Yes, Lord; you

know that I love you". He said to him, "Feed my
lambs". A second time he said to him, "Simon, son of
John, do you love me?" He said to him, "Yes, Lord,
you know that I love you". He said to him, "Tend my
sheep". He said to him the third time, "Simon, son of
John, do you love me?" Peter was grieved because he
said to him the third time, "Do you love me?" And
he said to him, "Lord, you know everything; you
know that I love you". Jesus said to him, "Feed my
sheep" (Jn 21:15–17).

The Church is given us

That which builds up the community stems from the authorities
whom the Lord instituted. It is not *made* by the community, but
given to it. This is the deepest meaning of authority in the Church.
"He who hears you hears me" (Lk. 10:16). (More will be said
362–363 about this in the chapter on the pastoral priesthood.) To recognize
this is one of the fundamental Christian joys. What binds us
together is the gift of Christ, not our work alone.

The Church as the "sacrament" of the kingdom

104 Christ spoke more frequently of the lordship of God than of the
Church. Are they different things or the same thing?

The Church is the community in which the signs of the
kingship of God—the sacraments—are found in their abundance.
It is also the community in which the message about the kingdom—the gospel—is heard clearly. It is the place where many
try to live the life of the kingdom. In a word, it is where the
kingdom of God is visible and audible. The Church may be
called the "sacrament" of the kingdom of God, that is, the sign
which signifies and realizes God's lordship as it makes men one
with each other.

351–352 But there is also the misery of sin and obstinacy. There the
kingdom of heaven is often found like someone who casts good
seed upon his ground—with the strange result that sometimes
weeds grow. The Church is not possession of the kingdom, it is
the struggle for it. But it is a struggle consoled by the promise
that the gates of hell will not prevail against it.

WHO IS THIS MAN?

The quest for the "life of Jesus"

How can one best describe Jesus' personality, as it is preserved for us in history? The first thing to do here is to try to avoid fanciful reconstructions. Uninhibited scientific research, untrammelled by Church tradition, which from about 1800 to 1920 tried to see the life of Jesus with new eyes, and which was often inspired by sincere admiration and a questing faith, did not on the whole succeed in avoiding fantasy. Innumerable "Lives of Jesus" appeared in this period, filling out the gospel record with fine descriptions of nature and above all with seemingly acute and penetrating descriptions of Jesus' psychological development. Our Lord appears simply as a great man, who began to teach in the enthusiasm of youth but ended in disappointment or embittered strife.

One result of this research was that attention was concentrated very much on Jesus as a man. This was not in itself harmful, because, as we have seen, the believer is often inclined not fully to realize the truth Jesus is both God and man.   80–82

Another welcome result is that these efforts, after a century and a half, have proved themselves to be utterly inadequate, and so have once more opened up the way for a more direct approach to Jesus as we find him in the gospel. We can now see very clearly, as we survey the efforts formerly made to analyse the "life of Jesus", that the enthralling psychological descriptions mirrored not so much the mentality of Jesus as the spirit of the age in which each of the writers lived. During the Enlightenment, Jesus was seen as a teacher who spoke with great insight of God and virtue. In the age of Romanticism, he appeared as a "religious genius". Where Kantianism was influential, he became an ethical teacher similar to Kant. In times of social upheaval, he was seen as a champion of social reform. And so on.

All these descriptions are now outmoded and are obviously one-sided or untrue. After the efforts of a century and a half, the gospels are still there for us, inviolate, in their firm, sharply-contoured and yet impenetrable simplicity, and the false pictures woven from their contents have been largely blown away. They remain in themselves more modern and astounding than each of the descriptions of Jesus which in their time seemed so up-to-date. But we are still left facing the same persistent mystery: who is this man? Though the old-fashioned views are still being widely circulated as "scientific", modern biblical scholarship, including that of exegetes independent of the Church, is fully aware that we should not allow ourselves to indulge in such fantasies. It is recognized that the sources offer no justification for them, being too little interested in "biography" and "psychological development", and being primarily testimony, re-presentation, and challenge.

No ordinary biographies

We know the human traits of Jesus primarily from four books. Each of these "gospels" contains the whole of the "good news", the whole "eu-angelion", evangel.

47–53
72   Because they are first and foremost a message, they leave
207–208   unanswered many of the questions the curious might ask. Such questions do not form part of the message. Thus we are never given the least indication of what Jesus looked like. And the gospels are not interested in the precise sequence of events of their exact topography. It is impossible, for instance, to tell from the gospels whether Jesus' ministry lasted one, two or three years. Then, when we compare the gospels with one another, we find that while on the one hand, Jesus' words were very carefully preserved, they were also transmitted with a certain freedom, in variants which were adapted to the situation of the community for which the evangelist wrote.

These characteristics are due to the fact that the gospels are not so much cherished memories of someone who is dead and gone, as books filled with the presence of One who lives. This explains a certain freedom in the rendering of his words. Christians knew that Jesus was still with them in the preaching.
60   And so the Gospel of John speaks of this explicitly, affirming that
207   the Spirit helps to bring things to mind (Jn 14:26; 15:26; 16:13).
208   This certainly must not be taken merely to mean that the Spirit of Jesus acted as a sort of tape-recorder or newsreel. He helped tradition and the writers to see the profound significance of the events—some of which were in fact related with great precision —and to bring out this meaning in terms familiar to the community.

As regards the description of the events, the gospels must not be taken too mechanically as a continuous narrative. A certain sequence is undoubtedly provided for the course of Jesus' life, but such particles as "after that" or "at that time" are often merely conventional elements of style, which we must not take literally in the sense we normally give them.

The gospels are rather constructed in an episodic style, that is, as a series of short passages, pericopes, each of which is a sort of prism through which the whole person of Jesus can be seen. The events narrated are not so many stages in chronologically unfolding development, as in an ordinary biography, but each of them is rather a complete presentation of the Lord. The result is that we encounter Jesus in the gospels in a different way from other figures of the past. We often know more details of their lives. But they are of the past, and raise no challenge. The person of Jesus is given a quite different treatment. He is there in his entirety in each pericope, and he calls to us. Hence a story from the gospel is not something that we can sit down and listen to in a detached way, with our legs crossed, as it were. It is something through which we are summoned to stand up.

The way in which the Church inserts the gospels into the eucharistic liturgy corresponds remarkably well to the literary form of these writings: they are read in pericopes, and listened to standing up. (On the New Testament, see also the section, 206-210 "The origin of the gospels".)

Of his time yet outside it

The fact that the Jesus of the gospels cannot be interrogated by modern man about his psychology, but on the contrary himself questions and challenges modern man, does not mean that his person is wrapped in the mists of obscurity and remoteness. Indeed, how could he question and challenge us if he did not present himself clearly? We have here in fact a characteristic which escapes no one who comes in contact with the gospels: the closeness of the events. The whole world in which Jesus lives is depicted in strong, clear and authentic colours. Priests and doctors of the law, Pharisees and publicans, the rich and the poor, the healthy and the sick—all are vividly drawn in the great events which constitute the encounter with Jesus—an encounter which each of them experiences in his own way.

We cannot fail to be struck by the fact that he is fully a part of the real world of his day, while observing also that he is completely distinct from it.

He is the preacher who announces the coming of the kingdom, and hence he is a *prophet*. "This is the prophet Jesus from
Nazareth of Galilee" (Mt. 21:11). But at the same time he is
quite different. A prophet was expected to show his credentials
by reciting the story of his call and above all, by prefixing to his
message the statement that declared its origin: "Thus says the
Lord". But Jesus never appeals to a call, and speaks simply in his
own name. There is a little word which is very characteristic of
Jesus' way of speaking. It is a Hebrew word which through trans-
literation is preserved in the Greek text. It has sometimes been
given in English as "so be it", and more frequently, in modern
translations, by "truly", which is not very expressive. The word,
is, of course, "Amen". It is a term used to re-affirm or confirm
what has been said: "it is so!" We still use it to join in a prayer, or
rather to show our assent to it.

But Jesus' way of using the word is completely unique. He
puts it, not after, but before the statement. He begins with the
confirmation. Further, it is not followed by a "Thus says the
Lord", but "I say to you". Thus for instance we read: "Truly
[amen] I say to you, whoever does not receive the kingdom of
God like a child shall not enter it" (Mk 10:15).

The prefixed Amen is not an arrogant way of speaking. It
displays the calm, humble consciousness of his mission in one
who is sent with full authority, one who of himself can speak
in the name of God. It sounds like an assent to the will of the
Father of which he has been notified.

Along with the traits of a prophet, Jesus also has those of a
teacher (rabbi). He appears as one who has discussions with his
disciples and with other teachers. He travels about and gives
instruction in synagogues. Strictly speaking, his profession is
that of a rabbi. And hence he is often addressed as such.

But just as his prophetic ministry had an entirely novel
expression, so, too, his way of teaching. The very fact that he
united in himself the roles of prophet and teacher was completely
unheard of. And as regards his way of teaching: it was the rabbi's
duty to appeal to the authority of Scripture and to quote other
rabbis. But in Jesus, God teaches directly. Even Scripture, as we
saw, is perfected on Jesus' lips.

Furthermore, all this is done in very simple words, which do
not demand preliminary studies, but can be immediately understood. Man is addressed in his actual situation—his ordinary life
97 and his ordinary experiences. This we have seen from the parables.

148

Then there are the short sayings of Jesus, which are of such startling lucidity. "Let the day's own trouble be sufficient for the day" (Mt. 6:34). "Men do not light a lamp and put it under a bushel" (Mt. 5:15). "When a woman is in travail she has sorrow, because her hour has come; but when she is delivered of the child, she no longer remembers the anguish" (Jn 16:21). "Truly, truly, I say to you, unless a grain of wheat falls into the earth and dies, it remains alone; but if it dies, it bears much fruit" (Jn 12:24). Through such words as these, the impression is gained from all four gospels that a great directness was characteristic of Jesus. There is no beating about the bush, no dreaming of the past, no escape into the future: "The kingdom of God is in the midst of you" (Lk. 17:21); "Blessed is he who takes no offence at me" (Mt. 11:6).

Everyone he meets is brought up sharply against the fact of God's Today. He brings God's Today along with him. This 122 gives his person an incomparable and tranquil authority.

"Every scene depicted in the gospels brings out the amazing sovereignty with which Jesus, while adapting himself to the people he meets, dominates every situation. This is clear from the many doctrinal controversies in which he sees through his adversaries, disarms their objections, answers their questions or even forces the others to answer. He can make his adversaries speak or he can 'silence' them (Mt. 22:34). It is the same when he meets the needy: marvellous forces flow from him, the sick press round, and their friends and families beg for help. Very often he does what he is asked, but he can also be unwilling or make the petitioner wait or put him to the test. Sometimes he refuses (Mk 1:35ff.), but he often makes the first move, and he is ready to act when the sufferers rely on their hope in him (Mt. 8:5ff.; Lk. 19:1ff.). He feels free to disregard the conventional attitudes which have been rigidly formulated by tradition. This is apparent in his dealings with his disciples. He calls them with a word of sovereign command (Mk 1:16ff.) but some would-be disciples he deters (Lk. 9:57ff.; 14:28ff.). Again and again, Jesus' attitude and behaviour is in sharp contrast to what people expect of him or to what they hope for themselves. He places himself out of reach, as John narrates, when the crowd wishes to make him king (Jn 6:5). A trait that is repeated again and again is that Jesus knows the men he meets and reads their thoughts. The gospels often present this as a miracle. The two sons of Zebedee experienced it when Jesus rejected their ambitious desires (Mk 10:35ff.)." This was written by the Protestant exegete Günther Bornkamm, to whom we owe several observations cited throughout this part of our exposition. (The above-mentioned traits also stand out in, for instance, Lk. 7:36–50; Jn 8:1–11; Mk 10:17–22).

143   This last story speaks of the gaze with which Jesus could attract people. This is mentioned several times. It was characteristic of him. The stories themselves show that it was not a sort of hypnotism or a sentimental look. He places men before a liberating decision, but leaves it to them to decide.

We see Jesus surrounded by all sorts of people, all authentically drawn: good men with their virtues, sinners with their faults, the possessed with their frenzy, the sick with their afflictions, the learned with their arguments. And all show themselves to Jesus as they are. Then he calls them to declare themselves.

Authority

The gospels have a word to describe this sovereignty, the unassuming and unquestionable majesty of Jesus. The word is "authority". It could also be translated "power". "They were astonished at his teaching, for he taught them as one who had authority, and not as the scribes" (Mk 1:22).

This word expresses the most strikingly characteristic trait of Jesus' person. It can be recognized in every pericope, in every saying and in all that is related about him. This is what makes his personality in the gospels not something remote and vague, but clearly and indeed imperiously present.

We must not think of the "authority" of his personality as a dignified aloofness or an equable mildness. Let us forget for a moment the pink and white plaster statues, and think of Jesus' sharpness as he drove out demons: "Jesus rebuked him, saying, 'Be silent, and come out of him!'" (Mk 1:25); of his just anger when cleansing the Temple (Jn 2:15), of his passionate interest in all he did, as when a leper begged for help: "Moved with pity, he stretched out his hand" (Mk 1:41). And the little incident of the blessing of children is also full of feeling. "He was indignant", we read, with the disciples, but "he took [the children] in his arms and blessed them" (Mk 10:13–16).

We should not be doing justice to Jesus' "authority" if we only saw in him a great pastor and preacher. This would not

explain all the data with which the gospels provide us. These
point to something else: the event of the coming of the kingdom. 106
He perfects all that went before him with words more enduring
than heaven and earth, which must pass away (Mk 13:31). God
reigns definitively through him. This is what gives him his
authority: the unique and final coming of God's infinite lordship
and revelation.

At the same time, however, it is that authority of him who
in the Jordan and in the desert had dedicated himself to humility, 91–93
death, insignificance and servitude. It was the authority of the 97
hidden kingdom of God. But this is why it affected the hearts
of men so simply and so deeply.

The names of Jesus

Having tried to describe the person of Jesus as he appears from
the events of the gospel, let us now use another method to
express who he is. One by one we shall go through the various
names which the early Church used to speak of his excellence.

Some have already been mentioned. There is his proper name, 72
Jesus—"Yahweh saves". There is the name he had from his first 89
calling, *Carpenter*—which is not without significance in the
order of salvation.

Then there is the name from his later calling, *Rabbi, Teacher.* 148
He is *the* Teacher or Master, of life itself, compared to whom
other teachers hardly merit the name. "Neither be called masters,
for you have one master, the Christ" (Mt. 23:10). This is an
excellent title to use when addressing Jesus in prayer, especially
when one's way is not clear and one needs light and wisdom.

We have seen that Jesus was sometimes called a *prophet*. He 148
himself also refers to the fact that he is the successor of the prophets, as may be seen from the parable of the wicked husbandmen
(Mt. 21:33–38) and from the saying: "I must go on my way
today and tomorrow and the day following; for it cannot be
that a prophet should perish away from Jerusalem. O Jerusalem,
Jerusalem, killing the prophets and stoning those who are sent
to you!" (Lk. 13:33–34).

The Church uses the title *Anointed* very frequently. Our
Messiah corresponds to the Hebrew, while the Greek is *Christos*
(in capitals, XPICTOC, abbreviated XP or ℞). This was the title 95
of the long-awaited king who was to replace foreign rule by the
lordship of God. It was a dangerous title, because it was con-

151

taminated by short-sighted nationalistic expectations. If the Lord had used the title, people would have wanted "to make him king" (Jn 6:15). Hence Jesus avoided it in his public preaching, as may be seen from the gospel of Mark. But this gospel also describes how Jesus finally professed himself the Christ, officially, before the Sanhedrin (Mk 14:62). But it was in a deeper and loftier sense. His kingship is not of this world.

In the other gospels, Jesus' reserve with regard to the title of Messiah does not appear so faithfully. By the time they came to be written, the title had in fact lost its misleading connotations and so it became the title in normal use in the transmission of Jesus' life and words. It was the name in which God's fidelity to his promises was embodied: he had sent his Messiah. It also expressed a truth which became more and more apparent in the contemplation of Jesus' life: that the kingship of God radiated from his person, that he was its central point—the king whose kingship was not of this world. The name "son of David", by which he was sometimes called, means more or less the same as Christ.

To indicate his messiahship, Jesus himself chose a word which had fewer associations in men's minds with earthly lordship. It came from the prophecy of Daniel. There a down-trodden people, threatened with destruction among powers portrayed as beasts, is shown a Saviour:

> I looked then because of the sound of the great words which the horn was speaking. And as I looked, the beast was slain, and its body destroyed and given over to be burned with fire. As for the rest of the beasts, their dominion was taken away, but their lives were prolonged for a season and a time. I saw in the night visions, and behold, with the clouds of heaven there came one like a son of man, and he came to the Ancient of Days and was presented before him (Dan. 7:11–13).

This heavenly Son of man brings the definitive kingdom of God. The gospels give *Son of man* as the name which Jesus used to speak of himself. It signifies, not his humanity, as one might expect, but his heavenly origin. Son of man is not a title which Jesus used in order to speak of himself modestly. It is the title of majesty which he adopted to indicate that his messiahship was of another order than the earthly. He therefore substitutes this title for that of Christ. "Again the high priest asked him: 'Are you the Christ, the Son of the Blessed?' And Jesus said, 'I am'". (Thus he does not deny it; but he goes on:) "And you will see the Son of man sitting at the right hand of Power, and coming with the clouds of heaven" (Mk 14:61–62). The title does not occur in the epistles of the apostles, and in the gospels it appears exclusively on the lips of Jesus. Obviously, it was remembered as the title by which the Lord spoke of himself. It is a term very rich in meaning. As well as indicating Jesus majesty, it also suggests the strange lowliness of his messiahship, its "otherness". And the very formula shows something of his unity with mankind. Son of man (Ben Adam) is a Semitic phrase of which the strict meaning is ordinarily "man". He is the Man, the Adam, uniquely so.

Then there is the title *Son of God*. This title was used often enough to describe a certain relationship of men to God. But Jesus is simply "*the* Son" (Mk 13:32). That his sonship is of an entirely different order to other men's, we have already seen 115–116 when examining his way of speaking. He never says, "our Father", but "my Father and your Father". How uniquely this man was Son of God may also be seen from the parable of the wicked husbandmen (Mt. 21:33–40). First servants are sent—the prophets. Then comes "the son"—"the beloved son", according to the parallel in Mark 12:6, the words used at the baptism in the Jordan and at the transfiguration.

It is not impossible that "Son of God" may have been used also as a title of the Messiah. In the Old Testament the king, the predecessor of the Messiah, is occasionally spoken of in these terms. But like the title of Messiah, "Son of God" was given an unexpectedly sublime and heavenly meaning by Jesus. No title renders so faithfully the mystery of his person. This is the ultimate root of his "authority". He who brought the 150 kingdom of God was no outsider, but the Son, who had his glory along with God before the world came into existence. As we read in the gospel of John, "Truly, truly, I say to you, before Abraham was, I am" (Jn 8:58). "God so loved the world that he gave his only Son" (Jn 3:16).

Certainly, before Jesus' resurrection, no one suspected how 77–82 unfathomable this title was. And even in our own case, it is 498–502 well not to think at once of a mystery in God far away from this world. Otherwise the title might seem empty and remote and far too great for us. It is well to share the groping efforts of the disciples as they tried to grasp the profound significance of this title. Only then shall we be able to discover the richness of the divine Sonship: we must think of his obedience, of his saying "Abba", of God's "delight" in his "beloved Son".

41–45   The name *Son* is replaced in one passage of the gospel of John
77–79   by the term *Word*. When speaking of Jesus' birth we mentioned this title, along with other sublime descriptions such as are found in Heb. 1:3, where he is called the Reflection of God's glory and the Image of his being.

In the New Testament, Jesus is also designated very frequently as *the Lord* (Greek, *Kyrios;* Latin, *Dominus*). Christians spoke of him thus after his resurrection. This was not merely an implicit protest against the divinization of the emperors, who also called themselves "the Lord". The title meant more than this. It was the title which was used throughout the Old Testament for God. This is the title which the primitive Church deliberately gave the glorified Jesus. In fact the glad tidings, the whole of the gospel, can be summed up with the utmost brevity in the magnificent formula, "Jesus is Lord" (Rom. 10:9; 1 Cor. 12:3; Col. 2:6).

Finally, there are some places in the New Testament where Jesus is called *God*. "The only-begotten Son" of John 1:18 is the "only-begotten God" according to some ancient manuscripts. But there is no doubt about John 1:1, "And the Word was God", or Thomas' "My Lord and my God" in John 20:28. In Romans 9:5 by far the most obvious translation is "Christ, who is God over all, blessed for ever". And Paul several times ascribes divine attributes to Jesus, as well as the divine title of "Lord".

There are several other titles in the New Testament which Christians occasionally used, out of the fullness of faith, to describe the majesty of Jesus. Thus, for instance, he is called *the Alpha and the Omega* (A and Ω), which indicates that history begins and ends with him (Rev. 1:8; 22:12); and, as John the Baptist cried out in the fourth gospel, "*Lamb of God*, who takes away the sin of the world" (Jn 1:29, 36).

Strangely enough, among all these names the simplest is also the most venerated: his proper name, *Jesus*. Paul could already write "that at the name of Jesus every knee should bow" (Phil.

154

2:10), and in the liturgy, the head is bowed only at this name. It is of course, sad to say, the name which is used in cursing and swearing. When intent on mischief, man grasps at what is most sacred.

In the ordinary life of Christians, a handy term has been current for a long time: *our Lord*. But as a piece of currency it is beginning to be worn out and the image is being rubbed off. What exactly does it mean? The Father of Jesus? This is the sort of lazy confusion which can easily occur among Catholics. At a given moment we do not know whether we are addressing Jesus or the Father. But we have seen how careful were Scripture and the Church in preserving the great titles of Jesus. We should also pay great attention to our use of his names. They comprise, in a narrow compass, the whole mystery of his person.

THE WAY TO EASTER

Jerusalem

Jesus' decision to go to Jerusalem was undoubtedly a turning-point in his life. Luke, who has already recounted two visits 88–89 to Jerusalem which Jesus made as a child, speaks of it in the 89–90 following solemn fashion:

> When the days drew near for him to be received up,
> he set his face to go to Jerusalem (Lk. 9:51).

These words tell of a determined resolve to face a grim reality. 114–115 What Jesus initially envisaged at the age of twelve, he now accepts fully and deliberately as a grown man. He goes to the city which he called on one occasion "the city of the great King" (Mt. 5:35). The kingdom of God must be made manifest there, as the prophets had predicted:

> It shall come to pass in the latter days
>   that the mountain of the house of the Lord
> shall be established as the highest of the mountains,
>   and shall be raised above the hills;
>
> and all the nations shall flow to it,
>   and many peoples shall come, and say:

"Come, let us go up to the mountain of the Lord,
    to the house of the God of Jacob;
that he may teach us his ways
    and that we may walk in his paths."
For out of Zion shall go forth the law,
    and the word of the Lord from Jerusalem.

He shall judge between the nations,
    and shall decide for many peoples;
and they shall beat their swords into ploughshares,
    and their spears into pruning hooks;

nation shall not lift up sword against nation,
    neither shall they learn war any more (Is. 2:2–4).

These are the symbols which the prophets used to affirm that God's kingship would proceed from Jerusalem. What precise 40 form it would take, they did not then know. But now the time 58–59 has come. Jesus sets out on his way to reveal the kingdom. The disciples who accompany him along the road are still full of hopes of seeing the prophecies being fulfilled in an earthly 95 way (Lk. 19:11). They look forward, for their own part, to having important places in the kingdom (Mk 10:37).

To suffer

But Jesus is fully aware that things are going to be very different. He asks the two disciples who were so eager to be awarded the places of honour: "Are you able to be baptized with the baptism with which I am baptized?" (Mk 10:38). The baptism in question 92 is the full reality which the baptism in the Jordan signified: 246–247 obedient service unto death.

Once, when he was warned in Galilee that Herod was determined to kill him, he answered: "Behold, I cast out demons and perform cures today and tomorrow, and the third day I finish my course. Nevertheless I must go on my way today and tomorrow and the day following; for it cannot be that a prophet should perish away from Jerusalem" (Lk. 13:32–33). The disciples felt the chill of fear.

And they were on the road, going up to Jerusalem,
and Jesus was walking ahead of them; and they were

156

amazed, and those who followed were afraid. And taking the twelve again, he began to tell them what was to happen to him, saying, "Behold, we are going up to Jerusalem, and the Son of man will be delivered to the chief priests and the scribes, and they will condemn him to death, and deliver him to the Gentiles; and they will mock him, and spit upon him, and scourge him, and kill him; and after three days he will rise" (Mk 10:32–34).

Jesus is to die at the hands of men. From the very start his unconventional teaching had been repugnant to many. He was set up to be the fall or the rising of many, so that the different attitudes of men might be brought to light. 88–89 102–104

Those who held off were from many different groups. There was the able political group of the Herodians; the Pharisees with their rigorous loyalty to the law; the laxer class of the Sadducees, the priests who held the reins of government; and then the lay aristocracy who were known as the ancients or elders of the people. Since they closed their hearts to the overwhelming originality of Jesus, they failed to hear the voice of their own God speaking (Jn 8:19). They sinned against God's holy Spirit (Mk 3:28–30), that is, they frustrated within themselves the possibility of inner conversion. They were to be followed by many of the ordinary people in Jerusalem.

"O Jerusalem, Jerusalem, killing the prophets and stoning those who are sent to you! How often would I have gathered your children together as a hen gathers her brood under her wings, and you would not!" (Lk. 13:34). At the climax of his task, at the very moment when he brings God's kingdom to God's city, the sin of mankind—and not only that of the Jews—strikes him down. The struggle which he waged so long with the weapons of preaching, healing and exorcism becomes a duel to the death in Jerusalem. He looks evil in the eye. He was to say at the moment of his arrest, "This is your hour, and the power of darkness" (Lk. 22:53).

How does Jesus fight this duel? By responding resolutely to his call, his Father's will, in obedience and love. He knows that out of his death the Father can bring the kingdom of God in power, like the stalk of wheat from the grain that falls into the earth and dies (Jn 12:24).

There is to be a triumph which the boldest of the prophets had not foreseen: the conquest of death. This was to be begun in Jesus and to be granted then to all mankind. These were the things for which he went up to Jerusalem. The events to come are called in the gospels his "departure" (literally, "exodus", Lk. 9:31), his being "received up" (literally, "assumption", Lk. 9:51), his "finishing his course" (literally, "being perfected", Lk. 13:32), his "glorification" (Jn 13:31), his "hour" (Jn 2:23).

One might ask oneself what would have happened if Jesus had not been rejected by men and put to death. Perhaps the kingdom of God would have been manifested in a totally different way in Jerusalem. But there is no point in discussing this here, since in fact the manifestation came through Jesus' death in agony.

The Old Testament contained clear allusions to what was to happen. There were descriptions of sufferers who were saved
175 by God (e. g. Ps. 17:22, 69). There was even a passage which
280 showed somebody taking upon himself the sins of others (Is. 52:13 – 53:12).

> He was wounded for our transgressions . . .
> All we like sheep have gone astray;
>   we have turned every one to his own way;
> and the Lord has laid on him
>   the iniquity of us all.
> He was oppressed, and he was afflicted,
>   yet he opened not his mouth (Is. 53:5–7).

The Jews had never dared apply such words to the Messiah. But Jesus made it clear that God's Anointed was to be a servant even to this extent. As he himself said: "The Son of man came not to be served but to serve, and to give his life as a ransom for many" (Mk 10:45). (The enigmatic word "ransom" will
281 be discussed in the chapter on the redemption.)

Let us now simply bear in mind the fact that Jesus comes
175–178 very close to us men in his death. He took on himself our sin-blighted life, our life-heading-for-death, and shared it right to
281–282 the end. "Greater love has no man than this, that a man lay down his life for his friends" (Jn 15:13).

It was not easy for him. He felt like someone before a serious and terrifying operation—though also looking forward to a uniquely splendid recovery. "I have a baptism to be baptized

with, and how I am constrained until it is accomplished!"
(Lk. 12:50).

Lent

The Church spends forty days in preparation for the events
which are to take place in Jerusalem. During this time a particularly urgent summons to repentance goes out to Christians.
"Behold, now is the acceptable time; behold, now is the day
of salvation" (2 Cor. 6:2), as the liturgy quotes on the First
Sunday of Lent. The forty days are already signalled by the
names of the preceding Sundays, Septuagesima, Sexagesima
and Quinquagesima, but they only begin on the following
Wednesday, Ash Wednesday. Before Mass, people's foreheads
are marked with ashes in the outline of a cross to the accompaniment of the words, "Remember, man, that you are dust
and to dust will return". This is the only time that the liturgy
addresses the faithful, not as "brothers" or by their own names,
but simply as "man".

The words come from the story of the Fall, and bring us
down to earth—to our misery. The cross of ashes is a symbol
with a profound truth, and we should not fail to attend this
Ash Wednesday ceremony. It heralds six weeks of honesty
with ourselves. We stop pushing awkward facts out of our
mind, we recollect ourselves and reflect, "Remember, man".

It is also a time for trying to better our lives—a time of conversion. It is a time of penance, when we defend our inner
freedom against all that curtails our attitude of service and love.
On the First Sunday of Lent, the gospel of the day tells of the
temptations in the desert, where Jesus overcame the efforts 92-93
to turn him from his task in life—total service.

What are we asked to do in Lent? Not so long ago the answer
appeared to be much clearer than it seems now. There was
a definite fasting law which gave people the impression that
at least they were doing something. But now the value and
wisdom of its indiscriminate practice have become doubtful.
The nervous strain imposed on many people by their work, our
view of the body-soul relationship, our eating habits (in many
cases by no means excessive), are responsible for our changed
attitude to this traditional Lenten penance. The fasting laws
have already been considerably relaxed, and they apply now

on so few days (Ash Wednesday and Good Friday) that fasting cannot be the main thing in Lent for most people. What then should take its place?

Lent is a time of sober realism, not a time of feasting. "Watching", in the spirit of the gospel, we turn the spotlight of honesty on ourselves, try to renew God's lordship in ourselves in solidarity with our Lord who is going to his passion. This can mean something different for each of us, according to the love which inspires us. For some of us it will be a matter of what we smoke and drink. For others it will involve a strict review of our duties at work and at home, a new effort to be patient under difficulties, greater attentiveness to the needs of others. An extremely 430–436 realistic and important thing is to give money to charitable causes, especially when one could make very good use of it oneself. We have a warning and an exhortation to this effect at the beginning of Lent, in the gospel of the first Monday in Lent, where we read the words, "As you did it to one of the least of these my brethren, you did it to me" (Mt. 25:40). (This 434–437 is further discussed in the section on "Help in need".) In all Lenten exercises, a greater insistence on prayer is necessary. 307–308 Morning and night prayers must be reviewed. All the family 314–316 must unite to make grace at meals less of a routine affair. There 331 are Lenten services in the churches, meditations on the passion, and so on. Lent is above all the time for a well-considered and 456–463 sincere confession.

There should also be a certain soberness in our general style of life. The feasts are suspended in the liturgy, and marriages are not celebrated without special cause. It is also well to omit festivities in the ordinary affairs of life. Though this may perhaps cause us some embarrassment it is also possible for good to result when we are seen to abide sincerely by a certain style of life.

The liturgy of Lent is remarkable for its choice of Scripture readings. It has three main subjects: penance to obtain forgiveness (especially in the first week), reflections on baptism (especially in the third and fourth weeks), and the passion of Christ (especially in the fifth and sixth weeks). The second week has no such special characteristics.

Passiontide begins with the Fifth Sunday, when the liturgy is centred on Jesus' going to his passion. The images of the saints, which could evoke the thought of heavenly glory, are covered with purple cloth. Even the crucifix, which in many ancient models already hints at the glory of the resurrection, is shrouded in purple. The gospels of this week are taken from the painful disputes between Christ and the Pharisees. The Church concentrates on Jesus' struggle.

ARRIVAL AND STAY AT JERUSALEM

All four evangelists find it important to relate how the promised envoy entered the city of the promises when he brought it the kingdom of God. He came riding on an ass. The ass was the mount of the humble rulers of Israel in earlier times (Gen. 49:11; Jg. 5:9; 1 Kgs 1:38). The horse had become the symbol of the arrogant, warlike kings (cf. Is. 31:1; 1 Kgs 1:5). Hence the prophet Zechariah had proclaimed that the future Messiah would come riding on an ass and that he would rid the country of horses (pride, self-will).

> Rejoice greatly, O daughter of Zion!
>   Shout aloud, O daughter of Jerusalem!
> Lo, your king comes to you;
>   triumphant and victorious is he,
> humble and riding on an ass,
>   on a colt the foal of an ass.
>
> I will cut off the chariot from Ephraim
>   and the war horse from Jerusalem;
> and the battle bow shall be cut off,
>   and he shall command peace to the nations;
> his dominion shall be from sea to sea,
>   and from the River to the ends of the earth
>   (Zech. 9:9–10).

Jesus, of course, was not bound to fulfil the promised signs literally. It was their spirit that mattered—simplicity and peace. But here he chose to conform to the external details. We have, therefore, the unforgettable picture of the king who makes his entry riding on an ass, greeted by the crowd as the Son of David as clothes, palm-branches and bunches of greenery are strewn along his path. To the horror of the Pharisees the children run after him up to the Temple where they continue their demonstrations of joy.

161

Thus Jerusalem did react to some extent to the arrival of Jesus and the beginning of the kingship. But the true beginning was to be different. It was to come through death.

Palm Sunday

The liturgy follows the gospels in laying special stress on these events. On the Sixth Sunday of Lent, a week before Easter, Mass is preceded by a procession, with hymns in honour of Jesus as king. Branches of greenery, or real palms, blessed for the occasion and carried in the procession, are taken home by the faithful. The palms are hung up in the house, a sign that we are sharing the gesture of love and reverence made by the Jews. Sometimes these sprigs are used to sprinkle holy water, as for instance at the blessing of the house before communion of the sick or the sacrament of the anointing of the sick ("extreme unction").

After the procession of Palm Sunday comes the most important part of the liturgy, the Mass. This does not speak of the entry into Jerusalem, but of the passion. As the gospel of the day, the whole passion according to Matthew is read. It can also be sung, to a grave and noble Gregorian melody which is deeply impressive.

In Holland it has become the custom to mark this day also by a public performance of the Passion according to St Matthew, as set to music by the eighteenth century composer, J. S. Bach. His *Matthew's Passion* is one of the great works of Christian art.

Days of menace

Between Jesus' entry into Jerusalem and his arrest, the gospels relate various sorts of discourses delivered by Jesus: in disputes with scribes, Sadducees and Pharisees, parables about judgment, the vehement denunciation of the scribes and Pharisees, and finally the prediction of the destruction of Jerusalem, an event which was to signal the end of Jewish existence in the promised land. Jesus saw this final destruction as a symbol of the catastrophes and the end of the world, which he brings into the perspective throughout the discourse, though without fixing "that day and hour" (Mt. 24:36).

Jesus, therefore, speaks like the prophets who were put to death in Jerusalem before him. But he is the last, the beloved Son

(Lk. 20:13). And even more than in the case of the prophets, his vehemence was a last effort to win the people: "Would that even today you knew the things that make for peace!" (Lk. 19:42).

His days in Jerusalem are a last and most decisive encounter with evil, the Evil one, in men. The counsel which he commends again and again to his disciples is: watchfulness, readiness. They are days of grim seriousness, a symbol of all decisive hours in the life of the Church and of each one of us.

The conflict rises swiftly to a climax. Jesus has no other weapon than the words which his Father gave him to speak, the works which his Father gave him to do, the unique authority of his person and the testimony of the Father in men's hearts. The Pharisees and authorities choose force. His arrest is decided on.

The liturgy commemorates the days before Jesus' passion (Monday, Tuesday and Wednesday of Holy Week) by reading very moving and personal passages from the prophets. For instance,

> I gave my back to the smiters,
> and my cheeks to those who pulled out the beard
> (Is. 50:6).

The gospel of Monday describes how Mary, the sister of Lazarus, poured a pound of costly spikenard on Jesus' feet. Unknowingly—Jesus explains—she did it for his future burial. On Tuesday the whole passion according to Mark is read, and on Wednesday that of Luke.

THE LAST SUPPER   332–347

On the last evening of his life, Jesus took a festive meal with his disciples.

That he chose a meal as a farewell gesture is consistent with all that he had said and done. He had often pictured the fulfilment of the kingdom of God as the common celebration of a banquet (Mt. 8:11), and the many meals he had himself eaten with friends and strangers were already joyful prefigurations of it.

163

The gospels let it be seen that the farewell meal was the passover or paschal meal.

The Jewish pasch, the commemoration of the liberation from Egypt, was a meal accompanied by stories, prayers, blessings and chants, in a word, a meal which was a thanksgiving, or to put it the other way round, a thanksgiving which was a meal.

Jesus had longed for this moment. It was his last supper before the eternal marriage feast in the kingdom. "I have earnestly desired to eat this passover with you before I suffer; for I tell you I shall never eat it again until it is fulfilled in the kingdom of God" (Lk. 22:15–16).

The washing of the feet

How the last supper began is narrated by John. Jesus, to the astonishment of his disciples, ties a towel round his waist and washes their feet like a servant. It is an expressive symbol of the service through which the kingdom is to be established (13: 12–17). Thus the passover does not merely signify that the kingdom will one day come in glory. It also shows how it is 91–93 to be built up: through service, as will be exemplified the next 112 day. John's picture of the events alludes to the great gift which will be given in express terms in the course of the meal: the Eucharist, in which Jesus loves his own gives himself, utterly and renders service unto death.

Betrayal

But there is a grim shadow across the friendship of the meal. 264 One of the twelve is in league with the enemy. Why? The roots 450–451 of evil are always obscure. The evangelists indicate that his unbelief is connected with avarice. And Judas had been Jesus' friend.

> It is not an enemy who taunts me—
>> then I could bear it . . .
> But it is you, my equal,
>> my companion, my familiar friend.
> We used to hold sweet converse together,
>> within God's house we walked in fellowship"
>> (Ps. 55:12–14).

Even my bosom friend in whom I trusted,
who ate of my bread, has lifted his heel against me"
(Ps. 41:9).

Even Jesus' allusions, clear though they were, could not restrain Judas. Thus the Scriptures were fulfilled. Psalms which told of the cruel disappointments a man could suffer from his friend's hands seemed to describe clearly Jesus' fate. This, too, was a pain which he had to suffer along with mankind. Judas went out. It was night, as John says.

Farewell discourse

John calls attention, in a way peculiarly his own, to the highly charged atmosphere of that evening. He shows Jesus radiant with the glory which was to be made manifest later. It is the whole Jesus that we see.

Jesus' farewell discourse, as given by John, records the memories of a disciple who was a young man at the time, and who carried with him for the rest of his long life the memory of that evening. They were memories nourished by the life and liturgy of the Church, where the glorified Lord remains present through his Spirit.

The discourse centres on love: love between Jesus and the Father, between Jesus and ourselves, between the Father and ourselves and between Christian and Christian. The conclusion of the discourse is Jesus' great and comprehensive prayer, which is known as the high priestly prayer.

"This is my body for you"

At this evening meal, Jesus showed his disciples how he was to die. He performed a prophetic action. We have an account of this unforgettable moment which comes from a source earlier even than the gospels. It is in one of the early epistles of Paul.

> For I received from the Lord what I also delivered to you, that the Lord Jesus on the night when he was betrayed took bread, and when he had given thanks, he broke it, and said, "This is my body which is for you! Do this in remembrance of me". In the same way also the cup, after supper, saying, "This cup is the

new covenant in my blood. Do this, as often as you drink it, in remembrance of me". For as often as you eat this bread and drink the cup, you proclaim the Lord's death until he comes (1 Cor. 11:23–26).

The gesture is not in itself extraordinary—to break the great round of bread in order to share it among the company. The distribution, along with a blessing, was one of the rites of the passover meal. But the breaking of the bread was given a startling significance when Jesus accompanied it with the unheard-of words: "This is my body." Now the breaking of the bread signifies the breaking of his body. It means his death.

This is even clearer from what Jesus says over the cup, which contained, as the rite laid down, red wine. The separate mention of the blood is in itself an indication of a violent death. But, as we read in Matthew and Mark, Jesus adds that it will "be poured
281 out". He is offered as a victim in sacrifice.

Thus the bread and wine show how he is to die. But they do more. They also show why he is to die.

38 Jesus speaks of "the new covenant" when taking the cup. The great new covenant of which Jeremiah had spoken six hundred years earlier, the covenant of the heart, is now established (cf. Jer. 31:31–34). And just as the ancient covenant was confirmed in the blood of sacrificed animals (Exod. 24:8), so, too, the new covenant in the blood of the Son. And this blood is poured out "for many". The word "many" echoes the words of the song about the suffering servant of Yahweh, in which we read:

> By his knowledge shall the righteous one, my servant,
> make *many* to be accounted righteous;
> and he shall bear their iniquities . . .
> Because *he poured out his soul* to death . . .
> yet he bore the sin of *many*,
> and made intercession for the transgressors
> (Is. 53:11, 12).

The sacrifice is "for many for the forgiveness of sins" (Mt. 26:28). In Aramaic, the language used by Jesus, "many" is used to mean "all".

Jesus' aim, however, is not merely to demonstrate this reality. He was not content merely with letting something be seen. It was also his intention to enable his disciples to make *bodily contact* with his sacrifice and the covenant. Hence this solemn act was not introduced by a call to hear and understand, like his parables, but by an invitation to eat. "Take, eat" . . . "Drink of it, all of you". By responding to this invitation, we can share in the blessings of the covenant and of the covenant sacrifice. Through contact with the body of Jesus, once dead but raised to new life, we have contact with the redeemed world, with the kingdom. "The bread which we break, is it not communion in the body of Christ?" (1 Cor. 10:16).

We see, then, that the striking symbols of broken bread and red wine are not only the means of suggesting a memory, they also present a reality: the body and blood of Jesus. (Here, too, we must remember that when the word body is used in a Semitic language, the whole man is meant. This is also true of the word blood. It signified the whole vital force. Thus we receive the whole of Jesus' person.)

This extreme gesture of Jesus' love, his giving of his body and blood as food and drink, is spoken of in the gospel of John in terms which are familiar to all Christians: "For my flesh is food indeed, and my blood is drink indeed. He who eats my flesh and drinks my blood abides in me, and I in him" (Jn 6:55–56).

When this was said—it occurred about the time of a paschal feast (Jn 6:4)—no one had understood how it could be possible. Many had had all sorts of crude ideas about what was supposed to happen. "This is a hard saying; who can listen to it?"

But then we read the words of our Lord: "Then what if you were to see the Son of man ascending where he was before? It is the spirit that gives life, the flesh is of no avail; the words that I have spoken to you are spirit and life" (Jn 6:62–63).

This evening meal which Jesus took with his friends shows what was meant: the glorification of the Son of man, his new spiritual existence, makes it possible for him to be so intimately among us that we "eat his flesh".

But was Jesus then already glorified at the last supper?

Our Lord offered himself up at this meal. He performed a prophetic action which not merely foreshadowed what was to happen, but already made it a reality in the signs. He really offered himself. The last supper was already part of that supreme event which is the suffering through which he is glorified. The celebration of the last supper already included the sacrifice of his life.

Thus Jesus changed the ancient feast of national liberation into the remembrance of a new liberation. The eating of the paschal lamb, with its saving blood, became the eating of his body, with its saving blood. Thus he gave his Church a meal which is a thanksgiving or a thanksgiving which is a meal. And this makes present to us the most loving action which he performed: the offering up of his life in sacrifice, with the glorification which this sacrifice already contained.

It is a meal, a thanksgiving and a sacrifice at once. The simplest of gestures, the giving of bread and wine, and the simplest of words, "this is my body . . . my blood", focus for us all that Jesus is and gives. There is more here than the Christian can realize at one time: the expectation of the kingdom; the memory of Jesus' farewell; the presence of Jesus' sacrificial act; the covenant between God and us; forgiveness of sins; thanksgiving (in Greek *eucharistia*)—and the sign and efficacious creator of mutual love in the Church.

These various meanings have been the subject of much thought ever since the time of Paul. But much more important than the meditations of the Church is the obedience with which the Church follows out the command, "Do this . . ." Because of this "doing", the Church has been accompanied, nourished and constituted by the Eucharist throughout the ages, down to the present day. Thus from the dawning of the light of reason, at the age of six or so, till literally the last hour of our lives, Jesus' 332–347 sacrifice is in our midst—till he comes. (A later chapter will take up once more the riches of meaning in the Eucharist and the way of celebrating it.)

The liturgy of Holy Thursday

It is not surprising that on the day of the Last Supper a sense of joy breaks through in the liturgy. The day is called Holy Thursday or Maundy Thursday.

The Eucharist is not celebrated in the morning, except in the cathedral church of the diocese. It is celebrated with twelve priests, seven deacons and seven sub-deacons. The oils for the coming year are blended and consecrated at this Mass. During the morning, the deans of the diocese come to fetch the oils from the cathedral. The parish priests and rectors fetch them in the evening from their local deanery. In this way is displayed the

solidarity of the whole diocese in the administration of the 258
sacraments. There are three sorts of oil. First there is the chrism, 360
by far the highest in rank, since it symbolizes the anointing by
the Holy Spirit. In ancient times a lamp was kept burning before
it. The symbolism of the chrism was originally its fragrance,
which represented the Spirit's filling all things. The materials
are very fine and precious balsams, mixed with olive oil. It is
with this that the Christian people is anointed as a "royal people" 256–257
(1 Pet. 2:9), and for this reason the chrism is used in the anoint- 245
ing after baptism, at confirmation, and at the consecration of a 363
bishop; and also at the consecration of a church, an altar, a church 255
bell and a chalice.

Then there is the oil of the sick. The symbolism here is the
use of oil as a healing ointment. This is the oil used in the sacra- 469–470
ment of the anointing of the sick (formerly called extreme
unction).

Finally, there is the oil of catechumens, the symbolism of
which comes from the use of oil by athletes, who, used to rub 244
it on their limbs to make them supple and strong. It is used at 363
the anointing before baptism, for the anointing of the hands of
newly-ordained priests, and at the consecration of baptismal
water, churches and altars.

The preparation of the oils has taken place on Holy Thursday
since ancient times, because solemn baptism and confirmation
were mostly administered at Easter.

That the celebration of the Eucharist on Holy Thursday takes
place in the evening should surprise nobody. There is only one
celebration of the Eucharist in each church on this day. No priest
offers Mass alone. All are together for the one Eucharist.

The epistle of the day is the most ancient text on the Eucharist
(1 Cor. 11:20–32). The gospel is the story of the washing of the
feet (Jn 13:1–15), which, as we have seen, contains impressive
allusions to the Eucharist. Immediately after this in the liturgy 164
follows the literal execution of Jesus' figurative command
(mandatum), "[so] you also ought to wash one another's feet".
The priest washes the feet of twelve of those present. The choir
sings the canticle "Where there is charity and love, there is God".

In the Canon of the Mass, after the words "the day before he
suffered", the celebrant inserts "that is, today". The liturgy of 70–71
all great feasts brings in this word, "today". This prevents us 343
from losing touch with reality by merely dreaming of the past.

169

The salvific event which we celebrate is present among us. Such is the holiness of the liturgy.

Afterwards, silently and without any liturgical action in common, some of the faithful try to meditate profoundly on Jesus' agony in the garden of olives. It is the evening on which he said to his friends, "Could you not watch one hour with me?" This hour-long prayer should not be entered upon in the hope of having pious and consoling feelings, but simply to be with the Lord and to watch with him as best we can. Even if we find nothing else to think of except that kneeling is uncomfortable, we are still showing our love of him and our desire to be one with him, not sentimentally but in steadfast presence.

THE DEATH OF THE JUST

The prayer in the garden

Jesus was arrested in the place where he was at prayer. This was in a quiet olive orchard on the slope of the hill facing the city. He knew what was going to happen to him and suffered much during his prayer. "My soul is very sorrowful", he said to his disciples, "even to death" (Mk 14:34). "His sweat became like great drops of blood falling down upon the ground" (Lk. 22:44). His prayer, perhaps the most beautiful ever uttered upon earth, was expressed in the words, "Abba, Father, all things are possible to thee; remove this cup from me; yet not what I will, but what thou wilt" (Mk 14:36). Jesus never showed himself so much one of us as here, where he was "distressed and troubled" (Mk 14:33) and "in an agony" (Lk. 22:44). But the will of the Father was a cup that strengthened him (Lk. 22:43). His disciples slept.

By the time of his arrest, Jesus had regained his calmness. A friend whom he had loved and chosen, Judas, put his face close to Jesus', who knew every trait of his features, and kissed him. A short while before, Jesus had said to his Apostles, "Watch and pray that you may not enter into temptation".

The arrest forms a poignant picture. It is not Jesus and his followers on one side, and his enemies massed on the other. What we see is Jesus left alone, facing his enemies, with one of his disciples at their head. The others have fled. One of them struck an awkward blow with a sword. But this disciple, Peter, was very shortly to assert, "I do not know this man".

The testimony before the judge

Jesus had predicted that his apostles would be called before the courts to give public testimony. Now Jesus is there himself, the first to bear testimony.

The question put to him in front of the Sanhedrin is, "Are you the Christ, the Son of the Blessed?" The "Son of the Blessed" here is probably the equivalent of "the Christ", "the Messiah". Jesus, well aware that the title had a nationalistic ring, confessed nonetheless that he was the Christ, but used his own special 152–153 term, the Son of man: "I am; and you will see the Son of man sitting at the right hand of Power, and coming with the clouds of heaven" (Mk 14:62; cf. Ps. 110:1 and Dan. 7:13).

Jesus gives the same testimony before Pilate, the Roman governor, when the charges are submitted to him. We read in John that Jesus said, "My kingship is not of this world . . . I am a king. For this I was born, and for this I have come into the world, to bear witness to the truth. Everyone who is of the truth hears my voice" (Jn 18:36–37).

Pilate, who is a cultured man, retorts, "What is truth?" and hands Jesus over to the primitive soldiery, who treat his kingship with derision. First they subject him to the humiliation of a thrashing, the scourging, then they throw a purple cloak around him, put a crown—of thorns—on his head, and for a sceptre thrust a reed into his hand.

While Jesus was testifying to his messiahship before the Jewish court, Peter was denying him. Judas went and hanged himself. The warning which Jesus gave him at the Last Supper leads us to suspect the worst: "Woe to that man by whom the Son of man is betrayed! It would have been better for that man if he had not been born" (Mt. 26:24). But even here we have no certainty as to God's final judgment.

Crucifixion

From prison and tribunal Jesus is led out to die. The sentence is carried out at a place of execution close to the city, on a slight rise of ground called Golgotha.

An inhuman form of death penalty, which the Roman Empire had learned from the East, and reserved mostly as a suitably cruel form of death, for the punishment of slaves, was inflicted on the Son of man. The evangelists record the fact soberly. "And they crucified him" (Mk); "when they had crucified him" (Mt.); "they crucified him" (Lk.); "there they crucified him" (Jn).

But the gospels stress the fact that two psalms of terrifying content here reach their fulfilment, Psalm 22: "My God, my God, why hast thou forsaken me", and Psalm 69: "Save me, O God! For the waters have come up to my neck." At times even details are verified—the offer of vinegar, the division of the clothes, the bystanders wagging their heads contemptuously, Jesus' cry—"I thirst".

More important than such details is the fact that these psalms come true as a whole: human misery at its worst, and divine salvation. From the depths of his pain and distress, Jesus himself intoned the first of these psalms. Possibly he recited the prayer to the end. We do not know.

Along with the first words of Psalm 22, the evangelists record six further sayings of Jesus while dying on the cross. They are utterances which throw light on the events. There are the two in Luke which are a continuation of the essence of Jesus' preaching. He prays for his executioners, "Father, forgive them; for they know not what they do". He promises the criminal who is crucified along with him, "Today you will be with me in Paradise". Right to the end Jesus is very much himself.

We know from the fourth gospel that our Lord looked towards John and then said to his mother, "Woman, behold your son!", and that he said to John, "Behold your mother!" After this the disciple took her to his own home. Since the Gospel of John is highly charged with symbols, we should not see in the gesture merely a sign of Jesus' filial love, an effort to make provision for the mother who would otherwise be left solitary. He is bestowing a new Eve on believers, who are represented by "the disciple whom Jesus loved". At the moment when new life is coming into the world, men are given another mother, a new mother of all the living. It is an hour of birth pangs. The atmosphere shows signs of the last days: darkness at midday.

Jesus cries out: "I thirst".

After hanging on the cross for about three hours, our Lord died about three in the afternoon. He uttered a loud cry. His mind remained clear to the end, and he gave his life in full consciousness of what he was doing. Luke then gives the content of Jesus' cry in the words of the psalm, "Father, into thy hands

I commit my spirit" (Lk. 23:46; cf. Ps. 31:5). John recalls Jesus' last gesture—how he deliberately bowed his head, the head still perhaps crowned with thorns. He gives as Jesus' last words, "It is finished".

The baptism of death, to which Jesus had been consecrated in the Jordan as the Servant of Yahweh, for which he had anxiously longed, is now fully accomplished. The kingdom of God is come through his blood.

91–93

279–282

The glory of the cross

The gospels tell of signs which indicated the significance of Jesus' death: an earthquake (the world-shaking import of this death), the rending of the veil of the temple (the end of the old covenant), the apparition of men from the dead (an enigmatic mention by Matthew, of which nothing further is said in the New Testament, and which is not interesting as an event. But as a sign, its meaning is clear—the life-giving power of this death).

And from this moment on there is the sign of the cross. It is silhouetted against the evening sky. From now on it is to renew the world. But no one could see this at the time. Golgotha was a dreadful hill covered with the bodies of the dead and dying—the place of the skull. But John's memory, looking back on this moment, could discern there signs of glory. No bone of this new lamb was broken, just as the bones of the paschal lamb remained unbroken. And above all, he remembered how Jesus' side was opened by the thrust of a lance (to make sure that he was dead) and how blood and water flowed out. This was what had been said: "Out of his heart shall flow rivers of living water" (Jn 7:38), and "My blood is drink indeed" (Jn 6:55). Hence John mentic · the water and blood on the cross. They signify the Spirit-giving baptism and the life-giving Eucharist, the sacraments of the Church. The gospel also alludes to the fact that Jesus' last breath signifies his supreme gift. In John, it is stated much more deliberately than in Matthew, "He gave up his spirit" (Jn 19:30). The Spirit is the gift which now begins to proceed from him. And so three days later, the Lord will breathe upon his Apostles and say, "Receive the Holy Spirit" (Jn 20:22).

Thus we can already see on the cross the sources of the Church's life: baptism, the Eucharist and the Holy Spirit. John mentions

20

them again in his first epistle: "There are three witnesses, the Spirit, the water, and the blood; and these three agree" (1 Jn 5:8). They are a unity, because they proceed from the core of Jesus' person, from his heart, from which flow streams of love, grace, salvation and healing: water, blood, breath—baptism, Eucharist, Spirit.

And above the sign of the cross, on which the body hangs which is the new temple with the unfailing fountain (Jn 2:21; Zech. 13:1), there is the glorious inscription, intended as cruel human irony, but now become the healing irony of God: Jesus of Nazareth, king of the Jews.

"Truly", said the centurion of the guard, "this was a son of God!"

The bodies of executed criminals were to be put aside somewhere in a pit, without funeral rites or procession. Through the courageous intervention of a noble councillor, Joseph of Arimathea, a request to Pilate for Jesus' body was granted. It was laid in a new grave which had been hewn in the rock.

Good Friday

It has been the custom since ancient times to commemorate the day of Jesus' death without the full celebration of the Eucharist. This was reserved for the Paschal vigil, when all the aspects of Jesus' achievement could be celebrated.

The name of the day, Good Friday, is in itself an echo of the feelings which dominate the liturgy. In spite of a deep sense of grief, there is a dawning joy at the thought of all that Jesus has accomplished. The structure of the liturgy is like that of the Mass. It starts with the liturgy of the word and prayer, and ends with the communion. In between, the "adoration of the cross" takes the place of the Eucharistic sacrifice.

The liturgy begins with the celebrant, deacon and sub-deacon prostrating themselves silently before the altar. Immediately after, two passages from the Old Testament are read, Hosea 6:1–6, which expresses confidence in God's power to give back life, and also the conditions for such a gift—conditions fulfilled by Jesus; then Exodus 12:1–11, which speaks of the paschal lamb and the saving blood. Then we hear, as the reading from the New Testament, the Passion in which Jesus' glorification is most in evidence—the Passion according to John.

This is followed by a series of solemn prayers on behalf of

mankind. The petitions are very simple and ardent, and probably go back to the time of the persecutions under the Roman emperors.

Then comes the adoration of the cross. The covering of purple cloth is removed from the crucifix in three stages. This is accompanied at each stage by the chant, "Behold the wood of the cross, on which depended the salvation of the world". This is sung on a higher note each time. The response sung by the congregation is: "Venite adoremus", "Come, let us adore". When we then kiss the cross, which can be a very beautiful and even festal crucifix, we adore the Lord in the sufferings which he bore and the glory which he attained.

During the adoration, the "improperia" ("reproaches") are chanted, in a tone so full of personal feeling that they cannot be matched elsewhere in the Roman liturgy. Finally, after the *Our Father* in common, we receive Holy Communion through which we participate in the Lord.

Another way in which Jesus is commemorated on this day is the following of the way of the cross, "the Stations of the Cross". In contrast to the liturgical celebration, the Stations may also be done as an act of private devotion. It is a very human way of praying, and also a very evangelical one, since we follow step by step the passion of our Lord, which is one of the high-points 72 of the gospel. Of themselves, the Stations of the Cross are not so comprehensive as the liturgy and the gospel, where the glory of Christ shines through more clearly.

Christians of the Reformation commemorate Jesus' death very specially on this day by the celebration of the Lord's Supper.

All Christians keep Good Friday in the greatest possible recollection and thankfulness.

DESCENDED INTO HELL

The psalms which speak of Life   55–56
                                                    319

It was not only Jesus' sufferings which were foreshadowed in the psalms. They also celebrate his deliverance and his glory. And they are in fact the same psalms—Psalm 22, of which Jesus uttered the opening words on the cross, Psalms 16, 69, 118, and

175

many others. "I shall not die, but I shall live, and recount the deeds of the Lord" (Ps. 118:17).

When we consider such texts carefully, we can see that they speak of being rescued at the very threshold of death—from mortal illness or some other grave menace. Such escapes were in fact only temporary. In the end God would allow death to come. Nonetheless, there is a remarkable transparency in the words through which the full life is clearly envisaged. God is much more than someone who, like a doctor, wards off death for the moment. He is the giver of life, and is proclaimed as such without reservation. But since the Old Testament had no clear 8 view of the immortality of man, this fullness of life could be given no adequate expression. The psalms have an intuition which they do not succeed in voicing. They remain half-way on the road to their goal, but their deepest purpose is reflected again and again in their utterances.

60–61 This only became fully clear with the coming of the fullness of revelation. Jesus fulfilled the psalms of deliverance in the same way as he fulfilled the prophecies of the Kingdom: by giving effect to the deepest sense of what was written. Deliverance at the threshold of death now becomes deliverance beyond the threshold of death. Thus the psalms were fulfilled in Christ.

470 *The land of the dead*

Jesus passed through the dark gate from which no one returns. He really died. This is the mystery of Christ which is celebrated on Holy Saturday. We confess it in the *Apostles' Creed* in the words, "He descended into hell".

This is an affirmation on which we are not inclined to dwell nowadays. It is an article of faith which remains very much in obscurity. We should understand why this is so. The language used reflects a picture of the universe which is not ours. For the Jews, and also for the heathen Greeks, death meant disappearing into "Sheol", "Hades", "the underworld", "the realm of the dead". This is what is meant here by the word "hell". It is not the place of evil-doers, but the realm of death where all are imprisoned, good and evil alike. The dead were thought of as shadowy beings confined to a certain place where everything was different from this world—since it was "dead".

In the mind of believers at the present day, the state of death

176

is not linked so definitely with any given place. Normally, we do not try to picture it. The dead exist—but where?

Hence the expression "descended into hell" is obviously composed of elements which are no longer part of our world of thought. But the truth of faith which lies behind the concept still remains. We must try to express it in terms of our present picture of the universe. And then there are two truths to be noted. One is more closely associated with Good Friday, the other is rather in the sphere of Easter.

The first truth is that Jesus truly died. By saying that he "descended into hell", Christians affirmed that he was really dead. It meant the humiliation of being dead, of being cut off from life, of ceasing to belong to the world which continued on its way.

Since Jesus went through death, we have the consolation that we cannot fall so deeply and darkly into the abyss of death but that Jesus, who has been there, shows that through it eternal life is to be found. In the Old Testament, it was thought that God no longer cared about those who were confined in Sheol. It is now revealed that the Lord is with us even in death.

This is the first meaning of "descended into hell", the mystery of faith of Holy Saturday. But there is another aspect to be considered. Jesus was "gathered to his fathers", that is, he joined the great mass of the dead. And so the Church began to think of the millions who had died before Christ, and for whom God also cared Jesus was imagined as announcing the redemption, immediately after his death, to the mass of the dead. "He went and preached to the spirits in prison, who formerly did not obey . . . in the days of Noah, during the building of the ark" (1 Pet. 3:20).

Judgment and redemption are for all mankind. The dead who "waited" receive their salvation. In ancient times it was said that they waited in the underworld. Later, it was said that they waited in limbo, "the limbo of the Fathers". We now generally say simply that they waited, but we do not claim to know where or how. Scripture speaks very sparingly of the matter.

What we do know today is that humanity is very ancient, and that great multitudes of men have lived and died since primitive times. And hence this truth of faith has taken on wider dimensions for us than it had for Christians of earlier centuries. Still, it was perhaps never so beautifully depicted as in the old Byzantine and Russian icons which portray the resurrection. They show our Lord bending forward over an old man, to take him by the right hand and lift him up. The old man is Adam, that is, humanity. Even to our modern ways of thinking this gesture still fully expresses the mystery of Holy Saturday. Having entered into death, our Lord stoops down to mankind's dead, to give them life for ever.

RISEN AND STILL WITH YOU

What scientific history can say of Jesus' resurrection is this: that the disciples testified to it. No human eyes saw the actual resurrection itself. It escapes historical observation. And the appearances of Jesus after his death were confined to his encounters with friends and disciples. Hence history can take us no further than these witnesses. It can weigh the credibility of their testimony. And Christians must do this. They may not "believe without good reason" (cf. 1 Cor. 15:2). Nonetheless, the final step which is demanded of them is faith.

184–185

No testimony is more unanimous in the New Testament. From the oldest to the latest writings the climax is always the same, that God "raised his Son from the dead" (cf. 1 Thess. 1:10), that the Apostles "have seen the Lord" (Jn 20:25).

The corner-stone of faith

That Jesus rose from the dead was not the opinion of a few, which gradually gained the upper hand and became the view of all. From the very beginning, this conviction was the centre and cornerstone of all preaching: "Whether then it was I or they [the other Apostles], so we preach and so you believed" (1 Cor. 15:11).

The faith stands or falls with the resurrection. "If Christ has not been raised, then our preaching is empty and your faith without foundation ... your faith is futile and you are still in your sins" (1 Cor. 15:14, 17).

Without the resurrection, Paul goes on to say, we Apostles are liars and you are most miserably deceived, since "if it is for this life only that we have set our hopes on Christ, we are of all men most to be pitied" (1 Cor. 15:19). Rather than set his heart on an imaginary Christ, he would associate himself with the cry of those whose merriment is always tinged with sadness "Let us eat and drink, for tomorrow we die" (1 Cor. 15:32).

All the first witnesses share Paul's attitude. Obviously, they are not men beset by fears and fantasies who take refuge in an illusion because they are unable to face the hard reality of life. No, they will do anything except build their lives on a lie. There is only one thing that they can affirm, in all simplicity: "But in fact Christ has been raised from the dead" (1 Cor. 15:20).

Our oldest written testimony of the resurrection, as of the Eucharist, is that of Paul. And here too he begins by affirming 165–166 with special emphasis that he also has received the testimony from tradition. Thus what he writes reflects a more ancient affirmation. Here we have reached the oldest stratum, the bedrock of the New Testament:

> "For I delivered to you first and foremost what I also received, that Christ died for our sins in accordance with the scriptures, that he was buried, that he was raised on the third day in accordance with the scriptures, and that he appeared to Cephas, then to the twelve. Then he appeared to more than five hundred brethren at one time, most of whom are still alive, though some have fallen asleep. Then he appeared to James, then to all the apostles. Last of all, as to one untimely born, he appeared also to me" (1 Cor. 15: 3–8).

This message, this "kerygma", is fully in accord with what is 209 known of the first preaching of the Apostles from the Acts of the Apostles.

We can deduce from Paul's account that Jesus probably appeared first to Peter. This first apparition is also mentioned in passing in Luke 24:34. But it is not narrated in detail in any of the gospels.

The first Sunday morning

All the gospels begin with a very simple and unassuming story, that of the women at the tomb on Sunday morning. One of the key-words for a full understanding of the story is the mention of the colour "white". They see a "young man" (Mk), "an angel" (Mt), at the tomb. He is clothed in white. White is the colour of God's holiness, of the time of the end, when God is to reign— 40, 59 the colour of the "Day of Yahweh".

Now, immediately after the sabbath, the first time in world history that the sun rises on a Sunday morning, a "Lord's Day" (Rev. 1:10), a few women are greeted by someone clad in the white of the last days. Their reaction is terror.

In Mark the whole scene is pervaded, down to the last word, by this sense of bewilderment; in Matthew, the mention of the angel is accompanied by the mention of his coming, at which an earthquake had taken place; in Luke the women bow their faces to the ground. It is the reaction of man in face of God's entry into this world. But all this is still only the outer shell of the true reality, the setting in which the real diamond of the story gleams, the words which spell peace and gladness: "He is risen". It is the same Easter message as we find in Paul: the Lord lives!

All four evangelists give the message of Jesus' resurrection in the form of narratives. When they are compared with one another, it can be seen at once that they display far more differences than do for instance the stories of the passion. The various writers often report different apparitions, and they often diverge in details where they are recounting the same fact.

From this, biblical scholarship can deduce that the stories in question were given a stereotyped form somewhat later than the preceding passion narratives. Thus, while the Easter message is the most ancient and central, the narratives were not given their fixed form so early. This is readily understandable. The passion was one single event. But the paschal events were many: "To them [the Apostles] he presented himself alive after his passion by *many* proofs" (Acts 1:3). Neither Paul nor any of the evangelists attempt to give all the events. They make their choice, no wider than is necessary to proclaim fittingly the one paschal message. Under these circumstances, a *fixed* form of narrative about the resurrection was not established so quickly. Several lines of tradition were formed with divergencies in detail.

The story of the empty tomb comes under the same head. Mark and Luke speak of three women at the tomb, though not the same three. Matthew mentions two, John one—though she says: "*We* do not know" . . . (Jn 20:2). Then Mark says: "They said nothing to anyone", while Matthew has: "They ran to tell his disciples." The command to go to Galilee is missing in Luke.

Matthew and Mark speak of one angel appearing. Luke and John say two. But in John the angels appear at the second visit, and they do not give any message. In Matthew, the angel is seated on the stone, while in the three other gospels the angel or angels are inside the tomb.

After the finding of the empty tomb, Matthew adds an apparition of the Lord to the women, which probably took place on another occasion.

It is clear enough that the four accounts are far from being well co-ordinated. Nonetheless, they agree on the main themes: the empty tomb, the appearance of the angels and above all on the heart of the message—the Lord lives. Their differences reflect perhaps something of the bewilderment shot through with joy which that morning brought, when life was proclaimed where death was expected. Undoubtedly, their differences demonstrate the assurance and the honesty of the early Church, which did not slyly smooth out the discrepancies but was confident enough to allow them to stand. But what remains crystal clear, in spite of these differences is the unity and priority of the paschal message. This is what the stories are concerned with—just as, indeed, as we have seen, Jesus' whole life is given in the form of a message.

We have dwelt a little on this question, because it is concerned with the central message of our faith, the basis of our assurance. And in this we are following Paul's counsel—"not to accept the faith without reflection" (cf. 1 Cor. 1:2).

The apparitions

Meanwhile, we have hardly mentioned the apparitions of Jesus. He does not appear in the story of the empty tomb.

How does he appear? As a burning fire? With shouts of triumph? 69–70

The joy that now begins takes on no grandiose forms. God did not will to manifest it in overwhelming dimensions, but in simple, human, almost idyllic terms.

Mary Magdalen thinks that he is the gardener. But all he needs to say is "Mary", to reveal himself. He bids the women a gentle good-morning—"Hail!" He takes a walk with two disciples. Among his Apostles at Jerusalem, he breathes upon them, eats fish and honey with them and says, "Peace be with you". He shows himself upon a mountain in Galilee, approaches and speaks to them. He breakfasts with Peter and some others by the lake. He also shows himself to Paul, in a blazing light in this case, but still with the very human words, "I am Jesus, whom you are persecuting".

He appears as a friend imparting consolation. All whom he meets are shattered men.

In all these apparitions we can see very clearly the regular contrast between what God does and what man does. Man is represented by the Apostles, the women, the witnesses who stand for us. They are all terrified, helpless, gone into hiding together. They have lost all confidence and do not know where to turn. Their hopes are dashed to the ground.

> This means that we should have to turn all the Easter stories upside down, if they were to be summed up in the words of Faust: 'These men are celebrating the resurrection of the Lord, because they themselves have risen from the dead'. No, they were not the ones who rose again. What they experience—first in fear and trembling and then in joy and jubilation, is this: that they themselves at Easter were marked by death, while it is he who was crucified and buried who lives (G. Bornkamm).

It is therefore impossible to think that the resurrection is to be explained by the inward attitude of the Apostles. It cannot be said that they spontaneously transformed their expectations into visions. To come to this conclusion, one would indeed have to turn the Easter stories upside down. The texts show clearly that the Apostles had no hopes at all. The allusions which Jesus had made to his resurrection had remained beyond their grasp, both at the time that he had made them and still more after his death. After one of these predictions we read in Luke: "But they understood none of these things; this saying was hid from them, and they did not grasp what was said" (Lk. 18:34).

Other suggestions which have been put forward to explain the resurrection of Jesus as a human invention are still more improbable. A deliberate fraud on the part of the Apostles or disciples fits in very badly with their character, as depicted by the gospels. A fraud engineered by others who stole the body and so deceived the Apostles, is in conflict with the nature of the events recounted. In any case, it was not the empty tomb but the apparitions which convinced them.

Another theory has been put forward, to the effect that we

have here the creation of a myth of spring, centred on the coming of new life. This can be excluded without further examination because the thought is completely non-biblical. 82–83

Finally, the suggestion that Jesus did not really die is contradicted both by the passion narratives and by the way in which Jesus appeared once more among his disciples. His mode of existence is different. His body is not in the same condition as it was during his earthly life. He is seen, and then suddenly seen no more. Closed doors cannot keep him out.

It was not a human work, but a work done by God which began to change human history. Jesus' bowed head is lifted up for eternity. The kingdom of God is unfolded in a man who is made anew.

Visible apparitions and invisible presence

There is a strange phenomenon to be noted in the stories of the apparitions. The disciples do not recognize him at first. Nonetheless, they discover that it is he. This fact is profoundly significant. Firstly, it is of course one more proof that the sight of the risen Lord comes to them from the reality and was not created by their imaginations. It takes some time before they recognize him. But it also demonstrates something deeper, something that is part of Jesus himself—his newness. He is no longer simply what he was before. The apparitions do not mean that he is continuing his earthly life for a few weeks more, but that he is initiating his disciples and his Church into a new form of his presence. The apparitions form a transitional stage. He uses them to show that he will always be with them. The fact that he suddenly appears in the midst of his disciples is not to prove that "he can pass through closed doors". It is a sign that he is always present, even when they do not see him. The risen Lord is the new creation in our midst. The apparitions are implicit indications of his *permanent presence*.

Meeting Mary in the garden, his disciples in the upper room, on the mountain or by the lake, he discloses himself through *his words*. This is very clear in the story of the two disciples on 322–332 the road to Emmaus. He walked along with them in person, but it meant nothing to them. But then, "Did not our hearts burn within us . . . while he opened to us the scriptures?" (Lk. 24:32). They encounter him in the word.

Another means of recognition is a certain gesture which he

makes: "the breaking of bread". Whether or not Jesus then celebrated the Eucharist with the two disciples is unimportant. 332–347 In any case, the gesture was meant to refer to the *Eucharist*, in which from then on he was to make himself known. The honey and the fish which Jesus ate are also allusions to the Eucharist. In early times these were sometimes eaten in connection with the Eucharist. They are allusions to his presence in the Eucharist. Thus in his visible apparitions he instructed his disciples as regards his invisible presence.

287–289 So too he also breathed upon them and gave them *the Spirit*, through whom they were to encounter him from that time on. 357–370 Further, Peter's *pastoral office* and the apostolic power of *for-* 454–463 *giving sins* are also spoken of in the apparitions. All are forms of Jesus' enduring presence.

124–127
289–297

Contact through faith

This presence is to be recognized through *faith*. This is also demonstrated by the apparitions. We observe that the disciples on the road to Emmaus only recognized him when they began to open their hearts in faith. It was not the eyes of the body but the eyes of faith which brought about the real recognition.

No doubt we read in the gospel of John that Thomas recognized Jesus while he was still "unbelieving". But let us examine the matter closely. This is not a man who refuses to give himself to Christ, but the Thomas who said, in the same gospel, "Let us also go, that we may die with him" (Jn 11:16). And the story of the apparition ends with the words, "Blessed are those who have not seen and yet believe" (Jn 20:29). This is the real point. Everyone who gives himself to Christ the Lord can know that the Lord is with him, even when he does not see him. Indeed, what Thomas confesses is not what he sees with his human eyes, but what is brought home to him by the light of faith. He says far more than his eyes can see: "My Lord and my God".

We must never forget that he is the risen Lord, and therefore the new creation. To come into contact with him, we need the organs of sense-preception which are proper to the new creation, the surrender of the whole man to the Spirit of God—faith.

Those who were not prepared to believe would not have recognized Jesus through his apparitions. There is an allusion to this truth in what is said about the brothers of the rich glutton in the parable, "If they do not hear Moses and the prophets, neither will they be convinced if some one should rise from the dead" (Lk. 16:31). This is also the key to the problem of why Jesus did not appear to the Pharisees and to the whole people. He would not have been recognized. (And even for us, the proof provided by apparitions to the whole people would not have been more convincing. It would have been dismissed as mass suggestion.)

It is encouraging to remember that faith was demanded even from the eye-witnesses. Thus they are not unlike ourselves, who have received the sign of the prophet Jonah, which is primarily the preaching (Lk. 11:30) and his resurrection (Mt. 12:40) *in* the preaching. A cold eye alone is not adequate to perceive truly the reality of Christ's resurrection, the new creation. Something more comprehensive is needed here—the whole man. 125–126

One more question might be put here. Why did not the Lord remain with his Church in visible form? We shall take up this question when speaking of the mystery of the ascension, which 192–193 will disclose to us the universality and closeness of his spiritual 343 presence. (The significance of the resurrection of Jesus for our resurrection will be explained in the chapter on the new heaven 470–476 and the new earth.)

THE CELEBRATION OF EASTER

The iconography of the resurrection

Christian art loved to depict moments from Jesus' risen life of glory: the women at the empty tomb, Magdalen in the garden, the disciples on the road to Emmaus, Jesus and the "Twelve", Jesus and Thomas. It was only very late in the Middle Ages that artists began to depict Jesus' leaving the tomb, which is not described in the gospels. Possibly it is a happier thought to confine oneself to the apparitions in which Jesus meets his friends than to depict a resurrection where he terrifies the guards.

One particular way of indicating the resurrection is to depict the Lord on the cross, but in such a way that the figure represents the risen Lord as well as the crucified. The glory of Easter already radiates from Calvary.

Separate pictures of the risen Lord, with his wounds visible, clad only in a mantle, are rare in northern lands, but commoner in southern Europe. We are of course familiar with images of the risen Lord in which his heart is shown. This theme, which goes back ultimately to John 19:34 (the opening of Jesus' side), has up to the present inspired few works of real art.

173

From the earliest times we have the picture of the Good Shepherd, the first representation of Christ in Christianity, which shows a young and still beardless shepherd, symbolizing Jesus' timeless person, through whom man is delivered from death.

Finally, there is a composite symbol of the resurrection, of great simplicity and beauty, which has survived from Christian antiquity. It is composed of the first two letters of the word Christ in Greek (XPICTOC), surmounted by a triumphal wreath on which doves are feeding (the souls of the faithful). Underneath, two guards are sleeping. This is a symbol which might well be given a place of honour in the Christian family during paschal time. Since many households have a crib at Christmas to depict the birth of the Lord, it is only reasonable that there should also be a special sign for Jesus' resurrection.

The signs of the resurrection

But the most important signs of the resurrection are not those of art, but the signs which Jesus himself gave: his words, baptism, the forgiveness of sin, the Eucharist and the experience of his Spirit among us—our Easter joy. When the Church recalls Jesus' resurrection, it also makes use of these signs.

183
343

The resurrection is celebrated at night. These are the most sacred hours of the year. If ever the faithful should keep watch, this is surely the night.

When the liturgy begins, the church is in darkness, to remind us of the darkness in which without Jesus we should be buried, lacking the hope in God which he brings. Outside the church a fire is kindled, from which a single great candle is lit, representing the Lord, whose light shines in our darkness. The column of wax with its burning wick is then carried into the church, and all the bystanders light their own candles from it. The whole church becomes a sea of lights. Each holds in his hand what he has inwardly become, a pure light, not of his own making, but through Jesus.

The candles remain alight while the voice of the deacon is

raised to sing the *Exultet*, the long cry of jubilation, unique in text and music, which celebrates the resurrection of the Lord.

Then a much quieter period follows. All sit down to listen to the Scripture readings, which alternate with chant and prayer. This is the genuine vigil style. In ancient times, the whole night was often passed this way. All the readings are from the Old Testament. The words pronounced under the old covenant, now that they have been fulfilled, are a means of recognizing Jesus, as they were for the disciples on the road to Emmaus. The first reading on this night of the new creation is Genesis 1:1 – 2:2, the poem of creation. Then Exodus 14:24 – 15:1 gives the greatest of the "wonderful works of God" in the Old Testament, the passage through the Red Sea, the destruction of the Egyptians, the end of slavery. It is a symbol of baptism, in which our sins are buried and we are rescued by Jesus to become children of God. The third reading, Isaiah 4:2-6; 5:1-2, predicts the restoration of Jerusalem. The prediction is fulfilled spiritually in us by Jesus' kingdom of heaven. Finally the testament of Moses is read, Deuternomy 31:22 – 32:4, as an exhortation to fidelity to what has been given us.

These readings are a preparation for the part that now follows, baptism. From ancient times, baptism was conferred in this night of the new light. It is still the privileged time for the reception of this sacrament. Hence in the next part of the solemnities, first the baptismal water is consecrated, and then, if there is a catechumen or a new-born child, baptism is administered. All present then renew their baptismal vows—the true answer, ever new, to the coming of the light.

The baptismal solemnity is introduced and ended by the first and second halves respectively of the litany of the saints. The whole of redeemed mankind is invoked.

Then the Eucharist is celebrated with all possible splendour. In the liturgy of the word, between the epistle which speaks of our rising with Christ (Col. 3:1-4), and the gospel of the empty tomb, the first Alleluia (*Halleluja*, Hebrew for "Praise Yahweh") is sung. Three times, in ascending keys, the melody rings out in which so much joy, peace and sense of liberation is expressed that it has been described as the first beat of the wings of the Dove—the Holy Spirit.

Then the actual liturgy of the Eucharist begins. We are invited by the risen Lord, and we recognize him in the breaking of bread. It is the climax of this holy night.

This solemnity, the most joyful in the Church, was gradually transferred to the morning of Saturday in the years following A.D. 1000. In the course of time, it thus lost to some extent its high dignity. But in 1951 it was restored to its rightful place, the night of Easter. The celebration no longer consists, as it did once, of keeping vigil through the whole night. However, we know that even in antiquity the congregation did not always remain in Church the whole of the night. During the baptisms, it was customary to go home to take a meal.

To go to Mass on Easter Sunday is, of course, to celebrate Easter. But now the great central celebration takes place at night. It is a holier night than Christmas, in as much as the fulfilment is more glorious than the beginning.

When we take part in the Easter vigil, we should not expect to feel the same moods and emotions as at Christmas. Christmas, with its treasury of striking melodies, has a character of its own. Easter, with its richer and deeper symbolism has also its own special character. If we try to sum up the mood of the birth of the Lord, we might say it was peace and tenderness. But then we should call the mood of Easter peace and joy.

The joy of Easter

Joy is what Easter calls for—an attitude to life which is difficult to achieve. It may be difficult on Good Friday to summon up a mood of grief if everything around us is prosperous and gay, but it is still more difficult to share the joy of Easter in spite of the cares and sufferings among which we live. Easter joy demands of us great unselfishness and strong faith, all the more so because this joy is not the pleasure, for instance, of a carnival, a mood in which we put many things out of our minds or only look on them from the brighter side. The joy of Easter is more sincere. It looks all reality in the face, including death, because it is founded on Jesus' life, on the other side of death. "O death, where is thy sting?" (1 Cor. 15:55).

One special feature of this joy is that it is linked with the forgiveness of sin. Baptism, or confession, the "second baptism", has brought forgiveness to those present. "If there is joy anywhere in the world, it is the joy of him who is pure of heart" (*The Imitation of Christ*).

The joy which Easter gives is the purest that exists in this world. To express something of it, Jesus compared it to the joy

101–102

of a mother soon after giving birth to a child (Jn 16:21–22). It is one of the fruits of the Holy Spirit. It is linked, therefore, to the gentle gesture of Jesus when he breathed upon his disciples on Easter Day. It is a sign of his presence among us, like his baptism, his word and his repast.

Like every gift of the Spirit, this joy is also open to earthly influences. Revelation does not eliminate the natural but fulfils it. Hence this experience can be modified by all that influences our moods, from physical health to music. But at the centre there is a peace whose origin is the risen Lord himself: "Peace I leave with you . . . not as the world gives do I give to you" (Jn 14:27).

One sign of the divine quality of our peace is that it is ineradicable. In pain, perplexity and fear, and even when we feel abandoned by God, there is still something of this peace in the depths of our heart, an assurance at its core. "And no one will take your joy from you" (Jn 16:22). No doubt there are certain moments when we are almost totally overwhelmed and we can hardly call it joy any longer. But at least it can still be called peace, stability: a peace barely perceptible, deep under all disturbance, a stability barely tangible, deep under all doubt. 293–294 318–319 487

Since peace is the work of God, it can be felt only in the measure of God's gift. We cannot therefore count on its being there on the night of Easter. Some great servants of God experience profound desolation on the great feast-days, and their inward joy is buried far from sight beneath doubt and depression. But the great holy-days are mostly holidays of joy for those who turn sincerely to the Lord.

But we should not go to the Easter vigil (or to midnight Mass at Christmas) to taste the joy of it. We go to encounter the Lord, whatever befalls. He will know what he is doing.

Easter Sunday

Easter Sunday is the day which has given us our Sunday. Our Lord rose from the dead on the day after the sabbath, and Christians made this day their weekly feast. Since then, every Sunday is a commemoration of the resurrection. There is no better way of sanctifying Easter, the Sunday of Sundays, than by a new Eucharist, a new communion, celebrated with new readings (1 Cor. 5:7–8, and Mk 16:1–7), chants and prayers. 320–322

This choice of new texts for Mass is continued throughout

the whole of Easter week. It is one long feast. Every day of this week was a real "Sunday" in former times. The newly-baptized continued to wear their white clothes, which they only put aside on the Sunday after Easter. The great feast of Easter ends on Low Sunday, as it is called in contrast to the "high-days" preceding it.

But even then the jubilation is not ended. Up to and including the week of Pentecost, fifty days after Easter, the *alleluia* resounds ceaselessly in the liturgy. The Sunday gospels speak of the Good Shepherd and of Jesus' promise of his presence through the Spirit.

AT THE RIGHT HAND OF THE FATHER

The resurrection as the exaltation of Jesus

Where was Jesus during the forty days after Easter, when he appeared to his disciples? Was he alone in a certain place in Palestine, from which he sometimes came to his disciples? No, he was with the Father. It was "from there" that he made himself visible and tangible to his own.

Did Jesus then ascend to heaven at the moment of his resurrection? Let us consider his meeting with Mary Magdalen on the morning of Easter. Jesus tells her not to cling to him. Things are no longer as they were before. The ordinary intimacy of earth is over. Jesus' place is now with the Father. He speaks of his ascension. "I have not yet ascended . . . Go to my brethren and say to them, I am ascending to my Father and your Father, to my God and your God" (Jn 20:17).

These words leave room for various explanations, but their central message is clear. Resurrection implies being with the Father. There are other texts in the New Testament from which we can also deduce that by the very fact of his resurrection our Lord is at the right hand of the Father.

It is Luke above all who gives the story in which this state of being with the Father is visually expressed. In his account, after the farewell words and the farewell blessing, our Lord does not suddenly disappear, as in the story of the disciples on the road to Emmaus. He ascends on high. All the other paschal stories stressed his "I am with you". But the last story calls attention to his "I go to the Father". But he has been there ever since his resurrection—and even now he remains with us.

The story of the ascension is very simple. There is no magnificent apotheosis (grand finale) as in pagan myths or in the theatre, but only a modest indication of where Jesus was going: to the Father. He ascended for a short while, till suddenly a cloud hid him from sight. The cloud signifies the presence of God 76 (cf. Lk. 9:34–35 and many Old Testament texts). There is also an allusion to the "clouds of heaven" on which the Son of man is to return.

Here the message of the gospel is not that Jesus, after being hidden by the cloud, went on up through the atmosphere till he finally came to the Father. Christ's glorified humanity does not pass through distances as we do. And then the Father, or heaven, is not "above". The notion of "above" was chosen because the vault of heaven with its light, its spaciousness and its freedom, is a splendid symbol of the place of God. But the Father to whom Jesus went is not bound to any place (Jn 4:24).

We must, therefore, leave aside our spatial representations. What we know is that Jesus as man is with the Father. He is a man, and he has a body, though not an earthly one. We do not know what is the nature of this existence, which is the beginning of the new creation. We do not yet live fully in the new creation, and the states and qualities which it involves are unknown to us (see the paragraph, "En route to the resurrec- 472 tion"). Hence we must be satisfied with the scriptural expression, "sitting at the right hand of the Father". Even this is a metaphor. The Father has no "right hand". But it is not hard for us human beings to understand the glory and love which are indicated by this expression.

To sum up: Jesus, by virtue of his resurrection, is with the Father. This is demonstrated vividly in the last of the apparitions by a symbolical gesture, the ascension. As regards Jesus' present existence as man, we know that he is in the love of the Father.

The crown of creation

Paul writes in the epistle to the Ephesians that Jesus "ascended ... that he might fill all things". The man Jesus is the crown of God's 499–500 creation. All that grows in the world, everyone who grows in the world, tends towards him, because God has appeared in him. This is expressed by Paul in the hymn:

He is the image of the invisible God,
the first-born of all creation;
for in him all things were created,
in heaven and on earth,
visible and invisible,
whether thrones or dominions
or principalities or authorities
—all things were created through him and for him.
He is before all things,
and in him all things hold together.
He is the head of the body, the church;
he is the beginning,
the first-born from the dead,
that in everything he might be pre-eminent.
For in him all the fullness of God was pleased to dwell,
and through him to reconcile to himself all things,
whether on earth or in heaven,
making peace by the blood of his cross (Col. 1:15–20).

His abiding presence

There is another question which may be asked as Jesus departs from earth in his visible form. Why did he not remain visibly among us?

The answer is: "It is to your advantage that I go away, for if I do not go away, the Counsellor will not come to you; but if I go, I will send him to you" (Jn 16:7).

Jesus' human form is replaced by the presence of the "Helper", the Holy Spirit, and, as Jesus says, this is to our advantage.

The Spirit within us brings us into closer contact with Jesus than his human form could bring about. The Lord can now penetrate us more profoundly and be more widely present in the world. Hence it is not "clinging" to his human form, as Magdalen wished to do, but the reception of his Spirit which now guarantees his presence. The Spirit is the Spirit of Jesus. "He will not speak on his own authority . . . he will take what is mine" (Jn 16:13–14).

The attentive heart leads us to him, not the easy gaze of the eyes. "Blessed are the pure in heart, for they shall see God" (Mt. 5:8).

Now that he no longer lives and works among us as a single individual, but abides within us all, he gives us a very special task and opportunity. Now it is our turn to glorify God through our human lives.

The whole life of the Church—its preaching, sacraments, Holy Spirit, sorrows and joys, strength and weakness, life and death—continues, falling and rising, the life of Jesus. Hence it would not be quite correct to say that our Lord is now invisible. He is seen now in a different way. His risen life in the world is reflected visibly in the life of men. What we really are is not yet fully manifest, of course. "Your life is hid with Christ in God" (Col. 3:3). Christ will be fully manifest only when our life reaches its total fulfilment, in the new creation.

We should not be too quick to call this fulfilment "the second coming" of the Lord. The expression is not found in the New Testament. He does not actually "return", since he is already with us. When he does "come", his presence will be completely manifest.

At Mass on Ascension Thursday, the paschal candle is extinguished after the gospel. It had been lit during Mass on each of the forty days after Easter, to symbolize Jesus' apparitions.

But then the Church looks forward for nine days to Jesus' new presence through the Spirit. It is the nine days which the Apostles, according to Luke's account, spent in prayer along with Jesus' brothers, the women from Galilee, and Mary. These nine days prayer and expectation led to the custom of praying for special intentions during a period of nine days. Such a period of prayer is called a novena. The novena for Pentecost is the most important—the prayer for the good Spirit.

I WILL SEND YOU A HELPER

The promise of the Spirit

"'If any one thirst, let him come to me and drink, he who believes in me' ... Now this he said about the Spirit, which those who believed in him were to receive" (Jn 7:37–39).

The Holy Spirit is like refreshing water; and also like burning fire. The word "spirit" also means in Hebrew, the language of the Old Testament, "breath"—and also, a breath of wind.

The material symbols of water, fire, breath and wind all indicate the impression made by God's own Spirit when given to man.

The Old Testament already used the word to indicate God's gift. His creative power—above all, in the giving of life—is described as the breath or spirit of God. Apart from this, "Spirit of God" was used above all to speak of a special personal gift by which someone was enabled to bring deliverance. Even the physical force of Samson was called the Spirit of the Lord coming "mightily" upon him, since it was the force which united the people (Jg. 13:25; 14:6-19; 15:14). The gift of prophecy was the action of God's Spirit on man (1 Sam. 10:6; Ezek. 11:5; Zech. 7:12). The wisdom of the elders who administered the law came from God's Spirit (Num. 11:17). The king is one who has been anointed by the Spirit of God (1 Sam. 16:13). These stirrings of the Spirit were often, as in the case of Samson, of a very primitive character, in keeping with the inward and outward circumstances of the times. And they always affected individuals separately. They were not given to the people as a whole.

But Israel awaited a gift of the Spirit which was to be more sublime and profound, and which would be bestowed on the whole people. A young man once ran to Moses, to tell him that two men were prophesying, not in the sacred tent but in the profane precincts of the camp. Joshua's reaction was to ask Moses to forbid them. But Moses' response was, "Would that all the Lord's people were prophets, that the Lord would put his spirit upon them!" (Num. 11:26-29).

And then, when in the days of the prophet Joel a plague of locusts brought to mind the coming Day of Yahweh, the prophet predicted for this Day not just judgment and calamity but a gift of the Spirit for all:

> And it shall come to pass afterward,
> that I will pour out my spirit on all flesh;
> your sons and your daughters shall prophesy,
>   your old men shall dream dreams,
>   and your young men shall see visions.
> Even upon the menservants and maidservants
>   in those days, I will pour out my spirit (Joel 2:28 f.)
> In Mount Zion and in Jerusalem there shall be those
>   who escape (ibid. v. 32).

The whole people is to be animated by the Spirit of God. Joel is thinking of prophetic visions and special charisms, which are to be the lot of all.

Ezekiel foresees a less sensational but more profound effect. "I will put my spirit within you, and cause you to walk in my statutes . . . A new heart I will give you, and a new spirit I will put within you" (Ezek. 36:27, 26). So too Jeremiah: "I will make a new covenant . . . I will put my law within them, and I will write it upon their hearts . . ." (Jer. 31:31, 33). The Spirit will teach gently from within and lead men to recognize in peace and joy what is the will of God. ⌐

These words of Jeremiah and Ezekiel are the spiritual climax of the Old Testament. They describe the gift which Jesus is to give as the fulfilment of his work of salvation, his last action in the setting up of the kingdom of heaven.

The giving of the Spirit

Jesus gives the Spirit. Immediately after his redemptive death the Spirit flows out from him. "Let him drink, he who believes 173–174 in me" (Jn 7:38). The water which signifies baptism also signifies the Spirit. Water and Spirit "are one", or "agree" (1 Jn 5:8).

On the evening of Easter Sunday, Jesus very explicitly gave this Spirit to his Apostles by breathing on them.

Many examples of the outpouring of the Spirit are recorded in the early Church. But great emphasis was placed on the first, which took place fifty days after Easter, on the day on which the covenant of Sinai was celebrated, the Jewish feast of Pentecost. This gift of the new covenant was then bestowed very palpably on the Apostles and their friends. The noise of a rushing wind was heard, fiery tongues were seen and foreign languages were spoken in ecstasy.

Was this the "speaking in tongues" of which Paul writes in 1 Corinthians 12 and 14—an unintelligible utterance which the ecstasy produced? Or was it a language which each of the hearers heard distinctly in translation? This is difficult to decide, and it is not of great importance. What the passage intends to convey is the unity which was suddenly brought about between all men. Luke names all the peoples expressly, in a long list. In the story of the tower of Babel we read of 261–262 estrangement and hostility, symbolized in the multiplication 230–231 of languages. These conditions are reversed at Pentecost. Men 349, 356 are now "of one heart and soul" (Acts 4:32). 421, 426

The impression was that of drunkenness. When this was remarked, Peter observed soberly, "These men are not drunk, as you suppose, since it is only the third hour of the day" (Acts 2:15). But the reaction shows the impression which was made: that of men who were beside themselves. Paul writes later to the Ephesians: "Do not get drunk with wine, . . . but be filled with the Spirit" (Eph. 5:18). Here, too, the gift of the Spirit is associated with the effects of wine. It was something by which a man was seized and rapt into ecstasy.

1 Corinthians 12 and 14 gives us glimpses of these ecstatic
59 gifts of the Spirit as they were experienced in the early Church:
317-318 an excess of joy and rapture which was manifested in astonishing sounds. Since all the gifts of God are given form and influenced by earthly conditions, we must also allow for the influence of racial peculiarities and existing religious customs in this case. Hence we must not be fascinated by the extraordinary aspects of the gifts. This would lead us astray when we go on to ask where is the Holy Spirit now.

The ordinary gifts of the Spirit

The special gifts, speaking in tongues, prophesying, healings and so on, are less frequently in evidence nowadays than in early times. This is because of the difference in religious customs, as we have said. It may also be due to the fact that at the laying of the foundations there were needs which were not felt as the building went up. The present-day fruits of God's Spirit are more "ordinary"—lucid, instructive, useful, serviceable gifts.

They are so ordinary that they fit in easily everywhere—in
287-304 the kitchen and the living-room, at school and in the factory. But these are the very gifts, as Paul explains in 1 Corinthians
59 12 and 14, and above all in the famous chapter 13 in between,
317-318 which are the most valuable and the most sublime. Ecstasy is less important than interpretation, since it is the latter which builds up the Church more effectively (1 Cor. 14:5, 19). Speaking
132 in tongues is less than charity: "If I speak in the tongues of men and angels, but have not love, I am a noisy gong or a clanging cymbal" (1 Cor. 13:1). Thus the Holy Spirit is present in the most "ordinary" thing of all, Christian charity, because there is nothing greater than this most "ordinary" thing.

The clearest description of the work of the Spirit is given by Paul in the epistle to the Galatians: "The fruit of the Spirit is love, joy, peace, patience, kindness, goodness, faithfulness, gentleness, self-control" (Gal. 5:22).

This list could be lengthened by a description of the whole of Christian life: unobtrusive loyalty, self-forgetful kindness (such as in lifelong nursing of the sick); duty done without fuss or parade (as by mothers rearing families); the sinner's unshakable confidence that God's heart is greater, steadfastness in temptations, kindness and sympathy towards a brother in need, ardent perseverance in silent prayer, patience under suffering, the joy of a good conscience. This is the work of the Spirit today. (See further on the sacrament of confirmation.) 258

It is customary to speak of the seven gifts of the Holy Spirit. The expression was occasioned by Isaiah 11:1–3, which speaks of the spirit of wisdom, understanding, counsel, fortitude, knowledge, piety and fear of the Lord which is to rest upon the Messiah.

The manner in which the Spirit works in us is determined by our temperament, customs and heredity, just as it was among the Corinthians. But it is precisely through and with our own qualities that the Spirit works in us, even where men do not know that there is a Holy Spirit.

The special gifts of the Spirit

But the extraordinary and striking gifts of the Spirit still exist today. They are there, as in the early Church, to build up the community in an exceptional way and to set special movements on foot. Though it is true to say that the ordinary Christian life is the primary gift of the Spirit, or "charism", the other more striking gifts are called "charisms", or gifts of the Spirit, in a special way. They take on different forms than in the early Church because the needs are different. They include, for instance, exceptional pastoral gifts, enlightened teaching (theology), prudent government, discovery of artistic forms, education (by parents and others), and finally, the ordinary Christian life lived in an extraordinary way (by the saints).

Sometimes such gifts are infectious, so that they animate groups rather than individuals. Sometimes there are places which are particularly open to the action of the Spirit, not on account of the places as such, but on account of the dispositions with which Christians visit them—Bethlehem, Lourdes, Rome 475 and so on.

It is to be noted that the first who received the Spirit, at Easter and at Pentecost, were Peter and the other Apostles, 136, 143–144 that is, the leaders of the Church. The ordinary government is the primary way of the Spirit, and no one can estimate highly enough the charity, gladness, peace, patience, friendliness, kindness, loyalty, gentleness and self-control which have been spread throughout the world by means of the rulers of the 360 Church in their power and in their humility. The ministry of orders itself is a regulating charism which must test the others for purity. As Paul says, "If anyone thinks that he is a prophet, or spiritual, he should acknowledge that what I am writing to you is a command of the Lord. If any one does not recognize this, he is not recognized" (1 Cor. 14:37–38). Order belongs to the gifts of God's Spirit: "God is not a God of confusion but of peace" (1 Cor. 14:33). The pastoral office watches over the charisms and discerns the spirits. This can be particularly true at a general council. But the charisms often form a complement, provided by the ordinary faithful or ordinary priests, to the work of the Church's rulers. One instance may be seen in St Francis of Assisi, who was of no higher rank than deacon, but pointed out new ways to a Pope.

But the charisms can sometimes come into conflict with one another. The fact that spiritual gifts are divided and distributed means that one person lacks what another has and vice versa. Hence a special charism generally brings suffering with it. With all the good will in the world we never manage to understand fully what another is sure of, where another is within his rights. Each one's gifts are limited and challenged by those of another. The important thing is to be patient and steadfast and gentle and not to give way to bitterness. Otherwise one who has received special graces may tend towards defeatism or egocentric rebelliousness. What began with the Spirit may end with self-centredness. The gift of God must be constantly verified. As Jesus said, all must "watch". It may happen that someone endowed with special grace does not remain true to his mission. But this does not mean that the charism was not genuine. The beginning may have been good, and the people of God can continue to build on it.

It might seem that we see very little of the Holy Spirit in the world. But it should now be clear that we constantly experience him. It only means that we use other terms— Christian love, charismatic persons, the hierarchical office. 287-289 And every time that we use the word "grace", we are really speaking of the work of the Holy Spirit of God.

The unobtrusive Spirit

If the Holy Spirit were withdrawn from the world, we should realize very clearly what his presence meant. The world would be like a land from which the water has vanished. Water is not very remarkable, but once it is gone, everything changes. Green fields wither into desert.

This is in fact the metaphor which the Church uses when it prays to the Holy Spirit. It chooses a text from Psalm 104 in which the life of natural things is described as the breath or spirit of God. All living beings exist through this spirit:

> "When thou hidest thy face, they are dismayed;
> when thou takest away their breath, they die
> and return to their dust.
> When thou sendest forth thy Spirit, they are created;
> and thou renewest the face of the ground"
> (Ps. 104:29–30).

The liturgy of Pentecost and of the rest of the Church year

The Holy Spirit is seldom addressed in the prayers of the liturgy. The visage which the Holy Spirit shows us is the visage of Christ. The Church does not pray so much *to* the Spirit as *in* the Spirit, through whom Jesus is present, through whom we cry "Abba" to God. Nonetheless, we can turn to him. The liturgy does so sometimes, especially at Pentecost (Whitsuntide). The celebration of Whitsunday—in red vestments—combines a note of joy and of supplication.

The Church year then continues with a long period of quiet meditation on the kingdom of heaven: the season "after Pentecost", which lasts till the beginning of Advent. The vestments used at the Mass of the day are a sedate green.

The season begins, however, with three mysteries which have still to be commemorated because—as the Christian people found—full justice was not done them during paschal time.

First of all, on the First Sunday after Pentecost, there is the mystery which was unfolded in Jesus' work of salvation, the mystery of the triune God—the Father who sent the Son, the 498–502 Son who was sent, the Spirit who was given by both. This is Trinity Sunday.

163–170   On the following Thursday the mystery of Holy Thursday
332–347 is celebrated once more in a very special way. It is the feast of
our Lord's presence in the signs, Corpus Christi, the feast of
the Blessed Sacrament.

173–174   On the Friday week following, one of the mysteries of Good
186 Friday is recalled once more, the pierced heart. This is likewise
a mystery of the resurrection, since it is the core of Jesus' person,
radiant and overflowing. There is also the custom or devotion
of recalling this reality of the faith on the first Friday of each
month.

    Thus certain mysteries of the redemption are celebrated anew.
This is reasonable, because Pentecost does not mean closing the
70 cycle of redemption. It brings Jesus and all the mysteries of his
343 salvation into our history for all time.

214   The work of God's Spirit in the lives of men is celebrated in
474–476 the liturgy by the feasts of the saints—their "birthday feasts",
which are here the day of their death. Personalities of the most
various types are thus commemorated in the liturgy of the
Church year. The feast of all those who allowed themselves
to be led by the Holy Spirit is celebrated on a single day, 1 November—"All Saints". These are the "hundred and forty-four
98 thousand sealed", the "multitude which no man could number"
of whom the epistle of the day speaks. The gospel is that of
the eight beatitudes.

    When depicting Pentecost, Christian artists often put Mary
76 at the centre of the picture, where she is seen with the flame
above her head. She is the type or image of the Church, filled
with the Spirit of Jesus.

    We are allowed to live in a Church of men, which is warmed
and lit by the Spirit, and summoned to go forth on its way by
the Son of man.

PART IV

THE WAY OF CHRIST

The joys of the first days

After describing the descent of the Holy Spirit and the words
of Peter, the Acts of the Apostles goes on to say:

> Those who received his word were baptized, and there
> were added that day about three thousand souls.
> And they devoted themselves to the apostles' teach-
> ing and fellowship, to the breaking of bread and
> the prayers. And fear came upon every soul; and many
> wonders and signs were done through the apostles.
> And all who believed were together and had all things
> in common; and they sold their possessions and goods
> and distributed them to all, as any had need. And
> day by day, attending the temple together and break-
> ing bread in their homes, they partook of food with
> glad and generous hearts, praising God and having
> favour with all the people. And the Lord added to
> their number day by day those who were being saved
> (Acts 2:41–47).

In such simple terms the coming of God's deliverance is
described. There is a group of men in Jerusalem who believe
that death has been overcome in Jesus, the Spirit has descended,
sin has been forgiven. Quietly and unpretentiously, like so
many great things, salvation stole into the world.

We can already recognize the Church of today in the description given by the Acts: the crowds; baptism; doctrine; the
breaking of bread; awe—the conviction that God is present
and active; the apostolic leadership; mutual aid; community
of goods—now realized in various ways, from collections to
the vows of poverty; joy; a Church in which outsiders have
a certain confidence.

Many problems did not of course exist, if only because the numbers were so small. Everything was fresh. The Church has always looked back nostalgically to the joy of those early days. Particularly in periods of renewal does the Church look back at its beginnings, as it did in the thirteenth and sixteenth centuries and as it is doing now. We draw inspiration from the simplicity of the Church's beginnings.

133–134
223–226
228–229

The difficulties of the first days

But the Acts of the Apostles and the epistles of Paul also show that even in the first days there were difficulties in plenty from within and from without. Here too we can recognize the Church of today. There have always been problems.

One of the greatest problems posed at the start was the attitude to be taken to the ancient revelation, the Jewish religion. It became steadily clearer that non-Jews could be accepted as members of the new people, the Church, on an equal footing with Jews, without being obliged to keep the Jewish law. At the same time it became tragically clear that the great majority in Israel would refuse to recognize Jesus. Though the Church is built upon Israel, though Jesus, Mary and the Apostles were Jews, the chosen people as a whole refused to enter the Church. Nonetheless, they remain the people of God's first call. Their existence comprises a mystery, of which we can feel the force in chapters 9 and 11 of the Epistle to the Romans, which was written by a Jew, Paul. Paul is convinced that good will come of it, even for the Jews. They are still called. "For the gifts and the call of God are irrevocable" (Rom. 11:29). As a people, they are more closely related to salvation than any other. As the Second Vatican Council expressly declared, it is impossible to deduce from Scripture that as a people they are rejected or accursed.

There were a number of Christians in the first century who were of Jewish origin and who wished to make all Christians obey such Jewish customs as circumcision and the food laws. This led to a division which persisted for some centuries. It was the first of the many divisions (schisms) from which the Church of God was to suffer. The existence of false doctrines (heresies) is also mentioned in the New Testament. The life and growth of the Church, as we can see, was a groping quest beset by difficulties and discord. Here, too, it was in order that "thoughts out of many hearts might be revealed" (cf. Lk. 2:35). This does not of course mean that everyone who broke away or taught false doctrine was wholly guilty personally, but that there could in fact be a certain amount of pride or obstinacy in the errors in question. This is the verdict of the New Testament writers. We sense here the high value which the Church attached from the beginning to the preservation of the apostolic faith in its purity, and how much it detested any misapplication, impoverishment or distortion of revelation.

The Church has to guard on earth a message which is not of 365 this earth. It may not shirk this responsibility, even if it wished to. It may not adulterate the truth, which is from God. Any compromise would do harm to believers and unbelievers alike and deprive them of light. At the same time, the Church is always bound to think out the truth afresh and give it new forms of expression in each age. How revelation is preserved purely and fully, how it is thought out afresh with open mind, may be seen from the way in which the books of the New Testament were produced in the bosom of the Church.

The Old Testament in the early Church

When the Church began, there was only the Old Testament. So far from rejecting it, Christians saw that it could only now be fully understood. With their "hearts burning within them" 183 they saw that, though in veiled terms, it was Jesus who was 60–61 referred to. They read there, for instance, of the manna which provided food for a single day. But after Jesus' coming, they saw that the manna was a prefiguration, a preparation for Jesus' gift, which was to abide for ever. "Your fathers ate the manna in the wilderness, and they died . . . If any one eats of this bread, he will live for ever" (Jn 6:49–51). The whole of the Old Testament was read in this way. Under the letter, Christians sought the Spirit who was already preparing in the ancient books that which was to come into the light of day in the new gospel (see 2 Cor. 3). And for this reason the Church still reads the Old Testament as the word of God when it gathers for worship: Jesus has made it all new. So, too, the early Church 175 continued to chant the psalms. 319

The origin of the gospels

Thus the Old Testament was the first book which the Church possessed. But very soon it felt the need of books which would relate "the things which have been accomplished among us" (cf. Lk. 1:1). This was the origin of the gospels, which are four in number.

Our knowledge of the life of Jesus is derived, in fact, not from one but from four parallel writings, something unique in the history of literature. Each of them comprises the good news (the *eu-angelion*) as a whole. That is why they are called the gospels. They are called after their authors: Matthew, the tax collector who became an Apostle; Mark, a young disciple from Jerusalem, in whose mother's house (where perhaps the Last Supper was held?) the community came together (Acts 12:12); Luke, the companion of Paul, "the beloved physician" (Col. 4:14); and finally John, "the disciple whom Jesus loved", who lived to be very old.

According to a very ancient tradition, Matthew wrote the first gospel. This was probably in Palestine, or Syria, about A.D. 50. But this gospel was only given its present form at a later date. Hence the oldest gospel which we possess is that of Mark, which was written in Rome about A.D. 63. The definitive form of Matthew, and the gospel of Luke, written in Greece, are generally dated about 70 to 80, while the gospel of John is put at about 100, and supposed to have been written in Asia Minor.

The first three, which are called the synoptic gospels, sometimes agree with each other word for word. This shows that they are connected with one another in some way.

It has been suggested that Mark had the first edition of Matthew before him when he was writing. (According to a very ancient testimony, one of the sources of Mark, however, is the preaching of the eye-witness, Peter, in Rome.)

When our present Matthew was written, the author had Mark before his eyes as well as the original Matthew, and also a written collection of "sayings of Jesus".

Luke used the same three sources "to write an orderly account" for an illustrious Greek, the "most excellent Theophilus", —"having followed all things accurately", as he says, so that the reader might "know the truth concerning the things of which you have been informed" (cf. Lk. 1:3–4).

As well as these sources, each of the evangelists had, of course, his own recollections and (or) the testimony of oral tradition, as delivered "by those who from the beginning were eye-witnes- and ministers of the word" (Lk. 1:2).

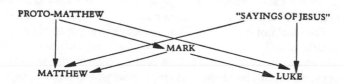

Little influence of the synoptics can be traced in John, which is a very personal gospel. It is a new account from an eyewitness, penetrated by more than sixty years' experience of Jesus through 112, 146 the Holy Spirit. 164-165

These books testify to the carefulness of the Church in pre- serving the message. But they also show how the message was adapted to the mentality of the milieu in which it was preached. Each of the gospels shows in its own way what a given community of believers found most important. Matthew, writing for Jews, composes five great discourses out of sayings of Jesus, parallel to the five books of Moses, so that Jesus appears as the new law-giver. Mark's chief interest is the revelation of Jesus as Messiah and Son of God, which took place in such a short space of time. Luke, writing for cultured Greeks, depicts a historical development (which is why he also wrote the Acts), and stresses Jesus' preference for the poor, for sinners, for wo- men—as people held in little regard. He also speaks constantly of the Holy Spirit and of prayer.

Sometimes the vocabulary is examined, to reveal the sort of community in which a gospel was preached before it was committed to writing. No doubt an effort was made to retain the words of Jesus in the form in which they were uttered, to which Jesus' rhythmic and picturesque language readily lent itself, but it remains true that they were transmitted by means of a living tradition. This means that they were sometimes formulated in clearer terms or adapted in some way to their 47-53 situation. We saw that Matthew replaces Jesus' "kingdom of God" by "kingdom of Heaven". But this freedom in rendering 95 the words of Jesus is most remarkable in John. We can recognize in Jesus' utterances the vocabulary of the circles in Asia Minor in which John was preaching. For instance, the phrase "the kingdom of God" is hardly ever used in John. It would not have had much meaning for the readers. "Light" and "life" were far more evocative to them. Hence these terms occur again and again in Jesus' words as given by John. The Apostle considered that, given the background of his hearers and readers, they were the best way of expressing what Jesus meant by the kingdom of God.

This does not mean that Christians gave free rein to their imaginations and created an image of Christ to their own taste. The evangelists did not set out, of course, to give a precise report of events month by month. Their purpose was to write a gospel, that is, pass on the good news. But for this, it was of the utmost importance that events should really have happened and words should really have been spoken. If nothing happened, there was no good news to give.

And here it can be seen that the fourth gospel can sometimes be very precise in its account of events. This is one of the reasons for attributing the testimony, late though it be, to the aged Apostle John. For instance, the "pool with five porticos" (Jn 5:2) remained a puzzle for a very long time. What did it look like? The architecture of it seemed almost impossible to imagine. It was suggested that the description was purely symbolic. But now excavations in Jerusalem have revealed the remains of a quadrangular bathing-pool, with a fifth portico joining the two longer sides at the middle. The information supplied by John was therefore accurate.

There was importance in the actual occurrence of certain events. But it was not less important to give the truth of what happened, the peculiar character of Jesus and his ministry. Modern biblical research has shown how deeply concerned the gospels were with this reality. At a time when many of the eye-witnesses had disappeared from the Church, and legalistic or free-thinking deformations were menacing oral tradition, the Church strove to establish the pure tradition of what Jesus really was. This is the origin of the gospels and of the other writings of the New Testament.

In its concern for the true picture of Christ, for the preservation of the exact faith, the community was guided by the Spirit. But the Spirit did not do this work outside the life of the community and outside the human process of authorship, but inside it. (See on this point, "Scripture the work of the Spirit".)

How truly the different gospels present the same Lord may be seen from the unmistakable originality of Jesus as he appears in all four gospels. Clearly, they have one real source—the person of Jesus of Nazareth. (On their distinctive style, and the directness with which they present Jesus through this style, see the section, "Who is this man?")

145–151

The four gospels are not our only sources of information about Jesus. Letters were also written in the early Church. They come from the pen (or the sphere of influence) of Paul (fourteen), James the Less (one), Peter (two), John (three), Jude (one). There is also a prophetic book under the name of John, the Book of Revelation or the Apocalypse.

Paul

Paul was a Pharisee with the benefits of Greek culture and Roman citizenship. He was present and gave his approval when the first martyr, Stephen, was put to death. Stephen prayed for his persecutors, and his prayer was answered. Shortly after, Paul, while hunting out Christians, was surprised by a vision of Jesus. Jesus called him to be an Apostle. He preached to the heathens and also played an important part in determining the attitude of the Church to Judaism. Paul also displays the two characteristics of preaching: reverence for the traditional truth and the endeavour to think it out anew. His letters, apart from being human documents of intense interest and amounting to a profound theological investigation of Jesus' mission, also contain the oldest written testimony to Jesus. Some of them are earlier than the gospels. The two letters to the Thessalonians (in Salonika) are from A.D. 51 or 52, and the letters to the communities at Corinth, Rome and Galatia are only a few years later.

The most ancient testimony to Jesus

Biblical research has discovered comparatively recently that within these letters there are parts which are still older. They are the summaries which describe briefly Jesus' work as a whole. Paul seems to have taken them over almost word for word from the oral tradition. The vocabulary which they use is different from Paul's ordinary formulations. The most beautiful of such cases is, no doubt, 1 Corinthians 15:3–5 (see also Rom. 1:1–4; Thess. 1:9–10, etc.). They affirm that Jesus ful-

179

filled the Scriptures by dying, being buried and rising again, that he has been exalted to the right hand of the Father for our deliverance. This ancient summary of the whole mystery of Jesus is called the *kerygma*, that is, the proclamation (of a herald). We find a similar structure in the apostolic discourses in Acts.

The scientific demonstration of the presence of the earliest form of the *kerygma* was not unimportant. There had been a theory that the Christian faith was nothing but the myth of a dying and rising god, involving originally no historical person. It had been attached only later, it was said, to Jesus of Nazareth. Then there was another hypothesis which affirmed that the life-story of Jesus of Nazareth had once been an ordinary narrative, without any significance in the order of salvation. The redemptive character had been attached to it only gradually in the course of meditation on it.

But the ancient *kerygma* shows that both the historical facts and the suprahistorical significance are at the heart of the message from the start. "Died and was buried"—historical; "according to the scriptures", "risen" and "exalted" for our salvation—suprahistorical. The whole Christian message was there from the beginning.

We shall be brief about the rest of the New Testament for, as was said at the beginning of this book, it is vital that you have a Bible in your home to use in conjunction with this book.

The epistles were written as particular occasions demanded, and therefore reflect spontaneously the life, tribulations and thinking of the early Church. The Acts of the Apostles provides us with a number of facts which illustrate the transition from a local community in Jerusalem to a world Church. The Apocalypse (Book of Revelation) reveals in visionary symbols the background of history. It contains, no doubt, allusions to actual persecutions, but its interest is not so much in history as in the great struggle between good and evil which is behind all history. Once can get a sense of the book and feel its impact without being able to understand all the details.

The Bible as permanent basis

The apostolic age is not only the beginning. It is also the fundamental period, when the eye-witnesses are alive, and the Spirit "leads the Apostles to all truth" (cf. Jn 16:13).

Hence this period has a unique and unsurpassable value, since it was the time in which all that Jesus brought was gathered in. After this period the revelation which had begun with Abraham and reached its fulfilment in Jesus was finally "closed". Since then, the Church has passed through emergencies in which it gained a deeper insight into the message, and this has often been accompanied by a sense of newness. But nothing essentially new has been added. And for the same reason the writings of the New Testament are of incomparable value. The Church established the list (canon) of its sacred books about A.D. 150, 46–47 having first sifted out very carefully inauthentic or falsified 322–323 gospels and writings.

In drawing up the canon the Church had the infallible guidance of the Holy Spirit, as it believes, this being a matter of vital importance. The Reformation also acknowledges the New Testament as covering the same authoritative books. About the same time the symbols of the four gospels (not the evangelists) were adopted, the four living creatures of Ezekiel 1 and Revelation 4, four mighty forces and four voices through which the one Jesus acts. At present the symbols are: the man for Matthew, the lion for Mark, the ox for Luke and the eagle for John.

Priestly authority

Thus the basic writings need not be replaced. It is different with the original leaders. Writings survive but men die. It was the will of the Lord that his presence should be embodied in a permanent ministry, to serve the Church but also endowed with authority. Peter and the Apostles passed on their office of rulers to the bishops, in its fullness, and to priests and deacons in part. Their office of being founders they could of course not pass on. The service done by their successors is to govern, to preside over the Eucharist, to forgive sins and to give instruction. (More will be said about this in the chapter on the pastoral office.) 357–370

One with the risen Lord

Thus the Church enters history to live out the kingdom of God on earth. It knows that it is the object of Jesus' love, and as his bride, the Church awaits him: "He gave himself up for her . . . that the Church might be presented before him in splendour" (Eph. 5:25–27).

Indeed, the unity of Christ and the Church may be expressed with even greater force. Paul continues: "No man ever hates his own flesh, but nourishes it and cherishes it, as Christ does the Church, because we are members of his body" (Eph. 5:29–30). The Church is so closely united with Jesus through the Holy Spirit that Paul can call it his body, with all the inward and outward endowments which it has received from Jesus. And to remain the body of Christ and become so more truly, it eats
339 and drinks every day, inwardly and outwardly, through our
351 mouths and through our hearts, the Eucharist, the body of Jesus.

Mary as image of the Church

The early Church had the mother of Jesus in its midst. As apostolic times go on, the Church speaks more and more about her. The latest gospels, Luke and John, speak of her at the most important places.
75–76   At the Annunciation she symbolized the people of Israel. As
172 At Pentecost she appears as the symbol of the new people of God the woman who after her birth-pangs thinks no more of her pain (Lk. 2:35; Jn 19:25).

The Church of which Mary is thus the image consists of all of us. In this sense, Mary is our sister. But the Church is also a mother for each of us. And in this sense Mary is our mother, since she is the living personification of the Church.
475–476   We can address her with confidence, if this helps us to see Jesus with new eyes and reach him more easily. The life of the people of God in the East and in the West has, in fact, shown that this has been a way to the Lord. The believer hears Jesus saying to him, Son, behold your mother. But there are also the words, Mother, behold your son. Mary cherishes the children of the Church. Our salvation is not only sublimer, but also more human, than we think.

History moving towards a goal

The Church now becomes part of history. How long is history to last? Jesus gave no answer. Christians thought at first that the end was close. The Bride watched, impatiently. But even during the lifetime of the Apostles it was evident that human history had a long course to run. Still, the Church remained watchful. We see this also in the last page of the Bible, which

212

ends with the words: "The Spirit and the Bride say, 'Come'. And let him who hears say, 'Come'. And let him who is thirsty come ... He who testifies to these things says, 'Surely I am coming soon', Amen. Come, Lord Jesus!" (Rev. 22:17–20). This longing and this certainty will give history consistency and direction. History is not a cycle which repeats itself endlessly, 40, 51 nor a helpless movement towards destruction. Humanity makes 82 its way towards an encounter in love.

THE HISTORY OF THE CHURCH

Till 311. Persecutions

The adventure has begun. The world in which the message began to spread was, as Paul says, "heartless, ruthless" (Rom. 1:31). But it was also true that there was an intense search for God, however misguided this was at times. Indeed, humanity, which comes from God, had reached a certain degree of culture and refinement. In a Latin poet for instance like Virgil, 382 one discovers a genuine longing for goodness and piety. And the State was so well organized and unified that communication was possible among many men, thank to the *Pax Romana*.

But persecution was the first reaction to the presence of Christianity in the world. The Roman Empire realized that a force was at work, loyal no doubt, but with an authority which ultimately did not come from the State. With a whispering campaign in which the slander was put about that Christians were responsible for the burning of Nero's Rome in A.D. 64, persecution flamed out.

A document of the years 111–113 shows how Roman law, for all its refinements, could come to grief—as it had already done under Pilate. All is beautifully correct when one of the best of the emperors, Trajan, writes to the younger Pliny, a governor in Asia Minor: "You have taken the right line, my dear Pliny, when examining the cases of those denounced to you as Christians. And no hard and fast rule can be laid down which would be applicable everywhere. They are not to be sought out. If they are denounced, and the charges proved, they are to be punished. Nonetheless, if they deny that they are Christians, and prove this clearly, by invoking our gods, they are to be given a free pardon in view of their recantation, no matter how suspect their past may be. Anonymous accusations are to be left completely out of consideration when a charge is being examined. Anything else would be a very bad precedent, and quite out of keeping with our times."

This judicious letter was in answer to a letter of Pliny, which may be summed up briefly as saying, "I find no fault in these men". Nonetheless, they are to be punished, because of their "obstinacy" and "superstition".

Christians were persecuted and put to death, on various excuses and for various reasons, for three hundred years, with intervals of peace. There are stories of senseless cruelty and of heroic steadfastness. But in the underground passages where
111 the dead were buried (the catacombs) the commonest word
485 to be seen is *pax*, peace.

A number of letters have been preserved from the aged Bishop of Antioch, Ignatius, who was thrown to the beasts, about A.D. 100. He writes: "I am the wheat of God and I am to be crushed by the teeth of wild beasts, to be found as pure bread of Christ . . . Fire, cross and fighting with beasts, laceration, tearing apart, breaking of bones, wrenching of limbs, shattering of the whole body, cruel torments from the devil—all may come upon me, if only I may go to Jesus Christ . . . Allow me to receive the pure light; once I have reached that point, *I shall be a man*" (Ignatius to the Romans).

200   The martyrs were envied and revered. They were not
474–476 considered as figures of the past, but as living in paradise, wherever this was thought to be. Christians asked the martyrs to intercede with God for them. Thus the honour paid to the saints grew out of faith in regeneration. The day of their death was called their birth-day.

These centuries also produced a number of great writers, the first great effort of reflection on the message by Christian thinkers.

About A.D. 200 there were Irenaeus of Lyons, who had to defend the gospel against heresies, Origen at Alexandria, a great Scripture scholar and the greatest Christian thinker of his day, Tertullian, a lawyer of Carthage with a vitriolic pen, who fell away later into uncompromising schism, and Cyprian of Carthage, once his disciple.

The government of the communities will be described
357–370 briefly in the section on the pastoral priesthood.

214

After 311. The Church integrated into society

After three centuries, a Roman emperor became a Christian. This was Constantine the Great (in 311). The Church began to be associated with a world-wide empire. It was an event of striking importance for the history of the people of God.

The first thing that meets the eye is the number of magnificent churches (some of which are still standing) which were constructed from that time on. They were not, like the heathen temples, throne-room for an idol adored by the people from outside, but spacious buildings principally decorated within and able to accommodate the crowds—"the first democratic architecture". For the people of God is the true place of God's presence, of the Body of Christ.

The church where Paul is buried (St Paul outside the Walls), and Santa Maria Maggiore in Rome, and also the basilica of Bethlehem are examples of church architecture from this time. The Hagia Sophia Church of Constantinople with its magnificent dome is only a little later, shortly after A.D. 500.

Great thinkers discussed the message of Christ on the highest level of the thought of their age. These are called the Fathers of the Church. In the East there were Athanasius, Basil, Gregory of Nazianzus, Gregory of Nyssa and the sympathetic figure of John Chrysostom, with his rich and popular eloquence. They were at once learned men and the rulers of large dioceses. They remained in constant contact with the people of God as they pondered God's works and his nature.

In the West, also, the greatest thinkers were administrators and pastors: the sturdy Ambrose, who took over much of Origen's thought, the very human Augustine, whose spiritual adventure is brought so close to us in his magnificent *Confessions.* Among the many questions which he discussed and clarified in the light of tradition, perhaps the most important is the truth that man cannot of himself free himself of sin. The grace of God is absolutely indispensable. Jerome, the great biblical scholar with the sharp tongue was the only one of these great figures who was not a bishop or administrator. They all lived about A.D. 400. Pope Leo the Great, who confronted Attila, wrote very profoundly on the incarnation of Christ (*c.* A.D. 500). Pope Gregory the Great, who reigned about A.D. 600, collected and summarized much of the wisdom of the earlier ages of the

215

Church. He was an outstanding administrator, and he was the Pope who sent missionaries to England.

The lives of these men were so thoroughly consistent with their doctrine that they are revered as saints.

Councils were called to solve grave questions. The three most important of this period have already been mentioned in the course of our discussion of the person of Jesus. We see here the sort of questions with which the Church was kept busy. And the Church was not spared schisms and heresies. Nearly every opinion rejected by a council still found a group of supporters. Both sides helped at times to obscure the issues, by their human faults, tactlessness and national pride. The most extensive division 79 was undoubtedly that caused by Arius. Centuries later Arianism was still a force.

Now that the Roman Empire was supporting the faith, it was clear that the message of Christ could be spread and developed not only under persecution, but also in time of peace.

But help from the Empire could also bring mortal peril with it. Emperors intervened in the explanation of the message. Non-Christians suffered disadvantages. Wars were fought in the name of Christ. The Church was menaced with identification with a certain world power, and thus with loss of the simplicity and catholicity of its message.

81–82 There was of course an impact in the opposite direction. The 233–234 Church taught a good deal of wisdom and tolerance to the society of the day. But the identification of Christ's way with a political 419 institution was a threat which could not be fully realized. Everyone knew that ultimately the Roman Empire was not the same as the kingdom of Christ. And when the Roman Empire was destroyed in the West, the faith continued along other paths.

After 400. Expansion among the Germanic peoples

The gospel took root among the Germanic nations which overran Europe. The Franks were united with the universal Church by about 500. And their rulers, of whom Charlemagne, about 800, was the supreme figure, aimed at establishing a strong connection between Christianity and the secular State. Some beneficent effects ensued, as well as such evils as forced conversions. But once more, total identification of the Church with the

State was not possible, if only because the Church was obviously more extensive than the Frankish kingdom. Ireland, which had been converted very early, lay outside it, as did England and South Italy, parts of Spain and the whole of Eastern Christianity. And even within his territory, Charlemagne knew that his leadership in the Church was only exercised in conjunction with the Pope and the bishops.

As regards the Pope: the city of Rome and the surrounding districts had been given by a predecessor of Charlemagne to the successors of Peter. Hence the Pope exercised temporal power there. One result of this donation was that since then the centre of the Church was never subject to any other government. This was perhaps of benefit to the freedom of the gospel, but it was also at times the occasion of grave harm.

The Church in the East

The Roman Empire continued to exist in the East, centred now on Byzantium (Constantinople). The spread of the gospel outside the boundaries of the Empire was soon checked by a tragic barrier to the east and to the south. About 600, a man called Mohammed appeared in the Arabian desert, preaching a very simple and manly form of monotheism, Islam.

Here we come upon one of the most painful enigmas in the life of the Church: how faith in Christ can disappear from whole territories. In North Africa, the home of Augustine, nothing was left of the Christian communities. The Muslims were very difficult to win to the message of Christ, as they still are today. Though they are our brothers in faith in the one God, they remain divided from us on the point of God's humanity which 31 was revealed in Christ, and consequently, with regard to man's task on earth. (See further the chapters on "Islam" and "Redemp- 271-272 tion".) The Byzantine Church spread very widely when it 285 preached the gospel towards the north, as far as Russia. But that was much later, about 1000.

c. 900–1000. The Dark Ages

After Charlemagne, grim days followed for the West. Society was shattered by the inroads of Asiatic tribes and Scandinavian and Saracen pirates. At Rome, the choice of the bishops, and hence of the Pope, came under the control of quarrelling ducal families. Never did such unworthy men sit upon the chair of Peter. The century from 900 to 1000 was probably the darkest of the Dark Ages.

Hence it was not merely on account of a mis-reading of the symbolic passage of Revelation 20:1–10, but also because they thought they saw the West collapsing around them, that many people expected the end of the world in the year 1000. The estate was bankrupt, history·had run its course. This was the time for the Lord to come.

After 1000. Development

He came, but not in the way in which he was expected. There was a second spring. One of the writers of the day said: "It was as if the world put aside its old clothes and clad itself with a snow-white garment of churches" (Rudolf Glaber). New building, often in bright-hued stone, signalled a new power of holiness in life. A new spirit was abroad.

An important factor was the Benedictine monastery of Cluny, founded in eastern France in 909, with the aim of realizing the full monastic ideal in all its purity. One of its special aims was to ensure that secular authority did not interfere with its spiritual life. Hence the monastery placed itself directly under papal authority. This *libertas*, freedom from interference by worldly interests, was evidently precisely what Christian life needed at the time. Many similar foundations followed, till finally Benedictines of the Cluniac Congregation were spread all over Europe. It had no desire to form a political movement, but the ideals which it embodied could not but have an effect in the political field. A general effort was made to separate worldly power and ecclesiastical organization.

One of the first results was the freeing of the papal elections from the domination of the emperor and the Roman nobles. Then came a conflict with the temporal power in the matter of "investiture", the giving of the insignia of episcopal office, including the appointment of the bishop. It was the constant practice of the princes to invest the bishops with the temporal administration of their dioceses, since as they had no dynastic interests they were less open to temptations of disloyalty. This meant in fact that the emperor or the king simply appointed the bishop. These exorbitant claims were reduced to more reasonable proportions in 1122, when it was agreed that the cathedral chapter should designate the bishop, with an imperial envoy present at the election. This did more justice to the fact that the bishop was primarily a man of the Church, while it also protected the interests of the Empire.

1054. The break between the East and the West

This new freedom, with the Church more independent of earthly authority and the Pope a much more outstanding figure, brought certain dangers with it. It emphasized the difference in mentality and atmosphere as compared with the Church of the East, where links between Church and State had always been very close.

Relations between Rome and Byzantium had often been strained in the previous centuries. Unity was difficult to maintain in the face of differences in theological formulas (the procession of the Holy Spirit from the Son), liturgical practice (leavened or unleavened bread) and spiritual authority (what was the primacy of the Roman See?). All these questions were complicated by political circumstances and the differences in language and culture.

Separation ensued in the eleventh century. 1054 was the fatal year. Since then the Eastern Church, with its doctrine unimpaired and with valid orders, has not been in union with the See of Peter.

In 1965, at the end of the Second Vatican Council, the mutual excommunications proclaimed in 1054 were lifted as a sign of reconciliation. This has not cleared up the differences in outlook between the Churches, but it has been a step, as we all hope in the direction of unity. 230–231

The tradition of the Eastern Church is marked by an immense reverence for God's majesty. Its refined and gentle vitality appears clearly in the liturgy. If space permitted, we should be happy to say more about its crowded history, but we must continue with that part of Church history which inevitably concerns us more closely.

Twelfth and thirteenth centuries: a climax

The West went its separate way, less cultured than the East, but with great vitality. It was inspired by new ideas, such as those of the humane Archbishop of Canterbury, Anselm (c. 1100). Newly discovered texts from Greek antiquity, especially those of Aristotle, demanded to be confronted with Christian thought. Hosts of Christians marched on Palestine in their impetuous zeal to free the Holy Land from its Muslim over-lords, in a series of "Crusades" from which high idealism was not lacking, though its expression was of course medieval.

Magnificent cathedrals and monastery churches were built, beginning with the sturdy, clean-lined style which is called Romanesque, which soon developed in France into the ex-uberant Gothic style of architecture.

A new insight into the simplicity of the gospel was attained. Men who had themselves become more humane discovered Jesus' humanity in a very particular way. Such were Bernard of Clairvaux and Francis of Assisi. A breath-taking encounter between faith and reason took place before the eyes of Western Christians in the profound and crystal-clear system of Thomas Aquinas, who used the thought-forms of Aristotle to speak of the message of Christ which is for all times. The urban civiliza-tion now arising produced a new type of man who had to 81–82 practise the faith in the new situation of city life. Serfdom, which 233 had already been greatly restricted, practically vanished with the Crusades.

The thirteenth century does in fact seem to have been a time of grace in the history of the Church of Christ in Europe. There was then a king who was a saint. Himself an impartial arbiter between kings, he actually ceded territory on his own initiative, out of a pure sense of justice (the end of the first Hundred Years War). This king, St Louis of France, died on a crusade which he had not undertaken, as so many others did, for the sake of booty and adventure. The Sainte Chapelle in Paris commemorates this king, who constructed the building as a shrine for the crown of thorns supposed to be that of Christ.

Some of the phenomena which we find appalling in the later Middle Ages appeared only on a very restricted scale in the thirteenth century. The burning of witches, particularly prevalent in the Germanic lands, only came to the fore about 1500, though it persisted in its ravages till well into the eighteenth century. Also the predominance of minor logic and juridical thinking in theology only came about in the later Middle Ages.

The Inquisition

Nonetheless, even in the thirteenth century appalling things happened. The occasion of some of the worst was as follows. A society which was living in practically total harmony of mind and spirit was challenged by another form of thought, whose devotees were well organized and worked vigorously to spread their ideas all around them. These were the Cathari, of whom the Albigenses formed a special group. There was a fundamental opposition, they thought, between Good (the pure souls) and Evil (the rest of all existing things). They declared marriage and the procreation of children an invention of Satan, rejected the oath of fealty (then the basis of society), and also the sacraments, the pastoral office in the Church, feast-days, the building of churches, and so on.

The whole of society reacted against such movements, civil administration as well as ecclesiastical authority. It happened often, before 1200, that captured heretics were lynched by the people, "because they were afraid", as we read, "that the clergy would be too mild".

About 400, a bishop like John Chrysostom could condemn the killing of a heretic as an unforgivable crime. (He was not, however, against prohibiting meetings or speeches in order to prevent the spread of error.) Bernard of Clairvaux (c. 1150) was against the death penalty for heresy, though not against imprisonment. But after 1200, when the menace of the Cathari was at its height, leaders of Church and State combined to take cruel and unjust measures against false doctrine. Since the movement in question was based on religious views, the bishop or a judge appointed by the Pope had charge of the examination (the inquisition) and passed sentence on whether the accused was heretical or not. The temporal government was then responsible for the sentence of condemnation and its execution (mostly by burning). Clearly, both were responsible for the death sentences, and not merely the "temporal arm". The teachers of false doctrine were regarded as spiritual forgers, which was held to be worse than ordinary forging of money, for which the penalty was already very severe. The conviction that the follower of a heresy was bound to perish eternally implied that the teacher of false doctrine was also a murderer of souls.

This may perhaps help us to understand why great and holy

men did not raise their voice against such procedures. Even Thomas Aquinas approved of the Inquisition. But we ask ourselves with astonishment how Christian society could proceed against divergent views with the same rigour with which the Roman Empire persecuted Christians. We see once more how an identification of the interests of Church and society, such as was then very complete, can harm the simplicity and gentleness of the gospel.

There are other examples of this besides the Inquisition. Many aspects of the Crusades, and the existence of religious, military orders of knights, show the weaknesses of the medieval situation. It shows how the Church is a very human thing which has to grow in God. But the growth may be seen. Associations for the 232-234 care of the sick and for the prevention of feuds and war were constantly springing up in these times. Members of the third order of St Francis—laymen—renounced the bearing of arms, which was then a very great sacrifice to make.

c. 1300–1500. The Later Middle Ages

Respect for papal authority reached a highpoint at this period. The Christian countries looked to the supranational element in Europe. There was a threat at one time that the newly emancipated Church might come to dominate even regions or aspects of society in which the secular government was the responsible agent. But from 1300 on the national consciousness 419 of the various States grew stronger. France now had the Pope residing within its borders, the papal residence having been transferred to Avignon from a crumbling and faction-torn Rome under German influence. Through an unfortunate combination of circumstances (a contested papal election) there were two Popes at the same time, one in Rome and one in Avignon. Great uncertainty ensued. There were saints on both sides. A council was held, but helped little, because the third Pope whom it named was not accepted by all. By the time the question was finally settled at the council of Constance (1417), after almost forty years of confusion, the Western Church had suffered serious damage.

But it was also a time when there were great mystics who also left their experiences in writing, and a time of many examples of heroic sanctity.

The religious orders aimed at greater simplicity and strictness.

But there was so much wealth in the hands of the Church, and so many ancient institutions had lost the meaning which they once had, that many of the rulers of the Church were infected by a spirit of worldliness and sloth. Rich benefices accumulated in the hands of individuals who were not equal to the responsibilities attached to them. Modern research has shown that these things were not universal. But their very existence was bad enough. The cry for reform became urgent.

But no reforms came. In Italy, with the Renaissance that set in after 1400, a new and glittering page of history began. And some Popes devoted themselves so enthusiastically to the new humanism that they paid too little attention to the misery and discontent which was so widespread, especially north of the Alps.

The sixteenth century. The parting of the ways

A calamity then came upon the Church which, along with the 204, 216 departure of Israel, the rise of Arianism and the tragedy of the 219 Eastern schism, must be counted one of the greatest which ever befell it. It was the division which Martin Luther set in motion. Luther was a man of profound religious sentiments, speaking in the passionate tones of a prophet, who set on foot in Germany, about 1517, a movement which found itself unable to remain within the universal Church.

Others followed with somewhat different views and viewpoints. The most outstanding are the Swiss, Zwingli, and the austere and level-headed Frenchman, Calvin, a man deeply penetrated by the notion of God's absolute majesty.

The words Reform, Reformation and Reformers are used in connection with the great sixteenth-century movements launched by Luther, Zwingli and Calvin. The term Protestant is used to embrace not only the Reformation Churches but also the other Christian communities which are connected directly or indirectly with the Reformation of the sixteenth century.

The Catholic community was by no means blameless in the matter. Too many Catholics, including the leaders of the Church, had remained slaves to ambition, sensuality and riches. They had watched very badly over Christ's Church. Nonetheless, there were still many wise and holy men in the Church, in the hierarchy as well as among the people. These were to provide the forces which were to bring about reform from within the Catholic community.

Among them was the priest Erasmus of Rotterdam, the humorous spokesman of gentleness, common sense and a refined humanism. It was a middle way which came at the wrong time to compete with the religious fire of Luther. But Erasmus' evangelical tolerance has much to teach us today. In England the noble figure of Sir Thomas More was prominent, though not as a reformer, and our generation is rightly drawing valuable inspiration from the Christian vigour and goodness of this family man, statesman and martyr.

Very different from Erasmus was the limping Spanish nobleman, Ignatius of Loyola. From 1521 on, shaken by spiritual crises, and filled with joy by God's Spirit, he had learned to see the world in a new light. His original intention had been to preach the gospel among the Muslims, without the use of force. He did not yet think of counteracting the Reformation in the north, though he was aware of its existence. But the times in which he lived forced him to co-operate with a three-fold task of a different nature: (1) the reform of the Church in the conviction that the bishops remain the rulers appointed by God; (2) the prevention of the further spread of the existing divisions; (3) the preaching of the gospel in the new worlds which had been discovered. But Ignatius was only one of many. Other great names are Charles Borromeo in Milan, and Peter Canisius, who was born in Nijmegen.

But the great desire of the Church was to see a Council convoked. One was finally convoked and it assembled in Trent (1545–63). It propounded the Catholic doctrine, going deeply but without polemics into the questions which the Reformers had raised. It also abolished abuses in the Church. Possibly many of the lines it laid down were too hard and fast.

Meanwhile the aristocratic Renaissance had developed into a culture with many popular and pious traits: the Baroque.

Was it the triumphal brilliance of this style which blinded so many to the sobriety of the natural sciences which were then making their first great strides forward? The foolish action taken against Galileo about 1600 in Rome was in any case a symptom of blindness to the values here involved. This is all the more regrettable, because at this very time, the foundations were being laid, by Ignatius among others, of a Christian way of life (spirituality) which discovers God in the earthly reality (see his vision at the river Cardoner). This lack of response is all the sadder because the Bible and Christian tradition had the vision of the world from which the natural sciences did in fact develop: a world which is not divine and inviolable, but the creation of God. This vision is sometimes spoken of as the desacralization of the cosmos, ridding it of special spirits, good or bad, which purported to make certain regions inaccessible to science. In Francis of Assisi's *Song to the Sun*, the sun is not a father but "brother sun". It is a world of reality, not of mere appearances, 270–271 though still going through its birth-pangs, and a world, finally, 271–272 which is not ruled arbitrarily by a Supreme Being, but has been given its own intrinsic values and laws.

It is hard to imagine that it was accidental that the natural sciences were developed in the part of the world which had been penetrated by the Christian faith. Indeed, there may be more truth than at first sight appears in the view that the spread of technological culture is already an element of the extension of 278 Christian redemption. (See further the chapters on the redemp- 426–430 tion and on work on the world.)

A new type of church architecture, in which there are no pillars to interrupt the view, was developed in the sixteenth century. The churches thus became more like public assembly halls than ever. The Gesù and the nave of St Peter's in Rome are of this type.

The Catholic revival is sometimes called the Counter-Reformation, not a very happy term. The Church was not primarily "against" something, but strove to renew itself. But there was in fact a strong defensive reaction as a by-product. Much that was valuable was regarded with suspicion in the Church because its importance was also stressed by the Reformers, who were no longer Catholics.

The differences have been exaggerated by both sides. Both groups of Christians subscribe to the same Bible, and profess the same twelve articles of faith in the Apostles' Creed. Both cherish 323–325 the ecumenical movement. And hence it is only with reluctance that we mention the points on which we differ. Nonetheless, we must dwell on them for a moment.

The most profound difference may perhaps be described as follows. Catholic Christianity believes more firmly that salvation is embodied in the most ordinary things: the bread on the altar, the voice of an assembly at Rome, the words of absolution. In these ways God comes to the Church.

God is encountered in all this only in so far as we are ready to meet him with faith. But as regards his offer, we are certain that the bread is Christ's body, that absolution is forgiveness, that the word of the universal Church is truth. This belief in God's being palpably present is intrinsically connected with the conviction that worldly reality, not excluding man, is ultimately good. So good, in fact, that in spite of our sins and defects, God can use these things to come to meet us.

252-256 The Reformation, on the contrary, was certain from the
292-293 start that God cannot be so palpably attained in the sacraments
364 and in the authoritative word of the contemporary Church.
454 Salvation for them is more spiritualized. The things of earth are not such that they can be said to contain salvation within them. Contact is made with God above all in the word of sacred Scripture, and in the creeds of the first great Councils. Special attention is paid throughout to the inner experience of the individual.

456-463 We may illustrate this by the forgiveness of sins. For Catholics, confession is a perceptible guarantee from the side of God, even if the confessor were himself a sinner who had gravely fallen. The Reformed Christian seeks the assurance of forgiveness in an inner sign from God. The marvellous thing is that the Catholic, who does not concentrate so much upon the inner experience, very often has the experience of peace and repose in abundant measure through this very everyday process. And those who seek assurance in inner experience often receive this peace only very partially. But there is a deep and true Christian feeling in this restless search for a sign of God's good will.

This has produced another type of man. The Reformation has made men more alert, more individualized—but also more restless and sometimes more sombre. In the Catholic Church, peace can be felt as very natural and obvious, which brings with it the danger of our being too easy-going with God, men and things. Nonetheless, it would be ungrateful of us not to see a sign here—not of our excellence, but of the gifts of God's presence—love, joy and peace. But it is impossible to estimate the immense amount of goodness and holiness which the Reformation, even in what is most peculiarly its own has to offer all Christianity. The Catholic Church cannot do without the Reformation.

We have dwelt a little on our differences in order to make it clear that the Reformation is concerned with a serious question.

It is something which lays hold of man and changes him at the very roots of his being: his attitude to sin, the world, Christ and God. The believing Protestant will agree with us here. The Reformers did not fight for a chimera. Happily, this is not the end of the story. But we shall take up the rest later, when dealing with the twentieth century and the ecumenical movement. 230-231

When this division took place in the Church, it was still generally held that each commonwealth or kingdom should have more or less the same religion. The reformed Christians were persecuted by the Inquisition. This is a dark page in the 221-222
history of the Church, just as the killing of Catholics and of dissident Protestants, are dark pages in the history of the Reformation. We can only pray that the blood of all will be fruitful.

The underlying notion, that one society must have one religion, entailed other disconcerting measures. Once the Reformation had made great headway, it was decreed in Germany and elsewhere that subjects should follow the religion 419
of their rulers (*cuius regio, illius et religio:* "whose the region, his the religion"). Those who refused to conform had to emigrate. This shows how difficult it was to adjust to the presence of opposing beliefs in the one society.

Before men learned to live with this new state of affairs, many an international and civil war was fought. Here, too, national feelings and opposing interests played their part, often much more effectively than the religious motives, as may be seen from the Thirty Years War. Hence it is wrong simply to label all these conflicts as wars of religion, though the religions of the various States did play a part. For centuries there were countries with a "ruling" and an "oppressed" religion— England, the Netherlands, Italy, Spain, Scandinavia, etc.

The modern age. A world-wide religion

Still other views of life were soon to make their presence felt. After 1600, and especially after 1700, there were men who denied that they were Christians, did not accept revelation, but professed belief in God (deism). After 1800, there were also many thinkers who totally refused to accept the notion of God (atheism).

Thus more and more different views came to be represented within society. This was a matter to which both Church and State took a long time to adapt themselves. The solution which

gradually suggested itself was that Church and State should
419 become more and more separate from each other. This, to say
420 the least, is not in conflict with the gospel message. The State
did not support religion *a priori*, but entered into contact with
it as the *de facto* conviction of a certain percentage of its subjects.
Hence the Church has spread much more in recent centuries
37 *among* people who hold different views (the diaspora situation).

But it has also spread over the whole world, and finds itself
in a world-wide framework. This was not the case formerly,
when the message was preached only to a small part of the
world. But at the time when the unity of medieval thought
started to disintegrate, the rest of our planet came into view
through the discoveries of Columbus and Vasco da Gama.
They were followed by irresponsible plunderers, but, also by
missionaries who brought the gospel. The most important
thing in the sixteenth century is not the unhappy divisions
within European Christianity but that the Church began its
momentous journey to the ends of the earth.

355–356 Efforts were made to implant the message of Jesus in the
language, clothing and ritual of the peoples who were now
evangelized. An example of such efforts is de Nobili in India.
Unfortunately a large number of missionaries made the great
mistake of identifying Christianity and European culture. They
vigorously opposed the notion that the evangelized peoples
should develop forms of thought and action appropriate to
their indigenous culture. These events of the seventeenth and
eighteenth centuries in Asia are known as the "Chinese (or
Indian) Rites Controversy". It was settled in favour of the
European forms. The missionaries who had advocated the
rejected opinion now obeyed the new ruling. However, since
the end of the last century, missionary methods have been more
and more inspired by attitudes such as those of de Nobili.

The Church in modern times

It is impossible, in this short space, to do justice to the events,
tendencies and great personalities of the last centuries. The
reader is referred to the plentiful existing literature on the
subject. More than ever, the fate of the Church is interwoven
with that of all mankind. This brings new difficulties with it,
353 and also brings out such virtues as tolerance without disloyalty,

228

independence withou loss of solidarity with men of different views around us. The w situation also creates new possibilities, such as constant self-criticism and the clearing-up of misunderstandings. There are, of course, still countries which favour a particular notion about God to the detriment of those who hold the opposite opinion. Thus the idea that God does not exist is favoured exclusively by the State in large portions of the world. Here Christians are persecuted or discriminated against. Unfortunately, there have also been countries up to the present day where the Catholic has to some extent persecuted or discriminated against others.

Nonetheless, the world as a whole seems to be moving into an era of greater openness and more contacts. 195-196
426

The Second Vatican Council concludes its *Declaration on the Relationship of the Church to Non-Christian Religions* by saying that love of God and of man who is made in his image cut the ground from under "every theory or practice which leads to a distinction between men or peoples in the matter of human dignity and the rights which flow from it. As a consequence, the Church rejects, as foreign to the mind of Christ, any discrimination against men or harassment of them because of their race, colour, condition of life or religion. Accordingly, following in the footsteps of the holy Apostles Peter and Paul, this sacred Synod ardently implores the Christian faithful to maintain good conduct among the Gentiles (1 Pet. 2:12), and if possible, as far as in them lies, to keep peace with all men (cf. Rom. 12:18) so that they may truly be sons of the Father who is in heaven (Mt. 5:45)".

Church buildings no longer always tower above the surrounding houses. This is also a result of the diaspora situation. The population as a whole no longer looks to these buildings for its worship. Churches are now very often built on a small scale, and Christians like to think of them as open and yet intimate, representing Christ as a pure leaven among our dwellings. Theology sets itself the task of answering the questions posed to it both from inside and from outside the Church—by biblical research, evolution, new ethical viewpoints, and so on.

It was an important event in the history of the Church that modern methods of travel and communication were developed, such as the aeroplane and television. These are media through which the non-Christian comes physically close to me as my neighbour. Other people's opinions are literally brought home to me in my sitting-room. Christians both listen more and are more listened to.

The ecumenical movement

A movement has been forming among Christians since 1910 which runs counter to the splinter-tendency of the previous ages. When the World Council of Churches was established at Amsterdam in 1948, the movement—the ecumenical movement—began to take on definite contours.

This World Council does not claim to be a new all-embracing Church or a World Church, but, as it was ultimately put in the New Delhi formulation of 1961: "The World Council of Churches is a fellowship of churches which confess the Lord Jesus Christ as God and Saviour according to the Scriptures and therefore seek to fulfil together their common calling to the glory of the one God, Father, Son and Holy Spirit." The Council envisages the union of all Christians in their common call, which is a call to testimony, fellowship and service for all mankind (*martyria, koinonia, diakonia*).

349–350

Nearly all non-Catholic ecclesial communities have joined the World Council of Churches. Initially the official attitude of the Catholic Church was hesitant, chiefly as regards making contacts with Protestants, though less so with regard to dialogue with the Eastern Churches. Of course there have always been individuals and groups deeply and actively concerned with unity.

Since the great Council summoned by Pope John, the longing for unity has been constantly given clearer expression and greater opportunities. The establishment in 1960 of the Secretariat for the Unity of Christians is an instance of the Church's sincerity. The conviction is steadily gaining ground that the ecumenical purpose need not mean indifference in seeking for God's truth, but rather attentiveness to the truth which links us all. As the Second Vatican Council said: "Catholics must be ready to acknowledge gladly and reverently the genuine Christian values from the common heritage which are to be found among our separated brethren. It is good and salutary for us to recognize the riches of Christ and virtuous works in the lives of others who give testimony to Christ, sometimes even unto the shedding of their blood" (*Decree on Ecumenism,* par. 4).

For centuries, as we have said, the tendency among Christians was to split into smaller and smaller groups. Now it seems as though the tendency is dramatically reversed, and that they are 219 coming together again, according to the prayer of Christ: 323–325 "That they all may be one". Openness to this movement comes through prayer, through constant reform and renewal, through studying the sources of the faith and each others' traditions, through readiness to abandon our well-loved forms, through honest and patient dialogue, through the seriousness which avoids easy evasions, through love of the least and poorest of men in one's own and in other Churches and communities, through co-operation in the service of mankind. And this openness brings with it the tranquillity and joy which is of the good Spirit.

A Church history in brief: the religious life

This survey of Church history dealt with such questions as the relation of Church and State, divisions and unity among Christians, and so on. Many other aspects have been passed over in silence. Nothing was said, for instance, of that special way of dedication to Christ which took its start from the words of Christ: "If you would be perfect, go, sell what you possess ... 410–417 and come, follow me" (Mt. 19:21). Let us now try to see brief-ly what this has meant.

The counsel was followed out in very different ways through-out the centuries. It was always combined with imitating Christ in his not being married. In the early Church ascetics and virgins lived the ordinary life of the community. Later, even before the Peace of Constantine, some withdrew to the desert (Anthony of Egypt). Very soon, they started to live together in groups, that is, the monastic life began to take shape. Mutual charity and a freely chosen obedience were thus naturally added to poverty and chastity (Pachomius of Egypt). Rules of deep evangelical wisdom were drawn up for community life. The Rule of St Basil became predominant in the East, that of St Benedict in the West. Augustine also drew up a Rule for priests living in community.

Those who followed Benedict's rule of life contributed a great deal to the beginnings of European culture (agriculture, learning), and also to the missionary work of the Church, following in the footsteps of the Irish monks. The missionaries Pope Gregory the Great sent to England in 590 were Benedictines. But their greatest contribution lay elsewhere. It was what they themselves conceived of as their great work: prayer (chanted) in common.

This is what chiefly distinguished the Benedictine type of religious life from that of the two great and vigorous orders which were founded in the thirteenth century, the Franciscans and the Dominicans (Order of Preachers). The latter took up residence in the towns, and their primary activity was preaching. The Franciscans stressed the life of poverty, of an unassuming simplicity before God and man, as one of their main ways of proclaiming the gospel, while the Dominicans stressed the life of study and the actual work of preaching. Thomas Aquinas was a Dominican. Later, in the sixteenth century, Ignatius Loyola developed a form of religious life which was still more closely involved in "the world", in as much as the office chanted in choir and other major characteristics of monastic life did not feature in the life of the "Society of Jesus", as he called his order.

In modern times, newly founded congregations and secular institutes are even more fully "in the world" while still living according to the evangelical counsels.

In these matters, the initiative was practically always taken by men. But women were never lacking to found their own congregations, constructing them according to the needs of their times. They may perhaps have fallen behind since the sixteenth century, due to the fact that two efforts to gain freedom of movement (by Mary Ward and Angela de Merici) were thwarted.

The foundation of new orders in the Church has never brought with it the disappearance of older ones. In as much as they preserved the spirit of their founders, they did not on the whole grow obsolete. The world of the twentieth century needs the Benedictine *pax*, the Franciscan joy, the Dominican interest in truth, and so on.

At Taizé in France a community of Reformed Christians has been founded in recent years, international in composition and highly ecumenical in spirit.

Very often the message of Christ has come to us through the

work of a religious congregation, in the parish, the school or
some other form of encounter. We are involved in their history.

The humanization of the world since Christ

58, 60–63

We have not yet touched on all the dimensions of Church
history. Hence we now return for the third time to stress one
aspect of Christ's message in history which is difficult to determine exactly but is of profound importance. The Christian faith
started on its way in a society in which ruthlessness and ine-
quality were generally accepted principles, as may be seen from
the discrimination between slave and free man, fellow-country-
man and barbarian, even man and woman. Jesus' doctrine
destroyed the foundations on which such attitudes were based.
Before God, all are equal. As Paul says, "There is neither Jew
nor Greek, there is neither slave nor free, there is neither male
nor female; for you are all one in Christ Jesus" (Gal. 3:28).
This was a sort of time-bomb, which made its impact bit by
bit down the centuries to the present day. The conclusion that
slavery should be abolished was not immediately drawn even
by Paul. But as men, slaves and free men were absolutely equal
from now on (cf. Eph. 6:5–9). So, too, were rich and poor:
"For if a man with gold rings and in fine clothing comes into
your assembly, and a poor man in shabby clothing also comes in,
and you pay attention to the one who wears the fine clothing
and say, 'Have a seat here, please', while you say to the poor man,
'Stand there' or, 'Sit at my feet', have you not made distinctions
among yourselves, and become judges with evil thoughts?"
(Jas. 2:2–4).

81–82
134–135
216, 220
222, 224
248
277–279
316–317
337
351
356, 376
388, 418
424
434
455

This had to be made come true in history. Progress was
uneven, with economic circumstances sometimes favouring,
sometimes counteracting slavery. Before it was abolished
altogether in the Christian world it went through various
milder forms. The process was a long one and in one or two
non-Christian parts of the world slavery still exists.

81
220

Democracy and social justice also seem to be connected with
the fundamental equality proclaimed by Christ for man as he
meets God, that is, in the core of his being. Men have also
become less harsh and cruel in their treatment of one another,
as in the case of condemned criminals and even in the bringing
up of children. They are less insensitive even when dealing
with animals. There is still, no doubt, a great deal of cruelty

421

and evil, but it is for the most part done covertly, there being some awareness of the fact that it is out of order.

Mankind has been acted on by the Christian spirit as by a leaven. Others may claim that this development is simply a sign that the normal evolution of man is in the direction of humaneness. But this need not be a contradiction of what has been said. Man has been so created that his development is orientated 501-502 towards the type of life which Jesus calls for and inspires.

And here it often appears that non-Christians have been the 286 champions of greater equality and tolerance. They concentrated whole-heartedly on the truth which they saw, and thereby often hastened the development. This does not mean that the development was always harmonious.

Nonetheless, as a historical phenomenon, it is remarkable that the struggle against misery and the conviction of human equality have developed precisely in that part of the world where the Christian message has penetrated the consciousness of men, where men had most understanding of Christ as the companion of their way.

Another view of the history of the people of God

We have observed three great lines in the history of God's message: striking events, the foundation of religious orders, and the continual growth of humane qualities. But one still feels that the whole history has not yet been properly grasped. After all, these are only narrow paths which we have traced through the land of the past. Invisible to the eyes of the historian, there lie on either side of these paths the regions of human life whose goodness is forgotten. An immense people advancing slowly across the vast plains—at times intolerant in its ignorance, at times cruel to man and beast, at times afflicted by superstitions from its heathen past, confused at times by prejudices, but always striving, with greater or less success, to prove the message true— such is the people of God.

This striving for a life of prayer, self-mastery, kindness, pure love, for fidelity in marriage or for virginity, for peace and patience is the real history of the Church.

Who constitute this people? They are those who encounter Christ in the Catholic Church, that living call to their conscience. These we call the Church.

But we may not refuse the name of Christ's Church to those who have found Christ while living in schism or error. It is only along with these that we can speak of the Church in the fullest sense.

Further, there are many who have not the name of Christian, but whose lives are in fact directed by the message of Christ and aim at kindness and love. They may reject the name of Christ because they do not know who he is, but they live in a climate created by Christ and do in fact sincerely strive after 234 values which Christ has brought. In a broad sense we may 403–404 perhaps also apply the term Church to them, because they belong to the people which in the course of history transmits something of Jesus' message to mankind.

Finally, there are those whom history has never brought into contact with the message, but who have listened to the voice of God in their conscience and their laws. These, too, should not be excluded in our minds from the people which is travelling towards the light which is Jesus, though they never heard of his name. For it is the Spirit who gives the heart its readiness, 249 its unspoken desire for illumination and re-birth such as Jesus gives. This seems to be a legitimate affirmation, for reasons indicated in the chapter on the general priesthood. And hence it is sometimes thought that the name of Church should not be denied these men either. But then the word would be used in a very broad sense indeed. Perhaps this is better avoided, so that the term Church in the broader sense is only used where there is a historically demonstrable link with Christ's message.

The deepest level of history

By evoking the history of nameless, unremembered acts of kindness, love and patience, have we perhaps reached the inmost kernel of Church history? No, not yet. We can go still deeper.

Beneath the surface of this goodness each man contains within him the history of sin and grace. This is what lies deepest: the treachery (apostasy, schism), the harshness (war, inquisition, feuds), the scandal, the indifference, the unbelief, the despair,

235

the hatred, to which God responds again and again with grace. Time and time again he has renewed his gift to us of the Holy Spirit. This is the true dimension of the history of goodness. This is an aspect of history buried deeper in obscurity than any other. The secret of countless lives is buried in the grave or 259–270 rather, hidden in God's eternity. It is the history of the power 270–286 of sin and the greater power of grace. If there is anything to signalize those who have tried to live out the life of Jesus in the ranks of humanity, it is the fact that they have been penetrated 349 with the sense of their own insufficiency and of the glory of God.

124–127   FAITH COMES BY HEARING. CONVERSION

289–297   *A message not invented by man*

Faith comes by hearing. It is not something one discovers for oneself. It cannot be attained by analysing the nature of man. No, one accepts something that one has not seen. One hears what Christ imparts from the Father. One hears it through the word of the Church.

288–289 No doubt we are already created "for Christ"—orientated to him. The whole of reality, including our own selves, is always in contact with him. Thus our spontaneous instincts, our sound reasoning, our talent for love, our human progress already contain something of Christ. But we cannot entirely rely on our own powers and development. Again and again revelation points to where our thinking fails us. The gospel 376 contains the unexpected. The gospel is a message which constantly forces us to revise our thinking. It turns us into some- 69–70 thing new. This is what is meant by "conversion".

Passing the threshold

Man has difficult steps to take before he arrives at faith—and indeed, to grow constantly in faith once he has found it. The approach is different for each man. But the difficulties are ulti- mately rooted in factors which are common to all men, and hence we may try to describe some of them.

The first difficulty is undoubtedly the desire to be master of all things, to subject everything to our will, including man himself. There is no room for admiration or reverence. The

236

one thing we ask ourselves is: what is there in it for me? There is no mystery about things, to make us pause reverently and ask: where do they come from? We simply work out how we can 12–15 be safe and try for that. The unexpected or incalculable is taboo. 445–449
Our attitude to men is the same. We do not treat others as other centres of love and freedom, each a unique and irreplaceable "I" with his own personal life. We see other exclusively as something that may be useful or desirable for us, otherwise they mean nothing to us. We manipulate men and things and are blind to their mystery.

This is true to some extent of all of us. In this age of technology, which can survey and measure so well, we are especially inclined to restrict ourselves to such approaches. But even in former times men were just as limited, in their own way. Covetousness, cold and hard, often mixed with pride, is a disability which lies deep in all of us, no matter how friendly we may be in our contacts.

This is a threshold which we cross when we take the step of really loving. Our fellowman then ceases to be the object of sentimental pleasure or cold utility. He is really a person like ourselves and other than ourselves, with his own depths and unexpectedness. We cease to calculate and foresee everything. We now see that the only way to know the other as he is is to let oneself be won over, to give oneself, to trust, to believe. Without belief there is no love. This belief in the other is not a lower form of knowledge but a higher. It is the one way of knowing the greatest thing on earth: another person. A cold psychological description, no matter how intelligent, does not reach the *self* of the other person. But knowing him in love does. Hence, "I believe in you" does not indicate uncertainty, as when we say, "I *believe* that it will rain tomorrow". It means grasping and knowing in the finest way of knowing which exists on earth: knowing another in his unique selfhood. And this is done only in admiration, reverence and love. Genuine love does not make men blind, but clear-sighted.

But those who have tried to live out mutual love to the uttermost sometimes come to summits where they feel that "the best is yet to be". They feel that they have been given to each other.

How? By whom? What is the ultimate mystery which binds us, which makes us exist? Our very powerlessness to hold on to the summits opens up the question: where does this immense longing come from, this ever unfulfilled desire? Is it that something or someone knocks at the door of our heart, greater than anything that we know? This is a question from which men can shrink, a threshold which they may refuse to try to cross. They can remain enthralled by the wonder, awe and love which this world inspires, refusing to go into the question which it poses. The question is this: if our love is not the ultimate, if the marvellous immensity which seems to be signalled in it really exists, must I not then reckon with the fact that it may reveal itself? To refuse such openness is to remain in a tragic state of impotence. But one can also try to listen. Questioning, searching, groping, the human mind forms an idea of what the Other, the Transcendent, should be. We depict a "God of the philosophers", and a great deal of truth begins to show through. But we still have not found the way to Christ. There is something that holds us back—the lowness of the lintel. We can only cross this threshold if we are ready to stoop. And we stoop when we do not shrink from the fact that God's speech is so ordinary. God himself has spoken in Christ, in a very human way. It is a humiliation to acknowledge this. And also a conversion.

16-17

Even then there is something that may make us hesitate. We are prepared to acknowledge that Jesus brought God within our hearing and our grasp. But we are not prepared to admit that he still does this in such humanly external things as the sacraments, the word, the office and the fellowship of his Church. It is understandable that we should shrink from this. But then we may be only partially open to what God gives. Contact with the Lord is not a purely invisible and individual matter. It is only in the fellowship which is the body of Christ that man really perceives God as the Other, and not as a product of his imagination.

There is a signpost outside: the unfolding of Christ's message, and a signpost within: the peace that the world cannot give. Together they point to the door, which is there for those who are ready to bow their heads. The house to which it leads is then seen to be wonderfully high.

Many men throughout the world come to believe as adults. But in our country the ordinary way by which the faith is first preached is through the mother who points to the crucifix, through the father who sets up the crib, through all that is said about the faith as the child sees and hears it.

It is sometimes said that this is wrong, that children should not be brought up in any given religion, but be allowed to choose for themselves as adults. The second is true, the first not. It is true that when one becomes an adult one must make one's own personal choice. But this does not prove that parents should not help to pass on their religion to their children. All who genuinely believe will spontaneously agree.

Firstly, can one imagine Christ refusing to speak to children of their heavenly Father? We read in fact of his mentioning "these little ones who believe in me".

This answer which springs spontaneously to the lips of believers is reasonable and responsible. We need only consider human nature. Man is in all respects an "animal educandum", a creature who has to develop by being trained. Parents give the best they have in every human sphere—their culture and their convictions, as for instance that animals should not be treated cruelly or that the better life is to be found in freedom and not under a tyranny. The most striking example is no doubt language. If a couple of babies were brought up without contact with adults, they would be something very inhuman. It was once thought that these conditions would produce the perfect language and the purest morals. But there would in fact be no language, no thought and no morals. Scientists are more and more convinced that the child gets his humanity or civilization from those around him, and especially from his parents. This means that the parents transmit to the child the best of their human qualities. Those who gratefully acknowledge the faith as their greatest possession, the deepest truth they know, cannot but wish to pass it on. After all, no one says, that children should be wary of the language they speak or the culture they adopt till they are twenty-one and then choose their own language and style of life. This point was strongly emphasized by the great Thomas Aquinas, defending in the Middle Ages the right of Jewish parents and guardians to bring up their charges as Jews.

We may put this argument in another way. Parents bring

their children into contact with persons whom they esteem—grandparents, good friends and so on. If they love our Our Lord, if he is really someone important in their lives, someone whom they prize above all, they cannot but teach their children to speak to him.

Secondly, children copy their parents. If the parents are believers, which is never a purely interior matter, the children automatically join in. There is, in fact, nothing more effective than example. Even if one tried to conceal one's faith, saying nothing of it, doing nothing to display it outwardly, one would still not leave the children free from all influences. Even then one would be nourishing the conviction that the Christian faith is a matter of indifference or at least that it is a matter of values which are never translated into visible action.

But when the child grows up, he has his moment—or period —of "conversion". It is the moment for him to choose whether or not he will accept the heritage which is there for him to take. The decision and the convictions of the twenty-one-year old cannot be based simply on the fact that his parents were Catholics (or non-Catholics). There is a personal threshold which he must cross. The child who has been reared as a Catholic will 408-409 mostly find this easier and more obvious than the child without a Catholic upbringing. But sometimes the very fact that so much is taken for granted is a hindrance to making a personal decision. In that case, it is well that the proclamation of the gospel should come as a shock and that young people should feel how little it should be taken for granted that God has become man and speaks to us in the Church. But even then the child who has been brought up a Catholic will be in a better position to make the decision.

There are certain prejudices from which he will not suffer. And he will already have tasted peace. As a child, he has often spoken to God. This has an effect somewhat like that of a normal affective life. At twenty, one can be loving and affectionate, because one's parents have been loving, and have not been sparing in giving signs of their affection. This helps us to recognize the way in which God gives faith. Faith, like every other 288-289 human thing, is something of a social act, something done together. Israel believed together. The faith of one influenced the faith of another (cf. Lk. 22:32). The Church believes together.

240

The faith of the parents and of the community affect the faith of the child. This does not mean that his faith is not personal. He simply acknowledges as his own the riches which have come to him in common with others. All it means is that faith is not isolated or individual. We believe along with the Church. And the recognition of this fact also contains a true, deep act of humility.

To the question, therefore, of whether the parents determine the faith of the children the answer is yes and no. No, because once he has come to adulthood, the child must determine his own attitude in face of Christ. One does not automatically become a fully mature believer, without the definite intervention of a free act. But it remains true that the parents' choice has influenced the children. This is inevitable and good and willed by God. It is in the nature of faith to be given to men in common.

When a young person gives up the faith of his parents, this can be because of his faults and the hardening of his heart. He 127 does not desire conversion. But it can also happen that everything has become obscure to him. Circumstances may have shrouded the visage of the Church so that the Church—and hence Christ— has become unrecognizable to him. To leave the Church for a while under such circumstances may sometimes signify spiritual progress. It may be an effort to take God more seriously. And finally, there may be a combination of both of these factors. But in all three cases parents have to leave the child more and more freedom as he grows up. Faith can be urged but not imposed. It is 320–321 necessary that parents should have an increasing respect for what the child sincerely believes, even if they think it is wrong. In any case, a child who has "left the Church" must never be shown the door.

Needless to say, it is hard for parents not to be able to pass on the riches of their faith. But this can be an occasion for making a new effort to live out their own faith. Sometimes they have been preaching what they did not practise, or their heart was not in what they said. The tragic situation of the child can help them to give effect in their own lives to the words which have failed with the child.—The parents who see a new Pentecost taking place in their growing children can call themselves blessed.

"THE WASHING OF WATER WITH THE WORD"

"They were baptized." The story of Pentecost ends with these words (Acts 2:41). Baptism is the visible sign under which we enter the people of God. We shall first follow step by step the ceremonies of the solemn celebration of the baptism of adults. Then we shall speak of the baptism of children.

The beginning of the catechumenate

The first ceremony is the admission of the candidate for baptism as a catechumen. This takes place outside the door of the Church, which is itself significant. The purple stole worn by the priest is also a sign that the candidate is still far from his goal. It is the colour of Advent and of Lent. So too the rest of the ceremonies down to the last detail are full of symbols. The place, the colour, the gestures and the matter used are all eloquent and can be understood without deep study.

The reception begins with the question: what is your name? The second question is: what do you want? The answer to this, on the lips of mortal man, is overwhelming: "What I need for eternal life". First and foremost, this is faith. The candidate comes because he believes, but he still asks for faith. It is like the prayer in the gospel, "I believe, Lord. Help my unbelief!" (cf. Mk 9:24). It ultimately points to the fact that faith is something that one is given, not something that one produces oneself.

After a mention of the works that are to be done, there is an interrogation about the candidate's preparedness. Then the priest performs Jesus' paschal gesture. He breathes upon the candidate, and orders the evil spirit to make way for the Holy Spirit.

This sort of "exorcism" of the wicked spirit occurs frequently during the solemnities of baptism. The evil which threatens man 109 is told to go away, always addressed as a person—the devil. But the words envisage all evil, including the influence of the sins 482 of others, the evil inclinations of the subject, and his previous errors as regards God. Only the harmful elements of his misconceptions about God are mentioned in the ceremony, which is starkly uncompromising throughout, showing nothing but light against darkness.

And it is well that it is so, because the ceremony is a brief and vigorous re-statement of a vital hour. The struggle for life, the conversion of the candidate, is summed up without nuances with a biblical succinctness and profundity. We see the temptations, 294 the dilemmas, the darkness, the despair which have presented themselves and will be there again; and we see over against them each time God's peace and goodness and joy. In a word, it is the expulsion of the evil spirit and the coming of the good.

The rite continues with the priest making the sign of the cross on the candidate's body—on his forehead, ears, eyes, nose, mouth, breast and shoulders. The whole body is lit up by the cross, to the accompaniment of good wishes and prayers.

The Church cannot give the Eucharist at this first meeting, but it gives some salt. This signifies preservation against corruption. It also means that the things of God are to be full of savour and not prove insipid: *sal sapientiae*, the tang of things. Finally, there is also the notion of making one thirst for water.

Then the candidate departs. The catechumenate begins, which sometimes can last for years.

The last step but one

The second ceremony also begins by depicting the struggle between God and Satan in the catechumen. The candidate says the Our Father, his sponsors (godfather or godmother) and the priest make the sign of the cross over him, and a sharp command bids evil depart. Then the catechumen is led into the church, where he remains for a moment in quiet thanksgiving.

Then he says out loud the Apostles' Creed and the Our Father. 114–116 He calls God his Father. He affirms publicly, before the com- 121 munity and before God, all that he has experienced in an inner process and in the instruction given him in private. This is a threshold that one could find hard to cross. But it is part of the sacrament. It is not an interior monologue in which Christ alone addresses the catechumen. It is a dialogue where man answers audibly in the framework of the ecclesiastical community.

Then again Christ speaks and acts through the Church. After another exorcism, the great gesture of Jesus' touching the ears of the deaf man with saliva is repeated. Jesus' miracles, after all, were symbols of the profound healing which he 111–112

243

confers in the sacrament. The priest says "Ephphatha", that is, "Be opened" (from Mk 7:34), and also touches the nostrils, as a sign that the candidate is to receive the sweet odour of Christ. (The actual touching can be omitted for reasons of hygiene where necessary.)

At the end of these solemnities, the privileged catechumen is anointed between the shoulders, with the oil of catechumens, 169 which signifies suppleness and strength for the combat. This too is an answer from Christ, given through the sign performed by his Church—the strength to be steadfast.

Baptism

But we are not yet at the baptism. This can be conferred at any time in the year, but one night is particularly appropriate for it, the night on which Jesus arose to eternal life.

Hence at the Easter vigil the baptismal water is hymned, and consecrated to its sacred purpose. Water is the element used in baptism. The prayerful chant of the Easter vigil goes right through the whole of Scripture to meditate the tremendous significance attached to this element, from the primeval waters over which God's creative Spirit passed, through the floods of the deluge and of the Red Sea, to the water which flowed from the side of Jesus.

The liturgy pauses to reflect on this element. And modern psychology has disclosed once more that it is one of the most fruitful symbols in the soul of each man. Modern science has discovered that all life on earth came out of this element. (In primeval times, all life, ours too, was in the sea.) Modern obstetrics has shown that the human embryo is born from the amniotic fluid, and that this fluid has the same composition as sea-water. Our life comes from water.

This, the most motherly of all elements, has been set aside by God to be the efficacious sign of our heavenly rebirth. "May the Holy Spirit descend upon this water, which has been prepared that man may be born again, and make it fruitful by mingling with it his mysterious power; so that a new heavenly race, conceived by sanctification, may be reborn as a new creation, and arise from the immaculate bosom of this divine source" (From the chant of consecration of baptismal water on Easter night).

The new birth

We enter the Church by a birth. And we should often put to ourselves the question of Nicodemus: "'How can a man be born when he is old? Can he enter a second time into his mother's womb and be born?' Jesus answered, 'Truly, truly, I say to you, unless one is born of water and the Spirit, he cannot enter the kingdom of God'" (Jn 3:4–5).

The baptized receive new life "of water and the Spirit". Hence baptism is much more than being inscribed on the rolls of a community. The Holy Spirit makes us be born, makes us new—in and through the community. Birth is never a purely individual matter, and certainly birth from God is not.

Just before baptism, the catechumen is once more asked about his faith. Then he is expressly asked whether he has come freely: "Do you wish to be baptized?" Immediately afterwards, the priest pours water on the catechumen while saying the words, "I baptize you in the name of the Father and of the Son and of the Holy Spirit" (cf. Mt. 28:19). The water signifies birth, the words specify what birth it is, namely, that the Holy Spirit enters into us, gives us life and makes us children of the Father.— Immediately after baptism there is an anointing with chrism, which signifies the good odour of the Spirit. 257

Through the Spirit who sanctifies, we are Christ—and Christ is in us. We are filled with sanctifying grace.

Thus this mystery can be expressed in three different ways: to receive the Holy Spirit, to receive sanctifying grace (be in the state of grace), to be in Christ. They all mean the same thing.

"In Christ." Just as those who love each other grow more and more like each other, take the same inward attitudes, have the same preferences and in fact live one and the same life, so too it is with us in Christ, only on a far deeper level. We live his life. This is made possible by the Spirit through whom he is present. And thus we begin to share in the new creation.

Cleansing

Sin has no place in the baptized who have been taken up into Christ. The flowing water signifies cleansing as well as birth. Baptism washes away the sins that a man has actually committed in his previous life. Even the roots of sin, original sin (on which 259–270 see later) are conquered through this contact with Jesus. (This

454–457 conquest cannot be separated from our whole life-struggle, as is explained in the following chapter.) Though a man's sins are as red as scarlet, Christ now makes him whiter than snow. He is friend of God. He makes a fresh start in all purity. Light has conquered. (Baptism is also called "illumination".)

After the anointing with chrism, the baptized are given a white garment and a burning candle, to symbolize purity and light. Two magnificent blessings accompany this rite, with which the ceremonies of baptism end.

Baptism is not to be repeated. It is once and for all, as is expressed by saying that baptism of water confers a character which can never be effaced. This of course does not happen where the will not to be baptized exists during the baptism. We 250–251 shall speak of child baptism later.

Buried in baptism

Like all the great symbols of mankind, water has a double significance, meaning both salvation and destruction. Water does not just signify life, it also signifies the deluge; along with drinking, washing and swimming it can mean drowning—the water that "comes up to the lips". Hence we cannot close this chapter without examining this aspect of baptism. As Paul writes, "Do you not know that all of us who have been baptized into Christ Jesus were baptized into his death? We were buried therefore with him by baptism into death . . ." (Rom. 6:3–4).

This symbolism is clearest when baptism is performed by immersion, as in the East. The "old man", man imprisoned by egoism, licentiousness, laxity, blindness, pride and obstinacy, is given over to death. He dies and vanishes, along with Christ's death. This means primarily, as we have seen, the forgiveness of sin. But it also means a transformation of life.

To see the full meaning of this, we must go back to the banks 176–179 of the Jordan and then to Calvary. Christ was baptized.

And he was baptized unto his death. He was consecrated at his baptism to submission, to sharing the common lot, to being 156–159 a servant and finally to obedience unto death. (Hence his temptations invite him to take up the opposite attitude—to refuse to serve.) He twice calls his future death "a baptism" (Mk 10:38; Lk. 12:50). This death is the climax of service. It is his real baptism.

This is also true of those who are baptized into Christ. We affirm our solidarity with his way—of service, humility and obedience, even unto death. We accept the baptism of life: service, suffering and finally death. Our death is our truest baptism. We accept it like Jesus, with Jesus and in Jesus. The fact that our Lord has redeemed us does not mean that he has set us beyond sin and sufferings. It means that we must join him in redeeming ourselves and others, in *his* way. And this way is described by Jesus in the words: "Are you able to drink the cup that I drink, or to be baptized with the baptism with which I am baptized?" (Mk 10:38). It is through his strength, after his example and wholly in his Spirit. But it is thus that we overcome our sins, by being humble and serviceable, peace-makers and poor of spirit. Death is the last act of our service, and it sets us wholly free—"the baptism with which Jesus was also baptized".

Is this a sombre thought on the happy day of baptism—that one is thereby dedicated to death? But is there anything more consoling? We are reminded that our mortal life is to be, 486–487 along with Jesus, not absurd but fruitful. God has turned the woes of mankind into the birthpangs of new life. When we 357 enter the water, it is a symbol of death; when we leave it, it is the symbol of resurrection and rebirth. That is why baptism is conferred on the happy night of Easter.

A people whose life is transformed

Baptism is not a purely individual contact with the Lord. The contact takes place because we are taken into the Church. Baptism builds new stones into the Church; it builds up the body of Christ. "For just as the body is one and has many members, and all the members of the body, though many, are one body, so it is with Christ. For by one Spirit we were all baptized into one body—Jews or Greeks, slaves or free—and all were made to drink of one Spirit" (1 Cor. 12:12–13).

Without distinction of nationality, income, intelligence or anything else, we are adopted into the fellowship which wishes to be a servant along with Jesus. Together we pass through the Red Sea, to be obedient to our call and to place our little lives and our death under the sign of service. We become little ones by joining in with God's little ones, just as Christ joined in and became a common man along with us. And likewise—together we break with the opposite attitude to life.

Does this mean that the sacrament of fellowship sets up a division in mankind? In one sense it does. "He that is not for me is against me", Jesus said. But we must pay great attention to where the line of demarcation runs. It runs between those who make Christ's baptism unto death come true in their own lives, by a life of service (which is always a sort of baptism, even if it 249-251 cannot be performed with water; see below), and those who make Satan's temptations of power, immorality and spiritual slackness their way of life (even though they have received the sacrament, which, however, they do not make come true). The division is between those who try to live according to the word of the Holy Spirit, "I am ready", and those who live according to the word of the tempter, "I will not serve".

There is therefore a dividing line. But let us look still more closely at where it runs. It runs straight through my self. Part of me says, I will not serve, and part of me, I am ready. The good spirit and the evil spirit have their front lines in me. There may be men who are almost entirely possessed by the spirit of evil, but we cannot and must not try to be judges of persons. Who knows what spark of goodness and helpfulness, and hence of contact with Jesus, is smouldering in many seemingly recalcitrant, selfish and corrupt lives? Jesus will not quench the spark.

Is one noticeably changed by baptism? Often there is an experience of a sudden growth, of a greater purity. But again, no change may be perceived at the moment. But that does not matter. One must not view baptism in isolation, apart from the whole life of which it is the start. And this life in turn must not be viewed in isolation, apart from the life of the whole Church. But then we discover that the centuries have been marked by a broad, deep stream of quiet goodness and unassuming service. 232 The new innocence which the Spirit has created, the new personality into which so many millions have been born, have really changed the face of the earth. We cannot imagine what the harshness of mankind might have been without the baptism brought by Jesus.

It is ancient Catholic doctrine that Christians baptized outside the community of the Catholic Church really receive baptism. Apart from our common humanity, this is the most profound and solid foundation of the ecumenical movement.

The non-baptized

We must now take up a point which has been mentioned above. We spoke of the goodness of the unbaptized, as manifested in their acceptance of life and readiness to serve. Can this readiness mean a redemptive contact with Jesus, without baptism of water?

The unbaptized make contact with Jesus in any case by the fact that they have been born. *They have Jesus as their fellow-man.* 80–82 The Church is convinced that if they are men of good will they share in the blessings of Jesus' redemption. Loyalty to their task in life, service to the end, baptizes them with the baptism with which Jesus was baptized. When an unbaptized person is put to death because of Jesus, explicitly, he is said to have received the baptism of blood. In other cases there is the baptism of desire, which can include unconscious desires. Every one who is prepared to be "obedient unto death" is touched by Christian baptism. This "baptism of the unbaptized", however, is not purely interior. It is the readiness to serve which is expressed in the whole of their lives and in their death. 289

This does not mean that the efficacious sign, the baptism of water, may be omitted. It *shows* that we need the forgiveness which it brings. It *proclaims* that the Lord is in contact with us. It *gathers* us, visibly and tangibly, as one people to which the Spirit is given and where forgiveness is at work.

These are not indifferent formalities. They mean that baptism is part of the great whole made up of the Christian preaching, choice of life and the intensity of Christ's forgiveness. Thus it *brings about* a reality; it places a leaven in this world. What would otherwise remain vague and full of error takes on shape and intensity where the Church of Christ is visibly at work in the world, through baptism. Hence those who believe in Christ and know of the existence of baptism may not treat it as of little account.

The baptism which makes new Christians also shows what 287–289 God wishes to do and is beginning to do with others. When your child is baptized, this is also for many others. Though they do not receive baptism, they live in a humanity—or a milieu— where baptism is conferred. In a certain sense, Christians are also baptized for them.

Infant baptism

Though we have taken the example of the baptism of adults, because the meaning is clearest there, infant baptism is far and away the most common. It has been in use since the earliest times.

239-241 We saw in the previous chapter that Christian parents take it for granted that they should bring their children up as Christians, and we also saw why this should be so. It is not surprising that Christian upbringing begins with the sacrament of initiation. The parents declare unmistakably that they wish their children to be received into the Church and to grow up there.

But the question is how can the child receive the sign of conversion and faith while it is still incapable of conversion and of the dedication of faith, for lack of mental equipment.

The answer is that it receives the sign in the way in which it lives—in dependence on adults. Christ made his salvation a community matter, a social thing. He did not give it to individuals in isolation from each other, but to a people. Just as the herd has its calves, each living people has its children, beings whose existence as men is totally sustained by the adults around them. Hence the baby is not baptized because it believes, but because we naturally wish to pass on our faith. We bring the children within the circle of our own faith, into the faith of the Church.

344 Here too we must remember that baptism must not be detached from the whole. Children are filled with grace and the Holy Spirit in their own way at baptism, incorporated into Christ and consecrated to their sort of redemptive service, to a redemptive death and an eternal life. All this is to be unfolded in the Christian education which follows, from which it may not be detached, either in our minds or in reality. One may well ask oneself whether children who have been baptized presumably because of the prevalent custom, but then grow up without conscious Christianity, should really be called Christians and members of the Church. The Church asks for a guarantee of Christian education.

240-241 Nor may baptism be viewed in isolation from the growing
408-409 independence of the child. We have spoken of this already. In the long run, there must be a "conversion", a giving of oneself. One sign of this is the solemn renewal of baptismal vows made by the child as it grows to maturity. This can take place, for

instance, along with adults at the Easter vigil, when all Christians present renew these promises together. But the real renewal can come later and be more part of everyday life. It may consist of an answer given publicly to a colleague or friend, of resistance offered in secret to a temptation, of a life of goodness, service and acceptance of death.

The child is christened at baptism. He is given the name of a saint, under whose particular protection he is placed. This is not because Christ's grace is insufficient, but because Christ wills to come to us through the fellowship of the Church, including the Church triumphant, whose intercession is invoked.

The Church as a whole is involved at each baptism, as well as the parents. The infant is "presented" by a godfather or god-mother. They hold (or touch) the child during the baptism, when it is not in its mother's arms or the father's. Godfather and godmother represent, after the parents, the wider fellowship of the Church, and share in the responsibility for the Christian upbringing. Godparents must be at least thirteen years old.

Unbaptized infants

What we said above about the relationship of baptism to 250 mankind, is also true of infant baptism. The baptism of a child is a sign of God's impatience. He is impatient to show that *every* new-born child is under God's call.

Every child is for God. But then what happens to children who die without baptism? We said above that the unbaptized 249 adult can be saved if he fulfils faithfully his task in life and so shares although unconsciously in Christ's service. But unbaptized children are incapable even of this "baptism of life". What happens to them?

There was great uncertainty in the Church for a long time as regards the fate of unbaptized infants, because theologians considered the necessity of the baptism of water too *exclusively* from the point of view of its individual importance. Augustine, in a letter to Jerome, shows how keenly he felt the problem: "When the question of the punishment of children is raised, it troubles me sorely, I assure you, and I am at a loss what to answer."

This was about A.D. 400. The great and humane Anselm was still uncertain about 1100. He cannot see how the infants can be saved, but he goes on to say: "I have spoken to the best of my capacity, making suggestions rather than affirmations, in the hope that at some time in the future God may teach me something better. But if anyone has a different opinion to put forward, I shall accept any view for which good reasons can be adduced."

In the course of the centuries, the Church has drawn on the ancient treasures of the faith to elaborate such reasons. It has become more and more clearly convinced that three truths must be borne in mind if the question is to be properly solved. The first is that God wills that all men should attain eternal blessedness. This certainly includes children, who are seen in the gospels as the special objects of God's love. The second truth is that Christ was born and died *for all*. And finally, we know that no one is lost except for sins which he has personally committed. In view of these truths, there must be a way by which unbaptized infants are saved. We do not know exactly how. But we know in any case that they are in Christ.

Baptism as part of a totality

Here too it is important not to isolate baptism and envisage it only as something individual and momentary which takes place between God and the soul. As soon as the baptism of water is taken out of the whole great context, strange problems arise, as the history of the Church has shown. Just as the hand is only really a hand in the totality of the body, so too baptism is only a genuine sign of Christ in the totality in which he gives it to us: the totality of our life and death, the totality of Christian upbringing, of the fellowship of the Church and of mankind.

SYMBOLS OF LIFE

Now that we have spoken of baptism, we may dwell for a while on the fact that such signs exist, outward signs in which Christ wills to meet us. The Church enumerates seven of them in all, and calls them sacraments. Let us see what can be said of them in general.

The shaping of the great moments of our life

From time immemorial, men have given the high-points of their existence a festal or significant form. When someone is born or reaches his majority or gets married or dies, the event is signalled by a celebration which contrasts with the greyness of everyday life. There is a spontaneous effort to create forms which will show what life really is. We think of what we are and celebrate our existence.

The sacraments too are ways of celebrating our existence, 352 given to us by the Lord in his Church. Key-points of our existence are given significant forms, to say that we are redeemed and given a new life. But there is more than a mere affirmation. The sacraments are just symbols, which are efficacious signs. They do not merely speak of redemption, they bring it to us.

This they can do because the Redeemer comes to us in them. The central sign of all was shaped very personally by our Lord 163–170 himself on the night before he suffered. He used our human 332–347 custom of eating together (a significant trait which constantly recurs) to manifest and to bring about his unity with us. He took bread and said, 'This is my body for you'.

But it is not only in the Eucharist, the great sacrament of his presence, that he acts upon us. When a child is born or a man 242–252 received into the Church, there is baptism in Christ. We have 256–259 confirmation for the moment of Christian maturity. When a 392–393 man and a woman pledge their troth, their consent is a sign of Christ's presence. The giving of the pastoral charge is a gesture of Christ, consecration. Nowhere has the Lord left us without a 363 sign of his life, not even where we fall and sin, since he is there for us in the sacrament of penance. And in those critical moments 456–463 of our lives when we are gravely ill, he is with us in the anointing 469–470 of the sick, extreme unction.

Some sight of God

When we consider the place taken by these signs in the work of salvation, we may sum up by saying that in Christ God became visible and tangible. That in the Church Christ, and hence God, 193 remained visible and tangible among us. And that the Church in 111–112 turn becomes visible and tangible in the seven signs. They are Christ's hands which now touch us and Christ's words which now ring in our ears. They are his way of being palpable today.

183-184 We have already seen that the Easter apparitions were prefigurations of this new way by which he was to become visible—
through the signs.

249, There is nothing inward in man without its corresponding
288-289 outward sign. There is nothing inward in Christianity without
its corresponding outward sign. Hence there is place for the
226 very human and reassuring reality of the sign in Christ's work
today. It is he who works in the signs. Beyond the ministers, the
Lord is active in the community of his believing Church, even
when he must act through a sinful man.

The sacrament does not work, so to speak, automatically,
independently of the inner attitude of man. The holiness of the
minister is not of decisive importance, but the faith and good will
of the recipient of the sign play an indispensable part. The
sacrament is an encounter with the Lord, and there cannot be an
encounter on one side only. The sacrament is an affirmation
that the Lord is faithful. But without us he can do nothing.

The simplicity of the signs

To signify these encounters with Christ at key-moments of our
244, 246 lives, very simple and fundamental elements of our existence
341, 347 were chosen. God, Christ and the Church become visible in
108-109 water, bread, wine and oil, in the touch of a hand, in the sound
148-149 of a yes, in a confession of guilt. They are as simple and accessible
as Jesus' appearance in Palestine.

Signs taken from our everyday existence become signs of the
risen Lord, of the new creation.

Their link with earth may be stressed by the conspicuous and
elaborate way in which the minister of the Church presents them.
But at the same time, it must be seen that their reality is orientated
to a new life. And this is shown in their refinement and reserve.
An ordinary thing is turned into a sign. Baptism is not a bodily
washing, the Eucharist is not the satisfaction of hunger. We are
washed in the new world, we eat in the new creation.

Part of each sacrament is the uttering of certain words, terse
and full of meaning. But it is these words which make it a real
sacrament. They determine the meaning of the gesture, give it
its orientation and make it perspicuous.

458 The shape of the sacraments is not rigidly fixed. It has developed in the course of the ages and is to some extent subject to change.

The sign is expanded by meaningful ceremonies, or it is stripped down just to the core. Changes can occur, because they are not magical formulae which only work when the combination is perfect down to the last detail.

The Church has preserved these signs faithfully, since they are gifts to be handed on, but also flexibly, since they are signs to be presented meaningfully.

Sign or reality?

It might be asked whether the sacrament is a symbol or a reality. Is the Eucharist, for instance, or baptism, "a sign" or is it "genuine"?

It is both. To begin with, it is a sign. The bread signifies Jesus' desire to nourish us, to be assimilated by us. The water signifies new birth. The sacraments are the signs which indicate symbolically Jesus' presence (that is, the Holy Spirit, grace).

But that is not all. What they indicate, they also give. They actually accomplish what they signify. The Eucharist *is* nourishment through Jesus' body. Baptism *is* re-birth. What is indicated symbolically is really given.

166–167
245

Sacramentals

Finally, a few words about sacramentals. From ancient times the Church has pronounced its blessings over men and over what men do or use—a new task, a new house, tools, food and so on. Blessings are prayers addressed to God, asking him to grant well-being, grace and blessing. Such prayers are not made by the individual as such, but by virtue of his right to represent the community. When, for instance, grace is said at family meals, it is said by the father or mother. Blessings which are given expressly in the name of the whole community (generally in a form to be used universally) are reserved to those who have been ordained priests.

When the blessing is used to set certain objects apart for God (a church, a church bell, a chalice, water, a rosary) it is often called a consecration. The prayer used on such occasions asks that the objects in question may be the bearers of blessing for those who make use of them, that they may be places of meeting with God. We are entitled to look for God's holiness through such things, because Jesus' sacraments show that the things of this earth can be linked with the kingdom of God.

We must, of course, remember that the sacramentals do not bring about the deep and certain contacts of the sacraments, and that they are not permanent as these are, since they come and go. They are the small change, as it were, of the sacraments, the fringes (often picturesque) of sacramental life, and very much conditioned by local culture.

We are very often more responsive nowadays to the signs of God which are not linked to consecrated places but are found everywhere. We see the ordinary water as a sign of him, the sun shining into the kitchen or the light falling on a basket of greens or the sea lapping against the beach. It follows from the existence of the sacraments that we may see in such things something of God's glory.

This discussion has been perhaps rather brief for such an important subject as the sacraments. This was to allow as much space as possible for each of the sacraments in particular, so that each sign may be displayed as the very special encounter with God which it is.

CONFIRMATION

The liturgy of confirmation

To impose hands on someone in the name of God means to transfer him into the sphere of God. This is the gesture with which the Apostles gave the Spirit of God to Christians. Peter and John "laid their hands on them and they received the Holy Spirit" (Acts 8:17). Christians still receive this sign as they grow to maturity. Confirmation, strengthening, is the sacrament which in some ways perfects baptism.

The bishop stretches out his hands over the candidates and says: "Almighty and eternal God, you have granted your servants to be born again from water and the Holy Spirit and have forgiven them all their sins. Send them your Holy Spirit from heaven, the Consoler, with his seven gifts. Amen. The Spirit of wisdom and understanding. Amen. The Spirit of counsel and fortitude. Amen. The Spirit of knowledge and piety. Amen. Fill them with the Spirit of your fear, and vouchsafe to seal them with the sign of Christ's † cross unto eternal life."

The candidates now come forward one by one and stand before the bishop, who lays his hand on their head and anoints

196–197

their forehead with chrism. The chrism is the symbol of the good odour of the Holy Spirit which penetrates all, and anoints them as full members of a "royal priesthood, a holy nation, God's own people" (1 Pet. 2:9). 348

The bishop then gives each candidate a light slap on the cheek, which is a medieval custom which may signify persecution and contempt to be borne for Christ. The words which now accompany the gesture are "Peace be with you".

The most appropriate time for the conferring of confirmation is during Mass, after the gospel. Then it ends with the *Credo* being sung together, and the Eucharistic liturgy. This is a sequence full of meaning, as baptism, confirmation and the Eucharist together have been the sacraments of Christian initiation from the most ancient times.

The connection with baptism

What does it mean, it might be asked, when we say that the Holy Spirit is given at confirmation? Have we not already received the Spirit at baptism?

But there is no contradiction. The gift bestowed in baptism is strengthened in confirmation, which is the "Pentecostal finale" of baptism. Originally confirmation was given soon after baptism, as is still the case in the East. Just as Jesus was anointed by the Spirit just after coming out of the Jordan, and just as he breathed the Spirit upon his disciples soon after rising from the dead (and just as, in fact, people were anointed with perfumes after bathing) so too, after the purifications on which the emphasis is laid at baptism, the joy and strength of the Holy Spirit are celebrated once more very specially at confirmation.

The close connection between the two sacraments may be seen from the fact that though confirmation has ceased to follow at once upon the administration of baptism in the West, the gift of the Holy Spirit is still alluded to at the end of baptism, by a ceremony of the same type. The newly-baptized child is anointed with chrism. This is not confirmation, but the resem- 245 blance is clear.

The gift of the Spirit

If we wished to explain fully the precise grace of confirmation, we should have to repeat here the whole chapter on Pentecost, which really has a place here also. 193–200

But we may add here a few words. Firstly, the sacrament should not be viewed as an isolated sort of magical action which 252 has power over the Spirit. It is like baptism, which should be viewed only in the context of the whole life of the Christian. The ceremony without corresponding education and preaching has very little point. As we said apropos of baptism—it might well be asked whether children who are baptized or confirmed just to conform to the prevalent custom but who then grow up without any specifically Christian conscience, can really be called Christians or members of the Church.

Another remark which we may add to the chapter on Pentecost is this. Confirmation should be viewed in connection with those gifts of the Holy Spirit which are related to Christian maturity: the power to forget one's own interests and to bear witness to Christ. "Whatever you wish that men should do to you, do so to them" (Mt. 7:12). "When they deliver you up, do not be anxious how you are to speak or what you are to say ... For it is not you who speak, but the Spirit of your Father speaking through you" (Mt. 10:19–20). — Confirmation gives every Christian the mission of bearing witness and serving the word. It makes them mature and responsible, each in his own state of life.

Some details

The fact that confirmation is only given by the bishop (except in danger of death, when the parish priest or the chaplain of the hospital may give it) has a special significance. The bishop is the divinely-appointed channel of the Spirit and the ordinary, proper minister of the sacraments.

He confers the sacrament of the Spirit, the completion of baptism. One result of this is that when the bishop comes, once every few years, confirmation is given to large groups at the same time, and is not linked with any particular season or time of life. Hence it is not an occasion which stands out very strongly. This is all the more reason why parents, teachers and priests should surround it with proper explanations and an imposing liturgical setting. Confirmation is mostly given to primary school children.

251 Local custom includes the adding of a new name at confirmation. It would be more sensible to devote special attention to the

baptismal name, the saint invoked at baptism. The custom of having godparents at confirmation has probably little meaning unless it means inviting those who had already stood for the child at baptism. This would be very sensible.

This sacrament is received only once. One may not remember much of one's confirmation, or one may know that one paid little attention to it at the moment of reception. But it remains certain that it is a gift which continues to develop. Once it has been received, it grows through life in the Spirit of God.

THE POWER OF SIN   449–454

Up to the present, we have been describing the coming of our salvation, from the beginning of history to our own participation through the sacraments of initiation, baptism and confirmation.—The Eucharist, the third and greatest sacrament of initiation, will be discussed later when we speak of the fullness of Christian life.—It is now time to look back over all that has been said, to recapitulate and to try to realize as clearly as possible what our salvation means. This will be the task of the next two chapters. In the first, the present chapter, we shall speak of sin, and in the second, of redemption.

Redemption co-extensive with sin

Sin is never seen in a pure state, so to speak, in the world. Humanity has never existed except as the race of men into which Jesus was to come or has come. Even in the most barbarous society of the past or of the present, man was always a fellow-man of Jesus, the Son of God.

A newly-born child, as yet unbaptized, has been ushered 249 into a world where redemption is at work. From the very beginning, he is a fellow-man of Christ and called to his friendship. And as regards adults—no matter how morally bankrupt a life may be, no matter how much evil a man permits himself, no one is proscribed, no one is excluded from the call of the good God.

Universal guilt

But this does not mean that one cannot suddenly experience in one's own life and in that of the world around a mysterious sense of guilt. We are oppressed by the inevitability of wars which break out like ulcers, though nearly everybody is against them; by the natural arrogance of capitalism and colonialism; by the poisoning of the atmosphere by racial and class hatred. Six million men perished in gas-chambers, on the highly civilized continent of Europe.

Our selfish incapacity to love one another, our failure to change our life and thinking is part and parcel of all this. We too do harm to men. We play our part in the great evil of the world. Our hands are not clean. "So the whole world may be held accountable to God" (Rom. 3:19).

It is sometimes suggested that it may all be explained as retarded development—not sin, but immaturity. Sometimes it seems that crimes are simply a matter of mental illness. But though there is some truth in these explanations, they are too smooth, too hygienic, to cover all that man experiences in his moments of truth: his tremendous, universal, inevitable and yet inexcusable incapacity to love.

"I realized that it was simply impossible for a human being to be and remain 'good' or 'pure'.

If, for instance, I wanted to be attentive in one direction, it could only be at the cost of neglecting another. If I gave my heart to one thing I left another in the cold ... I came up against my human shortcomings again and again, my failure precisely in the qualities which would enable me to realize my ideal of a perfectly pure and perfectly responsible moral life. I could see an immense distance between moral insight and actual practice. No day and no hour goes by without my being guilty of some inadequacy. We never do enough, and what we do is never well enough done ... except being inadequate, which we are good at, because that is the way we are made. This is true of me and of everyone else. Every day and every hour brings with it its weight of moral guilt, as regards my work and all my relations with my fellow-men. If I could only tell myself, well, you are no saint (supposing that holiness is above all human defects)—so you might as well be content with yourself the way you are. But it would not help, because I am not content. I am constantly catching myself out in my human failings, and in spite of their being implied in my human imperfection, I am conscious of a sort of check. And this means that my human shortcomings are also my human guilt. It sounds strange that we should be guilty where we can do nothing about it. But even where there is no set purpose, no deliberate intention, we have a conviction of our own shortcomings, and of consequent guilt, a guilt which sometimes shows itself all too clearly in the consequences of what we have done or left undone" (Anna Blaman).

"*If* there be a God, since there is a God, the human race is implicated in some terrible aboriginal calamity. It is out of joint with the purposes of its Creator. This is a fact, a fact as true as the fact of its existence; and thus the doctrine of what is theologically called original sin becomes to me almost as certain as that the world exists, and as the existence of God."

(John Henry Newman)

The message of Genesis 1–11

Sacred Scripture speaks of "original sin". It appears most clearly in chapters 1–11 of Genesis and above all in chapter 5 of the Epistle to the Romans. The first eleven chapters of Genesis tell of the origins of mankind—Adam, Cain, Noah and Babel. We know that they are not descriptions of disconnected historical facts. They go deeper. The narratives are symbols in which the kernel of all human history is described, including that which is still to come. Adam is Man. Cain is to be found in the newspapers and may be seen within our own heart. Noah and the builders of Babel—they are ourselves. Chapters 1–11 of Genesis describe the basic elements of all human encounter with God. It is only with chapter 12, where Abraham appears, that we begin to make out historical figures in the past. What is the message of the first eleven chapters? There are four points:

1. God creates and gives growth, as we learn from the poem of creation (Gen. 1) and the genealogies (which are not to be taken literally).

2. Man is clearly meant for friendship with God, as appears from the story of paradise (Gen. 2).

3. Human sin is the third element. From its own bitter experience, the faith of Israel had come to recognize the con-

425–426
40
51–52
389, 35

stancy of this element in human history. Hence the primeval history recounts a Fall four times over: the eating of the forbidden fruit, the murder of a brother, the corruption of Noah's contemporaries and the building of the tower of Babel.

4. But God does not leave man to his fate. He shows himself a God of undreamt-of mercy in Israel. This is also shown in the stories of the origins. Every fall is succeeded by a gesture of grace. When Adam and Eve are banished from paradise, God gives them clothing and promises them that the offspring of the woman will crush the head of the serpent. Cain is given a sign which will prevent his being killed. In the story of Noah, the process of deliverance takes up nearly all the narrative. And after Babel comes at once the story of Abraham, which is the beginning of the great restoration which the Son of God was to bring.

The primeval histories are a message of permanent relevance about the basic elements of our life with God: 1. creation. 2. election, 3. sin, 4. restoration.

The message of Romans ch. 5

In the New Testament there is a better comprehension of the fact that God's message contains these elements. Paul in particular, in the fifth chapter of the Epistle to the Romans, brings it out in its profundity. At first sight it seems that his intention is to stress the fact that it was through one man that sin came into the world. But the repetition of the word "one", occasioned by the view of the world history as it existed in Paul's time, is only part of the literary dress, not the message. What this difficult passage teaches is that though sin and death ruled over mankind, grace and eternal life, the restoration, has come in greater abundance through Jesus.

The Fall a message about man, not about the beginning

Of all these texts, the biblical story of the Fall is the one which is most deeply impressed on our minds. But we must remember that, as we have said, the following chapters contain the same message. It is no doubt particularly striking in the story of Adam and Eve. The whole glory and misery of human life are here summed up in a few short and graphic words. This most moving text of Scripture can never be replaced as a summary

of how man stands before God. But it can and must be replaced 9–12
as a description of the beginning of mankind.

We shall now dwell for a moment on the question of what
we are to think of the beginnings of sin.

In earlier times, indeed, until recently, our picture of the
world was primarily static, or stable. Things persisted the way
they first existed. If one wanted to say something about the
basic elements of existence, one showed how things were at
the beginning. The explanation lay there.

The explanation of the very existence of things was that
God had created them. He was spoken of like a carpenter who
had made something and left it there.

The existence of sin was explained primarily by the fact
that man had sinned.

But now our picture of the world has changed. We can see 488–489
further into the distant past. It helps us to see that the world
is involved in an upward movement, in a process of growth,
one way or another. Our view of the world is no longer static
but dynamic. This means that the authentic enlightenment is
to be sought not in the beginning but in the course of things
and their culmination. It is better to say, God creates, than to
say, God created. To put it in very human terms: if he were to
withdraw his creative hand from us for an instant, there would
be nothing there. God is not a carpenter who can go away. The
whole universe exists in God and depends on God. Creation
grows in his hands. The whole course of history is his work,
and it is only the whole that will explain it all and show that
"everything was very good" (Gen. 1:31).

Hence the beginning is less important to us than it was in
earlier days. This is also true of sin. The meaning of the first sin
needs to be pondered deeply. It is not of supreme importance
that man sinned and was corrupted. He sins and becomes
corrupt. The sin of Adam and Eve is closer than we imagine. It
is in our own selves.

The entry of sin

Nonetheless, with regard to sin in particular, we cannot but
continue to ask how it began. We expect some sure answer from
the beginnings, which will explain how this incredible mistake
crept into God's work. No matter how slow and gradual we

imagine the beginnings to have been, sin must have had a beginning at one time or another. The answer will be, as it was when a different picture of the world obtained, that sin has to do with human freedom. Freedom grew in man and hence sin.

But does not this seem to suggest that sin was inevitable?— All that we can say is that sin is committed with a certain freedom—otherwise it would not be sin—and freedom means that one could have done otherwise. But this does not necessarily mean that all sins in general could have been avoided. That any particular sin is committed is not inevitable, but that evil takes place is perhaps inevitable in practice. We do not know. 449-451 Our mind is always impotent when it comes to understanding the beginning of evil—even in our own lives. When we have really sinned, we know deep within us that we have done so. We know we are guilty, and yet we ask ourselves in astonishment—how could I have done such a thing? And indeed evil is not comprehensible. It is the great absurdity, the great irrelevancy. And hence its origin in world history remains incomprehensible.

But evil exists, and against God's will. Nonetheless, he has power, as we believe, to bring greater good out of evil (see the last chapter of the book).

Not inculpable imperfection

Before we go more deeply into the nature of evil, we must be clear on this point: it is of our sin and our guilt that we shall speak. This is different from the fact that man happens to be an imperfect being in a developing world, lacking in understanding and beset by wild passions. Primitive man on the 25 steppes and in the forests and in the caves had still to grow into 10 a humane being. He had to leave the beast behind him. He was still very far from perfect. But this of itself is not sin. Sin mingles, no doubt, inextricably with the passions and instincts through which it works, but sin is precisely that element of the instinct which is not animal, since it is real guilt.

In a world of ascending evolution, sin is often nothing but the refusal to grow in the direction which conscience reveals.

The common evil

Let us return to holy Scripture and see what it says elsewhere about human guilt.

In a certain sense, Scripture is a history of sin. The stories of Gen. 1–11 are followed by the history of the chosen people. Again and again it is seen to be obstinate, apostate, "adulterous"—a faithless spouse (Hos. 1–3). Here it should be noted that the people *as a whole* is described as sinful. Later parts of the Old Testament stress, no doubt, the responsibility of the individual. But there is still the feeling that sin is a matter of collective responsibility.

Jesus too points to a certain common responsibility in sin when he says, for instance, to the Pharisees that they commit their crimes (so) "that upon you may come all the righteous blood shed on earth" (Mt. 23:35). And when we read in John, "Behold, the Lamb of God, who takes away the sin of the world" (Jn 1:29), we see that the evil committed by man is taken to be one great sinfulness. It is the sin, not the sins, that is taken away.

We shall now try to grasp this collective character of evil by noting the various degrees of contagiousness which attach to our sins.

First there are the painful consequences. One man can injure another. This is a terrifying thought, but still more terrifying is the fact that one man can infect another with evil, with sin itself. There is the bad example by which the good is withheld, and in which evil is shown to be feasible. Where evil example is accompanied by deliberate perversion, we have the worst form of scandal, which led Jesus to make one of his most impassioned utterances: "But whoever causes one of these little ones who believe in me to sin, it would be better for him to have a great millstone fastened round his neck and to be drowned in the depth of the sea. Woe to the world for temptations to sin!" (Mt. 18:6–7).

The contagion of sin may also be seen in the undermining of men's sense of values. In a covetous family, children find it natural to be grasping, in a selfish society, individuals are easily selfish, colonialism produces exploiters and racism produces racists.

This envisages certain groups. But if we look further afield, we see that the whole world forms one single breeding-ground.

And it is the teaching of Scripture that sin reigns in the world. The whole of humanity is in a condition in which its values are obscured. And worst obscured of all is the supreme value, that of love.

Reluctance in face of Christ

This condition is man's own. It does not come to man from outside himself. It is really within him, because to belong to mankind is intrinsic and essential to each man. And each man has deep down within him, prior to his personal acts and colouring all of them, an unwillingness to respond to God, a refusal in face of real love. This does not mean that we will to do evil all the time. But we cannot fail to recognize, as we look towards Jesus' cross, that our life is not a life of love. Where God shows his love and his heart, we feel that we fall short, and indeed are unwilling and rebellious. We resist.

There is something Satanic about this (cf. Mk 8:33). We are not attentive to what God wills, but to what men desire. We do not wish to have the greatest possible love for him and for each other. We refuse God's intimacy, we want nothing of God's paradise, and of ourselves we are powerless to be otherwise.

This impotence is not inculpable. The possibilities of freedom are impaired. But a certain freedom remains ours, and we use it to set ourselves against the divine life, the joy and love, to which we are called. This solidarity in guilt is something which is never fully perspicuous to man. Evil is always obscure. Even in former times, theologians did not claim to have understood it fully. They looked to "human nature" which was propagated by bodily generation since sinful Adam. But this explanation of the collectivity or "oneness" of sin is not something which has been directly revealed. It is not part of the direct intention of revelation (what is *per se* revealed). The unity of the human race, according to Scripture, is not based on propagation ("Greek, barbarian or Jew") but on the call by the one Father. The oneness of sin is to be sought on the same level, though here in man's refusal. It reaches us, not merely by way of generation, but from all sides, along all the ways in which men have contact with one another. The sin which stains others was not only committed by an Adam at the beginning of man's story, but by "Adam", man, every man. It is "the sin of the world". It includes my sins. I am not an innocent lamb which is corrupted by others. I help in the work of corruption.

At the time of Augustine, *c.* 400, this general sinfulness which we know both from Scripture and experience was given the name of *peccatum originale*, original sin. The Greek Fathers of the Church used the word "death", the death of the soul. The stress laid on the fact that this inheritance of original sin came by way of generation from one's parents led to much discussion of original sin in infants. But when we take a more complete view of the contamination, and see it as coming from all mankind, the stress is rather laid on adult man. Original sin is the sin of mankind as a whole (including myself) in so far as it affects every man. In every personal sin, the original sin of man is basically present and active and contributory.

We must always remember that this "original sin" is not a sin in the ordinary sense of the word. It may be said that it only takes on concrete form in our personal sins. Hence no one is condemned for original sin "alone", but only for the personal decisions by which he ratified original sin, so to speak, and stood over it. (So too baptism is also initiation into a life-long struggle against personal sin.)

247
248

The sin of the world came to a climax in the crucifixion of Christ. This is the Fall in the most radical sense: the killing of the uniquely Good, the expulsion of God. Every man takes part in it. Those who carried out the sentence and handled the hammers knew perhaps less of what they were doing than many of us. All mankind has a hand in it.

The greater power of grace

This, the greatest of all sins, was redemption on the part of God. The most brutal No was answered by God with the most incomprehensible Yes. It made good stronger than evil in the world.

The flood of sin was surpassed by the greater flood of grace. Since such a Redeemer is our fellow-man, we can be sure that throughout humanity, from the earliest times, the good has been stronger and more pervasive than evil.

This we may also deduce from Scripture. It is no doubt a story of the contagion of sin, but it is still more the story of the attractive power of grace. We are inclined to think that the good we do is our own totally individual responsibility. But we must pay attention to the truth that our own goodness is also to a great extent a collective possession, in a solidarity which we hope is stronger than that of sin.

This is why the authors of this book—if they may be allowed

289
290–291
240–241

to mention themselves for once—were encouraged to write it. Though they knew that some of their heritage of sin and aversion from God might be reflected in the text, they were still more confident that the forces of truth and grace which flow to them through mankind and the Church, would work superabundantly in the pages before you.

Because the power of grace is the greater, the Christian revelation is rightly called gospel or glad tidings.

This happy conviction of the superiority of grace is brought out very forcibly in a truth which only became clear to the Church in a long, slow process. Thomas Aquinas and Bernard still could not see how it could be properly asserted. But the Church arrived gradually at this truth by meditating on the whole of revelation and solemnly defined it in the last century. It is the truth that Mary was free from the guilt of original sin. She was conceived immaculate. Living in a sinful world, she shared the pain of the world, but not its wickedness. She is our sister in suffering, but not in evil. She overcame evil completely by good. This was of course entirely due to Christ's redemption.

76–77   It is not surprising that the life of perfect obedience, which was lived by Christ, should also be lived in the greatest perfection by a woman. "Male and female he created them" (Gen. 1:27). The true Eve is created along with the true Adam. Mary is part of the mystery of Christ.

What is of faith here?

What then, in brief, is the divine message which this chapter passes on? It is the biblical message that mankind 1, was created by God; 2, that it was called to participate in a special way in his life; 3, that collectively and culpably it fails to respond to God's purpose; 4, that God wills to free and heal us. His salvation is to make us whole, to restore us.

This message has been propounded in the light of our present view of the world, as a world in a state of growth and evolution. The biblical authors gave the message in terms of the world as they knew it and the present exposition follows the present-day picture of the world. This is legitimate, because in both cases the same four elements are present, the same divine mystery which has been revealed to us, the same biblical message.

Was the world changed by original sin?

A question which may still remain in the minds of some is one on which some stress was laid formerly in religious instruction: the perfection of the world in the "original state of nature" before sin.

Thomas Aquinas said long ago that to believe that wild beasts were then tame was a sign of "a feeble mind"—though this opinion could still be heard in our schooldays. There is no reason which compels us to believe that creation was different before man sinned. There may always have been thorns and thistles.

And as regards man himself, we need not imagine that he once existed in a state of paradisiac perfection and immortality. We have seen what the story of paradise and the fall intended to convey: the purpose of God, as realized in the whole, and above all in the end. We really know nothing of the actual beginnings. The imagery of the curse under which man was banished from paradise (Gen. 3:16–19)—thorns and thistles, birth-pangs, the sweat of the brow and the tragic conflicts of marriage—simply affirms that these things are not part of God's most profound and ultimate intention. It also says that sin is connected with such things.

Sin makes the world less good. Where sloth reigns, the 492 fields grow thistles and the dykes collapse. Where there is hatred, a city is brought down in ruins. But gravest of all: a humanity in sin finds the world a heavy weight to bear. Everything looks darker to those who are inwardly ill at ease. The thistles and thorns are within man himself.

Sin and death, forgiveness and life   279–283

There is a very special and mysterious connection in our minds between sin and death. Holy Scripture sometimes expresses this by saying that through sin death came into the world. But since the beginnings are obscure to us, the beginning of biological 9–10 death is also obscure. What we do see, when we look at the 263–264 course of the history of salvation, is that along with sin death lost its sting. The resurrection of Jesus proclaims not merely forgiveness but eternal life. The consummation of human history will bring with it, as well as the complete conquest of sin, the complete conquest of death. Every member of the human race who allows himself to be saved from sin, will hear what the criminal heard from the lips of Jesus: "Today you will be with me in Paradise."

THE REDEMPTION

Our misery was described in the previous chapter. Our salvation is proclaimed in the present chapter, though it has really been described already. The Old Testament, Jesus of Nazareth, the life of the Church—they all constitute the immense process of salvation in which we believe. But in this chapter, we shall try to indicate the intrinsic nature of redemption. We start with a very roundabout approach, by examining first the major efforts of mankind to attain redemption, outside the Christian religion.

Man in fear and misery

To a certain degree, every man experiences life as a misery. If he is happy, he is afraid that his happiness will not last. If he is in distress—then he is certainly none the happier. "Is it serious, doctor?" or, "It is driving me mad". "No one ever cared for me" ... "Did I ever love anybody?" ... "I am all tensed up inside" ... "I do everything wrong" ... "I am no good" ... "Why had the only person that I loved to die?" ... "Think of it, you have to die" ... "Just imagine, the car ran up on the foot-path".

We all have our own way of trying to deliver ourselves from distress, discontent and insecurity. We try taking thought for the morrow; or hard work; or music; or looking for the real meaning of all that happens; or just not thinking, but simply living. We try the sunny, optimistic view, or perhaps a deliberately pessimistic one, to lessen the shock of the inevitable disappointments. We try to hold on to happiness by being selfish and reserved; or by being simply kind and open. There are countless personal attitudes which are all an effort to find deliverance in the midst of our human deficiencies.

Some major redemptive religions or attitudes have appeared among mankind, and have provided some sort of satisfaction and security for millions of their followers. The most important are Hinduism, Buddhism, Islam, western humanism and Marxism, and then Judaism and the Church of Jesus Christ.

We shall discuss each briefly, asking ourselves each time whether they really redeem the whole man or whether part of our being is left with its desires unsatisfied, hence unredeemed and abandoned to destiny.

We put this question as Christians and believers. But while answering it we shall try not to call expressly on the Christian faith as a criterion. We shall try to answer simply on the basis of our human nature—though as it has been enlightened by Christian values. As Christians, we have no other approach.

Hinduism and Buddhism

27–30
283–285

We have already given a brief outline of Hinduism and Buddhism in Part II, where we hope that something of their riches and depth appeared. Both of these religions are ways of redemption. They start from the basic experience of life as pain—the misery of the masses on the tropical sub-continent of India. But misery is not accepted as an inevitable doom. Liberation is sought through contemplation, asceticism or the eight-fold way. What is striking about Hinduism is the courage with which this is done. Buddhism further reveals an intensely personal note.

But in another way, Hinduism and Buddhism teach men to bow to fate. Though men are taught to hold themselves spiritually erect, unshaken by desires and conflict, misery itself remains as an inevitable doom. The sadness of the human lot may not be felt so keenly within the purified heart, but it remains just as great in the world. The world is regarded as mere appearances. And there is less incentive to work at its improvement. And the eternity which may or may not be hoped for is not the encounter of love, the expansion of the personality, but the impersonal dissolution of the self into the All.

501
284

In a word, the Hindu or the Buddhist, along with others (whom they spare their attentions), accepts the misery of this world as a necessity, resigns himself to the non-development of his personality, and seeks repose in the notion that he will not abide for ever in face of a conscious, personal love.

Islam

31
191
285

The attitude of Islam is very different. The earthly lot is no mere appearance. It comes from the hand of One who is merciful and bountiful, Allah, the one God. He is living and conscious, all-powerful and good. He is perfectly one (unitary, not triune).

501

271

Everything depends on God. This is also Christan doctrine.

449 But in Islam it means, in contrast to the Christian view, that no natural object has an activity or causality of its own. According to traditional islamic theology the laws of nature on earth, the laws of good and bad in the conscience, have no intrinsic structure or activity implanted in them by Allah. He moves and guides everything directly, and completely arbitrarily. If his will changes tomorrow then everything will behave differently tomorrow. There is nothing to hinder him except his own will. Thus the moral law is not found initially and fundamentally in the heart of man. It comes straight and exclusively from the will of God. And there can be no question of a deep sense of sin or of grace in Islam. Certain well-defined obligations are to be carried out, that is all.

As regards man's earthly lot, faith in the Merciful and Bountiful promises primarily joy. The good Muslim is lord of all things. Life is not merely illusion or pain, as it is for the Buddhist.

Thus Islam can create an atmosphere of joy. It inspires its followers to try to bring the world to the worship of Allah. High forms of culture flourished under Islam.

This joy is still further intensified by the promise of a happy eternity to believers, which will be an ideal continuation of earthly existence.

But Islam cannot escape from fatalism. Islam, whose name signifies surrender (to God), takes this surrender to a point which we must call fatalism. The idea that Allah has endowed men and things with no initiative of their own often leads to lack of effort to improve one's lot. Allah not merely guides the destiny of rich and poor, he has also determined the place and state of each. The Muslim must accept unresistingly his own and his neighbour's earthly lot.

This is to some extent due to the fact that the Koran, unlike the Bible, gives concrete directives about life in society and this is regarded as the will of Allah. There is little room for progress. Hence, just as under the religions of India, the human lot of man on earth was left mostly unchanged, in suffering and destitution.

The question may well be asked as regards Islam: cannot the theological basis for progress be found in the Koran? It is indeed being sought for in various Islamic countries. But it may be said that up to the present an element of fatalism is included in Islam's notion of God and the universe.

The religions of redemption which we have just described have few followers in our country. They are of Indian and Arabian origin. Is our part of the world too firmly committed to earthly realities to allow for such other-worldly faiths? Or are there other reasons why they have not spread much in the West? In any case, in our part of the world, apart from Christianity, a quite different attitude has developed to pain and misery, under the name of "humanism". The existence of God is neither denied nor affirmed. But it is said to be too uncertain to be used as a basic principle for one's life. Humanity must rely on itself to attain happiness and goodness. Misery and suffering must be attacked with all the means at man's disposal, science, technology and intelligence. We must not bow to fate like the Muslim. We must not hamper the development of our work and love like the Hindu or the Buddhist. We must take our hands out of our pockets and set to work. This sober and courageous attitude seems to leave little place for fatalistic submission to destiny.

Nonetheless, the problem of life remains just as great, indeed greater, for the consistent humanistic sage as for the eastern saint. It remains unresolved, because though the demand to live more fully, and to be more fully, wells up from the depths of our being, humanism asserts that man is only man. The question of eternity, of a perfect love, of the All, is said to be baseless. While Hinduism and Islam at least offered some sort of way out, humanism disowns such evasions.

But man still demands to know why he has come into existence   3–19
and what is the purpose of life. He feels the question all the more urgently the more clearly he recognizes life as something great and good. A humanist once came home after a long night's argument, during which he had succeeded in preventing a neighbour from committing suicide. Bone-weary, in the early dawn, but filled with a great sense of joy, he said: "I felt I needed someone that I could thank. Is that what you call God?"

The humanist has the problem of good. Where does all the good come from, and what is the purpose of it? Is it there just to disappear in death? Is the whole universe a pointless joke? How can we free ourselves from an existence which asks more than it gives?

Humanism does man the honour of allowing him to be man,

but it also leaves man with no other fate than to be man. Man is there the measure of redemption. It offers no other prospect than the gradual upward evolution of man, but of a humanity which perishes each time in each person who dies.

32
285

Marxism

One very distinctive form of western humanism is Marxism. It claims explicitly to be a doctrine of deliverance or redemption. This is not unconnected with the fact that Marx' parents were of Jewish origin, members therefore of the people which still awaited the coming of a Saviour. Like the Buddha, Marx was moved by the sight of human misery. The inhuman treatment of the new proletariat which the industrial revolution had created in the first half of the nineteenth century was the main object of Marx' concern.

Unlike the Buddha, Marx did not seek deliverance in individual detachment, impassibility or dissolution; nor in the effort to "go on being just a man", like the humanist. He saw deliverance in a very definite material process, in a return to the original relationship of man to the work of his hands. In early times, in the state of nature, man remained in possession of his product. He had put "himself" into his work, and so lost himself in it. But he retained the use and enjoyment of it, and so he held on to himself. As far as that was concerned, he was not alienated from himself. But with the growth of civilization, and the resulting mechanization and division of labour, a new condition arose. Some men own immense means of production on which others labour. The capitalist grow richer and richer. He owns things which he did not make. His own personal self is absorbed in these things, which are extensions of his person. His own person then becomes a sort of an alien thing. He becomes a stranger to his human self. He is "alienated".

The exploited worker becomes just as alienated, and in a still more painful way. He puts himself into the work of his hands. If he could hold on to his produce, he could remain himself. But he must surrender it—receiving less for it than it is worth. So the worker is also alienated.

The necessity of escaping this condition is felt primarily by the worker. Hence salvation and the future is with the worker. Their condition will become intolerable, because—in Marx' view—the gap between rich and poor with continue to widen —

till the explosion comes, the proletariat takes over, the means of production are socialized and the dictatorship of the proletariat installed. A society will then be formed which will be a city of salvation, in which the state of nature will be restored. Men will once more enjoy the work of their own hands. The proper relationship to nature will be restored. Each man will do the work which he wants to do: "In the communistic society, where the individual has no exclusive circle of occupation, but can develop in whatever task he chooses, production in general is regulated by society. And this makes it possible for me to do one thing today and another tomorrow. In the morning I can fish, in the afternoon hunt, in the evening breed cattle and also criticize the food, without being a hunter, fisherman, livestock farmer or critic, but just as I wish to be" (Karl Marx, *Die deutsche Ideologie*, 1845; E. T. *German Ideology*, 4th impression, 1956).

How this is to come about, Marx does not explain clearly. But a new day of joy is to dawn. Man will no longer put questions about life, death and God. He will not be alienated by allowing himself to be absorbed by such futilities. His life will be unimaginably harmonious and happy. He will be a new man, no longer alienated from the world, no longer alienated from his fellow-men.

The re-birth is to take place in a crisis, in pain. The proletarian masses must be utterly miserable if they are to dare to revolt. Hence extreme Marxism is against laws which improve the condition of the worker, since they only hold back the necessary development. The main thing is to promote the inevitable course of history by making the proletariat realize its condition, to preach the revolution and to encourage class hatred.

Man can lend himself willingly to the task, but in any case the process is inevitable. The evolution of mankind follows laws whose necessity is absolute. Hence it is not a matter of sin or of human goodness. It is a matter of having recognized the process of history. The capitalist is not a bad man, but he is something 298 that must disappear. The proletarian is not a good or holy man, he is where salvation lies.

We put once more the question which engages our attention in this chapter. Can this proclamation of salvation overcome man's fate?

The "historical materialism" of Marxism which we have

just outlined offers, 1, a future emancipation, 2, a fascinating theory, 3, a possibility of action now. Man can come to grips at once with fate.

But can it be said that it is conquered? Let us start with the last assertion. Man is a link—neither good nor bad, strictly speaking—in a historical process. It is a determinism which reduces each man to a pawn in history. The irreplaceable "I" is lost in the totality. The "I" in Marxism is really only the millionth part, say, of a million men.

In practice this means that the pawn can *be* sacrificed for the whole—which is quite different from the Christian notion of self-sacrifice for the whole. And this arouses misgivings. A human society which sets so little value on the individual that it can sacrifice him must ultimately destroy itself, because no one is safe. The course of history may make it necessary that anybody be liquidated. The course of history is the fate which no one escapes in Marxism. Here too it remains true that man is no more than man. Who is to set him free? The city of salvation? The welfare state?

In any case, if it does arrive can it release man from his fate? The brighter the city, the sadder death will be. And after death, nothing is offered but darkness. Nonetheless, the question will always be there: why all the splendour—from whom does it come, whither does it go? Will man one day be so different that the question will no longer be asked?

The great Netherlands socialist Troelstra wrote in 1915: "Historical materialism may be of great value in helping to build up a new view of the world, but it cannot claim to be a complete philosophy of life. Its basis is too restricted and its methods too one-sided. It throws light on changing methods of production in so far as they affect society, state, class and party, but the cosmic processes in general and the deeper instincts and longings of the human person lie outside its sociological perspectives. Hence it leaves unsatisfied the most intimate desires of the soul and views the human person from one aspect only, that is, as a function of social forces. This easily leads to a sort of fatalism which declares itself satisfied when it has given a *sociological* explanation of certain facts. It can lead to the 'acknowledgment' of the 'necessity' of certain facts which offend the human conscience ... In the long run, it cannot satisfy the *religious* disposition of man."

Marxism has, no doubt, a sort of religious inspiration. It has taken over various themes from the Jewish-Christian revelation. There is a "sacred" future which is a return to the original purpose of things. There is a message in which one "believes", a party which is a sort of "holy people", a "now" which is viewed as the "fullness of time", and a "suffering saviour", the proletariat. But all these themes are given a sociological content. They do not point to an answer to the ultimate questions.

The free man before God

Let us now try to observe how God's revelation of himself has affected human destiny. We believe that he has shown himself in Jesus. What processes have been set on foot by this event? Have we been enabled to break through the iron laws of destiny?

In the light of God's revelation of himself, we are disclosed as we really are. Jesus' holiness and his love of the Father show us how inexorably we are dominated by our egoism and cowardice. Our fate is rooted in our selves. And the first gift of God's revelation is a clear diagnosis. No fatal necessity is forced upon us from outside—no decree of Allah outside ourselves, no iron law of Karma, no law of human nature or historical dialectic. Our destiny is outlined by something that is part of our common but free responsibility—sin. There is no necessity imposed on 449–450 man from above or from below. He stands in the space of freedom along with his own deeds, which can make him happy or unhappy now and for eternity. This is man seen fully as he is. In this sense, sin is a concept unique to the Jewish-Christian 39 religious world, with only vague affinities outside Scripture.

Our powerlessness to save ourselves

349
235–236

As well as telling man that he is responsible for his destiny, 266 the Christian faith also teaches that man is of himself totally incapable of effecting his own deliverance. Contact with our foundation, God, has been broken off by sin, and we cannot re-establish it without him. This is the second great feature of redemption: man alone is not the measure of his salvation, as humanism and Marxism affirm. These latter doctrines cannot free us from being simply men, or men in a state of evolution. But Jesus raises us up from our impotence by the gift of his Spirit, which contains a new birth: the conquest of sin, life with God and salvation out of death.

Our struggle against sin and misery

God's intervention does not condemn us to renounce our responsibility or our development. On the contrary, it sets us free to intervene with all the love, kindness and efficaciousness we dispose of, in order to overcome sin, evil and misery. God permits us no fatalism. Neither sin nor misery may be accepted with resignation as the necessary human lot, or as something to be respected as God's will. It is God's will that we overcome them. This is the charge which he lays upon mankind as it marches onwards in history.

233-234   The Christian is no less called to be interested in earthly development than the humanist or Marxist. Indeed, the love taught by Jesus, and the conviction that goodness comes from God, makes the Christian more at home on earth than any one 426-430 else. He struggles against life's miseries with all the forces he 434-437 commands.

It may be true that in fact Christianity has sometimes encouraged a sort of fatalism as regards man's earthly lot. The prospect of heaven has made many feel that their primary duty on earth was the conquest of individual sin rather than human misery as a whole. In particular (though they were not the only ones) some Protestant groups have been extremely fatalistic in their behaviour—refusing vaccination, refusing to fight flooding. Christians were often not alert enough to the seriousness of man's call to progress on earth. At the present day, now that a broader historical vision has brought evolution within our perspective, we understand better how strongly the doctrine of sin, love and responsibility impels us to "subdue the earth", that is, make it a more human and tolerable place. (We shall speak 286 later of the possible influence of other views as Christians became clearly conscious of their task.)

This was something which had always been implicit in the 388 Christian faith. They believed that the world was man's to rule, and that it did not belong to gods or spirits or a divine lordship which ruled out the will of man. Thus forces which might have been blocked were released. And we are convinced that it is not accidental that it was in the Christian part of the world that 225 the very definite control of the forces of nature was gained, which we call natural science and technology. Sometimes believers have been opposed to scientific progress, but it owes more to the Christian vision than believers or unbelievers often realize.

"*The lifter of my head*" (Ps. 3:4)

There are tragic moments of life, however, when the word progress can do no more than call out a bitter laugh. It is better not to mention progress to a father whose little girl has just been killed in a motorcar accident. And we know that absurdities, evil and new miseries (such as nervous and psychical troubles) go side by side with progress, like the weeds with the wheat. There is always sin and suffering, where man in spite of all his efforts and all his progress cannot help. Does Jesus' message also free us from this fate?

The answer can be given in one sentence—the first and most ancient affirmation of Christianity, as we have seen. Jesus did what neither Buddha nor Mohammed nor Marx nor any one else ever did, he rose from the dead. The message given in this book is that Jesus lives. Sin and death have been overcome. The dead child will live, not dissolved into the All, but one with God and men in its own life and love. 178–185

Without the resurrection our faith is futile, and we are the most miserable of all men, liars about the most important thing of all. The resurrection of Jesus means that what began here on earth will be taken up into glory. 428

Redeemed by Jesus' death

But there is something more to be said. What we hear in the gospels is not merely that we are redeemed by the resurrection of Jesus, but also by his death. In our lives of suffering and mortal anxiety, this is a new source of comfort. How are we to explain that a death can be redemptive?

God created a human life which in the full simplicity of service fulfilled the real end of creation. It was the life of his Son, his Image, who in this loveless world was love. 77–82 / 155–159

The mission of the Son was difficult. The life of Jesus shows us how hard he found it. In a crooked world his life had to be upright, in a disobedient mankind he had to remain faithful, in an egoistic mankind he had to be love.

This was so intolerable that he was put to death. It was the climax of absurdity in evil, and from the very beginning the Church sought for explanations in the Old Testament. It found in Deutero-Isaiah a number of chants (the Servant of Yahweh Songs), which speak of a life ending in calamity, which appeared afterwards to be a source of happiness and goodness (cf. Is. 42:1–9; 49:1–6; 50:4–11; 52:13 – 53:12).

> "A man of sorrows, and acquainted with grief,
> and as one from whom men hide their faces
> he was despised, and we esteemed him not.
> Surely he has borne our griefs . . .
> Yet we esteemed him stricken . . .
>
> But he was wounded for our transgressions . . .
> All we like sheep have gone astray;
> We have turned every one into his own way;
> and the Lord has laid on him
> the iniquity of us all.
> It was the will of the Lord to bruise him . . .
> he makes himself an offering for sin" (Is. 53:3–6, 10).

We do not know what was the occasion in the past which gave rise to these mysterious chants of innocent and fruitful suffering. But they affirm something which was only fully realized in the death and resurrection of Jesus. They helped the Apostles to understand that this death had its place in God's plan.

But how can someone's hardship and pain and death redeem us?

There is a mystery here which cannot be fully defined in conceptual terms, well as we understand the central point with which it is concerned. We must examine it a little further, because so many of us have grown up with wrong ideas on the subject.

In the Middle Ages and for a long time afterwards, even in present-day preaching, stress was laid on the following aspect: The Father had been offended, the order of justice disturbed, and a penalty had to be exacted. The Son was the victim who paid the debt in full. Thus the right order was re-established.

This view starts from a rather one-sided concept which we can no longer entirely make our own. It is the medieval notion that sin or an offence upset the just order of things. But this could be corrected by punishment and the infliction of pain. This is a feeling which we ourselves often share. A wrong-doer will equivalently say—hit me, I have deserved it. But on the whole, at the present-day, we take a more personal view of guilt and evil. It is not a right order of things but a person who is injured and offended. This is not put right by the infliction of pain and punishment, but by regrets, works and love.   455–456

Scripture also seems to point in this direction. The redemption accomplished by Jesus is not seen primarily as the pain he suffered to restore a right order, but the service and goodness of his life, which made satisfaction for us. The Father did not will the pain and the death, but a noble and beautiful human life. That it ended in such a death was due to us. Jesus did not shrink from it. His death was his total obedience. And so in fact he made satisfaction for us. In this sense, his death was the will of the Father. That suffering and death appear precisely at this moment of rendering satisfaction is a great mystery which no one can fully explain. But it would be wrong to explain it by saying that the Father willed that "blood should flow".   269–270

The New Testament has a set of terms to describe all this: redemption or ransom, reconciliation, righteousness or justice, blood, sin. They are very often taken to mean that an order of justice was restored by the shedding of blood. But is this necessarily so? We must examine the terms one by one.

Jesus *ransomed* or *redeemed* us by his blood. The word reminds   158
us of how God "redeemed" Israel out of Egypt. No price was paid. It means that the people once more "belonged to God". In the same way, we belong to God once more through Jesus' death. The covenant is restored.

It is also said that we were *reconciled* to God through Jesus' death. We must note the expression. It does not say that God was reconciled *to us*. It is not an angry God who has to be reconciled to man, but evil man who has to be reconciled to God. Here too the covenant is restored.

This restoration is brought about through God's justice or righteousness. This is not, as might be imagined, the rigour of retributive justice which demands its pound of flesh, but the creative power of God which makes us righteous (just) and good.

Then there is *blood*. At the last supper, Jesus said, "For this is my blood of the covenant, which is poured out for many for the forgiveness of sins" (Mt. 26:28). Blood is an important word in the explanation of Jesus' work. It is an allusion to the blood of the covenant on Sinai. The animal offered in sacrifice is given   38–39
to Yahweh, but its blood, which now belongs to God, is given   166
back to be sprinkled over the people. The blood is a gift which   339–340

comes from God and is bestowed on Israel. There is one blood —or life—shared between God and Israel. They are blood-brothers, or, as one might almost say, blood-relations.

Thus Jesus' blood is not so much a gift to God as a gift from God. Jesus does not give his blood to a demanding Father who calls for vengeance, but to us. God's blood is our blood. We are linked as allies, in the new covenant in his blood.

Finally, there is the word *sin* in the passage from Paul, "For our sake he (the Father) made him to be sin who knew no sin, so that in him we might become the righteousness of God" (2 Cor. 5:21). This terse statement is also not to be taken to mean that God acts "as if" Jesus is a sinner and so brings down punishment upon his head. It means, on the contrary, that Jesus entered fully into this world which is characterized by sin and death. He became part of our world so that he could there give us his righteousness or holiness. He is reduced to the state of malediction of one hanging on the cross, in order to free us from the curse of our trespasses.

All these expressions signify Jesus' obedience, his service unto death. Hence they do not mean that the Father needed Jesus' sufferings as punishment undergone in our stead. God needed his life as vicarious love which would stand in our stead. But anyone who wishes to love in this world finds himself faced with an existence where love is rejected.

The great mystery is that the kingdom of God to come even when men, all of us, put him to death. Jesus and the Father did not turn away from us then. But the greatest love was shown from the midst of the greatest sin. Thus we are redeemed by Jesus' death.

And hence we believe that calamity and death are not the end, not a grim and fatal destiny, since God has shown that he can bring life out of death. And hence it is the task of the Christian to work and have confidence while it is day. For he has been given the hope that when he can do no more, in calamity or death, he remains one with his Lord, giving and receiving life.

Summary

We shall now try to sum up briefly how our Lord has redeemed us. He did so by attacking the root of evil, which is sin, through his obedience unto death. "With his stripes we are healed."

There *is* a good man in the world. His Spirit wills to pursue this work in us. He brings about in man the beginnings of a new birth. And thus he sets men to work against sin and misery. At the same time, he delivers us from being merely men. Even calamity is not a lonely fate, since it means that we pass through it along with Christ, our Lord and fellow-man. Suffering does not cease to be hard. But it loses the character of blind fate. It is 428–429 something which first of all we must fight against with all the strength we have. And secondly, where we can do no more, we still know that it is redemptive. Our Lord made it so by going through it.

If we contemplate carefully a figure of the Buddha, with the reposeful face which makes the escape from pain almost visible, and then suddenly turn to a picture of the crucified, we may notice, with a shock, how ordinary the latter is. He is an ordinary man on the gibbet. He feels pain, he dies. Such is the redemption in which we believe. The Redeemer did not escape pain by asceticism. He went right through it and turned it into love. He turned it into the holy cross, the outstretched arms of one who was to rise from the dead. The resurrection is the confirmation of Jesus' whole triumph over fate. The cross becomes through the resurrection the divinest symbol ever known by man. It means the final unfolding of life in love.

We are not to disappear in death, as humanism and Marxism teach. We are not to dissolve into the All, as Hinduism and Buddhism are inclined to think. Nor are we to lead a sort of earthly life for eternity, but far from God, as Islam imagines. We are to be absorbed in personal love in each other and in God.

In the last chapter we shall try to show how this promise is 498–502 ultimately linked with the revelation of the triune love in God.

The other doctrines elevated by Christ?

We cannot close this chapter without another remark about the other religions and ways of redemption. We have discussed their fundamental positions. But these religions and philosophies contain something else which is worth noting. There are certain forces at work in them which are difficult to harmonize with their basic attitudes and the explanations which they offer of their own doctrines. We mentioned this in the second chapter. 28, 29–30 We must now consider the matter for a short while.

About the beginning of the Christian era a new inspiration

which had been prepared for earlier appears in Hinduism. Hinduism, whose notion of God is so manifold and vague, now often attains to belief in one God. In one place the god Vishnu, in another Shiva, is adored as the One God.

So far, the basic tenets of Hinduism are not affected. But all is radically changed by the marvellous fact that men's hearts begin to be moved by a personal love of the one God. This is expressly said in the famous Bhagavadgita and is difficult to reconcile with the idea of a world in which everything, including the human "I", is to be considered mere illusion. Further, such personal love is inexplicable in terms of an All into which men's personal consciousness dissolves and disappears. Love involves some sort of encounter. The new attitude gave rise to some noble poetry. We may quote the words addressed to Vishnu by the seventeenth-century poet, Tukaram:

"You hold my hand and guide me wherever I go.
While I move on and lean on you,
    you bear my heavy burden . . .
You give me always new hope,
    and lead me to a new world.
In each man I see a friend, in each encounter a kinsman.
I play in your lovely world, O God, like a happy child.
And everywhere, says Tuka now,
    your goodness is outpoured."

This attitude of joy and love, for which Hindu wisdom provides no basic principles, can be well harmonized with the message of Jesus. Does it not seem possible to say that here the Spirit of Jesus has not left itself without testimony?

There was also a change in Buddhism. Strictly speaking, its object is to redeem man by suppressing all desire—including love, which can make man suffer so much. Benevolence is good, but merely in order to attain peace. But to surrender to another for the sake of the other would hinder the way to Nirvana.— Nonetheless, the Mahayana Buddhism (the Great Vehicle) really recognizes the value of caring for others. The ideal man is not the ascetic in his retreat, but the preacher, the "Boddhisattva" who dedicates himself to others. The Boddhisattva really desires the deliverance of the other. Instead of quietening and quenching the desire and so reaching Nirvana, he plunges once more, for the sake of the other, into the stream of appearances and change. This attitude reveals a love which cannot be derived from the teaching of the Buddha. The message of Jesus—personal love between God and man, and between man and man—provides the key.

In Islam too love breaks through marvellously. There is, no doubt, in the Koran one verse which speaks of love between God and man, but it is a love in pure obedience, not in fellowship. Such fellowship is not one of the basic tenets of Islam. God is inaccessible.

But early in the middle ages a mysticism of love appeared in some of the great and pious men of the Islamic world. Thus Al 317-319 Hallaj, who was put to the torture in 922 for his doctrine, and died praying for his enemies, left the poem which runs:

> "I am he (God) whom I love, and he whom I love is I.
> We are two souls who dwell in one body.
> When you see me, you see him, and when you see him,
> you see us both."

These Islamic mystics often sought to link up with Christ through contemplation. On the other hand, as late as 1953 the periodical of the Islamic University at Cairo could assert that there was no such thing as Islamic mysticism as such. There were no grounds in Muslim doctrine for a mysticism of love. We believe that the message of Jesus does provide such grounds.

Above all, we must not underestimate the Christian values which are contained in humanism and Marxism. There is no need to look very far to find Christian elements in humanism. They are often put into practice there in most attractive ways. But humanism itself is powerless to explain the deepest reasons for such values. We have already spoken of the problem of good in humanism. It contains much which can only be properly based on Jesus' message.

There is a constant tendency in Marxism, and one which is strictly speaking contrary to its theories, to treat the individual, and especially the oppressed individual, as possessing a personal dignity and worth of his own, and not merely as a fraction of mankind as a whole. May we not see here the trace of the Spirit of the Lord, who took one stray on his shoulder, leaving the ninety-nine in the desert?

There are religions and philosophies outside the Christian faith which contain elements which are strictly speaking foreign to such views, but which are wholly in the spirit of Christ.

Christians evangelized by non-Christians

But there is still more to say. It seems that the truth of Christ is also at work in the elements proper to the religions and philos-234 ophies in question. Sometimes portions of the general Catholic
352-353 faith appear there in very strong light. At times they are one-sided, but at times so much more intensely put into practice that they leave us ashamed. The total dedication of the Hindu, the gentleness of the Buddhist, the self-surrender of the Muslim, the care of the humanist for the things of this world, the Marxist's eagerness for justice and concern for social development are of this type.

It may therefore be said that in a certain way, non-Christians hold up to us in a new way certain portions of the truth of the gospel. In this sense it may be said that we are sometimes evangelized by them.

27   Melchizedek, the heathen priest of the "Most High God" in the polytheism of Canaan, may be taken as a symbol of all who seek God and the good way in the world for man. Melchizedek is mentioned reverently every day in the celebration of the holy Eucharist, immediately after the consecration.

Election

Finally there is the question: by what right or merit were the lands around the Mediterranean, and Europe, the first to possess the Christian revelation, and the only ones for a long time?

One might just as well ask: how did Abraham merit to be the first to be called? Why were the Jews the chosen people? The answer is always the same, God's loving choice. But we
249 must also remember that salvation is *for all men*. It is not merely given to the Church, but through the Church. Christians are
289 called to be the "city on the hill", to demonstrate clearly by their forbearance that Jesus fulfils the deepest and greatest longings of all who desire to banish fate, of all who desire to be fully redeemed, of all who desire to be pure, true and good, of all who desire that love should be the ultimate of all that is.

LIFE IN ABUNDANCE

What is known in love is full of holy mystery, but it is not 445–449
complicated. This is the way that a father or mother knows
the child whom they come to cover late at night: full of mystery,
but close to them and familiar. The child knows its parents in
the same way: full of undiscovered regions, but still not strange,
still familiar.

So too we hope that when we speak of God's unfathomable
gift in the following chapters we may not seem abstruse. The
subject that we take up is none other than the infinitely simple
Spirit of God, who brings not confusion but peace. 193–199

Grace

God desires us to have his Spirit. This desire was active throughout the whole of man's upward effort, but it was particularly
evident in the history of Israel. It was most fully revealed when
Jesus, our fellow-man, gave the Spirit. 173–174

The riches of this gift are indicated in Scripture and tradition
by many descriptions, which all point in the same direction.
We receive divine life, we are children of God, we are in Christ,
God dwells in us, we are members of Christ's body, we receive
grace. In each case, light is thrown from different angles on
the one truth, that the Holy Spirit is in us.

We must say a few words in particular about the term "grace".
In religious instruction, a distinction is often made between
sanctifying grace (the state of grace) and actual or helping
grace (the grace given for each particular act). Those who bear
this distinction in mind must not forget that we are concerned
with the one grace, which is the presence of the one Spirit.

The Spirit who comes to us is a living Spirit. Thus it is wrong
to speak of grace as an impersonal "quantity" or "entity".
This might suggest, if one may say so, that God's gift was a sort
of supernatural invisible fluid or again, a sort of proof of member-
ship of the Church. Grace is being known and warmed by the
Spirit of Jesus and the Father.

"Grace to you and peace." Nearly all the epistles of the
New Testament begin with this greeting. It is practically the
first written word which we have of the good tidings: "Gratia
vobis et pax" (1 Thess. 1:1).

In the scriptural languages, Greek and Hebrew, grace has a wide variety of meanings. First of all, it means God's response to our sins, that is, mercy, overlooking them, forgiving them—"granting grace".

454-456

290-300 The word also implies that it is the free gift of God, the initiative of God which does not depend on what we have accomplished. It is "gratis". Grace finally implies that man has been made well-pleasing, good and presentable: compare "graceful".

All three words connected with the gift—grace, gratis, graceful, taken from the sphere of law, business and ordinary intercourse respectively—have a comforting sound. Hence the word grace tries to signal all the riches of God's gift to us. The three meanings are developed most fully in the epistles of Paul. Again and again he proclaims his thanks for what has been granted to the Christian people: 1. deliverance from the doom of sin, 2. by way of an utterly free gesture, 3. which makes us new and pure. The doctrine is developed with most fire and permanent appeal in Romans 1–8, to which the reader is referred directly, and eventually to the commentaries on this most forcible of texts on grace.

Where can grace be seen?

Grace is not merely inward. It is also external, interwoven with all the realities of our life. For instance, Christ's grace in a wife can be a grace for the husband. Then she is herself a grace, a gesture of God's liberal, redemptive love. Parents can be a grace. And this is why it is not quite correct to say, as is often done, that after God, I owe everything to my father or mother. God is not just prior to or beside my parents. The Spirit of God comes to me *in* them, as elsewhere. It would be better to say, if one really wants to put it into words, that my parents are truly a grace for me.

But situations and objects can be graces for me, as well as men. God's redemption can make use of all that is. Those who have God's Spirit within them meet his friendly presence everywhere. "We know that in everything God works for good with those

4-63 who love him" (Rom. 8:28). Everything is good—nothing is exempted from the influence of Christ.

5-6 The most important way of the Spirit is through other men.

288

Indeed, this must be affirmed even more clearly, by saying that 240, 267
the Spirit is always given to us together. It would be a false 291, 304
individualism to think that the Holy Spirit is given to each one 318, 330
independently of the others. We have together *one* Spirit. The 373, 431
Spirit brings us together and unites us and forms us into a
"Church". It is in the Spirit that we are "in Christ" and brothers 456
of each other. For this reason, too, we all eat of one bread. It is
only through life in community with believing men that we
possess the life of God.

Even outside the visible Church, where the Spirit works
though men cannot believe in Christ (but where they try to
live according to their conscience, remaining open for God), it
is not a matter of separate individuals experiencing something
that is wholly inward. Here too the Spirit is in their mutual love, 249
which it reinforces.

In the following chapter we shall try to discern the basic
effects of grace in us. But here we shall not follow Galatians 5,
as in the chapter on Pentecost, but we take up the division given
in 1 Corinthians 13, which has become so deeply rooted in
Christian thought: faith, hope and love.

FAITH 124–127
236–241

What faith is and is not

The gospels show Jesus speaking more frequently of faith than
of love. Faith is the gift of the Spirit which enables us to give
ourselves entirely to him who is greater than we, and to accept
his message. Faith does not consist of mere reasoning. If it did, 125–126
it would be simply the registration of results and not faith.
But it is also not the result of a superficial feeling, which should
induce nobody to go beyond the bounds of intellectual reasoning. Faith is neither mere reason nor feeling. We are brought 445–449
very really and profoundly into contact with reality—the
story of Israel, Jesus of Nazareth, the existence of his Church. 34–236
Together, they form a testimony which places us before a
choice. Our intelligence considers it. But the Lord who bears
witness cries out to us: though it is true that no one should believe
inconsiderately, I ask of you the gift of yourself, if you really
wish to know who I am.—Faith is a leap, but not an irresponsible

one. It is justified by the leap itself. In the act of giving ourselves we experience the truth that life, growth, and the way lie here. If this could be calculated scientifically, it would not be so truly and profoundly human and vital.

It is like what happens when we learn to know what is most worth knowing in the world: our fellow men. Here too reasoning falls short. When people get married, it is not because they have fully analysed each other, but because they have faith in each other. It is the mode of knowledge whereby we attain all that is great and comprehensive in our lives. Hence it is through faith that we know (and much more truly) the Creator who reveals himself to us.

Then, we have deep within us, even deeper than our conscience, the conviction that it is good to believe. What is more profoundly valuable is also the most profoundly true.

As our ears listen to Scripture and our hands touch the Church, something in the deepest core of our person comes into play, something that has an intimation of God. This comes about in the same way that our conscience experiences something of God: it is veiled and indirect, but it is something that guides our whole life and grips us more deeply than any other reality. It can be shouted down and even stifled. It can be interpreted in various ways according to the education we have received and the views we have formed. But it still exists, and as soon as silence forms around us, or a vital decision looms up, we sense this consciousness, this voice, the Spirit of God in the depths of our being.

We have already spoken of faith when considering the life of Jesus. One of the marvels of faith, as we saw, was that it put the simple on the same level as the learned. It was not a matter of intelligent reasoning, but of personal dedication. A woman who is met on her doorstep by the preacher of a strange religion and only says, "We already have our religion" can be expressing a deep and genuine faith. People who grow up in an entirely Catholic country, and so practically never ask, "Is it true?", can also have very genuine faith.

Faith means partaking in God's life. Hence the light which we receive is not our doing, but the work of God, a freely-given grace. It is not, of course, something which works independently of man. Man lays himself open for faith. But this attitude is not at all equivalent or in proportion to what

237

125-126

288

290

God gives. The ways along which God sends grace are many: education, encounters and so on.

It is true of the grace of faith as of every other grace: it is not given apart from other men. Faith is something which we 288–289 have in common. We believe together.—We also believe *for* 286 others. This is the only answer when we ask ourselves why we believe and others do not. That which is given to us without 249 any merit of ours also means something for others, in many 352 ways.

Faith means to say Yes to God's revelation. It would be wrong to view this revelation as a vast system of cut and dried propositions and truths. It is primarily a message and a light: 365 God's light on our life, on history, on good and evil, on death, on God himself, on love as the last word. When this revelation is proclaimed, it has to be done in words, in a certain sequence and connection. But this should not be allowed to give rise to the impression that God's revelation is a system of isolated pieces of valuable information. It is rather God's view of our reality. To see with the eyes of faith is to see with the eyes of God.

> As it is written,
> "What no eye has seen, nor ear heard, nor the heart of man conceived, what God has prepared for those who love him." God has revealed to us through the Spirit. For the Spirit searches everything, even the depths of God. For what person knows a man's thoughts except the spirit of the man which is in him? So also no one comprehends the thoughts of God except the Spirit of God. Now we have received not the spirit of the world, but the Spirit which is from God, that we might understand the gifts bestowed on us by God. And we impart this in words not taught by human wisdom but taught by the Spirit, interpreting spiritual truths to those who possess the Spirit. The unspiritual man does not receive the gifts of the Spirit of God, for they are folly to him, and he is not able to understand them because they are spiritually discerned. The spiritual man judges all things, but is himself to be judged by no one. "For who has known the mind of the Lord so as to instruct him"? But we have the mind of Christ (1 Cor. 2:9–16).

Faith as a task

Our faith will not remain without our effort. It is something that we can attend to and foster, or neglect. It is a task. When we have acknowledged inwardly the revelation given by God, we still have a long road to travel. We have to make living, concrete realities of a truth which we believe profoundly without seeing and often without feeling. It is a leap in the dark which must be taken again and again. When we are almost overwhelmed by the seduction of a temptation, it is a leap in the dark to make our faith a reality and to say no, that is, to say yes to those to whom we have sworn to be true, and indeed, to say yes to God. On a day of bad weather on the road, disagreeable colleagues at work and quarrels at home, it is an act of dedication to believe in the Holy Spirit and hence in the possible goodness of others and of oneself. When one is almost overwhelmed by suffering, it is an act of great faith to bring 492–498 home to oneself God's faithfulness and the meaning which Jesus gave to suffering.

Hence faith is not just belonging to the Church without perceptible effects. Faith always affects the present instant. It believes that God is now powerfully at work on our behalf. 495 That he has power to ordain the course of events. That he is in 112 fact able to work a miracle in his love. "And he awoke and rebuked the wind, and said to the sea, 'Peace! Be still!' And the wind ceased, and there was a great calm. And he said to them, 'Why are you afraid? Have you no faith?'" (Mk 4:39–40). Faith means that we overcome distrust of God's world. It is one of the great forces for progress in mankind. It is not surprising that Jesus so constantly urged men to take this leap which carries them out of themselves.

The reasonableness of faith

This conquest of despair is not *un*-reasonable. Though the intel- 125 lect cannot penetrate so far, it can recognize that believing (as we have seen) is the proper way of knowing the great 237–238 realities. Further, the way to faith is not such that the intellect is forced to keep silent all the time. The chapter on the resurrection and many other sections of this book will show how great a role rational reflection plays. It is a typically Catholic perspective to see faith and reason as related to each other. (The 226 Reformation, with its constant attitude of reserve towards the

292

salvific possibilities of the earthly, emphasizes the otherness of
faith.)

As regards the relationship of faith and science, many false
problems have been raised because of false notions of what was
of faith and what was scientifically proved. Revelation has no
teaching to give on the course of the stars, the evolution of
the world or such matters. Science has no teaching to give on
the deepest reality of our life or the ultimate origin of the world.
Since faith and science deal with the same reality, conflicts are
always possible. But the conflicts are only apparent, since
there is but one truth.

220
224–225

In the fields where science has a really serious contribution
to make, it always has the priority in such cases of conflict—
in the measure of certainty which is appropriate to science,
which is often that of the hypothesis. If believers have thought
differently up till then, it was because conclusions had been
drawn from revelation which should not have been drawn. The
story of creation, which is a poetic description of the origin of
mankind, did in fact give rise to the opinion that evolution was
to be excluded. But this was not part of the divine message contained in the story. So too opinions were often formed about
the literal meaning of the Old and New Testament which
seemed obvious enough, but did not belong to the divine
message.

439–440

261–263
47–53
206–210

Is faith surer than science? It has a certainty of a different sort.
It may be affirmed that the assent of faith is attached to the
most profound of our faculties. This makes its certainty the
most profound and the strongest that we know upon earth.
But at the same time it is the certainty of dedication, of love,
of love towards God who is only known in this act of dedication.
Thus we are not, so to speak, entirely on our native soil. And
hence the certainty of faith is essentially accompanied by
difficulties or "doubt".

Doubt

If one falls back on one's own resources, one can always ask:
"Am I deceiving myself? Am I not being deceived?" Periods
of certainty can be succeeded by periods of disarray. Some men
are almost always at peace with their faith. Others are in a
constant state of questioning. (The word "doubt" in the title
and throughout the section means every temptation or diffi-

culty against faith. Thus we do not take the word in the sense in which it is often used in religious instruction, as hesitancy or refusal to assent to the faith. We have spoken of the sinfulness 126–127 of such refusal "Unbelief", a paragraph in Part three.)

The presence of doubt says nothing about the certainty with which we believe. We can be torn by doubt and still be fully dedicated, with a faith firm as rock. Indeed, strong faith can 318–319 often be accompanied by great doubt. The more one loves, the more one surrenders oneself, the more one has abandoned one's own ground. More is at stake.

A faith that is challenged can remain a full faith. True faith is always full. One is not half believing, half unbelieving. As long as one says, Yes, I wish to believe, one is fully a believer. No one ever fell away from his faith unless he wished to.

The man who cried out to Jesus: I believe, help my unbelief, had a full faith. And Jesus therefore healed his son. Thérèse of Lisieux had painful doubts against her faith before her death in the convent at the age of twenty-three. All that was left of her faith was the ultimate surrender: I wish to believe, help my unbelief! And this young girl was canonized. She could well take her place among the heroes of faith mentioned in Hebrews 11. In the midst of the great crisis of faith which her contemporaries were going through in Europe, from the intelligentsia to the workers, she shared their pangs with the utmost self-surrender in love, day after day for two periods of nine months each. No doubt there was life for many in such love and faith.

And we must look at our Lord himself as he is tempted in the desert and utters his cry of grief on the cross. Here we can see best of all the certainty which is not eliminated by the worst of difficulty or "doubt". His gift of himself was at its most total at the temptations and on the cross.

Scripture constantly shows us men in a crisis of faith and confidence. We can read again in this light the story of Abraham (Gen. 22), the people in the desert (Exod. 17:4–7), the prophets (1 Kg. 19; Jer. 15:10–21), the people after the destruction of Jerusalem (Is. 49:14), men crushed by illness (Ps 22) and men in positions of responsibility (Lk. 22:31).

The crisis of faith takes on a different form in each age. There were times in the history of the Church when darkness fell 299 rather in the form of despair. People thought they were eternally lost, that God would not save them. Or again, people suffered long periods of torment of conscience ("scruples"). Nowadays it is very common for people to feel that the existence of God and Jesus' Spirit is a complete illusion.

This doubt is occasioned by many difficulties: how can the 492–498 cruelty of the world be reconciled with the goodness of God? Or, the salvation which I hear of brings me no deliverance at all. Or, God is no part of my existence; he means nothing in 3–22 my experience. Or, men without faith live just as well, if not 270–286 better. Such questions are discussed elsewhere in this book, 351 apropos of divine revelation. Here we confine ourselves to seeing what a Christian should do in times of doubt.

The combat against doubt

It was once quite common to advise people suffering from doubts "not to think about them". This advice was no doubt correct where people were troubled by misgivings about their own damnation. But it seems less helpful today. Nonetheless, we can begin by deriving one wise counsel from it. This is that we should not let ourselves become the plaything of every thought that crosses our mind or the slave of compulsive notions. It can often be very advisable not to go into the difficulties at the precise moment that they occur to us. One should simply go on with one's ordinary believing life, and fix a time in one's mind for dealing with the doubt—this afternoon, tomorrow, next month. When the time comes the difficulty should be seriously examined, possibly with the help of pen and paper.

Above all, it is well to discuss the doubt with someone else from the community of the faithful—a priest, a friend, a teacher. 288–289 If one is disappointed by an evasive answer or faulty reasoning from one, one tries another. In a matter of such importance, it is not too great an imposition to have to enquire further.

One often discovers that the impressiveness of the doubt, which sometimes seems so obvious and plausible, is superficial rather than real. One is fascinated by a certain thought, which then loses its force when the whole of the reality is taken into perspective. Hence facing things fully and clearly can be a great help in doubts about the faith. This may, indeed, involve the discovery that some things which we thought were Catholic faith were not fully and really so. Then we learn to know better the actual truth of Jesus' message. For this reason it is well to consult learned men and competent writers.

But a clear diagnosis is not always a cure, because difficulties with the faith generally lie deeper than the intellect. We are downcast by the absurdity of suffering or we feel that God means nothing to us and so on. Here too, no doubt, a better knowledge of our faith can throw light on our questions and worries, as for instance if we recall that God is fighting on our side against evil, or if we can recognize his presence in our daily joys.

Nonetheless, knowledge is not enough. There may be other things to consider. Our faith can waver because we are not living up to it and because we are allowing it to be choked "by the cares of the world, and the delight in riches, and the desire for other things" (Mk 4:19). We may perhaps have taken a decision which is against the dictates of conscience. And this may have led us to try to fit our convictions to our decision in the long run. Our vision of God may have been obscured by some inward trouble; by our being unable to bring ourselves to love others; by our indulging in hatred of a parent and so on. Thinking alone is not enough in such matters.

What is to be done?—Sometimes we must just try to live according to the truths of our faith, and humble ourselves in so far as we find ourselves unable to do so. At other times, we need to be more open and perceptive, to try to be more alert to the presence of God's strange otherness in all that happens. Then there is prayer, which is a much more vital act than reflection—to pray to the God in whom we believe, even when our faith itself is under attack. But here we must watch out for insincerity, and not allow ourselves to be talked or prayed into something. Sometimes the only honest prayer possible is to say, "Lord, if you exist, let me know it somehow". This is sometimes more honest than to go on thinking without praying. Mere reflection might mean that we are persuading ourselves not to pray, because it might mean that we exclude even the possibility of our prayer being heard.

Sometimes the conquest of doubt lies in an entirely different approach. It involves coming out into the open with one's fellowmen. The man who is always taking offence, who never really gives himself, who is in a state of isolation—possibly through no fault of his own, simply because he has no faculty of communication—can sometimes find faith an impossibility. And even if he does believe in God and Christ, nearly everything is often missing which should go to make up the warmth and quality of his faith. The thought of God is only a way of remaining in isolation. Very often the only way out for such a man is that others should meet him with warmth and love, and thus enable him to believe once more in life itself—to believe in others, to believe in the Lord.

It has been said that there are as many types of prayer as there are men. The same may be true of difficulties against faith. Hence it is impossible to give advice which will cover all cases. Thus there may be men who should just cease to concentrate on God, and free themselves from a concentration which has become an obsession, simply holding out, and allowing their uncertainty free rein. "If God exists, and Christianity is not an Ilusion, faith can well stand doubts" (H. M. M. Fortmann). One then tries only to be sincere towards others. One's only way of praying is to keep oneself open.

"When he came back, he stood at the doorstep and whistled for a while—something he never did otherwise." This is how the mother of a student described her son's return from a visit to a priest, who had given him the sort of advice just mentioned above. It shows that God is a God of peace and joy.

One of our reasons for delaying so long upon doubts against the faith was that they help in their own way to show what faith is. Difficulties are part of faith. They have a positive function. They force the believer to bring the message of Jesus more clearly to mind. They make dedication a more conscious act. They purify faith from accidental motives. They make it wider and deeper, because newly discovered realities and values—the sources of many doubts—are seen to be not outside our God, but within him. (See for instance how magnificently this was demonstrated in the crisis of Israel's faith during the Babylonian captivity, Is. 40–55.)—In a word: in the hour of crisis our contact with God grows more intimate and intense, because it is a moment of the history which we live along with him.

HOPE

It might seem unnecessary to go on to speak of hope after faith, since faith, if lived out to the fullest, includes hope. Nonetheless, it is well to explore more deeply the warmth and joy of the dedication of our faith. For hope is just that aspect of faith which makes us certain that the world is cared for and loved by God. Hope is not vulgar optimism, not just the looking at the sunny side of things and saying, "Let's hope for the best, after all". This sort of outlook may be due to a happy type of mind, but it may also be due to superficiality.

True hope is possible only if the ultimates in life give grounds for hope. The grounds of Christian hope are God's eternity and Christ's resurrection, and also God's goodness—that he will not abandon us, for whom Jesus lived, as long as we cling to him. Such confidence is not something which we can produce in ourselves. It is a gift of the Holy Spirit.

Hope is not contrary to soberness and realism. It can go along with a clear and hard-headed view of our own inadequacies and those of the world. The form it takes will depend on our character and disposition. In some people, it will be a deep and joyful thankfulness for everything that happens. In others it will be a struggle against innate pessimism. In others again it will be the ability not to become embittered and full of rancour. It is not merely a matter of being confident that our own eternal destiny is in good hands. It also means that we are sure that the life of the world is in good hands. God has good things in store for all men.

Hope for mankind

The Church believes that God means well with man. Thus there is a people upon earth which believes in man. No man is excluded from God's grace. The persecutor can become an apostle, the blasphemer a saint, and we can trust that the ignorant are in good faith. The adversary may not be destroyed. He must be invited in, and no doubt with more joy in heaven than for the ninety-nine just. In a word, each and every man is destined for bliss. No one is reprobated. This is not as obvious as one might

275–276 think. Communism, for instance, which holds out happiness for all mankind, admits that many of those alive today are excluded from happiness for good. A capitalist cannot become a proletarian. He has to be eliminated. He can never be converted, since, as it is assumed, he cannot change. All mankind is not trusted. But not so in Christianity. Any communist can become a Christian, and possibly a very good one. And again, to take up a very different point, the greatest villain who asks to be received into the Church of Jesus cannot be refused.

Many humanists have a very encouraging confidence in   273-274
mankind. But they have no faith in a resurrection, and hence
are to some extent "men without hope". And their confidence
in mankind lacks the anchor which holds Christian hope
unshakably: the goodness of Jesus, which can give all men
a new birth. Man in humanism is dependent entirely on himself. A humanist who realizes his own and others' badness—
like many of the French existentialists, for instance—have no
firm grounds for hope. Man is absurd, and utterly inauthentic.

A Christian who believed that God has excluded some men
beforehand from his love, would be a heretic. That is, he would
be affirming something as divinely revealed which God did
not proclaim. Hence predestination to evil is an unchristian
notion which warps and obscure one's relationship to God
and to man.

Catholics, no doubt, have often failed to try to recognize   251-252
how for instance God could bestow bliss on someone who died
a Muslim. This failure has in fact often obscured Christians'
hope in the eternal happiness of all mankind. But even then
there was always at least the certainty that every man received
sufficient grace. This hope has been growing steadily clearer
and stronger in the Church, and must grow clearer still. It is
a great force for good among men—this conviction that
mankind is moving towards God, who is not a God of the dead
but of the living.

The temptation which besets this attitude to life is despair,
distrust. Despair means that we assume that our sins are mightier
than God's love. God does not save us! Such distrust of God's
love can be a very grave temptation. To give way to it fully
would be to deny and disavow God's most proper attribute,
and would be a very grave sin. But it is one thing to be overwhelmed by the sickness of despondency, and quite another
thing to reject the saving hand of God.

Patience

Patience is very close to hope. It means to be on the watch,
lovingly but soberly, to note every spark of goodness in the
acts of others and every spark of truth in their words. It is
without bitterness and without rancour. Patience is one of the

227–230 loveliest virtues of our times, where so many opinions, grudges and resentments clash and fight it out. Our hope in God should give us the patience not to break off relationships and not to grow hard.

For we believe that in the groping efforts of mankind God's visage is gradually revealed more clearly, as we move towards the great revelation of Jesus, who is the human visage of God for us. He will call forth from mankind the kingdom of peace
478–487 and goodness. This is our deepest hope. "Come, Lord Jesus. Maranatha."

132   LOVE

"God's love has been poured into our hearts through the Holy Spirit" (Rom. 5:5). By "God's love" Paul does not of course mean love given to God but love from God. He affirms that we men are given a spark of the great divine fire. Hence Christians should never begin by telling themselves that they have to love. Prior to all such efforts is the fact that they do love. The fact that they belong to Jesus means that they already have love within themselves. We are men who love, not through our own
288 merit, but through a gift beyond our reach, a gift of God.

To recognize that we love calls for a great act of faith, of which there is only one thing to say: do it. Believe that God has created you and renewed you in such a way that you love. Believe it and you will discover that it is true.

The gift of love is likewise a duty: "You shall love the Lord your God with all your heart, and with all your soul, and with all your mind. This is the great and first commandment. And a second is like it, You shall love your neighbour as yourself" (Mt. 22:37–39).

The heart of Jesus' message

We have now come to what is most sacred in Jesus' message. It cannot be propounded in a few pages. A few remarks are all that can be given in this chapter. The whole book actually tries to be a discussion of Christian love. As we said when speaking
104–105 of the kingdom of God—this is what the whole catechism is about. The same may be said of other subjects such as faith, Jesus, Church, Holy Spirit, grace. But we say it in fact only of

300

the kingdom of God, because it is the core of Jesus' preaching, and of love, because it is his great commandment. The kingdom of God and the commandment of love are, in fact, the same message. The reign of God is the reign of love. To say, "Thy kingdom come" is as much as to say, "Thy love come". Love is discussed especially in the chapters "The Will of the Father", 132–135 "I will send you a helper" and "The second commandment 196–197 which is like the first". 371–381

"Love, and do what you will"

It is well to dwell for a while on the truth that love is the greatest of all virtues. It is not the greatest in the sense in which one tree is greater than others. It is the greatest in quite a different way, by being present in all other good qualities. Perseverance, temperance, friendliness, obedience, service—they are only valuable in so far as they have love within them, in so far as they are a form of loving. Augustine put this very forcibly when he said, "Love, and do what you will" ("Ama et fac quod vis"). If we love, we wish to do only what is good. Love is enough, because it is everything.

Augustine was speaking of the true love which goes out of itself and throws itself open. We all know how easily our love abandons the gold standard, so to speak, how easily it begins to be self-seeking, though not professedly so. To prevent our making mistakes, there are therefore other commandments in the preaching of Christ and the Church. But they do not come to stand beside love. They are rather directives for the purity of love. Every commandment is a commandment of love. Jesus' commandment, that we should love the Lord God with all our hearts is accompanied by the commandment of the Church which bids us to go to Mass every Sunday. Jesus' 320, 452 commandment, that we should love our neighbour as ourselves, is accompanied by his prohibition of adultery. (See further the 401 chapter, "The second commandment which is like the first".) 372–378

Jesus also explained what pure love is when he included enemies among those who are to be loved. "For if you love 135 those who love you, what reward have you? Do not even the tax collectors the same?" (Mt. 5:46). Our model must be the heavenly Father, whose sun shines on all alike, good and evil. "You, therefore, must be perfect, as your heavenly Father is perfect" (Mt. 5:48).

378-379   Love is so divine that we can say not only "God is love" but "Love is God". Wherever there is some element of pure love—even where men do not know God—God lives there and divine life.

All those who love add to their human stature, as will be seen in the hereafter. But this makes some of us dubious. We conclude that after all love is always concerned with oneself, aiming at self-development and a reward here and in heaven. True and perfect love for the sake of the other does not exist. But this is not quite just. No doubt, God is so truly love that all who love draw closer to him. It cannot be otherwise, since this is the very structure of things, as we recognize with delight. But this does not mean that love cannot be pure and disinterested. Jesus Christ did not love us in order to profit by it, but simply for our sake. And we cannot but believe that the great saints really left their own interests out of account to a great extent. Their self-improvement or their attaining heaven mattered not

131-132   at all at any given moment. On reflection, no doubt, they must have recognized that the reward was there, inevitably. But love is precisely something quite different from merely reflecting on oneself and turning in on oneself. It is action and self-abandonment. Hence Paul could write: "I could wish that I myself were accursed and cut off from Christ for the sake of my brethren, my kinsmen by race" (Rom. 9:3). It was an impossible wish, but it shows how far true love is ready to go. Love is not primarily a feeling but action. Feelings are no doubt very helpful if love is to be warm and human and tender, but its real aim and the touch-

56   stone is what we are really ready to do. The words of the Song of Solomon, speaking of bridal love and of the love between Yahweh and his people, and which are understood by the Church of the love which Jesus brought, show how little

388   sentimentality there is about this love: "Love is as strong as death" (Song 8:3).

133-134   *The norm of love*

But should not love be tempered by right reason?—Real love is not moderated by right reason, but helped and made concrete. Right reason, seeking for the most effective ways of being good, is the great aid to love. It helps us to "identify" with others, to start from their point of view. It helps to achieve the impossible—

reconciliation in long-standing feuds, help in helpless cases. It helps to make possible what is humanly foolish—the putting of others' interests before our own. This is because we take the others' point of view, and that we make their desires our own—like the good Samaritan.   133

"Right reason", however, which takes its own interests as its starting-point, standing up for its own rights (and family ones) refusing to let anything go, cannot make the desires of another its own and so cannot seek out a possibility where all seems impossible. Its principle is that true charity begins at home, meaning in fact that true charity stays at home. The consequences are the grave sins of failure to help, and of persistent feuds among Christians and Christian families.

To love means to go out of oneself. Hence it is something quite obviously "not in our line". We are afraid of it, both of love of God and of love of man. We are no longer fully sure of our lives. To unredeemed mankind love appears as folly, such as is pointedly expressed by Jesus in the sermon on the mount: "If any one strikes you on the right cheek, turn to him the other 130 one also" (Mt. 5:39). No doubt, when Jesus stood before Annas and received a blow in the face, he did not turn the other cheek. But that is not the point. We are not dealing with a precise law. What is described here is an attitude of the spirit. "If any one would sue you and take your coat, let him have your cloak as well" (Mt. 5:40). In other words, if someone wants your jacket, let him have your overcoat as well. And if someone demands that you should go with him for a mile, go along with him for two miles. All this sounds very strange. Nonetheless, this is Jesus' message. Paul indicates the very same attitude when he writes: "Do not be overcome by evil, but overcome evil with good" (Rom. 12:21).

To respond with good to evil puts one's conduct at once on a new and higher level. A force of unknown power is let loose on the other, "for by so doing you will heap burning coals upon his head" (Rom. 12:20). This is the way to break down barriers and to make men ready to give themselves to one another.—We are all beginners in love. Egoism and bad faith, the inhibitions of inner disabilities and immaturities, all make us men who have still to learn nearly everything. We cannot learn the lesson by overtense effort. The foolishness of the gospel is calm. All overanxiety is unevangelical. No doubt we learn love by an effort of the will, in so far as our will forces itself to be free and detached and self-sacrificing. But the way it takes to find love may just as well be that of joy, good humour, good relationships 432 and even rivalry. Anything that opens up man's heart can be the beginning of grace.

It is truer of love even more than of faith, that it is given to us 289 in common. It is something that must be done together. Love cannot always remain one-sided. This is not meant as a piece of good advice to guide our actions. As far as we are concerned, we must do everything. But it remains true that love in return, love from the other side, can be a powerful help to us. Then we in turn receive burning coals on our head—"a most vehement flame" (Song 8:6, literally, "flames of Yahweh").

Though we are afraid of love, it remains the deepest craving of our being, and of the Spirit who lives in us. It is a great relief to remember that our whole life is meant for one thing only: 501-502 for loving. Without this, the rest is immaterial:

"If I speak in the tongues of men and of angels, but have not love, I am a noisy gong or a clanging cymbal. And if I have prophetic powers, and understand all mysteries and all knowledge, and if I have all faith, so as to remove mountains, but have not love, I am nothing. If I give away all I have, and if I deliver my body to be burned, but have not love, I gain nothing. Love is patient and kind; love is not jealous or boastful; it is not arrogant or rude. Love does not insist on its own way; it is not irritable or resentful; it does not rejoice at wrong, but rejoices in the right. Love bears all things, believes all things, hopes all things, endures all things" (1 Cor. 13:1–7).

CHRISTIAN PRAYER

Before God

Man is the only creature on earth that can turn to its origin, its ultimate ground. The birds seek their food and nourish their young, the cattle graze and sleep and produce their calves and milk and finally die without ever thinking of their creator. Man can turn in adoration to the mystery of his origin. There is a sense, no doubt, in which the beasts also praise the basic mystery of their existence, by living it out. The poet Guido Gezelle sees the little waterbeetle writing God's name on the surface of the pools as it whirls and skates. And the psalmist says:

> "Thou makest darkness, and it is night,
>   when all the beasts of the forest creep forth.
> The young lions roar for their prey,
>   seeking their food from God" (Ps 104:20).

But it is man who knows this and says so. He realizes that the roar of the lion in the tropical night is an answer of life to the creation of life. The cries of the beasts only become cries to God in the "animal rationale" which is man. We alone are before him with heart and mind. Hence the ancient summary of how to be a good man, the ten commandments, begins with three 371-372 commandments on the relationship of man to God.

> "I am the Lord your God, who brought you out of the land of Egypt, out of the house of bondage.
> You shall have no other gods besides me.
> You shall not make yourself a graven image, or any likeness of anything that is in heaven above, or that is in the earth beneath, or that is in the water under the earth; you shall not bow down to them or serve them; for I the Lord your God am a jealous God . . .
> You shall not take the name of the Lord your God in vain . . . Remember the Sabbath day, to keep it holy" (Exod. 20:1–5, 7–8).

Thus man is invited to keep some time free for God. He turns away from his daily round and from visible things. He joins his hands and rests. He lets his eyes rest, to see what is deepest in men and things, the ground of their being. His whole body shares in the elevation of his mind to God. Standing, sitting or kneeling, it takes on a fitting posture, the posture of giving oneself, of leaving oneself behind. His thoughts try for some firm footing from which to contemplate the unfathomable mystery. The imagination fixes on something, or possibly on a vanishing point. A special place is sought, alone or with others.

All these things are ways of trying to bring home to oneself the presence of God: a place apart, posture, thoughts, and imaginations. Music may help, a church, the stillness of the country-side, the openness of the heavenly vault. Thus we seek symbols within and without ourselves, to be intent on him who is "higher than my highest flight, more intimate than my inmost depths". He is outside our power and possibility. We can say of every 489–490 symbol that it is not he. Nonetheless, we are orientated towards him in the depths of our being.

But if we continue on these lines alone, we shall never reach Christian prayer. We should remain within the bounds of purely human religion, or not even there. For we have been speaking merely of part of prayer, and indeed the smallest part, that is, how we try to speak to God. But prayer is above all listening to God. This is the greatest part of prayer: the fact that he speaks.

The ways of prayer

What then does God say to us?—In the Son who is from the earth, and who is also Son of the Father, the Father gives us access to himself. The first and most important thing is to see what ways and what symbols God gives us in Christ. And what are they? They are everything in which we find Jesus Christ: 300 our love for one another in his Spirit; the words of Scripture, 322 inspired by his Spirit; baptism and the other sacraments, and 252–256 especially the gift of the bread and wine.

This is the heart of Christian prayer—the Eucharist. Here we receive the whole Christ: his word, his body, his Holy Spirit. We find in his words how we are to speak to God. His sacrificed body is the one offering that we can bring. His Holy Spirit teaches us what we are to say and ask for, interceding within us with unutterable sighs to God.

We must then ask ourselves how we are to join in properly at the celebration of the Eucharist, and how we are to pray at the supreme moment of our prayer. And the answer is that we are to follow out all the points which the celebration itself involves: coming together, listening, remembering, thanking, offering ourselves with Christ, eating and so on. We shall speak more 332 fully of this in the next chapter.

But there is one quality of prayer which we may already emphasize here. It is that the supreme form of prayer obviously

takes place in common, and not in isolation. The Eucharist is an
assembly. It should not be surprising that this can cause us
difficulties. There are two reasons for this—that being in company, praying and singing together is a distraction, and that
the others are not dear to us. As regards the first point, we may
say that it involves an error stemming from the time when the
altar was far away and the prayers were in Latin. The faithful
then used the time of Mass for silent, interior prayer. Such prayer
is excellent, but it is not the primary end and object of the
Eucharist. It was not instituted to provide a setting in which we
could forget our neighbour, but in order that we should
remember our solidarity with him.

As regards the second difficulty, that we do not care for the
others, the solution is not to withdraw entirely. It is better to try
to enter into the mind of the others—why they are so and why
they act so. From this point of view, going to Mass is a whole
undertaking. It imposes a duty on us—but a duty given us by
Christ. It is a marvellous truth—that the supreme prayer, the
Eucharist, is also a reunion with our fellowmen in love. When
we break away from our daily routine and elevate our minds to
God in the Eucharist, we find once more our neighbour, our
husband or wife, our children, those who are closest to us.

This is where Jesus' message points. Hence the confession of
sins at the beginning of Mass is also a prayer that our indifference
and hostility may be overcome.

The liturgical "hours"

Hence the Eucharist and the other sacraments are not, so to
speak, individual performances. They come from the Church as
a community.

The celebration of the Eucharist is also enshrined by a form of
prayer which is uttered by the Church as a community. This
prayer is "the canonical hours" of the liturgy, also known as the
hours of the breviary or the office (in choir). It has been called
"a treasure-house of purest prayer". The canonical hours
developed out of the morning and evening prayers which used
to be said in common in church in the early centuries of Christianity. The liturgy or worship of the Church consists of the
sacraments and these canonical hours. (There are also a number
of blessings, prayers for journeys and forms of grace at meals

which have been established for universal use and form part of the liturgy.)

The kernel of the canonical hours is still morning and evening prayers—Lauds and Vespers. In the course of time, other elements were added in monasteries and cathedrals: Matins, mainly composed of readings from Scripture and from the great Christian writers, which are sometimes recited at night; then Terce, Sext and None, short prayers for the third, sixth and ninth hours after sunrise; finally there is Compline, late in the evening.

The structure of Lauds is as follows: it begins with a number of psalms taken from the most striking songs of praise and thanksgiving; then a very short extract from Scripture is read. Then there is a hymn, followed by the Benedictus (the Canticle of Zachary, Lk. 1:67–79), and finally a short prayer.

This ancient form retains a wonderful freshness. Morning prayers composed at a later date are often overladen, while Lauds always offers something new. This is also true of Vespers, which has the same structure. The psalms, however, have a more intimate and suppliant tone. Hence Lauds and Vespers can be a help to all Christians, and not just to the priests and religious who recite them in their entirety every day.

One of the most striking features of these prayers is that so little attention is paid directly to man. The praise of God displaces all thought of self. Lauds scarcely ever speaks of the coming day, nor Vespers of the day just gone by. It is just the hour itself which is consecrated.—The variety is also a help. New psalms are recited each day of the week. The text of Scripture varies with the season of the year, and so too the closing prayer.

Those who are interested, as groups or individuals, in the form of their prayer might well follow the structure and variety outlined above. They could begin with a psalm in praise of God, then a text from Scripture, part of the canticle of Zachary and end with a prayer in their own words.—Some general information about the psalms is given at the end of the chapter.

Between Lauds and Vespers every day comes the climax of the Church's liturgy, the celebration of the Eucharist. The most important celebration of the Eucharist each week takes place on Sundays. The Sundays of the year form a great cycle in which the mysteries of our Lord's life, death and resurrection are brought close to us in all their variety. Hence the Mass of each Sunday is 343 composed of different readings of Scripture, chants and prayers, to bring out each time a different saving fact, another aspect of our Lord's coming. On weekdays, the Eucharistic celebration corresponds to the liturgical season, to which Lauds, Vespers and other canonical hours are also adapted. Thus the whole yearly liturgy is one great reminder of the mystery of our redemption, with the Sunday of Sundays, Easter, as its climax. It is not necessary to dwell on the liturgy here, since we all in fact take part in it.—There is also common prayer composed by individuals. It will mostly be inspired by the liturgy, as when for instance the family makes its own evening prayer or when the parish 448-449 spontaneously prays in time of need.

Private prayer

Then there is the prayer offered in silence. Jesus speaks of it when he says: "When you pray, go into your room and shut the door and pray to your Father who is in secret" (Mt. 6:6). Jesus did this himself—in the desert, among the wild beasts, on a mountain. And we also practise this form of prayer. We withdraw to seek the deepest parts of our existence. After a hard day's work, we "recollect ourselves", "lift up our hearts". This sort of prayer is as much part of the Christian life as is the liturgy. The liturgy keeps our prayer in touch with the great stream of Church life. The prayer offered freely by private inspiration gives us a very personal experience of the fact that the same living relationship—not without the community—exists between God and ourselves. Without such prayer, our liturgy would be reduced to a merely formal worship.

It is true here too, as it is in the liturgy, that God is the first who speaks. His word came first, the gospel message, on the lips of those who brought us up and instructed us in the faith.

This divine revelation reminds us that he began his discourse even earlier. The universe, the plants, mankind—father, mother and the rest—are all a gesture, a word from God. Indeed, I can 9-17 go back still further. My own existence is his first word to me. 382-383 "In him we live and move and have our being" (Acts 17:28). This takes us very far indeed. My parents did not want "me", but "a child", "a boy", "a girl". It was only God who knew and willed "me".

Thus prayer is first and foremost to note thankfully, with the eyes of faith, all that God does with us. It is only afterwards that prayer means trying to give an answer to God with all our heart.

God always greater

When we speak of an answer to God, we suggest that we can talk to him and turn to him as to a person. And in fact the most profound truth about the world is that reality is ultimately personal. Love between one another is the most profound reality. And we can say nothing truer of the mystery of our origins than that the ultimate was not a primal nebula, an impersonal gas or fluid, but someone whom we can address as You. As the Curé of Ars said, the best way of conversing with God is to speak to him as if he were a man. Christ made this possible for us. He
114–115 called God Abba, using the familiar word of the child for its father. Indeed, in Christ himself God has become still more
497–502 accessible. God appears to us with human visage in the Son.

Nonetheless, it must be remembered that God is more than what is expressed by the human term You; he is not just "someone". If we think of "someone", only one aspect of his truth strikes us, a limited aspect, from one side or the other, showing him as one person among others, so to speak. But the You which God is is with me from all sides, from the roots of my being and of those of others. He is the source which flows in upon me from all sides.

Hence it can happen that we do not directly address God in prayer, but simply remain in his presence without the sound of words or even of thoughts, so to speak, while "our heart watches". This is an effort to acknowledge the greatness of God, that he is
490 infinitely more than "a person"—that he is immense like the ocean. This is also true in another way of Jesus Christ. God is before us fully and personally in Christ. And he too is more than a man. He too comes to us from all sides. And hence we ex-
81 perience in prayer the mystery of the God-man in person. Ultimately, the true Christian prayer must discover again and again that the awe-inspiring surmise with which the whole world fills us is in its profoundest reaches "Someone". This can be seen nowhere more clearly—as Christians believe—than in

the opened heart of Jesus of Nazareth, the only-begotten Son 173
of God. 318

"Lord, teach us to pray"

The request is made again and again: Lord, teach us to pray, in
these days of constant pressure and tumult, in spite of all the
distractions of work, visits, radio, newspapers, traffic, colleagues
and children. How are we to pray now? The difficulty is not
perhaps that we have less time nowadays. The working day
was very much longer in former times. But the whole rhythm
of life is faster and more exhausting. Prayer seems beyond our
strength.

And then there is another difficulty. When we do manage to
speak to God, during a quiet walk, in a church to which we turn
aside or in our bedroom, our prayer is very often not our real
life. It is a world apart, into which in fact we have just withdrawn for a moment. But our real existence, we feel, is in our
family, our work, in the events around us, in the progress of
our country and the world. We must ask the Lord to teach us
how to speak to him with vital sincerity, with joy and frankness.

Many of us must certainly address such requests to God, to
ask for a gift of prayer which will remain part of our ordinary
life. And not be like a museum-piece, possibly visited only
rarely. Can there not be prayer which is a real answer to God's
first word, which is my existence? Yes, of course, there must be.
And the first step is to remember that our first and greatest
answer to God is our life as it is lived: in our care for our family,
our work, our study, our love, our perseverance, our patience
and above all, our obedience to his will. Some saints have
emphasized very strongly that our whole life is a prayer. And
Jesus himself says: "Not every one who says to me, 'Lord, Lord',
shall enter the kingdom of heaven, but he who does the will of
my Father who is in heaven" (Mt. 7:21).

To try to live well—is that prayer enough? It is already a
great deal. And some people do in fact restrict themselves to this.
A day of demanding duties leaves them with little peace. They
manage no more than a prayer which they find fleeting and
unreal. Then they find it more in keeping with God's infinite
mystery to let their ordinary life itself be their answer. This is at
least honest.

But is it fully human? And is it possible in the long run? Is it human to be always silent where we really care for someone? And is it possible to persevere thus in faith and obedience? At the most difficult moment of his life, Jesus gave the warning: "Watch and pray that you may not enter into temptation; the spirit indeed is willing, but the flesh is weak" (Mt. 26:41). We cannot do without watchfulness. Otherwise obedience will deteriorate into self-will. The sense of the presence of God will vanish, and at the moment of trial we will forget his will and disregard it. There can be no work without contemplation, no expansion without exploration in depth. Love cannot exist without self-expression. We saw in the life of Jesus himself how 112–113 he hid himself from men and their sick, in order to pray. After his prayer he was clear about his task—to preach the good news still more widely.

We too have need of prayer, and much more so. We need to speak to God in the depths of our heart. Otherwise we run the risk of imagining that something is our task which is really not our business. We are inclined, after all, to consider our work and our love as much more indispensable than they are. Prayer can teach us that God has other ways. Prayer means detaching ourselves from our prejudices and seeing our existence in the light sent by him who gave us our life.

113–114
344–345 *Prayer and life*

But prayer may not in fact be detached from our daily lives. There can be no religious world apart from our genuine existence. It is therefore necessary to insert our prayer into the real rhythm of our life with all its ups and downs. Our existence is not homogeneous progress. There are times of expansion when all goes well. And there are times of recession, when we are ignored or old or disappointed or sick. There are times of decision and times of just going ahead with our routine. Our way of speaking to God must grow spontaneously from our way of life.

We must not be too ready to imagine that we have mastered this attentive spontaneity. We know it all too little. We sometimes think it means that we should only pray in the way our feelings suggest. But it need not be so. When we consider before God a way of life to be undertaken, or a decision to be made, or when we wrestle with God in our doubts, or even when we are full

of glad thanksgiving—all genuinely in line with our real life—
it may well be that we first have to overcome some indifference
or antipathy. Superficially, we seem to have no taste for it at all.
Nonetheless, our prayer forms spontaneously a unity with our
being. It springs from our real life, and links up with a deeper
"sense" within us. It may well be, indeed, that during our prayer
we experience distaste, restlessness, inner emptiness, distraction
and dryness, while still realizing that we must persevere. Everyone who tries to pray will undoubtedly meet with such difficulties
in prayer. Possibly it is just some such struggle to make contact
that lessens the danger of our constructing a religious world
beside and apart from the real one.

The continuity of prayer and life may mean that we sometimes
just follow routine, sometimes make petitions, sometimes make
thanksgiving, sometimes rejoice, sometimes admire, sometimes
are watchful, and sometimes complain. There may be times
indeed that we cannot even lament, but just remain submissively
dull. Or again we have to try to overcome a distaste for the
things of God which lames our faith and our prayer—a distaste
occasioned by disgust and desolation, or by some faulty attitude
which we refuse to give up.

But ultimately the inner attitude must always be obedience
and love. All flows from this—including our prayer of petition. 116–117
(On this last and on the hearing of prayer see the chapters 119–122
"The teacher of prayer" and "God".) 495–497

Our bodily posture is an expression of our inward attitude,
and can also affect this, so closely are the inward and the outward
united. No attitude is excluded, but kneeling and standing, which
involve the maintaining of equilibrium and a slight discomfort,
are good symbols of readiness, watchfulness, and love. Sitting
on an ordinary chair at table can be a better posture than with
crossed legs in an armchair. Some people find that they can
meditate and pray in calm when they lie down at night, before
going asleep. Still, it is well to have knelt down beforehand to
say a prayer. Some can give their whole heart to the divine
mystery while they take a quiet walk. Many factors have always
to be considered. It is certainly not true that the most comfortable
position is always the best. It is a matter of how to meet God with
the utmost sincerity.

The many ways of prayer

Let us now examine briefly the various ways in which we can pray.

Those who love God will sometimes interrupt their day to say a short word to him. Just as there are many who curse unthinkingly, there are many (or perhaps the same?) who often turn deliberately to God to say "Help me" or "Give me patience" or "Thanks". They are all ways of expressing briefly the great basic attitudes of faith, hope and love. Some men have a quick sense of God's peace in the midst of a fierce rush of business, in a traffic jam or at a party.—And it can also happen that those who have not really spoken to God for a long time, suddenly find words during the repose of their holidays.

A very simple and common way to create a space of peace is to recite set prayers. We must not despise this form of prayer. In a busy life, fixed forms can be a help and an inspiration, as when we say the Our Father and the Hail Mary to ourselves. The sign of the cross before and after are like two doors, between which we are free for God. Even little children learn to be quiet then. Obviously we cannot think of each word during vocal prayer at such times. We have just been cutting bread, the children have just been quarrelling—in fact, there just has been no time for recollection. But the whole gesture is a little pause for peace, an indication of the Other who is among us, an act of thanksgiving.

A greater inward peace is brought about by a longer vocal prayer, as when we use a prayerbook, or recite one or more psalms. Here too one cannot always think of all the words. But they create an atmosphere of peace, so that we can let God's light in on our lives, or say how sad or how grateful our existence makes us.

This is also true of the rosary. The words are so beautiful and monotonous that they make a space of a quarter of an hour in which one can be quiet before God. It was, of course, never intended that we should think of all the words. We can think of the mysteries—or of a troublesome child, a dying neighbour, a newly-married couple for whom we wish to pray.

308–309
160
Early morning is a privileged time for prayer. Many of us would be happier if we got up half an hour earlier and went more quietly about everything each day. The morning hours are golden. And prayer is part of this gold.

Nonetheless, there are many of us who never manage to say morning prayers. Still, we wish to begin the day with God. Many of us will find that the good morning with which we greet one another is something to which the Lord listens attentively. Our love for each other comes from him and ultimately goes to him. We can also utter a short prayer directly to God, and thereby associate ourselves with those who have —or take—time to remain longer with God in the morning.

"Make a joyful noise to the Lord, all the earth!
Serve the Lord with gladness!
Come into his presence with singing!
Know that the Lord is God!
It is he that made us, and we are his;
We are his people, and the sheep of his pasture."
(Ps 100:1–3).
This is part of Sunday Lauds.

Many have the habit of offering each day to God expressly each morning, and this can in fact be a very good thing. But we must bear clearly in mind that it is not the formula nor even the intention but only our obedience to our real task in life that makes our day a day which belongs to God.

Very often, evening prayers well said fit in better than morning prayers in the rhythm of our life. Night-fall is the time of recollection. It is the hour to give thanks, to reflect, to ask pardon, to read some Scripture or some other book. What reason can there be for married people not to pray together to him in whose name they have been married? It can be a very good practice to make night prayers consist in part of a fixed form of words, such as part of a gospel or a psalm, and in part of one's own words, even though very few. Set prayers, as we have seen, form a haven of peace for busy men, while one's own words do much to make prayer real.

As well as morning and night prayers, there is grace at meals. We bless our food before eating and give thanks afterwards. It is one of the ways by which human eating is distinguished from that of the animals. We should not let ourselves grow slovenly at this good family custom. And if it has become slipshod or 160 even disappeared, we should restore it. The form used should not be too babyish. The children pray along with their parents, not the parents with the children.

Holy Mass, as we have seen, is not primarily an occasion of
306-307 private prayer. Nonetheless, there may be moments of stillness
345 in which we can raise our heart to God—along with the congregation, no doubt—in our own words.

A retreat may be an undreamt-of surprise and time of renewal. A retreat means that we ask for the hospitality of a monastery for a few days, or that we retire to a retreat house where we will find suitable books, calm, and men who know the gospel well and are ready to be of service to all who come. A retreat is strongly recommended when one is not satisfied with one's way of life or when one faces a decisive hour in life.

Contemplative prayer

Those who desire to know God better will start to ponder on him reverently. They kneel down. They ponder a prayer word by word—the Our Father, a psalm—or an episode from the gospel, or an attitude to life, such as patience, readiness to be of service and so on. They speak of it to God, and thereby gain insight, force and love. This form of prayer is called meditation, and no one can ever know how much this has meant for the progress of mankind and for goodness in the world.

Those who have made meditation regularly for years (or have tried to meditate, as they will at once say), come to a moment when they cannot do it at all. They try to concentrate their thoughts, but do not succeed. But they want to pray. Their heart wishes to be with God and to be attentive to the divine depths of reality. It sometimes happens that they meet
189 with dryness, or even that they feel distaste or bewilderment.
318-319 Still, something in them wishes to remain at prayer. They feel very strongly that they are doing nothing, but that something is happening to them. And then it sometimes happens that they are filled with the peace of God. They are, as it were, rapt. They feel that God is with them.

This prayer, in which there is much less discursive reasoning, is called the prayer of quiet. Meditation has turned into contemplation. Those who persevere a long time at meditation arrive at this stage. Some think that even then they must continue to reflect and produce thoughts. They fail to realize that they have come to another type of prayer. Here a good adviser can prevent much disturbance and suffering. He will explain that it is not regression but progress. There is no need to try to form thoughts and pronounce words. One is just with God.

Mystical prayer

But the way towards a still greater experience of God's closeness is not yet at an end. Contemplation, with its ups and downs like all love, its periods of light and darkness, grows to a deeper and deeper simplicity. The sense that it is not oneself who acts but God becomes stronger and stronger. This form of prayer is called mystical, though we should not allow ourselves to be misled by the term. It does not mean anything vague and nebulous, but the experience of the closeness of God's power and love. History shows that mystical prayer has often been the centre from which a wide and beneficent activity radiated. An experience of this type is described in Isaiah 6: a mystical experience from which stemmed the whole life and message of the prophet. This chapter describes in external images the unforgettable moment which is the inner source of the whole book of Isaiah, the prophet face to face with God's manifestation. It still echoes in all the liturgies of Christianity, since nowhere in   56 the East or the West does the canon of the Mass begin without the "Holy, holy, holy" of this experience of God.   335

The history of the Church shows us many great men and women who tried to impart the mystical experiences which they had received. In many, like Augustine, Gregory and Bernard, such great graces of prayer do not seem to have been accompanied by miraculous phenomena. To others, such as Teresa of Avila and John of the Cross, they seem to have been familiar. One such by-product is that the body ceases to see or feel. The mystics who have gone through such experiences say   195–196 little about them. They are certain that these extraordinary symptoms are not of the essence. They are concomitant phenomena which may eventually prove a hindrance. No doubt, they were also conditioned by the times in which the mystics in question lived. But they show us, in any case, that powerful forces were at work.

But what the great mystics describe as the supreme grace of prayer is always something different from the miraculous phenomena. It is a sublime ordinariness. Teresa of Avila wrote a book in which the interior man is represented as a castle with seven mansions. Mansion after mansion leads deeper and deeper till we reach the seventh chamber, where God, that is, Christ, dwells. His presence may be sensed throughout the whole castle, but when one reaches the centre, deep at the heart of reality, one is fully pervaded by the quiet sense that God is in one. One lives in the earthly reality, but this has become full of splendour, since one has realized how God is the unutterable core of all reality.

289   Must mysticism be always an individual experience?—No mystic considers himself emancipated from the task of loving mankind. Further, mysticism often flourishes in a religious milieu, where others are also seeking in the same direction. It is something they speak of together.—But mystical rapture in common is rarely described. Augustine tells in his "Confessions" how while he was staying at Ostia, the port of Rome, he had along with his mother a moment of intense experience of God. If we return to the sources we find mystical experiences in
196–197   common at the first Pentecost. And the Easter apparitions, unique though they are, need not be disassociated from the
183–185   history of mysticism. They were, after all, encounters with the risen Lord of a very specially unmistakable type.

Mysticism need not go hand in hand with great holiness, that is, with the greatest possible charity. Many saints seem to have had little experience of mysticism. Some men who were not so holy have been richly endowed with such experiences. And mystical prayer is not found only within the Catholic Church. The chapter on the redemption speaks of mysticism in
285   Islam.

Finally, there is the question as to whether mysticism is out of reach of the ordinary man and woman. There are human lives which at first sight have nothing remarkable about them, except their great goodness. But it may well be that God often elevates their prayer to such a deep and simple joy that it should be called mysticism—if they knew the word. But the term makes little difference.

Sine dolore non vivitur in amore. There is no living in love without pain. Those who tread the lightsome regions of mys-
293–297   ticism must pass again and again through dark valleys of doubt

and near-despair. Even the more ordinary believer who knows the green hills of joyful prayer has passed through foggy and chilly plains. Prayer is not a gentle pastime. Love is put to the test. We must not think of such trials as very outstanding events. 468 They are often unexpectedly banal: the common distaste for prayer (though still with some desire for it), being rather isolated in one's environment, constant doubts and melancholy.

"Even though I walk through the valley of the shadow of death, I fear no evil; for thou art with me" (Ps 23:4).

The psalms   55–56

If we wish to see described briefly all the riches of human attitudes in prayer we may take the hundred and fifty psalms of the Psalter. Some of them are addressed to God, while some of them are meditations on God. They contain lamentations, petitions, hymns of jubilation and thanksgivings. We find there again our security and our insecurity. The language at first sight is strange and antiquated. (The oldest psalms are nearly three thousand years old). But if one perseveres, one sees that nearly all the words and images are still familiar nowadays: helping hands, watchful eyes, gladdening light. The psalter is the collection of poems most often read by the human race: and read with such great intensity! "If I had not had the consolation of the psalms to enliven me, I would have perished in my misery", said the poet Vondel.

The psalms were written before the coming of Jesus. But this does not render them useless for us. In the Old Testament itself their meaning was already being broadened and deepened. Jesus fulfilled them completely, and brought out their deepest 175 truth. We can now pray the psalms along with him, in him, to 60 him, through him and about him. This is something which must be tested by experience.

Sometimes we get no further than a few words in five minutes of the psalms, at other times we go through them speedily. Each of us should find after some time a group of five or six psalms which are very dear to us and will become our own words to God.—Many of the psalms are in the first person plural. And the whole Church prays and sings the psalms together every 113–114 day. This may help us to remember that Christians never come 288–289 before God without at the same time bringing others, as it were.

SUNDAY

437-438 Not to have to work is an almost divine feeling. Sunday, the Lord's Day, is meant in this way. It is to be a day of festival, of being something more than human, of knowing what one works for, of thanksgiving for what one has got. It is a breathing-space in the atmosphere of God. Not to have to work is a sort of divine experience. "The sabbath was made for man, not man for the sabbath" (Mk 2:27). Since New Testament times, Christians have chosen the day of the resurrection as the Lord's Day. The day after the sabbath was when they came together and celebrated the Eucharist, and later, took their solemn weekly rest.

The day of the Eucharist

Sunday still means the same to us. And hence Catholic Christians keep one hour free for the celebration of the Eucharist, as the kernel of the Sunday. This excellent practice is confirmed by a Church precept for which many are grateful, since they know that it has helped them to be faithful in making this very obvious gesture towards God. An hour a week is not too much for those who believe that their lives and happiness come from the hands of God. The existence of the obligation to go to Mass on Sunday 301 does not mean that one does not come with love. The precept is often an assurance against slovenliness and carelessness. It sets one free to do something in which one finds one's real joy.

But we must not measure the faith of others by their frequency in going to church. If a Christian remains for some time blind to the value of Sunday and does not practise the excellent precept, we must not pass judgment on his Christianity. It may be, for instance, that a young person is trying to break with routine. One seeks for a valid motive and hence misses Mass some Sundays.—But it may also be that one stays away for want of 452 confidence in God and generosity. There are many such cases. But dislike of those who go to church is mostly a bad motive. It often goes hand in hand with the thought that the truant is a good man, while the others are not.

What is to be done when growing children come to the stage when they refuse to go to Mass on Sunday? The point is discussed 239-242 in more general terms in the section "Conversion" and "Educa- 408-409 tion for independence". One should let the children see clearly that one takes the matter very seriously, though not fanatically.

At the same time, faith in Christ is free, and cannot be enforced. Where there are younger brothers and sisters, the older ones may be asked to keep them in mind, which they are mostly quite ready to do.

The rest day

Sunday being a festival and a day of rest, the term "servile work" was used in earlier times to define what was to be avoided on Sundays, so as to preserve its proper character. Servile work meant hard manual toil such as digging or hammering, looking after heavy machines and so on.—We do not find the word "servile" very appealing. But we must remember what social protection it signified for slaves and manual and farm workers, that the Church prevented their working one day a week.—Work which appears less heavy, such as painting, doing accounts and so on, has been considered lawful.

But at the present day it is becoming harder and harder to make clear-cut distinctions. We may say as a general rule that anything which disturbs the general atmosphere of the Sunday should be omitted. The Sunday rest is a social and public affair. Sunday is not kept by the individual so much as by the family and the country. Certain types of gardening in muddied boots may well be contrary to the spirit of the day, while social pottering around in the garden may not be. Children again will need other rules than adults. The limits are to be fixed by our own common sense and the general feeling.

It is, in fact, necessary to take the feelings of others into account. There is no reason not to, unless they are making really foolish demands, such as are in fact put forward by those who still insist on bearing the yoke of the ancient covenant in these matters.—Hence we must transpose to Saturday whatever is not suitable to Sunday.

Sunday may therefore be the day on which to go more deeply into the meaning of life and its joys. As well as Mass, there may be a sermon etc. ("liturgy of the word") or a baptism in the afternoon. Sunday may be a day to take up a book which goes more deeply into matters, or to visit a friend, to be with one's wife and children, to make an excursion with them etc. It is the day on which a father can perhaps listen calmly to what his son or daughter has to say, or on which a wife can pay more attention to her husband. It should not be a day of selfish relaxation when we demand extra comforts and consideration. Anyone who takes up this attitude will find that everything disturbs him. Sunday is rather a day on which we should be alert and attentive. It should be a day of greater resilience than the rest of the week—especially the resilience of love. "Where there is love and affection, there is God."

WORDS OF ETERNAL LIFE

183-184 The Easter apparitions show us how the Lord wishes to remain among us always. Hence in the gospel of Luke, the risen Lord explains the Scriptures in his own words. He wishes to remain with us also through his word. And we can always sense the sound of his voice and the purpose of his Spirit among us in the
60 Old and New Testament. The word is among us as an efficacious
208-209 sign from the Lord, just like the other symbols of life which he gives, the sacraments—which are in fact not administered
252-256 without words. Hence it is possible to speak of the "sacrament of the word".

A household book

And like the seven sacraments, we find God's word in the community of the Church. It is entirely a community matter. Let us look at the life of the early Church. It was consoled by the words of Jesus which were handed on by the eye-witnesses: "The Lord said . . .";—or rather, their attitude was slightly
146-147 different: "The Lord says . . ." He was the living Lord. And through his Spirit he reminded Christians of what he had said, and taught them what he still wished to say.

Here and there such preaching was written down. Along with the oral tradition written records were made of it. The writings belonged to the community. They had grown out of it. And when many years later fantastic and heretical books began to circulate about Jesus, the Church determined which books were
211 reliable. The Church established the canon, that is, the official list of the books of the New Testament, as we know it. This was about A.D. 150.

When we reflect on the matter, it must seem a very remarkable event. The teaching and authoritative community passes judgment on the Bible—deciding what belongs to it or not. Did it do so because it had carefully investigated what books contained reliable tradition? The Church did in fact make careful enquiries, which were directed by the fact that the books were in use in the Church and by the convincingly apostolic character 208 of their contents. But the ultimate certainty did not stem from such examination. It came from the authority of the Church itself. In other words, it came from the conviction that in such important decisions the Church is not abandoned by the Spirit of Jesus. When the Church speaks expressly as such, through a council gathered along with the successor of Peter, or through 365–368 the words of the successor of Peter alone (but never disconnected from the other bishops), we believe that the Spirit of God does not mislead us.

But then, if the Church can clearly speak in the name of God's Spirit, is not the Bible superfluous? On the contrary. The Church knows—because it has determined so itself in obedience to the Spirit—that Scripture contains its fundamental rule and standard—the word of God from which it cannot stray a hair's-breadth.

What all this means is that sacred Scripture is the household book of the Church. If the book is separated from the Church, enormous difficulties arise. A vital bond is broken. This is the tragedy of the Reformation. Since the Church was denied its authority as the court guaranteed by the Spirit of God for the interpretation of the Bible, the word of God has been understood in the most diverse ways, and many ecclesial communities have sprung up, each with their own explanation.

The word of God in the Reformation

While we are discussing these matters, we must say a word on the place which the Bible holds in the minds of Christians of the Reformation.

1. Sacred Scripture did not lose its power outside the Catholic Church. It remains the consoling word of Jesus' revelation. Just as baptism is efficacious among other Christians, according to the doctrine of the Catholic Church, so too it recognizes that they listen to God's word.

2. On closer inspection, it appears that the Reformers happily took more with them than the Bible. They took, for instance,

part of a Church fellowship (that is, good men in the tradition of Christ), and also some authoritative oral tradition. The Reformation is not just a shelf of books. To say so would be a caricature of it. Young Protestants do not find the Bible in a library or by the roadside or dropped from heaven. They get it from their parents and preachers—in a word, from the living community, from which they derive both text and interpretation. There is nothing to be ashamed of in this. On the contrary, it means that the word of Christ is never isolated from a living, speaking Church fellowship.

3. Hence the Churches of the Reformation, even as bodies, are not left without Christ, without his Spirit. They continue to uphold and develop Christian truth and goodness. "The Christian way of life led by these brothers is nourished by their faith in Christ, and strengthened by the grace of baptism and the hearing of God's word. It is a way of life which is manifested in personal prayer and meditation on the Bible, in a Christian family life and in the worship of the community when it assembles to praise God" (Vatican Council II, Decree on Ecumenism, no. 23).

Does this mean that, as is sometimes said, it does not matter whether one is Protestant or Catholic? That all that matters is the one Christ?—This is often said by people who are not Christians, and hence only superficially affected. It is also often said by those who apparently at least do not take very seriously the full message of Scripture. It is heard less often from those who try to belong to Christ with their whole heart and soul—whether Protestant or Catholic. Those who try to remain really attentive to the words of Jesus, and really try to live according to his Spirit, see ... of course, that there is only one Christ. They recognize the words of Jesus among the others. But at the same time, they see precisely that there is a difference. Men are not united by denying the existence of divisions, but by overcoming them. More was said of this in the chapter on Church schisms.

222–227

4. However, there is more to be said here. The fact that men know Christ outside the Catholic community does not leave Catholics unaffected. It is not as if the tree continued to grow triumphantly as though nothing had happened. There remains a wound, a void. Certain elements of life develop outside the Catholic Church. It misses ecclesial elements that would enrich it. In the sixteenth century, it felt the loss of Luther as prophet

and doctor of the Church. This loss was all the graver because the Church showed itself hesitant about certain values simply because they were emphasized by Protestants, such as a certain biblical spirituality, certain particularities (such as the vernacular) in the liturgy, a certain personal responsibility for the faith and a certain freedom—and even certain music: the Protestant hymnals.

Hence it is not only the Reformation which must be looked on as suffering from the loss of the truth of the Catholic Church. The Catholic Church also shows traces of not exploiting fully the truths of the Reformation. This "has made it harder for the Catholic Church to realize the fullness of Catholicity in every aspect of the reality of life" (Vatican Council II, Decree on Ecumenism, no. 4). Candidly, we may say that the Church at present does not perhaps look as if it were capable of absorbing the Reformation. We all have to evolve together, towards a new Catholic, that is, universal Church. This does not mean a Church 230-231
where the wine of Christ's truth is watered down. But it means a Church where forms and opinions which are not essential will be transformed and remoulded. We must try gradually to learn the joy of not merely expounding the truth to each other, but of seeing each other's truth and receiving it from each other.

We know that we never possess the truth neatly wrapped up in a closed compartment. The times are always new, the Church must always seek further for God's view of the human world. The Bible is always full of new life. What we know as Catholics is that the direction in which we are going is right. The signposts are placed correctly. This is the confidence which we have in the Spirit who leads the Church throughout the ages. 365-366

We have thus spoken of the two forms in which Christ's words resound among us: the living word of sacred Scripture and the word of the living community, the Church. It is sad that on such an occasion we have to speak of a division among Christians. But we must face the difficulty. Jesus too had to discuss scriptural questions and defend the authority of his mission. But our wish is that the world could see us less as divided, and more and more as working together. "The co-operation of all Christians is a vivid expression of the bond which already unites them and manifests more clearly the visage of Christ, the servant of all" (Vatican Council II, Decree on Ecumenism, no. 12).

The sects

We have not yet spoken of the sects. By these we mean groups of Christians who do not feel at home either in Catholic or in Protestant ecclesial communities. We have no room here to discuss such movements exactly and adequately. We prefer to refer our reader to the existing literature on the subject.

It may be said in general that one of the most striking features of the sects is that they interpret the Bible very literally, while attending mainly to one or only a few aspects of the biblical message. Very often, they concentrate intensely on the imminent return of the Lord. They mostly recruit among the more simple of believers. They mostly form small groups, and recognize no special priestly functions in any of their members. Anyone can come forward and all are equally competent. Some sects, like the Jehovah's Witnesses, have a tendency to turn against society and against existing Churches and ecclesial communities. The Mormons and the Seventh Day Adventists are also sects, and there are many others. The Pentecostal movement cannot always be called simply a sect. It often includes groups of a more ecclesial character, aiming at evangelization and revival. Sometimes they include ecumenical movements, which are totally lacking in the sects as such.

The existence of all these sectarian groups is a challenge to the Church which may not be lightly dismissed. They seem to offer something that is missing in the Church as known to many people—a closely-knit community at a local level, with opportunities of sharing, enthusiasm and self-sacrifice. The sects have been described as the Churches' unpaid bills. They are made up of men who have suffered from the routine and one-sidedness which are to be found in the Churches at all times. The sects seek to solve the problem by forming splinter-groups or at least separate ones. But is this the way of fruitful reform? One initial answer is to look at the monastic communities and other groups which have based themselves on the evangelical counsels. These were efforts to live together on a footing of equality before God. Since there is no marriage, no one ever becomes a member of the community by being born or by following convention, but only by vocation and conversion. The religious congregations with their various forms of spirituality are a response to the constant wish to live the message of the Lord freshly and intensely and in small groups. They provide a concrete opportunity of great dedication to God and men. One can only hope that they will draw inspiration from the daily life of the faithful in general and renew themselves constantly so as to preserve their first youth. They will then be a divine yeast in the living Church, and a call to all Christians to realize in suitable forms the self-sacrifice and joy of the first community in Jerusalem.

The word as food for all times

Apart from the question of what the word of God means as a whole, the main lines of which are propounded by the magisterium, there is the other question about the meaning of Scripture: what does the word of God say to me and to us here and now? The Bible is an ancient book; its language is solemn and remote. How can I rediscover the message of Jesus in its constant relevance for each age?

Here too the primary answer must be: in the community. There the word is explained and distributed, as bread is broken and distributed. The language of God is rendered anew in modern words and fresh terms. This too is the way Jesus speaks in the Church.

Such modern commentary shows us, for instance, how the Old Testament was already a preparation for Jesus. We see how the fulfilment was already latent therein—like the tulip hidden in the bulb. The Old Testament stories can be seen as symbols of Jesus' work. Jesus himself constantly alluded to them in this sense. The Church makes free use of them. (See also the paragraph, "The spiritual sense of Scripture".)   60–61

We then found we were justified in speaking of God's word as Christ's word. The whole of Scripture, including the Old   322 Testament, has become a message about him ever since his coming. Things that were remote and material in the old order have become, through him, profound, close and spiritual in the new. The manna is now his body which is for us. The promised land is his promises to us. The brazen serpent is his salutary death for mankind. The preaching of the Church searches the ancient scriptures in this way, to make them new and relevant for us.

It is important to emphasize that this modernization is always spiritualization. Some people miss this point and then the wars

in the Old Testament are seen as symbols of the wars we are fighting. In the New Testament, however, the great battle is
61 not against flesh and blood, but against the forces of evil in ourselves and others. This is the ultimate meaning of the wars of the Old Testament.—It has also sometimes been thought that the curse laid upon Ham and his eldest son was to be taken in its material sense. Slave-dealers appealed to the Bible by quoting, "A slave of slaves shall he be to his brothers" (Gen. 9:25). This was to forget that the New Testament says that all men were slaves to sin but were saved by grace, so that there is no longer slave or free in the sight of Christ, but only a new creation. Thus the whole Bible became in this way, through the New Testament, a message about Jesus. The letter—which kills—has become spirit. (Here we may read the difficult but profoundly vital considerations of Paul in 2 Cor. 3:6–18.)

But even the New Testament has to be constantly read anew (strange as it may seem) in a way which will make it relevant and topical. Even in the New Testament it is possible to remain involved in the letter which kills. The preaching has to show us how every passage speaks of us. A lame man is cured. But what does this mean to us? Jesus himself suggests during the
111 cure that sin is the greatest paralysis, and that he has come to cure this. This was the end and object of his coming, and it still concerns us.

Sooner or later we discover that every page of Scripture concerns us. I am Adam, we are the family of Noah, we are the Apostles on the stormy lake, we are, just like Jesus, on the way to Calvary and the resurrection.

As we thus go slowly through God's word, we discover how our life appears in God's eyes, what are the real dimensions of our life. We can see how safe we are, how imperilled, how sinful, how loved and how greatly filled with grace.

51 The preaching cannot proclaim this profound meaning of Scripture unless it also proclaims that events really took place. This is what is done by the first cry of the heralds, the first kerygma (see the paragraph, "The most ancient testimony
209-210 to Jesus"). The Christian faith is not a myth. That is, it is not a sort of fairy-tale which comprises deep truths about human life without proclaiming facts which occurred in history. Scripture contains a reality which is valid for us because it contains things which actually took place. The language in

which the story is told is really interwoven with the inexpressible reality of God's manifestation in history. When reading the Bible, we must try to register faithfully the tensions, the emphasis and the movement which are intrinsic to the text itself. In this way we shall come all the more easily and adequately both to the elements which are valid for us and to the real history (the inexpressible experience) of those days.

51
208

The Church's care for the preaching

365

The explicit approbation of the whole Church is not, of course, demanded for every word of interpretation. But care is undoubtedly taken that the official explanation remains linked to the magisterium. This is done as follows. Before a preacher goes into the pulpit as part of the liturgical office he must have permission from the local bishop, that is, from the successor to the Apostles in the place. Further, he must have been ordained deacon or priest. But if one of the faithful who is not ordained preaches a sermon with the permission of the local pastor, this need not be regarded as a breach of the great traditional line. This link with the hierarchy, and thus with the whole, safeguards the Christian people against interpreters whose words might run contrary to the Spirit of God. The responsibility of the bishop is very great in these matters. The official interpretation through priests and deacons is the norm for the more ordinary exposition, which takes place in books, periodicals, lectures, theological societies, biblical associations and the discussions of the ordinary faithful among themselves and with those of different beliefs. It is also the guiding line for one's own further investigation of what one has read in the light of faith in the Bible.

365

361-362

Hence our reading and discussion of sacred Scripture outside the liturgy, in the family, in the monastery, in clubs or alone, can be sure of the help of the Holy Spirit. As regards the great lines of the message, one knows that one is united with the fellowship of the Church which is filled with the Spirit. As regards the meaning of God's word in our daily lives, we may trust that the Spirit of Jesus will enlighten and inflame us when we ourselves search the Scriptures. We must not be afraid of applying the words personally to ourselves. It was formerly the custom in religious instruction to warn people emphatically against private interpretation—really against the wrong use of free enquiry to explain the great lines of the message apart from the fellowship of the Church. But this made many of the faithful afraid to seek personal consolation and spiritual understanding directly from the source of God's word. We must have confidence that what we ourselves find will strengthen us, even though our interpretation may well be capable of improvements.

At present there are many excellent books and periodicals available for the study of Scripture. It costs some trouble to begin, but the result is often great peace.

The word and the community

When we read the Scriptures with the eyes of faith, we feel one of the great forces that flow from the word: that it makes us one. On the first Pentecost, three thousand men—and men of 195–196 many different nationalities—were united by the words which Peter spoke in the Spirit of Jesus. It was the opposite of what happened at Babel. The word of God has still preserved this unifying force. We are not listening in isolation, each of us concentrating silently on the voice in his own heart. We are 125 listening together for the voice of one who is present for us all 288–289 together. The Church as a whole, the parish where one listens, a religious house which worships together, even the tiny society of man and wife reading together a page of the Bible in the evening—they all know that they are united more closely in the love of Christ and in the love of each other, by the word of God.

This does not mean that the word works automatically. Some Christians fancy that there is a sort of magic in the word. If the Bible is just read aloud, something good has taken place; if the Bible is merely sold, good has been done. But this is not true. The Bible is the book of the Church. This means that there must be fellowship, a common bond, some communion of spirit, before one is allowed to utter the word of God. This is also true when dealing with non-Christians. When we take up the word of God, there must be some sense and reality of community. Sometimes the Spirit of Jesus is more truly present when we talk about the weather, but really make contact with a lonely man, than when we quote a fine text of Scripture at such a moment. "A proverb from a fool's lip will be rejected, for he does not tell it at its proper time" (Ecclus. 20:20). But

330

some people can produce a word of consolation straight from the Bible, without seeming artificial. They can be a great help at such moments. Thus the word of God is a living thing on the lips of countless Christians. It is like the falling rain that does not dry before it has accomplished something, growth and new life, however slight.

We may add here a quotation from Erasmus, himself a wit and a humorist, which may help to preserve a balance where necessary: "There are people today who try to show how clever and humorous they are by turning the deep and mysterious words of Scripture into cheap jests. This is not only a lack of culture. It is also a lack of piety."

The liturgy of the word

We cannot end this chapter without saying a word about the most social aspect of the word, its presence in the liturgy. There are forms of worship where the word is used apart from the liturgy. Prayer, hymn-singing, reading and exposition 160 bring God's word to us. But the official liturgy of the word for all the faithful is that with which each holy Mass begins. Just as the Passover was a memorial which included the story of the escape from Egypt as well as the eating of the paschal 163-164 lamb, so too the liturgy of the word precedes the liturgy of the repast, to recall what God has accomplished among us. The liturgy of the word consists of an introductory chant and prayer followed by two or more readings from Scripture. The last reading is always taken from one of the four gospels, and the congregation stand up for it ("the gospel"). The other readings 147 are taken from other parts of the Old or New Testament, very often from one of the epistles of the Apostles (whence the general title of "the epistle"). A chant from the psalms is inserted between the readings. This commemoration of God's great works through Scripture is only complete when we discover how these works of God live on in us. Hence the gospel is followed at once by the explanation—the sermon or homily.

Readings and sermon together form the first great high-point of the celebration of the Eucharist. The atmosphere is that of attentive listening. All that breaks the stillness (such as the jingling of coins at the collection) is just as much out of place at these moments as during the canon of the Mass.

Listening is an activity. To commemorate the work of God

and to rediscover it in oneself is not a mechanical or passive performance, like letting a wireless set run on which has been switched on by accident. We need patience and faith. Otherwise one is interested only when from time to time a gifted speaker appears in the pulpit. But the point is to take something with one from the ordinary preacher, even the less gifted priest and indeed from the less inspired. He addresses us, even if he is somewhat too stilted or commonplace or highbrow or lowbrow for us. If we open our ears and our hearts, we shall hear the Lord speaking to us.

79 On Sundays and feastdays, after the sermon, the liturgy of the word is closed by the confession of faith (the credo), recited or chanted in common. It is our answer to the word of our Lord. Then the transition to the Eucharistic sacrifice is made by the prayers which express the needs of mankind and of the congregation before God.

163–168   THE EUCHARIST

"In memory of me"

It often happens in a new parish that when the congregation transfers from the temporary church to the great new parish church there is a slight sense of disappointment. The new church is finer, more solid and spacious, and no one would want to go back to the old one. Still, the little barn-like building had something special about it. Everything was awkward, but it sometimes seemed easier to pay attention to what was happening.

What was happening? What the Lord did. That is the important thing. In all that can be said about holy Mass, this must always be the first thing to dwell on. The Church does what the Lord did. On the night before he suffered, he took bread in his hands, the bread that was on the table, the Passover bread. Giving thanks and pronouncing words of blessing, he broke it and distributed it, saying: Take and eat of it, all of you. For this is my body. So too he also blessed the cup with the wine, passed it round and said: Take and drink of it, all of you, for this is the cup of my blood, of the new and eternal covenant, which shall be poured out for you and for many, for the forgiveness of sins.

When the action of Christ is re-enacted, it is not important to repeat his words exactly. The Lord did not leave us a sort of magical formula. Thus Scripture transmits the words in four different forms. The Church now uses a fifth formulation which is a combination of the four forms given in Scripture. But the meaning is the same in all five cases.—We have already spoken of the last supper in this catechism. We shall now rather consider how it is celebrated in the Church.

At the last supper, Jesus gave the command: "As often as you do this, you shall do it in memory of me." These words give us the deepest reason *why* the Church does what the Lord did. It is in order to think of him. This is the beginning of all initiation into this mystery. Let us suppose for instance that you have a child who is making his first communion and that you have to prepare him. Or that something has been explained at school, and that the child questions you about it. When answering, you may take it for granted first and foremost that a child does not need to understand everything. He may be far from understanding everything, but he can still go to communion. (In ancient Christian times, and up to the present day in the eastern Churches, one can see babies receiving communion in their mothers' arms.) It is only gradually that one learns the deeper secrets of this mystery. The question for the moment is how the child is to be given its first notions of it. This should be done by *narrating* what our Lord *did*. One must speak of 163–167 what happened at the last supper, of the Apostles, the bread, the wine, Jesus' death, and of how he rose again on Easter Sunday. One must recall that the Apostles met every Sunday to celebrate the Eucharist and so to recall his death and resurrection. One must say that this is what we are still doing today. With this, the kernel, the most profound part of the Eucharist has been explained.

Riches of meanings

Let us return now to the world of adults. Strictly speaking, we are all always children in face of God's mysteries. We go through the actions, but the mystery which is unfolded before us remains to some extent incomprehensible. The Eucharist has often been pondered, discussed and written about. And new light can still be thrown on it in each age. It is the focus of all the great realities of faith. Hence it is not surprising that in each period of Church history new facets and values are revealed in this so divinely simple gesture. At one time Christians stress their unity. At other times, thanksgiving to the Father. Then again, the sacrifice. Or Jesus' presence. And there must still be treasures as yet undiscovered within the mystery. Jesus is always new in his greatest mystery.

The Church has been charged to transmit and safeguard this gift. It is convinced that the Spirit of God will not permit it to
365 err in this matter. Hence in the course of centuries, councils of the Church have pronounced upon it. They did not aim at determining exhaustively and for all time all the truth of the mystery. The words they used were often formulations meant to defend very definite Christian truths and values at a certain period, against certain errors. To understand properly the teachings of the councils, one must always ask: what Christian and evangelical values were at stake at the time? When we know what was being defended, we must then proclaim the same truths in the language of our own day.

This we say to reassure some believers, who are disturbed when they hear truths of faith propounded in a different way, and above all, when they see matters that were once considered to be of primary interest now put in a less prominent place. For instance, in the Netherlands catechism of 1910 the real presence of Jesus was given as the first reason which led Jesus to institute this gift. The purpose of recalling Jesus' death came only second, to be followed in the third place by his desire to be our nourishment, and fourthly by the wish to leave us a sacrifice. The catechism of 1948, however, puts the real presence in the last place. This does not mean that it is denied. All it means is that at present the Church does not feel the need of contemplating this truth apart from the others, as did earlier Christian ages. It was perhaps necessary in former times, when there were errors which denied the presence. But now we prefer to look on the real presence less in isolation and more in the context of the mystery as a whole. At the end of this chapter further
342-345 explanations will be given on this point.

The process of celebration

After these introductory remarks, we take up the actual description of the Eucharist, beginning with the structure of the celebration. The Eucharist proper, the "service of the table", is always preceded by the "service of the word"—discussed in the previous chapter under the heading of the "liturgy of 330–331 the word". The Eucharistic service itself consists of three parts— the offertory, the canon and the communion.

There are really only two parts, since the offertory is merely a preparation for the canon. During the offertory the ministers at the altar and the people in the church go, so to speak, their own different ways. The priest prepares bread and wine and washes his hands. The congregation is often preoccupied with the collection. The effect is somewhat disorderly, but this is no great harm. After the quietness of the liturgy of the word and before the attentiveness of the canon a certain relaxed atmosphere is permissible.

Previously, great stress was laid on the offertory as the offering of oneself to God. But it is a preparation for the canon, which is Christ's own offering, and ours in him. The inward attitudes proper to this preparatory stage are repose, prayer and recollection. A final prayer over the gifts forms the transition to the canon.—The canon begins with a set of greetings and a chant (the "preface"), ending with the "Sanctus", which is inspired by the words of Isaiah 6, and is found in all the liturgies 317 of the East and West. It indicates what the basic attitude is to be—one of profound reverence. The canon itself contains thanksgiving, sacrifice and an invitation to eat. It centres on the narrative of what Jesus did on the night before he suffered. This narrative is the climax of the Eucharist, as the Church believes. The church is silent. Some years ago, many of the faithful made the sign of the cross and beat their breasts, so as at least to have something to do at this moment. But now we only look upwards. Some say silently to themselves the paschal words of the Apostle Thomas, "My Lord and my God!". One could also repeat some of the words said on Calvary, such as, "This is indeed the Son of God". Or one need say nothing at all. The basic effort must always be to remember Jesus Christ. The consecration is a holy and privileged moment in the canon. But the whole canon shares in this holiness.

At the end of the canon comes the Lord's Prayer, which forms the introduction to the reception of the body and blood of Jesus at communion, that is, in the act of union.—Some prayers follow, and then Mass ends with the blessing and the dismissal of the congregation. This dismissory blessing was called the *missio* or *missa*, and strangely enough, it gave rise to one of the most common names for the Eucharist—holy "Mass". This short word which is so easily pronounced has remained the most common term for the Eucharist down to the present day.—Such is the celebration of the Eucharist in its main outlines. For the details, the reader is referred to the actual celebration itself.

This summary mention of offertory, canon, and communion has not really told us much. What do they mean when taken together as a unity? What is the point, purpose and essence of the whole? Is the whole Eucharist an assembly, or a repast or something else again?—We shall begin with what we see and hear, as we look for the significance of the Mass.

Together to remember

The first thing we see is that we have come together. This is not just a necessary presupposition. It is significant. We live alongside each other, but sometimes remain inwardly very far from each other. But now we come together to experience
253 above all that we are men together, saved and called by Christ. In other words, it is not just a working party, it is so to speak a festal gathering, a reunion. Christ is the host, and he invites us to come together, in the name of the Father. He often spoke of the kingdom of God under the imagery of a meal.

It is not accidental that the Eucharist begins with the liturgy of the word. We become one as we listen, as the unifying word
330 of God is read out to us (on which see the previous chapter). Even what takes place before the readings, prayer together, community singing, already forms a bond.

This opening is not a superfluous luxury. After all, we are
98–102 not so very much united when we come together from all "the streets and the lanes of the city", spiritually often "poor and maimed and blind and lame" (cf. Lk. 14:21), indeed, "both bad and good" (Mt. 22:10). We do not know one another. We are not interested in one another. There is a certain amount of aloofness, as between the great man and the common man, the shopkeeper and the artist, the eccentric and the sedate, between neighbour and neighbour and indeed between one member of the family and another. And if we include the clergy, there is another element of strangeness.

We find ourselves therefore before God, on the only occasion when we assemble as the Christian people, in some disorder. Can such a group become one? And can it be united in a place where there is so little intimacy, where everyone keeps his distance? Would it not be better to give up and go home and let each of us pray alone? Or at least to allow each of us to make his own silent prayer to God in Church?

This is not the mind of Jesus. The eighteenth chapter of Matthew's gospel contains various sayings of our Lord about the Church. It is a treasury of precepts about how to be and live together. The main points are as follows. Who is the greatest? He who is like a child.—Woe to those who give scandal.—There is more joy about one lost sheep recovered than about ninety-nine others.—How can I act fairly if another sins gravely?—We must forgive one another, because our own sin is greater.—And in the middle of the chapter comes one of the pearls among Jesus' sayings: "Where two or three are gathered in my name, there am I in the midst of them."

Jesus invites us to come together. This has in fact made much 233 unity possible and obviously desirable in the Christian Churches. Certainly, no one finds it strange that at our altar rails we see together such diverse types as the slum-dweller and the big business man, the school-girl, the house-wife and the sculptor. Before Jesus, we take it for granted that our differences disappear. He has made us children of the one Father. This is why our equality in the Church is taken so much for granted—though it is of course not uniformity. Each of us is called to develop along the lines of his own personal gifts.

Eucharist as thanksgiving

But we have not yet come to the real purpose of the Mass. Why have we thus come together? We must look at the actual celebration.—From beginning to end it is a prayer to the Father. This is not accidental, because at the centre of the Mass we find the gospel narrative which relates how Jesus took bread and *gave thanks*. In some prayers of the liturgy which have been preserved since ancient times, but have now fallen into disuse, this element of praise and thanksgiving was much clearer. In our present canon, which is in fact very ancient, there are undoubtedly many prayers of petition and offering, but the jubilant preface with the Sanctus at the opening of the canon, the narrative of the last supper in the middle of it, and the whole atmosphere of prayer there itself, makes the Mass for us an act of praise and thanksgiving. The canon ends, for instance, with the words: "Through him (Christ) and with him and in him is to thee, God the Father almighty, in the unity of the Holy Spirit, all honour and glory, for ever, Amen." Hence the Greek name for the whole celebration is *eucharistia*, that is, thanksgiving.

Prayer of petition is also uttered in the course of this thanksgiving. We pray for the Church, for the needs of those present and the absent, of the living and the dead. There is a custom of putting some special "intention" before God at Mass—of asking for some particular thing.

The common meal

We have thus found what we were looking for: the real purpose of the Mass, which is thanksgiving. But there are also other elements. We come together in a place where a table is set, with bread on a dish, and wine ready in a cup. During the canon we hear the words, Take and *eat*, and then people do eat and drink. Hence Mass is an assembly in the form of a meal. The body of Jesus is offered to us.

342 We shall speak later in the chapter of the way in which our Lord is present in this sacrament. Here we note above all that it is to a meal that we are invited, where Christ is not only the giver of the meal, but the food itself. And the food is also a memorial of his death.—The broken bread is his body. The wine consecrated separately is his blood poured out. In biblical thought, both blood and body signify in a certain sense the whole man. Both by eating and drinking we receive the whole Jesus.

The Eucharist as a meal signifies: 1. that the Lord nourishes us; 2. that he thereby makes us one with himself; 3. that he makes us one with each other. These three things are intrinsically connected.—The element of nourishment in this meal is strongly emphasized in John 6. "He who eats my flesh and drinks my blood has eternal life" (Jn 6:54). His life, his Spirit, strengthens us and makes us live and grow through this gift.

Our union with Christ is also described in John. "He who eats my flesh and drinks my blood abides in me, and I in him" (Jn 6:56). This too is the work of the Spirit.

Finally, we are united to one another as we eat. We read in 1 Corinthians 10:16, 17: "The bread which we break, is it not participation in the body of Christ? Because there is one bread, we who are many are one body, for we all partake of the same bread." Thus our assembly is suddenly given a bond of union all its own. By eating his body, we remain—and become still more—his body. This too is the work of the Spirit of Christ. 211-212

But a question remains. Is there not something strange about this combination of a meal and a thanksgiving? Are they not mutually exclusive? One may eat or one may praise God, but not do both at the same time! But we saw in the chapter on the last supper that the Jewish passover combined the two things. They sang and gave thanks as they ate, in memory of the liberation from slavery. So too at Mass, we give thanks during a repast, in memory of the liberation from sin. We are still accustomed to combine laudatory remarks with eating and drinking when we drink a toast to somebody. At Mass, he who is addressed is the ultimate source of the joy which we commemorate: the Father of Jesus and of us. 163-164

"The new testament in my blood" 165-166
281-282

Thus we have a meal in common and thanksgiving in common. Have we seen all the aspects and meanings of the Mass? If we continue to gaze and to listen, we shall find still another aspect. We hear in the canon words which signify that a sacrifice is being offered. What does this mean?

At the last supper, Jesus already made present the sacrifice of his life. It was a prophetic action—an "anticipatory memorial". It was a memorial which already made the death on the cross really present in the symbol. The broken bread was Jesus' broken body. And every time that the Church does this, and so proclaims Jesus' death, Jesus' one sacrifice is there in the Church.

Man's desire to offer sacrifice, which existed "since Abel", has here a sacrifice which he can put before God without being ashamed. Friendship between the Father and us is definitively restored by this sacrifice—the new friendship, the new covenant or testament. The covenant of the old friendship was concluded by means of sacrifice—on Sinai, at the Exodus. The new friendship arose through the offering of a life. The ancient passover was a memorial of the old friendship, but only a memorial. When we, on the other hand, recall our new friendship, the sacrifice of the covenant is really there among us. We 38 are enabled to partake in mankind's definitive sacrifice—not a goat or an ox, but the Son.

> If the sprinkling of defiled persons with the blood of goats and bulls and with the ashes of a heifer sanctifies for the purification of the flesh, how much more shall the blood of Christ, who through the eternal Spirit offered himself without blemish to God, purify our conscience from dead works to serve the living God (Heb. 9:13, 14).

To join in the celebration of Mass is to partake of this sacrifice and to be associated in the making of the covenant between God and his people. It takes place not amid the thunders of Sinai, but with the joyful and festal simplicity of bread and wine, in thanksgiving and among beloved companions.

Our attitude as the offerers of sacrifice is a very special one. The sacrifice has already been offered. Strictly speaking, we offer no other sacrifice than the sacrifice of Christ. No other offering is demanded of us. We join in with the one sacrifice—especially by eating. The repast and the sacrifice are not to be separated. The sacrifice is a repast; that means that we receive it, taking and eating. "Take and eat"—these are the words with which it was given. What we offer is offered to us.—But are not the bread and wine which we offered some sort of sacrifice on our part? No, the offertory was merely a preparatory gesture, setting things apart for the one true sacrifice which is the body and blood of Jesus.—With this, we have undoubtedly named all the significant aspects of which the Eucharist is composed.

Many meanings, one experience

But we must still note that each of the meanings embraces the *whole* of the eucharistic process. Each of them comprises offertory, canon and communion at once. Thus the whole celebration is a repast, a thanksgiving, and a sacrifice. And the basic factors which form the profound background of the whole—memorial and covenant—also take in the whole Eucharist, and also all its three aspects.

An element which we have merely mentioned incidentally, and which we shall discuss further on in this chapter, is the presence of Jesus in all this. His presence gives depth and background to repast, thanksgiving, and sacrifice.

A practical question might be this. Is not the multiplicity of meanings in this sacrament somewhat confusing? Strictly speaking, this raises the question as to whether Jesus really intended so many meanings. As regards this last question, we are convinced that it must be answered in the affirmative. The deeper a symbol is rooted in the realities of everyday life—eating 254 and drinking, body and blood—the greater the multiplicity of meanings that it contains. And we also believe that the Spirit of 246 Jesus does not allow the Church to err in its interpretation of this gift. We firmly believe that each of the meanings given above was implicit in Jesus' intention.

But there is the practical question, of whether we can realize all these meanings at once. There are so many structures combined in one, and pervading them all the factors of memorial, covenant and presence. It does not seem feasible to try to keep them all in mind at once. There is no doubt one element which, it would appear, should never be quite lost sight of: the memory of what our Lord did. He himself insisted on this. But as we think of the Lord, one or other aspect of the great riches present will stand out. Some will always have one main structure in mind, such as eating together or giving thanks. Others will now think of one aspect, now of another, sometimes of some aspects at the same time. And as they do so, they will be affected each time to some extent by different aspects of the background—memorial or covenant and so on. Others will simply allow the mystery to penetrate them. It is all a matter of personal preference, of the form of the celebration, of one's education, and even of the age in which one lives.

Some further questions arise about how we celebrate the Eucharist.

Does it follow from the fact that one goes to communion that one always experiences Mass as a repast? This does not necessarily follow. One may, for instance, accept the gift very specifically with thanksgiving and so experience the whole of Mass as thanksgiving. And one can also use communion to unite oneself very specially with Jesus' sacrificial death and with his resurrection. One may also do nothing special after communion except look at the others, with whom one is at one in Jesus. Thus one makes Mass an experience of fellowship. (This can be a very difficult form of prayer, which may demand self-conquest.) And so on.

341

Now let us take the same question the other way round. Can someone who does not communicate experience Mass as a meal? He certainly can. When we consider Mass as a meal, we must not concentrate on the food, but also include our being together. At a family meal, or at a banquet, the fact of being together, the social element, is often as important as the food. Hence it may well be said that one who does not communicate can still join in the Mass as a meal, under a certain aspect. This is all the truer, because ultimately the food at the Eucharist is Jesus. One makes a certain contact with him by participating even if one does not communicate.—But the more one thinks of it, the stranger it appears to go to Mass without going to communion. Jesus intended the Eucharist to be, as he said, taken and eaten. One must not be too ready to think that one is not worthy enough to receive Christ. We are never worthy, but still he invites us.

Jesus present in the signs

We could close the chapter here, if we had not left one of the great realities practically untouched. It is a reality which, as we have already said, permeates the whole: the presence of Jesus. We must therefore try to penetrate further into this unfathomable mystery. Let us begin by taking a very human and ordinary point of view.

101   When the Apostles ate together with Jesus during the time of his earthly existence, there was something between them all. The presence of someone like Jesus is not a minor element. When he was dead, they were together for his sake. He was the bond which linked them together. There was still "something" between them—that which was there when the Lord ate with them, something of his presence. All the more so, since they knew from his apparitions that he was alive. All the more so, since they had received power from his Holy Spirit. All the more so, because they knew they had to remember him in this way: by repeating his words and by taking bread and saying what he said at the last supper.

Thus there remains, when his Church assembles—even today—that special, beneficent element, the presence which was there when the Apostles ate together with Jesus in Galilee and Judea. This presence is linked with the bread. His words proclaim it: This is my body. And the bread itself shows it. He is as close and life-giving as food, in his presence. Hence bread is

the symbol in which he is among us. Ordinary bread has become 255
for us bread of eternal life: Christ.—But then, what happens to
this bread? It remains the same as regards outward appearance
and taste. Otherwise the symbol in which he wills to be among
us would disappear. What then is changed?—Before the Middle
Ages, no special thought was given to the matter. There seemed
to be something obvious in the fact that the reality of Jesus'
presence should be there in the sign. The Middle Ages examined
the question more deeply. The believing mind then found the
following way of expressing the mystery. The "accidents",
that is, the form or species (colour, taste etc.) of the bread
remained, while the "substance", that is, the reality or nature of
the bread did not, but became Christ himself.

When we consider the matter in terms of present-day thought
one should therefore say that the reality, the nature of material
things is what they are—each in its own way—for man. Hence
it is the essence or nature of bread to be earthly food for man. In
the bread at Mass, however, this nature becomes something quite
different: Jesus' body, as food for eternal life. Body in Hebrew
means the person as a whole. Bread has become Jesus' person.—
This is a mysterious presence. We must not imagine, for instance,
that Christ's body enters our mouth in a very small edition, so
to speak, just as in Nazareth he entered the house of Mary in
actual life size. We must be equally on our guard against the
opposite explanation, which would be purely "symbolic", as
though Jesus were not really present. It is better to say that the
bread is essentially withdrawn from its normal human meaning
or definition, and has become the bread which the Father has
given us, Jesus himself.

Jesus present in the cycle of the year

70, 83
86, 169–170
186, 308–309

In the celebration of the liturgy, the Church has always in its
midst the Christ whose mysteries it recalls throughout the year.
He is risen. He had been consummated. His whole life is there
within him. He contains his past, much more fully than anyone
here on earth who carries his past with him on his visage and
in his bearing. The life of Jesus was upright, consistent, without
twists or turns. For instance, he never betrayed the child within
him, as we do. And his life, through his death and resurrection,
is more perfect and unified than the life of any man on earth.
The new-born child, the twelve year old, the carpenter, the

teacher, the dying man—the signs of the wounds!—the risen Lord, the giver of the Spirit: all this lives on in his risen person, and hence in the Eucharist. This is the deepest reason for our being able to celebrate each feast in the annual cycle as a present reality, as "today".—Because the risen Lord is among us along with Christmas in the Eucharist, something of the child in him is among us, and we may kneel before the crib. This is the truly Christian way of celebrating the mysteries. To remember is to re-present.

250
312

Not an isolated element

We must not see Jesus' presence in the Eucharist as something apart, in isolation. It must not be disjoined from the other factors such as covenant, memorial, thanksgiving and sacrifice. And we should not isolate it from the other modes of the Lord's presence among us, from his presence through the word, and 286–289 above all, from his presence through his Holy Spirit in the hearts and the mutual relationships of men. In a certain sense, it may be said that this last form of presence is the greatest. It is the form by which Jesus is most among us, by which we have him most continually in our circle.

The Church teaches that those who do not possess the Holy Spirit (who are not "in the state of grace", who are cut off from God) have no real contact with Jesus, even though they receive the Eucharist externally. We then speak of a "sacrilegious communion". But anyone who has the Holy Spirit within him is undoubtedly in contact with Jesus, even though he does not receive communion. It is not the purpose of Jesus that communion should ever be sundered from our whole life as Christians.

This consideration also provides the answer to the difficulty: that I go to communion, but that it does not help; or again, they are always going to communion, but are not one bit the better of it. Do not such difficulties stem from the fact that we are too much inclined to regard the Eucharist as a magical device which stands apart? Communion is not magic, but food, consolation, companionship, and realization of what we are: sinners who have been called by Christ. Through this very tangible presence of Jesus among us, which we can celebrate so realistically, we *live out* the fact that Jesus is among us through his Spirit: He is really the man Jesus, who died and rose again, not something shadowy and unreal. We have now been given what we men are so desperately in need of: a symbol through which the reality really becomes present.

The duration of the Eucharistic presence

There is another small question which we may discuss here. When does the Eucharistic presence of Jesus cease? It ceases when the form of bread is no longer there. It is not a matter of deciding how long it can still be called bread from the scientific point of view (indeed, one might well ask whether bread was a scientific concept). But some theologians did try to think along scientific lines, and then came to the opinion that the presence ceased a quarter of an hour after eating. But the conviction today is that the matter can be dealt with more simply and humanly. Bread is something to eat. As soon as it is eaten, it is no longer called bread. The form or species of bread remains till the host has been eaten. Then it is no longer something to eat. It has already been eaten. So too a piece of bread which has been reduced to dust is no longer called bread. Hence little particles which may have been left behind on the altarcloth are not in any sense the presence of Christ. The point is this. What would still be called bread by ordinary, sensible people? As long as it is there in that sense, Christ is present. In a word—bread must be taken as an anthropological and not as a scientific term. As soon as we have received the body of Christ, the Eucharistic presence is transformed into that which it is meant to bring about: an intenser presence in us through the Spirit.

To think clearly and gratefully of this, it is very often advisable to remain for some time after communion. One does not need to run away at once from something great and important. One does not need to depart at once after a banquet. We can linger on awhile. This "staying to pray" is all the more important nowadays because our way of life leaves us with so little time for quiet prayer and recollection. Prayer after Mass provides a unique occasion. One does not need to make special efforts to bury oneself in tranquillity and recollection. One is there already, through the preceding celebration. One has met the Lord and one speaks to him for a while. This is perhaps a time for reading part of the Bible—John 6:48–71, for instance, on union with him; or chapters 14–17 of John, Jesus' farewells; or Psalm 34, the favourite communion chant in Christian antiquity; or the psalm which expresses the utmost confidence, Psalm 23.

Some find that at such times they can experience very particularly the spiritual fulfilment of the Song of Solomon.

What we have just said about the cessation of the Eucharistic presence may seem to be in conflict with ancient "miracles of the Blessed Sacrament", such as the medieval story from Amsterdam. It tells of a host which was vomited up by a sick person. Out of reverence, an effort was made to burn everything, but the host remained suspended above the fire. What are we to think now of such stories?—The first point to note is that marvellous events can correspond to a certain form of the experience and understanding of the faith. The second point is that the fact that such a miracle took place in the Middle Ages is not, of course, a truth of faith. A certain amount of mis-apprehension and imagination may have been at work, but the general reverence, the silent awe, still remains meaningful. What really matters is not the minor miracle of the host suspend-ed above the fire, but the great miracle of Jesus' presence in spite of the flaming passions and discords of our human existence.

The reservation of the Eucharist

The body of Christ is "reserved" reverently even after the Eucharistic celebration is over. Thus it can be given to the sick at any time. It is usually kept on an altar in church, in the "taber-nacle". Thus even when there is no Mass being celebrated, our Lord remains among us in this way. All that has been said above about his presence remains true here. It is a visible sign that the Lord is as personally close to his Church as he was among his Apostles. We should try to remain reverently and thankfully aware of this presence whenever we enter church. It is an excellent custom to genuflect or kneel when we enter or leave. The constant presence of Jesus here can be honoured by silent prayer, as when a housewife takes a few minutes off a shopping expedition to pray and give thanks for her husband and children, or by public veneration, as in processions or benediction of the Blessed Sacrament.

But as regards public veneration, we are now becoming more and more convinced that the great solemnity must always be the Mass. Possibly veneration for Jesus' mysterious abiding presence will be more and more a matter for private and silent prayer. And even here we shall always have to be attentive to

: bread, that is, to be
l celebration of the
, the symbols of his
ong us as the sacrifice

vely for our earthly
. And this is true in a
ory is already among
gels is food on earth.
f man on earth has
a word, something of
ady here. As we think
ste of his glory. And
-halls through which
A holy presence makes
e bread and wine, the
ally. Apart from the
ense will suggest, the
y by the consecrated
g of God's holiness is

pomp and pageantry. 254
simple and silent. The
ring a table with bread
whom the precept is
of our celebration of
derstand how it corre-
e Eucharist is of course
meal. But the form of
eminded that the Mass
he holy climax of our
e our eating, praying,
rist.

NAME

ADDRESS

CITY/STATE

PHONE

St. Mary 1985 Western Days Festival

SERIES D

№ 08726

№ 08726

St. Mary Parish

WESTERN DAYS

Griffith, Indiana

FESTIVAL

August 15, 16, 17, 18, 1985

GRAND PRIZE — 1985 FORD ESCORT

2 Dr. Hatchback, Pwr. Steering, Pwr. Brakes, Air Cond.
AM/FM Stereo, Automatic Transmission

DRAWING SUNDAY, AUGUST 18th, 1985

Donation $1.00 - Ticket

Winner Need Not
Be Present

SERIES D

Tickets Courtesy of Konnie Kuiper
Kuiper Funeral Home

347

THE PRIESTLY PEOPLE

"God's own people"

"Come to him, to that living stone, rejected by men but in God's sight chosen and precious; and like living stones by yourselves built into a spiritual house, to be a holy priesthood, to offer spiritual sacrifices acceptable to God through Jesus Christ. For it stands in scripture:

> 'Behold, I am laying in Zion a stone,
> a cornerstone chosen and precious,
> and he who believes in him will not be put to shame'"
> (1 Pet. 2:4–6).

This is how the first epistle of St Peter speaks of those who are followers of Christ. Indeed, the whole epistle is concerned with the fact that the Church as a whole is "a royal priesthood" (1 Pet. 2:9).

The Christian priesthood is primarily the sacerdotal quality which all the faithful possess as priests—a quality given them in baptism and confirmation. This makes the Church on earth "God's own people" (1 Pet. 2:9). With profound faith, Christians recognize that they have been called "out of darkness into God's marvellous light" (1 Pet. 2:9). At first Christ seemed a worthless contribution, a rejected stone at the building of mankind. But he is clearly the most important stone. Those who 235 adhere to him are invited to a life where everything is purer, where men have "purified their souls by obedience to the truth" (1 Pet. 1:22). We are linked by the strongest bonds which ever bound man: we who "once were no people, now are God's people" (1 Pet. 2:10).

This is not something that can be stored quietly away. It is a charge and a task—to be priests together among mankind. But how are ordinary people to do this?—It may be said first of all 249 that of ourselves we do not know exactly what it means. Christian education, the institutions of an ancient Christian society, the gospel preached from the pulpit, the celebration of the Eucharist—these are ways through which the Spirit of God influences us more than we often realize. Christians find things normal which would elsewhere be found strange. The lamp of God's redemption is often held in unsuspecting hands.

The realization of our impotence

The first thing that we as Christians have to realize—as is proclaimed again and again by the gospel, the liturgy and the preaching of the Church—is our inadequacy. This is the primary task of Christians in the world. They must realize that "once they had not received mercy, but now have received mercy" (1 Pet. 2:10). In other words, they are called to know and to proclaim that man is of himself incapable of any good actions, but that we constantly receive light and strength from him who loves us. This is the first element of sanctity in the Church: to know how much we fall short. The great saints almost exaggerated (we feel) their recognition of their shortcomings. But they saw clearly what should be accomplished in the line of love, faith and kindness.

Those who sense this insufficiency share the true fundamentals 277 of holiness in the Church. Through it, dedication to the Infinite takes shape. For there are no bounds to the call of the sermon on the mount, to the call of love. Self-complacency is emptied of meaning, arrogance is tamed. This gives man hope, because it offers support and perspectives which are above man's closed circle, and still leaves the task in our hands. Babel is silenced. The task of serving is there to be done.

Service

The people of God is priestly because of its readiness to serve. It is invited to make the most spiritual of all sacrifices (cf. 1 Pet. 2:5) —its own life.

> Sacrifices and offerings thou hast not desired,
> but a body thou hast prepared for me;
> in burnt offerings and sin offerings thou hast taken no
>   pleasure.
> Then I said, "Lo, I have come" . . . (Heb. 10:5–7).

There is nothing depressing about this task of rendering service in the Spirit of Christ. It means a reversal of values. Power and standing cease to be primary, and we are freed to adopt a new attitude, which will correspond to the profoundest desire of 93 each of us.

Our earthly task

In our Christian service, we are summoned to work at this earth's tasks. Each of us will find there a task which is truly his own. The writer, the housewife, the manager, the trade unionist—in a word, everyone who is deeply involved in his earthly task, who is skilled in the sober wisdom of his own particular work, brings about something real which he offers to man and God. (In this sense we may speak of the priestliness of every calling. And here it is not enough that we should have a pure intention—working
428 only for the sake of God and man. This has often been put forward as the only permanent value: as if only the pure intention,
439 the love involved, bore fruit for eternity, while the earthly
483–484 things themselves perish for ever when God makes all things new.

We are learning to see more and more clearly that our work on material things influences strongly the development of man and hence makes the possibility of love greater. And hence it influences eternity. Our work on earth is therefore cooperation with what God promises us for eternity—because it helps to create an atmosphere where love can flourish. And we are in fact justified in asking whether the new creation will not also take up and continue our earthly work itself.

In view of all this, it is not only important that we should have a pure intention in our work. It is also important that the work should be done well according to its intrinsic laws and according to the values contained in each calling. Hence the preaching of
288–293 the gospel must always remain alert to what the Spirit says, as it speaks from the depths of reality, of the experience, prudence and habit of mind born of all natural knowledge and skill.

The message of love and service remains throughout as the precious and inspiring contribution of the gospel. But we must
432 not take a one-sided view of this service. It may well be that some serve by suppressing their own idiosyncrasies. But it may also happen that some must emphasize strongly their personal independence and peculiarities, as for instance the artist, who takes a strong line which few perhaps understand. As long as it is honest work at earthly things, it is service of mankind in the end. What constitutes service is not that one brakes or gives free rein to one's personality, but that one tries humbly and joyously in what one does to be outgoing, to give oneself, as our Lord did.

The holiness of the Church

When Christians perform this task of love slothfully, they betray their priestly election among mankind. Where glory has been given, its refusal is gravest. Where man is most clearly revealed, laxity and hardness show up most clearly. In the countries and families where the gospel of love has been preached and the body of Christ given in communion, discord and injustice cry out loudest to heaven. Nonetheless, they do happen there. It may well be that a so-called Catholic country or family is not in fact so truly Catholic in faith as its own folklore or traditions suggest. But it remains true that in the midst of defects there may be a warmth and a reservoir of kindness of which respectable people have no inkling. This does not mean that the sins of Christians may be dismissed lightly. They are all too obvious, and they are a hindrance to the message of the Lord.

Undoubtedly, goodness, by its very nature, must always be less striking than evil. The brightness of the city on the hill can only be fully recognized by the Father who sees in secret. Who can tell all that is accomplished in the Church by people of whom one never hears—by the "common man", in whatever 233 level of society he or she may be, by the pious child, by all the hidden lives which have been praised by Jesus in the eight beatitudes. We do not notice them. They do not appear in the newspapers. But the Church is a Church of the small and poor, and 37 hence of saints. It is not because the dome of St Peter's is so vast that the Catholic Church is the Church of Christ, but because so many common men have been declared blessed or saints under that dome. They are a sign of countless others who remain nameless.

The holiness found in the Church is, of course, not a purely human achievement. This spiritual sacrifice of service is completely one with Christ's service, with his radiant outgoing to all the world which is celebrated in the daily Eucharist. Everything through which Christ is in the Church makes the Church 212 this people of service among mankind. To develop this point, 252 we should have to speak of many things such as the sacraments, 322 the word, prayer and so on; but they are discussed elsewhere in 304 this book.

The proclamation of the truth

365
258
One further priestly task must be mentioned, the preaching of the truth. Here too the great message of the Church is human insufficiency. It proclaims a truth which no man can discover or fully comprehend, a truth which has to be *given* by Christ,
291 the Word of God. It does not consist of a bundle of propositions which have been neatly and clearly communicated. But all the
33 surmises of the human race about its creator have been gathered
497 up in Christ's revelation, purified, and above all, totally renewed and changed by his passion and resurrection.

When God gave his revelation about himself, he also gave us purer forms in which to articulate the depths of our own being. Both the gospel preaching and the sacraments (the ceremonies which give form and contour to all the great seminal moments of our lives) reveal what man is and what man's way must be.

We may put this in very ordinary terms. If in no. 3 there is a Catholic family, and in no. 5 a family which claims to have "no religion", then no. 3 has been provided with a means of being
249-250 fully human—through faith, forgiveness, prayer, marriage,
253 first and last communion—which corresponds to the truest human desire. It corresponds to the profound desire to see one's life and capacities, both social and individual, really bear fruit. It corresponds to the longing to live in such a way that one is pleasing to God and hence to oneself and to others. Even if no. 3 falls short of the ideal of the Christian life, it is still true that it possesses the means whereby the truly human longings of no. 5 can be expressed.

"Know, Christian, thy dignity." This dignity is only really significant—as we must remark at once—if no. 3 effectively believes and is really inspired in life and in death by the divine message. It is only then that no. 3 really forms part of the "royal priesthood" in its environment.

235 *Non-Catholics*

But there is something else to be considered. If there are
323-325 Protestants living in no. 7, they share the same Christian truth to a great extent and are in this sense part of the "royal priest-hood", even though they have not adopted certain precious

elements which we believe Christ intended for his Church. But if they are sincere believers, they belong to a great extent to Christ's work and Church.

But we can go still further. The family at no. 5 which claims to have no belief, but which lives in a society where Christians live and have lived for centuries, will have undergone in a thousand unconscious ways the influences and challenges which are contained in the Christian faith which is preached, lived and solemnized around it. Hence if this family sincerely tries to live well, it is not entirely disjoined from the Church. In a broad sense it belongs to the class of men who have been touched by the Christian message. Indeed, it can often shame the people in no. 3 and no. 7. 234

This does not mean that we are ready to compromise about the truth revealed by God and admit that it is the same everywhere. All we wish to do is to recall that the Christian truth exists outside the Catholic Church—especially among the Christians with whom we hope to be re-united—at many levels and in various forms, where the voice of Jesus may be heard. And it is part of the priestly task of the Church to become a source for these currents, by remaining true to itself. 356

And then the Catholic will sometimes realize that the others in turn have something to say to him—something Christian. Outside the Catholic community men have sometimes been fired with marvellous enthusiasm for certain values—philanthropy, social justice, integrity, a sense of earthly realities. Thus we hear from men that stand far off certain echoes of the Christian message. In this sense, the others are priests for us. 286

Tolerance 228–229

Here we may insert a few words on tolerance. This does not merely mean that we respect the Christian element in the opinions of those whose beliefs are different. It also means that we respect the convictions of others even where their tendency is away from Christianity, when, therefore, we find that they impoverish men instead of enriching them. The question of tolerance is not an easy one which can be dismissed with a few catch-words or slogans.

The difficulty is not so much that another possesses such convictions in his own mind. The Church recognizes that faith is a free act and hence that force or pressure may never be used to 408–409

bring men to believe. Thus the inner freedom of others is clearly recognized as a principle. And the Church emphasizes just as
374–375 strongly that each man must follow his conscience. The difficulty begins when a conviction becomes the subject of propaganda and tries to impose itself with all the means it can dispose of. Take for instance the typically non-Christian racialism of the Nazis. No amount of respect for the opinions of others should prevent us from airing our distaste and disagreement.

May we also call in the law of the land? If the conviction which is being put about is not merely unchristian but inhuman, criminal, then this may be done. But who is to decide ultimately that an opinion is such? The law of the land? But if so, no revolution would ever be possible or permissible. Then who decides? It is impossible to define this clearly, and hence tolerance must always be something which must be worked out in each particular case by society.

The Church has the ten commandments, which therefore provide a help. But one cannot use these without more ado as the norms for what human society should regard as inhuman. (For instance, it would not do to impose the first commandment on atheists.) The Church must defend these commandments with all its might. But what we are concerned with now is whether society may impose them as the norm to decide what is criminal and what is not and hence upholds them by its laws and sanctions.

Hence it is obviously difficult to describe in theory the limits of tolerance and define them sharply. But this should not make us underestimate the value of this virtue. We must make the greatest possible tolerance of the convictions of others an ideal after which we strive. Love, the gentleness of the gospel and reverence for the uniqueness and freedom of the other demand
81–82 this of us. We must be proud to see responsible functions in a
130 practically fully Catholic society placed in the hands of those of different beliefs. We should be proud of the fact that in such a society other convictions can freely exist and exercise their attraction and find nothing opposed to them except the clear light of truth and the patience which comes from the Spirit.

270–286   *Why the missions? The young Churches*

"Go therefore and make disciples of all nations" (Mt. 28:19). The gospel is meant for all men. Jesus brought help and food and healing. Jesus did not fail to proclaim the truth. These two ministries are also imposed on the Church. No commentary on the charge is needed for those who really believe. Because Jesus healed, the Church tries to help where help is needed. Here women above all have been the instruments of Christ, the thousands of nuns and others all over the world. Because Jesus spoke, the Church goes forth to spread the truth.

One of the strongest motives of the missions was the fear that the pagans would suffer eternal damnation if they were not brought Christ's truth and power. At present the conviction is clearer and more general (see the chapter on baptism) that we do not know how God judges where men are ignorant of Jesus' way. We are very much in the dark about the eternal salvation of non-Christians, and the Church—led, no doubt, by the Holy Spirit—is much more tranquil about it. In the New Testament the word "salvation" is not confined to the securing of the perpetual happiness of the individual. It has a wider set of meanings. It signifies that a people has been gathered together to live in the joy of the kingdom. This includes the joy of being able to await with confidence the coming of the Lord, and this includes his perpetual, hidden and gladdening coming in our daily existence. To be open to this is salvation for man.

It is for this that the missionaries go out. They set up the fellowship where the kingdom of God begins to take shape. The deepest longings are given their true direction. The real root of evil is exposed, lovelessness. The fountain of forgiveness is opened, the resurrection proclaimed, the good news that the ultimate reality is not the brutal necessity of fate but love. Men develop under the consolation and strength of the Spirit and their whole existence becomes more fruitful. Our Lord comes to them. Hence the lives of the missionaries form a splendid chapter in the history of mankind, known only to the Father who sees in secret.

Jesus' command to preach meant for centuries to go abroad. And the foreign missions are still an important factor. But they bring with them the difficulty that along with the Christian message a dose of European culture can be imposed on other peoples contrary to their natural genius. Each people which becomes Christian has a task of its own within the people of God. This was sometimes realized in earlier times, but sometimes ignored. We should not go to romantic extremes and act as if every people had a vital and flourishing culture to offer.

299

248–252

20–22

277

282–283

228

The technical culture which has penetrated everywhere has often partly replaced the ancient culture and reduced it to insignificance—just as the same technology has done in Europe with ancient European cultures. Nonetheless, the missions must always try to bring out what is proper to each nation, each family and each man. Even here on earth God does not wish to lose anything that has come forth from his hand.—It follows at once that each nation must have its own bishops and priests. It is only then that the Church is really implanted in a people.

And even if men do not join the visible community of the Church in large numbers, they will not be untouched by its influence, if they are men of good will. Very often, they will stress the most Christian elements in their own religions and philosophies and put them into practice as well as possible, so as not to suffer by comparison with Christians.

195 The Christian missions can also be the profoundest factor in 233 the unification of mankind. They proclaim Jesus, whose doctrine was service, not power, whose answer, when shown all the kingdoms of the world and offered power over them, was the refusal: "Begone, Satan!" They proclaim Jesus, whose preaching of the kingdom of God opened and still opens men's hearts to one another. It is the Jesus who said: "They will heed my voice. So there shall be one flock, one shepherd" (Jn 10:16). He meant all men, since he wished "all men to be saved and to come to the knowledge of the truth" (1 Tim. 2:4).

230-231 In this missionary preaching which goes out to the ends of the earth, the ecumenical mission, to which the Spirit impels Christians in these days, is of course particularly important, particularly difficult and particularly pressing.

As the Church is planted in every people, the missions will 228-229 perhaps mean being the leaven in our own people rather than going abroad. We shall carry out this mission by prayer and kindness, by giving the message of human insufficiency and hence that of human potentialities.

"The afflictions of Christ"

277-279 It is no easy, triumphal task to be God's people. Jesus said that the gates of hell would not prevail against his Church. But he also asked: "When the Son of man comes, will he find faith on earth?" (Lk. 18:8). Much of what is to happen remains an open question . . . put to us. "I came to cast fire upon the earth; and would that it were already kindled!" (Lk. 12:49).

We were not promised that it would be easy. But we were promised that suffering would also produce life, like the sufferings of Christ. In this way too the Church is priest. "For while we live we are always being given up to death for Jesus' sake, so that the life of Jesus may be manifested in our mortal flesh. So death is at work in us, but life in you" (2 Cor. 4:11–12). Paul is so convinced that this is part of the Christian life, that he feels he has not yet contributed his share, and he writes: "Now I rejoice in my sufferings for your sake, and in my flesh I complete what is lacking in Christ's afflictions for the sake of his body, that is, the church" (Col. 1:24).

These "afflictions of Christ" are the birth-pangs of new life 172 and hence are not purposeless: "You will weep and lament . . . but your sorrow will turn into joy. When a woman is in travail, 247 she has sorrow, because her hour has come; but when she is 487 delivered of the child, she no longer remembers the anguish, for joy that a child is born into the world" (Jn 16:20, 21).

Hence we conclude this chapter with the words of the first epistle of St Peter, which contain a consolation "always ancient, always new":

> Beloved, be not surprised at the fiery ordeal which comes upon you to prove you, as though something strange were happening to you. But rejoice in so far as you share Christ's sufferings, that you may also rejoice and be glad when his glory is revealed. If you are reproached for the name of Christ, you are blessed, because the spirit of glory and of God rests upon you. But let none of you suffer as a murderer, or a thief, or a wrong-doer, or a mischief-maker; yet if one suffers as a Christian, let him not be ashamed, but under that name let him glorify God (1 Pet. 4:12–16).

THE PASTORAL PRIESTHOOD   135–144

Service

Those who represent the Lord by holding office in the Church are men set free to be ready to serve with all their might. "For what we preach is not ourselves, but Jesus Christ as Lord, with ourselves as your servants for Jesus' sake. For it is the God who said, 'Let light shine out of darkness', who has shone in our hearts to give the light of the knowledge of the glory of God in the face of Christ. But we have this treasure in earthen vessels, to show that the transcendent power belongs to God and not to us" (2 Cor. 4:5–7). There are many such statements in the New Testament which tell us that the pastors of the Church are not like the kings of the nations, but servants. The care of the Churches, and hence the great authority, which the Lord gives to men is to be understood against this background.

The office of the Apostles

Jesus was "as one who served" among his Apostles, and at the same time was the authority at the centre of the little flock. In the same way, he gave these Apostles the charge of being servants of God's people and at the same time his own authoritative representatives. The task which he conferred is described in such words as these: "Truly, I say to you, whatever you bind on earth shall be bound in heaven, and whatever you loose on earth shall be loosed in heaven" (Mt. 18:18). We have already 139 explained that loosing and binding signifies authority, both to govern a community and to decide questions. During the last supper, he also gave his Apostles the mandate, "Do this in memory of me" (Lk. 22:19). And after the resurrection, the gospel shows him breathing upon his apostles and saying, "If you forgive the sins of any, they are forgiven; if you retain the sins of any, they are retained" (Jn 20:22). To govern, to teach, to administer the signs of the Lord—it was with such authority that the Apostles were equipped.

The transmission of the office

The New Testament also gives us a glimpse of the care which the Apostles had to transmit their pastoral office after their death. Paul, who was also an Apostle, through the explicit mandate of the Lord, said to the leaders of the communities of Asia Minor: "And now, behold, I know that all you . . . will see my face no more . . . Take heed to yourselves and to all the flock, in which the Holy Spirit has made you guardians, to feed the church of God" (Acts 20:25–28). He wrote to Titus: "This is why I left you in Crete, that you might amend what was defective (in the organization), and appoint elders in every town as I directed you" (Tit. 1:5). The heads of the communities thus indicated are mostly called presbyters (elders) or bishops (*episcopi*, overseers) in the New Testament. The communities were governed by a group of bishops or presbyters, who were helped by deacons, while the Apostles retained supreme authority. It might possibly be deduced from the comparison of 1 Timothy 3:1 (singular) and 3:8 (plural) that even then there was sometimes only one head of the community, and that *episcopus* (bishop) was the name given to this monarchical governor.

At any rate, this is certainly true of the end of the first century, immediately after the death of the Apostles. This is clear from the letters of Ignatius of Antioch, which reflect the situation 214 about the year 100. He writes for instance to the Church of Smyrna: "Be obedient to the bishop, as Jesus Christ was to the Father, and to the presbyterate, as to the Apostles. Have reverence for the deacons, as charged by God." We see here three different degrees, deacons, presbyters (presbyterate) and one *episcopus*, "bishop".

There is also another way to trace the existence of the episcopal office in the ancient Church. When an appeal was made towards the end of the second century to the tradition of the Apostles, it was a tradition or succession of bishops, whose names are listed. 214 Thus St Irenaeus in his "Against the Heretics", a work written about 180, names the bishops of Smyrna and of Rome from the times of the Apostles down to his own time. Similar lists exist for Alexandria, Jerusalem and Antioch. The occasion for mentioning the lists—the preservation of the purity of the message against heretics—also reveals perhaps something of the circumstances in which the office took precisely the form it did. The one supreme (monarchical) ruler was the guarantee of the unity of the Church in each place.

Men as representatives of the Lord

We can learn from the letters of Ignatius of Antioch what were the feelings deep down in Christians with regard to the pastoral office which existed in the Church. He says of the bishop, when writing to the people of Tralles, that "you are subject to him as you are to Christ". Hence it is not a matter of serving men, but of exercising obedience to the Lord by obeying the bishop instituted by the Church. The most profound description of this attitude of the faithful is given by Ignatius in the words already quoted: "Be obedient to the bishop, as Jesus Christ was to the Father." The existence of the bishop makes possible in Christians the same mind which was in Jesus Christ (cf. Phil. 2:5). Obedience to God takes on full life and warmth in obedience to the bishop. He is appointed to be one "who presides in the name of God" (Ignatius to the Magnesians). He is helped by the priests and deacons. The living Lord wills to be present through living men.

The shepherd gives his life

The pastors are called in order to share Jesus' messianic consciousness—that the good news must be preached to the poor. They have been sent, in order to become like the Servant of Yahweh, 91 who gave his life. This is not the place to discuss how far they have been successful in their task in the course of history. Their shortcomings are often mentioned, and rightly. But such comments are also an expression of a lofty expectation, of which in fact something has always been fulfilled. It is significant that many bishops have been canonized, and that some bishops are looked upon as saints even in their own lifetime. It would be ingratitude towards the Lord to overlook all the goodness which has come into the world through the successors of his Apostles.

This shepherd gives the life of Christ

With this description of the call of the bishops to a Christ-like life we have not yet completed the story of their office. It remains to be said that their office is a sacrament, that is, that through it Christ remains present among us, even though the pastor seems to fail seriously in his human qualities and abilities. He is given a mission and an authority which are greater than man's. Bishops, priests, and deacons are the bearers of something through which Christ is among us. Even if the personality of a priest had nothing of service about it and no life-giving quality (a state of affairs which would be a tragic split in his life), his office would still be life-giving, because Christ's work for his Church is still done through him.

The bishop

The fullness of pastoral power and authority is given to the bishops. They are *the* priests of the Church.

360

In the solemn ceremonies at the consecration of a bishop, we read the following words: "May his preaching and speaking be not with the plausible words of human wisdom, but with demonstration of the Spirit and power. Give him, o Lord, the 197-198 keys of the kingdom of heaven, so that he may exercise his authority without glorying in it, since you bestow it not for destruction but for edification; so that all that he binds on earth may be bound also in heaven, and all that he looses on earth may be loosed also in heaven; so that the sins that he retains may be retained, and those that he forgives may be forgiven." The meaning of such words is that the powers of the Apostles (except of course the power to be founders) are transmitted to the bishops. The bishops too are given authority to feed the 211 flock of Christ by governing it, teaching it and distributing the sacraments. These three tasks have to be performed in different ways in various ages. Hence Christ left his authority among us embodied in living men.

The episcopal government is of course not a political element, 197 but a spiritual ministry. As such it is really authoritative and 419-420 directive. The service which the bishop performs on behalf of the Church is in fact to govern. That this leadership is service means not only that the bishops are ready to help, but that they are open and alert to the voice of all Christians.

The teaching office of the bishop has a protective and a 365 creative aspect. It is protective because the bishop is responsible for all that the priests put forward as Catholic doctrine before the faithful, in writing or preaching. The bishops still share the anxieties which Paul expressed to the pastors of Asia Minor: "I know that after my departure ... from among your own selves will arise men speaking perverse things, to draw away the disciples after them" (Acts 20:30). The office is also creative, since it is that of the householder who brings out of his treasure what is new and what is old (cf. Mt. 13:52). Each age puts new questions to the gospel, and the gospel throws new light on each age.

The office of administering the sacraments is performed by the bishop when, for instance, he consecrates the oils for his 168-169 diocese, when he ordains priests and when he confers confirm- 363 ation (thus completing the baptism of all the Christians in his 256 diocese). Further, he is responsible for the correct administration of all the sacramental signs in his diocese.

Bishops as envoys

The just fatherliness of episcopal authority is determined constantly by the gospel directive: "You are all brethren. And call no man your father on earth, for you have one Father, who is in heaven" (Mt. 23:8–9). It is not merely a question of feelings. Before the Father, the bishop is just as much the receptive believer in the Church as the smallest child going to communion. Further, he receives his mission and his authority within and in the name of the whole people of God. (When we speak of the "people of God" in the biblical sense, we do not of course exclude the bishops and priests.) It is true that the way in which power comes to the bishop is not the way which we see in democracies. There is a special significance in this fact.—Incidentally, it may first be noted that the *choice* of the person to be bishop, the designation, can happen in various ways, as for instance by the voice of the whole people, as was often the case in former times.

But the authority itself is not transferred because the majority confer it on one of their number, the bishop. Those who have already received authority hand it on. A bishop is consecrated by another bishop. (To show that it is a charge given by the Church universal, three bishops impose hands at the solemn consecration.)—This way of transmitting the pastoral office is not meant as an assertion of overlordship from on high. The real meaning is that the pastors are *sent*. Mission and authority were given by the Lord to the people of God by his putting this mission and authority in the hands of the Apostles. The Apostles passed on the authority to those whom they in turn sent. Thus the episcopal office contains in this way the trait of a sacramental mission from the Lord. It is a window open on the origins. Men did not confer on themselves the status of a priestly people. It was given them by the Lord. This is the profound significance of the pastoral office in the Church: that to be the people of God is something that has been *given* us.

The priesthood of Christ, of the people, of the bishop

It might seem that the "general priesthood" of the people of God has now been reduced to a very secondary thing. There seem in fact to be merely a few mediators. But this is not so, because the relationship between the general and the pastoral priesthood is on another level. There is only one priesthood,

Margin numbers: 140-141, 368, 367, 137, 348

that of Jesus Christ. The people of God shares this one priesthood. Hence the general priesthood is truly the central and
important thing. The people of God receives it through the word
of preaching and the sacraments. But the word and the sacrament
are handed on by those to whom the Spirit gave the relevant
office, the bishops. Thus the priestly office whereby the bishops
govern the Church is a service through which the people of
God is priestly and is constantly renewed in its priesthood.
And hence the bishops are to be regarded as "servants of Christ
and stewards of the mysteries of God" (1 Cor. 4:1).

Since the pastoral office in the Church is a sacramental sign   252–256
of Christ, if follows that episcopal consecration is a sacrament.
It takes the following form. Three bishops impose hands on
the head of the bishop-elect and pray that the Holy Spirit
may descend on him. This is the kernel of the ceremony. It is   254–255
surrounded by symbolic actions: the anointing of head and hands
with chrism, the giving of the crozier and ring, and the laying
of an open book of the gospels on the head of the bishop-elect,
to ask that the Spirit may descend upon him from the word
of God.

Priests and deacons

Along with the episcopal office there are other grades of the
priesthood. The bishop has priestly helpers, those who are called
priests, and the deacons.—The ordination of a "priest" also
consists of prayer to the Holy Spirit and the imposition of hands.
This is done by the bishop, and also by all priests present. The
ordination is surrounded by illuminating ceremonies: the
anointing of the hands with oil, the giving of the chalice and
the golden plate (the paten), officiating with the bishop for
the first time in the concelebration of the Eucharist. At the end
of Mass the bishop imposes hands once more and says: "Receive
the Holy Spirit. Whose sins you shall forgive, they are forgiven
them. Whose sins you shall retain, they are retained" (cf. Jn
20:22 f.).

The powers here conferred on the priest include that of
celebrating the Eucharist and of forgiving sins sacramentally
(hearing confessions). The priest also shares the charge of
preaching and giving guidance, according to his situation.
He is attached either to a diocese or to a religious order or
congregation (which will practically always be international).

In the first case, he is called a diocesan or secular priest and in the second case he is called a member of the regular clergy (regular—bound by rules of an order). Generally both are addressed as "Father".

Normally, the task of the priest is to look after a certain part of the diocese called the parish. Those who are in control of a parish are known as the parish priests. His helpers are known as curates or assistant priests. Many priests, especially religious, are not attached to parishes but serve the Christian people in other ways. All these priests, secular and regular, are the workers in the vineyard with whom Christians and non—Christians have most contact. Not many of those who work in parishes have been canonized, though a large number of excellent novels have taken this type of clergy, the secular, as their subject. It is a sort of modern canonization of this type of priest by the *vox populi*, and a recognition of their truly Christian answer to grace.

For many centuries, ordination as deacon had no other function than to be an introductory ordination to the priesthood to be received later. The deaconate is also conferred by the imposition of hands and the invocation of the Holy Spirit. The Acts of the Apostles (6:1–6) describes how this office originated in Jerusalem. The Apostles appointed seven men for the distribution of "relief" *(diakonia)*. It is clear from Acts 6:8 and 8:26–40 that the deacons were also active as ministers of the word and of baptism. This remains the task of the deacon: to help, to baptize and to preach. The Second Vatican Council has restored the office as a life-long function.

The consecration of bishop, priest and deacon forms together one sacrament of different degrees. The ceremonies of consecration are of impressive beauty. They consecrate the subject for ever. The sacrament can never be undone. Though the actual exercise of the office, say, of a priest, may be given up under certain circumstances, in case of necessity he can still perform his office.

The office among other Christians

226 It is not surprising that the Reformation took another view of this office in particular. It shrank from admitting that Christ's salvation was so earth-bound that it could be found in men with holy orders. No doubt the Reformation admits that the office

is given by the Lord. But the office-holder receives Christ's mission not from the bishops of the Church but directly from the people. The manner and the measure in which the Reformation regards, the office varies according to the different trends. The Lutherans have bishops, though not in our sense of the word. The Calvinists recognize no hierarchical office above the local preacher. The office of bishop is conceived to a great extent in the same way as ours in the separated "Anglican Church" and also in the small group of "Old Catholics" in the Netherlands, which stems from a sad division in the eighteenth century. In particular, the Churches of the East which are still not re-united to the See of Peter in Rome, have a real episcopal office going back to the Apostles.

The college of bishops and infallibility

We now come to the place where we must speak of the great unity of the Church of Christ. Up to the present we have spoken only of the individual bishops. But they are not separate entities. A bishop is not merely the ruler of his diocese. He is also one of the rulers of the universal Church. Together, the bishops constitute the supreme pastoral office in the Church. When they assemble, they form a council. The place of the bishop of Rome in a council is very special. His office goes back to Peter. Of this we shall speak shortly. The bishops together are the guardians of the Church and of the truth of Christ. In this "college of bishops" the infallibility of "God's own people", which is never abandoned by Christ, finds expression. Hence a council is infallible, when it affirms expressly that it speaks as such.

Truth and dynamism

81–82
205, 291
306–307
323, 329
334, 352
361, 442
448–449

Infallibility implies to a certain extent the static and smoothly rounded off. But it is the expression of a reality which is many-coloured and dynamic. It signifies that the Spirit of God does not allow the Church to err in its search. "The faithful as a whole, who have received the anointing of the Holy One (cf. 1 Jn 2:20, 27) cannot err in belief" (Second Vatican Council, *On the Church*, no. 12). In the past, infallibility was undoubtedly regarded too much like a cash-book: it was entered or not, and that was the end of it. Truth was regarded as a rock, and if it was not a rock, it could not remain faithful to itself. Too little attention was paid to the fact that we never deal with the truth as such, but only with the expression of the truth. The same truth must always be said in new ways and adapted to new conditions, if it is not to grow stale and wither.

Modern conditions of life and thought have made this still more evident. But the result has been that some people have lost all sense of direction. Something that they thought was fixed now seems movable: the expression and adaptation of the truth. And they cannot recognize the unchanging and absolute nature of God's message in such movement.

Nonetheless, it is there, just as much as it ever was. Those who have become familiar with a more dynamic way of thought find little difficulty in this. They know that a fixed point need not be an immovable point. For instance, the fixed point in the existence of a calf is not the hedge or the tree, but its mother, which moves and runs. Or to take an even better example, the mother of a very small child, say, on a farm, is the fixed point for the child. But it is a very movable point, because a living one. At one moment she is in the farmyard, at another in the kitchen; at one moment she is laughing, at another serious. A fixed point in the deepest sense of the word is something that lives and moves. And so too is the authoritative teaching of the magisterium, precisely when it remains true to the gospel and to its own past. It is not a rigid system, but a living voice. It interprets the gospel truths for each new age. This is because the interpretation remains capable of improvement.

The bishops, listening to the universal Church, searching along with the whole Church of God on pilgrimage, confident that the light of Christ will not be withdrawn from them, are the teachers of the truth of the gospel. The light of Christ which they hold out to us is the ancient, imperishable light, *lumen Christi*, which like the paschal candle always has stamped 186-187 on it the date of the year in which it now shines.

Unity through the successor of Peter

But here we must put a very obvious question, which will throw some further light on Christ's gift to the Church. The question is this. Where are we to turn if there is a division in the Church, among the bishops? We take this question as the occasion of speaking of the mandate of the bishop of Rome.

Jesus made Peter the head of the Apostles. Three times our Lord said to him, "Feed my sheep". To say something three times in the Old Testament meant to confirm it with the greatest possible force. We have spoken of this Galilean fisherman and the charge which the Lord gave him in the chapter entitled "The Messiah and his Community". The pastoral 141-144 office of Peter was transmitted to his successors. Peter died in Rome under Nero in 64 or 67. The first thing we hear about the city after that is about 100, in the letters of Ignatius of Antioch and Clement of Rome. It is clear from both writers that the Church of Rome already held a special position among the Churches. This continued to be so. This involved at first no special organization. But undoubtedly, before important decisions were taken, the other Churches sounded this community.

Was this perhaps because the city had world-wide prestige as the administrative centre of the empire? This is improbable, because the primacy just then was not an administrative one at all. What made the bishop of Rome the first among his brothers was not primarily the authority of the capital of the empire, but the authority of the ancient apostolic community going back to Peter. To be in unity with the community of Rome was a sign that one was in union with the Church as a whole.

The special task of the bishop of Rome is that of Peter: to be the principle of unity in the Church, to keep it one in faith and life. For this purpose, the bishop of Rome is the authoritative head of the college of bishops. He is not placed above the bishops, but as the first among them and the one who gives directives. In this sense, he is of course above them, just as a head belongs to the body and still is above it. He has been called Pope (i. e. Father, from the late Greek *papas*), since the fourth century. As ruler and teacher, he is the head of the Church.

The rule of Rome became in the long run, especially after 222 the fourteenth century, very active and centralized. This had disadvantages as well as advantages. It is possible that the Spirit is now leading the Church once more to a greater local autonomy under the presidence of the Pope.

At present the bishops are ultimately designated by the Pope. 362 He can interfere in a diocese. And when a bishop can no longer exercise his functions he can even appoint an apostolic administrator in his own name.

The development has been that in the course of time the

far-reaching central government has been exercised by the Pope with the help of the Roman Congregations, all of which together make up the Curia. They are like the various ministries in a State. Important helpers of the Pope are the cardinals. They were originally the bishops, priests and deacons of prominent churches in Rome and the surrounding districts. Since the eleventh century they have elected the Pope. The composition of the college of cardinals has become steadily more and more international. The bishops of many important dioceses belong to it. Other cardinals work in Rome, as heads for instance of the various Roman Congregations.

The unifying function of the Pope entails an important task as teacher. As head of the infallible college of bishops, he possesses infallibility in a special measure. He is the beacon. This does not mean that he can proclaim dogmas apart from the Church. He can only declare what the Church universal believes. He takes counsel with all the Catholic bishops, particularly with the Synod of Bishops instituted since the Second Vatican Council. But since union with the Pope is the touchstone for belonging to the unity, an utterance of the Pope is certainly full of the truth of God's Spirit, at least when he affirms explicitly (which happens very rarely) that he is speaking infallibly
197–198 and binding all Christians. This charism (freely-given grace of the Spirit for the general good) is linked with the office of being first among his brothers.—As regards the faith of the Pope,
140–141 he is a believer who receives his faith, even as Pope, from the
362 fellowship of the Church in which he has such an important task to perform.

Many directives and pronouncements of the magisterium (the teaching authority) make no claim to absolute infallibility. This does not mean that they are therefore without the Spirit of God. They are utterances which call for extreme respect and are highly authoritative.

Fellow-workers with the faithful

Of the apostolic task, Paul wrote: "Not that we lord it over your faith; we work with you for your joy" (2 Cor. 1:24).
91–93 It is very significant that every priest and bishop is first ordained deacon—server. It remains a basic element in his life, that he should be the least of his brothers, for the good of all.

Disinterested service is something that is always too little verified in any society. Hence it is one of the functions of the priest of which he will not easily be deprived. As far as he can, he retains something of the absolute detachment and freedom of the Lord. He is set free in order to be bound to the people of God. He is left without cares, so that he can be laden with the cares of the Churches.

This is why the Church of the West has adopted the custom of ordaining as priests only those who are ready to remain unmarried. At the same time, there is the conviction that a priest 416 should not be rich. This latter element is not defined by any laws, and the former need not always remain a law binding on all. But both elements crystallize the Christian conviction that a priest, charged with Christ's own messianic task, must be an outgoing man, someone who gives all his life.

At the same time the faithful who have no office are asked to share some of their means of livelihood with their priests. The faithful have the duty of providing for the material needs of the priests, since, as our Lord said of the preachers of the gospel, "the labourer deserves his hire" (Mt. 10:10). The priest is also dependent on the affection, the demands, the faith and the sincerity of the faithful.

No one can say beforehand what the life of the priest will be in the future. For example someone ordained in 1970 will still be a priest in 2000. We do not know what will be the circumstances under which priests will then exercise their ministry. And many priests will cry out to God at difficult moments, like Jeremiah, "O Lord, thou hast deceived me, and I was deceived" 320 (Jer. 20:7).

Priestly vocation

This text of Jeremiah has often been translated with the word "seduced", and it is true that the priest is "seduced" by God, because ultimately it is God who has called him. How does this vocation come? There are many stories of vocations in Scripture. 91 They describe vividly and colourfully something that happens inwardly and has been repeated again and again down to our own times. It is undoubtedly significant that personal vocations have been such favoured subjects in Scripture. It proves how stimulating such stories were for the people of God. Perhaps it is also a proof of how much God himself likes the theme—not merely of calling mankind, but of calling men.

How is one to know that one is called? By the discernment of joy. If the thought of becoming a priest evokes joy and peace, there is every reason to believe that God is calling. For God is not a God of disturbance but of peace and joy. We used the word, *discernment* of joy, because there can be two sorts of joy in conflict: the joy at the thought of not being a priest, and the joy at the thought of becoming a priest. But one of the two joys will appear deeper and more peaceful. We must steer by the deeper joy.

This may point to what one finds hardest to do, or perhaps not. The basic attitude throughout must be one of tranquillity, openness, and at the same time self-forgetfulness: the attitude which says, "Lord, what would you have me do?"

Such considerations should not be kept to oneself. It is well to seek the fellowship of the Church, in the person of a good and intelligent priest. He will rather increase the questioner's liberty than diminish it. He will be quite sure that only a free choice can be a fitting preparation for the office.

The community plays, however, a part in the vocation on a still higher level. The Church, through its hierarchy, determines whether the candidate is apt, and then gives him his mission. Thus the definitive vocation is given by the Church of Christ, no doubt at the very moment of ordination. But even when one goes back to the beginning of a vocation, the community will always be found to have been at work: the family, the 405–406 parish, the school where the child was educated, or people he met later. They all open up the perspective of a life filled with the service of mankind and with the spirit of friendship with Christ.

If one goes back to the beginning of a vocation one will often find certain motives at work there which were not fully valid or noble. But no one begins with fully matured motives. The first purification and self-examination takes place during the time of probation, before the candidate utters his definitive Yes—somewhat like the time of betrothal. But life itself, the very fact of growing mature and old in the service of God can make the motives purer and deeper. There is of course a continuity between the first determination and its realization. But the great continuity is the Living, the Unexpected Lord with whom one has set out. The priest tries to work with him at his most living and unpredictable creation, man.

THE SECOND COMMANDMENT LIKE THE FIRST

The previous chapters have spoken chiefly of our relationship to God. They showed man full of reverence and love towards the mystery of his origin. In the next chapters we shall consider our relationship to the world. They will show man full of reverence and love towards the mystery of "the earth and the fullness thereof, the world and those who dwell therein" (Ps. 24:1). This is the division made in the ten commandments, of which the first three speak of God, the other seven of man. 305 Hence we shall now discuss the subject-matter of the last seven commandments, though we shall not always follow exactly the order of these seven.

Origin of the decalogue

We offer a preliminary consideration of the word "commandment". Many understand by this a burden imposed upon man from outside. They imagine that they would behave quite differently if there were no commandments. But this way of thinking debases the commandments to something that would be concerned with matters of no value in themselves. Honesty, reverence for life, material fidelity, respect for others, would not be valuable in themselves, but merely precepts imposed by a God who could have chosen others. Such attitudes are often the result of an education where the good is too strongly emphasized as a system of well-defined precepts; of a general atmosphere where too much stress is laid on the extrinsic "must" and too little confidence placed in the intrinsic and spontaneous sense of values in both pupils and educators. The result is that the truth 405–409 that the commandments are good in themselves is lost sight of. We people forget that they are in themselves most profound and vital values, which are already anchored in the nature of man and of the world.

This does not mean that "hence" the commandments do not come from God. On the contrary—all creation with all its values comes from God and moves towards him. By living according to these values we live according to the will and commandment of God. At the same time, we should be clear that this clear grasp of the voice of conscience did not originate spontaneously from the confusion of human error, arrogance and selfishness. The commandments were only grasped fully

and clearly where God had begun to intervene very specially
38–39 with man—in Israel. The story of Sinai is the succinct expression
(and a very splendid one, cf. Exod. 20 and again, 33) of a long
historical process. Once God had begun to reveal himself so
effectively and so personally in the faith and history of Israel,
the proper attitude to be taken towards him became clearer and
33 clearer and was enshrined in the ten commandments. Hence
the commandments are both an expression of our deepest
376 longings and God's critical verdict on our unworthy actions.

The commandments are couched in a primitive terseness. We
simply read, for instance, "You shall not kill". But this comprises
all reverence for life. Hence we shall not dwell here on the
provisional element of "harsh law" in the ten commandments,
but concentrate on their deep and permanent meaning: that in
ten sayings, which can be counted on the fingers of two hands,
the whole conscience of mankind is contained at once.

The commandments in social life

The sense of values expressed in the commandments has to be
adapted to human societies of the most diverse stages of culture
and over vast regions of time. A translation, an application is
361 necessary. The magisterium of the Church has as one of its
365–368 special tasks the duty of interpreting these profound values for
the faithful. "Whatever you bind on earth shall be bound in
heaven, and whatever you loose on earth shall be loosed in
heaven" (Mt. 18:18). These words which our Lord addressed
to his Apostles also hold good for their successors. To bind and
loose, a function which contributes to the building up of the
community, also comprises the function of declaring what is
and what is not permissible. This is discussed in the chapter,
135 "The Messiah and his Community". How the government of
the Church reflects the instinct of faith in the whole Church is
365 explained in "The Pastoral Priesthood" and will also be treated
in this chapter when we speak of conscience. Here too we shall
speak of the greatest value of all, love, the principle by which all
rules are to be guided.

We must always remember here that every effort at adaptation
bears the stamp of a certain type of society at a given epoch.
Elements which are conditioned by their times and elements
which are perpetually valid are always interwoven. No formulation ever renders the value in question in its purity and in its

372

perpetual validity. There is always a growth of insight into good and evil, into the actual adaptation of eternally valid commandments.

This is not to deny that there is a really authoritative rule and government in a real society. From the community in which God's revelation is at work we obtain—gropingly, in growing measure—light and guidance for our conduct. Here the eternal values are interpreted.

Conscience and the commandments

This interpretation is not isolated from our own sense of values, from that organ of perception for the good by which each one is personally led: conscience. Man has within him (or rather, 15–16 he is) a living sense of what he ought to do.

Commandments and conscience interpret the same values. We should be very much mistaken if we tried to make our conscience a purely private matter, our own special secret, without any links with the community. This would estrange men from one another. It would be inhuman.

It is therefore very short-sighted to affirm, as one sometimes hears, that in former times men lived by the commandments (they did what they did because they had to) while now they live by their conscience (they now do good freely). Even in former times men did not act without reference to their conscience, and even at present they do not act without reference to the commands of the community. The two go together. The emphasis may be different at different times, but that is another question, which we shall deal with later. Here we confine ourselves to the unity of conscience and commandments.—It would be well to get rid of the bad habit of thought by which people are apt to see "person" and "society" as 240 primarily opposed to each other. More basic and primordial than any conflict is the fact that justice can only be done to either of them when both are taken together. The more a being is itself, the more it is together with others, the more open to give and receive, even the things of God. And vice versa, 288–289 the more a being is open to others, the more truly it is itself. (Plants are less themselves, and hence less together, than men). "Self" and "together" are not ultimately opposites, since creation is there for love.

A good law and a well-formed conscience are therefore a

help to each other. The personal conscience does not exist in isolation from the conscience of the community. Hence it is still true that "A wise man will not hate the law, but he who is hypocritical about it is like a boat in a storm" (Ecclus. 33:2).

Conscience against the commandment

This discussion has helped us to see the primordial and profound unity of conscience and commandments. But there is another element to consider. They can and must come into conflict with one another. The law, the precise precept, cannot foresee exactly all circumstances. Cases will arise where one must do more or less than the law prescribes. Conscience, with its instinct for what is good here and now cannot simply let itself be guided by the letter of the law. It must sometimes even depart from the law in order to affirm in certain cases the ultimate moral values.

Another reason for a laudable tension is the development of our sense of values. There is a constant growth, as we saw, in our appreciation of good and evil. What at one time was the best possible expression of the great values of life (that is, of the ten commandments, which are radically unalterable) is seen later to be unsatisfactory. Conscience tries to reform and re-state the law.

This is of particular interest because we are speaking of the commandments as they are expounded in the Church, the community of God, that is, in the community where conscience plays a particularly important role. What matters to the Church, after all, is how man stands with regard to his God. "Whatever you bind on earth shall be bound *in heaven.*" The role of conscience is essential in the Christian life, so much so that the Church affirms that even "an erroneous conscience" is binding. Thus Saint Paul said: "Whatever does not proceed from faith (i.e. conscience) is sin" (Rom. 14:23); St Thomas Aquinas (13th century): "If one professes faith in Christ or the Church when he has come to the conviction that it is wrong, then he sins against his conscience." Cardinal Newman (last century): "I have always firmly held that obedience to one's conscience, even if the conscience is erroneous, is the best way to the light."

These thinkers are well aware that the question is not solved by a purely subjective decision. The challenge of the law, of the conscience of the authentic fellowship, cannot be lightly

139-140

dismissed. Medieval thought, which was very objective and strongly orientated to society, even laid stress upon this element. One has the impression, for instance, that St Thomas cannot imagine how one can come to have an erroneous conscience through no fault at all of one's own. St Augustine's view (4th century) was even more strongly opposed to the possibility of an inculpably erroneous conscience. Nonetheless, it remains the constant teaching of the Church that each man must be guided by the profound law of his conscience. The council says that "Fidelity to conscience is the bond which links Christians with all mankind in the search for truth" (*The Church in the World*, no. 16).

The Church is concerned with the relationship between one's self and God. Hence the laws of the Church are of a different order than those of the State. The laws of the State are concerned with public order and do not claim to have to do with conscience. This does not mean that they cannot bind in conscience. But that is not the business of the State. The laws of the Church, however, claim to bind in conscience, because they are supported by conscience. There is no outward coercion, but an inward call. Those who do not believe are not bound by the laws of the Church as such. 418

The forms in which Church law is articulated should display more and more clearly what is proper to Church law: that they are different from the laws of the State.

The formation of the conscience

There are many reasons why at the present time greater stress is laid on the personal verdict of conscience. There is a growing sense of the uniqueness of each man and of his situation. And we are living in a special period of transition when our sense of values is being very definitely renovated.

The question is all the more urgent where an antiquated sense of values is also an over-narrow one, or when laws which reflect an antiquated notion have gone too deeply into details. In such cases it is our duty to take counsel with our own instinct of faith, our own sense of what is good. (This of course will not be a solitary process. In the community of God, indeed, in the whole of mankind, one asks for advice, one discusses matters with others and one notes how a new notion takes form in consciences.)

Hence we find ourselves today faced with a very special task. On the one hand, the government of the community continues to call for humility and obedience, virtues without which the Christian spirit and peace cannot exist: "Think not that I have come to abolish the law and the prophets", said 129 Christ (Mt. 5:17). On the other hand, we have the duty, as friends of God, with tranquil and courageous consciences, to consult men of good will and not to evade the responsibility of personal decision where this is called for. This is the attitude 129 which Jesus called for when he said: "Have you not read what David did, when he was hungry, and those who were with him; how he entered the house of God and ate the bread of the Presence, which it was not lawful for him to eat, but only for the priests?" (Mt. 12:3–4). Then there is the fact that Jesus himself did not regard the commandments as rootless, isolated precepts, merely dictated by an arbitrary command of God. He shows that at the heart of the commandments there is 132 a living core from which each has value and significance. This he does when he says, "On these two commandments depend all the law and the prophets" (Mt. 22:40). The two commandments are: "You shall love the Lord your God with all your heart and with all your soul, and with all your mind. This is the great and first commandment. And a second is like it, You shall love your neighbour as yourself" (Mt. 22:37–39). The whole source and purpose of the law is love. The ten commandments, the first three as well as the last seven, are comprised in this. Here they are given their profoundest meaning: love of God, love of man.

Love of neighbour as a mystery of faith

132–135 We are left therefore with one commandment—love, one which is full of divine demands. Is this the revelation of something that should be taken for granted in any case? We are sometimes inclined to think so, unconscious as we are of how 232 deeply our attitudes have been penetrated by twenty centuries of the preaching of the gospel in the Church of God. But Teilhard de Chardin could write, feeling himself once tempted to regard struggle and power as the greatest forces in the universe, that the revelation of the charge to love seemed to him the revelation of a mystery. The arrogance of the strong and the rancour of the weak melt away under this commandment.

It is God's mysterious criticism of our actions—a criticism which heals and gives life. It is essentially nothing less than the revelation that God is love. Hence love of God and of man cannot be separated. 372

Love of the neighbour, to the disregard of God, is so much contrary to the message of Jesus that it is not even mentioned in the gospel. The lordship of God, to whom we are converted in love, is the kernel of the preaching of Jesus. His prayer, the Our Father, speaks first of the name, the kingdom and the will of the Father. The Father is prior to all, totally and obviously. This is not surprising. How can one be firmly convinced that love is the greatest of all things if he has closed his heart to God? How does he know, for instance, that self-preservation is not the first law? Or that everything is not simply meaningless? Only if we believe that the universe is ultimately and most profoundly based on love, that is, on God, can we know that love of others is the one thing that matters for us men. 93–105 121–122 501

But are there not men of great and authentic love who are without God? Let us consider the various possibilities. There are men who find that friendliness and kindness are the most rewarding ways of dealing with their fellows. This is the best way to avoid clashes. Things go smoothly along these lines. And such a conviction may be held without God. But it is easy to see that in such cases, love is a means to something else, and this something else (esteem, comfortable relations) is looked on as the greatest good. But Jesus' message, love of the neighbour, is something different. It means that everything must be a means to love. This is the supreme and only serious end.

But are there not men who regard love really as the one important thing, and still despise God? Are there not men who cherish a sort of grudge against God, and hence feel themselves on terms of comradeship with mankind? Linked in a sort of conspiracy? But how can this be possible? If they despise deliberately the greatest love, how can they arrive at authentic love? It is impossible. It would end up as a collective lamentation. And there would be no good reason for ever restoring unity if it ever broke down among them. It would, in a word, be Babel.

But it will be maintained that there are men who live such a life of love. They regard the Mystery of the Origin as unhelpful and uncertain, but still they manage to build up some sort of solidarity among themselves. They despise God and love their neighbour.—But it is not in fact so. What they despise is a caricature of God, incorporating, for instance a blind urge to create, or a cold hard fate—a silly old man in the clouds, a tyrant, but not God himself. And then, with the homing instinct which each good man has, they seek the purest and finest thing on earth. They find that this is love of the neighbour. Wherever true love is genuinely discovered and lived, something of God's self is discovered and experienced, even where men think that he does not exist. "Where there is love and affection, there is God."

But then should not such good men come sooner or later to an explicit faith in God? Very often they do. But here on earth this must not always be the case. The caricature of God may be so profoundly impressed on men's minds by their education that they never succeed in picturing the true and living God. But their openness towards man, the crown of creation, will undoubtedly have given them an openness for the whole of existence. They will be watchful for the mystery which reveals itself behind and in love. They will listen to see whether the mystery of existence may not after all be a mystery of love. There is no pure love of the neighbour without openness for the true and living God.

12–17
445–449

38–39

God in our neighbour

And vice versa, there can be no love of God without love of his most beloved creature, man. "He who does not love his brother whom he has seen, cannot love God whom he has not seen" (1 Jn 4:20). It is undoubtedly possible to *appear* to care much for God and still fail to be good and kind to others. One can pray very often and very fervently, and still behave badly to others. But then either the prayer is not real prayer, but simply preoccupation with a God of one's own making, without listening to the word of God in the Church and in creation. Or the person in question is not really such a failure as he appears to be. He may simply be very hot-tempered or introvert by nature, but ready when the need arises to do all he can for others, calmly and soberly. Or he may have been brought up with very one-sided ideas of what Christian life should be, which have led him to neglect some of the ordinary ways by which goodness is attained, such as joyfulness and naturalness. He may have learned little of the connection between the message of Christ and the spontaneous goodness of man (on which see above, in the

296

134–135

discussion of "Love" in the New Testament). Such neglect is a serious matter, and it is to be hoped that no one will pass on such attitudes when it is his turn to be an educator. But meanwhile, by sincerely concentrating on God, he may have developed a really steadfast and solid goodness.

Psychology and temperament enter so much into all these matters that they call for lengthy discussion. But we can at least note some directives in our own regard. Each of the two loves constitutes a check on the other. If we wish to check our attitude to God, we should examine our attitude to our fellows. And if we find that our love of them is sincere, it will often be evident that we are open to God. And again, those who are trying to unite themselves more closely to God may often be helped by turning their attention to their fellows, while those who find it hard to love others can be helped and enlightened by turning to God. The unity of the two great commandments brings with it growth and freedom.

Law without limit

The commandment of love is beyond human forces. Self-preservation and self-interest often remain our profoundest motives, deeper than our love. Nonetheless, we must love our neighbour "as ourselves", that is, with the same energy that we 133 put into self-preservation. Hence the law of love knows no limits. We can never say we have accomplished it. This we have already noted, in the discussion of the Sermon on the Mount. We dwelt at some length on the fact that while Jesus maintained the law, he let it be seen that there was more in it than the rigid: thus far and no further. Jesus made all the law a task of love, and love never says, It is enough. The law became thereby a 129-131 more serious matter, as may be seen from Jesus' description of the judgment in Matthew 25:31–46. Since Jesus came, all human failure is failure in love, and this is the most serious failure of all.

But at the same time everything has become personal. The law is no longer an impersonal set of regulations bearing with them their automatic sanctions. It has become a task in which we are personally and warmly involved, since to break it is to offend others—and God. Hence the task is endless. But this also means that our weakness is taken into account. It is graver to fail, but we can always try again. All we have to do is to continue to hunger and thirst after justice and love.

> "But if anyone has the world's goods and sees his brother in need, yet closes his heart against him, how does God's love abide in him? Little children, let us not love in word or speech but in deed and in truth" (1 Jn 3:17–18).

No one can define exactly what it means to be good to his fellows, so that he can say contentedly, yes, I have done it. It is a task with which one is never done. It is a gift for which we must always long more and more.

Will-power and neat resolutions are not enough to make such goodness flourish. Love also needs openness, reverence, thankfulness and other attitudes with which will-power has little to do directly. It is something to be strained after with all the fibres of our being. If it is to be full and genuine, it must be the outcome of all the perceptivity, the gaiety and seriousness, the tranquillity and tension of our spirit. All profane and sacred sciences and skills are needed to find ways to express it. We must always pray for it humbly with all our heart. It is prayer for God's own Spirit "who washes what is unclean, waters what is withered, bends what is rigid, warms what is cold and heals what is wounded". "Without his power there is nothing in man that is not harmful"—as we say when we sing the hymn, "Come, Creator Spirit".

300-302

The Church in the World

373 "God so loved the world." Christians are called to love like God, that is, with a love that goes out to the whole world. We are now happy to have the constitution "The Church in the World" of the Second Vatican Council, because it describes this task of Christians in pages which direct the disciple of Christ not only to the world of ideals, but to the actual world of workaday life, with its daily round of duties, the place where men buy and sell and contend according to their own rules and values, the universe as it actually evolves. This is where our God is to be found.

In the following chapters all this will be discussed more fully: family and married life, the religious life of the evangelical counsels, political life, reverence for life and all that work, property, altruism, culture, leisure and the quest of truth involve.

MARRIAGE AND THE FAMILY

One of a family

If I am asked who I am, I give my surname as well as my Christian name. I am identified by my family. Even something so much our own as our name includes those who are nearest to us. It shows how little we can really be separated from our family. The colour of our hair, the traits of our character and the very fact of our existence are derived from others. To be human is to be born of other men, to be woven with fibres from other lives. There was a man and a woman, and a family behind each of them. Two currents of humanity came together in my parents' marriage, and at a given moment, there was I.

We may well say, at a "given" moment. Neither my father nor my mother could say with certainty that a new life would come to be. The fecundation is always to some extent unpredictable, and in it there are forces at work which human ingenuity cannot imitate. Human beings are responsible for having children, but the result goes so far beyond them that the parents feel that the child is given them rather than procreated by them. Psalm 127, 74–75 "Unless the Lord builds the house, those who build it labour in vain" says of the conception of children: "He gives to his beloved in sleep. Lo, sons are a heritage from the Lord."

It may still be affirmed, however, that though new human life comes about according to laws that we have not made, we can still study these laws and to some extent gain control over them. But there is still one thing which remains an inviolable wonder outside all human control: that it was precisely "I" who was to be born. Why did the union of two people, on a certain day, say, in Amsterdam in 1930, result exactly in this "I"? Why did this I not come into existence in the African mountains ten thousand years B.C.? Why not in the next parish? Why not a thousand years ago? Why not—never? Who sorts this out?

The creation of man

Each human person is so unique that as he comes into existence we see very well that we should not say, "God created all things", but, "God is creating all things". It was once usual to say that God created the world and preserves it in being, but creates each soul directly each time. But this manner of speaking failed to do justice to two things, one, that creation itself is a reality which strives upwards, and two, that body and soul are not to be divided. Hence it seems better to express the same truth in another way by saying that God's creative power causes reality to be and to grow at each moment. The beginning of a new human life is a sacred moment in which this creative power is particularly evident. After all, my parents could not have wanted "me". At best, they wanted "a boy" or "a girl". Only God wanted "me". An "I" which could say "You" to God, have a direct personal relationship with him, is called into being through human heredity, and hence by the hand of God. These two things form together one action. Hence the power to cooperate with God is bestowed on parents as they give new life to a child. This cooperation does not end at the birth. It is completed in the education of the child. God nourishes, loves and guides the new human life through its parents. They have a serious and a joyful responsibility.

488–489

239–240

The family as the cell of love

The family is where the first smile is seen—the child knows its mother, and smiles—which no animal can do. "Incipe, parve puer, risu cognoscere matrem"—"Smile, little one, as you begin to know your mother", as the poet Virgil sang. The child's human consciousness is formed in the family, and there he discovers that he counts, that he counts along with the others. Father, mother, brothers, sisters, friends, neighbours, grandparents and so on, are all discovered on the basis of the family. One grows as man by discovering other human beings, since man is made for love.

213

The first to be known as "others" are father and mother. Nothing has a deeper influence in life than the relationship between parents and child. It can never be undone. We are always the children of our parents. And it is in the family that the way to the Other begins, who comes to us in all others. God who created and gave growth to the child through its parents is also known first and foremost through the parents. The child cannot know God through its own efforts. As it plays, cries and sleeps, it feels at home in its little world which is very great to him, and in which goodness, omnipotence and omnipresence are represented by father and mother. The way we have learned to know our parents is of immeasurable importance in our image of God. No doubt the parents are not the only ones who help to form the image. Everyone whom we encounter in later life and who loves us, reflects for us once more the goodness of God. Much that may have been warped by the incapacity or indifference of parents may be put right in this way—all the more so because there is something in man which is always looking into a farther distance, beyond father and mother, beyond any other man. God is not the mere extension of father 115-116 or mother or of anyone else. He is the infinite goodness for which the human heart was ultimately made. He is the most truly "other", in whom our heart is the less disappointed the better we learn to know him, that is, to know him in Jesus, the companion 497 of our route and our God.

The erotic element

All human life is giving and taking, serving and being served, 385 giving and accepting love, giving and accepting inspiration. 390 Without it, we are dead; with it, we move among new life, new 401, 410 forms, new thought. All that is human, from lonely work to 501 companionable talk or saving someone's life, is in one way or another giving and receiving and hence life-giving and fruitful. Whether married or single, man shares in the process of birth. Being man or woman is a special instance of this basic rhythm. Husband and wife, man and woman, does not designate an absolute difference, but the giving and receiving has a different emphasis in each: the male is more active and outgoing, the female more passive and receptive. This is intrinsic to the whole man and can even be deduced from his outward appearance. Hence bodily giving and receiving is also happy and joyful, in a very comprehensive way: the whole man is affected, from his most inward depths to his most tangible earthliness. This mutual giving and receiving is fruitful and life-giving in the highest possible measure: it brings forth new human life. It is a force which mankind discovers within itself with rapture and awe as each man discovers it anew. He recognizes that he is accomplishing more than he could consciously follow with his mind.

To say that the erotic is good would be inadequate. (We use "erotic" here for sexuality in all its facets—physical, psychic etc.) It is a marvellous and creative force in us. But it is likewise terrifying, on account of its force. When erotic desires are detached from human values as a whole, and especially when the most bodily aspect of them, genital sexuality, is isolated from human erotic as a whole, unsuspected depths of evil can be revealed where all seemed delicate and endearing.

It is only when integrated in the totality of man's being that we can see how good and lovely the erotic is. Everyone knows how dear the beloved is to the lover. The attractiveness of another is seen and activated. Something of the infinite shines through the beloved, something to which one is drawn to give oneself totally. This is not an illusion. The eyes are opened to a beauty which is really there. In our estimation of the world, many more erotic tendencies are at work than we often suspect. The source and the summit of them is love between man and woman.

To give oneself fully is to give oneself for always. It is not a matter of giving and receiving physically, and then going away without meeting again, as with the lower animals. There is also more in human love than the temporary companionship of the higher animals, who stay together fondly to bring up their young. In human love, the man and the woman wish to belong to each other wholly.

The homosexual

There are a certain number of people whose eroticism cannot be directed to the other sex, but apparently only to the sex to which they themselves belong. Lack of frank discussion has allowed a number of opinions to be formed about them which are unjust when applied generally, because those who have such inclinations in fact are often hard-working and honourable people.

It is not the fault of the individual if he or she is not attracted to the other sex. The causes of homosexuality are unknown. In their human isolation, they look for friendship. But even where they find true and loyal responses, the perfect fulfilment of their human longings is not granted them. Ultimately all homosexual (or rather, homo-erotic) tendencies come up against the discovery that the sexual in man can only find its natural fulfilment—as may be deduced from human structure—in the other sex. Those who know that they are homosexual should discuss the matter with a doctor, a spiritual director or someone prudent and competent. They must also try to learn that the greatness of life consists of giving and receiving.

The very sharp strictures of Scripture on homosexual practices (Gen. 19; Rom. 1) must be read in their context. Their aim is not to pillory the fact that some people experience this perversion inculpably. They denounce a homosexuality which had become the prevalent fashion and had spread to many who were really quite capable of normal sexual sentiments.

383

390–391

Love and promise

We now take up the subject of marriage, and begin with the ordinary way to marriage. People begin to suspect that they are meant for each other when they experience the marvel of falling in love. A young man and a young woman discover something in each other that no outsider can fully see. The hope and the need of giving themselves to each other completely take shape and grow. The heart has its reasons which the reason does not quite know, according to Pascal, nor is it necessary that it should. But if one is to give oneself to another totally and for ever, one must make a decision with one's whole person. Hence reason and conscience cannot be left out. The enchantment of love opens the eyes to the uniqueness of the other, but it can also blind, if it remains a superficially sensual or romantic attachment.

The engagement allows the young people to see whether their first love is growing into real love. They confront each other either alone, in affectionate conversation, or with other young people, to compare themselves with them. In their families or at work they can witness each other's ups and downs, and gradually become acquainted with each other's background and interests. This is really necessary if they are to choose each other with the profound insight which such a vital decision deserves.

The parents stand more aside than they formerly did in most cases, and confine themselves to giving advice. The young people make the most important choice of their life quite freely. Love and prudence, not ambition (the hope of making money and a career), or resentment (against former loves or against parents) should guide them in choosing the proper partner. As they grow more and more sure that they are meant for each other, they grow towards each other, not merely as companions but as future spouses.—Sexuality, in the broadest sense of the term, plays an essential part in the engagement, both spiritually and physically. It is no longer the mere urge towards "the" male or "the" female. As the fully human eroticism develops, it is concerned with the You alone, and any third person is automatically excluded as a threat.

> "Arise, my love, my fair one,
> and come away;
> for lo, the winter is past,
> the rain is over and gone.
> The flowers appear on the earth,
> the time of singing has come,
> and the voice of the turtledove
> is heard in our land.
> The fig tree puts forth its figs,
> and the vines are in blossom;
> they give forth fragrance.
> Arise, my love, my fair one,
> and come away.
> O my dove, in the clefts of the rock,
> in the covert of the cliff,
> let me see your face,
> let me hear your voice,
> for your voice is sweet,
> and your face is comely" (Song of Solomon 2:10–14).

Gradually the young people recognize that they are responsible for each other's future. Genuine love will prevent their courtship from becoming an "égoïsme à deux", an effort to "get all they can out of it". Such attitudes during the engagement can so predominate over all other experiences that they sometimes do not really know each other well before they marry.

Timidity and anxiety are also out of place. The fact that they are in love enables the young people to speak honestly and conscientiously about the caresses they may indulge in at the various stages of courtship. This will make them ready to adapt themselves to each other's wishes, and make them prepare prudently for any situations that may arise. The great guide in these matters, better than hard and fast rules, is the chastity of courtship, which is characterized by an intimacy which still keeps a healthy distance from the total surrender of marriage.

The provisional element

Ideally, people should marry as soon as both are decided. But this ideal date has to reckon with difficulties from two angles. One is the fact that marriage might come too early, because the young people are too immature spiritually to guarantee that they have chosen each other calmly and seriously. And there is also the overhasty precipitation if a child is on the way—as if a "shot-gun" marriage was the best solution. The other difficulty is the prolonged wait for housing or for the completion of studies. In this case the young people will be well-advised not to allow themselves to adopt too quickly the attitude of future husband and wife. As long as the bond has not been confirmed by Church and State, it is not definitive. Hence, though the young people may have become very intimate, sexual intercourse in such a situation is irresponsible. The reason is that it has by its very nature a definitive character. It implies that it is "for good". If they surrender themselves to it, there is an inner change in the young man and the young woman. From then on they experience each other as husband and wife, and each act of union conjures up one to follow. This brings with it on the one hand the sense of being married, and on the other, the conflict of knowing that they are not married. And a step backwards —at any rate if a long period is involved—is only possible at the cost of profound inner tensions.

From all these human reasons we can deduce God's will and law—that only married people should live together. That it is the will of God will be a welcome and strong motive for the believer. Failures need not cause inhibitions, but may be occasions for new courage, once the will of God is acknowledged. It will broaden our whole outlook on life by reminding us that "we are not our own". In difficult situations this can be a thought which people can use to encourage each other.

The history of marriage

We begin our discussion of marriage with a glance at the history of human marriage. We see a gradual evolution. More and more, marriage came to be looked on as the union of one man with one woman. This has gone hand in hand with the fact that the mutual dedication has become more profoundly human and that each of the partners has come to stand more and more on the same footing as the other. Parallel to this evolution is the tendency —very clear in our own day—to set up a family which will be complete in itself, and not just part of a wider group of clan or family. People now launch out in twos. It is an adventure which offers the possibility of great and profound intimacy. Another development which is just as clear in our own times is that the number of children is no longer left to the blind forces of 402 fertility, but has become rather a matter of personal responsibility.

These features, which allow of, and call for, a greater humanization of marriage, have certainly not developed throughout the ages without the Spirit of God. But the development has 402–403 drawn strength, inspiration and clarity from the divine revelation in the Old and New Testament, as we shall now see.

Marriage in the Old Testament

One of the oldest and most striking texts on marriage is the 56 Song of Solomon (Canticle of Canticles). The core of the Song goes back to the ancient period of the monarchy. In erotic poetry of high quality, and without the least embarrassment, it sings the love of two young people. Why was it adopted into the canon of the sacred books? Some suspect that it was already there even before it was given the deeper meaning of the love between Yahweh and Israel. It could have been admitted because it described love as a human reality, not as a sort of murky participation of the adventures of the gods and goddesses of 36 fertility (the Baals and Astartes). To reveal the true meaning of the erotic, it was necessary to rid it of the dubious "sacralization" of the pagan rites. That love reveals something of God himself we shall see later. For the moment it suffices to say that the 224–225 erotic is earthly and human, that is, a gift of creation from the 278 one God.

The creation narratives breathe the same spirit. Genesis 1 261–262
emphasizes fertility: "Male and female he created them . . .'Be
fruitful and multiply'." Genesis 2, which is older, puts more
stress on love (the first encounter after Adam's awakening!) and
on the similarity of man and woman. Perfect equality is not yet
to be found in this narrative. But there is an obvious preference
for monogamy. Though monogamy was not commanded,
the preference for it can be noted frequently in the Old Testament.—The making of Eve from the rib of Adam is of course
not a historical description. But it has its significance. It means
that the woman is of like nature with the man, and loved by
him. (The Arabs still say of a close friend that he is "a rib".)

In Genesis 3, the story of the fall and its punishment, the Bible
also speaks of the tragic element of marriage, obviously in connection with the whole of human sinfulness. There the woman
appears also as seducer, the man also as tyrant. But the story also
includes signs of confidence that God will redeem and restore
mankind—God's giving them protective clothing, his promise
of the conquest of the serpent.

In the prophets, and under the pen of the writers who re-
worked the Song of Solomon, marriage appears as an image of
Yahweh's love for his people. This shows how highly Israel
esteemed the perfect marriage. And there is great human
tenderness behind this regulation of the Israelite law: "When a
man is newly married, he shall not go out with the army or be
charged with any business; he shall be free at home one year, to
be happy with his wife whom he has taken" (Deut. 24:5).

Marriage in the New Testament

The fact that our Lord was not married does not mean that he
gave the least hint of lack of esteem for marriage. On the
contrary, when the Pharisees asked him whether a man might
divorce his wife, he sent them to the intuition which was already
contained in the creation narrative, and concluded: "What 128–129
therefore God has joined together, let not man put asunder"
(Mk 10:9). And later he said: "Whoever divorces his wife and
marries another, commits adultery against her; and if she
divorces her husband and marries another, she commits adultery"
(Mk 10:11–12).

Thus Jesus makes the marriage bond indissoluble. Man and

woman give themselves to each other. This is how seriously they must take one another. And Jesus does not intend it merely as an external institution. He goes deeper. The whole man, even in his inmost depths, is to keep himself free for the other. Hence

129 Jesus says: "You have heard that it was said, 'You shall not commit adultery'. But I say to you that every one who looks at a woman lustfully has already committed adultery with her in his heart" (Mt. 5:27–28). Jesus aims at giving love its greatest possible and most enduring opportunity.

The New Testament has still more to say about marriage. The Epistle to the Ephesians compares marriage to Christ's love for the Church. It goes so far as to say, when dealing with the unity of the married couple, that "husbands should love their wives as their own bodies. He who loves his wife loves himself. For no man ever hates his own flesh, but nourishes and cherishes it, as Christ does the Church" (Eph. 5:28–29). "As Christ loves the Church" is the important point. To grasp Paul's intention, we might go through this chapter, which is used as the epistle at the nuptial mass, and underline the word "as" with red every time we meet it. It would then be clear that it is the same comparison as that used by the prophets when they compared Yahweh's love for Israel with married love; only that here, on account of Christ's humanity, the comparison has become much more striking. Further, the comparison is now reversed and thereby given a much deeper meaning. It is not that Jesus' love for the Church is like married love. It is that marriage is like Jesus' unity with the Church. The real and ultimate thing is the divine love—a giving and receiving between Christ and mankind. Marriage is so sacred a mystery that it may be compared with this love. When we then recall that the love between Christ and mankind is in turn a reflection of the love between the Father and the Son—"As the Father has loved me, so have I

383 loved you"—we realize that the giving and receiving in marriage is an image of the love in God. Marriage, that gift of creation, manifests on its own level something of the unfathomable

501-502 depths of giving and loving, of mutual absorption and satisfaction within the divine being itself. Newly married couples who use the word divine during the honeymoon are very profoundly justified.

This does not mean that marriage is the only way to participate in the mystery of God's love. All love and kindness among men participates in this mystery, all giving and receiving, all the more so the purer it is. And its purity is measured by the way it corresponds to the love which Christ taught us and gave us through his Spirit: love of God with our whole being, and of our neighbour as ourselves. Indeed, the comparison between human marriage and the union between Christ and the Church is only verified in so far as our family shows the sort of love which Christ taught and inspired. It must be love of the other as of oneself. It is the love—and now a decisive word must be spoken, the one word which can really place us in the New Testament—in which the cross has its place. Thus it is a love which is proof against disappointment, a loyalty which is proof against failure—failure to come up to each other's expectations, to make joy full, to find love satisfying. It is love and loyalty which persist even where humanly speaking there seems to be no reason for it—just as the cross of Jesus was humanly speaking hopeless, but brought salvation and goodness. It is only faith that makes Christian marriage really an image of Christ's love for his Church. This alone is wholly "marriage in the Lord" (cf. 1 Cor. 7:39). When Christ is there, marriage is not the anxious adventure of isolated people living together. He is with them. `282-283`

He has not promised that everything will be pleasant. He tells us that our love must be forgetful of self, more attentive to giving than receiving. "It is more blessed to give than to receive" (Acts 20:35), he said. But he does not merely ask this of us. He also gives us power to strive for it, through his Spirit within us. `300` And this is a promise that every failure, every collapse, every pain has its meaning as the way towards the total happiness given even to human love when it is in God. The crucifix in the house becomes more than an ornament. It signifies that ultimately nothing is hopeless, where an effort to love has been made. It also means that the absolute indissolubility of marriage —even though it seems absurd in what are, humanly speaking, hopeless cases—still retains its profound significance, as participation in Christ's love even in the crucifixion. Because he did not abandon mankind and the Church when he was nailed to the cross, every marriage "in the Lord" retains the indissolubility `282` of the bond between Christ and the Church, even where it has become a crucifixion.

Hence Jesus' presence in Christian marriage does not mean that there will not be clashes of temperament, mistakes in choice of partner, troubles with children, strained nerves, illness, boredom and even necessary and final separation. But it does mean that for Christians there is always a third person present, the Christ who strengthens, consoles, and gives hope, and reminds them that it is better to give than to receive. Those who allow themselves to be penetrated by this faith on their good days will be able to live by it in evil times.

That the cross has a place in Christian marriage should not be taken up wrongly. It does not mean surrender to unhappiness and failure. Christians will always make every effort to build up and preserve a happy family life. But it means that even the misfortunes which befall a family can ultimately have a meaning, like the cross of our Lord.

By holding forth these hopes and making these demands Christ has visibly elevated the status of matrimony in the course of history. In an age-long process he redeemed human love. He taught man and woman how to treasure each other's dignity. He freed love from the tyranny of untamed forces in sexual matters, and opened men's eyes at the same time to the holiness of married love, in spite of the puritanical inclinations which 221 constantly re-assert themselves.

Marriage as a sacrament

The holiness given by Christ to marriage is seen very clearly from the fact that the conjugal union of the baptized is a 252 sacrament. This means that marriage itself is a sacred sign through which Christ gives us his Holy Spirit. What does the sign consist of? It is the simplest imaginable: the mutual promise, and the life in accordance with this promise. This is the sacrament. Hence the form of the sacrament is no particular juridical formula taken by itself, nor the marriage ceremony by itself, but the will to belong to each other in love and freely-chosen loyalty, till the day of death. Hence all the love, tenderness, help and counsel that married people offer each other is a source of grace, of Christ's presence, of the Holy Spirit. This is the nature of the marriage which Christians enter into before God.

A public act

Such a bond needs to be notified to society. The union must be entered into publicly, before the community. This everyone

392

recognizes. No one wants to get married in secret—except for very special reasons, which are not always very pleasant ones. A girl wants to appear as a bride before her family and acquaintances, before anyone who wants to look. And no one wishes to get married without having his marriage ratified and protected by the law. A good law is not contrary to love, but signifies the recognition and protection of the bond of love in the public sphere.

The public nature of marriage varied at different times. In the middle ages marriage was contracted in the family, according to the forms and laws of the local community. If it was desired, a priest was asked to pronounce the marriage blessing, but this was clearly only a "sacramental". The sacrament itself was the 255 mutual consent to marriage of man and wife, confirmed by the physical consummation of the marriage. After the Council of Trent in the sixteenth century, precise legal forms were instituted 223–225 for marriage in canon law. (This was possible because the Church is the guardian of the sacraments.) It was laid down that marriage must be contracted before the parish priest (of the bride) and two witnesses. This juridical form was a condition for the validity of marriage.—But even in this solemnization of marriage the sacrament itself remains the mutual consent of the man and woman. The parish priest does not marry them. They marry each other by making their promises before the priest—when they say, I will. This is best done at the nuptial mass. The blessing given by the priest emphasizes the fact that it is a promise "in the Lord".

The laws laid down by Trent—which can admit of exceptions, however, as in danger of death or when it is foreseen that a priest will not be available for some time, in which case the presence of two witnesses suffices—were a far-reaching intervention, but necessary. Since there was no system of registering marriages, the number of "clandestine marriages" (mutual consent before two witnesses without registration or publication) had grown to disquieting proportions, opening up the way in many cases to infidelity and bigamy. This gave rise to the demand for fixed public forms, under pain of invalidity. We must also remember that the State did not register marriages at the time. At present, now that the State does so, the Church may under certain circumstances dispense the parties from the legal form, and recognize as ecclesiastically valid a civil marriage, as for instance in certain exceptional cases of marriage between a Catholic and a non-Catholic.

Civil marriage

It is understandable that the State, following the example of the Church, should provide legal security as regards marriage. This led to the introduction of civil marriage. Some countries avoided the double ceremony by admitting the religious ceremony as legally valid. In other countries they remain distinct. Where a civil ceremony does take place before the religious marriage, such a promise of mutual faithfulness before the national community, represented by the civil officer, is more than a formality, even for the Catholic. It is essentially a subordinate part of the total consent, which is only fully given by the Catholic when he also pronounces his Yes before the representative of the Church. For this reason it is wrong to let too much time elapse between one form of consent and the other.

The marriage of non-Catholics

The Church laws concerning the form of marriage affect only marriages where one or both of the partners are Catholics. As regards non-Christians, the Church law is based on the supposition that their marriages are and remain valid, even when one of the partners becomes a Catholic. But if the non-Catholic partner then refuses to live in peace with the Catholic, the "Pauline privilege" (cf. 1 Cor. 7:12–15) can come into play in canon law.

The marriage of two non-Catholic Christians is of course also a Christian value. One may be sure that wherever Christians wish to be married "in the Lord", Christ is present. Hence the marriage of baptized non-Catholics is sanctified and of a sacramental nature. Hence too it is indissoluble.

Protective laws

Let us return for a moment to the canon law of marriage. It serves as a public protection for the values of marriage, even where it speaks of impediments. The State sets up impediments as well as the Church. The Church has the power to do so in as much as marriage is a sacrament in its fellowship. The impediments stem from the very nature of marriage: a marriage bond already in existence; one or other of the pair being too young; compulsion or fear; too close a degree of blood relationship; physical impotence. They set out in detail what each of us feels is contrary to the nature and dignity of marriage.—For other cases and for marginal cases the experts should be consulted. Here we give only the main outlines.

Cases undoubtedly occur where the mutual consent was not humanly complete.—This can happen where the partners are spiritually non-adult, not entirely free, and not clear enough about what they are undertaking by getting married. But they still want to get married—for instance, because there is "a child on the way". The marriage is just a way of legalizing a situation which would otherwise excite too much attention among the talkative members of the community and above all leave the woman in an intolerable position. The sincere but over-simple judgment of society then practically obliges the man "to accept the consequences" and so get married officially. It cannot of course be maintained that such a marriage has been entered into clearly and demonstrably under compulsion by third parties, since the two parties themselves mostly take the decision which has become necessary. They accept the consequences which are based chiefly on a social sense of obligation. Often they do care for each other. But no one will maintain that a union entered upon so hurriedly and unexpectedly corresponds to the idea of matrimony in a truly human perspective, much less in the Christian one—which is the responsible acceptance of a free union for life which must be able to stand the test of misfortune and disappointment. These "shot-gun" marriages often give the impression that they have been entered upon without due consideration, though no one can say that they will necessarily fail. Still, many such unions are entered upon by those who are spiritually immature, and practically forced into them by the pressure of social judgment.

In canon law, such marriages cannot later be declared null and void, because no one can provide clear proof of lack of freedom when the marriage contract was being made. Here we have a conflict between a just law which is based on correct 374–376 principles but can lead in some cases to the continuation of an injustice. On the one hand, there is public order in the Church, for which the Church, as witness to Christ, must always be the champion, even as regards marriage. And on the other hand, there is the individual conscience—assuming that this is not the cloak of purely selfish interests but the recognition of God's supreme lordship. The result is a tragic inner discord. In such cases a thorough discussion with a prudent priest can free people from many unnecessary anxieties. It may even happen that a Christian—after sincere consideration and prayer—will come to the conclusion that his marriage does not bind him in conscience and that a second marriage would not therefore really mean "living in sin"—though it might be termed so, understandably, by others. In such cases he is suffering the consequences of his earlier imprudence. But he is also bearing the burden of a law which is not quite perfect (as even canon law is not) and also the burden of a social verdict which is often harsh, hypocritical and certainly not fully Christian. Strictly speaking, Christians should not pass judgment on each other in such matters, much less condemn each other, because it is not granted us to know infallibly who is really married in Christ and who is not.

A still more difficult case arises where marriages which were contracted freely with all reasonable precautions later turn into really intolerable situations, even for the children, no doubt through the fault of the partners, or possibly because they only learned to know each other too late. There can be no question of an initially defective marriage consent, as in the cases given above. It is simply that a marriage which according to the general consensus began well afterwards broke down.

From the earliest times, the Church has acknowledged the right of the partners to a separation *a mensa et thoro*. But then there is the difficulty that they are obliged to go through life alone, without a new marriage partner. Many, who are nonetheless conscientious in their general behaviour, find this too heavy a burden and enter upon a second marriage—outside the Church.

What are we, as Christians, to think of such situations? Prescinding from the fact that a better preparation for marriage might well have prevented such conflicts arising, it remains true that we should never judge such people harshly. Whether they are necessarily and perpetually to be excluded from the fellowship of the Eucharist can only be judged by God who

knows all things. In particular cases a wise priest will be able
to help them to come to a conclusion themselves on the matter.
In such a discussion, for instance, their actual obligations, in
terms of the situation which has now arisen, may become
clearer. It may, for instance, be their duty, in a situation possibly
brought about by sinfulness, to do the best they can with their
lives and the lives of those for whom they are now responsible.

In this world of failures, the sacraments are given to men to
nourish and strengthen them.—Though the priest can help
them to form their conscience, he cannot take over the duty
of making the decision. Here too it is true that the final certainty
of conscience is achieved by the individual himself.

Needless to say, all this does not mean that marriage is not
indissoluble according to the faith of the Church, or that it
must always be declared null and void where this would suit
difficult situations. On the contrary, the Church has not only
the right but the duty of proclaiming the indissolubility of
matrimony before God and man. It must base its marriage
laws on this truth, and will always continue to do so. And the
individual, who believes in Christ and in his presence in the
Church, is not permitted to put aside the commandment of
Christ and make his own laws.

The matters raised in these pages simply mean that it is not
granted to us men—even where legislation is at its most subtle,
and most strongly orientated to practical life—to decide in
every instance whether this or that marriage is really contracted
in Christ. In these matters we must always start from the normal
presuppositions. But Church law, as it reflects them, must
become steadily more precise, subtle and dexterous. Canon
law does not stand still. Nonetheless there will never be, on
this earthly pilgrimage of the Church, a total identification
between law and conscience, canons and love, regulations and
faith. According to Christ's word and Paul's preaching, it is
a very Christian thing to keep this tension between law and
conscience well in mind. Otherwise the sad consequence will be
that the official Church may appear to be tainted by Phariseeism,
while the individual faithful starts to interpret in purely arbitrary
fashion the law given by the love of Christ.

Hence the last thing we wish to do is to tamper with the
absolute indissolubility of the full Christian marriage—an
indissolubility "even to the death of the cross", endured for
love. What God has joined, no man may put asunder. We have

128-129 spoken of tragic marginal cases in defective marriages. Full Christian marriage "in the Lord", in him who loves unto death, is an unbreakable bond of fidelity "for better or for worse".

Mixed marriages

By "mixed marriages" Catholics understand marriage between someone who belongs to the fellowship of the Catholic faith and someone who is not a Catholic. Clearly, there are many possible cases. Marriage with a convinced Protestant is very different from marriage with an unbeliever. And we must not forget that even inside the Catholic Church there are many ways and degrees of professing the faith. There are "good practising Catholics" and some very careless ones. But in canon law what counts is whether or not one belongs to the
289 Catholic Church. For the faith lives in a fellowship which—
135-139 in the mind of the gospel—is wider than that of the family.
336-338 It is by this fellowship that faith at home is given its concrete
252-254 form—in the celebration of the Eucharist, the sacraments,
144 the recognition of a mission from Christ and so on. If man and wife do not agree on these points, it is here—where their convictions try to express themselves in the concrete—that the longing for deep unity causes an almost unbearable tension. After all, they would wish to be together in their experience of the great values of life. Hence it often happens that a mixed marriage means that the partners grow away from each other in the most essential things. There is also a serious danger of growing indifferent to the things of faith.

Nonetheless, the situation can be envisaged in which two people, and especially two Christians, can accept each other's convictions with reverence, love and tolerance. And it is likewise conceivable that the faith of one of them can inspire and help the other, as Paul writes: "For the unbelieving husband is consecrated through his wife, and the unbelieving wife is consecrated through her husband" (1 Cor. 7:14).

But where everything founders, where even canon law to some extent founders, is on the child. Husband and wife can find a compromise and perhaps even a solution. But in the child marriage comes to a climax in one single human being. And there is really no more room for compromise.

And even where a compromise must be sought, the solution

398

is never fully satisfactory. Let us examine the possibilities. If the child is brought up a Catholic, the non-Catholic partner refrains from explaining fully his own attitude to life—from which silence all kinds of difficulties can ensue, even for the child. To leave the children "free" means in fact that the parents have made a very definite choice (see the chapter on faith and 238-240 conversion). Some have spoken of a "non-sectarian" or "general" 357-362 Christian education. But what would this consist of? To bring 352 up the children without any genuine connection with one of the really great Churches which have received a mission and authority? Would this be evangelical? In the eyes of the Catholic, a good Protestant education would then be preferable. But in 323 this case there is the difficulty that the Catholic party does not impart his own faith to the children, and this can be a still greater difficulty than elsewhere because the Catholic Church admits practically all that the Reformation believes, while the opposite is not true. We must not underestimate the amount that is common to all Christians which is held by the Catholic Church.

Where the partners take little interest in their faith, a mixed marriage need not cause much strain. It is then rather a result of religious indifference. But where Christians try to live out their faith sincerely, the compromise will weigh heavily on the child.

This is a delicate situation, and the canon law which caters for it is complicated. On the one hand, respect for the human person demands that each one must be as free as possible to choose whom he wishes to marry, even if the choice involves grave difficulties. On the other hand the community may make an impediment of whatever runs counter to marriage. To do so is not an encroachment upon the intimacy of the bond, but the official protection and support of the bond. No human value ever belongs just to one or two individuals alone. It only exists as part of a wider fellowship. Because the marriage of a Catholic is also a sacrament of the fellowship of the Church, the Church has a right to intervene in it. It can make a declaration of incompatibility with its task, if there is something which is really in conflict with its message.

These are the general principles. But how do they apply to mixed marriages? On the one hand, the Church will pay the greatest possible reverence to the great value of free choice of partner, by not refusing a dispensation where a mixed marriage in church is asked for. On the other hand, the difficulties must be clearly envisaged, and one question in particular must be declared as incompatible with the message: that a Catholic's children should grow up outside the community of the Catholic faith. According to the existing regulations, the Catholic is asked to promise to bring up the children as Catholics. The non-Catholic must be informed of this obligation of the Catholic, and is also to be asked whether he (or she) is prepared to put no obstacle in the way. If he agrees, the bishop can give the dispensation, and then marriage can be celebrated with nuptial mass. If the non-Catholic partner has difficulties in conscience about making this declaration, or if there are even difficulties about the marriage being performed in the Catholic Church, the dispensation is not to be refused, but the matter is to be referred to the Congregation for the Doctrine of the Faith. Thus the possibility remains of paying due reverence to the principle of the free choice of partner and of a marriage outside the Catholic Church being eventually recognized by the Church. It is easy to see that these are marginal cases.

In a country where the population is of different religions and there is constant and intense contact between people of different faiths, mixed marriages will of course be much more frequent than elsewhere. But here too, and indeed here above all, it must be affirmed and re-affirmed that marriage between two (convinced) Catholics is an inestimable blessing. It may be said in general that it is in such marriages that the faith flourishes most spontaneously and harmoniously. Those who envisage a mixed marriage must not take refuge behind the excuse that this will further the cause of union of the Churches. On the contrary, they are transferring a tragic situation of Christianity into a marriage, and indeed, into the one human person of the child. It is of course true that the partners of a mixed marriage are suffering in particular under a division for which the blame rests on Christianity as a whole.

There are no doubt mixed marriages where good will and self-sacrifice have led to genuinely evangelical results. But it cannot be right to close one's eyes to the fact that in most cases, even where everything seemed most promising before the marriage, the task turns out to be too difficult to be performed well. And young people should pray to God that the partner on whom the choice of their heart falls will share with them their faith in the one Catholic Church—for the sake of union in their own lives and in that of their family. This is a very realistic prayer.

Chastity

Married people give themselves so fully to each other that only death can undo the bond. All sexual contact with others is a betrayal of this self-dedication, even if one's partner condones it, even if it were not to damage or ruin any other marriage. It is always a breach of faith as regards the marriage in Christ which one has entered into with one's husband or wife. This fidelity is the primary form of married chastity.

Marriage gives the partners—as it is perhaps too materialistically formulated—"the right to each other's body". But if in the exercise of these conjugal rights sexuality is aimed at apart from the person of the other and without desire of the other, this can hardly be called chastity. We come here to the deepest form of married chastity: that both together, as full human persons, live out the experience of marriage. Sexuality does not exist apart from the other, as fully a person; it cannot be isolated from the whole of married life and from the countless attentions which married people pay each other. The body which toils to perform the common task is cherished in mutual tenderness. Sexuality is the language of love.

Fruitful love

When we survey the history of marriage, the question cannot but be raised: why did man and woman come together and stay together in marriage in the first place? Was it to give themselves to each other or to have and to educate children? But this is a question which puts asunder things that are united and should remain united. Fruitfulness is something that naturally springs from love, and love is always life-giving— 383 even in other realms of human life. Where there is love, there is always new life.

But the characteristic of sexual love is that it is intrinsically connected with a particular and lofty form of fruitfulness— the origin of new human life. This is so intimately connected with married love that a marriage where the condition is laid down from the start that a child must be excluded is not regarded as valid by the Church. Obviously, this does not mean that sexual intercourse is only right when it is directly intended for the begetting of children. No one holds that. But it means that in the projected matrimony as a whole the child may not be expressly excluded.

Family planning

The propagation of the human race is not a task that falls at random to the lot of the family. Children are called into life in conscious love. Health, housing, personalities and countless other factors help parents to decide how large their family should be. No outsiders can really tell.

One consideration of a more general nature is that the family should not be increased without a deep sense of responsibility towards the family itself and towards the world. But it must not be thought that this responsibility can be determined in any special way which would be valid for one and all. Another consideration is that we must not regard the coming of new life into the world primarily as a threat. Our first reaction to new life should be joy. Even the child who has not been planned for, who is born "by accident", must be welcomed heartily, with all the Christian self-denial and joy that we can bring to bear.

But once more, this tells us nothing about the number. Ultimately, it is a question of how well and lovingly the family can get on—how in this particular family love of each other and love for society can be best realized (the optimum birth-rate). The effort to attain the greatest possible fruitfulness in love, free from all egoism, will lead in one married couple to quite a different form of family planning than in another. People must remain free in the matter.

As everyone can ascertain nowadays, there are several methods of regulating births. They are all at one in the effort to make intercourse between man and woman possible without conception ensuing. The Second Vatican Council did not speak of any of these concrete methods as such in the relevant chapter of the constitution on the *Church in the Modern World*. This is a different standpoint than that taken under Pope Pius XI, some thirty years ago, which was also maintained by his successor. We can sense here a clear development in the Church, a development which is also going on outside the Church.

The fact is that we can now know more about all the processes involved in human conception than formerly. Men now have a more sovereign control of their fecundity. Further, there is now a growing sense of the independent human value of sexuality. Sexuality and fertility are seen more clearly as values which are combined in the one totality of life, rather than as factors simply arranged in the relationship of means to an end. It would of course be absurd to think that this element was not realized before our times. Possibly it was experienced in a profounder and more human way than among ourselves. Who knows? But we are now speaking of a definite realization of the manner in which sexuality and fertility are embodied in the totality of human values. And this greater clarity, which, as the last council also testifies, did not come about without the Spirit of God, can in fact be of great benefit to our lives.

Are all methods of regulation of births of equal value to the Christian conscience? The council gave no answer to this question. It does, however, call on married people to ask themselves conscientiously whether the practices in question do, or fail to do, full justice to the great personal values which should be expressed in sexual intercourse and in the whole of married life.

Therefore when there is question of harmonizing conjugal love with the responsible transmission of life, the moral aspect of any procedure does not depend solely on sincere intentions or on an evaluation of motives. It must be determined by objective standards. These, based on the nature of the human person and his acts, preserve the full sense of mutual self-giving and human procreation in the context of true love. (*The Church in the Modern World*, n. 51).

It is advisable in such matters also to approach a doctor who can take all the varying circumstances into account and after due discussion can decide what is medically the best for each particular case.

The last word lies with the conscience, not with the doctor or the confessor. But reverence for life undoubtedly demands that no practices be chosen which could be harmful to health or the affective life.

"Honour your father and your mother"

From the very fact of our birth it is obvious that men are dependent on one another. It is part of our human nature. We have *received* our life. This is the deepest reason why in spite of all

403

development of our selves and of our own wills, obedience remains part of our nature. The child learns by experience that it is good, and in accordance with conscience, to be obedient. And hence the fourth commandment is: Honour your father and your mother. This does not primarily set up conflicts in the child. He finds it peaceful and joyful. No doubt conflicts and friction ensue, and here precisely obedience comes into play. But even when the word is not used, and everything is going smoothly, the normal obedience is being exercised in which family life develops. "We should rather love obedience than fear disobedience" (St Francis de Sales).

359-360
418 Since I always remain a person who has received and still receives life, obedience in one way or another forms part of every stage of my life. To recognize this is liberating—because it is the truth.

But in fact all our relationships of affection, authority and dependence are also permeated by weakness, tyranny and distrust, and from our earliest days. We keep a careful eye on each other. Fear is a bad counsellor for authority. "What is worse than a reign of terror?" "A terrified reign."—And then there is the primitive urge of the will to power. For all these reasons, authority, like every other human value, is in constant need of redemption. To have power and authority, no matter how worthy of reverence (in family, society, or Church, through experience or by virtue of a mission), and no matter how fascinating (through press, radio, television, eloquence, daring or talent) is something that needs deliverance. Christ delivers and redeems power by teaching that it must be service.

164 It will not be a pretence of service which makes use of kindness to hold others in its power psychologically and prevents their reaching adulthood. It will be a service which helps men to find themselves. "Let the leader become as one who serves" (cf. Lk. 22:26).

Now that we are on the subject of Christ's attitude to "authority", we may take up a question which arises out of the epistle of the nuptial mass. We read there that "the husband is the head of the wife as Christ is the head of the church" (Eph. 5:23). Is it the teaching of Scripture that the husband must normally be master in the family, ruling over the wife?—Strictly speaking, this is not the meaning of the text. As we have already had

390 occasion to point out, the word "as" needs to be specially

noted in this epistle. Paul's background is a society in which
in fact the husband is the head of the family. But this is not part
of his message. His message is that in the family the relationship
should be such as exists between Christ and the Church. By this
he means love, the giving of self. Hence the Apostle is not
concerned with making a statement about the relationship of
authority in the family. What he affirms is that this relationship,
in whatever form it is determined by society, must be permeated
by Christ's Spirit, of service and of love.

Education to love

132–135
435

Education is service. To treat children as unimportant is to
be self-seeking. To regard children as things which can be
turned into copies of one's own person and desires, is also
self-seeking. Each child has something special and unique about
it. It is a new human being, not a repetition of ourselves. The
parents should serve this new life, to set it free to be itself.

It is a service which takes in fact the form of giving directions.
It cannot always give way, because then the child would not be
itself but a slave to itself. But it becomes itself as it grows into
the liberating commandment of love: love of God, the cause 132
of all, love of other people. The mother will try to explain
in whose hand all human life is held and guarded. She will
teach the child to pray reverently along with her. She answers
questions about the crib and the cross. She begins cautiously to 315–316
explain what is right and what is wrong. But more important
than what she says is the atmosphere of the family, the sincerity
of its faith, the reality of its love.

Nowhere else will the parents feel themselves so powerless,
when they see the evil that they pass on, unwittingly and 267
unwillingly, in this situation of original sin. But as Christians,
they are also confident that they can share with their children
something which is mightier than sin, a redemption which
means that life is ever more fully penetrated by faith, hope
and love.

We see something similar in the education of children for
love of the neighbour. The egoism of the parents—for nobody
is free from it—is passed on to the children. But it is still truer
that they can also pass on their goodness, by their consideration,
patience and helpfulness towards each other, towards their

426 children and towards other men. Education for love may
468 perhaps be summed up as teaching the children the art of being
happy with the joy of others. And then they will also stretch
out their hands to the sufferings of others. This may even lead
to a vocation to place their whole life in the service of mankind
369 and the kingdom of God. Those parents are blessed who can
easily keep their hearts open to such a possibility in the lives of
their children.

Education for manhood and womanhood

Education for love also means guiding the child to a mature
erotism. This sexual education—in the broadest sense—is not
a matter for strangers but for those who have at heart the whole
education of the child, namely, its father and mother. Here too
the atmosphere in the family is decisive to a great extent.

Where relationships between the parents are warm, and where
the children have the joy of witnessing spontaneous expressions
of affection, the most important element of sexual education
is assured. The children grow up in an atmosphere where love
between man and women is taken for granted.

It is quite different in a family full of taboos, with a stifling
atmosphere of prudery which denies or represses the sexual and
thereby isolates it from human love as a whole. The child is
allowed to see only the "higher love", the spiritual contact
between his parents, while he is given a few intelligible hints
about physical love only in a few awkward minutes on a sudden
impulse.

If a child is to be educated for morality, if he is to learn to
live without undue or unsound emphasis on bodily sexuality,
then he must be allowed to see with his own eyes how his father
and mother can be calmly and respectfully affectionate towards
each other, and how their attentions and caresses fit naturally
into the whole life of the family. Their whole life, giving and
receiving, must demonstrate love to the child. Later information
about their most intimate intercourse, which is also a form
of giving and receiving, will not be shocking revelations.
Against this background it can then be explained to the child,
when it is older, that chastity is simply reverence for what is
good and lovely in marriage.

This calm will be preserved if, for instance, small children
discover their own bodies and start to play with them. The

406

parents will not treat this as the behaviour of adults and react violently. They will just distract the children's attention and given them other matters to occupy them, which is part of the normal education to morality.—If another birth occurs in the family, the parents need not be afraid to supply enough information, so that the children need not look for it at the street-corner. At about the age of ten, children may ask about the difference of the sexes. It should be possible to answer, without superfluous biological details, on the basis of the love between father and mother. Shortly before puberty, at a time when the child is still very receptive for all that is beautiful, and strongly curious, it will react gratefully with more questions as it learns more about parenthood.

The period of questioning at about twelve years of age is the best time to give fuller information as occasion offers. As soon as puberty begins, the child is affected by sexual feelings and his knowledge is too much of a personal experience for it to continue to put questions without being embarrassed. It closes up, goes its own way and avoids confidences, especially under pressure. Hence it should have been prepared earlier for its own personal experiences and for what it will undoubtedly hear and see elsewhere.

It is therefore realism and common sense that parents should have prepared their children beforehand for what is going to take place in their physical constitution. They will find that they can talk to their son about masturbation almost without any awkwardness, at this uncomplicated stage—it being a delicate question for them rather than for him. This does not mean that the discussion will preserve him from all future difficulties. But it will possibly spare him needless anxieties and guilt feelings. It can also give him the quiet assurance that his parents will understand him. He need not then at once see masturbation during puberty under the sign of sin. In this emotional and unstable phase, there is often too little freedom for guilt to be present. (Indeed, even in adults freedom is more often absent in this matter than was admitted formerly.) It is well to bear in mind that the phenomenon is mostly due to affective tensions from which the child is suffering: disappointments in his contacts with others, lack of friends, anxiety about shortcomings in his school-work and so on. The child going through the stage of puberty is ready enough to talk to his parents of his disappointments, in the hope of finding understanding. But he prefers to keep silent about the major and minor problems of sexuality—problems which may last for years; and when he does speak of them, parents are usually content to try to soothe his conscience. They must emphasize above all the aspects of his character which promise most. With the sympathy of his parents and the more direct guidance of an understanding confessor, the boy will sense, even in this phase of life which is normally the most individualistic, that he ought to grow out of his egoistic desires in all respects and hence that he must not remain immature and isolated even in his physical experiences. He begins to have a lively sense of the truth that sexuality is exclusively "the language of love". For he has learned from his youngest days, having had experience of a family devoted to each other which let their mutual interest be seen by the attentions they paid each other, that he can live for others with his whole being, body and soul.

This is of course true of girls as well as boys. There are a number of girls who sooner or later content themselves. But in the case of girls, the connection between masturbation and physical maturity is less direct. It is not therefore advisable to bring up the subject when the young girl is being prepared for the onset of menstruation. In a large number of young girls sexual feeling is absent or very vague and masturbation unknown. Neither the girls who have such feelings nor those who do not are abnormal. Girls of both groups can grow up into well-integrated women.

The above discussion may have gone more thoroughly into the subject than the preaching demands directly. But sound information is not something foreign to the gospel message. The short sketch that has been given here may provide considerations which may be further developed through the study of the relevant literature. Those who find that it has all been seen through rose-tinted spectacles—mutual understanding, love, harmony and so on, must remember that the intention was to provide a spacious and inspiring perspective, which could only be partially made concrete here.

240–241   *Education for independence*

The parents provide the child with all the security and affection which it needs. But surprisingly soon, very often, it strikes out on its own both in its conduct and in its religious views. This can be a period of disappointment, misunderstanding, distress and loneliness—on both sides. The Christian message does not tell us that all conflicts can be avoided. But it does suggest that the dialogue should be maintained, and that parents should humbly recognize that the difficulties on the other side are greater. Interest, openness and sympathy are no less important at such times for education in the faith than the positive religious directions given the child hitherto—which for the moment he rebels against. More than he admits, the child likes to see his father and mother sincerely practising their faith—rather than urging pious practices upon him.

The child is now particularly sensitive to the natural values which he sees realized in his parents: kindness and steadfastness, 438 warmth and thankfulness, a sense of responsibility and industriousness. In his phase of religious indifference these values form a precious contribution to his development into a mature adult and a mature Christian.

It is a blessing to grow up in an open-hearted and hospitable family where there is room for friends and which readily offers the possibility of spontaneous meetings between boys and girls for recreation and hobbies. This openness enables the family to assure to a great extent the social development of the children and prevent over-affective links with parents or friends. The intimate and yet open atmosphere of the family makes it possible to learn the standards of other parents of sound views, and guards against rigid and absolute norms. Where there is a healthy flexibility and a sense of what is merely relative, psychic calm is the rule and unnecessary conflicts are more easily avoided.

Sound and rich personalities can develop in families where trust and understanding predominate over the extrinsic relationship of obligation. This is where the foundation is laid for the future happiness of young people in their own families. They will be strong and upright in love because they have known and practised it from their earliest days. The memory will not grow dim, even when they leave their parent's house.

A new era now dawns for the parents. They are together once 467–468 more. Marriage, "the whet-stone of human existence" now comes to its true fulfilment. Husband and wife will be there for each other more than ever. They have never been so radically

409

together. They can then perhaps display together a new ideal of goodness, openness, sense of reality and deliberate self-effacement. There is something divine even about self-effacement. God is so marvellously withdrawn and reserved though he is so close to all things. The Christian never comes to the end of his task.

Finally, one will see the other to the end of the road and then remain alone. Circumstances will often compel the aged to seek a new environment. The fullness of a tranquil life is mostly granted to those whose heart is in contact with others and with God.

231-233   THE EVANGELICAL COUNSELS

Man is ordained for marriage according to the structure of his mind and of his body. But there are people who deliberately and gladly remain unmarried. They do it "for the sake of the kingdom of heaven" (Mt. 19:12).

Man is allowed to call certain things in this world his own. He needs them to be independent, as a human being should be. But there are people who undertake to possess nothing personally.

Man develops by being able to follow his own initiative. But there are people who freely vow obedience.

Those who renounce these three human values are trying to
123-124   follow the example and counsel of Jesus. Hence the name of "the evangelical counsels". Those who model their lives perpetually on these counsels are called religious.

Celibacy for the kingdom

383   The unmarried state is not a state without love. On the contrary, the only motive for its existence is love. And it is not an existence without a body. The man cherishes no woman and begets no child. The woman embraces no man and bears no child. But the body after all is there for many other things besides sexual intercourse. It is there to be kind, to utter the truth, to be a sign in a thousand-ways of all that man can be, to be the starting-point of the service of many and thus too to be fruitful. Ultimately the body is there to be with God. "The body is . . . for the Lord, and the Lord for the body. And God raised the Lord and will
478   also raise us up by his power. Do you not know that your

bodies are members of Christ?" (1 Cor. 6:13–15). These words 486 (which do not speak of the unmarried state, but of avoiding unchastity) tell us that the ultimate purpose of the body is not sexuality. Hence celibacy for God need not ultimately signify a denial of the body.

But it remains true, it will be said, that they do not get married. The growth of the seed, the waiting womb, the heart to be given to another—all is in vain. No—it is not in vain, but simply a subordinate part in the totality of being a fully-grown man or woman. Religious renounce marriage but not the development of their human personality. A nursing sister, a teaching sister, does her life's work as a woman. A missionary does the work of a man. Physical sex is not exercised, but it must of course be there to make someone a real man or woman, so that they can have the real goodness of an adult person. In this sense no faculty of body or heart is superfluous. We understand that Christ was fully a man. It was as a man that he brought the good news to mankind.

Those who are unmarried for the sake of the kingdom try to be fully prepared, through prayer and work, and so to be fruitful in ways for which others are often not free. Their heart is given in many ways to many different men, through whom and in whom they find the one, the constant and the true. This shows how essential faith is in the religious life. For how could anyone choose to love many, without giving his heart to one?

Without possessions

The second evangelical counsel is to live without personal property. All things are possessed in common. This does not mean that the link with earthly things is given up as if they were evil. In a certain sense, the religious feels himself particularly at home with all things. Since he calls nothing his own, the whole world is his home, just as St Francis of Assisi, when he rid himself of all things, called all creatures his brothers and sisters. Peter once said to Jesus, "Lo, we have left everything and followed you". Jesus answered, "Truly, I say to you, there is no one who has left house or brothers or sisters or mother or father or children or lands, for my sake and for the gospel, who will not receive a hundredfold now in this time, houses and brothers and sisters and mothers and children and lands, with persecutions, and in the age to come eternal life" (Mk 10:28–30). In this marvellous text Jesus explains how much one who has lost everything receives even here on earth. But it does not come to him as a peaceful possession, but rather as a gift constantly bestowed, new each time with persecutions in between. The religious has the use of goods without having them in his power. He mostly lives without personal property in a community to which everything belongs, so that he remains personally detached from things. The community too must remain detached. For this, constant soberness is needed. Only what is needed for its work should be retained. This is how Jesus behaved. The rest is for those who are worse off.

Obedience

The third evangelical counsel is the renunciation of one's own will in obedience. The religious seeks very explicitly one will, 122 the will of the Father, because that was what Jesus always did. It is of course true that every good Christian seeks to do the will of the Father. But when Christians began to live the life of poverty and celibacy in communities, they also began to see in the commands of the superior a very concrete and direct expression of the divine will. They then vowed to obey their superiors, in order to live a life as Christ-like as possible.

373–375 This is not a renunciation of one's conscience, which would of course be impossible. If anything sinful is commanded, the religious may not obey. This principle is laid down in the most ancient rules as something to be taken for granted, which is an explicit rejection of the plea, say, of ·war criminals, that they were only following orders. Further, obedience is not the renunciation of initiative and of one's critical faculties, though the religious is prepared if necessary to give up his own plans if the superior, having heard the case, decides otherwise. This can involve great hardship, especially where the superiors do not know their job well, go too much into details, allow too little scope for initiative—in a word, have all the defects which all 404 other authority can also have. But the religious is not deterred. He knows that there is a great mystery in obedience. It means oneness with Christ's obedience to the will of the Father, sometimes obscure but always the bearer of brightness. Much peace has been brought to this world by the deliberate meekness of the obedience of such men.

412

The undivided heart

The following of the three evangelical counsels is the dedication of a whole life, promised to God in a three-fold vow. This life is a very special type of human experience. Paul had a word to describe it. When he speaks of remaining unmarried for the sake of Christ, he says that this makes it possible for the Christian to give his "undivided devotion to the Lord", while not distracted by "anxieties" (1 Cor. 7:35–38). This experience, which Paul put forward as his personal opinion, has been confirmed by the experience of countless others down to the present day.

The Christians who are not called to the evangelical counsels will find a difficulty here. Does it not imply that they are "divided"? Is there something wrong about marriage, property and being one's own master?—Of course not. The Christian faith regards these things as ways in which the human being is developed, as ways to God. From the joy of the first loving kiss, from the pride of the first hard-earned wages, from the adventure of the first great independent decision, these values can be an encounter with God. But since we are sinful men, there is always something wanting. Our love does not attain the other fully, remains somewhat egoistic and is thereby distracted from Christ. We do not always let ourselves share (and realize) God's generosity in our possessions. Our own will 430 sometimes runs counter to the will of God. In a word, all these ways to God—which they are and remain—are not outside the situation of original sin. They do not lead to God without any 259–270 obstacles. Hence there are people whom God calls, through the mystery of his Church, to dedicate their lives to him as simply and with as little complications as possible. This does not of course mean that they *are* in fact at once "undivided". It is their abiding task to become so. As the singleness of their intention is realized in life itself, they become men who have something of the simplicity and freedom of Christ. It sometimes seems as though they had taken something with them from their youth which others have often lost. It is not a trace of childishness— though that can happen, in religion as well as in marriage—but an unpretentiousness, an uprightness and a singleness of heart.

Freedom for the new creation

Another motive given by Paul as well as undivided devotion is that "the form of this world is passing away" (1 Cor. 7:31). He thought that this was to happen quickly. The fact that the process is slower makes the motive less obvious, but not invalid. Religious are called by the evangelical counsels to orientate their lives as directly as possible towards that which is to abide: 486–487 love of God and of all men, the kingdom of God, the will of the Father. It is true that in marriage, possessions and self-determination one directs one's heart to that which abides. It is done in and through these earthly values. Religious are called to a certain freedom from these valuable earthly realities, to keep their eyes fixed on the eternally valuable core which is promised in these realities.

The religious is no doubt a man with a task on earth and human feelings. Indeed, by being free from such valuable things as family and possessions he can be specially close to all earthly things and to all men—as were Francis of Assisi, Paul and indeed our Lord himself. But in spite of this, or rather, on account of this, religious take a certain joy in what will abide most fully in the new creation, trying to experience in all things in a very special way what the Lord has promised for ever. Hence these communities, if they live up to their ideals consistently, and are not isolated from the rest of the faithful, can be a symbol of what marriage, possessions and self-determination are ultimately concerned with. They are a sign that all these things can only satisfy the heart of man if they are lived out "in the Lord", that is, in self-forgetful love, faith in the cross and hope of the resurrection.

In order to follow the counsels, religious abandon the normal ways to God. Hence they also give up the grace which is proper to these ways. This involves a risk. One abandons certain cares and joys which can make one good and holy. It follows that married people have a task with regard to religious. They must show the goodness, prudence and self-denial that go with the ordinary lives of Christians. This is a counterpart which the religious needs, just as married people need the religious. It will be a comfort to each to know the joys and cares of the other.

Christ as model

The third motive for the counsels is not mentioned by Paul. It is clearly present throughout the whole of the evangelical message. It is the fact that Christ was unmarried. He, the ideal man, the one man of really undivided heart, lived unmarried and without possessions. This does not mean that he regarded marriage and possessions as wrong. It was evidently because his message came most clearly and simply to us in this way, in a world where sin reigns. His message was the reign of God. On the model of Jesus, others may also renounce marriage "for the sake of the kingdom of heaven" (Mt. 19:12). The permanent presence of the Lord in the Spirit makes this life livable. Religious know whom they have given their hearts to.

123
279
192–193
288–289

Faith

These motives are all founded on faith. Without faith this sort of life is absurd, an empty dedication. But the faith which it involves is often a very evident and joyous one. The experience of living as one of "the poor of Yahweh", child of God, brother of Jesus, set free to do good, to preach the faith without distraction, makes this type of life profoundly and harmoniously human. This is already an indication that one is not building on sand. There can of course be times and situations which are full of difficulties. Here as elsewhere there can be frustration, through one's own fault, through the fault of others, through circumstances. In such cases the sign is less appealing, from the human point of view. Nonetheless, there is still something impressive—the faith. In a certain sense it is more impressive than ever. They know that they are called to such situations. Faith, confidence, and love still burn under the ashes of many failures. And very often one sees in such men or in such communities a new inspiration dawning after dark hours, to reward the faith with which they persevered.

37
84
316–319

The strongest signs of faith are perhaps provided by the communities whose work is very humble and practically all service, —religious congregations of nuns and brothers, and the brothers in the priestly congregations. It is very often evident that their work could have been undertaken and persevered in joyfully only for the sake of Christ. This is also true of the orders and congregations whose main task is prayer. Their faith makes their life meaningful.

The three evangelical counsels go together. They help to build up one definite sort of life and they are an aid to each other. This does not mean that they must always be found together in their entirety, but that those who strive to follow any of them will always realize something of the others.

369 *The celibate priest*

It has been the custom from time immemorial in the Church that the bishop is and remains unmarried. This also holds good for priests in the western Church, though in the eastern Church a married man can be ordained—though an ordained priest may not marry. We have already spoken of the notion which underlies this link between priesthood and celibacy: that the task of the leaders in the Church is to a very special service and one which is very fruitful. The link is therefore very meaningful. This does not mean that it could not be otherwise. The married priests of the eastern Churches and the ministers of the Reformation Churches are often very good pastors.

It is often said that unmarried priests should not give advice on matters concerning matrimony. But the facts seem to show that many are actually glad to speak to celibate priests on such matters. The priests have wide experience from their many discussions with the laity. (And is it not also true that the psychologist at a marriage guidance clinic bases his advice primarily on his studies and his practice, and not on his own experience of marriage? Much of what is most personal is very different in others.)

405–409 Religious and priests also seem very often to have special gifts
435–438 of grace for their work of education. After their many years of loving experience in education they can sometimes at least— apart from the loss of sensitivity which sometimes occurs— understand children in a way which not all parents can.

Diocesan priests promise obedience to their bishop, but take no vow of poverty. In fact they recognize, as does the whole Christian people, that a certain austerity goes with their life of administering the sacraments and preaching the gospel. Sometimes they live in great poverty, more than many religious who own nothing.

Together before God

The people of God waits for the Lord as for the bridegroom. He loves the Church and seeks her. She seeks him too. Every diocese, every parish, every religious house and every family joins in this search. Married people, in their mutual love, are an image of this mystery of Christ and the Church. But they also participate directly in the mystery, since their love also seeks Christ in their partner, the Christ who joins them both. Religious are called to participate in this mystery of Christ and the Church with especially undivided hearts. That this may be done in religious institutes of men and women has already been explained (see for instance the chapter on the "Word of God"). 326

The signs of vocation to the religious life are the same as for 369-370 the priesthood: the peace and joy whereby Christ attracts the soul, the confirmation of the vocation by the candidate's being accepted into a community, the constant deepening of the motives. Something has been said of the rich variety of orders and congregations in the chapter on Church history. 231-233

CHURCH AND STATE

The people of God lives in the world. It is not *of* the world—if we take the word "world" in the biblical sense of mankind in so far as it is estranged from God, in so far as we come in for God's criticism. But the word "world" has also another meaning, which is also biblical, and which is also more in keeping with present-day speech. It is the world in so far as it is called to be gathered by the Lord, "the world which God so loved", the world peopled by God, "the lover of all that exists" (cf. Wis. 11:24). In this sense, the people of God does belong to the world, and must be as much a part of it as possible.

In the chapter on the priesthood of the people of God, we 349-350 spoke of how the Christian and the earthly task coincided. We saw that the people of God is called to serve mankind by its help and its witness. The great problems of hunger, peace and knowledge do not leave the Church indifferent. Through the 230 mission which it has received, it is totally committed to such problems. We shall try in the following chapters to see our life in the world in the light of the gospel and of the charge it lays upon us. We shall discuss our life as it is to be lived outside the family—though without going into too much detail, since the precise application of the principles depends on so many sciences and circumstances. This first chapter will discuss briefly the relationship between Church and State—two very different societies, of which Christians form part without divided loyalties.

Loyalty

Men live together in society, where they are linked by ties of language, friendship, race, way of life, dependence, and responsibilities. The great organization for life in common is the State. Our relationship to organized society is one of loyalty and cooperation and obedience, according to the teaching of Scripture. "Let every person be subject to the governing authorities. For there is no authority except from God, and those that exist have been instituted by God" (Rom. 13:1). How are we to understand these words of Paul?

Obedience to the laws of society (as regards business, rights, responsibilities, traffic and so on) is a duty towards God. This does not mean that the authorities are designated by God. But it means that it is part of man's nature, as created by God, not only to grow up in obedience to his parents, but also to give his
404 loyalty to one form of State or other, and to the authority which has been chosen to rule it. This produces order, peace and happiness. These things are in keeping with the Spirit of God.

The service of one's country can call for sacrifices. At time of disasters, epidemics, hostile attack and so on, the forces of a
424–426 society are mobilized. Men give their lives. We feel more united than ever. In peace-time, one of the most radical duties is the payment of taxes. Those who pay less than their share, necessarily increase the burdens which fall on the lower-income groups, whose income can be precisely checked. Taxes should be paid in the way the State in fact expects. On this point Paul writes: "Therefore one must be subject, not only to avoid God's wrath but also for the sake of conscience. For the same reason you also pay taxes, for the authorities are ministers of God, attending to this very thing" (Rom. 13:5–6). On the meaning of the last sentence, see above on Romans 13:1.

Tension between Church and State

When all is well, Church and State live in harmony. Each society looks after its own sphere of interest and respects that of the other. But sharp tensions can arise. A totalitarian tendency, a desire to control everything, may creep into the State. It is irritated by the existence of an institution which will not submit to it entirely. The Church too can give way to the inclination to dominate the State. It is characteristic of the history of Christian Europe that the spiritual and temporal powers were never fully in one hand. There was always a duality, a tension, a "polarity": the Church with its zones in the independent State, the State with subjects who also obeyed the supranational Church. This brought about a freedom in the history of Europe which is unique on earth. This freedom was often threatened or restricted, but it never reached the vanishing-point of a stifling theocracy or a totalitarian State.

It is the task of the Church to maintain this tension, that is, not to try to dominate the State and not to be intolerant of other views, but to come forward with prophetic voice if ever the State menaces evangelical values. To be accommodating in such matters is a sin of which the Church could be guilty. It happens when the Church is so exclusively linked to the established order of things that in every conflict with the deprived it always takes the side of the powers that be. Even if the deprived classes are not entirely in the right, the Church ought not leave them on their own.

The "polarity" mentioned above has sometimes occasioned the complaint that Catholics are not whole-hearted citizens. They are accused of recognizing the authority of a foreign power. It is not, of course, true that they recognize the authority of a foreign power. Some non-Catholics like to talk about "the Vatican". And the Vatican is in fact a State, with the Pope as its political head. (The Vatican is also the hill where the basilica of St Peter stands. Hence the name of the council—the Second Vatican Council.) But the Church is not that Vatican State. The Church is the people of God throughout the world, the community of which the bishops, in union with the Pope, are the spiritual heads. Their authority is as little political as that of Christ. It is an appeal to faith and conscience. And it can in fact happen that a Catholic may and must say No to the State for the sake of his conscience. This is not a betrayal of one's country.

Non-Catholics too will sometimes say No as their conscience directs them. The Catholics will form perhaps a more unified block, but even so it is not treason. It is done for the sake of society. It can be the attitude of the youngest daughter of King Lear, who refused to say that she loved her father more than her future husband, but was more help to him than her sisters with their fulsome flattery.

424 The Church has probably taken up this attitude too rarely rather than too often. (It must also be recognized that the Church authorities, in their way of life and directives have clung at times to a material power and a disappearing culture, where the State had already advanced further.) Such historical mistakes are remarkable, but do not affect the essentials. The great principle is that the Church has gradually penetrated man's conscience with the message of Christ, and continues to do so, while presenting that message in a form which is always purer 233 and purer.

Different tasks

235 It seems as though the difference between the task of the Church and that of the State is being grasped more and more clearly. The Church is to be less and less on the style of the State, more and more spiritual—which does not mean invisible—while the State ceases to propagate any particular philosophy of life. There is a more thorough-going separation on the level of organization. This does not mean that there are no links between Church and State. They still deal with the same men, who cannot be divided up into "ecclesiastical" and "worldly" halves.

As regards the separation of Church and State, the question may still be asked: if a country is a hundred per cent Catholic, should there not be a total unity and combination of Church and State? The answer must be that even in such a case separation is desirable. The mandate of the Church is given it by revelation, and it is different from that of the State. And even in such a Catholic country the State must remain free to treat anyone who leaves the Church as a full citizen with all the rights due to all others.

The unity of mankind

Certain structures are now being set up to implement the unity of the human race. These initial efforts, still beset by so many difficulties and weaknesses, do not leave the Church indifferent. They are in harmony with the Christian message. The Church sees the unity of mankind as one of its tasks and sees peace as one of its ideals. It believes that unity is a blessing, while division is a mark of sinfulness (as at Babel), and unity a mark of grace (as at 195 Pentecost). Hence the council urged international cooperation in all spheres, affirming that this was the way to the universal peace which men desired (*The Church in the Modern World*, nos. 83–90). We shall take up the theme of peace at the end of the next chapter.

REVERENCE FOR LIFE

Life is something to be admired and marvelled at, even the life of a plant. Much more so the life of an animal, which is closer to man, and is sentient. The higher the type of animal, the more clearly is it a prefiguration or a reflection of humanity. Hence our attitude to animals is a reflection of our love for men. We may not kill, much less inflict pain, without due cause. We must avoid such actions for the sake of the animal itself, otherwise this attitude will not help to civilize or educate man.

When dealing with animals we must remember that their feelings are not like ours. They are more momentary and disconnected, and the animals are not conscious of themselves as we are. We project much of our own feeling into the animals that we deal with. As regards the slaughter of animals, we must note that the animal is not an "I", not a person. His dignity is not 275–276 absolute, like that of man. If necessary, it can be sacrificed for human ends, but not without due reason, and always as painlessly as possible. We can note a growing refinement in this matter. 233–234 This has not come about without the Spirit of God. "A righteous man has regard for the life of his beast, but the mercy of the wicked is cruel" (Prov. 12:10).

"You shall not kill"

Our reverence for life is shown most strongly in our respect for human life.—Men avoid what is harmful to life: cold, heat, 428

421

damp, bad air. Medical science has developed the means of hygiene. Our expectation of life is longer. A remedy has been found for very many illnesses. All this is excellent. God's sympathies are on the side of life, as the miracles of Jesus show. Health is a magnificent blessing.

The effort to provide enjoyable externals, good food, well-fitting clothes, comfortable housing and also mental hygiene is part of the proper care of life. But we must bear in mind throughout what is the real point—life itself. Jesus stated this very bluntly: "Is not life more than food, and the body more than clothing?" (Mt. 6:25). Otherwise such things enslave us.

Care for life is deeply implanted in us. Like God, man, or the best in man, has a care for all that lives. All this is comprehended in the commandment, "You shall not kill". It does not just forbid murder. It comprises all that should be done for the preservation of life. It forbids wounding, from the malicious injury to the effects of carelessness or stupidity. It also condemns everything that makes life less agreeable for ourselves and others: pollution of the air, dirt, breaches of traffic laws, the sale of bad goods, working too hard for one's living—ruining one's life and the life of one's family in order to live! It can also be contrary to 437–440 the due care for life to work too little—keeping oneself and others at too low a standard of living. Drinking too much destroys a man. Narcotics are particularly dangerous, because they begin by making life apparently more intense. They leave behind them tormenting needs. They must never be begun, not even out of curiosity.—Noise has ruined many people's nerves. There is no protection. One can shut ones eyes, but not one's ears.—There are many other harmful agents that could be mentioned, including those on the mental level. The bitter word, the direct insult—Jesus links such things with murder (Mt. 5:2). He extends the commandment "You shall not kill" 129–130 to include, "You shall not even hate"—a precept that we cannot fulfil of our own strength.

Possibly the ugliest and most abhorrent of all sins is envy—to be vexed at seeing other people being happy. This is really a sin against life. As the saying goes, people go green with jealousy— the colour which is most in contrast to the complexion of health.

One of our normal duties towards life is that one submits to medical treatment when one is ill or run-down, and more important still perhaps, when one feels mentally depressed or disabled. But it is also one of the rights of man to be free, if he wills, to refuse to put himself in the hands of doctors. Likewise, there is no absolute need to prolong indefinitely a life which has been despaired of, by means of medicines and machines, especially if the life in question is purely vegetal, without signs of human reaction. In the latter case above all, extraordinary means may be omitted and the natural process allowed to take its course.

On the other hand, it is wrong to put an end to life wilfully—to kill those who are incurably ill physically or mentally (by euthanasia, for instance) or to commit suicide. Our life has been given us by God and we cannot end it at will. The reason given for ending life is always that it has become meaningless and 282 valueless. This can never be accepted by the Christian faith, which believes in every life, from the first moment of conception. Abortion is a sin against life. As regards suicide, this is sometimes the result of complete hypertension or depression, and we cannot pass judgment on the guilt. It is very often to be laid at the door of others whose neglect, deliberate or not, has excluded someone from adequate social contacts. But there can in fact be cases where a person's conscience tells him that he has no alternative but to take his own life. What are we to think, for instance, of someone under torture, who knows the names of many whom he could endanger and knows that he will certainly betray them? There are always cases where the commandment must be fulfilled in its truest sense by the verdict of a personal decision of conscience.

Capital punishment. War

There are two situations where it has been generally held from time immemorial that it is lawful to take human life: in self-defence (which would include many wars) and in the infliction of judicial sanctions (capital punishment).

If I wilfully threaten the life of another—when the choice therefore has to be made between the aggressor and the victim—then the other may take my life. It is on this principle that the permissibility of fighting in war is deduced.—As regards capital punishment, the traditional arguments for it are based on the notion that the community has powers which an individual has not. Such powers have never been extended to include the killing of the innocent. But they are said to include the killing of the guilty. The sanction includes an element of retribution.

But how Christian is all this? Christ did not condemn war or capital punishment in so many words. The gospel would certainly have recorded it had he done so. But this does not mean that they are normally Christian, any more than slavery, which is also not abolished by the New Testament. Christ brought no organizational changes for which society was not yet morally or psychically or organizationally ripe. But he implanted a spirit which would cause such changes to come about. It is our duty to work together with all our power for Jesus' doctrine of equality before the Father, of turning the other cheek, of love of enemies—to make it more and more concrete and real in milder and juster laws and institutions.

Very often, no doubt, the Church has been so closely identified with the established political order that it lacked the enterprise and energy to make war and judicial sanctions evolve as they might have. The time is perhaps more than ripe to cast judicial sanctions in a different mould. The element of retaliation should be excluded more and more from all "punishments", according to the Christian notion. But here we must be alert to the fact that the element of retribution at least treated the delinquent as a responsible human being. If he is merely given "treatment", he is treated as a sick man, and this can very soon mean that he is deprived of his human rights.

Then there is the monstrous factor of "war". The principle of self-defence is not the last word. Our faith must be dominated by the thought of peace. The Christian conscience must always try harder and harder to draw stricter limits to the permissibility of war. Christians must try to implement such statements as those of Pope John in *Pacem in terris*: "Hence justice, common sense and a sense of human dignity demand urgently that the competition in armaments should cease; that the offensive weapons at the disposal of each country should be everywhere and simultaneously reduced, that atomic weapons should be forbidden and that finally all countries should agree to simultaneous disarmament with mutual and effective inspection" (part 3).

The total atomic war is an evil of unknown magnitude compared to other wars. The question of the lawfulness even

424

of defensive armaments with atomic bombs must be answered, at least by a passionate effort to make such weapons effectively, that is, on both sides, non-existent.

"We must obviously strive with all our might to prepare for the moment when all peoples will agree to forbid war of any type whatever. But the necessary condition for this is the setting up of an international authority recognized by all which will dispose of effective powers to guarantee security, justice and respect of the rights of all . . . Meanwhile the efforts already undertaken and being undertaken to avert the danger of war should not be underestimated" *(Church in the World, no. 82)*.

The sober considerations of scientists, who speak the same language all over the world, will perhaps play a role in the establishment of mutual confidence, which, as *Pacem in terris* says, is the one real basis of peace. But the prophetic passion of those whose eyes have been opened to the madness of war, and who are properly organized to prevent it, will be indispensable in alerting our consciences more and more thoroughly. The conscientious refusal of military service should be possible. As the council says, "Furthermore, proper provision should be made in law for those who refuse military service for reasons of conscience. Another form of service to the community may be envisaged in such cases" *(Church in the World, no. 79)*. The council, however, does not make this obligatory; it leaves it to the individual judgment. Hence it also has a word to say to those who work for peace while carrying out military duties: "Those who serve their country in the armed forces must also regard themselves as guardians of the security and freedom of their country, and contribute, by the proper fulfilment of their military service, to a real and stable peace" *(Church in the World, no. 79)*. The council has special praise for statesmen who work for peace: "We must support the efforts of the many men of good will who in spite of the burdens of high office, feel it their serious duty to strive for the outlawing of war, which they abhor, though they cannot alter the complications of the actual situation" *(Church in the World, no. 82)*.

The great symbolic stories about human life which are found at the beginning of the Bible, the story of Adam's disobedience, of Cain's murder of his brother, of Noah's survival of universal disaster, of dissension among grandiose pretentions at Babel, all take on terrifying dimensions in these

40
261-263

425

days of the threat of atomic war. The divine message of these stories is that the real roots of our calamities are in our sins, and hence that our only real deliverance must come by our being freed from sin, hatred and distrust. To work with Christ 278 here is to help to avert a conflict which would be suicidal for mankind. "The statesmen who are responsible for the well-being of their people and who must at the same time promote the good of the whole world, are in many ways dependent on the opinion and mentality of the masses. Their efforts for peace must always be thwarted as long as enmities, arrogance, distrust, racial hatred and ideological fanaticism divide men and set them against one another. Hence what is needed first of all is a re-education of public opinion. Those who are responsible for edu-405–406 cation, especially that of young people, and for the formation of 445 public opinion must regard it as a sacred duty to implant in all minds a new devotion to peace. We must all revise our attitudes to take in the whole world and the tasks which we can all perform together for the good of the human race.

And we must not allow ourselves to be deluded by false hopes. If humanity does not renounce enmity and hatred and does not succeed in concluding inviolable and sincere treaties to maintain world peace, the danger is already so great that in spite of the marvels of science mankind will experience the dark hour when there will be no other peace than the awful peace of death" (*Church in the World*, no. 82). Inspired by these grave fears, and 297–300 inspired also by the Christian hope in the future of mankind, the 195 council then expresses its conviction that international co-operation on the social and economic level (solidarity in the war on want) is the highroad to peace (*Church in the World*, nos. 83–90).

350 WORKING ON THE WORLD

Each of us has his own particular task in life. He has to face difficulties or boredom at school, the seriousness of an adult vocation, the tediousness of long hours, the repugnance of endless routine, the disappointment of a lowly position, the pressure of grave responsibilities, the strain of housekeeping. But there is also the joy of mastering one's trade and receiving a good salary. And behind it all is the sense of being at work producing something. In all our efforts, at school, at work or in

426

the family, we are producing something that would otherwise not exist, we are cooperating in a great whole through which human life is supported, happiness increased and menaces averted. In shops and factories, in schools and households, in hospitals and in the fields, society forms a great organization of effort, working at making the world a better place to live in.

Good hopes

There are moments in our lives—as when parents look at their growing children or when someone contemplates a piece of work well done—that we sense that our work is in fact working with others on this world, that is, on God's creation. And this is in fact the first thing that the Christian message has to say about work. God did not create the world long ago. He *is* in the act of 488 creating the world, and he also does it through us. It is not of course true that God makes the countryside and man makes the cities. The cities are almost even more his creation, because man, the climax of God's creation, expresses himself in them. What man makes is God's creation. The Christian need not think of this all the time, but it supplies a background of certainty that we are working along God's lines in our daily task and in our families.

Another value which the Christian eye can discern in work is that it unites man. Working with others increases solidarity and contact in a very special way, differently in each calling. The fact that husband and wife work together for their family has a definite effect on the unity of this little group. Work also makes men one because it is done for others: the husband works for the wife, the wife for the husband, the baker for the consumers, the architect and brick-layer for the future inmates, the docker for so many that he will never know or see. Society is a system of services in which we all take part. Often we do not see those for whom we are working and take little interest in them. Nonetheless a sense of "belonging" is in the background, and affects our lives more than we think. If we pause for a moment and look at the walls or windows of our home, or take up something, and think of all who have worked at it from the time that the materials were still in the earth or elsewhere, a whole army is conjured up before our eyes. Even the smallest object, a book or a clock for instance, embodies the work of our

fellow-men, sometimes from two or three parts of the world.
On our furniture as a whole thousands of hands have worked.
Our own work in turn is often a contribution to the life of
thousands. Human work is an element of human oneness and
solidarity.

Thirdly, the Christian message also affirms that in their work
350 Christians may have a good hope for eternity. Our work helps
men to be more themselves, and hence to put more love into
their lives. And we take with us into eternity our love and all it
has grown into. Hence work on this world has its consequences
in the new creation. And who knows but that after the ressurrec-
tion of the body the new world will show in its own way
traces of the best that human work has achieved? Our work
may be of eternal importance.

282-283   *Deliverance from the yoke*

But we are not yet done with the gospel message about work.
We found three gladdening points of view. But the most usual
and striking thing about work is the difficulty, boredom,
slavery, stupidity and shortcomings which it involves. Christians see that the imperfection of this evolving world—an
269 imperfection aggravated and provided with a sting by the sin
of the world—also makes work a burden. As the Bible says, "In
the sweat of your face you shall eat bread" (Gen. 3:19). Work
can be hard, dull, or oppressive; it can make men harsh or
unfeeling; it can cause discord; it can be crippling or distorting
or limiting in a thousand new ways each day. Like all great
human values it needs to be redeemed.

The Christian message affirms that this redemption has been
accomplished. It sees it in the three elements through which our
creator and redeemer is acting: the growing mastery of resources,
growing unity, and the resurrection of our Lord after his passion.

The first reality is that our work is more and more humanized
by the mastery of resources which God has created and which
man discovers. Progress in skill, technology and ease of work
are part of the humanization of it and are really a redemption.
421-422 God is on the side of the joy of life, health, and the lightening
of burdens. This is also revealed by Jesus' miracles—his healings,
106 his effortless feeding of the multitude, his easy catch of fish.
In so far as technology produces cures, food, and ease, it is in
line with God's purpose.

428

Closer to the heart of the Christian message is the redemption of work by love, which makes light of heavy tasks. This love is found in affection for one's family, comradeship, and organizations in one's work or in one's profession; responsibility and service with regard to the society for which one works.— In later chapters dealing with property and mutual aid we shall 431–432 treat of the demands of justice. All we need to say here is that 433–434 the duty of goodness and love which is as clear as day in the gospel is not a sentimental project. And it does not exclude in the least the formation of groups in which men struggle vigilantly for greater justice, for deliverance from the impositions of injustice. But it means that both in the family and at work and 303–304 in the whole of society love and goodness are a redemption for work. In the family it acts through mutual comprehension and readiness to help. In the working community it acts through honesty and solidarity. In human society as a whole it acts through the fact that in spite of all conflicts of interest men still recognize their fellowmen as such. No individual or group may be proscribed and declared irreconcilable enemies. The gospel affirms in all seriousness that not hate but love, a love that excludes none, is the only way of redeeming our life and work 298 together on earth. It is a task that takes the long view, but one at which all men may work unsentimentally and hence all the more seriously. And there is hope that we may see it actually making headway in society, as the progressive redemption of work is accomplished.

These two ways of redemption suppose real progress. But has the gospel nothing to say to those who have still very little experience of growing prosperity and more human relationships? Has it nothing to say to those whose progress is very slow, slower than a human life-span, to those whose work is still deadening to the spirit and unhealthy for the body, to those whose life-work is a failure? Must the failures console themselves with the thought of a future happiness which they will not share? In Marxism, this is undoubtedly the only prospect left to misery. It can indeed be a hope, and a very real one for good men. But it is too little. It means that the individ- 81–82 ual is unimportant. He may have to lead a futile life, but what matters is the whole, mankind as a whole.

Christian faith also recognizes that the whole of mankind is important, but affirms that no member of it may be neglected

279-280 or contemned. It believes that even a life which is humanly
499-502 speaking a failure can possess personal value and joy and peace.
For it believes that through calamity and disaster the Lord attained
life for himself and for others. Hence it is confident that in him
even human failure is not devoid of hope, though it seems to
overwhelm us. The crucifix in our room has a meaning for
our work. It affirms that though our work is drab, hard, unimportant, and oppressive, though it gives us little share in the
prosperity, comradeship, and love for which we strive, still,
this meanness and hardship can bring forth peace and joy. For
99-100 the Lord has promised that those who are poor, mourning, meek,
and persecuted will harvest along with him joy, both for
themselves and for others, both now and hereafter.

278   Faith in the redemptive cross should not make us slacken
our efforts to redeem work by improving its conditions, above
all, where others are concerned. It is only the three together,
progress, mutual kindness, and faith in the resurrection of Jesus
from catastrophe, that make up the Christian redemption of
work on the world.

POSSESSIONS ON EARTH

Those who are without possessions are totally dependent on
others. But it is essential to each man to have a certain amount
of independence and freedom. Hence it is necessary that each
man can have possessions. There are some things of which he
must be able to dispose freely. There must be a part of the world
which belongs to us. It is well that men should have possessions.
The growth of prosperity is from God. It gives man more
chance to develop. And God is on the side of life.

The contamination of sin

The better a thing is, the worse is its corruption. The corruption
which affects possession is particularly diabolical. Men are
"possessed" by their possessions. They think that they are
worth more than others, not by what they are but by what
they own. Standing in front of his house or sitting in his car,
a man can feel that he is as great as the house or the car. He tries
to be more of a man than others, not by being better, but by

having more property. This is one of the most common illusions of mankind. We are all more or less affected by it from childhood, even so-called good men. It is one of the main 99 breaches through which the "sin of the world" pours through. 413 It is one of the grimmest obstacles to the kingdom of God.

The redemption of possessions

Hence too there must be a redemption at work in matters of ownership. The means is the recognition of the social nature of ownership—that we own things together, and not just as 288–289 individuals. It is like all human existence. We are ourselves, independently, and at the same time we are together with others, not just perforce, but by a profound desire. It is the same with ownership. Ownership means that I may dispose of my possesions freely. But a certain dependence remains. Nothing is purely and simply mine. I may use and consume, but not abuse. I may not make use of my expensive piano by pushing it out of the top window for fun. There are people who could make good use of it.

Just distribution

It is all a question of justice—not only of "commutative justice" which says that each one must be given his own in business and the like, but of "social justice". Social justice demands that the goods of this world should be distributed rationally. Mankind possesses the world in common. And just as there is a certain equality among men—as we see more and more clearly since the coming of Christ—so too men have a right to a certain equality in the distribution of the world and its goods. It is not good that some should be very rich while others are very poor. It is a matter of justice that this should be changed.

The process is a slow one. The law does not make much provision for it, sometimes practically none at all. Social justice, in so far as it involves the re-distribution of property, is only expressed to a very limited extent in law. The sense of social 434 justice and the possibilities of it must grow. Very often this sense is most developed in the deprived classes. They struggle for their rights. This is sometimes interpreted as avarice. But the struggle for a fair share of property is ultimately the struggle for a fair share of the dignity of being a human being. It is not

434

303–304
350

a matter of having, but of recognition, which is expressed in possessions.

The social struggle and the self-interest there involved are not against the Christian message. But a society where constant struggle and vigilance are needed to preserve the right of all to a fair distribution of property is not a truly human society and certainly not a redeemed one. Something deeper is at work as a juster distribution is aimed at. Behind all the struggles, there is the growing conviction that the object is just. There is some joy on both sides that things are moving in that direction. There is some love at work. (In the economic field, love is translated as a juster distribution.)

99–100
129–131

The spirit of the Sermon on the Mount

Such mutual joy, good will and love, slowly and painfully gaining the upper hand in the conflicts of society, cannot exist without the spirit of the Sermon on the Mount. There Jesus demands that men should be inwardly free as regards possessions, poor in spirit, seeking their happiness not in having but in giving. This corresponds to our deepest longings but runs counter to our immediate inclinations. We are always menaced by being possessed by our possessions. Hence the vigilance which permits a society to enjoy the fruits of the earth is directed ultimately not against one another's avarice, but against our own.

It is difficult to be inspired in a fight for one's own rights by the spirit of the Sermon on the Mount, which calls the poor and the persecuted blessed. There is a tension between the two. But it is Christian to endure this tension. This is done by reminding ourselves that the authority we feel we must maintain is just, and hence ultimately must content what is best in our opponent. Ultimately, for instance, all Netherlanders will be glad that the people of Indonesia are not nobodies from a colony, but their equals as nationals of a great state.

And every Christian fighting for lawful authority must remember that this must ultimately end up as what seems the opposite: as service. A truly Christian and redeemed society can only grow through mutual service. Jesus lived poor and as a servant to bring out this truth. Some have been called to follow him here as literally as possible.

Are our hands clean?

There is something further to note. We have seen that social justice is gaining ground. But this can mean that we may now have a vague sense of living in an unjust structure of society.

There is for instance the difference in welfare between our own and some other countries. Working on a plan for social justice is a matter of years or centuries. We must long for it and strive for it. But meanwhile the situation in which we live is wrong.

Jesus has addressed a word to all men—and all nations— whose hands are not completely clean. "Make friends for yourselves by means of unrighteous mammon" (Lk. 16:9). The parable where this saying is found is anything but an invitation from Jesus to make ourselves rich with ill-gotten gains. But it contains an invitation to individuals, nations and even churches, if they have possibly doubtful gains, to do as much good with them as they can, without self-complacency. 434–437

Stealing

To end this chapter, a word about offences against commutative justice. These include stealing, receiving stolen goods, fraud, damaging another's property, not paying one's debts, not giving back things found or borrowed (including books), wasting time for which one is paid, not paying for services rendered (excluding voluntary help offered in friendship), plagiarizing the ideas of others and so on. Such faults can also be committed with regard to the property of the State or of proprietors unknown to the offender.

What is called for here first and foremost is to restrain our covetousness. Dishonesty is a shameful thing, while everyone feels that unimpeachable honesty adds to a man's stature.—In extreme necessity—such as danger of death by hunger, as has been admitted from the most ancient times—one may take other people's things without asking permission. The earth is so much the common property of all that all have a fundamental right to have as much of it as they need to continue existing on it. "Those who are in extreme necessity have the right to provide for themselves from the riches of others" (*Church in the World*, no. 69).

HELPING THE NEEDY

132-135 *Human rights*

The first and fundamental way of showing love to the needy is to try to give them their due rights. The rights of man are still only very partially committed to writing in codes of law and institutions (see the previous chapter). In this sense, love is 431-432 the advance-guard of justice. Love first discovers what will later be a matter of justice.

The United Nations Organization has been much preoccupied with the rights of man. As Pope John wrote: "The progressive views of this organization are clearly attested in the *Charter of Human Rights* which was ratified 10 December 1948 by the General Assembly of the United Nations ... We have not failed to note that certain points of this charter have aroused just criticism in some quarters. But we think that the charter must be seen as a move in the direction of the political and juridical order which has yet to be created by all nations together. The charter solemnly affirms the dignity of the human person in all men without exception and recognizes the right of each one to seek the truth unhindered, to follow the prescriptions of morality, to exercise his just rights, to demand a standard of living befitting human dignity and the other rights which this involves... We hope that the time is at hand when this Organization will be able to protect effectively the rights of man, those rights which are universal, inviolable and inalienable because they are based directly on the dignity of the human person" *(Pacem in terris,* part 4).

As well as we are able, according to our state of life, we have to guard and further human rights. For each of us, personally, this is the primary duty of charity.

Giving to those in want

But we are also called to intervene with charity where con-433 ditions are still not ideal. The gospel often speaks of this. It remains an unending task, because the law will never cover everything. There will always be unforeseen cases and situations. Love will always be indispensable, as the perpetual corrective of existing laws and well-defined rights.

How much?

It is well to give away some of our goods. The New Testament speaks of the widow who gave "out of her poverty" (Mk 12: 41–44), of earning money so as to have something to give away (Eph. 4:28), of giving from one's riches (Lk. 8:3; 18:22), even from ill-gotten gains (Lk. 16:9). Giving is to be anonymous (Mt. 6:3) and cheerful (2 Cor. 9:7). How much one gives varies from a "cup of cold water, which will not be left unrewarded" (Mt. 10:42), to "the half of my goods" (Lk. 19:8) and even to "all you have" in situations of special grace (Lk. 18:22). In between there is the Baptist's advice to give away certain things of which one has a double supply (Lk. 3:11). The good Samaritan gives what is necessary to be of real help; and also his precious time and his personal attention (Lk. 10:30–37).

Thus the gospel lays down no fixed rules. Nowhere does it say that one's charity should be such that it does not interfere with one's standard of living. One need have no scruples if one's giving leaves one somewhat poorer. It is a blessing to put so much into the health, holidays and development of others—in a word, into the collection boxes and plates—that we have a cheaper car, or no car at all, less exclusive clothes, shorter travels and cheaper toys for our children. The children who adopt this as the normal attitude from their parents are 405–406 also to be envied. We may ask ourselves whether children who have not been given such an example have not been deprived of something essential.

Giving is something that we are never done with. Jesus said that we must love our neighbour as ourselves, and this is an 133–134 endless process. Some Christians, in consequence, have a strong feeling that strictly speaking they should give up everything, in order to be like Christ and the poorest of their fellowmen. But there is a danger in such vague feelings. In practice, they are always rejected as impracticable by sound reason and by our sense of responsibility towards our family. The result then is that one does nothing.

It is much better to be convinced that one must give *something* and at the present moment. This is what Jesus depicted, immediately after the commandment of love—the considered help given by the Samaritan who had to travel further the next day. When such help has been given, there is still more to be done,

everywhere. It is brought home to us that we cannot do everything, and this reminds us that we are "unworthy servants"
(Lk. 17:10).

In present-day society giving is best done through qualified
relief officers, that is, by subscribing to collections. There is less
chance of our being deceived. Fund-raising has become an
essential minor part in Christian life. Paul devotes chapters to
such efforts in one of his letters (2 Cor. 8 and 9). It would also
421 be well to refer once again to nos. 83–90 of the constitution
426 *The Church in the Modern World*, as we did when speaking of
world peace and world unity.

It would, however, be wrong to think that Jesus meant us
to look twice at every penny we spent, because of the existence
of poverty. Jesus also praised the lavish generosity of Mary of
Bethany (Jn 12:7–8). Each of us has to find his own style in
such matters. Some are more spontaneous, others more inclined
to calculate and plan. We shall always find an endless road
opening up before us, and we must tread it if we are to be good
Christians.

Giving one's life

But the first gift and the last gift which we have to give to others
must not be forgotten, and that is our life. There is only one
gift which is really enough to satisfy our fellowmen, and that
is ourselves. We must care for those around us, we must be *for*
them. We must not imagine that this has nothing to do with
the need of the world. It is obviously a help to the world close
by, but it is also a help to the world afar. No one knows the
paths which goodness travels on earth. Behind every working
volunteer in the underdeveloped countries are other men
through whose goodness these volunteers have been inspired.

To be good even to those near us is an endless task. There
are lonely people to be visited or invited. There are neighbours
and especially busy mothers who could do with a helping hand.
There are services that we can do without always demanding
payment. We need perhaps to overcome our shyness or laziness
or surliness or self-absorption to show some interest in others.
Life is given a very special warmth by the natural and companionable way in which some men are always ready to help.
(There are others, however, who "practise charity" with

officious cordiality. Still, they often do much good. It does not seem genuine, but it often is.)

There is a connection between love and courtesy or politeness. It is said that St Francis of Assisi took as his example here the "courtesy" of God, who lets his sun shine each day on the good and on the bad. Could it perhaps be said of us that our climate does not allow us to keep this divine example always before our eyes?

Pope St Gregory the Great wrote that what the woman did who anointed the feet of Jesus is an example of what we can do for others. She did not merely wash them with her tears (sympathy) but dried them with her hair (practical help). And this would have remained incomplete without her further action of kissing his feet (her love). Otherwise, he said, it may happen that "the needy we succour are a burden to us, and while we help with our hands, love grows cold in our hearts" (Matins of Ember Friday in September).

Those who try to put this into practice, that is, not only will "not hurt a fly" but really and lovingly help where help is necessary, will always discover that there are more who need help. They will feel that they fail both as men and as Christians. They will not lightly say that they are kind to all. They will understand how much they need to be redeemed and delivered from the evil that they do through neglect or lack of generosity. They will even understand that they need to be redeemed from 260–261 the evil that they do not clearly know of. For our guilt is deeper than we sometimes think. Or, to put the same idea more optimistically: there is a generosity for which God can set us free of which we hardly suspect the existence. Our failure must 277 not dishearten us, but impel us to seek strength not in our own 299 excellence but in God's good Spirit, whom he will not refuse us if we ask.

THE BUSINESS OF LIVING

"Work is serious, but leisure, recreation and art are not." "We are put here to work." "Business before pleasure."—Is this really so? Is the time which we give to productive work (or studying for it) more important than the rest? Most people feel and think otherwise. People live with an eye on the clock, waiting for the week-end, counting the days to their holidays.

437

They work to live. A very real and human life is lived in the times when we are "free". Work and leisure together make up our lives. Leisure, recreation, just being casual are necessary for the truly human life. It brings us together disinterestedly, just for the sake of companionship. It gives us time to recover from the onesidedness imposed on us by our calling. It allows us to be ourselves. Much of our education takes place in our leisure hours. They bring husband and wife, boy and girl, parent and child together. Leisure is the time of love.

Leisure occupations

We shall have more and more free time. The five-day week will not be the end. Mass media have been invented for filling up our leisure hours in common, especially with television. They make us all one. Ten million hearts beat together at the sight of a football match, a play or a piece of news. This can in fact be an ennobling and a unifying factor. But such ways of occupying ourselves can also be stultifying: the father does the same as his small child, the skilfull the same as the awkward, the inventive the same as the dull. Hence the need will always be there to devote some of one's free time to things which demand effort, insight, originality, skill and creativeness, whether they take the form of sport, carpentry, playing a musical instrument, studying some interesting subject, building up a collection, taking a responsible part in an association or whatever it may be. This is also necessary for the sake of the children. When the
409 parents steep themselves, so to speak, in reality on their own initiative, the children also learn to know the world independently, to admire, to be happy there. They become alert and responsive instead of unimaginative. It is only in such circum-
445 stances that one can judge critically what television and other mass media offer, and hence enjoy them properly.

The arts and the sciences

Leisure occupations and non-utilitarian pursuits were also at the origin of the arts and sciences. From the time of the earliest dances, songs and stories, from the cave-paintings of Altamira and the first descriptions of the plants and the stars, men have always tried, as soon as they had a breathing-space from life's cares, to trace and systematize the profound order of the world.

This growing power of thought and definition distinguishes man from animals. Man asks for answers, whether it be as to how electricity works or as to the meaning of existence. He tries to represent order and beauty, disorder and ugliness, through music, words, dancing, colour, and form. It is true of art and science as of work: that they influence the life of man and hence 350, 428 his love, and love influences eternity. And here we can also ask whether their only permanent result is in their harvest of love. Is it perhaps thinkable that something of the forms in which science and art now exist on earth may remain for ever in the "new heaven and the new earth"? If what is best in man rises in incorruption, why not also the best of his creations?

Independent values in science and art

Science and art cannot be divided cleanly from work and religion. Are science and art subordinate ministers to productive work and to religion? No, they are valuable in themselves. They are in themselves reflections of God, and hence follow their own laws. In practice, science and art are often linked with production, and also with public worship of God. Then there can be a mutual interaction of the various laws. But in their supreme expressions in particular, it is clear that science and art follow only their own laws. If these are implemented without inter- ference, they cannot come in conflict with the faith. What is 292-293 true according to science cannot be contrary to faith. What is truly art brings out as such real beauty and truth, and cannot as such be evil.

But art is more closely linked to the living man who produces it than science and hence gives rise to many complications. In a certain sense, the role of the artist can be compared to that of the priest. The true artist has the task of mediating the brightness of truth and beauty to the world. This he can only do though his own personality, though he is concerned with values and effects which far transcend his own person. In this sense he may be compared to the priest, to whom it is granted 348 to transmit through his person something that is far greater 360 than himself. The priest may be a bad man, but he still transmits salvation. But the good he does is tainted in so far as his personal evil is also reflected there. So too the true artist always is trans- parent to God's beauty, deeply and truly. Though he describes lies, he is authentic. Though he describes sexual perversions, he shows man as he truly is as a whole, and not in the seductiveness of a romantically isolated element. But along with the penetrating insight and the inexorable message of the artist in man, there can also be the mistakes, baseness and cowardice of the man in the artist to befoul his work. Or there may simply be his truth and goodness as a new and beneficent force in his work. The laws proper to art and its oneness with life are inextricably woven together.

Mature and cultured men often have a certain facility in distinguishing the one from the other. Those who are not fully mature and have had less practice will not be so adept. Along with the clean air of the human and the beautiful, they drink in some dirty water. It is particularly sad when young people's introduction to the world of human articulateness is saturated with such things. They suffer not so much from what they take in than from what they are deprived of during their first fine period of receptivity. Educators—parents and teachers—must not meet the situation with sheer prohibitions. It is more important to teach young people—and themselves—how to read and look at things properly. A people is not given its writers to leave them unread.

Jesus and culture

The gospel says little about culture. Jesus does not reject art or science. Neither does he counsel them. He refers to the flowers by the wayside, which he finds more beautiful than the magnificent clothes worn by Solomon. When his disciples admired the architecture of the temple, he had its destruction before his mind's eye. But on the other hand, his parables are so simple and 97, 148–149 telling that he must be counted among the greatest wielders of the word among mankind. As a man, he was one of the greatest forces in human culture. But this came automatically. He did not explicitly devote himself to science or to art, and he did not give any instructions on the subject. The one thing that dominates his mind is the lordship of God, the leaven of the world which is 91–93 for its peace. He accepted so fully God's preference for poverty 99–100 and service that he gave his whole life to these things. They were the greatest beauty and the greatest truth that he knew. It is a vocation and a privilege to share with him this passionate 369–370 singlemindedness. It often goes hand in hand with a life according 413 to the evangelical counsels.

Words are part of our greatest achievement. Language can open
up life. It can change our existence. The most intimate com- 38
munication between men takes place through language. Love
is spelt out in words. Language is a great gift, greater than we
realize—more awesome and more lovely. The one power which
can explode the atom bomb—as indeed it manufactured it—is
the human word. And on the other hand, it is only the human
word that can immobilize it. And we all know the power of
even a single word to make a man deeply warm and happy.
Christ carried out his mission as he spoke. He himself was called
the Word. There is a great mystery at the heart of language.   44-45

Conversation; speaking well or ill of others

The background of all our speech is conversation: sitting
companionably together and chatting of unimportant things.
This is one of the basic structures of our existence. It is a way in
which we learn to know each other without hypocrisy or
suspicion. Those who always take over a conversation and give
others no chance are destroying something. There are women
who wear out their whole families talking. To let someone talk
himself out, to encourage him by our attention, can give great
happiness.

It is sometimes well to try to turn a conversation into something
more than mere chat. We can try to explore some truth together.
Or try to say something that has not yet been said. It sometimes
happens than one can talk without insincerity about really great
matters, even about God. It is wrong to chatter superficially all 330-331
the time, with nothing but idle words. There are people who do
so. But that is not what language was given us for. It is also well
to speak to give people encouragement, to praise them openly
or even to utter just reproach (Mt. 18:15). There are times when
a tongue-lashing is in place, if the shock effect will bring home
to others the seriousness of their situation (Mt. 23).

It is wrong to say hurtful things and also to flatter for selfish
ends. Silence is a very sharp weapon—ignoring disdainfully the
words or the very existence of others. This can be a grave sin
(or a pathological condition), if one persists in ignoring someone
with whom one lives under the same roof or in the same community.

To recount another's faults is particularly grave. It destroys something that we all desire and which we all have a right to—a little esteem from others, our good name. We feel it at once if people are gossiping about us. Those near us freeze, their eyes fill with suspicion. If the faults revealed in fact exist ("detraction") the damage done is practically beyond remedy. If faults are falsely attributed (slander, calumny), this is even more unjust. And how can one defend oneself?—The opposite is very much of a blessing: to stress the good points of others. This enriches both the hearers and object of our praise. There is something creative about the good word.

Sincerity

One of the great glories of the word is that it can reveal the truth. To speak the truth makes a man great. All admire a man who can be trusted: not the *enfant terrible* who blurts out everything, but the man whose word can be relied on. This is what speaking the truth is for: to show oneself trustworthy, not to lessen our trust in one another. It goes with the inner habit of thinking honestly. This means no emotional prejudices, egoistic self-delusion, stupid bigotry, fashionable clichés from exclusive groups, blind conservativism. It means giving reality a chance in our thinking. It means integrity. This is an endless task. A basically upright faith in Christ can be disfigured all too often by one or other of the tendencies just named.

One aspect of sincerity is to recognize how often we fail, and that there is much good that we are quite unequal to. This helps us to feel át one with other men. Phariseeism on the other hand is dishonest, because it makes itself a special case in its pretension of excellence. It is one of the greatest obstacles to receiving help from God.—Allowing our viewpoints to harden can also be fatal. We can have right on our side and still not be quite honest. A little humour can sometimes help the truth without breaking any bones. It can help people to relax and see things again in their proportions.

Lying

The lie is opposed to the truth. It is a distortion of reality. It makes a person unreliable. Hence in truth or lying we are concerned with the mutual trust and confidence by which we rely on one another. A complication arises from the fact that mutual confidence also involves the keeping of secrets. There is a natural feeling of reserve about personal matters affecting oneself or others. People do not tell all-comers about everything that happens in their homes. Each of us has a right to a certain privacy. Hence, for instance, there is also the professional secret. Doctors and others whose duties bring them into contact with the private lives of other people are bound to secrecy. They may not speak of what they learn in this way to unauthorized persons. A priest is absolutely forbidden to speak of what he hears in confession. It is a matter of mutual trust to be able to count on secrets being kept. People cannot but respect those who refuse to tell others what they have no right to hear. The respecters of secrecy gain our confidence.

It may sometimes happen, however, that there is a risk of a secret's being revealed, as when tricky or impertinent questions are asked. Only an untruth can preserve secrecy and hence our reliance on one another. If for instance someone asks a doctor in a certain case, from which clear deductions can be made, whether he has had a visit from a certain patient, an evasive answer might only mean, Yes, he had. In such a case the doctor may or must simply say No. There are many possible instances of this sort of thing.

Are such untruths contrary to the fabric of mutual confidence? Certainly not. It is of the nature of language that men should be able to conceal something from others, and this is something that everyone knows. There is no breach of mutual confidence. And hence it evades the charge of lying. It is not a real lie.

This does not mean that we have a free hand to play fast and loose with the truth. It merely means that purely verbal accuracy is not a real and human norm for truthfulness. The norm is mutual reliability.

"Fortune-telling"

We may say a few words here about a form of contact with reality which cannot be definitely attributed to any one of our senses, because it may be a matter of direct perception in the mind or conscience. We mean such phenomena as presentiments, second sight, feeling that someone is looking at us, telepathy (transference of thought), clairvoyance, fortune-telling, astrology ("Your stars this month"), palmistry and so on—all of which may be summed up under the head of "extra-sensory perception". They represent only a small selection of very diverse phenomena, very few if any of which have been properly explored from a scientific point of view. This is a pre-scientific region of experience which makes us suspect that creation, and our perception of it, is richer than we can define. All these are matters which need further investigation.

Meanwhile they can give a very definite impression of the existence of something mysterious, as though the curtain before the mystery of life were lifted a little for a moment. It is something that we can spend hours talking about. It is also something to which people cling to have some sort of hold on the uncertainty of the future.

This sense of the mysterious and the uncertain can be exploited as a money-spinner by tricksters who are complete frauds, and by others who have paranormal or parapsychological gifts, which they combine with a lot of humbug. There are, however, people with such gifts who honestly try to serve mankind with them.

The love of truth with which this chapter is concerned demands that we should not deny at once without investigation the existence of such types of phenomena, and also that we should not lose our heads and think that we can solve the ultimate mysteries of life along these lines. Our faith tells us that God has revealed nothing greater than the Son of man, who led us along the way of obedience and love. It is not twilight mysteries, but 196–197 the mystery of something as ordinary as goodness and love, the mystery which does not vanish with the dawn and can face the glare of midday, which shows the way to life. And it is not a sleight-of-hand which will enable us to know our predetermined destiny. The responsibility to which our creator calls us in our freedom gives us the truest contact with reality. There is nothing of the magician about Jesus. His miracles show marvellous 108–112 powers, but the great sign that he gives is the dedication of his life. He is mysterious, but not a dealer in the occult. And the signs of his power among us, the sacraments, are not mysterious glimpses into another world but encounters with him in faith. They are not magical contacts which work automatically, but a summons to man's heart, to the whole of his life in the broad daylight. All that is truly evangelical breathes this spirit. The true mystery never involves anything less than our whole selves.

444

We do not therefore exclude the possibility of the existence of parapsychological experiences; and they may be the means of unravelling some of the enigmas of nature. What we are against is the unhealthy notion which one might form, that one could reach the profoundest reality along these lines. There is no substitute for the one great way to himself which God has given us: the love and dedication of the free man under grace.   499–500

Service of the word

Those who work for the press, radio or television are the great agents for spreading the truth. They are servants of man's right to good information. Their profession gives them great power over human beings. There is an immense task to be done here. An ethic of service must be constructed which will be more and more in keeping with the gospel, while corresponding also to   426 the intrinsic demands of this calling, which are not at once evident to the outsider.

Parents must try to train themselves and their children to a critical and detached view of what is offered in publicity. And all who are engaged in education, from kindergarten to uni-   438 versity, are in the service of the truth in their lives and think-ing. Something of Christ's message should appear both in their own persons and in their approach to what they teach. This will for the most part be done through the scale of values which they represent, rather than by direct preaching. (We have spoken briefly of art and science in the last chapter.)

Mystery, not riddles

12–17
236–238

Those who seek and preach the truth are intent on clear concepts and exact understanding. The culture which we are part of has for centuries been storming the citadels of natural phenomena: rain, tempest, electricity, atomic particles, cells, psychic structures, sociological laws—more and more of them have been explained, and hence have become more and more manageable. Our knowledge gives us a mastery of reality, in meteorology, technology, the treatment of bodily and mental illness, sociological planning and so on. Our education and society as a whole have thus learned to concentrate on what can be measured and put to use. And this has given results, as we can see. It has also brought with it a sober and objective frame of mind which can favour the development of the balanced and integrated man, honest with his neighbour and with God. But as soon as this desire for "clear ideas" begins to exclude every other point of view, we see the human spirit beginning to close in on itself and disregarding anything that cannot be calculated and made use of. There are the seeds of this attitude in us all. The conviction of the mystery in all things, the sense of wonder in face of life, can be pushed away into the background as irrelevant. The scientific attitude is in itself not responsible for this. The great founder of modern physics, Newton, compared his work with that of a child playing on the strand, preoccupied with shells and pebbles, while the noise of the immense ocean rings in its ears. Newton was firmly convinced that he was working only on the fringe of God's infinite mystery. Neither science nor technology need stand in the way of the sense of mystery—on the contrary.

Nonetheless, it seems true to say that our capacity for recognizing the mystery has in many ways been restricted. This is true even of religious instruction, as may be seen from the way in which the word mystery was explained in the nineteenth century and later. Some of us may remember the definitions from our school-days. It was common to describe the mysteries of faith as "truths revealed by God which our reason is (unfortunately) not yet able to understand, but of which we shall be granted understanding later". The mysteries of faith were presented, so to speak, as lines which disappeared behind a curtain. Our hearts will be at rest when the curtain is raised and we see all clearly.— In this approach, the mystery is really reduced to a riddle, an unsolved problem, which annoys us as long as the complete calculation is not presented. Riddles and problems (which are often in fact termed mysteries) can in principle be solved by diligent enough use of our intellect. With proper means and application we can tell the distance of the stars, the structure of matter, trace a burglar, evaluate an employee, find out the secret which the silent conceal. But the great mystery is on an entirely different plane.

Where are we to seek it? It is in our own home. The beings around me—men, plants and even objects—are a mystery which grows as I penetrate their nature. My own thought, my "I", my feelings and the life of other men all escape my comprehension, and every science which explains part of them leaves us with a greater sense of admiration for all that is discovered and described. And the more clearly a thing appears as a living unity, the better it can show itself, the better does it reveal itself as mystery.

Let us try to see for a moment what this means to us. The man who works all day in industry, administration or government approaches reality as something to be comprehended and calculated, no matter how complicated the problems which it presents. But when he comes home and greets his wife, there is something there which refuses to be simply the object of mental or computerized calculations. And the fewer the secrets they hold from each other, the more they are at one, the greater is the mystery. It is the mystery of the human being, which cannot be set out on squared paper. Does this disturb them or give them a feeling of being strangers? No, everything is much more natural and familiar than one might imagine. They do not say to themselves—What a mystery you are to me! but — How well you look, or, How tired you look, or, How late we are for supper. They do not stop to ponder that the other is a living "I". But they feel it so — as a presence and a warmth which changes everything and makes everything secure. Secrets which another keeps from us may perhaps disturb us; the secret which another is for us, gives us peace. We are happy, because we are encountering that which is greater than ourselves, that for which we were made.

The mysteries of faith are expressions given us to name the inexpressible which is revealed in all things and in all men. The believer may thus recognize that the mystery of existence is a mystery of friendliness and security, of life and light which will stream out upon us, the mystery of the Father, the Son, and the Holy Spirit. (In this last sentence we have indicated the four great mysteries of faith, the Trinity, the incarnation, grace, the beatific vision.) We encounter that for which we are made and which becomes all the more mysterious the more familiarly it is revealed. The word mystery meant in Greek something reserved for initiates, not disclosed to the profane outsiders. Where we encounter the mystery, we are being initiated into the household secrets of God, we are being given a foretaste of the peace for which our purest nostalgia longs. 42–44 499–500

Our mind is made to see and understand, and it is a duty never to tire in the effort to attain clarity. The duty remains with regard to the mystery. But the most profound and essential desire of our spirit is to put everything we have, our mind and

125 all the forces of love and goodness within us, into our admiration, our adoration of what is greater than man. It is in this act that man is most himself, that the spirit is most fully conscious of itself. If he were to lose this faculty, he would be less of a man, no matter how close and clear his analyses. What is complicated we shall manage to disentangle and make use of; with what is simple we shall never feel fully at home. The fountain of life remains infinitely far away. In recent years, certain mental illnesses have been deciphered as the result of our restricted concentration on the clear and utilitarian in education, society and religion. The effort isolates the intellect from man as a whole. It also isolates the will and makes it its own end. And what is taught is how to gain the upper hand, to earn money, to hold on to what we have—with or without a good intention. Thus we are to try to go through life without living, to be real without roots, to show affection without having love, to do good without our heart being involved, to practise religion without self-surrender. But it is only those who welcome the mystery into their lives who can learn to admire, to let themselves be gripped, to give themselves, to believe, to give, and to serve. And it is only they who find the fountain of life.

"Everyone who is of the truth hears my voice" (*Jn* 18:37)

97 No one evokes our mysterious goal as much as Jesus. He begs us not to be blind when seeing or deaf when hearing. Again and again he cries out: "He who has ears to hear, let him hear." "O that today you would hearken to his voice! Harden not your hearts" (Ps 95:7–8). In him, as we believe, God's mystery
79-80 has appeared. The words with which the Council of Chalcedon expresses the mystery are not the formulation of a riddle but the statement of a mystery: that through him we really come home, in him in whom we are really initiated into the mystery of God and of creation. This is the meaning of the dogma that he is truly one of us and truly Son of God. What the intellect in isolation cannot conceive, the intellect in union with our whole being is enabled to believe. Not just one faculty, but our whole soul, our whole mind and all our forces are stirred to say Yes to him. We experience in the Son of man that the unfathomable secret of the world and of man is ultimately not something
310-311 abstract, but someone. For his Spirit makes us cry out, "Abba".
Hence part of our search for truth is humility, faith, hope and

448

love, personal prayer and communal liturgy. As we celebrate
the cycle of the Church year we can experience the mystery of
the world: the Son of God with us. To those who celebrate it 343
together the truth is very close.

THE FAILURES OF CHRISTIANS. SIN

The preceding chapters were meant as a statement of the
Christian task in life. Every Christian will have his own response
to his task. It will be the story of an effort to live according to
the light, and of failures. None of us can claim to have not failed
at times, not to have fallen short in faith, hope and love. We
discussed the common sin of mankind, the evil which is ordin- 259–270
arily termed original sin, in the chapter entitled "The Power of
Sin". The following chapter takes up our shortcomings again,
but this time from the more personal point of view.

Both the gospel and our own experience tell us that we need
Jesus as redeemer as well as teacher. He is rarely so clearly
characterized as the manifestation of God as when he forgives.
There are many stories of forgiveness in the gospel: the paralytic 111
who is let down through the roof; the woman who pours her
perfume over his feet; the murderer on the cross and many
others. He sees in all of them their deepest misery—sin. And
the first recorded words of the New Testament (1 Cor. 15:3) 209
affirm that his dreadful death was connected with our evil.

The nature of sin   39

What does the Christian revelation teach about evil? It says
that the great fault of man is not ultimately the fact that a cog-
wheel is in the wrong place (as Marxism holds) but that his 274–276
will is freely set on evil. It says again that evil is not ultimately
just the imperfection of a free creature, which can be corrected
by intelligence and energy (as Buddhism is inclined to hold) 29
but man's turning away from God, which cannot be set right
by man. Then, the ultimate wickedness is not the transgression
of a cold, lofty law (as Islam generally holds) but an offence 271–272
against personal love. Finally, it is not just an offence against man
(as humanism holds) but also an offence against our creator 273–274
and redeemer. All this is implied in the connotation of the word
sin in Christian revelation. It is a deliberate offence, which

449

cannot be made good by man, against divine and human love. The four main attitudes to evil mentioned above—that it is only imperfect evolution, misconduct to be corrected by one's own efforts, transgression of the law, an offence against man— are not incorrect. Sin is slavery and impotence, and at the same time a challenge to self-conquest; sin is harmful to man, and at the same time transgression of God's law. But true as this is, it does not touch the true point of the revelation. The true nature
379–380 of sin is that it is the refusal of love of others and of the Other. There is something of this in each really sinful act.

492–498   *The mystery of iniquity*

This sounds abominable. But sin is abominable. The message
102–104 of Scripture—including Jesus' words about eternal damnation— leave no doubt about the seriousness of evil. It is not an accident that the Our Father ends with a plea to be delivered from evil.
453 When we sin, we try to attain something contrary to the love of God and of the neighbour. We violate the order of love, in one way or another. This does not mean that we seek evil purely for its own sake. In every sin, we also seek something which is of itself not evil. A man who slanders and insults another is perhaps seeking more spiritual living-space, which is not in itself bad. But he seeks it contrary to the rights and living-space of another, and that is bad. A woman who lives with another's husband, contrary to the rights and interests of others, and contrary to her own conscience, does not intend just evil thereby. Nonetheless, it is sinful.

The fact that some good is involved helps us often to realize how one comes to sin. It is sometimes an excuse. But it also shows the corruption and sacrilege of sin: something true and good, something from God, is misused. We can sin with what is good in ourselves and others. We seek ourselves apart from the whole, apart from God.

Augustine has left us the following profound analysis of sin: "Impelled by love of his own independence, man turns away from the universal whole to the individual part. If he had followed God's guidance in the general course of nature, he would have been led along the best ways by God's laws. But now in his apostate pride, which is the beginning of sin, he tries to grasp something that is greater than the whole. Striving to master it by his own laws, he is thrust back into caring for a part. There is nothing greater than the whole. Hence when he desires something greater, he grows smaller" (*De Trinitate* XII, 14).

How does one commit sin? Is it not folly and blindness? 263-264
Is it really done knowingly? Is the will really free? Sin is after all so incomprehensible, so impenetrable. We recognize, nonetheless, that it exists. Something in our Christian experience tells us that it is more than things taking an unfortunate turn, an upset extrinsic to ourselves. Something within us tells us that in sin we have acted against our better judgment (and hence knowingly) and of our own volition (and hence freely), to choose the wrong direction, away from God's love. We are weak, enslaved and impotent to some extent, but the sin is there.

But it cannot be fully explained. Intelligible sin would be a contradiction in terms. Sin is absurd and obscure. One asks oneself: how could I have done it? *I ought not to have done it.* The good is comprehensible, in order, in harmony with God and man. Evil is not in order. It is a breach of good order and a discordant note. Hence one cannot do evil with as full knowledge as one does good. The one sure thing that remains is the "I" that did it. Sin is a circle from which one cannot break out. The only way to be set free is to make the honest confession: "I did it."

I myself did it. But I was not quite alone. There is a contamination there from the sins of others. This has been explained in the chapter on the power of sin. Through the sin of the world, 259-270
we have been placed in a position in which we are influenced by the evil of man as well as by the good which he does. The sin of the world is revealed in our own sin, but it is also—if it is really sin—our own personal sin. (We shall take up once more the mystery of iniquity in the last chapter.) 492-498

Serious and less serious sin

There are degrees of gravity and seriousness in sin. The amount of clear knowledge and inner freedom can vary from one period of life to another, from situation to situation, from man to man. Further, the actions themselves are different. Of itself, a blow is less serious than murder.—In the first Christian centuries, no lists had been worked out in which serious and less serious sins were distinguished. It was admitted, of course, that some sins were graver than others. Apostasy (idolatry),

458 murder and adultery were treated as very grave matters on account of the open scandal which they gave. But there were also much less precise distinctions between "great" and "small" sins. In later centuries, to facilitate confession, lists were drawn up to signal the sins which had to be confessed before going to communion. They were actions which were of themselves so much of an aversion from God that their doers were unworthy of communicating along with the Church. They were inwardly cut off from God. They were worthy of damnation.—The sharp division between "mortal" and "venial" sin contributed in no small measure to the education of the peoples, to the moral elevation of mankind. It is a way of expressing the seriousness of sin—which is not concealed in Scripture.

But a too precise juridical definition of the difference has also its disadvantages. One can be so preoccupied with it that the attention becomes exclusively fixed on the action while little heed is taken of the attitude of the heart, which remains, how-

127–128 ever, as Jesus said, the real source of all evil (Mk 7:14–23).

A second disadvantage of precise definition is that it is mostly concerned with acts seen in isolation which can be readily described and recounted, while much less attention is paid to the whole inner attitude which is revealed in a series of acts and the whole manner of life. For instance, missing Mass on Sunday was listed, but nothing was said of the icy indiffer-

301 ence which might have been the cause or the result of missing

320 Mass.

What this means is that it is not easy to say what is grave sin and what is not. There are certain outward acts which are clear indications that something is badly wrong within. The fact that the Church calls something mortal sin means that a human and a Christian value is at stake. Some things are so clearly bad that everyone feels at once that they are gravely wrong: murder, adultery, deliberate blasphemy, leaving someone to die without trying to help and so on. But even then the wickedness depends ultimately on the inner attitude.

Aversion from God

In mortal sin, the inner attitude is the will to break with God as he is encountered in our fellowmen and in our conscience. It is a serious break with God, which does not merely mean hatred of him, but also the refusal of something that is essential for faithfulness and love. A husband offends his wife gravely not only by hating her, but also by infidelity in what is essential to love.   450

We must not be too ready to think that this has happened in any particular case. Mortal sin is no trifle. If one starts to turn minor matters into mortal sins, one ends up by turning mortal sins into minor matters. As St Alphonsus Liguori said, If an elephant comes in, you notice it at once. Grave sins are not committed inadvertently. It can also happen, however, that we are so preoccupied by the picture of our apparent holiness that we miss the really great harm that we do. This happens for instance when we are almost scrupulous in keeping various minor laws, but offend against the great Christian precept of kindness. Jesus calls it straining out gnats and swallowing a camel (Mt. 23:24). It is sobering to read Matthew 25:31–46, where Jesus shows what he has in mind when he says this.

If a man lives in grave sin, is he an enemy of God and will he be damned if he dies in such sin? Yes, if he perseveres in a wilful estrangement, in a deliberately total indifference, he is at enmity with God. And if he persists in this attitude till his death, the state of eternal hardening or obstination sets in, which   480–481 is hell.

But here we must recall what we said above, that real sin is above all an inward attitude. The deed taken in isolation does not tell everything. We may have done something dreadful, so bad that we do in fact regard it—not least because of the breach of inner loyalty—as a grave sin. But it is still possible that God sees that there was much good in our attitude and that his judgment is milder than our own.

And even if someone is so hardened in evil that he lives in total enmity with God and is really worthy of damnation, there is still hope as long as he lives. He has turned away from grace and goodness. But God still desires that he should unbend, be converted, repent. He never ceases to offer opportunities of conversion (cf. Jer. 1:2–3). Hence we prefer not to use the word "mortal" sin. Mortal sounds too much like fatal, incurable. We prefer to speak of "grave" sin, as one speaks of a grave illness which is not yet mortal, though it can lead to death.

Nonetheless, grave sin sets men's feet on the way to eternal obstinacy. Hence it is a terrible thing to live at enmity with the goodness of God. This should give us pause. It is not to be lightly dismissed. That is why Jesus repeated so often, as his Church repeats after him: "What I say to you I say to all: Watch" (Mk 13:37).

FORGIVENESS

His own authority to forgive was given to the Church by our Lord as an Easter gift. The fourth gospel describes how on the day of his resurrection Jesus breathed upon his Apostles and said: "Receive the Holy Spirit. If you forgive the sins of any, they are forgiven; if you retain the sins of any, they are retained" (Jn 20:22–23). Jesus is among us through the Holy Spirit. Forgiveness comes to us through the Spirit. The liturgy of Pentecost puts this even more strongly when it says: "He himself is the remission of all sins."

196–199 288–289 The gift of the Spirit, and the Spirit himself, are always present. Forgiveness is present. Our whole life bears the stamp of forgiveness. Indeed, all society bears this stamp. We are all, both Christians and non-Christians, so accustomed to the atmosphere of forgiveness which emanates from the gospel and the Church, that we do not realize that it could have been otherwise.

We live in an atmosphere of mercy as if it were the most natural thing in the world, because the Old and New Testament tell us again and again that God is wonderfully gracious even towards our worst sin. Possibly this consciousness of forgiveness 226–227 has penetrated most deeply into Catholic Christians, so much so that it has given occasion to a less pleasing phenomenon, namely that we no longer feel the seriousness of evil. Christians of the Reformation—and also non-Christians—sometimes have a profounder insight into the seriousness of sin and our impotence to remedy it. It is well that we should be fully aware of what happens when God forgives us.

Repairing the damage

We believe that our sins have really been blotted out by Christ's redemption. Forgiveness does not mean that we remain in a state of sin to which God turns a blind eye for the sake of Christ. We have been made new men.

But then a question arises which we sometimes pass by too easily. Sin does damage—to us, to others. Think of the case of someone who has ruined irretrievably someone's good name by revealing his faults. The Church forgives him, in the name of Christ. But the damage remains. The reputation is ruined. The sinful act continues its ravages. Can we really say that the sin has been blotted out? It has been destroyed in its kernel, the hardening of the heart against God and man. The sinner has been converted with the help of God's Spirit. He is once more headed in the right direction.

This is also the beginning of the elimination of the consequences of sin. Firstly because the thought of making reparation accompanies repentance and forgiveness. This can sometimes take a very practical form, as in restitution after theft. Where this is impossible, as in the sad situation of detraction, the penitent will try to make up for it in some way or other, by some good act. The offender also feels the desire to suffer for what he has done—to do penance. These things have been described in various ways in the tradition of the forgiveness of sins in the Church: reparation, restitution, good works, penitential works, the temporal punishment for sin to be expiated in purgatory.— In former times, the penance imposed could be replaced by useful good works. Instead of going on pilgrimage to Jerusalem, 233 the penitent built a bridge for travellers. There was a custom in still more ancient times of being released from some of the ecclesiastical penance on account of the sufferings of a martyr— by a sort of substitution. Such customs were at the origin of indulgences. A good work could replace penance, and later, "the temporal punishment due to sin", and the difference was made up from the "treasury of the merits of the saints", which the Church besought God to draw on. The element of faith of permanent value behind these antiquated customs is that the Church tries to bestow largesse as royally as possible from the treasure of Christ's forgiveness, and that we do something which embodies our good will.

The great act of reparation is our life itself with its end, death,

247 through which we are "baptized with the baptism with which Jesus was baptized". The criminal on the cross beside Jesus made good his whole life this way, through the grace of Jesus.

The point of it all is that we should not be too ready to believe that with the forgiveness of the Church everything is at once (automatically) over and done with. Forgiveness does not just mean that a load has been taken off one's mind. One has been accepted in grace, but this means to take part with Jesus in the struggle against the evil which one's own sin and the sins of others are causing.

But at the same time we must not lose sight of the greatest truth of all: that through Jesus, goodness is stronger than evil. Forgiveness—including our efforts at reparation—is truly
247-248 redemption, deliverance, renewal, new creation. But it will be a growth spread over years. It may be a different type of growth than we had imagined. Possibly we had foreseen the disappearance of our passions. But what has come about in fact is perhaps a growth in humility and goodness, imperceptible to ourselves, while our fits of temper still occur. The conviction that Jesus' pardon has made the good stronger than the evil should prevent us from spending our lives bowed down under a weight of sin and guilt. Cheerfulness, humility, calm, and even a certain assurance should be predominant, when we live with and work with the Spirit of God, who is the forgiveness of sins.

The Church as the channel of pardon

The Church is the place where God's pardon is given to men. The Church has been given full authority to forgive. Everything which identifies us more closely with the Church, everything through which we are more together with one another through the Lord, is a fountain of forgiveness. Our efforts to repair the
289 damage we have done, of which we have spoken above, make us more one, and hence are channels of forgiveness. As husband and wife, or two colleagues, make amends to one another, Jesus is among them and pours out his Spirit of forgiveness, since such acts go to build up the fellowship of the Church. (Even where Christ's name is unknown, we must believe that
249 sincere reconciliation brings about some sort of fellowship in his spirit.) The welding together of such broken bonds may be a costly and difficult process. But no forgiveness on the part of
122 God is conceivable as long as there is no forgiveness of one

456

another. Jesus speaks of this in the sermon on the mount. He tells us to abandon our offering in front of the altar if we are not reconciled with our brother (Mt. 5:23–24). And we ask our Father in heaven to forgive our trespasses as we forgive them who trespass against us. In the miniature rite of reconciliation with which Mass begins, we confess our sins publicly and to each other. To listen to the gospel together in the liturgy is a channel of forgiveness. Participation in the Eucharist, the great sacrament of fellowship, is immensely purifying. And it is not an accident that the sacrament of initiation into Church fellowship, baptism, also signifies and effects the washing away of sin. 245–246

Confession

But the great sign of forgiveness in the Christian life is confession. Confession is not isolated from mutual reconciliation and other acts of forgiveness in the Church. It is the climax of all such acts. If we ask why this sign was instituted, the answer is that the sacraments give form and expression to all the great realities of our life: birth, maturity, union of man and woman, vocation, repast and illness. Sin is another of these great realities. And here too the Lord has given a sign of his presence. He is ready to meet us there with his redemptive power. This is the first reason for going to confession—that the Lord has given his Church the authority to forgive sins in his name. Happily, confession is there for us. Further, it is only reasonable that our reconciliation with him should be given outward expression, when we make good our faults against each other. Every time we fail, in one way or another, to live up to our task in life, we also offend our creator and redeemer. Hence it is reasonable to ask and receive explicitly his forgiveness.

Another reason for confession is that we thereby acknowledge our impotence to set right the relationship with God and our fellow-men which we have distorted. Of ourselves we can do 266, 277 nothing. And hence confession is also an efficacious sign of God's power, as he forgives sin and restores what has perished.

It is significant that all this takes place by means of a sacrament of the Church. Serious sin, after all, is also a break with the fellowship of grace which is the Church. And a less serious sin does at any rate some damage to this fellowship, since as far as it lies in our power we thereby make the community less holy.

Forgiveness means the restoration of internal unity with this fellowship of grace. And this is the most profound significance of confession: the restoration of unity with the fellowship of the Spirit, the Church.

These reasons for going to confession are most urgent when one is conscious of having committed serious sin—a sin through which unity with the Church and friendship with God is broken off, so that one may no longer communicate. One may 459 only go to Holy Communion when the act of reconciliation has crystallized in confession.

Thus in Christian forgiveness the fellowship of the Church plays an indispensable role. Authority has been given to the Church to forgive sins. "If you forgive the sins of any, they are forgiven." Through this mandate of the Lord, the Apostles and their successors possess a special fullness of the Holy Spirit which they can pour out on others—it is not for themselves, since a 360-361 priest cannot absolve his own sins. The ministers of this sacrament 357-358 are the bishops and priests.

The historical forms of the sacrament of penance

254-255 The sacrament of penance has taken on very different forms in the course of history. This is a very clear proof that Christ did not prescribe the sacraments in detail but left it to the Church to give his signs different forms according to circumstances and the needs of the faithful.

In the first Christian centuries the sacrament was administered far less frequently and under much stricter conditions. It was 452 envisaged only for three offences: apostasy or idolatry, murder and adultery (to which three theft was later added), if they were publicly known and hence gave great scandal. The other sins were forgiven through mutual reconciliation, prayer, private penance, good works and so on. But a Christian who had been publicly guilty of one of the sins named above had to confess it to the bishop and was officially classed as a penitent. He had to perform public penance and was not admitted to the Eucharist. Absolution was given on Holy Thursday. (Hence penance preceded absolution.) The sacrament was administered only once in the lifetime of each penitent. In the case of relapse, it was assumed that the first conversion had not been sincere. After penance and absolution there still remained very often an obligation to perform some penance.

The custom grew up, about A.D. 600, under the influence of eastern and Irish monasticism, of also confessing secret sins. At such confessions, absolution was given immediately after confession, privately and not publicly, and was not confined to any particular day of the year. The penance—which now came after absolution—also ceased to be public. It was performed in private. The sacrament could now be received several times in a life-time. This "modern" form of the sacrament of penance is a re-statement of the primal Christian truth that we are all sinners, not just the murderers or adulterers. Progress has been made here, it would appear. This is the form in which we still receive this paschal gift of Christ from the Church.

The frequency of confession

There are many liturgical and personal occasions on which it seems fitting to receive the sacrament: Easter, Christmas, before 160 a marriage or other celebration, or on the occasion of undertaking some important work. (At the building of some of the great cathedrals it was agreed that all the workers should be in the state of grace. Should it not also be so as we work together to build up society?) Confession is there above all for the times when we are deeply conscious of our sin, especially if we are living in grave sin. If we wish to break with our sin, a sincere, difficult but liberating confession—joined to the effort to make good the harm we have caused—is the surest sign of our sorrow and God's forgiveness. The Church supposes that a Christian guilty of grave sin does not communicate (does not share in the fellowship of Christ and the Church) before going to confession. Confession is still demanded, even where an inward and outward conversion has begun in view of a reconciliation with the Church and Christ. This needs to be completed by the sign of Christ's Church.

252–255

Some Catholics have the habit of receiving the sacrament frequently. If this is the result of anxieties, it is not advisable. But if it is due to a desire to meet Christ as the Lord who forgives, frequent confession can be a very evangelical practice. But individuals or religious houses should not be compelled to adopt this habit, especially as we are now clearer about other modes of forgiveness in the Church.

The liturgy of the sacrament of penance

There are three elements in the sacrament of penance: a contrite confession, absolution and the penance imposed. This form allows of wide variations.

It is possible to confess one's guilt in a common liturgical assembly, and this form has become very popular in our own day. It has the advantage that the preparation in common can help to set one free from an over-narrow and incorrect view of sin with which one may have been burdened since early childhood. It can also be used to speak of sins which might seem harder to mention in a private confession—our common shortcomings as regards the misery of the world. We ask God's forgiveness for our part in this immeasurable misery and promise to do all we can to set it right.—If such liturgical forms of penance are practised, they can end with a prayer for forgiveness uttered by the priest over all the congregation. This would not be sacramental confession. But the liturgy could be organized so that the faithful could make a private confession to the priests in church and receive sacramental absolution from them.

This liturgical rite of penance is quite different from the form which confession takes when it consists of a long talk in private in an ordinary room. This is followed by the imposition of a penance and the pronunciation of absolution in the name of Christ.

Up to the present, the most common form of confession has been something between these two extremes. It consists of preparation and confession in private, followed by a short word from the priest and absolution, all done in the confessional (in church). We now treat confession, penance and absolution under three separate headings.

Confessing

We confess our sins to a priest. This is not easy. Confession being one of the few things in life that we cannot watch others do to copy them, many of us keep to the methods which we learned as children, which is to recite a list of isolated faults. It is better to mention briefly some basically wrong attitude and one or more of the principle faults to which it gave rise. A confession would be incomplete if it were confined to saying, "I have sinned". For the integrity of confession, there must be mention of one's own personal evil.

What is the reason for this confessing? Why not just a prayer to God in the silence of the heart? The reason is that we are reconciled to him by means of reconciliation with the Church, the fountain of forgiveness. Our Lord has in fact entrusted his power of forgiving sins to the hierarchical Church. And it is also in fact a deep desire of man to confess his guilt, distasteful or forbidding though he may find the task. The confession of sins is not in conflict with the situation of the sinner. It is, on the contrary, very fitting.

All sins need not be mentioned in confession. But each grave fault should be mentioned. This is to be done in general terms, without going into details of description. Sometimes it is hard to speak of what one wishes to confess. But if one tells the confessor that one cannot find the right words, one has already made a start with the confession. It then generally turns out to be less difficult than one expected.

The confessor is not there just to listen passively. He has also, in a certain sense, a judicial function. As far as possible, this should not be exercised by putting questions which go beyond what the penitent wishes to confess. This is a matter which the penitent himself must decide on. But the confessor has an opportunity of correcting false views, as, for instance, when it appears that the penitent is convinced that God is interested only in chastity and in Friday abstinence. Then the confessor may well call the penitent's attention to the evangelical requirements of kindness, helpfulness and prayer. This can be liberating. We should not be easily satisfied with a confessor and we should try hard till we find the one who suits us.

Penance

After hearing the penitent's sins, the confessor imposes a penance. In the conviction of Jesus' overwhelming grace, the penance is usually disproportionately small. Jesus has made good our sins, not we ourselves. (We have already spoken of making restitution 455–456 for damage done.) Still, the penance should not be so small as to be comic. Three Hail Marys seems hardly fitting. If a penitent has confessed to speaking ill of his neighbour, he should be told to say something to correct the impression. If he has been secretly unfaithful to his marriage vows, he should be told to find some way of being specially good to his wife. A possible penance would be the reading of a part of Scripture relevant to the confession (the Sermon on the Mount, for instance). Sometimes the confessor will feel that he must put no difficult questions and say very little. The confession may then seem very paltry, but may thereby correspond well enough to the paltriness of our ordinary, sinful life. Nonetheless, it would be wrong for the confessor to take this as the norm, much less as the ideal. Confession must never become routine.

Absolution

Absolution, the forgiveness of sins, is given by the priest with the words, "I absolve you from your sins, in the name of the Father and Son and Holy Spirit". This is the direct exercise of the power conferred in the words, "If you forgive the sins of any, they are forgiven; if you retain the sins of any, they are retained". Hence the priest says authoritatively, "I absolve you from your sins". This is a power which clearly no one has of himself. It is God's Holy Spirit in him.

363–364

Contrition

The whole rite of confession is meaningless where there is no contrition, where there is no inward conversion. Since Christ, we can have sorrow for our sins. Contrition or sorrow is more than a moral hang-over, more than fear, remorse or disgust, more than the feeling of having done something despicable. Contrition includes the realization of having offended against the love of God. I have violated something that is not entirely my own. I have offended someone—God—who loves me. People can have regrets without faith. But contrition demands faith. Contrition includes confidence in forgiveness, the realization of God's mercy, and a desire to be reconciled through the signs of God's Church.

379–380
449

Our struggle against sin may seem to remain in vain. But this does not prove that our sorrow has not been genuine. There may be a long process of growth before us, growth towards the hour of grace, growth also towards other virtues than those we asked for. In all our lapses we must remember that our Lord does not break the bruised reed or quench the dimly burning wick. He spoke of the power of the good over the evil that has been done, as he was at table in the house of Simon the Pharisee: "One of the Pharisees asked him to eat with him, and he went into the Pharisee's house, and sat at table. And behold, a woman of the city, who was a sinner, when she learned that he was sitting at table in the Pharisee's house, brought an alabaster flask of ointment, and standing behind him at his feet, weeping, she began to wet his feet with her tears, and wiped them with the hair of her head, and kissed his feet, and anointed them with the ointment. Now when the Pharisee who had invited him saw it, he said to himself, 'If this man were a prophet, he would have known who and what sort of woman this is who is touching him for she is a sinner'. And Jesus answering said to him, 'Simon, I have something to say to you'. And he answered, 'What is it, Teacher?' 'A certain creditor had two debtors; one owed five hundred denarii, and the other fifty. When they could not pay, he forgave them both. Now which of them will love him more?' Simon answered, 'The one, I suppose, to whom he forgave more'. And he said to him, 'You have judged rightly'. Then turning toward the woman he said to Simon, 'Do you see this woman? I entered your house, you gave me no water for my feet, but she has wet my feet with her tears and wiped them with her hair. You gave me no kiss, but from the time I came in she has not ceased to kiss my feet. You did not anoint my head with oil, but she has anointed my feet with ointment. Therefore I tell you, her sins, which are many, are forgiven, for she loved much; but he who is forgiven little, loves little'. And he said to her, 'Your sins are forgiven'. Then those who were at table with him began to say among themselves, 'Who is this, who even forgives sins?' And he said to the woman, 'Your faith has saved you; go in peace'" (Lk. 7:36–50).

PART FIVE

THE WAY TO THE END

The unquenchable hope

No one has ever found or given enough love in his life, enough truth, freedom, beauty, goodness, and joy. We are always living for a new 'tomorrow'. Man recognizes no limit. This is the most profound urge of all life and progress. We live for the ultimate.

This is a marvellous thing—the existence of hope. It is marvellous that we hope for a humane humanity, for a welfare state, or at any rate for a brighter future. Because in fact the ultimate reality that looms up for everybody, inexorably, is the dark void of death. Nonetheless, all human life, even that of men who do not believe in an afterlife, and reduce hope theoretically to dread, is penetrated by the notion of progress and hope. Life is stronger than doctrine. Human nature has an intuition which refuses to be silenced, and one which is found not so much in our thought as in our very action.

Meanwhile, we are just as truly filled by the inexorable certainty of death. Death is served up to us piecemeal by life itself. A bitter disappointment, an affection which has cooled, loneliness, sickness, the brittleness of the body—these are all presages, cat's-paws from the storm of death, like the cobwebs of July which are an early sign of autumn. 486

The evening of life

Old age is the clearest sign of death. Our life takes a dreadful downward turn. Towards the end deterioration sets in—of our brains and even of our contacts. We drop out of things. The end is upon us before we have tasted life to the full. Indeed, it is just when we begin to know life and take it in as a whole and try it out more deeply that we find ourselves standing outside it.

The evening of life is one of the great tasks which men are set. 409–410

"Ripeness is all" (Shakespeare). It does not always happen, but sometimes older men are helped by their very age to rid themselves of all fanaticism, of all enslavement to ideologies or closed groups, to turn their mind and heart to man himself, who is so profoundly one and the same throughout all. They see Christ less as "the protagonist of an ideology" than as the redeemer who comes to aid man in his helplessness. They see him as the redeemer through love. There is a warmth and maturity here through which old men can sometimes give more strength and hope than others. The murmur of disappointment when the old man John XXIII was chosen as Pope was soon silenced by the joy which this truly human figure spread.

Very often, the greatness of old age comes into play only by fits and starts, between the cares, worries and loss of energy which old age brings with it. And there can only be greatness 406 where one has learned to find one's joy in the joy of others. The others who will live on have now become so many ways in which one's own joy and happiness radiate. One who lives at this level has surpassed himself, that is, has become great. (If the word "mortification" is to be used at all, it should be for this fullness of life, this living in others.) Such people do not push themselves forward, but they are still a source of joy. That age holds such blessings seems to be an indication that life does not end after death in the cold of nothingness, but flows on into a great warmth and love.

Illness

Illness is another onslaught on life. We sometimes feel, when we are ill, that we have lost hold of life. Everything which made up 293-297 life, contacts with men and things, seems to be dissolving. Even 319 our contact with God seems lost. Our concept of God belonged to the realities of our healthy everyday life. Now that that is gone, it seems that he has gone with it. We feel abandoned. We are left with only our pure, hard faith to live by.

But sometimes sickness can also mean a new perspective on men and things, a new relationship to God, at the moment when one is forced to leave the centre of things to cling to life in a 3-4 marginal area.

Visiting the sick is a duty often overlooked. Possibly there is something in us which shrinks from it in fear. The gospel praises this mark of consideration so highly (Mt. 25:36–43) that it is remarkable that we practically never make a point of confessing that we have missed visiting a sick friend, or that our visits were too rare.

It will be a very special experience for each of us when we learn at a given moment that this sickness which we are suffering from can be fatal.

The anointing of the sick

Just as the other great moments of life have been sanctified by 253 Christ through his sacraments, so too there is a sacrament for those in danger of death from sickness. This is the sacrament of extreme unction or of the anointing of the sick.—As soon as a sickness takes a grave turn, the priest should be called to anoint the sick. This is very often put off too long, for fear of frightening the sick person. But the administration of the anointing of the sick does not mean that certain death is impending. It means that there is a possibility of death, perhaps only very slight. Very often, on receiving this sacrament, the sick person actually experiences a revival of strength. As well as being a preparation for death, the sacrament may in fact be a preparation for life. But even if the sick person is going to die, one should not delay too long. It is usually a great blessing for the sick person to be able to receive the sacrament while his mind is still clear and fully conscious. Very often he experiences great calm and consolation afterwards. Obviously, the sacrament should be administered in the presence of the household, and of other members of the family, as far as possible.

There is an indication of this sacrament in the epistle of James, where we read: "Is any among you sick: Let him call for the elders of the Church, and let them pray over him, anointing him with oil in the name of the Lord; and the prayer of faith will save the sick man, and the Lord will raise him up; and if he has committed sins, he will be forgiven. Therefore confess your sins to one another, and pray for one another, that you may be healed" (Jas. 5:14–16). This sacred sign is also very simple in 254 structure. The priest anoints the eyelids, ears, nose, mouth, lips, hands, and feet (or in case of necessity, merely the forehead), saying at each anointing: "Through this holy anointing, and through his own loving mercy, may the Lord forgive all the faults that you have committed through your eyes (ears, nose, mouth, hands, feet)." The holy oil used is the oil of the sick.

The family should prepare a table, or the corner of a table, in the sick-room, covered with a white cloth on which there should be a crucifix and two lighted candles. They should also provide a little bowl of holy water and a sprinkler (such as a sprig of greenery), and another little bowl of ordinary water. The priest will bring the rest.

The anointing is a sacrament for the sick. It is not given when someone is in danger of death or faced with death from other causes, such as execution. In such cases the signs given by the Lord are confession and communion.

Like every other sacrament, the anointing of the sick is orientated towards the reception of the Eucharist. Hence after the anointing, the sick person is given Holy Communion. When the sick person receives Holy Communion again at home, it is fitting that as many of the household as possible should be present. The last communion of a person's life is called *viaticum*, "food for a journey".

175–177
246–247

Death

A dying person has nothing better to leave to those around him than signs of his love and signs of his hope. And proofs of love and hope are also the last thing that family and friends can provide for a dying man. Sometimes they can express these things in words; at other times merely through their faithful presence. As the hour of death approaches, the household can say parts of the "prayers for the dying". They can call a priest to say these prayers along with them. When the dying person has expired, the last part of these prayers are said: "Come, you holy ones of God, you angels of the Lord, come to meet him. Take him and bring him before the Most High." With this hopeful wish Christians take leave of their dead. The earthly man whom we have known and loved no longer moves, speaks or exists. The limbs remain sound for a while, but it is an outward form that is empty within. Man returns to the earth like 8–9 an autumn leaf or an animal. It is an intolerable mystery, which man cannot fathom. Death is not in man's nature.

Death is radical. It is not that just the arms, legs, trunk and head die. The whole earthly man dies. Here the deniers of immortality are right. Death is the end of the whole man as we have known him.—Our hearts bid us be reverent in the face of death. Silence falls. Even the Marxist who should believe that the spirit is only a by-product of the body-cells, does not hurry away the dead, but pays them honour. The human heart is filled with awe before this dark gate, as before a mystery. This is the profound intuition of mankind as a whole.

The Scriptures and the power of God

As we begin now to proclaim the good news which Christ gave about this mystery, we put a very human question. Does nothing of man really remain? Has the dead person utterly disappeared? Is the love and insight of a human life suddenly extinguished at death?—No; the warmth and light which some one has spread continue to live in others. It is marvellous how strong a person's influence can remain after death. Most creative of all is the effectiveness of a good life. And this continues in mankind even when the memory of the name and person has completely vanished. The good done by some one long ago to a child's grandmother can still be one of the factors moulding the child's life. The insights and affection of thousands long dead live on in the present day. The dead are still among us.

But surely not in person?—But perhaps they live on in this way more personally than we often imagine. After all what is more a man's own than the warmth of his love and the light of his wisdom?

This is uniquely verified in the life of Jesus of Nazareth. Since he died and was buried, his spirit has never ceased to be active. On the contrary, he still stirs men's conscience and 192–193 renews their lives by his love, his words and his power. He has a deeper influence on more men than any who are alive today. It seems as though his death does not matter. While our own great-great-grandfathers are often hardly even names to us, Christ remains a real person.

It may still be said that no matter how "personal" the influence of one who is dead and gone, it is still not the man himself. Surely the self, the person, has disappeared? Let us first consider Christ once more. He is not merely recalled and admired from afar, like Rembrandt or Madame Curie. He is spoken to and loved. When we remember him in our liturgy, he is among us. 146–147 We recognize that he lives, and lives in the truest sense of the 342–344 word. His influence on mankind is so deep and marvellous precisely because he *himself* is present through his Spirit. He is with us, to exhort, strengthen, and console.

This faith in the resurrection of Jesus is the heart of the gospel which is proclaimed in this book. No one who believes in the good tidings can say that no one has ever come back from the dead. We believe that the Lord showed himself after his death. In the midst of this mystery of dissolution which is death, 209-210 God has appeared. This is the foundation on which our hope is built: life is stronger than death. And this is true not only of Christ, the first-born from the dead, but for all those whom he knows as his own. They shall follow him. Man is not made to vanish like the beasts.

The reality which was manifested in power by the resurrection of Jesus was also expressly affirmed in his words. Answering the Sadducees, who denied the resurrection, he gave an argument in which the deepest truths of Scripture were embodied. It may take years for the significance of these words to reach us, but then, suddenly, we see the great truth.

"As for the resurrection of the dead", Jesus said, "have you not read what was said to you by God, 'I am the God of Abraham, and the God of Isaac, and the God of Jacob'? He is not God of the dead, but of the living" (Mt. 22:31–33). In these words, our Lord recalls the covenant made by the personal God with man. If God finds it worth while to associate himself with certain men definitely named and unique in themselves, if he 38-39 enters into friendship with them and shares a history with them, 309-310 will he then, the living God, let each of these unique lives disappear in nothingness? No, he has not created and called them as beings of a day who will disappear. He is not a God of the dead but of the living. To believe in the God of Israel and the God of Jesus means that we believe in the personal call of each man to eternal life. And if we find it hard to imagine that God is so good, that he finds us so important, we must take the reproach to heart which he often uttered on this matter: "You are wrong, because you know neither the scriptures nor the power of God" (Mt. 22:29). Faith in the power of God for whom nothing is impossible makes us confident that we are ultimately destined for life.

They are about to arise

The resurrection is promised. But if we ask "how" the dead exist, we notice that scripture mostly speaks of the resurrection of the whole man, of the resurrection of the dead with soul and body.—But is this not something that only comes later? And where are those we loved now, immediately after their death? The Bible does not go into this question. The inspired authors do not intend to give precise information about the "how" of the after-life. Their intention is to proclaim that God calls man to himself in death. Hence, in particular, they give no clear doctrine on the way in which man exists with God immediately after death. Nonetheless, it is a question which our heart puts unceasingly.

Up to quite recent times, a solution was often sought in the simple distinction between "body" and "soul". After death, it was thought, the soul continues to exist separately while the body perishes. At the last judgment, the body is gathered from the clay. This clear picture was an effort to render faithfully the data of the Bible. But an effort must be made to express them otherwise, for the following reasons. The new effort at expression is not a change in the faith, but a somewhat different way of interpreting the same faith. The reason is that the Bible itself never thinks of the soul as entirely divested of all corporality. And modern thought lies in the same direction. What we are is so strongly linked up with our bodies that we cannot think of ourselves as an isolated "I" disconnected from our body.

Let us therefore consider the texts without prejudice. What does the Bible say? It says of Jesus that he *is* risen, of the others who have died that "they shall be made alive" (1 Cor. 15:22), "they have fallen asleep" (*ibid.* v. 6). Then there is Jesus' word to the criminal on the cross, "Today you will be with me in Paradise" (Lk. 23:43). Paul speaks of his desire to be "at home with the Lord" (2 Cor. 5:8). Sometimes Jesus uses the word "soul". "Do not fear those who kill the body but cannot kill the soul" (Mt. 10:28). But he does not mean to refer to a human spirit which floats free, as it were, of the body. As elsewhere in the Bible, the meaning is rather "life", "the living kernel of man as a whole, body and soul". Our Lord means that there is something of man, that which is most properly himself, which can be saved after death. This "something" is not the body which is left behind. But our Lord does not say that this which is truly man is entirely disassociated from a new body. It is not biblical usage to speak of a purely disembodied soul of man.

How then are we to understand the texts? They speak of a "today" with reference to something which is not entirely without a body. And at the same time, they speak of those who

"shall live" after death. What message is to be read here? It seems to be that we are to think of the "today" as something that has already begun, and that it is not without the body. In other words, *existence after death is already something like the resurrection of the new body.* This body of the resurrection is not molecules which are buried and scattered in the earth, a point which we shall come back to again later. Man begins to awake
478–479 as a new man.

And at this point we must be silent. The "how" is unknown. And we do not know the relationship of this "about to rise" to our time and space. We speak of it as "today" and "in the future" at once. But this involves something which the human mind cannot picture clearly. And it is just as well that we cannot express precisely the greatness of God's promise. It is good to learn to live with the firm hope of the resurrection and at the same time with our ignorance of how it will precisely be. But then how are we to speak of it? We should keep to the words of scripture: "they have fallen asleep", "they shall be made alive", they are "at home with the Lord". They wait. They are about to rise. They are beginning to live with God. We can pass on in this way the message from God, and use such terms to speak of it to children.

The communion of saints

But may we not try to understand more clearly? May we not look further into revelation, to find the purest possible expression of how the new life is to be thought of, how we are to picture those dear to us who have died? If we do try, we find that revelation does not lead us away to a distant other-world. It points to our own. What, after all, is the greatest manifestation of the fulfilment of God's promises to us? It is the Easter appari-
181–183 tions of Jesus and his presence among us. We are shown how he is
192–193 a friend who strengthens and consoles, and that he has remained the same ever since in the life of mankind, giving new force and peace, new gentleness and love. This manifestation—the permanent influence of the risen Lord since the first Easter apparitions—is the purest indication that we have about the nature of eternal life, including that of those who have already fallen asleep in him. To find out something about the new life of one who has died, we may fix our attention on the good which lives after him on earth.

474

This, rather than any nebulous fantasies, will help us to sense what eternal life is: man's fulfilment through dedication and love. Just as we know the risen Lord through the force that flows from him, in the same way we must try to recognize our dead by their good influence. St Thérèse of Lisieux said that her heaven would be to let a rain of roses fall upon earth. She spoke in the sentimental terms of the nineteenth century. But she expressed a profound Christian truth at the same time. The good that lives after a man on earth is the finest picture that we have when we think of his after-life in God.

All who have died, belonging to the fellowship of the human 214 race and to the fellowship of the Church, all the good from the apostles, martyrs and saints to the least of believers, now live in God. And therefore the Church recognizes that they are joined to us in some way. In this union of life in God and with us, Mary has a very special place. This is not stated, to begin 76–77 with, as "doctrine", but simply as a fact which may be observed. In the Christianity of the East and of the West she is present more than any other person, except of course Christ. Her presence is to be felt even in our houses, not just through the icons with the expressive eyes or the pictures with the gentle smile, but above all because she is spoken to and because prayers to her are heard by God. And again—though this is to be seen rather as an added blessing than as the kernel—she has sometimes appeared at places which afterwards offered truly evangelical characteristics—peace, healing and amendment of life, as for instance at Lourdes. The Christian reality of what happens in 197 such places is sometimes explicitly recognized by the Church, though never in a specifically infallible utterance. It is more important that the Church as a whole has recognized her glory so much as part of its faith that it has expressly proclaimed that Mary has already been raised from the dead, body and soul. Of the other dead we may only say that they will be made alive, they are about to arise, but we acknowledge that Mary is already glorified. It is true that her glory—like that of Christ himself—will only be perfect when the whole of mankind is gathered together.

Just as Christ's resurrection is effective among us through his forceful, vivid presence in the life of the world, so too, we may say, the glory or the "Assumption" of Mary. This means that she is more in the world than any other woman. Cleopatra is remembered. Mary is addressed. She is the most closely present of all women. The risen Christ and Mary assumed into heaven—the true Adam and the true Eve of mankind—are not to be sought far away from us, as though heaven were an immense theatre full of purely spiritual souls where only two places were bodily occupied, those of Christ and Mary. Once again, it must be remembered that imagination in terms of space and time is powerless here. We can experience the presence of Christ and Mary by living on earth in the Spirit of Christ and by speaking to them in prayer.—The same may be said of the other dead. Some great saints and good men are more powerfully present than others. Does this perhaps indicate that they are already further on the way of resurrection?

Christians and the purification of the dead

A very human question has yet to be asked. Is there anything we can do for the dead?

The first thing that the Church—that is, any of us—does for the dead is to pray for them. The last rites for the dead are the focus of intense supplication. This farewell mostly takes place through the burial of the dead, but can also be done by cremation. A Christian funeral is accompanied by the celebration of the Eucharist, the remembrance of Jesus' death on the cross. The Preface is full of human tenderness and divine certainty: "In Christ the hope of a blessed resurrection shines upon us, so that we who are saddened by the inexorable law of death are also consoled by the promise of a future immortality. For life is changed, not taken away, in those who believe in you, O Lord, and when the house of this earthly dwelling is dissolved an eternal dwelling-place in heaven is bestowed on them."

It is not the custom, unfortunately, in our society—except in rare cases—that the remains are borne to the grave by the family, friends and neighbours themselves.—The last prayers and readings take place by the graveside, for the consolation of those present, and to offer supplications to God for the person who is being buried. Prayer for the dead is a tradition of the Church. Why is it offered? It is offered because there is still so much bad will, indifference and rebellion in man, even when he dies in grace. (Would any of us feel that he is ready to enter heaven just as he is?) There is still much ingrained egoism to be converted, cleansed away and purified. This takes place in death. To die is also to die to evil. It is the baptism of death

along with Christ, in which the baptism of water is completed. 246-247
The other face of this death—as the Church believes—can be
a purification, the definitive, total conversion to God's light.
How long does this process last? We must remember once
more that all this takes place outside time as we know it. We
cannot determine the time or the place. But from our point of
view there is a certain time during which we regard someone
as "departed". We help him by our prayers. How many months
or years it is we cannot tell. It depends on a man's life.

In former times efforts were made to visualize this mystery
as clearly as possible and it was all represented vividly in pictures
and plays. In the Germanic lands this purification (*purgatorium*,
purgatory) was given a name which meant "purifying fire".
It was depicted as a place, a fire, a certain length of time, with
an angel calling out the souls one by one, like patients in a
doctor's waiting-room. In this way, the unseen was brought
home to Christians, and fervent prayer was offered for the dead.
We must now train our imagination to return to the soberness
of Christian antiquity, and to consider the purification of
purgatory as connected with death. We must not make it one
of the "Last Things" in isolation. We must not make it too
independent an entity—all the more so, because scripture hardly
speaks of it at all. We read in 2 Maccabees 12:43–46 of a sacrifice
being offered for the sins of soldiers killed in battle, who were
awaiting the resurrection. The sacrifice in question was said
to be a sign of faith in the resurrection. It is a gesture which we
find readily understandable in the presence of death, since we
too believe in the resurrection.

The Protestant Churches do not pray expressly for the dead.
Their intense hope that the dead are with God takes the place
held by prayer among Catholics. The difference is in fact not so
great perhaps as we think. Protestants do not pray explicitly
for the dead, but the funeral is accompanied by prayer.

In the canon of the Mass every day there is a place provided
where the names of the faithful departed may be mentioned,
in the middle of the community's act of worship, in the middle
of the celebration of the sacrifice of the cross. After the mention
of those who are prayed for, the following prayer is said: "To
these o Lord, and to all who repose in Christ, grant, we beseech
you, a place of refreshment, light and peace." 2 November is a
day of special intercession of the dead.

The resurrection on the last day

We were created to be together. Hence, when Jesus speaks of the last things, he speaks primarily of humanity as a whole. What exactly is to take place we do not know. Christ gives the atmosphere, the grandeur and the awe of these events in words which he borrowed from the prophets: clouds, angels, floods, wars, false prophets and persecutions—as we find, for instance in Matthew 24 and Luke 21. And this is perhaps the place to say something which should be understood as said at many other places of this book. It is that this catechism tries to expound clearly the living truth of faith. But there is more force, life, truth and authenticity in the pages of the Bible.
47-53 The pages of the Bible seem to glow with the warmth of faith,
146-149 experience and divine revelation, with the warmth of Jesus' own words. Very often the Bible does not explain—it simply impinges on one, in the way that life itself makes its impact.

This is also true of the descriptions of the end. They depict in extremely vivid colours the calamities and miseries of all ages, the horrors of war, even catastrophes on a cosmic scale. And we hear at the same time the message that even then—and above all, then—God remains faithful. "Now when these things begin to take place, look up and raise your heads, because your redemption is drawing near" (Lk. 21:28). This is the statement which the horrifying pictures of the prophets, the evangelists and the apocalyptic seers make, for all ages. Hence they are not a description of the course of events at the end. They give us a general sense of the course of history and its consummation, affirming that whatever happens, God moves to his triumph in all things. It is a message of consolation among the menaces of all ages, even of that of the atomic bomb.
162-163 Jesus warns us to be on the look-out for him in all circumstances, to be watchful, above all by our faith (Lk. 18:8) and love (Mt. 24:12). He gives no precise indications of the time.
40-41 But the fact that scripture testifies so definitely that history as
328-329 a whole has an end and object indicates that it will also reach a consummation: that God will do with history as a whole what he did with the life of Jesus.

All men will then rise again like our Lord. The new birth will be completed. The Bible speaks, in splendid imagery, of the dead coming up out of the earth. This does not mean that the molecules of which our body was once formed will be reorganized as at the hour of our death. It is not a matter of re-constituting our earthly body. (In any case, what are "our" molecules? They are changing at every instant. Practically nothing of the material elements of the child's body remains there when he is grown up.) What takes place is the perfecting of our spiritual body, of which Paul speaks ardently and at great length in 1 Corinthians 15:31–50, showing that we must not think of the resurrection as a return to the flesh and blood of our mortal frame. Our present body is only a prefiguration of the great reality: "What is sown is perishable, what is raised is imperishable. It is sown in dishonour, it is raised in glory. It is sown in weakness, it is raised in power. It is sown a physical body, it is raised a spiritual body" (1 Cor. 15:42–44). We are not to think so much of the biological body as of the body which has the life of the new creation. The biblical phrase "coming out of the grave" means that we shall be our own selves—the same as before, but with a difference, just as Jesus after his resurrection was the same, but also different, so that his Apostles knew that it was the Lord, but did not recognize him 183 at first.

Judgment

102–104

When mankind has reached its full numbers and has been raised from the dead, everything will come to light. This is the kingdom of God. The thoughts of all hearts will be revealed. Here upon earth, "all that glisters is not gold". But when God manifests himself, everyone will be seen exactly as he is. This is judgment. The wheat and the weeds which could not be distinguished on earth will be then recognizable. The kingdom of God is like a fishing-net, says Jesus; the good will be gathered in, the bad rejected. Yes, the consummation means judgment, and this means that everyone who has not hardened himself against grace will be seen to have contact with Christ and to be like him. "Come, O blessed of my Father." But those who have steeled themselves against grace and call will be without link with or resemblance to Christ. They are severed from the one person who can save them. "Depart from me, you cursed." This is judgment: union with Christ (even though one has perhaps never heard of his name) or aversion from him (even though one has had his name on one's lips). It is unity with his Spirit of goodness, faith and service—or separation from his Spirit. Thus Jesus is the judge by his very existence, like a magnet which attracts or repels according to whether something is of its own nature or alien to it.

This judgment is already begun at death. When speaking of the resurrection, we said that men are about to rise immediately after death; so too we must say here that man is already being judged. And here too we must repeat that this takes place outside time as we know it. Hence we cannot speak of a time, in our sense, between judgment at death—the particular judgment—and judgment on the last day (the general judgment). We simply do not know how this can be, and it is not important to know such things, since it is ultimately the verdict pronounced by the same Judge.

472–474

Reprobation

Jesus speaks of the possibility of one's being eternally condemned. We read of "eternal punishment" (Mt. 25:46). This could be wrongly understood, as if a disaster or even an injustice then befell the damned, as can sometimes happen with punishments on earth. Hence we find it more enlightening to express the same truth by the term "eternal sin". The state of cold obstinacy has become eternal. They have become impervious to God, love, goodness, Christ and fellowship. But it was for these things that man was made. It is now a total perversion, sin brought to its fullest self-expression. To be lost means to be entirely closed in on oneself, without contact with others or with God. This is the punishment, the "second death" (Rev. 20:14). Scripture uses terrifying words to express it: darkness, gnashing of teeth, fire. They need not be taken as literal descriptions. They are apt expressions nonetheless of the dismay at having missed the end and object of existence.

453–454

We sometimes think that hell is impossible to reconcile with the love of God. But it is precisely those who have been profoundly penetrated by God's love who have believed in it. First and foremost was Jesus himself. He did not discuss the numbers involved, but when he questioned about whether many would be lost, he urged his hearers in the most solemn terms to take the way which leads to life. Each of us must draw his own conclusions here. The warning given by Christ is a blessing for us. Saints too have believed in hell, without finding it in contradiction with God's love.

102–104

For those who harden themselves, the tender warmth of God's love becomes for ever a fire of remorse and embittered resentment. In the scenes of the last judgment in the cathedrals of the middle ages the gesture of condemnation appears as Jesus showing his five wounds. It is the equivalent of saying: see what I have done; what more ought I have done?

St Thérèse of Lisieux also seeks the answer in God's justice. No one is there who ought not to be there. Man places himself in this situation willingly and knowingly. We must therefore avoid arrogating to ourselves judgment on something that we do not understand. We must not manufacture for ourselves a God of our own. We must believe in him as he has revealed himself in Jesus. In Jesus we see the love of the Father in its supreme expression, but we also hear such words as these from his lips: "Do not fear those who kill the body but cannot kill the soul; rather fear him who can destroy both soul and body in hell" (Mt. 10:28).

We need not avoid mentioning this doctrine of reprobation to children. But it would be wrong to use it as a threat, as if they too could go to hell. Jesus' warning is concerned with adults who harden their hearts. And it has only one purpose, the purpose of salvation. It is a call to abhor evil, to desire all that makes man good, to trust him who is the way to life.

The new creation

"No eye has seen, nor ear heard, nor the heart of man conceived, what God has prepared for those who love him." These words from 1 Corinthians 2:9 are easily applied to the glory of our eternal dwelling-place with God. But, surprisingly enough, they are primarily concerned with faith on earth. Our peace, our forgiveness, our stability in Christ—all this is the beginning of heaven. Something of eternal joy begins already amid the distress and fears of this life. This joy will flower fully in the paradise which God had in mind since he created man: "the kingdom prepared for you from the foundation of the world" (Mt. 25:34). 290–291

Are human beings the only creatures called to this love of God? Or are there other creatures also called who exist outside our space and time? And perhaps creatures from our own space and time who live on other heavenly bodies?

As regards the first, scripture speaks of such beings, the angels. They are the messengers of God, or powers stemming from God, "ministering spirits" (Heb. 1:14), who are often presented under human form in the Bible. They give concrete form to God's goodness, these great and good forces which work with us in this creation. Is their existence a supposition based on scripture's view of the world? Or is it part of God's message? In any case, the Bible presents them as fully involved in our history of salvation in Christ. And everything that is said about them in the Bible proclaims the marvellous truth: that God is concerned for us in a thousand ways. The names of the angels tell us this. Gabriel means "strength of God"; Raphael, "God's healing"; Michael, "Who is like God?"—The same is

492 true of Satan, but the other way round. It is the power that opposes, though not on the basis of equality with God, not with the same primordiality or power, as scripture expressly says. It is the horrifying wickedness which we see at work in humanity, often so much greater than individual wickedness that we ask

92-93 ourselves what forces can be at work here. Are they purely
109-110 human?

As regards the existence of beings on other planets, no answer can be given. But like the previous question, it makes no essential difference to the message about the final consummation of all things, that God will be one with his beloved creatures.

"Then I saw a new heaven and a new earth" (Rev. 21:1). When we think of the final consummation, the many millions of the human race come to mind, inspiring us with joy, but perhaps also with the feeling that there are unthinkable multitudes here. It seems to us impossible. But this is to think in terms of our own limited memories and interests. It tires us to see and meet too many people, so that our contact is less close in each case. This is earthly imperfection. But even on earth we can already see a manifestation of human development in the fact that someone can be open and good towards many. We may know someone who can take as much interest in a number of persons as others not even in one. In the new creation, as we hope, and as we deduce from Christ, there is a humanity which transcends the dead weight of numbers and the nameless

472 multitude. This is supremely true of the love of God himself. No one is merely a number to him. "To him who conquers . . . I will give a white stone, with a new name written on the stone which no one knows except him who receives it" (Rev. 2:17).

"And I saw no temple in the city, for its temple is the Lord God the Almighty and the Lamb" (Rev. 21:22). God, the infinite, the simple, the ever new will be all in all. An inexpressible unity will overcome all the confusion of multiplicity. God's presence in each and every one will be light and life. No temple or church will seem necessary to seek him in.—The fullest texts of scripture in which eternal life is described are to be found in the book of Revelation. There we see the ardent hopes of the early Christians, and we can inflame our own hopes there, even if we cannot understand each individual text. These passages from Revelation are echoes of the words of the prophets as they chanted the coming salvation of Israel in marvellous imagery based on the notion of paradise. The kernel of all the images is God's merciful presence, as appears above all in passages from the end of the book of Isaiah.

Scripture encourages us to look at the world around us and at our own life in God's hands, to form for ourselves an idea of the promises. We must think in particular of certain moments in which men suddenly feel themselves renewed, happy, absorbed in a great mystery, as can happen when listening to music or in the spring or when looking at the bright lights of a city in the evening. There is the security of a child when its mother dries its tears, the love of man and wife, the peace and consolation of prayer, liberation from a heavy menace, the intimacy of a family or friends eating together: so many hints of heaven.

All the imagery of scripture tell us that God pays man the honour, as it were, of letting him be himself. As Ignatius of 214 Antioch wrote of the time after his coming martyrdom: only then shall I really be a man. God wishes to make men of us. Does this characteristic of all God's action allow us to infer that our earthly life and work have an influence on the new creation? We know at any rate that the harvest of love in the world will be gathered in. But may we not also surmise that all the creativeness, truth, beauty, communication and authentic experience which were attained on earth will continue to be effective in God's eternity?

Now that we have learned to see more particularly how the 350 evolution of the world under our hands is a creative work of God, we may well surmise that the life and work of our history will indeed be transformed but need not be destroyed in the new creation. The achievement of Mozart can never be obliterated. That I have lived near someone who has touched me deeply, that I have helped someone or that someone has helped me—these are things that can never be undone, much less the fact that I have been a wife to my husband, a mother to my child. Jesus' words tell us that we must not imagine any more procreation in heaven, or that the exclusivity of marriage will persist. But this does not mean that love will not abide and grow between those who have been married. The gospel speaks so lovingly of brotherliness that we may suppose that the relationship of parents and children, and indeed that of all men, will be that of brothers and sisters. This begins already on earth when the children have grown up.

What are we to think of the age of the risen body? We know nothing of this matter. But here too we may believe that nothing of the loveliness of any age on earth will be lost. Perhaps, as has been suggested, we are given something of the age in which we were happiest, or in which we were most faithful to our purest love. Or is age a far too earthly concept? We do not know. "One dies there as a child, even if one is a hundred years old", as Isaiah's vision of the future may be interpreted (cf. Is. 65:20). But what can this mean in the place where there is no death? We cannot tell. We must not even ask ourselves, except to comfort ourselves, like the writer of Isaiah 65.

What the whole of revelation tells us is that existence with God consists of love, the full development of man who can cherish and give. Just as here on earth the survival of the saints 474–475 is manifested most clearly in the influences which radiate from them, so too in the new creation man is someone who lives to the full in giving, love, dedication and outgoing. Man's creative urge is involved, but in what form we cannot tell. We may suppose that in a life given by God the creative, there may exist something like a very great joy in creativeness.

What may certainly be excluded by virtue of God's promise is the notion of any boredom. A medieval legend relates that a monk once asked himself how that could be, as eternity went on and on. Bemused by his speculations on the matter, he wandered into a wood where a nightingale was singing. He stood to listen, enchanted. After listening awhile, he returned to his monastery. But when he reached the house, no one recognized him. He gave his name, and the name of his abbot, but even the abbot no one could recall. Finally, they looked at the annals of the abbey and there they saw what had happened. A thousand years had passed since the monk had left the house. While he was listening, time stood still.—Even modern man is still aware of this. In great moments of love and rapture time no longer counts. It is a foretaste of eternity, of a peace never to be eclipsed.

The witness of all scripture to God's eternal fidelity   472

When considering eternal life, we began with the texts of scripture whose purpose it is to speak of our future with God. But there is another way in which we can interrogate the scriptures about the new creation. This is to remember that God reveals his eternal purpose in all his dealings with man. The Church Fathers termed this approach to the Bible the "anagogical sense"—the sense "pointing upwards"—to heaven (*sensus anagogicus*).

This is one of the "spiritual" senses of scripture. It is based   60–61 on the insight of faith which tells us that what God has been for man in history, he will also be for eternity, and not only in the present age, as is affirmed by the ordinary "spiritual sense". Read with this conviction, the story of the passage through the Red Sea means not only the deliverance from Egypt in the past, and not only the liberation which Jesus brings us now in our present life, but also the eternal salvation into which we enter through death. Or, to take an example from the New Testament, the story of Jesus' touching the eyes of the blind man enables us to think not only of the healing which then took place, but also of our present enlightenment through faith, and also of the promise that God will be our light and healing for eternity.

This way of regarding scripture as transparent with God's promises is much less in the nature of precise description than any other. And this is what gives its upward thrust. It leaves unuttered that which is unutterable. It only shows that Jesus opened the eyes of the blind, and it remains within the terms of the image. The story then becomes a symbol or sign of our eternal hope in God. By the graves of the early Christians in the catacombs we find this story sketched in in a few lines—tiny pointers to God's life-giving faithfulness.

If we can use the whole of scripture in this way to fill our heart with joy and hope, we shall also sense this element of our heavenly happiness—that it is *liberation*. All the glory described by scripture is depicted against the background of the darkness which precedes it. It is rescue, joy after grief, the drying of tears. This is true above all of the joy which follows the day of Golgotha, the Easter apparitions. These remain for us the great pointers to paradise. Jesus stands for us, as the first to be freed, the first-fruits of the new creation. But he is also the saviour himself, who stands for God. And it is all very human. He addresses his friends by name. This mark of consideration is pregnant with the promise that salvation does not consist of a sort of 282–283 eternal sleep cast upon the human personality, but of its full 501 expansion in the light of the God of the living.

Life in hope

Are we concerned in all this merely with the future? Paul reminds us that we already begin to be one with Christ, the 245 risen Lord, through our baptism, and that we are therefore 346–347 already dead and risen in a certain sense. "Set your minds on things that are above, not on things that are on earth. For you have died, and your life is hid with Christ in God" (Col. 3:2–3).

There is a profound consolation in the truth that the new life begins in us because we have died with Christ. It is a life stronger than death. It is a life which proceeds from death. Hence it is also relevant to the "dying a little" which constantly happens us in the midst of this life—in disappointments, misfortunes, illnesses, losses and farewells. It means that this daily dying, accepted in the spirit of Christ, is also full of hope. Through God's power, each of our losses enshrines the beginning of resurrection, a hidden fruitfulness for ourselves and others.

410–411 The conviction that we already bear within us the new creation can sometimes take the form of a glowing confidence and gladness. But it can also take the form of awe, shot through with joy, as we realize the holiness that is already bestowed upon us by the Spirit. It is a holiness which also consecrates our body. Hence Paul can say, when warning against the sin of unchastity: "Shun immorality. Every other sin which a man commits is outside the body; but the immoral man sins against his own body. Do you not know that your body is a temple of the Holy Spirit within you?" (1 Cor. 6:18–19).

This faith that glory has already begun should not deprive the 350 world of its reality in our eyes. It should not give us an "escaptist"

486

attitude to life. This would be to misunderstand the real purpose of God's message, which makes the actual life we lead an important, serious and hopeful thing. The message is that life 414 has a meaning, that it is in the hands of God, and that all we do is important for this world and for the new creation. This is the profound meaning of the words, Set your minds on things that are above. They underline the perspectives, the confidence and the beauty that life holds out. And there are moments of repose and peace when this is brought home to us, and we realize deeply that creation is made for ultimate glory. In such moments we need not call on men and things—as we did above—to be signs of God's promises. By their very existence they begin to tell us that God will fulfil what he has begun in us. The flowers on 483 the table, the shout in the street, the hands of those dear to us, the courage of the dying, the faith of the missionaries, the cheerfulness of the child—everything that is good begins to speak by its very existence of a destiny too great for words, of a hope of being protected and secure in face of destruction, safe with God.

In less exalted moments, this hope takes the form of confidence that all is not in vain. And when the believer is invaded by a sense of the absurdity of everything and even by a sort of existential dread, this confidence remains the hard core from 189 which he derives strength. The passion narratives give us to understand that this hope was not quenched even when Jesus cried out: "My God, my God, why hast thou forsaken me!" St Paul writes to the Romans (8:18–25):

> "I consider that the sufferings of this present time are not worth comparing with the glory that is to be revealed to us. For the creation waits with eager longing for the revealing of the sons of God; for the creation was subjected to futility, not of its own will but by the will of him who subjected it in hope; because the creation itself will be set free from its bondage to decay and obtain the glorious liberty of the children of God. We know that the whole creation has been groaning in travail together until now; and not only the creation, but we ourselves, who have the first fruits of the Spirit, groan inwardly as we wait for adoption as sons, the redemptions of our bodies. For in this hope were we saved. Now hope that is seen is not hope. For who hopes for what he sees? But if we hope for what we do not see, we wait for it with patience."

GOD

"He who dwells in inaccessible light"

447–449 There have been Christians who have thanked God for the impenetrability of scripture. Such for instance was Teresa of Avila, when she laid aside the Bible in its difficult Latin to read the word of God in her mother-tongue, and still found much there that she could not understand. She then thanked God. She saw a sign of the greatness of his mystery in the fact that even in his word he could not be grasped, comprehended and fully surveyed. Graham Greene said that he would refuse to believe in a God whom he could understand.

There are no words of man, not even in the Bible, which succeed in naming God. Nowhere does the Bible attain an easy perspicuity. At every stage, from the dark wrestlings of the book of Job to the morning sunshine of the gospels, the mystery is just displayed, but never taken away.

A multitude of names for God may be gathered from the pages of scripture. They speak of his majesty: "He dwells in unapproachable light" (1 Tim. 6:16); of his thought of us: "Then the Lord God formed man of dust from the ground" (Gen. 2:7); of his being exigent: "Our God is a consuming fire" (Heb. 12:29); of his life-giving might: "The lifter of my head" (Ps. 3:4); of his love: "And he embraced him and kissed him" (Lk. 15:20).

These words may be mere stammerings, but they are of very great power. And if all that scripture says of God is taken in together, it provides a certain clarity—not a clarity which enables us to comprehend him, but one through which we undoubtedly attain a more correct orientation. For it is characteristic of the revelation given to Israel that pre-existing notions of God are cleansed of errors and pointed more directly towards
33 where God is to be found. This cleansing affects primarily the relationship of this world to God, in men's minds.

309, 427

382–383 ### *"It is he who made us"* (Ps. 100)

God's concern for his people, shown through the exercise of his sovereign power—this was Israel's earliest experience. It
39–40 first knew God as deliverer. It was only when the world took

on greater dimensions in their eyes that the people began to realize that it was from this saviour God that all things came. 40 God was then seen as the creator, as is splendidly expressed in the lyric of creation in Genesis 1.

The vaster the world appears, the greater our concept of God continually grows. Nebulae and light-years, microbes and nuclear particles, psychological depths and biological processes which are discovered by us mortals, enlarge day by day our concept of God's incomprehensible creative power. In our own days, our growing consciousness of evolution in particular has 9–12 given us a new vision of God's majesty. The "becoming" of the universe is unfolded before our eyes and we feel it in our lives. This gives sharper contours to a truth which had always been proclaimed but little attended to: that the creation of the world is not so much something that God has done as that he does. The beautiful biblical image of the creator as modeller 486–487 should not mislead us into thinking that after modelling the world God could leave it "alone". Creation is not making something as men make things. The carpenter makes a chest and goes away, but the chest remains in existence. The poet makes a poem and dies, but the poem remains. But if God were to withdraw his creative power for even one moment—we must allow ourselves this human way of talking—then nothing would exist. That God is creator means that all that exists is dependent on him, that all depends on him. To grasp the notion of God as creator, we should think not so much of the beginning as of the present and the future. He is now at his work of perfect- 261–263 ing all things.

The words "in the beginning" with which scripture opens (Gen. 1:1) and also the gospel of John (Jn 1:1) should not be taken as merely an indication of time, but as an indication of order and primordiality. They mean "at the origin" or "most profoundly", and proclaim God's "Priority". In the same way, Ruysbroec says that God is "the cause and origin of all creatures".

> *"As the heavens are higher than the earth"*
> *(The transcendence of God)*

In all this the biblical message never ceases to affirm from the start, and indeed from the times when Israel only considered God's sovereign power as saviour, that God is not part of this world. This is the first clarification of the relationship of the world to God. God is in no way absorbed by the world or included in it. This is what is expressed by the word "transcendent". God's transcendence means that he surpasses and remains above creation.—There is a tendency in human thought to deny God's transcendence. The tendency is called pantheism. In some forms the world is considered as a divine power, but in all cases the world and God are so closely identified that God is no longer seen as the one God who is himself outside and without us. It is not what pantheism recognizes that is wrong, but what it denies. It recognizes that this world is penetrated by God, and that it is good to ponder this truth more and more deeply. But it then rejects the mystery of God's independence with regard to creation. The biblical revelation is at work from the start at correcting this error.

The majesty, uniqueness and transcendence of God's being is inexpressible. We divine from his creation that he exists and of what nature he is, but we know that he surpasses infinitely all our thought of him. The beauty of a city, a child, a tree, is only a tiny spark of his fascinating loveliness. The holiness and goodness of the best men we know is only a faint reflection of his goodness and light. But we look for ways of speaking of God. Then we take earthly words and put "infinitely" before them: infinite truth, infinite person, infinite love. But here the words truth, person, love, beauty and so on remain derivatives of what we know on earth. We always include something finite in our understanding of them. Hence the human spirit must always proceed still further and consider that he is infinitely "other" than all that we can think of. Hence we should also say that he is 310 "not person", "not love", "not truth". By thinking in this way we are trying to throw these words open to the infinite. Then we receive them back once more in a way which enables us to use them in a higher sense and which reminds us that we must immediately purify them once more and continue this same process indefinitely. Thus the thinking spirit remains in continual movement, marvelling more and more at God's infinity.

"Israel, my child"
(God's immanence)

Scripture does not speak only of God's inaccessible distance. It proclaims still more insistently his closeness. "He is not far from each one of us, for in him we live and move and have our being" (Acts 17:28). He sustains the whole universe by his power and his love. This presence of God in all that exists is called God's immanence. The closeness of this intimacy can no more be comprehended by the human spirit than the sublimity of God's distance. And now that our knowledge of the world is becoming more extensive, the notion of this presence takes on a very special character. In earlier times men were inclined to see God at work precisely where the natural causes of things were unknown. It was taken for granted that he was at work in all that existed, but very often he was supposed to be most intimately present where strange and inexplicable things happened, such as the sudden onset or cessation of a tempest or an epidemic. His presence was felt in particular outside the ordinary course of events. Thus he was seen perhaps more readily in the blessing over the sick than in the skill of the doctor. We on the contrary feel ourselves called very specially to see him at work in the expert knowledge of the physician—not alongside of the doctor, or even as someone who guides his hand or prompts him with a whisper, but in the doctor who remains himself. The more a creature is itself, the more God is active in it. God's action does not consist of his pushing aside what he has created, but of his bringing it to be itself as fully as possible, and man most of all.

488–489

107
288–289

Scripture did not use philosophical terms to work out immanence of God. But the essential truth of the doctrine speaks to us from every page: "I am with you in all that happens to you." As we have already seen, the first truth that came home to the consciousness of believers was that God's help was near. He began this way—familiar and near at hand, and so he remained. As the people of Israel, exiled in Babylon, learned to understand more and more of his immensity and that before him "the nations are accounted as the dust on the scales" (Is. 40:15), he was still saying to them: "I, the Lord your God, hold your right hand; it is I who say to you, 'Fear not, I will help you'. Fear not, you worm Jacob, you men of Israel" (Is. 41:13–14). And he still says to us that he is not far from any one of us. What is amazing is not so much his transcendence in itself, but the fact that while he is so supremely exalted above all things, he still has care for the least of his creatures.

The truth in its purity

33 Here then are the two pointers which, taken together, lead to the light where the purity of God's revelation is unfolded. God is free of the world, but he is still at the depths of its being. God is independent of man, but he is still bound up with man. The combination of transcendence and immanence in God is a mystery before which human reason remains powerless, though the believer recognizes that this revelation manifests God's greatness. It would no doubt be an easier solution for human reason to think of God as absorbed into the world (pantheism) or as utterly aloof from us (deism). But the assertion of his distance and presence at once gives revelation the very tension, grandeur and impact through which man feels that God is 33 speaking. Our heart expands in the unfathomable mystery which 445–449 lies outside the paths of our thought. It finds peace. It was made for such a God.

The man Job speaks to God

But we are not yet at the end of his revelation. We are still tormented by the question which Job put: where does evil come from if everything depends on a good God?

The whole of revelation asserts most emphatically that evil 482 does not stem from a dark power which is as primordial and as potent as God. Nothing could be more alien to the message of the Bible than to divide the world into two equally balanced forces, God and evil. No, God, in whom there is no darkness, is the one origin of all things. But then the question of where evil comes from becomes still more awkward. If its source is not to be sought in some eternal force of evil, is its origin then God— and how can that be, since he is the eternal goodness? The whole of scriptural revelation attests that God is not the cause of evil but its antagonist. At the same time, the Bible teaches us where to look for the primary cause of wickedness and suffering: in the freedom of the free creature which corrupts its own goodness. Sin is revealed as the profoundest evil in the world. (See 259–270 also the chapter on "The Power of Sin".)

It is obvious, nonetheless, that there is pain and grief which cannot be connected in any demonstrable manner with sin, but which is produced by the growth, the becoming, of the world. The roots of misery are inextricably entangled in these two factors together: the evolution of the world and sin. But

492

this means that there is some misery and misfortune which we cannot place to the charge of sin. Does not this then come from God? And furthermore, though there can be no denying the fact of human sin, can we consider sin as entirely independent of him who holds all things in his hands?

When we start to ponder these things, it is well to begin by recalling the following point. When we affirm of each thing in itself and of each event taken in isolation that in each case it comes entirely from God, we are affirming more than we know as a matter of faith. We are producing our own concept of God's omnipotence by adding up everything that we can imagine and then saying: this is God's omnipotence—to be able to do all this. But then we have in fact constructed in heaven—if we may be forgiven the expression—a perfect robot, with the help of our own ideas. And this enables us to deduce precisely what God has neglected and hence why the world is so full of misery.

But how do we know that the infinitely omnipotent God is omnipotent precisely in the manner which we have thought out? Perhaps his omnipotence is more incomprehensible, more marvellous—more omnipotent—than man can realize.

From God's revelation we know as a matter of faith that *everything* comes from him. But this does not yet mean that we are justified in ascribing each particular event entirely to him. Men and things possess also a certain real efficacity of their own, go their own way also in a certain sense. And this can be an unfavourable one, a way which of itself is contrary to the whole. It can be an activity through which men and things when considered individually are not perfectly themselves. That is, they have not precisely the place and the mode of being which make them good in the whole. Hence, considered in themselves, they are not wholly full of God. Hence we may not affirm without more ado of an evil conjuncture, a catastrophe or a crime that it comes from God. Pain and evil as such are contrary to the whole, contrary to God's purpose. They are precisely contact with what is not God. (Another reason why it is so difficult to investigate evil is that it has so different a degree and type of existence from good. Evil cannot exist of itself. Evil is always combined with good. Evil is always corruption of 450 something good. It is just as real or unreal as a division or an amputation.)

If then we cannot ascribe evil things to God without more ado, what we know as a matter of faith is this: that he is powerful enough to bring good out of evil; he can guide it to good, that is, to the whole. In this sense we can be sure, even in pain and misery, and indeed precisely there, that "not one sparrow will fall to the ground without your Father's will," and that "even the hairs of your head are all numbered". This is the message of faith. Everything is in the hand of God. He will lead all things to the goodness of the whole, in spite of, indeed by making use of evil. In view of the whole, therefore, evil has in fact a place. But if we say that God is "therefore" the cause of it, we assert more than we are entitled to. God, whom we have recognized as the infinite goodness in what is best in us, must never be placed in the perspective of what is most miserable in us. He is the enemy of all pain and evil.

It is quite different with all that we sense as good and happy. Then we see things and man being themselves, in their right place, in harmony with the whole, God's whole, God's purpose. Then we recognize and thank God, the lover of all that lives (cf. Wis. 11:24), in all good things, even in the least of them.

> *"Thou hast loathing for none of the things*
> *which thou hast made"*

We see this divine revelation being unfolded more and more fully and expressed more and more purely, with certain correctives of earlier expressions. The purpose was always to describe God as saviour and as source of salvation, but this was first expressed sometimes in such a way that he seemed to be the source of evil for others. Thus we read that "the Lord hardened Pharaoh's heart" (Exod. 10:20). At other times the expression is more exact: "The heart of Pharaoh was hardened" (Exod. 9:35). So too in chapters 1 and 2 of the book of Job. We read on the one hand that "the Lord gave, and the Lord has taken away", while on the other hand the story indicates that it is precisely an evil power that "takes away". It is also very instructive to compare 2 Samuel 24:1 with 1 Chronicles 21:1.

This also helps us to understand better such sayings as "the Lord kills and brings to life . . . the Lord makes poor and makes rich" (1 Sam. 2:6–7). The real message of such sayings is not that God is the source of evil. They assert roundly that God holds the whole world in his hands, for no other purpose indeed but to produce salvation from it. The canticle 1 Samuel 2:1–10 as a whole makes this message clearly transparent, in spite of the primitive mode of its expression.

In the New Testament this joyful revelation becomes much more lucid, through the whole manner of acting and speaking 119 of our Lord—his parables, his healings and the word "Father" 115 which he teaches us to say. When we read the New Testament 115 with this in mind, we find the Father makes his sun shine on the just and unjust, but not that he sends calamities on anyone as 135 a punishment. Even the destruction of Jerusalem is not described in so many words as a punishment from God. Where such matters are spoken of, it is much clearer than in the Old Testament that it is evil which punishes itself. No doubt comparisons are still made at times in the New Testament with earthly punishments out of the Old Testament (cf. 1 Cor. 10:1–11 and 2 Pet. 2:1–10), but such texts refer here to eternal reprobation. This is proclaimed with all possible seriousness in the New Testament: 102–105 "He who can destroy both soul and body in hell" (Mt. 10:28). But we have seen that this is not a divine punishment which falls on man from outside himself, but the hardening which man has brought about in himself, while God always remains he who 480–481 wills to save. "He has loathing for none of the things which he has made" (cf. Wis. 11:24).

It may perhaps be said that the New Testament still uses expressions which could be wrongly understood—according to the letter, not according to the spirit. The petition of the Our Father, "And lead us not into temptation" might possibly give some to understand that it is God who may lead us into temptation. No doubt that is why we have the further petition in Matthew: "But deliver us from evil." The temptation comes from evil, not from God.—Scripture taken as a whole proclaims with increasing and unmistakable clarity that no evil proceeds from God, but only good.

"Whatever you ask the Father in my name"

There is a further possible question. If men and things have an activity of their own which can be unfavourable, an activity which we cannot ascribe to God, can God then really exercise an influence there? Can there be any sense in praying for the good Spirit? And there is another question which comes up even more frequently, about the elimination of disease and natural calamities. Can God interfere with these, intervene by violating the laws of nature? To begin with the last question: we have no reason to believe that our prayers are answered by divine actions which set aside the natural order of things. It is a matter of which we know nothing. All the forces at work in God's world are not known to us. We do not know the depth of creation. This we admit all the more readily since we believe, through Jesus' resurrection, that God is at work at perfecting this world, intent on bringing about a new creation.

Hence creation as a whole is vaster, deeper and fuller of perspectives than our explorations can reach. And what faith tells us about our prayer is this: when we pray, we make ourselves receptive to the activity of the risen Lord in creation. We are open to the new forces of the new creation. These forces do not thwart the existing world. They make it more its true self. They make it more alert to its true purpose of salvation and goodness. Thus we remove barriers to Christ's power among us, so that creation is enabled to display to us more clearly its ultimate purpose, as for instance in healings and even in good weather. Hence we may pray for such things. And they will take place, if it is part of the mystery of Christ that it should already reveal itself to us here and now in such ways. From the answer to prayer in the gospel, in the history of the Church and in our own lives we know that God hears the prayer inspired by steadfast faith.

"I will be with him in trouble" (Ps. 91)

But the urgent questions mount up. Why, for instance, is it part of the mystery of Christ that suffering is sometimes taken away and sometimes not? Why had this mother to die and leave her young family? Could he not have prevented this?—When Lazarus died, the question was also asked: "Could not he who opened the eyes of the blind man have kept this man from dying?" (Jn 11:37). What was our Lord's answer? It was to give a glimpse of a greater whole: the glory of God (Jn 11:4) and deeper faith on the part of men (Jn 11:42). Jesus' words tell us something about God, but so do his actions. Here he gives life, and a greater joy, glory and faith than if Lazarus had remained alive. Suffering is taken up and pressed into the service of the ultimate joy. But we see something else here as well, something that puts God's permission of suffering into a new light that we should never banish from our consciousness. We see also that Jesus wept. God does not conquer suffering by permitting it calmly and impassively.

It might, however, be objected that after all, God's glory was manifested at Lazarus' expense. He did die that day!—Let us watch then the Son of God himself in the garden of olives. One of his disciples reaches for his sword. This is our idea of power and rescue. Jesus says: "Do you think that I cannot appeal to my Father, and he will at once send me more than twelve legions of angels?" But this is not all that Jesus says. He goes on: "But how then should the scriptures be fulfilled?" (Mt. 26:53–54). There is a greater and more splendid whole, and hence no intervention of God's omnipotence can really be expected. It would be out of place. This is not calmly recognized and accepted. On the contrary, it cost Jesus a sweat of blood. In his own person he came to grips with misery, heavy-hearted, submitted to it and went through it. This is how his omnipotence shows itself. He weeps for his friend and sweats blood for himself.

Could it have been otherwise? Would an easier way have been better? Who can tell? The one thing that we can say with certainty is that God does not permit evil calmly, with folded arms, as it were. In Jesus, the image of the invisible, we see how God is. Even when he is resisting unto blood against suffering and evil we can hear Jesus say: "He who has seen me has seen the Father" (Jn 14:9).

"God permits suffering." The phrase is apt enough, as an expression of the truth that God can make good come out of evil. But it does not explain how, and hence it is misleading. It is better and truer to say that God fights against evil, that he rescues from evil. That is what he is doing. He invites us to fight along with him. In our love too, in our work, God is struggling against suffering and evil.

The unexpectedness of God himself

Was this the right place, at the end of the book, to put the question of evil? Ought it not have been raised earlier, so that this last chapter could have been all lightsome? No—because it is in the answer to the question of evil that God leads us to his true light. It is in Jesus' struggle with sin and death that the Infinite reveals the heart of his mystery. Left to ourselves, we are always inclined to think of God as a rarefied sphere of infinite power, love and truth. But in Jesus the omnipotence of God, at its supreme manifestation, is seen as suffering death unresistingly with us, and so overcoming death. God's beauty is seen to appear as pitiable ugliness: "We esteemed him as smitten"—like a leper 279–280 (Is. 53:4). God's holiness is not just infinite inaccessibility, but the company of sinners, where he mixes with those whom he 100–101 wishes to renew. God's truth, in Jesus, is not a cold omniscience, but a warmth which is one with love and confidence. (And this is also seen from the fact that God will not have himself found by 124–126 frigid calculation, but by the totality and warmth of such a dedication as that of faith). And God's omnipresence is not the homogeneous filling of the height and width of the universe, but 186–188 fellowship with our love and suffering: "Where two or three 192–193 are gathered in my name, there am I in the midst of them" (Mt. 18:20). Warm, human and friendly, but still full of the love that is as strong as death—this is how the true revelation of God shows itself. While we were trying harder and harder to explore his mystery in the heights and in the depths, he has led us to his presence in ordinary life with its ordinary joys and sufferings.

The living God

When we try to penetrate this revelation prayerfully, we begin to realize that our whole life is in the hands of an eternal love. Being brought to the Father by Jesus and filled with their Holy Spirit, we are perpetually involved in a mystery of love. Since we are privileged to be the family of God, the most magnificent glory is revealed to us.

This is something which we shrink from summing up briefly, since it is the mystery of the Father, the Son and the Spirit. We shrink from the task, because we know that in order to know God, we must not leave the ground where his revelation has brought us—our ordinary life, the world of men. We must not ascend to dizzy heights, because our imagination might at once be captured by some such figure as three interlocking circles. Or our thought might be preoccupied at once by combinations of the numerals one and three, and thus miss the riches of this revelation as given in the Bible. The Bible does not use the word "three" to speak of this mystery, any more than do the twelve articles of the Apostles' Creed, or the Nicene Creed. This does not mean that we must therefore avoid it. But it is a warning not to begin too readily with a brief formula in an attempt to proclaim the mystery which is so utterly comprehensive. In the religious instruction now given to children, attention is first fixed on the Son and on how he speaks of the Father and how he loves the Father. At Whitsuntide, the Spirit whom they send is spoken of, but it is only years later that the term Holy Trinity is used.

But we are even shy about speaking of this mystery in biblical terms. After a whole volume in which everything spoke of the Father, the Son and the Holy Spirit, a "treatment" in a few pages would be to set the mystery too much apart. It would rather be necessary to repeat all the shades of meaning that have been evoked as we spoke of Jesus of Nazareth, in his obedience to the will of the Father, his passion and his glory with God. The 122–124 destiny of Jesus comprises and signifies the eternal love between the Father and the Son. They send out the Spirit to the world, 153–154 the Spirit who is one with the Father (1 Cor. 2:10), one with the Son (2 Cor. 3:17) and indeed the mutual love between Father and Son itself, as is exemplified by the descending dove as the voice rings out: "This is my beloved Son" (Mt. 3:17). The 91–93 message of scripture proclaims so vigorously both the distinct proprieties of the Father, the Son and the Holy Spirit, and their divine oneness, that we cannot but confess one God in three persons.

"For in him all things were created"

We *live* all this out, by trying to be with Christ. When we try to live with him, through the Spirit which comes from him and the Father, we realize that the humble obscurity, as it would seem, of our existence, flows with him from the Father and to the Father. He, the Son, is "the first-born of all creation" (Col. 1:15). He and creation go together. It is because the Son is born in God that the world of men—and each man in turn— proceeds in him and through him from God the origin. Hence 382 it is to the triune love that we must look for a hint which may point to the answer to the question: why does the world exist? All things have been created because in God this Spirit of love of the First-born is breathed forth. "In him all things hold together" (Col. 1:17), in the Son. "All things were created through him and for him" (Col. 1:16). Let us think of the immensity of the universe. Let us penetrate in thought to the smallest particles of matter. Let us consider still more marvellous realities: the spirit of man and his consciousness, the heart of man and his love and warmth. Man, even scientifically speaking, is more wonderful and richer than the stars of the galaxies with their burning heat. Even the smallest child playing on a village street is a mysterious unity. It seems to be insignificant compared to the sun, but it can know the sun and be glad of it, while the sun cannot know the child or be glad of it. The child is alive and the sun is not. The sun is golden only because the child has eyes. The sun is beautiful only because man is responsive. A child may cry because it is not loved, but the heavenly bodies do not know what love is. A man is a richer reality, and indeed, more real, than the fiery explosions of the stars in space.

We must open our eyes to all that exists and open our hearts to the message which says: "All things were created through him and for him." He is the first to come forth. In all the silences by which creation speaks to us, he, the primal Word of God, is

42–45 always present. We believe that this Word, the Word of life, has become flesh and dwelt amongst us. In the creation which exists through and with him, he has revealed himself at the most intense focus of reality, where darkness can be most impenetrable and pain the severest, but also where light is most brilliant, life most beautiful and love really love, for he revealed himself in man.

He is the Son of man. This is his way of setting up fellowship with us. And hence he also became "head of the body, the church. He is the beginning" (Col. 1:18). By opening our hearts

82 to him we can live in fellowship of spirit with the source of all
447–449 things.

This truth of our being taken up into the flux and reflux of divine life is beyond what our mind can grasp and our words express. It is more comprehensive and more immense than we can fathom. But it does not reduce us to nothingness. On the contrary, it gives us life. God is "the lifter of my head" (Ps. 3:4). We are sons and daughters of the God of the living, brothers and sisters of the "first-born from the dead" (Col. 1:18). Thus the whole of revelation, and in particular the personal love of

472 Jesus for men in person, points to the fact that God will not let
28–29 us dissolve into an ineffable but impersonal Nirvana. He made man according to his image so that the personal consciousness which we received from his love should never be lost, but should continually develop, among our family today, in the instruction of our children, in our tasks, in our joy, throughout our suffering and through death into life.

God is love

Why this should be the end to which God leads his creation, we can surmise from what we believe about the life of God. In the mystery of God's triune life there is a revelation which throws light on the deepest question which concerns man: why we are such as we are, creatures who can know, produce and love; how 132–135 the idea of "knowing", "loving", "producing" could ever have arisen (—we can only speak in human terms, as we stretch out with profoundest amazement to the ultimate "why?"). But it is not a matter of how it could be. It is because God is love. He is not the merciful but isolated Allah. The mystery of God is not 271 a mystery of isolation but of fellowship, creativity, knowledge, love, outpouring and receiving, and that is why we are what we are. Human life is the possibility of cooperating with what God is: love.

In our everyday life, which can be drab or tragic or very complicated, where there are so many things which constantly claim our attention, the light which God offers us is love. This is the beacon by which we must set our course, if we are not to miss the real purpose of our lives. "Little children, let us not love in word or speech but in deed and in truth. By this shall we know that we are of the truth." "If any one has the world's goods and sees his brother in need, yet closes his heart against him, how does God's love abide in him?" (1 Jn 3:18–19, 17). We would be glad to end this book by rounding off the subject nicely, by putting the last touches to the painting in the sanctuary and saying: there is God. But it cannot be done this way. God himself steps out of the images and the icons to embody himself in the men who have need of us. And there he says, I am here. He conceals himself in the little ones of earth and says, Look for me here. Those who wish to live with God find that nothing is ever rounded off. There is always a fresh start to make, new with every day that dawns. The words of life and the symbols of life which the good news gives us on our way all tell us that we must love the Lord our God with our whole heart and our whole soul and our whole mind and—with equal force—that we must love our neighbour as ourselves.

There is none of us but feels powerless before this task. There is none of us but feels that he falls short in face of this God, not just as an individual, but also in common with his fellows, as a family, as a nation, as Church, as mankind. Yet there is no other way to life than love. Outside love, the Spirit of the triune God does not vouchsafe his encounter. But when we try with the Son of man to march along this narrow path of love, we may take as addressed to ourselves the words which follow the text of John quoted above:

> "We shall reassure our hearts before him whenever our hearts condemn us;
> FOR GOD IS GREATER THAN OUR HEART."

SUBJECT INDEX

504

F

Faith
— given by the outward testimony of Jesus and the Church and the inward testimony of the Father 124
— and our deepest knowledge 124–5, 289–90
— not a system, but a message and a light 291; *see also* Dogmas
— and miracle 111
— thresholds before man attains faith 236–8
— do the parents determine the faith of the children? 239–41
— is something we have in common 240–1, 250, 291
— is grace 291
— is virtue and task 292–3, 415–16
— and "brains" 125–6
— reasonableness of faith 292–3
— and doubt 293–7
— refusal 126–7, 377–8
— we need the faith to recognize the risen Lord 183–5
Faithful
— those not in holy orders, *see* Priesthood — of the people of God; and *passim*
Family 381–410
Family planning 402–3
Fathers of the Church 215–16
Forgiveness 245–6, 449, 454–63
Francis of Assisi 86, 198, 220, 222, 225, 232, 411, 414, 437
Freedom 6–7, 277, 450–1

G

Gifts of the Spirit, *see* Charisms
God
— the way to God through reason 16–17
— Jesus calls God "Abba" 115
— not our idea of God 19, 79, 90–91, 310–11, 376–8, 488, 497–500

— and evil 17–19, 118–19, 242–3, 269–86, 492–502
— the mystery of the Father, the Son and the Spirit 498–502
— really appeared in Jesus of Nazareth, *see* Jesus of Nazareth
Godfather 251, 258–9
Gospel
— the meaning of the word 67–68
— the literary genre 72–73, 146–7; *see also* Scripture
— the origin 206–9   [211
— the symbols of the four gospels
Grace 235–6, 286–9
— not given to an individual apart from other men 288–9
Guilt, *see* Sin

H

Happiness 5–6, 483–5
Heaven, *see* Resurrection, New Creation, Promise of God
Hell 102–4, 479–81
Hinduism 27–28, 271, 283–4
History of the Church 212–36
Homosexuality 384–5
Hope 297–9, 467, 486–7
Human impotence 277–8, 349, 437
Human rights 229, 434
Humaneness, growth of
— in Israel 58–61, 388–9
— in Israel and elsewhere 60–63
— by Christ's revelation 81–82, 224–5, 233–4, 389–92
Humanism 32, 273–4, 285–6
Humour 442
Hygiene 421–2

I

Illness — visiting the sick 468–9
Immanence of God 490–1
Incarnation of our Lord
— the doctrine of the three great Councils 79–82, 498
— the title "Son of God" 153–4
— Jesus' consciousness 90–91, 150

THE SUPPLEMENT
TO
A NEW CATECHISM

Edouard Dhanis, S.J., and
Jan Visser, C.SS.R.

On behalf of the Commission of
Cardinals appointed to examine
A NEW CATECHISM

This is a translation by Kevin Smyth of
"Aanwulling bij De Nieuwe Katechismus"

TABLE OF CONTENTS

PREFACE

The text of this Supplement to A NEW CATECHISM follows in essentials the modifications of the text of that book prepared under the direction of the Commission of Cardinals who were charged with the examination of the book. The modifications were then intended to be inserted into the text of the Catechism. But they are now presented separately.

This new form of presentation made certain adaptations necessary. Many corrections of details have been omitted which might have been adopted in a new edition of the book, but are superfluous in a separate publication of a series of modifications. Sometimes the actual modification is accompanied by a context which will make it more comprehensible. This takes the form of a reprint or adaptation of the context of A New Catechism itself. (Even in the first draft there were several places in which expressions, sentences and passages of A New Catechism had been retained.)

Further, the discussion of original sin has been shortened, though it is still extensive. Some references to very recent documents of the magisterium have been included. The draft of the previous year now also includes, apart from some minor editorial changes, a few improvements, in agreement with suggestions made by some members of the Commission of Cardinals. These suggestions refer primarily to complementary explanations on original sin. They do not comprise any new demands as regards the Catechism, but they help to make it more complete.

Then there was the question of arrangement. If it had simply followed the order of the pages in A New Catechism, in several cases modifications referring to the same subject would have been scattered here and there. Hence it seemed preferable to arrange the matter according to subjects, and the order chosen was that of the ten points indicated in the Declaration which was made by the Commission of Cardinals, 15 October 1968 (*Acta Apostolicae Sedis*, 60 [1968], pp. 685–91).

This decision made it possible to give the corresponding text of the Declaration before the changes with regard to each subject. This allows the reader to see at once the kernel of the doctrine which the various modifications strive to explain, and he can more easily distinguish the important from the incidental. However, the Declaration of the Cardinals is only a summary, and does not comprise all the indications which they themselves had given earlier for the revision of the Catechism. The result is that in the text given here some modifications are linked only indirectly with the contents of the Declaration. But this happens only exceptionally. In most cases, each of the changes suggested corresponds directly to an indication of the Declaration.

The new presentation of the modifications of the Catechism was prepared by the theologians who had composed the text of the previous year. But they had not, unfortunately, the valuable help of Msgr. Fortmann, who died 3 May 1968.

I. CREATION

DECLARATION (see AAS, 60 [1968], p. 687): *The Catechism must teach that God created, along with the visible world in which we live, a realm of pure spirits whom we call angels* (see for instance Vatican I, Constitution *Dei Filius*, ch. 1; Vatican II, Constitution *Lumen Gentium*, nos. 49, 50). *It must also be explained that the soul of each man, since it is spiritual* (cf. Vatican II, Constitution *Gaudium et Spes*, no. 14), *is created directly by God* (see for instance the Encyclical *Humani Generis*, AAS, 42 [1950], p. 575).

1. The existence of pure spirits: angels and devils

a) *Catechism text*, p. 482: "As regards the first . . . Are they purely human'?"

New text: As regards the first category, Scripture often speaks of such beings, angels. They are messengers, powers which come from God, "ministering spirits" (Heb 1:14). The Bible often presents them in human form. The angels give concrete form to God's goodness. They are created by him as beneficent spiritual beings who cooperate with us. Exegetes and theologians have not yet fully answered the questions which arise from the steadily growing place which the angels occupy in the books of the Old Testament, or from the history and further development of the doctrine of angels. But the existence of angels—as also that of devils—is a truth belonging to Catholic doctrine, and of which the Fourth Lateran Council, for example, speaks. These mysterious beings always appear as fully involved in the history of our salvation in Christ. And everything that is said about them proclaims the happy truth that God is concerned with us in innumerable ways. This is indicated by the angels' names. "Gabriel" means God's strength; "Raphael" God's healing; "Michael" "Who is like God?" We have here a glimpse of the mysterious connection between the various degrees of creation. (What we learn about Satan and the devils—created in holiness by God, but rebelling against him—attests the same connection, but in the opposite direction. The rebellion of the wicked spirits became a source of evil for our human world. The horrifying evil which we sometimes see at work in humanity goes so far beyond the evil of the individual that we ask ourselves: what power is at work here? Is it purely human?)

b) *Catechism text*, p. 242: "This sort of 'exorcism' . . . But the words envisage all evil . . ."

New text: This sort of "exorcism" of the wicked spirit occurs frequently during the solemnities of baptism. The evil which threatens man is told to depart. The personal term "devil" is always used for it. We have already encountered the figure of Satan or the devil in the Gospel. We shall come back to it later when dealing with the angels. In the exorcism in question the recipient of baptism is certainly not treated as one "possessed". What is envisaged here is a much less visible contact and influence of the adversary of God and Christ. It is seen as connected in some way or other with all the evil which is in man . . .

2. The direct creation of the human soul

Catechism text, p. 382: Section entitled "The creation of man".
New text: The creation of the soul

Each human person is so unique that when we consider his origin we must recognize a privileged case of the truth that "God is working still" (Jn 5:17) in the preservation and development of the universe. The created world is a reality in a process of growth, and at each moment the creative power of God imparts to it existence and activity. Under the impulse of God's power the world ascends, in the preparation and development of life, from the lower to the higher.

But the coming of a new human being into existence is a sacred moment in which God is active in a special way. My parents did not wish for "me". They wanted a boy or a girl. It was only God who willed "me". But there is much more to it than that. He willed me as a person, as an embodied spirit, an "I" who would be able to say "You" to God.

518

The existence of each human person follows from the transmission by the parents of a body which is ready for the soul and demands the existence of a soul. For the rest, the existence of the soul goes back only to God. The complete and direct transmission of the body by the parents extends indirectly in a certain sense to the soul itself, insofar namely as the body is for the soul and calls for it.

This is the ordinary way, though with some variations, in which the direct creation of the human soul is explained by theologians. Obviously, this doctrine does not forbid one saying that when a human couple produce a child they cooperate with God as regards the origin both of the body and of the soul. But the mode of cooperation differs as regards the body and the soul. In any case the cooperation is such that one can say that the parents transmit the human nature to their children. They are the parents of the whole person. They continue to be, as it were, in their children, as their heart assures them, and find themselves there again in a certain sense. Their cooperation with God does not cease with the birth of the child. It is completed in the upbringing. God nourishes, loves and guides a new man through his parents. It is a serious and happy responsibility.

II. ORIGINAL SIN

DECLARATION (see AAS, 60 [1968], pp. 687f.): *Though in consequence of the questions about the origin of the human race in its gradual development, the dogma of original sin now presents new difficulties, the New Catechism must faithfully reproduce the doctrine of the Church about man, who rebelled against God at the beginning of history (cf. Vatican II, Constitution Gaudium et Spes, nos. 13 and 22), with the result that he lost for himself and for all his descendants the holiness and righteousness in which he was placed, and transmitted to all a real state of sin through the propagation of human nature. Undoubtedly, discussions must be avoided which could give the impression that the individual members of the human family were stained by original sin only because they are exposed by their origin to the influence of human society where sin reigns and so find themselves from the beginning on the way of sin.*

Catechism text, pp. 261–9: From the section entitled "The message of Genesis 1–11" to the section called "Sin and death, forgiveness and life" (inclusive).

New text: The message of Genesis 1–11

The Book of Genesis speaks of the mysterious reality of evil, and probably most expressly in chapter 3, which must, however, be read in connection with the first eleven chapters, the story of the origins. They are not historical narratives in the sense of modern historical science, or in the sense of history as written by the Greek and Roman historians. To some extent they have a symbolic meaning. Seen in this way, Adam is man; Cain is in the newspapers and can be seen in our own heart. We ourselves are Noah and the builders of Babel. We find in these chapters the basic elements of the relationships between man and God.

But this is not all. Several of these ancient narratives aim at expounding certain aspects of our human situation or illustrate it with the help of primordial events. This is very specially true of the story of the fall of Adam and Eve. From the human point of view it is just groping and seeking. God made use of it to tell us something, not of course in detail, but still no doubt in some central facts, about the tragic beginning of the religious history of mankind.

After the first eleven chapters, Genesis, when speaking of Abraham, follows tradition concerning the special origin of the people of Israel. It is still not yet history in the sense of Greek or Roman writers, but one is closer to it. What then is the message of these first eleven chapters of Genesis?

1. God creates and gives growth, as we are told by the creation narrative, Genesis 1, and the impressive genealogies (which are therefore not to be taken literally).

2. Man is meant for friendship with God, as the story of paradise (Genesis 2) gives us to understand.

3. The third element is human sin. From its own bitter experience, Israel's faith had learned to know this constant in human history. It is not, therefore, strange that the story of the origins should describe four times how men sin: the first disobedience, the fratricide, the corruption of Noah's contemporaries, the building of Babel. These deeds are symbols of our grave sins.

4. But God does not leave man to himself. He already shows himself to Israel as a mysteriously merciful God. This is also shown by the story of the origins. After each fall into sin there is also a gesture of grace. At the flight from paradise, it is God who gives clothing to Adam and Eve, and promises that the offspring of the woman will crush the head of the serpent. Cain is given a sign which prevents him

from being killed. In the story of Noah, the theme of deliverance takes up practically all the space. And after Babel? Immediately after the story of the unfinished tower the history of Abraham begins, a first stage in the preparation of the great renewal which the Son of God is to bring.

5. Finally, through the story of paradise, God began to reveal to us that the human race at the very start took an ill-fated way in the direction of sin, and that this had grave consequences, though the perspective of deliverance was not excluded. But if we had only the story of Genesis, our exegesis would remain very hesitant. It gives us an indication. But how far has this indication the value of an authentic declaration? Later revelation, especially that of the New Testament, and the teaching of the Church, which has the assistance of the Holy Spirit, will have to give us the answer to this question.

The message of chapter five of the Epistle to the Romans

In the New Testament it has become very clear that God's message comprises the first four of the elements noted above. As regards the third element, sin, nothing speaks more eloquently of the greatness of the evil which is in the world than the sacrifice which the Son of God himself willed to offer "for the forgiveness of sins" (Mt 26:28). The Lamb of God came to take away the sin of the world (cf. Jn 1:29).

What does the New Testament teach on the fifth point? In chapter five of the Epistle to the Romans, St. Paul takes up again original sin and gives particulars about its consequences. The passage is very difficult and even today the exegesis is doubtful. But some points are established. The Council of Trent declared that St. Paul here teaches the existence of a sinful state in which all men are born, and which comes to them through the sin of Adam (5th Session, canons 2 and 4). Catholic commentators on the Bible find this doctrine in the whole passage (Rom 5:12–21), but above all in the following verses: "Therefore as sin came into the world through one man and death through sin, and so death spread to all men because all men sinned..." (v. 12), and again: "As by one man's [Adam's] disobedience many were made sinners, so by one man's [Jesus'] obedience many will be made righteous" (v. 19).

Does the symmetrical echoing of the word "one" include the fact, as part of the message of revelation, that Adam was one single individual? St. Paul thinks of Adam as the sinner of Genesis, and that he

521

was one single person did not form a problem. This was also the case of the Fathers of the Council of Trent. We are no longer in the same situation. Without precisely affirming that the ascent of life gave rise in the beginning to a number of men, palaeontology, along with genetics, nonetheless poses the question of polygenism (i.e. of this multiplicity). What direction will their conclusions take tomorrow? Is one bound to think that there is an original multitude of men concealed behind the figure of the biblical Adam? We shall return to this question later. In any case, the Second Vatican Council, linking up with Scripture and tradition, speaks several times of "Adam", of "men fallen in Adam" (cf. Gaudium et Spes, no. 22; Lumen Gentium, no. 2). Pope Paul VI spoke in similar terms (Profession of Faith, 30 June 1968), which we are also to use. Eve, of course, was always considered in the same terms as Adam. We shall also return to this point later.

In the same Epistle (Rom 6:12f.; 7:7 and 14–20), St. Paul speaks of an inclination to evil which is within us. He calls this inclination "sin", no doubt because he links it with the fall of Adam: "It is from sin and leads us to sin" (Council of Trent, 5th Session, canon 5).

St. Paul's interest here in the Epistle to the Romans is primarily to glorify Christ, who saves us from the evil which Adam caused. The sin of Adam is enough to make sinners of his descendants (Rom 5:12 and 14). They add their own transgressions to his rebellion (Rom 5:16). "But where sin increased, grace abounded all the more" (Rom 5:20). St. Paul also says that death depends on sin (Rom 5:12; cf. 6:34), but justification through Christ will give us back life (Rom 5:18, 21): "For as in Adam all die, so also in Christ shall all be made alive" (1 Cor 15:22).

The description of paradise and the story of the fall

Let us look once more at the description of the earthly paradise and the story of the drama which took place there. It is one of the passages of the Bible which are most deeply imprinted on our memory. A few words and pictures take in the whole glory and misery of our human condition. Nothing can ever replace this unforgettably telling passage of Scripture, as a summary of how man stands before God.

But we have learned to see life on earth, including that of man, as an ascending evolution. And we have come to recognize that the beginning of the ascent of human life was very modest. Then there came a period of extremely slow growth in the realm of civilization and culture. Have we not heard a period of hundreds of thousands of years mentioned in this connection? Then, a few thousand years ago, civilization made a mighty spring forward in some privileged parts of the globe. At present, technological progress is changing the whole earth at a quicker rate, and the era for inter-planetary travel has begun. Now that we know all this, can we still make sense of a paradise of brief duration at the dawn of history? And above all, can we still attach great importance to a sin committed in the distant and lowly origins of our race?

First we must say a few words about the "golden age" in paradise (leaving the problems of the gift of original justice and immortality till later). The description of paradise is undoubtedly naive, just as the description of the creation in six days is naive, in spite of its stress on the dignity of man and its teaching about the observance of the sabbath.

St. Thomas Aquinas said long ago that it "is not a mark of good sense" to believe that beasts of prey did not make a kill. Nothing compels us to imagine a different sort of creation before the sin of man. There may always have been thorns and thistles. But it remains true that sin brings on evil, even in the world outside man. Where sloth reigns, thistles grow in the corn-fields and the dykes burst. Where there is hatred, men and cities crumble to ruin. And above all, there is something which goes still deeper. A sinful humanity finds that the world weighs heavily on it. He who is inwardly ravaged sees everything blacker. The thorns and thistles are in the heart of man himself. Here, be it noted, the description of the lost paradise begins to teach us something.

This is done above all through the indications of the familiar intercourse with God which Adam and Eve enjoyed in the noble garden which had been planned for them. Here, too, there are a number of naive and anthropomorphic traits. But they give a hint of the great message, that man is called to live in friendship with God. This vocation is revealed more clearly in the history of the chosen people, and fully in the Gospel. Man is so highly elevated beyond himself that he passes from the situation of a mere creature to the state of sonship of God. This call given to the whole human family must already have begun, very modestly no doubt, at the beginning of our race. Under insignificant externals, there is a very great truth. Insofar as this can be done in this ancient story, the description of Eden points to the summons given by God to the human family in the springtime of its existence.

St. Paul speaks more strongly and precisely of the significance of the first sin than the writer of Genesis. But it should be clearly noted that already in the Old Testament and then very specially in St. Paul, the great emphasis is on the multitude of the sins of men. The Old Testament is in a certain way the history of sin. The stories of the first eleven chapters of Genesis are followed by the history of the beloved people. It appears again and again as obdurate, apostate, "adulterous". In the first three chapters of Romans, St. Paul describes in most sombre terms the wickedness of the pagans, then that of the Jews, and says finally: "So every mouth is stopped and the whole world is held accountable to God" (Rom 3:19). Did not Jesus also see the world in this way, calling Satan "the ruler of this world" (Jn 12:31; 16:11)?

Thus we gather from Scripture that humanity fully ratified the original revolt. And this perhaps enables us to suspect that without making Adam a strangely gigantic figure, without yielding to the temptation which led human fantasy in earlier times to the ancient Eastern myth of the "primordial man" or the Gnostic myth of the "heavenly man", we can undoubtedly attribute great significance to the first sin, in so far as it is intimately connected with the whole of mankind's sin. For the moment, this indication may suffice with regard to a point to which we shall return when dealing with original sin and the sin of the world.

The entry of sin into the world

But why then original sin, and why the series of sins committed by man which followed it? There can be no sin which is not committed freely. Freedom means that one need not have done it. No doubt sin is made easier through the lower inclinations of our bodily nature, especially after the loss of original justice (of which we shall shortly speak). But the healing grace of Christ did not only begin to be efficacious among fallen man when the Redeemer came. And we still ask, why original sin, and why the flood of sins after it?

From God's point of view, they were permitted with an eye to the salvation which Christ brings us. From the point of view of man, sin must be regarded as dependent on our freedom, which is why we cannot fully explain how it takes place. The explanation of a free choice by what precedes it, proximately or remotely, always remains only a partial explanation. We cannot fully explain a free choice, and still less an evil free choice. But when we have sinned, we know deep within ourselves that we have done so. I am guilty. Nonetheless, we ask ourselves in amazement, how we could have come to do that. Evil is not fully comprehensible. It is the supreme absurdity, the non-sense as such. All the more so, its beginning in the remote past of history is incomprehensible to us. And the many sins committed by the human race remain an enigma.

What does original sin consist of?

Though the first sin and the many transgressions cause us bewilderment, the mystery of sin is not yet exhausted. It has its climax in what the Church calls "original sin", the sin brought in by Adam, not only in himself but in all his descendants.

We have already seen that St. Paul speaks of the sin of Adam through which all men became sinners. The Council of Trent makes it clear that the sin of Adam is transmitted to us by the propagation of human nature—by way of descent, we may say—and exists in each of us (Session 5, canons 2 and 3). The Second Vatican Council speaks of the "sons of Adam" being deprived of "the divine likeness which had been disfigured from the first sin onwards" (Gaudium et Spes, no. 22). And Paul VI recalled recently that this disfiguration is transmitted by descent and that it is "a real sin" in us (Profession of Faith, 30 June 1968). We shall contemplate this doctrine reverently and try to give an explanation of it, insofar as this is possible with a truth which will always remain mysterious.

The Greek Fathers were more inclined to speak of "death" and "corruption" than of a "sin" transmitted to the descendants of Adam. But though their tradition with regard to original sin is less explicit than the Latin, the two traditions are not in conflict.

"Sin" is a theological term, which is primarily applied to an act which is morally evil (actual sin) and secondarily to the state of sin (habitual sin) which is a certain persistence of the malice of the sinful deed. By a sinful act, man turns deliberately away from God, whom he should love. He alienates himself deliberately from God. The Constitution of Vatican II on the Church in the World of Today speaks in this connection of man's misusing his freedom by setting himself up against God and trying to find his goal outside God (Gaudium et Spes, no. 13): "Against thee, thee only, have I sinned" (Ps 51:6). The state of sin consists of the fact that in consequence of a sinful act, the original deliberate alienation from God persists in the depths of the soul: "We have all become like one who is unclean" (Is 64:6). And this state persists till the merciful God brings the wicked heart of the sinner to repent, to come to him. "Blot out all my iniquities. Create in me a clean heart, O God" (Ps 51:9–10). The state of sin is a sin in a true but derivative sense of the word.

The sin of Adam which is transmitted by human descent cannot be anything but a state of sin: a certain persistence of an originally deliberate alienation from God. But here—and this is the whole mystery—the persistence which was once in the first sinner is prolonged and continued in his descendants. Every human being is born with this sin: "Men (have) fallen in Adam" (Vatican II, Lumen Gentium, no. 2). It must be said at once, incidentally, that it is a sin in a certain true sense, but in a very diminished one: in an "analogous" sense, as the theologians say. In this connection the Council of Trent speaks of a "death of the soul" (Session 5, canon 2), by which it means the absence of "the state of grace and adoption as children of God" (Session 6, canon 4). We may say: the absence of the spirit of sonship (Rom 8:15). It is the same as being deprived of sanctifying grace and love.

Trent also speaks of the absence of "holiness and justice" (Session 5, canons 1 and 2). It seems to be thinking here not merely of being deprived of the spirit of sonship but also of the absence of "integrity", of which it speaks explicitly a little later (Session 5, canon 5). These two gifts together—spirit of sonship and integrity—we call, with many theologians, "original justice". According to the common opinion of theologians, the original integrity of man is to be understood as the radiation and effect of the first grace of sonship on our sensible inclinations. Original sin implies the loss of the whole of original justice.

How then is the gift of original integrity to be more precisely explained? It is a sort of adaptation of our sensible inclinations to the demands of the spirit of sonship. These inclinations become obedient rather than indifferent to the voice of conscience. This gift makes man an inner unity rather than a person torn by anarchistic inclinations, so that grace and reason can reign. The condition of man deprived of original integrity is described by the Second Vatican Council in sober but telling terms: "What divine revelation makes known to us agrees with experience. Examining his heart, man finds that he has inclinations toward evil too, and is engulfed by manifold ills which cannot come from his good Creator . . . Indeed, man finds that by himself he is incapable of battling the assaults of evil successfully, so that everyone feels as though he is bound by chains" (Gaudium et Spes, no. 13).

It is understandable that the spirit of sonship in our first parents should have been quenched by their transgression. Their sin was incompatible with the attitude of childlike love for God which is proper to the spirit. It is also understandable that our first parents should also have lost their original integrity. For this was after all the radiance of the grace of sonship on their sensible faculties.

Good, it will be said, we recognize in this explanation the outlines of the traditional doctrine on original sin. But this brings up a number of formidable problems. Firstly: How can the deprivation of original justice be transmitted by way of descent? And how is this lack a sin in everyone who comes into the world? Further: What connection is there between original sin and the multitude of the sins of men? And what religious value can we find in this sombre part of the Christian message? In the next two sections we shall try to answer these questions.

How is original sin transmitted?

Up to this we have been able to reproduce the doctrine of the magisterium of the Church, filling it out only here and there. But to give an answer to the difficulties which this doctrine evokes we shall have to enter far more into the field of free opinions. There are different opinions here, old and new. This is not the place to discuss them. The solution which we present is based on one of these acceptable opinions, and it is capable of being filled out later and of being adapted anew.

1. How can the deprivation of original justice be transmitted from generation to generation by way of descent? We shall be able to answer this question more easily if we have first grasped how original justice itself was to have been transmitted by descent. Hence we shall first speak of the transmission of original justice and then explain how it was also lost for the descendants of Adam.

For original justice to be transmitted by way of descent from Adam, it was necessary and sufficient that it was bestowed on Adam by God not as a purely personal endowment but as an endowment of his nature, insofar as this nature was made to propagate itself in innumerable descendants. We take as our starting-point that original justice was bestowed on Adam in this way. In this case, supposing that innocence was preserved, the procreation of human beings would have been a transmission, along the way of descent, of human nature endowed with original justice.

"For the supernatural is itself carnal", as Péguy said. God had willed to elevate man in a marvellous way above his state of creature and to make him his son. But man is an embodied spirit, called (by nature) to people the whole earth by propagating himself. "Be fruitful and multiply" (Gen 1:28). We should rejoice at the thought that the original elevation was bestowed on man in such a way that he could transmit it, exactly like his own nature, by way of descent. The transmission of life by our first parents and by their descendants should have been, if they had remained in the state of innocence, a sacrament, as it were, of the transmission of grace.

But Adam lost this justice. Since he had lost it after it had been bestowed upon him to be transmitted by way of descent, he was no longer capable of imparting it to his descendants. He and his offspring could henceforth only transmit a nature deprived of original justice.

2. Can we now also see how the lack of original justice in each member of the human family is a state of sin? Yes. And we shall try to work it out more closely.

Firstly, it is easy to see why the loss of original justice in Adam became a state of sin. We know already that original justice comprised the spirit of sonship and in connection with this, original integrity, and that these gifts were lost by the original rebellion. In Adam, their loss was as it were the permanent echo of the rebellion, through which he turned away from God and alienated himself from God. But this is a state of sin. Have we not in fact described this as a sort of continuation of an original deliberate estrangement from God?

But how did the absence of original justice remain a state of sin in Adam's offspring? This is connected with the fact that it is transmitted by way of descent. Living beings strive to reproduce themselves in this way, in living beings which stem from them and are like them. The latter are both a continuation of them and a renewal of them. Hence propagation means to continue oneself and to renew oneself, the two together. This is true of everything which is transmitted by way of descent, whether it be human nature or its proprieties or a divine endowment of this nature and then, no doubt, the absence of this endowment.

It follows that the absence of original justice in the children of Adam is still in a certain way the continuation in them of a deliberate alienation from God which was originally the habitual sin of Adam. It can thus be seen that the lack of original justice corresponds to a certain degree even in the descendants of Adam to the notion of habitual sin or the state of sin. But it can also be seen that in every member of the human race the absence of original justice is renewed with human nature and as human nature. And this means that the continuing alienation from God, which was originally deliberate in Adam because of his own rebellion, can only be called voluntary because of its link with the rebellion of another, the sinner from the first beginning. Hence in us original sin is a state of sin only in a very weak sense of the term.

The God of justice, for these reasons, could have refused the whole race of Adam the infinite happiness of the children of God, which is a superabundant bliss. But he could not have refused them, on the ground of original sin alone, a final state in keeping with human nature. But we, who remain the work of God's hands, were not dealt with strictly by God. He invites us through his Son to the happiness of the children of God which has been marvellously restored.

When a man is re-born through the grace of Christ, he receives the spirit of sonship. This is the grace of complete justification. "There is therefore no condemnation now for those who are in Christ Jesus" (Rom 8:1). But he does not receive back the state of original justice, the spirit of sonship which also brings with it the gift of original integrity, and which could have been transmitted by way of descent. Original justice, the justice which Adam possessed, is lost for ever. Hence, as the Church teaches, "though the Christian parents are themselves sanctified, they cannot transmit sanctity to their children". Even in holy parents "the procreation of natural life has become a way of death (in the order of grace), along which original sin passes over to the child . . . But it is theirs to offer their children to the Church so that through this mother of a multitude of children of God they may be re-born in the waters of baptism" (Pius XI, *Casti Connubii*, AAS, 22 [1930], pp. 544).

Original sin and the sin of the world

We use the expression from the Gospel of St. John, "the sin of the world", to indicate the multitude of sins committed by men. The Bible, which speaks to us of original sin, also speaks, and much more frequently, of the sin of the world. St. Paul speaks of these two great miseries of humanity in the Epistle to the Romans. In the first three chapters he describes the ravages of the whole of the sins of mankind, then in the fifth chapter he considers the mystery of the sin which we inherited from Adam. We have already had to do with the sin of the world when we pointed to the number and gravity of men's sins. We now discuss it further, describing the collective dimension of the sin of the world, and defining more closely the relation between this sin and original sin.

By the collective dimension of the sin of the world we mean the interplay of causes through which the sins committed by men are influenced, at least in a certain respect, by a sinful environment, and through which they themselves in turn become components of this environment, helping to cause new sins. We shall now try to throw light on this dimension of sin by considering one by one the degrees of contamination which our sins involve.

It is terrifying to think that sin is infectious, that one man can spread the contagion to another, that he can pass on evil. Bad example is both a withholding of the good and a demonstration of the feasibility of evil. When bad example is further combined with seductive compulsion, we have the gravest form of scandal, which provoked Jesus to one of his sternest warnings: "But whoever causes one of these little ones who believe in me to sin, it would be better for him to have a great millstone fastened round his neck and to be drowned in the depth of the sea. Woe to the world for temptations to sin!"

The contamination of sin also appears in the loss of the sense of values. In a covetous family, children find it natural to be grasping. An egoistic society creates egoists, colonialism makes colonialists, racialism racialists.

This envisages certain groups. But if we look further afield, we see that the whole world forms one single breeding-ground. And the teaching of Scripture is that sin reigns there. The whole of humanity is in a condition in which its most authentic values are obscured. Love, the supreme value, is obscured most of all.

The sin of the world is the triumph of individual and collective egoism. It sweeps along like a great river. It is a social reality. The notion of an intimate bond between this sin and original sin is inescapable. One senses it. What is this bond?

Through original sin we have been weakened in our struggle against evil, since even those who have been re-born through Christ still suffer from the loss of original integrity. But it would be a mistake to see in original sin the total cause of the sin of the world. It would be wrong, not merely because sinful acts are always free and cannot be fully explained by their antecedents, but also because, as the Second

Vatican Council recalls: "(God) did not abandon men after they had fallen in Adam, but ceaselessly offered them helps to salvation, in anticipation of Christ the Redeemer" (Lumen Gentium, no. 2). Hence the sin of the world is not ordinarily the necessary consequence of the sin of Adam.

But there can be another bond between original sin and the sin of the world. When we consider the unity of the human race and the further unity of the divine plan of salvation, we cannot but think that God willed and foresaw from all eternity an order of things in which the coming of the sin of Adam and its transmission are permitted, so that the sin of the world is permitted at the same time. The sin of the world would have a place in this plan only in connection with the sin of Adam. Finally, we may say that God permitted the two sins so that the triumph of Christ's grace should be all the greater where sin had reigned in all possible forms.

In this perspective, belief in original sin combines with our experience of the sin of the world to attest a still greater universality of evil. All men are born alienated from God. There are no just and innocent here. From their very birth they need a Redeemer. The profound religious truth revealed in the dogma of original sin is that it shows us how we owe everything in this order of salvation to him who came "to seek and to save the lost" (Lk 19:10).

The Church slowly drew the conclusion from revelation as a whole, and solemnly declared in the last century, that Mary had not the guilt of original sin. God willed that the mother of his Son should commit no sin, and that she should even be conceived immaculate. Living in a sinful world, she was involved in the pain of the world but not in its evil. But this does not mean that she did not need to be redeemed. She, too, was saved by the merits of Jesus, but in her case in a completely singular manner. She was preserved totally free from all sin.

Original integrity and immortality

We must now return to two subjects which have already come up: the original gifts of integrity and immortality.

As regards original integrity, we must try to explain how we must consider the presence of this gift in man before he sinned, and how there can be room for this in a perspective of existence in accord with the findings of palaeontology.

Considering the discoveries of this science—and whatever view be taken of the way the primates fanned out in their progress, where the apparition of man is to be situated—we are justified in saying that man became more and more man in the course of very many generations. It was probably not immediately that he learned to pay less regard to his instincts and more to the new light of intelligence which had developed in him. This gradual progress may be compared—though only very remotely—to the development which children now go through in a few years, guided by educators and living in a highly formative environment. In the framework of such concepts, can it be accepted that man had original integrity at the beginning of his history?

Yes. Because it is possible that this gift made its influence felt at the beginning only in a restricted field. It makes the sensible inclinations, as we have said, obedient to the demands of conscience. But conscience regulates its demands according to the perception of moral and religious values. If man had remained innocent, he would have been enlightened in this knowledge, not merely by his intelligence but also by the spirit of sonship, and by apt supernatural illuminations—which we should properly think of rather as modest than brilliant. But even in this way he could probably have had only rudimentary insight into moral and religious values, and in a way open to further growth. In this way his moral life could have been holy but this holiness was that of a wholly primitive man, in whom original integrity could make itself felt only in a limited field.

The gift could also have been limited at the beginning in the order of intensity. There is no reason to believe that the obedience brought about by integrity in the lower inclinations was at once the highest degree of perfection. There must have been an essential obedience at the beginning, which could have grown more intense later.

But the growing inward harmony produced by original integrity was destroyed by sin. Its destruction meant that the development of moral and religious life was more dramatic, and subject to sad aberrations, in spite of the grace of Christ which was never wanting. But that is another story. It is enough for the moment to have pointed out that the gift of original integrity does not oblige us in any way to form a picture of Adam which would be out of place in an evolutionary perspective.

"Original immortality", even more than integrity, can appear perplexing. But there is an adequate answer to the difficulties to which it gives rise. It is a matter of understanding it better, not of denying it.

For St. Paul says explicitly: "Sin came into the world through one man and death through sin" (Rom 5:12, cf. 6:23). If St. Paul, as some think, looks beyond bodily to spiritual death, it is nonetheless true that he envisages primarily bodily death. The doctrine that death depends on sin forms an important part of St. Paul's Christology, according to which the death and resurrection of Christ free us from sin and death. The Councils of Carthage (418) and of Orange (529) took up this teaching once more. It is not astonishing that the Second Vatican Council, in the constitution on the Church in the Modern World, should have spoken of "bodily death from which man would have been immune had he not sinned" (Gaudium et Spes, no. 18). Pope Paul VI, in his Profession of Faith, 30 June 1968, also speaks of the state of justice and holiness in which "man knew neither evil nor sin".

But how are we to conceive of the first immortality? We see that the body of man is part of a mighty stem of living organisms which were all subject to the law of birth, procreation and death. Man, too, must be born and propagate himself: "Be fruitful and multiply, and fill the earth" (Gen 1:28). Would he then have had a wonderful gift in his possession which prevented the curve of his life being a curve towards death? Would the gift have made him immune to sickness and fatal accidents? Many theologians, including St. Thomas, have thought that original justice exercised such power over matter that the body became immortal. This would have implied a profound change in man's insertion into the world. This view of the relation between spirit and matter and between man and the world undoubtedly merits our attention. But was Adam in fact in such a condition? Did he have and lose such immortality in his person? Or is it perhaps sufficient to hold that mankind, if it had not sinned, would have been preserved from death, by such a gift of immortality, for instance, but without having already been transformed by this gift before sin? It is enough to believe that death in the human race is the wages of sin (cf. Rom 6:23).

We can gain some understanding of the matter in the following way. In spite of its cruelty, death remains a natural thing for man. But the grace of the sonship of God elevated man so much above his own proper dignity that if our human race had corresponded with grace it would have had, in God's eyes, to be preserved from death. A gift of immortality, as understood by St. Thomas, could have transformed man in this case. But it is best not to try to imagine what the order of God's providence would have been if sin and death had not reigned.

The endless possibilities of God's wisdom and power are hidden from us.

In the order of things which God foresaw and chose from eternity, the dignity to which the human race was raised by original justice was lost at the very beginning of history. Hence it was superfluous to bestow the gift of immortality on the first man in the form of a modification of his being. Rather, the promise of immortality was offered him, as it were, in the grace of original justice. By sin, he lost immortality in a definitive way. Sin entered the world and with sin death (cf. Rom 5:12).

Apropos of Adam

We shall now touch on two points which raise questions. The first concerns the bond between Eve and Adam. The second is the hypothesis of polygenism. The first point is incidental. The second is delicate and difficult.

1. Apropos of the doctrine of St. Paul about Adam, as the cause of the sin which is transmitted to us, we said that we must think of Eve as united to him. But how are we to conceive of this bond? Is it exclusively a matter of the sin itself, which was committed in common by both, or also of the loss of original justice, not only for themselves but for their offspring?

St. Paul spoke only of Adam as the cause of original sin. The tradition of the Church did the same, and we have followed their example. Our method of discussion may be understood simply as leaving the question of Eve aside, or as a definite exclusion. No one ever failed to recognize that Eve sinned. But scholastic theologians in general have thought that it was only Adam who lost original justice for himself and his offspring, because he alone had had to transmit this justice to his descendants. But their doctrine was based in part on a biological view which is no longer at a premium, according to which the woman plays a merely passive role in procreation, while the man is the only active agent in the transmission of nature.

Many modern theologians think that Adam and Eve received original justice as a single gift which they were to transmit to their offspring. In the state of innocence both would have transmitted original justice as well as life to their children, like a sacrament to some extent, as we have said. Their common sin ruled out this transmission, which would have bestowed so much happiness on the human race. But a sin committed separately by either of them would have done the same.

Here we add a brief remark. In connection with the idea that original sin is transmitted by way of descent, St. Thomas Aquinas said at least once that if Adam had not been a sinner, the men who would have probably sinned later would have transmitted original sin, each to his offspring. We can perhaps use this opinion as an introduction to what we shall now say about the problems presented to Christian thought by the scholars' hypotheses with regard to polygenism.

2. Hence we shall now touch upon our second question, that of polygenism. By monogenism we mean the existence of one single pair of human beings as the starting-point of all the generations of men. Polygenism means the existence of one or more "populations" of men as the starting-point of the series of generations. Palaeontology and genetics have not proved polygenism, and scholars do not affirm that it is proved. But from a purely biological stand-point—which is certainly insufficient in such a question, on account of its philosophical and theological implications—many scholars favour polygenism.

We have seen on the other hand that when speaking of original sin St. Paul, the tradition of the Church, the Council of Trent and the Second Vatican Council use formulas of which the obvious significance is undoubtedly monogenistic. This is true of Trent in a very special way. It is certain that these formulas contain in one way or another revealed truth. Hence they cannot be lightheartedly dismissed. But we should also avoid exaggeration, and not impose anything as absolute on faith which can perhaps be divorced from it. If science ever proves polygenism, we should have to conclude that the truth of faith which was hitherto expressed in monogenistic terms would have to be stripped of the husk of its apparently monogenistic meaning. The revealed truth would then remain intact. But is such a separation thinkable?

Various theologians have tried in recent years to determine whether this is possible, and with this aim in mind, have tried in various ways to describe the mystery of original sin on the hypothesis of polygenism. It may be useful to give one such attempt in outline here, not to invite the faithful to give up the doctrine of monogenism, but to ease their minds in the midst of the various questions which their faith has to undergo today.

Let us then suppose that "Adam and Eve" represent a first population of men (or a group of populations, which makes no real difference for our problem). It must also be supposed, as has already been done above, that for the transmission of original justice a pair of human beings is needed, both of whom remain innocent. How are we then to think of the case of the human race in "Adam"?

One would have to suppose that sin increased so rapidly and universally in the "Adamite population" that even after the first generation no human pair was capable of transmitting original justice to its offspring. But the hypothesis of this rapid and universal spread of sin raises difficulties. We should possibly then consider the matter in another way by supposing that the "Adamite population" comprised a number of generations (which in view of the future spread of the human race was extremely small). Bad example would have caused disaster in this population and the heritage of original justice would have been lost in a steadily growing number of persons, either because they themselves sinned or because they sprang from a human couple which was already stained with sin. Finally there would not have been a single couple left which would have been capable of transmitting original justice to their offspring.

In these two hypotheses regarding the origin of our fallen state, the traditional image of "sinful Adam" would be represented by the "Adamite population" which fell into sin: or rather, to put it more precisely, by the constantly growing number of human couples who—by reason of the sinful state of one of the partners—could only pass on to their offspring a nature deprived of original justice. This is certainly a gloomy picture. But is it much more gloomy than our experience of sin in the world? And it is, so to speak, not unthinkable.

Consequently all the descendants of the "Adamite population" which would have been the equivalent of the "sinful Adam" have been burdened at birth with original sin. They would all have "sinned in Adam". As regards this point there should be no new problems. But in the "Adamite population" there could have been men who remained innocent. Would this not be in contradiction to the affirmations of St. Paul and the Council of Trent about the sin of Adam which affects all men? One would have to say that these affirmations speak of all descendants of the sinful Adam. But here we would not be speaking of the descendants of the equivalent of the sinful Adam—the solid front of human couples which were gradually stained by sin—but of members of the "Adamite population" which preceded these descendants. (These sinless individuals would presumably have been subjected to death, because God did not will to preserve from death the human race in which sin was already rampant.)

Does this sketch do full justice to the revealed truth? In the present state of theological science it does not seem possible to answer this question with certainty. The Church remains attached to the monogenist perspective, and this attitude is wise. For it knows in fact that the traditional formulas about Adam and Eve and the human race fallen in Adam contain a truth of the history of salvation which has been entrusted to it—even though these formulas are not to be understood literally. But the Church is not able to affirm the same thing with regard to the polygenist formulas. Hence it preserves the traditional formulas and asks that they be preserved as the only ones which certainly safeguard the faith. But it does so without closing the door to questions which are raised by scientific findings. This is, it would seem, the meaning of the doctrine given in the encyclical Humani Generis (Denzinger-Schönmetzer, 3897). And when the Second Vatican Council and Pope Paul VI used the traditional formulas (see above, apropos of the 5th chapter of Romans) their doctrine followed the same line. But the Church allows theologians to continue their investigations and to go on with their dialogue with the students of the natural sciences.

The mystery of original sin in the teaching of the Church

The teaching of the Church, which is the kernel of our explanation of original sin and the sin of the world, is really the message of Scripture. It is the message which in the course of the development of tradition became clearer and more precise and was also enriched with certain elucidations. We have given above, briefly, the biblical message, at least insofar as it is contained in Genesis and the Epistle to the Romans. We shall now collect the doctrine of the Church out of our explanations as a whole, where it is combined with other considerations.

Man, who came innocent from God's hands and was elevated by him to the state of adoptive sonship, became sinful. The rebellion against God began at the start of history. It was the rebellion of our first parents. This was not merely the beginning of a series of sins. Adam lost for himself and for us original justice, that is, the spirit of sonship which he had received along with original integrity.

He had received this justice as a gift which he was to transmit along with purely human life to all his descendants. But having fallen from this higher state, he had simply a human nature to transmit, and one which was also fallen. This inward deterioration, which likewise estranges us from God, along with Adam and continuing his estrangement from God, is in us a state of sin.

Fallen man, even when he is re-born through baptism (through at least the baptism of desire) and thus united to Christ, remains inwardly weakened in the struggle against sin, since he does not receive back original integrity. But he is bound all the more to seek the healing grace of Christ, and when necessary new forgiveness, by receiving the sacraments and by humble prayer.

In spite of the grace of Christ, human history remains for a great part the history of constantly repeated rebellion against God. Original sin and the sin of the world together make up the mystery of sin. On account of original sin, followed by the sin of the world, God permits death to reign in the human race. Death is the wages of sin.

The whole drama finally ends in the triumph of the love of God, shown to us in his Son, our Redeemer. He is the good shepherd, whose stay upon this earth has brightened history for ever. He is the sacrificed Lamb, who takes away the sin of man through his blood. He is our innocent and adorable brother, in whom the elect will always glory before the Father.

III. THE BIRTH OF JESUS FROM THE VIRGIN MARY

DECLARATION (see AAS, 60 [1968], p. 688: *It must be openly professed in the Catechism that the holy mother of the incarnate Word remained always adorned with the honour of virginity. It must teach equally clearly the doctrine of the virginal birth of Jesus, which is so supremely in accord with the mystery of the Incarnation. No further occasion shall be given of denying this truth—contrary to the tradition of the Church in reliance on Sacred Scripture—retaining only a symbolic meaning, merely indicating for instance the gift inspired by pure grace, which God bestowed on us in his Son.*

1. The mystery of the virginal conception

Catechism text, pp. 74–75: "Jesus is the climax of all the promises . . . from God; from the Most High."

New text: Thus many children were given to Israel as the fruit of a promise. Jesus is the climax. When he came into the world, he was being prayed for by a whole people and was promised by a whole history. He was a child of promise in a unique sense. The deepest longing of all mankind was fulfilled in him. That is why, much more than in the birth of every human child, the fulfilment here surpasses all human possibilities. There is nothing in the bosom of mankind, nothing in human fruitfulness that can procreate him, from whom all human fruitfulness, all the birth of our race depend: for all things were made in him.

The mystery of this greatest gift of God to man in the person of Jesus can also be seen to be indicated by another event which is also mysterious, the virginal conception of Jesus, of which Matthew and Luke tell us in the Gospel. Jesus was not procreated by the intervention of man. He was conceived of the Holy Spirit, born from a young woman who was full of grace and chosen by God to be the holy mother of his Son. This doctrine of the evangelists is repeated by all the ancient creeds, and by the uninterrupted tradition of the Fathers of the Church and the magisterium. Under the guidance of this magisterium we all confess that Jesus "was conceived of the Holy Spirit, born of the Virgin Mary". The unique share which the Mother of God had in the mystery of the Incarnation explains the also unique role which she had, in dependence on her Son, in the work of our redemption.

When we consider these events, we must take care not to lose sight of the main intention of the gospels which proclaim this mystery of our salvation. It was supremely fitting that when the Son of God came into the world he should be conceived by means of the humble "Fiat" of a mother whose heart was given to God in virginity. It was also fitting that he who is from eternity the unique Son of God, and who, even as man, was to be more united in sonship to his Father than any other man, should have had no other Father in the full sense than God. Those who believe in the Incarnation of the Son of God will also find it possible to believe that the entry of Emmanuel into history goes together with an extraordinary birth, which is in harmony with this divine mystery.

It has indeed been pointed out that the virginal conception is only explicitly mentioned twice in the whole of the New Testament, while the death and resurrection, for instance, are proclaimed on every page. The first answer to this is to confess that the death and resurrection of our Lord are most certainly the good news beyond all else. As we have seen, the New Testament relates the youth of Jesus only for the sake of this primary message. But it is also well to note that the only two texts of Scripture which describe the youth of Jesus also relate the virgin birth of our Lord. It is, as it were, the centre of the infancy narratives of the gospels.

2. The perpetual virginity of Mary

Catechism text, p. 77: "Further, Jn 19:27 makes it highly improbable that Mary had other sons."

Add: The perpetual virginity of Mary is confirmed by the tradition of the Church, and presented by the magisterium to our belief.

3. Additional note

Since we are speaking of the mystery of Mary, we suggest two changes with regard to the knowledge which she had of the adorable majesty of her Son.

a) *Catechism text*, p. 77: "Did Mary fully understand . . . who he was?"

New text: Did Mary fully understand whom she was bringing into the world? She had an initial intimation of it. Her faith grew in clearness and depth. The resurrection of Jesus must also have thrown new light for Mary on the mystery of the Son of God.

b) *Catechism text*, pp. 153–4: "Certainly, before Jesus' resurrection . . . 'beloved Son'."

New text: To reveal clearly the unfathomable depth of this title, "Son of God", the resurrection of Jesus was needed, even for those who like the Apostles and above all Mary had in different measure come to see something of it. And even in our own case, it is well not to begin at once to contemplate this mystery in itself. It would appear too distant and abstract. It is better to learn it gradually, as the disciples did, through the life, death and resurrection of Jesus. Only then shall we be able to discover the riches of the mystery of the Son made man, expressed in such terms as: "Obedience", the cry of "Abba", "well pleased", "beloved Son".

DECLARATION (see AAS, 60 [1968], p. 688): *The elements of the doctrine of Christ's satisfaction which form part of the faith should be clearly given. God so loved sinful men that he sent his Son into the world to reconcile them to Himself* (see 2 Cor 5:19). *"We are reconciled with the God who already loves us"*, says St. Augustine, *"with whom we lived in enmity on account of our sins"* (In Joannis Evangelium, Treatise CX, no. 6). *Hence Jesus, as the first-born among many brothers* (cf. Rom 8:29), *died for our sins* (1 Cor 15:3). *Holy, blameless, unstained* (Heb 7:26) *he certainly did not undergo any punishment imposed on him by God, but obeying his Father freely and with childlike love* (cf. Phil 2:8), *he accepted for the sake of his sinful brothers and as their mediator* (cf. 1 Tim 2:5) *the death which is the wages of their sins* (cf. Rom 6:33; Vatican II, Constitution *Gaudium et Spes*, no. 13). *Through this most holy death, which in the eyes of God far outweighed the sins of the world, he caused the divine grace to be given back to humanity as a blessing which it had merited in its divine Head* (see, e.g., Heb 10:5–10; Trent, Session VI, Decree *De Justificatione*, chapters 3 and 7, canon 10).

Catechism text, pp. 282–3: The first part of the section entitled "Summary", down to "... by going through it"

New text: Redeemed by Jesus' blood

But there is something more to be said. What we hear in the gospels is not merely that we are redeemed by the resurrection of Jesus, but also by his death. In our lives of suffering and mortal anxiety, this is a new source of comfort. How are we to explain that a death can be redemptive?

God, St. Paul tells us, sent his Son in the likeness of our sinful flesh (cf. Rom 8:3), that is, in mortal flesh like that of sinful men. He sent him to "go about doing good" (Acts 10:38) and to live before the eyes of his Father as he with whom the Father was to be well-pleased (Mk 1:11). This was the earthly life of the image of the Father, of the unique Son who is in the bosom of the Father (cf. Jn 1:18). In this loveless world he was love.

His mission was difficult. His life shows us how hard he found it. In a crooked world he was to live uprightly, in a disobedient humanity he was to remain obedient, in an egoistic humanity he was to be love. He had also to make himself acceptable to his people as the Redeemer who had been announced by the prophets and on whom men waited.

In this he failed. The salvation which he brought was too pure. He disappointed those who clung to this earth, eager for national triumph, for glory and earthly riches. He was put to death. This horrifying drama, the climax of senseless evil, was recognized from the start by the Church as a profound mystery. Certain texts of the Old Testament guided it. One finds for instance within Deutero-Isaiah the "Servant Songs" (Isaiah 42:1–9; 49:1–6; 50:4–11; 52:13–53:12). They speak of a life taken away by the godless, but well pleasing to God and bringing sinners to him.

"A man of sorrows, and acquainted with grief, and as one from whom men hide their faces he was despised, and we esteemed him not. Surely he has borne our griefs . . .
Yet we esteemed him stricken . . .

But he was wounded for our transgressions . . .
All we like sheep have gone astray;
We have turned every one into his own way; and the Lord has laid on him the iniquity of us all.
It was the will of the Lord to bruise him . . . he makes himself an offering for sin" (Is 53:3–6, 10).

We do not know with certainty to whom these songs can have been applied, in a pre-figuration which they ultimately surpass. They say something about a mystery which was completely fulfilled only in the death and resurrection of Jesus. They helped the Apostles to see that his death had a place in God's plan.

But how can we be redeemed by someone's hardship and pain and death?

There is a mystery here which cannot be fully defined in conceptual terms, well as we sense the central point with which it is concerned. We shall dwell on it a little, since many of us have a garbled notion of the mystery.

From the Middle Ages on, theologians and preachers emphasized the notion of *satisfaction*. When properly understood it forms part of the message of faith, and the Council of Trent teaches that Christ "offered satisfaction for us to God the Father by his most holy passion" (Session VI, canon 7). It is true, nonetheless, that this has often been wrongly understood or at least expressed in very unsatisfactory terms.

God's attitude to man was not that of an angry king who seeks to appease his anger. He merely recognized that we merited punishment,

542

being at the same time decided to free us from it through his Son who was to reconcile us to him.

God did not will that his Son should offer satisfaction because he loved sinful men less, but because he loved them more. But he did not simply will to bestow the alms of forgiveness on them. He gave them the much greater grace of the coming of his Son, their brother, whose incomparably holy life was to compensate in God's eyes for all their sins. We have now access to the Father in humble confidence, and we can boast with holy pride of this "first-born among many brethren" (Rom 8:29). Further, the Son of God has shown us how immeasurable is the love of God for us. One who loves gladly dedicates and sacrifices himself for those whom he loves. It might have been unthinkable that God could show his love in this way. But he did so in Jesus, his Son.

We must not for a moment imagine that the Father imposed a punishment on Jesus. The innocent One is not punished by God. But his death was not "unsuitable" for sinful man, from which God would have freed man had he preserved his divine sonship. For "death is the wages of sin" (Rom 6:23). The Son of God became our brother by becoming man, a mortal man like us. He willingly accepted the death to which his preaching of the Kingdom and his testimony to his own mission led him. Through this humble acceptance and as representative of sinful men before his Father, he willed to confess their unworthiness for them and ask forgiveness for them. And by doing so he made up for sin in the eyes of God and merited that the graces leading to eternal life should be offered to sinners at all times. This holy acceptance of death was in accord with the good pleasure of his Father: he was "obedient unto death" (Phil 2:8).

The New Testament uses certain characteristic terms which describe this work of redemption. The chief are: redemption, reconciliation, justice, blood, sin. It is important to understand them properly.

Jesus *redeemed* or *ransomed* us by his death. The term recalls how God "redeemed" Israel out of Egypt. No price was paid. The people is recovered by God. In connection with our redemption by Christ mention is sometimes made of the price which was paid. St. Paul, for instance, speaks of our being redeemed by his blood (Eph 1:7; see Col 1:14). This is understandable, because Jesus gives us back to God by accomplishing a work which cost him much: the acceptance of his passion and death. Union with God is restored in this way.

We also read that we are *reconciled* with God through the death of Jesus. We should note this expression. It does not say that God is reconciled *with us*. It is not an angry God who is reconciled with man, but evil man must be reconciled *with God*. Here too the bond is restored.

The restoration, according to St. Paul, takes place through God's justice. This is not the justice which punishes or demands a punishment, but the sanctifying power of God which communicates to us his holiness and justice (Rom 3:21). Nonetheless, the sacrifice which Jesus offered to God had supreme value in the eyes of God, and through this it merited salvation for us. St. Paul says that "Christ loved us and gave himself up for us, a fragrant offering and sacrifice to God" (Eph 5:2).

As regards the blood, we must first note the words of the Eucharist, "For this is my blood of the covenant, which is poured out for many for the forgiveness of sins" (Mt 26:28). "Blood" is an important word for the understanding of Jesus' work. It is an allusion to the blood of the covenant on Sinai, where the sacrificial animal was offered to Yahweh. Then the blood, which now belonged to God, was sprinkled on the people. In this way the blood which was offered to God became the gift of God to Israel. A brotherhood was formed in blood, a "blood relationship", one might almost say.

So, too, the blood of Jesus is offered to God. This offering must not be understood in a wholly material sense. The blood has value only through Jesus' holy acceptance of his death, which has been spoken of above. This blood is offered to God for us and it is given to us at the Eucharistic repast. The sacred victim, accepted by God and glorified by him, makes us like to himself so that we also succeed in belonging to God. We are united to him. This is "the new covenant in my blood".

Finally, there is the word *sin* in the text of St. Paul which reads: "For our sake he made him to be sin who knew no sin, so that in him we might become the righteousness of God" (2 Cor 5:21). This terse sentence is not to be taken to mean that God acts "as if" Jesus were a sinner and so brings down punishment on his head. It rather means that Jesus entered fully into our world of sin and death. He became part of our world so that he could there give us his holiness (his righteousness). He is reduced to the state of malediction of one hanging on the cross, in order to free us from the malediction of our transgressions.

All these expressions signify Jesus' obedience, his service unto death. Hence they do not mean that the Father had to punish Jesus in our stead. God demanded Jesus' love for his Father and for us, and the

544

highest expression of this love: "Greater love has no man than this, that a man lay down his life for his friends" (Jn 15:13).

We learn from the doctrine of redemption that sin, death and calamity are not the end, because God shows that he can bring forth life from these things. Hence it is the task of the Christian to work and to have confidence as long as he can. For he has been given the hope that even when he can do no more, in death and calamity, he remains in union with his Lord, giving and receiving.

Summary

We shall now try to sum up briefly how our Lord has redeemed us.

He attacks the root of evil, sin. He does this by obedience unto death. "With his stripes we are healed."

God so loved sinful men that he sent his Son into the world of sin to reconcile it with himself (cf. 2 Cor 5:19). Jesus, the first-born among many brothers (cf. Rom 8:29), became obedient unto death (cf. Phil 2:8). Holy, innocent, unstained (cf. Heb 7:26)—never punished even by his Father—he freely accepted for his sinful brothers, and as their mediator (cf. 1 Tim 2:5), the death which for them is the wages of sin (cf. Rom 6:23). In this way he made satisfaction to God for their offences and merited that divine grace be restored to a humanity which had compensated for evil in its Head.

V. THE SACRIFICE OF THE CROSS CONTINUED IN THE SACRIFICE OF THE MASS

DECLARATION (see AAS, 60 [1968], pp. 688f.): *Jesus, to make good our misdeeds, offered himself to the Father as a sacred victim with which God was well pleased. "Christ loved us and gave himself up for us, a fragrant offering and sacrifice to God"* (Eph 5:2).

But the sacrifice of the cross is continued uninterruptedly in the Church of God in the eucharistic sacrifice (see Vatican II, *Sacrosanctum Concilium*, no. 47). *For in the celebration of the Eucharist, Jesus, as the principal priest, offers himself to God through the Eucharistic offering which the priests make and in which the faithful join. But this celebration is both an offering and a repast. The offering of this sacrifice is completed by the communion in which the victim offered to God is eaten as food, in order to unite the faithful with itself and to bind them to each other in love* (see 1 Cor 10:17).

Catechism text, pp. 339–40: The section entitled "The New Testament in my blood".

New text: Thus we have a meal in common and thanksgiving in common. Have we seen all the aspects and meanings of the Mass? If we continue to look and listen, we meet a third aspect. Some words in the eucharistic prayer indicate that a sacrifice is being offered. What does this mean?

During the last supper, Jesus himself already made present the sacrifice of the cross, in a symbolic action, an "anticipatory memorial". It was a memorial which already made the death on the cross present in the symbol. The broken bread became Jesus' body, the wine in the chalice his blood shed for us. Thus Jesus "instituted the eucharistic sacrifice of his body and his blood. He did this in order to perpetuate the sacrifice of the cross throughout the centuries until he should come again" (Vatican II, Constitution on the Liturgy, *Sacrosanctum Concilium*, no. 47). And each time the Church does this and so proclaims the death of the Lord, the one sacrifice is present in it.

Man's desire to offer sacrifice from ancient times, "from Abel", finds here a sacrifice with which he need not be ashamed to come before God. Friendship between the Father and us is definitively restored by this sacrifice—the new friendship, the new covenant or testament. The covenant (alliance) of the old friendship was concluded by means of sacrifice—on Sinai, at the Exodus. The new friendship arose through the offering of a life.

The ancient passover was a memorial of the old friendship, but only a memorial. When we, on the other hand, recall our new friendship, the sacrifice of the covenant is really there among us. We are able to partake in man's definitive sacrifice—not a goat or an ox, but the Son.

> If the sprinkling of defiled persons with the blood of goats and bulls and with the ashes of a heifer sanctifies for the purification of the flesh, how much more shall the blood of Christ, who through the eternal Spirit offered himself without blemish to God, purify our conscience from dead works to serve the living God (Heb 9:13, 14).

To join in the celebration of Mass is to partake of this sacrifice and to be associated in the making of the covenant between God and his people. It takes place not amid the thunders of Sinai, but with the serious and joyful simplicity of a religious meal. In this way Christ himself continues "in an unbloody way the sacrifice which was accomplished on the cross, and offers himself to the Father through the ministry of priests for the salvation of the world" (Congregation of Rites, *Instructio de cultu mysterii eucharistici*, AAS, 59 [1967], pp. 541f.). And the faithful join with the priest to offer this sacrifice of "thanksgiving, reconciliation, supplication and praise", through and with the priest and likewise with the Lord Jesus. Humbly, they also offer themselves, along with the sacred victim, so that there "be honour and glory for ever and ever to God" (cf. 1 Tim 1:17).

As regards the actual offering of the sacrifice, it would not be right to pay too much attention to the preparatory actions which have been given the name of the "offertory". This consists in the making ready and setting apart of bread and wine. The main thing is that it is all the sacrifice of Jesus' body and blood. For this the "canon" must be recited, with the words of Jesus at the last supper, and communion received. The communion is included because the way in which we fully participate in the eucharistic sacrifice consists in doing what our Lord commanded: "Take and eat". The sacred victim which we offer to God becomes in communion the gift which God offers to us, "the true bread from heaven" (Jn 6:32). In the celebration of the Eucharist "the sacrifice and the communion are so much part of the one mystery that they are united most intimately with one another" (Congregation of Rites, *Instructio*, p. 541). It seems that with this we have covered the full extent of the meaning of the Eucharist.

Note: See also above, IV. "The satisfaction offered by Jesus to the Father", especially the passage, "As regards the blood ... in my blood" (pp. 30 above).

VI. THE EUCHARISTIC PRESENCE AND CHANGE

DECLARATION (see AAS, 60 [1968], p. 689): *It must be said very clearly that after the consecration of bread and wine the body and blood of Christ himself are present upon the altar and are consumed in a sacramental manner at holy communion, so that those who approach worthily this divine table are spiritually nourished with Christ the Lord. It must further be explained that the bread and wine, with respect to their inward (not apparent) reality are changed by the utterance of the words of consecration into the body and blood of Christ and that therefore, where the species or apparent reality remains, the humanity of Christ himself is hidden in a very mysterious way, united with his divine person.*

After this wonderful change, which has been given the title of tran-
substantiation in the Church, the species of bread and wine undoubtedly
receive a new significance and a new finality, since they really contain
and signify Christ himself, the source of the grace and love which are
imparted in holy communion. But they receive this new significance and
this new finality precisely because transubstantiation has taken place
there (see the encyclical of Paul VI, *Mysterium Fidei*, AAS, 57 [1965],
p. 766; *Letter of the German bishops to all who are entrusted by the*
Church with the preaching of the faith, nos. 43–47).

1. The eucharistic presence

Catechism text, pp. 342f.: The first part of the section entitled "Jesus
present in the signs".

New text: The presence of Jesus under the eucharistic signs

We cannot end this chapter without first peaking explicitly of the
great mystery which is contained in what was said above, but not yet
discussed, the sacramental presence of Jesus and the change of bread
and wine into his body and blood.

When the Apostles ate with Jesus during his earthly life, he was
certainly present among them, visibly and in bodily form. But that was
not all. There was also "something" between them all. The presence
of God's Son among them was not without special effect. Along with
the external presence and activity of the Master went the feeling of an
inward and efficacious presence which united them to him. This
inward presence is a presence of the Lord through his action and the
action of the Holy Spirit. This is the presence of which St. Paul speaks
when he writes to the Ephesians that "Christ dwells in your heart
through faith" (Eph 3:17), or of which Jesus himself spoke when he
said: "Where two or three are gathered in my name, there am I in the
midst of them" (Mt 18:20). This is the presence which, along with the
words which Jesus spoke, set the hearts of the disciples on fire on the
road to Emmaus (cf. Lk 24:32).

When the disciples of Jesus came together out of love of him, after
his death and resurrection, he was the mysterious and efficacious bond
which united them. There was still "something" between them, just
as there already was when the Lord ate with them. This was all the more
so because they knew from his apparitions that "he lives!", and
because at Pentecost they had received the power of the Holy Spirit
in superabundance.

548

They also knew that they were to celebrate the memory of his supreme sacrifice and of his glorious resurrection by taking bread and wine and repeating the words which he had spoken at the last supper. They knew that at the celebration of this memory they received the Lord himself as food for their souls. They knew that what lay before them was no longer bread (and wine) in its deepest reality, but the body of the Lord, which one could not approach except in a worthy fashion (cf. 1 Cor 11:27).

Hence in the celebration which recalls the last supper, which is repeated continually by the Church, there is a mysterious presence of Jesus under the eucharistic signs. For what is on the altar, after the repetition of the words of Jesus, is only according to appearances—according to the "species" as the Church says—bread and wine. The profound reality not perceptible to the senses, the "substance" of bread and wine, is changed into that of the body and blood of Jesus. And the Church expresses this more precisely by saying that because of this change, the body and blood of Jesus—his holy, glorified and life-giving humanity—is present under the eucharistic signs in itself, and not merely through their activity or effects.

For what purpose is Jesus present in this way? In order to effect in us through the rite of communion—the sacramental meal—what this meal symbolizes. And the meal symbolizes our spiritual nourishment by him, the bread of life. Through this sacred refreshment, our union with him in faith and love is intensified. There is a greater union with our divine Lord who with the Father and Holy Spirit dwells in our heart.

Hence we re-discover in the Eucharist something similar to the twofold presence of which we spoke at the meals or conversations of Jesus with his disciples, an outward and an inward one. But when Jesus lived among his disciples his external presence was visible. In the sacrament of the Eucharist his presence on our altars is invisible and accessible only to our faith. In both cases the inward presence is the mysterious but supremely precious gift, towards which the external presence is directed.

The Lord already dwells in the heart of the faithful, before communion, even before the celebration of the Eucharist. He also works through the priest in order to offer the eucharistic sacrifice through the change of bread and wine into his body and blood. He is the priest preeminently. The priest who celebrates the holy sacrifice is only his minister. But in the community of the faithful and in the priest who

549

offers the sacrifice, the glorified humanity of our Lord is not present in itself, but through its effects. That which is present on our altars in a specially mysterious way under the species of bread and wine is his sacred humanity itself, and with it the divine person of our Lord. Hence we may and should, as the Council of Trent teaches, offer the Blessed Sacrament the adoration which is due to God. Like the Apostle Thomas before the risen Lord, but now illuminated only by faith, we say: "My Lord and my God"; and we also say: "Lord, I am not worthy."

2. The eucharistic change

Catechism text, p. 343: Second part of the section entitled "Jesus present in the signs".

New text: But what is the change which takes place in the bread? We have already said that there is no change in the perceptible reality of the bread, i.e., the reality which we see and touch and which is the subject of study in physics and chemistry. We have also said that Jesus himself brings it about, through the mediation of the consecrating priest, that what was bread becomes the body of Jesus. Can something more be said of this mysterious change?

It was discussed before the Middle Ages, but without trying to describe more closely the nature of the change. In the course of the Middle Ages a further step was taken in the investigation and explanation. The Council of Trent adopted the kernel of these explanations and it forms part of the mystery of faith (as regards the reality which is indicated, not as regards the formula used). Our senses do not attain all that is comprised in corporeal realities. In the perceptible and more or less changing reality of bread and wine something deeper and more permanent finds expression. And our mind aims at it and attains it—although vaguely—when we say as we perceive the visible phenomena: This is bread.

This deeper reality (non-phenomenal) of bread and wine makes place, by virtue of the words of Christ, uttered by the priest, for the very reality of the humanity of Christ (for the deeper reality of his body and blood). And we then say truly: Behold the Lamb of God, and, "The body of Christ". The deeper reality of which we have spoken (that of the bread and wine, and that of the body and blood of Christ) is called "substance" (the being) by the Council of Trent. In consequence, the Council calls the eucharistic change "transubstantiation" (change of being) and affirms that only the "species" of bread and wine remain.

What we have said is not an explanation of the mystery, but gives its content more precisely. The mystery is not laid bare. God is greater than our mind. But it is important to know that it is a mystery of love. It means that wherever there are communities of the faithful, the Church can unite itself with the sacrifice of its Lord, which continues on earth for all time. It also means that we can receive the Lord as nourishment for our souls in the very human way of a meal. God chose this touching way in order to display to us his love.

In modern times, many theologians have spoken of a change of significance and finality which comes about in the consecrated bread and wine. In the encyclical Mysterium Fidei, Pope Paul VI accepts this double change. But he sees it as the consequence of the change of bread and wine into the body and blood of Christ. By virtue of this change, the eucharistic signs contain Jesus, the bread of life, and therefore signify (change of significance) and bring about (change of finality) the fact that we are spiritually nourished (cf. Paul VI, encyclical *Mysterium Fidei*, AAS, 57 [1965], p. 766).

3. The duration of the eucharistic presence

a) *Catechism text*, p. 345: "There is another small question . . . an intenser presence in us through the Spirit."

New text: There is another small question to be discussed here, on which there can be different opinions. When does Jesus' eucharistic presence cease? The answer is, when the visible reality, the "species" of bread, is no longer there. Sometimes the solution has been sought along chemical or other lines of natural science. But should "species" here be understood in a scientific sense? Is it not better to ask oneself what is to be considered bread according to the general view or on the level of ordinary perception? This is the criterion by which we should judge the duration of the eucharistic presence. In any case, we receive the body of Christ so that this sacramental nourishment may intensify the indwelling of the Lord in our spirit and increase our union with him in love.

b) *Catechism text*, p. 346, "The body of Christ is 'reserved' . . . or benediction of the Blessed Sacrament."

New text: The body of Christ is "reserved" reverently even after the celebration. Thus it can be brought to the sick at any time. It is usually

551

kept on an altar well to the fore in church, in the tabernacle. Thus even when no Mass is being celebrated, our Lord remains among us in this way. All that has been said above about his presence remains true of this proximity. It is a mysterious and hidden presence of the very humanity of Jesus. We should try to remain reverently and thankfully aware of this presence whenever we enter church. Our external attitude should show our reverence for this adorable presence. It is an excellent custom to genuflect on entering and leaving. The constant presence of Jesus here can be honoured by silent prayer, as when a housewife takes a few minutes off on a shopping expedition to pray and give thanks for her husband and children, or by public veneration, as in processions or benediction of the Blessed Sacrament.

VII. INFALLIBILITY OF THE CHURCH AND KNOWLEDGE OF MYSTERIES

DECLARATION (see AAS, 60 [1968], p. 689): *It should be made clear that the infallibility of the Church is not confined to giving a correct orientation in an always progressing search. It indicates the truth which is to be preserved in the doctrine of faith, which must always be interpreted in the same sense* (see Vatican I, Constitution *Dei Filius,* chapter 4, and Vatican II, Constitution *Dei Verbum,* chapter 2). *"Faith is not only a search, it is above all a certainty"* (Paul VI, Sermo inauguralis Synodi Episcoporum, AAS, 59 [1967], p. 966). *Further, the readers of the Catechism should not be allowed to gain the impression that human reason can go no further than the verbal or conceptual reflection of the revealed mystery. Care should be taken to show that human reason and its concepts can truly attain and express the revealed mysteries even though only "in part" and "in a mirror dimly"* (cf. 1 Cor 13:12).

Catechism text, pp. 365f.: The section entitled "Truth and dynamism".

New Text: Truth and dynamism

"Infallibility" is a negative word, but it expresses something positive, the preservation and communication of truth. Of itself it says nothing of the development which is intrinsic to all truths which men possess. When applied to the Church it tells us that it is to preserve faithfully the treasury of revealed faith which has been entrusted to it (cf. 1 Tim 6:20), and that the Spirit will lead it without error as it penetrates further into the message (cf. Jn 16:13). "The body of the

552

faithful as a whole, anointed as they are by the Holy One (cf. 1 Jn 2:20, 27), cannot err in matters of belief. Thanks to a supernatural sense of the faith which characterizes the people as a whole, it manifests this unerring quality when 'from the bishops down to the last member of the laity' it shows universal agreement in matters of faith and morals" (Vatican II, Lumen Gentium, no. 12). But in what does the progress of the people of God towards the fullness of truth consist? The revealed message is so rich that it comprises aspects which were concealed at the beginning but which Christ willed to make known to the Church, his bride, in such a way that it was gradually to make progress in knowledge of them. Then, we attain revealed truths through the instruments of human modes of expression. These are words and formulas which are capable of change to a certain degree. We must also use images and concepts. These last can attain the mysteries in a way which is partly negative, always imperfect but nonetheless really true, and which retains its value in spite of all changes in culture and history. But the expression of truth in concepts can also comprise elements which belong to the world-picture of a given epoch.

We need not be surprised to find theologians distinguishing at times between the truth which is really intended and certain expressions of it. This is the distinction made by John XXIII between the deposit or treasury of the faith—the truths summed up in Christian doctrine—and the mode of voicing it (Opening Allocution to the Second Vatican Council, AAS, 54 [1962], p. 92). It should be noted finally that revealed truth must always be so presented that the hearers in any given epoch may be enabled to approach it in the light of their own mentality, knowledge and problems.

All this means that the preaching of the message of Christ by the Church, and its sound exposition by theologians and those charged with the care of souls, is not a rigidly fixed system, but a dynamic element, a thing in movement. This must not disturb our equilibrium. For the very small child, the mother is the fixed point, but a very mobile one—because she is a living being. She moves to and fro, in and out, now serious, now laughing. A fixed point in the deepest sense of the word is something with life and movement. This is also true of the preaching of the message. It changes and adopts new forms, while the content remains the same.

Theological thinking at the present day is very fully aware of this dynamism and these efforts to find new forms. Some theologians shrink from the necessary changes, others are in danger of failing to do justice to the unchangeable truth, or lay an undue stress on the dynamic element. Paul VI took up a position between the two extremes when he said at the opening of the Synod of Bishops (29 September 1967): "Faith is not merely a search, it is above all a certainty".

The hearer of the word of Christ which remains for ever, the Church, is on the way towards a knowledge, constantly renewed, of the same truth. It is the ancient and unquenchable light of Christ, "Lumen Christi", which, like the paschal candle, always bears the date of the night in which it now shines.

VIII. THE OFFICIAL PRIESTHOOD AND AUTHORITY IN THE CHURCH

DECLARATION (see AAS, 60 [1968], p. 690): *Care must be taken that the dignity of the official priesthood is not diminished, since it consists in participation in the priesthood of Christ in a way which differs not only in degree but also in kind from the general priesthood of the faithful* (see Vatican II, Constitution *Lumen Gentium*, no. 10; Instructio de cultu Mysterii eucharistici, AAS, 59 [1967], no. 11, p. 548).

When describing the task of the priest, more care should be taken to bring out his office of mediator between God and men, not only when preaching the word of God, instructing the Christian community and administering the sacraments, but above all when offering the eucharistic sacrifice in the name of the whole Church (cf. Vatican II, Constitution *Lumen Gentium*, no. 28 and the Decree *Presbyterorum Ordinis*, nos. 2, 13).

It should further be made clear that the power of government and preaching in the Church is given directly to the Pope and to the bishops in hierarchical communion with him, but not to the people of God, to be then transmitted from the latter to the former. Hence the office of the bishops is not a charge given them by the people of God, but one which they have received from God for the well-being of the whole community of the faithful.

It should appear more clearly that the Pope and bishops do more than sum up and confirm what the whole community of the faithful believes. The people of God is indeed inspired and supported by the Spirit of truth, and adheres steadfastly to the word of God. But it does so under the guidance of the magisterium, to which is assigned the authentic preservation, interpretation and defence of the deposit of faith. In this way there is a marvellous agreement between bishops and faithful in the spiritual reception of the traditional faith, its confession with the lips and its exercise in deeds (cf. Vatican II, *Lumen Gentium*, no. 11; Dei Verbum, no. 10). *Sacred tradition and sacred Scripture—which form a body of sacred truth which is both one and firmly defined—are so linked with the magisterium of the Church that neither can exist without the other* (cf. Vatican II, *Dei Verbum*, no. 10).

Finally, the authority by which the Pope governs the Church must be clearly presented as full, supreme and universal jurisdiction, which the Pastor of the whole Church can always freely exercise (see Vatican II, *Lumen Gentium*, no. 22).

1. The priesthood of believers and the official priesthood

a) *Catechism text*, p. 348: "The Christian priesthood . . . (1 Pet 2:9)."

New text: The Christian priesthood belongs in a true sense to the whole community of the faithful. They receive it through baptism and the anointing of confirmation. Hence the Church in this world is "God's own people" (1 Pet 2:9).

b) *Catechism text*, pp. 362–3: "It might seem . . . the mysteries of God (1 Cor 4:1)."

New text: The pastoral mediation, which re-presents the mediation of Christ, is therefore exercised by a limited number. Does this diminish the dignity of the general priesthood of the people of God, of which pastors are members along with the rest? No. It would be wrong to envisage the relationship between the general priesthood of believers and the hierarchical priesthood of bishops and priests in this way. Both partake of the priesthood of Jesus Christ. As Vatican II teaches (Lumen Gentium, no. 10), there is a difference of kind between the two. The hierarchical priesthood is higher, but this does not prevent its being a service. That the faithful are constantly born anew and re-born as a priestly people, is given to the faithful by the bishops and priests. These are servants of Christ and of his people and the dispensers of the mysteries of God.

2. The official or hierarchical priesthood

a) *Catechism text*, p. 361: "The meaning of such words . . . in living men."

New text: These words affirm that the powers of the Apostles (except of course their power to be founders) were passed on to the bishops. It means that they have authority to feed the flock of God, by teaching, by celebrating the eucharistic sacrifice (see Lumen Gentium, no. 26) and distributing the sacraments, and by giving guidance to the Church. These three tasks are to be discharged in different ways at each epoch. Hence Christ wills to be among us precisely in the authority of living men.

b) *Catechism text*, p. 361: "The office . . . in his diocese."

New text: This office of "minister of the sacraments" is discharged by the bishop (apart from his responsibility for the ministrations of the priests) by ordaining priests and administering confirmation—through which he completes the baptism of all the Christians of the diocese. He also consecrates or blesses the holy oils for the diocese. He also is responsible for the right and proper transmission of all sacramental signs in his diocese.

c) *Catechism text*, p. 363: "The ordination of a "priest" . . . of the Eucharist."

New text: The ordination of a priest also consists of prayer to the Holy Spirit and the imposition of hands. All priests present join in this imposition of hands, as a symbolic expression of the unity of the priesthood. Around this kernel, which is the essential rite of ordination, a number of illuminating ceremonies have been arranged: the anointing of the hands with holy oil, the handing over of the chalice and a gold plate (the paten), and finally the concelebration of the eucharistic sacrifice with the bishop for the first time.

d) *Catechism text*, p. 363: "The powers . . . situation."

New text: The power here conferred upon the priest is that of offering the eucharistic sacrifice and forgiving sins in the sacrament of penance (hearing confessions). He also shares the charge of preaching and governing, according to the situation which he occupies.

3. The authority to govern and instruct

a) *Catechism text*, p. 362: "Further, he receives . . . given us."

New text: Further, he receives his mission and his authority only in the midst of the people of God and for its well-being. (When we speak of the "people of God" in the biblical sense, we do not of course exclude bishops and priests).

The way in which this power comes to the bishop is not the way which we see in democracies. This has a deep significance, which we shall examine.

556

Meanwhile it may be noted that the *choice* of the person who is to be bishop can of itself take place in several ways, for example by the voice of the whole people, as happened no doubt in earlier times.

But the authority itself is not transmitted by its being conferred on the bishop by the majority, but by its being passed on by those who have already received authority. (The custom of two or more bishops laying hands on the bishop-elect may be regarded as an expression of the unity of the college of bishops, its collegiality).

The manner in which a bishop consecrates a new bishop shows that he does not receive his pastoral mission from himself, any more than the authority which it brings with it. Like the Apostles, the bishops receive their ministry and authority from the Lord. But by virtue of the will of Christ, these powers are transmitted to them by way of the apostolic succession. The consecration of a bishop opens up a window on the divine origin of his power. It is by God's gift that men have the charge of gathering together, feeding and governing the people of God.

b) *Catechism text*, p. 365, section on *"The college of bishops and infallibility"*: "The bishops together . . . it speaks as such."

New text: The bishops together—united with the successor of St. Peter—preserve the truth of Christ in the Church. Along with the people of God which they have to guide, they are moved by the Spirit of truth. And a Council is infallible when it declares explicitly that it is giving an irreformable (unchangeable) doctrine.

4. The authority of the successor of St. Peter

Catechism text, pp. 366 f.: Section entitled: "Unity through the successor of Peter."

New text: Unity through the successor of St. Peter

There is a very normal question which may be asked here, and one which helps us to understand better the gift of Christ to his Church. It may be formulated as follows: To whom must we turn when the bishops in the Church are divided? We may use the question as an occasion of studying the mandate of the Bishop of Rome.

Jesus appointed Peter the first of the Apostles. Three times he said to him: "Feed my sheep". To say something three times in the Ancient East was to give it the most solemn confirmation. The fisherman from Galilee and the charge given him by the Lord are discussed in the chapter entitled: "The Messiah and his community".

The pastoral office of Peter is handed down. The Apostle met his death at Rome, under Nero, in 64 or 67. Our next piece of information about the city comes from Ignatius of Antioch and Clement of Rome, about 100. Both make it clear that the Church of Rome occupied a special position among the other Churches. It retained this position. Initially this did not demand any special organization. But on important questions the Churches kept in contact with the Church of Rome.

But was this perhaps due to the fact that Rome was also the political and administrative centre of the Empire? Even on purely historical grounds this is unlikely, precisely because at that time the primacy as a whole was not an administrative office. What made the bishop of Rome the first among his brothers was not primarily the authority of the capital of the Empire, but the authority of the ancient apostolic community which went back to St. Peter. Since the fourth century the bishop of Rome was called "Papa", i.e. "Father". But he was not in fact the only bishop who was given the title at the time. It was reserved to him only later. To maintain communion with the Church of Rome was a guarantee that one was linked to the Church as a whole.

The special task of the bishop of Rome is the same as that of St. Peter: to keep the Church a unity, to preserve it in the unity of confession of faith and of life. This is the foundation of the "full, supreme and universal" power which he possesses as "Vicar of Christ and pastor of the whole Church" (Vatican II, Lumen Gentium, no. 22). This power strengthens that of the other bishops, does not impair it in any way, and does not make them simply vicars of the Pope. We do not say that he is above the college of bishops in the sense that he rules over it without being himself part of it. He is a member of the college of bishops, and also its head.

In the course of time the notion of the "primacy" which was bestowed on St. Peter and transmitted to his successors became more and more clearly defined. And the notion was still more precisely determined between the First and Second Vatican Councils. As regards the exercise of this charge, in varying historical circumstances it has taken different forms, and continues to do so. Hence from the 14th century on in particular, one can note a tendency to centralization or "concentration", with its inherent advantages and disadvantages. And judging by the developments since the last Council—a more conspicuous participation of the episcopate in the service of the whole Church, the emergence of a Synod of Bishops, the role of episcopal conferences, the assigning of broader powers to the heads of dioceses—we can already sense the impetus of the Spirit towards new forms: new ways of harmonizing unity with a new sense of the spiritual riches proper to the local Churches, a new sense of the responsibility which devolves on each bishop.

At present it is the Pope who in the last instance at least nominates bishops or explicitly confirms their choice. He may under certain circumstances intervene in the affairs of a diocese. Sometimes he appoints an "apostolic administrator" who acts in his name to take up for a time the functions of a bishop who is unable to exercise them.

In the course of centuries, the development has been that he exercises his wide-ranging central authority with the help of the Roman Congregations, under the general name of the Curia. They are comparable to the ministries of a State. The cardinals are important papal assistants. They were originally bishops, priests and deacons of the leading churches of Rome and its environs. Since the 11th century it is they who have elected the Pope. The composition of the college of cardinals is being more and more internationalized. It includes the bishops of many important dioceses. Other cardinals work in Rome, e.g., as heads of the various Roman congregations.

The unifying function of the Pope entails his charge of teaching and the charism of infallibility. "This is the infallibility which the Roman Pontiff, the head of the college of bishops, enjoys in virtue of his office, when, as the supreme shepherd and teacher of all the faithful, who confirms his brethren in their faith (cf. Lk 22:32), he proclaims by a definitive act some doctrine of faith or morals" (Vatican II, Lumen Gentium, no. 25). This does not mean that he could proclaim dogmas without being himself in unity with the Church. Rather, he proclaims and explains the content of the revelation which the Church received from Christ and the Apostles. For "this teaching office is not above the word of God, but serves it, teaching only what has been handed on, listening to it devoutly, guarding it scrupulously, and explaining it faithfully by divine commission and with the help of the Holy Spirit" (Vatican II, Dei Verbum, no. 10). In the exercise of his charge as teacher of the whole Church, the Pope remains constantly in contact with the faith of the Church and especially with his brothers in the episcopate, just as on the other hand all members of the Church believe in fellowship with him. When he clearly expresses his intention of imparting a doctrine to the whole Church as definitive, which is rarely the case, this utterance is certainly full of the truth of God's Spirit. To accept it is a touch-stone for full participation in the fellowship of the Church.

Many directives and utterances of the magisterium do not claim absolute infallibility. This does not mean that they are therefore without the Spirit of God. They speak with an extremely venerable and authoritative voice, which demands of the faithful a prudent, reverent assent of mind and heart *(assensus religiosus)*, in proportion to the intentions of the magisterium. These may be gathered from the type of documents drawn up, from the frequency with which something is taught and from the expressions chosen to communicate the doctrine (cf. Vatican II, Lumen Gentium, no. 25).

IX. VARIOUS POINTS OF DOGMATIC THEOLOGY

DECLARATION (see AAS, 60 [1968], pp. 690f.): *A more suitable way of speaking should be used with regard to the three adorable persons in God, whom Christians rightly contemplate with the eyes of faith and reverence with childlike love, not merely as they appear in the economy of salvation but also as they exist from eternity in their immanent life, the vision of which we await. In some places the effects of the sacraments should be described more precisely. The Catechism should not be allowed to appear to suggest that miracles can only be worked by God insofar as they do not deviate from the course of effects which can be produced by the forces of the created world. And finally, there must be a clear statement about the souls of the just who having been fully purified already enjoy the beatific vision, while the pilgrim Church still awaits the coming of the Lord and the final glorification* (see Vatican II, Constitution *Lumen Gentium*, nos. 49, 51).

1. Our knowledge of the mystery of the Holy Trinity

Catechism text, pp. 498–9: The section entitled: "The living God."
New text: The living God

When we try to penetrate this revelation prayerfully, we begin to realize that our whole life is in the hands of an eternal love. Being brought to the Father by the Lord Jesus and filled with the Holy Spirit, we are perpetually involved in a mystery of love. Since we are privileged to be the family of God, the profoundest glory is revealed to us.

This is something which we shrink from summing up briefly, since it is the mystery of the unity of the Father, the Son and the Holy Spirit. It is difficult, because as our minds ascend to immeasurable heights, our imagination may at once be gripped by some such image as three interwoven circles. Or our mind may immediately start to work on combinations of the numerals one and three, and hence miss the biblical riches of this revelation.

We must always contemplate God in the light of this world and the history of salvation in which he has given us a place. But we have received the Spirit, St. Paul tells us, who "searches everything, even the depths of God" (1 Cor 2:10). And it is well that we should gaze with the eyes of faith at the Father of our Lord Jesus Christ, at Jesus the Son, born of God before all ages, descending on earth to reveal to us the heart of God, and at the Holy Spirit who lives in the Church and with the Father and the Son is the guest of our souls. It is well to gaze at the one God in three persons, since in this fundamental mystery we are confronting an eternal exchange of love, and can hear the summons to unity in faith and love. "That they may be one even as we are one" was the prayer of Jesus to his Father (Jn 17:22f.). All our Christian life, from our baptism on, is under the sign of the Father, Son and Holy Spirit. When we make the sign of the cross, we confess that we belong to the three divine persons. And we walk in faith until we one day may contemplate the one God in three persons and abide for eternity in his love.

The tendency in the religious instruction of children nowadays is to begin by concentrating attention on the Son and how he speaks of the Father and loves the Father. At Pentecost the Spirit sent by the Father and the Son is spoken of. Later, the sublime term, the Holy Trinity, is introduced.

We shall not deal with this mystery at great length. A "treatment" only a few pages long would run the risk of falling between two stools. Either the doctrine of the Holy Trinity would be situated too much outside the history of salvation in which it is revealed, or it would be a mere summary repetition of what has been said throughout the book, which spoke all the time of the Father, the Son and the Holy Spirit. We shall not repeat here what has already been said about Jesus of Nazareth, his obedience to the will of the Father, his Passion, his glory with God, or how his lot in life revealed the eternal love of the Father and the Son. And likewise we shall not repeat what has already been said about the Father and the Son who send the Spirit into the Church to animate it, and into the world which the Spirit renews.

The message of Scripture brings so clearly to our minds both the special attributes of the Father, the Son and the Holy Spirit, and at the same time their adorable unity, that the Church makes us confess in the Creed: I believe in one God, the Father almighty ... and in Jesus Christ his only-begotten Son ... and in the Holy Spirit who is Lord and who gives life.

2. Our knowledge of God and of Jesus Christ

Catechism text, pp. 79 and 81: "As though we ... revelation"; "How God is ... in his Church."

New texts: As though we really knew who God is and above all what is in his heart! We only know it well through Jesus. It is Jesus who brings us a higher knowledge, a knowledge which is fully true and certain, in connection with our sonship. His appearance is the full disclosure of God's revelation.

The real God appears in a real man. And in this man Jesus, the majesty of God is revealed, so kind and so close, so full of pity for us, so much involved in the struggle against evil. Who is God? The Old Testament undoubtedly reveals his most beautiful traits, or at least allows them to be surmised. It tells us, and the Church teaches us, along with St. Paul, that it is possible for us to know God from his creation. But in Jesus Christ God reveals himself in an incomparable way, in Jesus who was born and died, who rose again and lives on through his Spirit in his Church.

3. The consciousness of Jesus

a) *Catechism text*, pp. 90 and 312: "... and feels with all the fibres of his being ... vocation"; "After his prayer ... more widely."

New texts: ... and with all the fibres of his being (the child Jesus at Jerusalem) feels, "Here I am at home". Jesus is so absorbed by this sight of the majesty of God his Father that he forgets, as it were, his parents. It is very like what happens to a gifted child as he has the first intimation of his calling in life.

In his prayer in solitude, where he sets us an example, he had a deeper sense of his mission and found he had the strength to fulfil his task: to preach the good news still more widely.

b) *Catechism text*, pp. 90f., the section entitled "Jesus' consciousness": "The question ... to us."

562

New text: Jesus' consciousness

The question might now be asked: "How can he be the Son of God, and hence know all things, and at the same time man, and hence grow in knowledge?" We are here confronted by a profound mystery. On a lower level, if one may use the term, of his human consciousness, Jesus like other men discovered himself through a progressive contact with reality. On this level of his consciousness, Jesus, like ourselves, looked out at the world and used human words, images and concepts. But at the same time even at this lower level there was a radiation and a penetration of the eternal limitless knowledge which Jesus had as Son of God. So too in the summit of his human soul where he was turned to the Father he felt this light. Its influence enabled the divine Redeemer to announce the mysteries of God in human terms, so that he spoke to us "the words of eternal life" (Jn 6 :69). In the words of Jesus as well as in his works the mystery of God became accessible. "No one has ever seen God; the only Son, who is in the bosom of the Father, he has made him known" (Jn 1 :18); "He who has seen me has seen the Father" (Jn 14:9).

4. The sacrament of baptism

Catechism texts, pp. 246: "Baptism ... during the baptism"; 249: "This does not mean ... at work"; 250: "All this ... education"; 252: "In the course of ... in Christ."

New texts: Baptism gives a certain participation in the priesthood of Christ (we shall speak again later of the general priesthood of the faithful). Something similar holds good for confirmation, and in a very special way for the sacrament of orders. Hence it is said that a "character" is conferred in these sacraments. A person is baptized, confirmed and ordained priest for ever. Hence these sacraments cannot be repeated. But if someone during his baptism explicitly wishes not to be baptized, he is of course not baptized.

The dignity of the baptism of desire should not make us draw the false conclusion that the efficacious sign of the baptism of water can be omitted. The sign had a three-fold task to perform. It shows that we have need of forgiveness. It proclaims that the Lord is in contact with us. It gathers us tangibly and visibly into one people, and hence causes our rebirth through the Spirit who lives in this people.

All this is to be unfolded in the Christian education which follows, from which the sacrament may not be detached, either in our minds or in reality. One may well ask oneself whether children who have been baptized presumably because of the prevalent custom, but then grow up without any Christian education, can be called Christians. The Church asks for a guarantee of Christian education.

As regards unbaptized children, the Church gradually came to recognize more clearly that other truths were to be taken into consideration besides the principle of the necessity of baptism for salvation. The divine salvific will extends to all men. God wills that all should attain bliss, and children are included in this will. Christ died for all. According to the doctrine of limbo, which became classical in the Church, the children who die without baptism are certainly not unhappy. But is there no way at all by which the grace of the baptism which they did not receive can reach them? Can it give them no access to the blessedness of the children of God? There are theologians who search in this direction and make guesses. It should not make us less concerned to have children baptized. But we know that they are not outside the interests of our Redeemer, or outside his love, or outside his power.

5. The sacrament of penance

a) *Catechism text*, p. 461: "The confessor . . . helpfulness and prayer."

New text: The confessor is not there just to listen passively. He has also, in a certain sense, a judicial function. He can cross-question. He must apply this function as a way of helping the penitent to fulfil his duty which is to confess his grave sins properly. He has also the opportunity of correcting wrong notions. If he notices, for instance, that a penitent seems to think that God is interested only in chastity and Sunday Mass, he may prudently draw the penitent's attention to the evangelical demands for goodness, helpfulness and prayer.

b) *Catechism text*, p. 455 (on indulgences): "The element of faith . . . our good will."

New text: These practices are good in themselves but can lead to certain abuses. The Pope has recently described very clearly the meaning and use of indulgences. We must try to recognize the profound faith which inspires the practice. The Church tries to bestow largesse as generously as possible from the treasury of Christ's forgiveness, and we do some good deed which embodies our generosity. Far from excusing us from a laborious effort, indulgences encourage us to intensify it (cf. Paul VI, Constitution on Indulgences, AAS, 59 [1967], pp. 5–24).

6. The nature of miracle

Catechism text, p. 107: The section entitled: "The nature of miracle."
New text: The nature of miracle

It is well to consider for a moment what the Bible understands by miracle. A miracle, according to Scripture, is something in which man sees God at work. He can be seen at work in the marvellous works of creation. Thus one of the psalms sings of the starry heavens: "Let the heavens praise thy wonders, O Lord" (Ps 89:6). But the term is chiefly used in the Bible for events in which God's saving power is very specially manifest. "Marvel" and "wonderful work" are used in the New Testament in connection with the special manifestations of Christ's goodness, which arouse men's wonder and possess a significance. They are called "miracles", "signs", "works" and "powers". The two last terms call attention to an intervention of divine power beyond the forces of man and nature.

It is quite natural that as men of modern times, whose knowledge of nature and its laws increases yearly, we should put the question: Are these signs "outside the laws of nature", beyond the forces of nature and of man? Though this question is not put explicitly in the Bible, it is not simply absent from the indications which it gives of the nature of miracles, as we have seen above. And it would be a pity to try to exclude from the gospels all the wonderful works of Jesus which might give the impression of not being explicable in terms of the forces of nature. There are not only providential facts in the world. There are also miracles which surpass the proper forces of created causes. The greatest of all miracles is the resurrection of Jesus, in which his earthly body was glorified and raised up from the tomb, and after which God showed Jesus (Acts 10:40) to his witnesses.

Miracles are not exceptional deeds from the point of view of God. They are simply special effects of the eternal divine act which sustains and moves the universe. "My Father is working still", says Jesus (Jn 5:17). Though the miracle surpasses the forces of nature, it may be that God uses these forces, intensifying their activity, to bring about the miracle. A miraculous intervention of this nature on the part of God is not a breach of the order of things and does not represent an arbitrary act. It serves the order of grace, being a sign which guarantees this order, and thus is comprised within the total order of creation, which is both natural and supernatural.

The fact that the miracle surpasses the forces of nature gives it a certain affinity with grace, which elevates us to sonship of God, and with the whole unique elevation by which the humanity of Jesus of Nazareth is the humanity of the Son of God, the humanity in which the Son dwelt among us (Jn 1:14). The miracle is also a signal and an initial realization of the new creation, the new heaven and the new earth, which the risen Jesus has entered and which we await from him. It is not a violation of the laws of nature but goes beyond them. It is in the line of the yearning and expectation in which creation exists (cf. Rom 8:22).

Man is amazed in front of the miracle, because the profoundest meaning of the world is disclosed to him there. It is seen as the place of the redemption and rebirth of sinful man, as revealed and granted to us by Jesus the Redeemer.

7. The mystery of life after death

Catechism text, pp. 472–4: The section entitled: "They are about to arise."

New text: Awaiting the general resurrection

We have been speaking of the promised life without explaining precisely what it is. If we then ask ourselves "how" the dead exist, we notice that Scripture mostly speaks of the resurrection of the whole man, of the resurrection of the dead with soul and body.

But this is linked with the coming of the Lord Jesus in glory which the Church awaits. Where are the faithful departed now, immediately after their death? The Bible does not give a detailed answer to this question, but only indications in various places. It is not the intention of the Bible to give precise information about the "how" of the next life.

We must examine the biblical texts without prejudice. We find that they say of Jesus: "He *is* risen". Of the others who have died they say: "All shall be made alive" (1 Cor 15:22), "They are asleep" (1 Thess 4:13). Jesus sometimes uses the word "soul". "Do not fear those who kill the body, but cannot kill the soul" (Mt 10:28). Our Lord means that "something", the most proper element of man, can be saved after death. This "something" is not the earthly body since this remains behind as a corpse. And it is not a pure spirit, freed from a body in which it had been a prisoner. It is the living kernel of man, created to live in a body and which must never be considered anything else. But it can continue to exist separated from the mortal body.

We also know the promise which Jesus gave on the cross to the good thief: "Truly, I say to you, today you will be with me in paradise" (Lk 23:24). St. Paul speaks of his desire to "be away from the body and at home with the Lord" (2 Cor 5:8). He himself, as he writes to the Philippians, desires "to depart and be with Christ" (Phil 1:23). In the Book of Wisdom we read: "The souls of the righteous are in the hand of God. ... In the eyes of the foolish they seemed to have died. ... but their hope is full of immortality. Having been disciplined a little they will receive great good" (Wis 3:1–5).

These and other texts tell us that we cannot simply delay the glorification of the elect till the coming of the Lord. In what state do they find themselves? "Blessed are the pure in heart, for they shall see God", says Jesus (Mt 5:8). St. Paul and St. John wrote for their part: "Then (we shall see) face to face . . . then I shall understand fully, even as I have been fully understood (by God)" (1 Cor 13:12); "we shall see him as he is" (1 Jn 3:2). Do the dead receive at once the bliss of the vision of God (after the completion of any purification which may be necessary, of which we shall speak shortly)?

The tradition of the Church was at first silent on this point, and then a long period of hesitation followed. But then it spoke definitively at least from the Constitution *Benedictus Deus* of Pope Benedict XIII on (1336). The magisterium which gives the authentic interpretation of the deposit of faith teaches that the dead who are fully cleansed already enjoy the "clear vision of God himself triune and one as he is", even before "the coming of the Lord" (cf. Vatican II, Lumen Gentium, no. 49). Nonetheless, this is not the full and definitive glorification. This takes place at the coming of the Lord (the parousia), along with the whole new creation (cf. Rev 21:5) of which the risen Jesus and his mother are the first-fruits. Then the Lord Jesus will "change our lowly body to be like his glorious body, by the power which enables him even to subject all things to himself" (Phil 3:21). We shall then contemplate God in a fashion more fully human than before. For we shall not merely see him unveiled in his unfathomable mystery, we shall also and above all see him—in a way adapted to the condition of our glorified bodies—in the adorable humanity of Jesus, and consequently in the innumerable multitude of the saints of the Lord, and finally in the new heaven and the new earth. And more than ever love shall reign.

Note: Another passage (p. 476, end of first section) may be modified in the same sense. One may simply say of the dead, with the exception of Mary, that they have the promise of resurrection. If some of them "are more powerfully present than others"—through the favours which they bestow on the faithful—this is perhaps due to their greater union with the risen Christ.

8. Judgment and the final purification

a) *Catechism text*, p. 480: "This judgment ... Judge."

New text: But was not this judgment passed immediately after death? This is true, but it takes place outside our time. The coming of the Lord and the general resurrection are to manifest the fulfilment of the first judgment. We are familiar with the scene in which Jesus pronounces the last judgment, as described in the Gospel of St. Matthew (Mt 25:31–46). In the Gospel of St. John Jesus speaks of a "resurrection to life" for the elect and of a "resurrection to judgment" for the reprobate (Jn 5:29). In view of the duration between death (along with the "particular judgment") and the coming of the Lord (with the "general judgment") our way of speaking should be sober. The duration in question is of a higher order than that of our time. The judgment will be the same, and it will be pronounced by the same supremely just Judge.

b) *Catechism text*, pp. 476f.: "There is still much ingrained egoism ... God's light"; "We must now train our imagination ... Scripture hardly speaks of it at all."

New text: There is still much ingrained egoism to be converted, cleansed away and purified. This begins to take place with death itself. Dying must also be dying to evil. It is the baptism of death along with Christ, in which the baptism of water is completed. But after death, as the Church believes, there is room for a final purification, purgatory, involving the total and definitive turning to God's light.

But we must now train our imagination to return to the soberness of Christian antiquity. We must simply hold that the purification which is part of death is completed by what lies beyond death. This sobriety is all the more called for because Scripture hardly speaks at all of this matter.

9. The mystery of the vision of God

Additional text, to be inserted on p. 483, before the sentence: "The fullest texts of Scripture ... in the Book of Revelation."

Scripture includes the words: We shall see God as he is (cf. 1 Jn 3:2). When we consider this promise, we may have the feeling that we are to be dissolved in the ocean of simplicity, love and brightness which is God. But contrary to what our mind or heart may feel, the Christian faith proclaims that man as a person does not disappear when he is admitted the ineffable vision of God, in his presence.

In the interpretation which the Church gives of this mystery, it has been careful not to water down the divine revelation. With the teaching of Scripture in mind, it has taught that the blessed do not disappear in the being of God but that God fulfils man and takes him into his own ineffable simplicity, so that each is granted the vision by which he knows God "face to face". It is an unfathomable mystery, a mystery of grace which is the inexpressible answer to the longings of our heart.

X. VARIOUS POINTS OF MORAL THEOLOGY

DECLARATION (see AAS, 60 [1968], p. 691): *It should be made quite clear that there are moral laws which can be so clearly known and expressed by us that they bind our conscience at all times and in all circumstances. Solutions of questions of conscience which do not take fully into account the indissolubility of marriage should be avoided. It is quite right that much importance should be attached to the person's fundamental moral attitude, but care must be taken to ensure that this attitude is not made too independent of deeds. The explanation of matrimonial ethics should be more faithful in rendering without omission the doctrine of the Second Vatican Council and the Holy See.*

1. The universal moral laws

a) *Catechism text*, pp. 372f.: "How the government of the Church ... values are interpreted."

New text: How the government of the Church gives directives to the moral conscience, along with the Holy Spirit who awakens and maintains the spirit of faith in the people of God, will be explained in the chapter entitled "The Pastoral Ministry". It will also appear in the present chapter when conscience comes up for discussion. And the supreme value, love, which is the norm of every rule, will likewise be discussed in this present chapter. It is necessary to bear in mind throughout that formulations and applications of moral laws can bear to some extent the mark of a given society and a given epoch.

Historically conditioned elements are then interwoven with the permanently valid. It also happens that the formula used does not do full justice to the value which is in question. Though new applications are made, the meaning of the commandments always remains the same.

For all these reasons, a really authoritative commentary is necessary for society. In the society of the Church which lives by God's revelation light comes gradually to guide our conduct more and more firmly. In laying down its norms, the Church allows itself to be guided by the universal moral laws. But it is obvious that the precepts of the Church are not always in the same necessary relationship to these laws. There are obligations which rather come under the heading of "good order", and can thus be subject to change. Other precepts are more direct applications of the natural law in changeable particular circumstances. And finally there are precepts which are the clearest possible expression of universal moral laws.

b) *Catechism text*, p. 374: "This discussion . . . the law prescribes."

New text: This discussion has helped us to see the primordial and profound unity of conscience and commandments. But there is another element to consider. Conscience and commandment are two poles between which a tension can and sometimes must arise. The law, the precise precept, cannot foresee exactly all circumstances. There are some divine laws so absolute in character that no exception is ever possible, whatever case may arise in the concrete. But the defective mould into which they are sometimes poured by human expression can bring about cases in which one must do less or more than is prescribed by the law, whose formulation aims at being universal. This is even more obviously possible in human law, since no human legislation, not even that of the Church, can foresee the concrete reality of all cases and circumstances.

Note: Text, p. 423 ("But there can in fact be cases . . . decision of conscience"): the Commission of Cardinals judged that this passage should be omitted.

2. The indissolubility of marriage

Catechism text, 394–8. The section entitled: "Protective laws."

Note: Apropos of this passage, the Commission of Cardinals, in the *Report* drawn up in view of the improvement of the Catechism, declared that "the solution given for two marriage cases should be omitted". The same passage is envisaged by the *Declaration* (of 15 October 1968), where it says that solutions of cases of conscience which do not fully take into account the indissolubility of marriage should be avoided (see the quotation from the Declaration, above, p. 55 under the heading: X. "Various Points of Moral Theology").

It is sufficient to have called attention to the request that the passage in question should be omitted. But we may also recall a remark which appeared in the *Report* mentioned above: "If the New Catechism still decides to deal with these two marriage cases, it will have to present a solution of a pastoral type *in* the framework of the moral theology of the Church. In some cases the partners of the invalid marriage will agree to live together simply in mutual friendship. [If they are seriously prepared to do this, and if the danger of scandal is completely excluded, they may receive the sacraments.] In other cases [if they do not make this resolution] they can take part, in humility before God in the Church's life of prayer, practising justice and love towards their fellow-men. This is no slight matter in the economy of salvation which the Lord Jesus announced".

3. Serious and less serious sins, inner disposition and acts

a) *Catechism text*, top of p. 452: "In the first Christian centuries . . . worthy of damnation."

New text: The descriptions of sin which we meet with in Scripture are often linked with an indication of their gravity in the sight of God and their consequences for man. Jesus himself, for instance, condemns the scandal given to little ones as one of the gravest of misdeeds (Mt 18:6; Lk 17:2). He points to sin against love of the neighbour as the great sin by which man brings down upon himself the condemnation to "the eternal fire which was prepared for the devil and his angels" (Mt 25:41). St. John returns constantly to the topic of the sin against love of the neighbour which prevents the love of God abiding in us (cf. 1 Jn 3:17). And St. Paul gives summary lists of sins which exclude from the kingdom of God (1 Cor 6:9–11; Gal 5:19–21). But these lists, which were certainly known and accepted by the early Christians, were not at the time given any precise expression in the practice of penance. No doubt apostasy (idolatry), murder and adultery were treated with very great seriousness, as public scandal, from very early times. A long period of penance was demanded before reconciliation with the Church was granted. Lists with more precise distinctions between "grave" and "venial" sins were drawn up in later centuries for the use of confessors, when private penance became the general practice in the Church. They were to be used in determining the penance to be imposed, and to define the sins which had to be confessed before receiving Holy Communion. The latter were sins which taken in themselves contained such an aversion from God that the sinner was not fit to go to Holy Communion with the Church.

b) *Catechism text*, pp. 453–4 (middle of the page): "Yes, if he perseveres . . . eternal obstinacy" (top of page).

New text: Grave sin, as we have said above, is a break with God, a wilful act of disobedience in a matter which is essential for love of him. It necessarily excludes friendship with God, makes a man one of the "children of wrath" (Eph 2:3) and consequently deprives him of the divine life of sanctifying grace and the loving indwelling of the Holy Spirit. It is spiritual death. This is why such sins received the name of mortal sins. And if a man is obdurate in his wilful estrangement, even in death, he passes into the state of eternal obduracy and deprivation of the divine friendship, hell.

But here we must recall what we said above, that real sin is above all an inward attitude. The deed taken in isolation does not tell everything. We may have done something dreadful, so bad that we do in fact regard it—not least because of the inward breach of loyalty—as a grave sin. But it is still possible that God sees how much good there still was in our attitude, and that his judgment is milder than our own with regard to the possibility of a reconciliation.

But no matter how bad and obdurate a person may be, no matter how completely he lives at enmity with God and how worthy of condemnation he may be, there is still hope as long as he is alive. Man has turned away from goodness and grace. But God still desires that he should unbend, be converted, repent. He never ceases to offer opportunities (see Jer 1:2–3). Hence when we use the term "mortal sin", we must not think of it as definitive and irreparable. Nonetheless, grave sin sets men's feet on the way to eternal obstinacy.

4. *The married state*

a) *Catechism text*, p. 389: "The creation narratives . . . preference for monogamy."

New text: The creation narratives breathe the same spirit. The first chapter of Genesis also lays the emphasis on fertility: "Male and female he created them . . . Be fruitful and multiply." The second chapter of Genesis lays the emphasis on love. See the first encounter when Adam awakes. And it also stresses that man and woman are of like nature. Genesis speaks of one man and one woman who together become one flesh. In the light of Christ's teaching (Mt 19:4–7), we are justified in seeing in these chapters the original intention of the Creator, which was to establish matrimony as monogamous. The Bible shows us that this intention was obscured in the minds of the ancient patriarchs. But it came to be recognized more and more clearly by the people of God, under God's guidance, and Jesus proclaimed it definitively for the new people of God.

b) *Catechism text*, p. 402: "The Second Vatican Coucil . . . outside the Church."

New text: The Second Vatican Council did not pronounce upon any of these concrete methods as such in the relevant chapter of the constitution on *The Church in the Modern World*. And thus it did not explicitly repeat the doctrine which Pope Pius XI had formally laid down some thirty years earlier, and which had been maintained by his successor. Nonetheless, this still may not be seen as a fundamental modification or change of standpoint as regards Church teaching. The reason why the Council kept silence was that Pope Paul VI had removed further discussion of the matter from the agenda, because the special commission which he had set up to study some new aspects of the problem had not yet finished its investigations.

An unmistakable development is taking place in our times, both in and outside the Church, in the views taken of man's sexual life.

c) *Catechism text*, p. 403: "Are all methods of regulation . . . the affective life."

New text: Are then all methods of regulation of births on an equal footing in the light of the Christian conscience? As we have seen, the Council gave no precise answer on this point. But it calls on all, especially married couples, to ask themselves conscientiously whether the practices in question do full justice to the high values which should be expressed in marriage and the familiarity of love. "Therefore when there is question of harmonizing conjugal love with the responsible transmission of life, the moral aspect of any procedure does not depend solely on sincere intentions or on an evaluation of motives. It must be determined by objective standards. These, based on the nature of the human person and his acts, preserve the full sense of mutual self-

573

giving and human procreation in the context of true love" (Gaudium et Spes [Church in the World of Today], no. 51). "The parents themselves", the Council affirms, "should ultimately make this judgment, in the sight of God. But in their manner of acting, spouses should be aware that they cannot proceed arbitrarily. They must always be governed according to a conscience dutifully conformed to the divine law itself, and should be submissive toward the Church's teaching office, which authentically interprets that law in the light of the Gospel. That divine law reveals and protects the integral meaning of conjugal love, and impels it toward a truly human fulfilment" (Gaudium et Spes, no. 50).

It is advisable in such matters to approach a prudent priest, but also a doctor who can take all the varying circumstances into account and after due discussion can decide what is medically the best for each particular case. But reverence for life also demands that within the limits of what is morally permissible everything should be avoided which might gravely injure health or the affective life.

Note: Since this is a matter of modifications which were made before the publication of the encyclical *Humanae Vitae*, no mention is made of the important teaching given there. In the *Declaration* of the Commission of Cardinals which was published 30 November 1968, we read: "The explanation of matrimonial ethics should be more faithfully in rendering without omission the doctrine of the Second Vatican Council and of the Holy See" (AAS, 60 [1968], p. 691).

CONCLUDING NOTE

Having cited the passages from the *Declaration* of the Commission of Cardinals which ask for modifications in the New Catechism, it is also well to cite the final remark of the Declaration, in which the merits of the book are acknowledged:

"Though the preceding comments are not negligible, either in number or in seriousness, they nonetheless leave by far the greatest part of the New Catechism untouched, with its admirable pastoral, liturgical and biblical character. So too they support the praiseworthy intention of the authors of the Catechism, which was to present the eternal good news of Christ in a way which is adapted to the mentality of the people of our times. It is precisely the high qualities with which the work is enhanced which make it desirable that the teaching of the Church should always be given without any shadows which might obscure it" (see ASS, 60 [1968], p. 691).